Systematic Theology

David F. Wells

"It would be difficult to overestimate the influence that this study has had and continues to have in forming evangelical beliefs."

Mark Noll

"It is satisfying indeed to possess an abridged version of Charles Hodge's *Systematic Theology*. Professor Gross's work of condensation has been careful and fair. The result is much easier access to a work that an early reviewer described as illuminating 'the great themes of the Augustinian system from an evangelical standpoint.' That 'system' and that 'viewpoint' were much appreciated when they first appeared in the early 1870s. Now adjusted to the quick read and the easily distracted attention span of our own day, they may do even more good."

James M. Boice

"For those unable to pursue the original edition, this abridgment presents the heart of Hodge's theology in an attractive and readable format."

Roger Nicole

"Charles Hodge, one of the foremost American theologians, exercised his influence through his long tenure at Princeton Theological Seminary and, long after his death, through his monumental, three-volume *Systematic Theology*. The sheer mass of the material constituted an obstacle, not to speak about frequent untranslated Latin quotations and fairly extensive developments that appear obsolete at the end of the twentieth century. It is therefore with joy that we salute the appearance of this one-volume abridgment, in which the full outline of the original work is retained, but the text has been cut down to about one-third of the 1873 edition."

Systematic Theology

Abridged Edition

Charles Hodge

Edward N. Gross, *editor*

With Study Questions

P.O. BOX 817 • PHILLIPSBURG • NEW JERSEY 08865-0817

© 1988, 1992 by Edward N. Gross

First edition 1988
Revised paperback edition 1992
Reissued by Presbyterian and Reformed Publishing Company 1997

Printed in the United States of America

Library of Congress Cataloging-in-Publication Data

Hodge, Charles, 1797–1878.
    Systematic theology / Charles Hodge ; Edward N. Gross, editor. —
Abridged ed., with study questions.
        p.   cm.
    Originally published: Grand Rapids, Mich. : Baker Book House, 1992.
    Includes indexes.
    ISBN 0-87552-224-6 (pbk.)
    1. Theology, Doctrinal. I. Gross, Edward N. II. Title.
[BT75. H6332   1997]
230'.51—dc21   97-18567

Contents

Part I. Theology Proper

Part II. Anthropology

Part III. Soteriology

Preface

Charles Hodge (1797–1878) faithfully taught at Princeton Theological Seminary from 1820 until his death. During that time he exerted an incalculable influence over the Reformed churches. He was named Professor of Oriental and Biblical Literature in 1822, taking a position beside Archibald Alexander and Samuel Miller as the third professor of the ten-year-old seminary. Upon the recommendation of his senior colleagues he studied in leading German theological institutions from 1826 to 1828. There Hodge saw firsthand the soul-threatening dangers of both mysticism and rationalism. He returned with added academic and spiritual insight which grew year by year as he arduously and selflessly labored at Princeton.

Hodge founded the *Biblical Repertory and Princeton Review* in 1825 and edited it for over forty years. His contributions to that journal dealt with a wide range of theological and practical subjects and were known for their knowledge, clarity, and fairness. The vast respect which he gained through this avenue may be well represented by a quote from Irenaeus Prime of the *New York Observer*, who a week after Hodge's death wrote: "We recall a case in which the General Assembly (Presbyterian Church), after one of the ablest debates ever held on its floor, came to a decision on an important ecclesiastical question with almost entire unanimity. Dr. Hodge reviewed the decision in the 'Princeton Review' with such masterly power, as to set back the opinions of the Church, and hold it on the other side to this day."

15

Hodge's exegetical aptitude was proven with the publishing of his first book, a commentary on Romans, in 1835. By the time of his death nearly twenty editions had been issued. In 1840 he became Professor of Exegetical and Didactic Theology. He was now to build upon his expertise as an exegete and develop into perhaps the greatest theologian in American history. In the opinion of Archibald Alexander, Charles Hodge was, more than any man he knew, like John Calvin, without his severity. William G. T. Shedd affirmed that "Dr. Hodge has done more for Calvinism than any other man in America."

Systematic Theology was Charles Hodge's magnum opus. The vast bulk of its contents were penned after his sixty-ninth year. The fruit of decades of intense theological study and teaching, they emit an authority and maturity unexcelled in American theological treatises. The precepts of *Systematic Theology* are convincingly Biblical. The *New York Tribune* early hailed its appearance, declaring, "This work everywhere exhibits the evidence of profound thought, acute analysis, and wide learning." The original work encompassed over twenty-two hundred pages in three massive volumes. As proof of its supremacy in the world of theological literature, it remains in print and is required reading in many Reformed institutions.

In honor of Hodge's fifty years as a professor at Princeton, a semi-centennial was celebrated in 1872. This historic event nearly coincided with the publication of his *Systematic Theology*. Hundreds flocked to Princeton from all over the United States and abroad to honor their teacher, example, and friend. The main speech of the day, presented by Henry Boardman in behalf of Princeton Theological Seminary, included the following words:

> And now there is superadded that which all your friends regard as the crowning mercy of your life, viz.: that health and strength have been given you to complete and publish the only comprehensive work of Systematic Theology in our own or any other language, which comprises the latest results of sound scriptural exegesis, discusses the great themes of the Augustinian system from an evangelical standpoint, and deals satisfactorily with the sceptical speculations of modern philosophy and science. In thus supplying what was confessedly, in the way of authorship, the most urgent want of Protestant Christendom, you have extended indefinitely the range of your beneficent power.
>
> Your Theology must soon become the Hand-Book of all students of the Reformed faith who speak the English tongue. Where you have taught scores, you will now teach hundreds; and where you have taught hundreds, you will teach thousands.

Systematic Theology properly involves the utilization of data from such other disciplines as Biblical, historical, and apologetical theology. I have attempted to retain those aspects of Hodge's Biblical theology which do not demand scholarly exegetical analysis of the reader. This abridgment is, then, in the main, Hodge's Biblical theology. The many sections of the original work which involved historical theology have largely been omitted; the exceptions are a few basic passages distinguishing truth from error in contemporary systems of thought. Hodge was keenly logical and cogent in his apologetics. However, many of the errors he confronted were influential only in his day, and thus not appropriate to include within the scope of the present work. This is especially true of those sections in his work challenging pre–Vatican II Roman Catholicism and nineteenth-century philosophical intricacies. Preserved are those timeless apologetical principles and illustrations which are ever needed in opposing the reintroduction of old fallacies via new forms.

Non-English quotes have been omitted from the abridgment, as have some large sections deemed either unnecessary or better suited for separate publication (e.g., the excellent chapter on the law of God). I have had to keep size in mind, and this has demanded omission of some very valuable data and almost all repetition. Some classic quotes are denied publication in our volume as they are touched on by previous material. Hodge was hoping to add a separate section on ecclesiology, but was hindered by death. Hence the abridgment is, like the original, deficient in this area.

Thorough fairness to the original work has been strenuously attempted. This can be illustrated in the representation of Hodge's eschatology. Hodge there admits his lack of certainty, but argues against premillennialism and amillennialism. I am a convinced premillenarian, but strove to represent Hodge's postmillennialism fairly.

Symmetry was also a goal of the abridgment. I did not want to give undue prominence to any chapter, removing the balance so carefully worked out by Hodge in the original. Hence, as a general rule, the longest chapters in the original remain the longest in the abridgment.

To inject a personal note, the work of abridging Hodge's *Systematic Theology* was not a tiresome task testing the bounds of Christian endurance. It has been for me, on the contrary, a labor of love. My father was converted at age forty. He grew in grace and faithfully witnessed through his vocation as a dentist in upstate New York. My four brothers and I saw tremendous changes occurring in our family. I remember our parents continually requesting one thing of the Lord: "Lead us into the full knowledge of thy truth." Eventually they decided to be-

come dental missionaries in Africa under the mission board founded
by the famous Princeton defender of orthodoxy, J. Gresham Machen.
It was through this contact with the Independent Board for Presbyterian Foreign Missions that we were introduced to the works of the
great Princeton theologians in general and Charles Hodge in particular. My deep love for the writings of Hodge stems from my parents'
sincere and simple request that God would teach us truth.

As a trained missiologist, I am aware of the accusation that all
theologies are culture-bound. It is true, of course, that all theologians
are inhabitants of certain cultures and write from the limited per-
spective of their individual backgrounds. This does not mean, however,
that a theology cannot be effective in a culture other than the one
which produced it. Some have argued that because Charles Hodge
wrote in nineteenth-century America, his theology is hardly suitable
for twentieth-century America, much less for foreign cultures. This
abridgment has been carefully designed with such criticisms in mind.
I have attempted to decontextualize Hodge's theology, preserving that
which is truly transcultural. Must we neglect Hodge's beautiful expressions of Biblical truth simply because he wrote in a different time and
culture? I am convinced that to do so is to reject a tried and proven
source of blessing at a time when there are few defending historic
Christianity.

Indeed, I have personally witnessed the dynamic relevance of Hodge's
theology both in my experience on the mission field and in my teaching at Faith Theological Seminary. The theories of those who would
refuse Hodge a prominent place in the current teaching of theology
have been disproved by the great use currently being made of Hodge
in cross-cultural situations. The power of truth as stated by this man
is something I have not only felt with my own heart, but seen with
my own eyes. I have often read a quote from Hodge to my systematics
class and been immediately compelled to worship God in prayer. I felt
helpless, completely overawed by the power of truth expressed by
Hodge. There was nothing that I could add. I knew that to say anything
would only detract. I could see that my students (Africans, Asians,
Americans) were responding in the same way. As we prayed and expressed our praise to God for some radiant aspect of His glorious
character never before so appreciated, or as we thanked Him for some
expression concerning His infinite grace to undeserving sinners, we
almost invariably would be led into a humble and tearful confession
of our own sin and unworthiness. Words cannot express the growth in
sanctification and knowledge experienced in such sessions. In the first
chapter of his famed *Institutes of the Christian Religion*, John Calvin
wrote, "It is evident that man never attains to a true self-knowledge

until he has previously contemplated the face of God, and come down after such contemplation to look into himself." It is possible for us to enjoy such an experience upon prayerful consideration of Hodge's exposition of Scriptural truths.

However, it is not only Charles Hodge's theological expressions that are spiritually powerful; his godly life radiates through his writings. Rarely are scholarship and spirituality so inextricably united in one man. A few remarks from William Paxton, a contemporary of Hodge's, will help explain why the Holy Spirit still uses his works to challenge and edify Christians:

> The teaching of some great and good Professors is purely intellectual; they develop splendid systems, reason with interest and force, and communicate abundance of instruction, but the impression which they make is purely intellectual. The students listen with a profound attention, just as students in other schools listen to lectures upon law and medicine— and go away, instructed, indeed, but without any spiritual or moral impression upon their minds or hearts. The reverse of all this was true of Dr. Hodge. His was not a dead theology. It was instinct with life. What he gave us was bread from our Father's table. It was life to his soul, and he dispensed it to us under the deep conviction that it would be life to us, and that we would make it the Word of life to others. His great intellect shone in every discussion, but it was accompanied with spiritual power, and made upon us a deep practical impression. He created an interest in the study of scientific theology, but his impression on us did not stop there; he made us feel that we were dealing with sacred things, and that these truths were to be to us and to others "savors of life unto life or death unto death." . . .
>
> I remember that as students under Dr. Hodge we were deeply impressed with the conviction that the thought most in his mind was Christ, the being nearest his heart was Christ, the centre of all his theology was Christ. Now that many years have passed, and I have heard other teachers and read other authors, the impression grows upon me, as I remember my early instructor, that no teacher, no author, so centralizes all things in Christ, or so uses all things to glorify Christ.

Charles Hodge speaks simply for the advancement of truth and the glory of God. His message is strong and compelling, Christ-centered and blessed by the Holy Spirit whose office it is to exalt the Son of God. Now no one thinks that, as helpful as the Princeton theologians are, they are substitutes for dependence upon Christ and His Word. But they are gifts of Christ, the Chief Shepherd, who has in love given them to the Church to help feed His tender flock.

Finally, I wish to give special thanks to my dear wife, Deborah, who, in the midst of caring for our four young children, was a constant support in this project through prayer, encouragement, proofreading, and typing. I also thank Ray Wiersma for his many helpful suggestions in editing, and Norman Manohar for his assistance in typing the abridgment. I am grateful as well to each of my students who responded so positively to the teachings of Charles Hodge and encouraged me to pursue the publication of this abridgment. May God receive all the glory for the good resulting from the publishing of this work, which aims to give the incomparable theological teachings of Charles Hodge an increased level of influence upon the mind and life of the Church during the latter part of the twentieth century.

Introduction

Chapter I

On Method

§1. Theology a Science

A. The Nature of Science

In every science there are two factors: facts and ideas, or facts and the mind. Science is more than knowledge. Knowledge is the persuasion of what is true on adequate evidence. But the facts of astronomy,

chemistry, or history do not constitute the science of those departments of knowledge. Nor does the mere orderly arrangement of facts
amount to science. Historical facts arranged in chronological order
are mere annals. The philosophy of history supposes those facts to be
understood in their causal relations. . . . If, therefore, theology be a
science, it must include something more than a mere knowledge of
facts. It must embrace an exhibition of the internal relation of those
facts, one to another, and each to all. It must be able to show that if
one be admitted, others cannot be denied.

The Bible is no more a system of theology than nature is a system
of chemistry or of mechanics. We find in nature the facts which the
chemist or the mechanical philosopher has to examine . . . to ascertain
the laws by which they are determined. So the Bible contains the
truths which the theologian has to collect, authenticate, arrange, and
exhibit in their internal relation to each other. This constitutes the
difference between Biblical and systematic theology. The office of the
former is to ascertain and state the facts of Scripture. The office of the
latter is to take those facts and determine their relation to each other
and to other cognate truths, as well as to vindicate them and show
their harmony and consistency. This is not an easy task, or one of
slight importance.

B. Necessity for System in Theology

It may be naturally asked, Why not take the truths as God has seen
fit to reveal them, and thus save ourselves the trouble of showing their
relation and harmony?

The answer to this question is, in the first place, that it cannot be
done. Such is the constitution of the human mind that it cannot help
endeavoring to systematize and reconcile the facts which it admits to
be true. In no department of knowledge have men been satisfied with
the possession of a mass of undigested facts. And the students of the
Bible can as little be expected to be thus satisfied. . . .

Second, a much higher kind of knowledge is thus obtained than by
the mere accumulation of isolated facts. . . . Without the knowledge of
the laws of attraction and motion, astronomy would be a confused
and unintelligible collection of facts. What is true of other sciences is
true of theology. We cannot know what God has revealed in His Word
unless we understand, at least in some good measure, the relation in
which the separate truths therein contained stand to each other. It
cost the Church centuries of study and controversy to solve the problem concerning the person of Christ; that is, to adjust and bring into

harmonious arrangement all the facts which the Bible teaches on that subject.

Third, we have no choice in this matter. If we would discharge our duty as teachers and defenders of the truth, we must endeavor to bring all the facts of revelation into systematic order and mutual relation. It is only thus that we can satisfactorily exhibit their truth, vindicate them from objections, or bring them to bear in their full force on the minds of men.

Fourth, such is the evident will of God. He does not teach men astronomy or chemistry, but He gives them the facts out of which those sciences are constructed. Neither does He teach us systematic theology, but He gives us in the Bible the truths which, properly understood and arranged, constitute the science of theology. As the facts of nature are all related and determined by physical laws, so the facts of the Bible are all related and determined by the nature of God and of His creatures. And as He wills that men should study His works and discover their wonderful organic relation and harmonious combination, so it is His will that we study His Word and learn that, like the stars, its truths are not isolated points, but systems, cycles, and epicycles in unending harmony and grandeur. Besides all this, although the Scriptures do not contain a system of theology as a whole, the Epistles of the New Testament do provide portions of that system. These are our authority and guide.

§2. Theological Method

Every science has its own method, determined by its peculiar nature. . . . The two great comprehensive methods are the *a priori* and the *a posteriori*. The one argues from cause to effect, the other from effect to cause. The former was for ages applied even to the investigation of nature. Men sought to determine what the facts of nature must be from the laws of mind or assumed necessary laws. . . . Every one knows how much it cost to establish the method of induction on a firm basis and to secure a general recognition of its authority. According to this method, we begin with collecting well-established facts and from them infer the general laws which determine their occurrence. . . .

The methods which have been applied to the study of theology are too numerous to be separately considered. They may, perhaps, be reduced to three general classes: (1) the speculative; (2) the mystical; and (3) the inductive. . . .

§3. The Speculative Method

Speculation assumes, in an *a priori* manner, certain principles, and from them undertakes to determine what is and what must be. It decides on all truth, or determines on what is true, from the laws of the mind or from axioms involved in the constitution of the thinking principle within us. To this head must be referred all those systems which are founded on any *a priori* philosophical assumptions. . . .

§4. The Mystical Method

. . . Speculation is a process of thought; mysticism is a matter of feeling. The one assumes that the thinking faculty is that by which we attain the knowledge of truth. The other, distrusting reason, teaches that the feelings alone are to be relied upon, at least in the sphere of religion. . . .

§5. The Inductive Method

A. *The Steps in the Process*

. . . First, the man of science comes to the study of nature with certain assumptions. (1) He assumes the trustworthiness of his sense perceptions. Unless he can rely upon the well-authenticated testimony of his senses, he is deprived of all means of prosecuting his investigations. The facts of nature reveal themselves to our faculties of sense and can be known in no other way. (2) He must also assume the trustworthiness of his mental operations. He must take for granted that he can perceive, compare, combine, remember, and infer; and that he can safely rely upon these mental faculties in their legitimate exercise. (3) He must also rely on the certainty of those truths which are not learned from experience, but which are given in the constitution of our nature. That every effect must have a cause; that the same cause under like circumstances will produce like effects; that a cause is not a mere uniform antecedent, but that which contains within itself the reason why the effect occurs.

Second, the student of nature, having this ground on which to stand and these tools wherewith to work, proceeds to perceive, gather, and combine his facts. These he does not pretend to manufacture nor presume to modify. He must take them as they are. He is only careful to be sure that they are real and that he has them all, or at least all that are necessary to justify any inference which he may draw from them, or any theory which he may build upon them.

Third, from facts thus ascertained and classified, he deduces the laws by which they are determined. . . . It is to be observed that these laws or general principles are not derived from the mind and attributed to external objects, but derived or deduced from the objects and impressed upon the mind.

B. The Inductive Method as Applied to Theology

The Bible is to the theologian what nature is to the man of science. It is his storehouse of facts, and his method of ascertaining what the Bible teaches is the same as that which the natural philosopher adopts to ascertain what nature teaches.

1. Basic assumptions to be brought to the task

In the first place, the theologian comes to his task with all the assumptions above mentioned. He must assume the validity of those laws of belief which God has impressed upon our nature. In these laws are included some which have no direct application to the natural sciences. Such, for example, as the essential distinction between right and wrong; that nothing contrary to virtue can be enjoined by God; that it cannot be right to do evil that good may come; that sin deserves punishment, and other similar first truths which God has implanted in the constitution of all moral beings and which no objective revelation can possibly contradict. These first principles, however, are not to be arbitrarily assumed. No man has a right to lay down his own opinions, however firmly held, and call them "first truths of reason," and make them the source or test of Christian doctrines. Nothing can rightfully be included under the category of first truths, or laws of belief, which cannot stand the tests of universality and necessity. . . .

2. Facts to be collected

In the second place, the duty of the Christian theologian is to ascertain, collect, and combine all the facts which God has revealed concerning Himself and our relation to Him. These facts are all in the Bible. This is true because everything revealed in nature and in the constitution of man concerning God and our relation to Him is contained and authenticated in Scripture. It is in this sense that "the Bible, and the Bible alone, is the religion of Protestants." It may be admitted that the truths which the theologian has to reduce to a science or, to speak more humbly, which he has to arrange and harmonize are revealed partly in the external works of God, partly in the constitution of our nature, and partly in the religious experience of believers. Yet lest we should err in our inferences from the works of God, we have in His Word a clearer revelation of all that nature reveals. And lest we should misinterpret our own consciousness and the laws of our nature, everything that can be legitimately learned from that source will be found recognized and authenticated in the Scriptures. And lest we should attribute to the teaching of the Spirit the operations of our own natural affections, we find in the Bible the norm and standard of all genuine religious experience. The Scriptures teach not only the truth, but what are the effects of the truth on the heart and conscience, when applied with saving power by the Holy Ghost.

3. The theologian to be guided by the same rules as the man of science

In the third place, the theologian must be guided by the same rules in the collection of facts as govern the man of science.

(1) This collection must be made with diligence and care. It is not an easy work. There is in every department of investigation great liability to error. Almost all false theories in science and false doctrines in theology are due in a great degree to mistakes as to matters of fact. A distinguished naturalist said he repeated an experiment a thousand times before he felt authorized to announce the result to the scientific world as an established fact.

(2) This collection of facts must not only be carefully conducted, but also comprehensive and, if possible, exhaustive. An imperfect induction of facts led men for ages to believe that the sun moved around the earth and that the earth was an extended plain. In theology a partial induction of particulars has led to like serious errors. It is a fact that the Scriptures attribute omniscience to Christ. From this it was inferred that He could not have had a finite intelligence. . . . But it is also a Scriptural fact that ignorance and intellectual progress, as well as omniscience, are ascribed to our Lord. Both facts, therefore, must be included in our doctrine of His person. We must admit that He had a human as well as a divine intelligence. It is a fact that everything that can be predicated of a sinless man is in the Bible predicated of Christ, and it is also a fact that everything that is predicated of God is predicated of our Lord. Hence it has been inferred that there were two Christs—two persons, the one human and the other divine—and that they dwelt together very much as the Spirit dwells in the believer or as evil spirits dwelt in demoniacs. But this theory overlooks the numerous facts which prove the individual personality of Christ. The same person who said, "I thirst," also said,

"Before Abraham was, I am." The Scriptures teach that Christ's death was designed to reveal the love of God and to secure the reformation of men. Hence Socinus denied that His death was an expiation for sin or satisfaction of justice. The latter fact, however, is as clearly revealed as the former; and therefore both must be taken into account in our statement of the doctrine concerning the design of Christ's death.

Illustrations without end might be given of the necessity of a comprehensive induction of facts to justify our doctrinal conclusions. These facts must not be willfully denied or carelessly overlooked, or unfairly appreciated. We must be honest here, as the true student of nature is honest in his induction. Even scientific men are sometimes led to suppress or to pervert facts which militate against their favorite theories, but the temptation to this form of dishonesty is far less in their case than in that of the theologian. The truths of religion are far more important than those of natural science. They come home to the heart and conscience. They may alarm the fears or threaten the hopes of men, so that they are under strong temptation to overlook or pervert them. If, however, we really desire to know what God has revealed, we must be conscientiously diligent and faithful in collecting the facts which He has made known and in giving them their due weight. . . . Science cannot make facts; it must take them as they are. In like manner, if the Bible asserts that Christ's death was a satisfaction to justice, the theologian is not allowed to merge justice into benevolence in order to suit his theory of the atonement. If the Scriptures teach that men are born in sin, we cannot change the nature of sin, and make it a tendency to evil and not really sin, in order to get rid of difficulty. . . . We must take the facts of the Bible as they are and construct our system so as to embrace them all in their integrity.

4. Principles to be deduced from facts

In the fourth place, in theology as in natural science, principles are derived from facts and not impressed upon them. . . . The investigator sees, or ascertains by observation, what are the laws which determine material phenomena; he does not invent those laws. Unless sustained by facts, his speculations on matters of science are worthless. It is no less unscientific for the theologian to assume a theory as to the nature of virtue, of sin, of liberty, of moral obligation, and then explain the facts of Scripture in accordance with his theories. His only proper course is to derive his theory of virtue, of sin, of liberty, of obligation, from the facts of the Bible. He should remember that his business is not to set forth his system of truth (that is of no account), but to ascertain and exhibit what is God's system, which is a matter of the greatest moment. . . . It is plain that complete havoc will be made of the whole system of revealed truth, unless we consent to derive our philosophy from the Bible instead of explaining the Bible by our philosophy.... It would be easy to show that in every department of theology—in regard to the nature of God, His relation to the world, the plan of salvation, the person and work of Christ, the nature of sin, the operations of divine grace—men, instead of taking the facts of the Bible and seeing what principles they imply, what philosophy underlies them, have adopted their philosophy independently of the Bible, to which the facts of the Bible are made to bend. This is utterly unphilosophical. It is the fundamental principle of all sciences, and of theology among the rest, that theory is to be determined by facts and not facts by theory. As natural science was a chaos until the principle of induction was admitted and faithfully carried out, so theology is a jumble of human speculations, not worth a straw, when men refuse to apply the same principle to the study of the Word of God.

§6. The Scriptures Contain All the Facts of Theology

... All the truths taught by the constitution of our nature or by religious experience are recognized and authenticated in the Scriptures. This is a safeguard and a limit. We cannot assume this or that principle to be intuitively true, or this or that conclusion to be demonstrably certain, and make it a standard to which the Bible must conform. What is self-evidently true must be proved to be so, and is always recognized in the Bible as true. . . .

Believers have an unction from the Holy One: they know the truth. This inward teaching produces a conviction which no sophistries can obscure and no arguments can shake. It is founded on consciousness, and you might as well argue a man out of a belief in his existence as out of confidence that what he is thus taught of God is true. Two things, however, are to be borne in mind. First, that this inward teaching or demonstration of the Spirit is confined to truths objectively revealed in the Scriptures. It is given, says the apostle, in order that we may know things gratuitously given, i.e., revealed to us by God in His Word (1 Cor. 2:10–16). It is not, therefore, a revelation of new truths, but an illumination of the mind, so that it apprehends the truth, excellence, and glory of things already revealed. And second, this experience is depicted in the Word of God. The Bible not only gives us the facts concerning God, Christ, ourselves, and our relations to our Maker and Redeemer, but also records the legitimate effects of those truths on the minds of believers. So that we cannot appeal to our own feelings or inward experience as a ground or guide unless we can show that it agrees with the experience of holy men as recorded in the Scriptures.

Although the inward teaching of the Spirit, or religious experience, is no substitute for an external revelation and is no part of the rule of faith, it is, nevertheless, an invaluable guide in determining what the rule of faith teaches. The distinguishing feature of Augustinianism as taught by Augustine himself and by the purer theologians of the Latin Church throughout the Middle Ages, which was set forth by the Reformers and especially by Calvin and the Geneva divines, is that the inward teaching of the Spirit is allowed its proper place in determining our theology. The question is not first and mainly, What is true to the understanding, but what is true to the renewed heart? The effort is not to make the assertions of the Bible harmonize with the speculative reason, but to subject our feeble reason to the mind of God as revealed in His Word and by His Spirit in our inner life. . . . The true method in theology requires that the facts of religious experience be accepted as facts and, when duly authenticated by Scripture, be allowed to interpret the doctrinal statements of the Word of God. So legitimate and powerful is this inward teaching of the Spirit that it is no uncommon thing to find men having two theologies—one of the intellect and another of the heart. The one may find expression in creeds and systems of divinity, the other in their prayers and hymns. It would be safe for a man to resolve to admit into his theology nothing which is not sustained by the devotional writings of true Christians of every denomination. It would be easy to construct from such writings, received and sanctioned by Romanists, Lutherans, Reformed, and Remonstrants, a system of Pauline or Augustinian theology such as would satisfy any intelligent and devout Calvinist in the world.

The true method of theology is, therefore, the inductive, which assumes that the Bible contains all the facts or truths which form the contents of theology, just as the facts of nature are the contents of the natural sciences. It is also assumed that the relation of these Biblical facts to each other, the principles involved in them, the laws which determine them, are in the facts themselves, and are to be deduced from them, just as the laws of nature are deduced from the facts of nature. In neither case are the principles derived from the mind and imposed upon the facts, but equally in both departments the principles or laws are deduced from the facts and recognized by the mind.

Theology

§1. Its Nature

If the views presented in the preceding chapter be correct, the question, What is theology? is already answered. If natural science be concerned with the facts and laws of nature, theology is concerned with

33

the facts and the principles of the Bible. If the object of the one be to arrange and systematize the facts of the external world and to ascertain the laws by which they are determined, the object of the other is to systematize the facts of the Bible and ascertain the principles or general truths which those facts involve. And as the order in which the facts of nature are arranged cannot be determined arbitrarily, but by the nature of the facts themselves, so it is with the facts of the Bible. The parts of any organic whole have a natural relation which cannot with impunity be ignored or changed. The parts of a watch, or of any other piece of mechanism, must be normally arranged, or it will be in confusion and worthless. . . . So the facts of science arrange themselves. They are not arranged by the naturalist. His business is simply to ascertain what the arrangement given in the nature of the facts is. If he is mistaken, his system is false, and to a greater or lesser degree valueless. The same is obviously true with regard to the facts or truths of the Bible. They cannot be held in isolation, nor will they admit of any and every arrangement the theologian may choose to assign them. They bear a natural relation to each other, which cannot be overlooked or perverted without the facts themselves being perverted. If the facts of Scripture are what Augustinians believe them to be, then the Augustinian system is the only possible system of theology. If those facts be what Romanists or Remonstrants take them to be, then their system is the only true one. It is important that the theologian know his place. He is not master of the situation. He can no more construct a system of theology to suit his fancy than the astronomer can adjust the mechanism of the heavens according to his own good pleasure. As the facts of astronomy arrange themselves in a certain order and will admit of no other, so it is with the facts of theology. Theology, therefore, is the exhibition of the facts of Scripture in their proper order and relation, with the principles or general truths which pervade and harmonize the facts themselves. . . .

Sometimes the word theology is restricted to its etymological meaning, "a discourse concerning God." . . . The word is still used in this restricted sense when opposed to anthropology, soteriology, ecclesiology, as departments of theology in its wider sense. . . .

We have to restrict theology to its true sphere as the science of the facts of divine revelation so far as those facts concern the nature of God and our relation to Him as His creatures, as sinners, and as the subjects of redemption. All these facts, as just remarked, are in the Bible. But as some of them are also revealed by the work of God and by the nature of man, there is so far a distinction between natural theology and theology considered distinctively as a Christian science.

With regard to natural theology, there are two extreme opinions.

The one is that the works of nature make no trustworthy revelation of the being and perfections of God; the other, that such revelation is so clear and comprehensive as to preclude the necessity of any super-natural revelation.

§2. The Facts of Nature Reveal God

A. Objections to Natural Theology

Those who deny that natural theology teaches anything reliable concerning God commonly understand by nature the external, material universe. They pronounce the ontological and teleological argu-ments derived from the existence of the world, and from the evidences of design which it contains, to be unsatisfactory. . . . Besides, it is urged that religious truths do not admit of proof. They belong to the same category with aesthetic and moral truths. They are the objects of intuition. . . .

All this is sophistical. For the arguments in support of the truths of natural religion are not drawn exclusively from the external works of God. Those which are the most obvious and the most effective are derived from the constitution of our own nature. Man was made in the image of God, and he reveals his parentage as unmistakably as any class of inferior animals reveal the source from which they sprung. If a horse is born of a horse, the immortal spirit of man, instinct with its moral and religious convictions and aspirations, must be the off-spring of the Father of spirits. This is the argument which Paul on Mars' Hill addressed to the cavilling philosophers of Athens. . . .

The second objection to natural theology is that its arguments are inconclusive. This is a point which no man can decide for other men. Every one must judge for himself. An argument which is conclusive for one mind may be powerless for other minds. That the material universe began to be, that it has not the cause of its existence within itself and therefore must have had an extramundane cause, and that the infinitely numerous manifestations of design which it exhibits show that that cause must be intelligent, are arguments for the being of God which have satisfied the minds of the great body of intelligent men in all ages of the world. They should not, therefore, be dismissed as un-satisfactory simply because all men do not feel their force. Besides, as just remarked, these arguments are only confirmatory of others more direct and powerful derived from our moral and religious nature.

As to the objection that religious truths are the objects of intuition, and that intuitive truths neither need nor admit of proof, it may be answered that in one sense it is true. But self-evident truths may be illustrated, and it may be shown that their denial involves contradictions and absurdities. All geometry is an illustration of the axioms of Euclid; and if any man denies any of those axioms, it may be shown that he must believe impossibilities. In like manner, it may be admitted that the existence of a being on whom we are dependent, and to whom we are responsible, is a matter of intuition; and it may be acknowledged that it is self-evident that we can be responsible only to a person; and yet the existence of a personal God may be shown to be a necessary hypothesis to account for the facts of observation and consciousness, and that the denial of His existence leaves the problem of the universe unsolved and unsolvable. In other words, it may be shown that atheism, polytheism, and pantheism involve absolute impossibilities. This is a valid mode of proving that God is, although it be admitted that His existence after all is a self-evident truth. Theism is not the only self-evident truth that men are wont to deny.

B. Scriptural Argument for Natural Theology

The Scriptures clearly recognize the fact that the works of God reveal His being and attributes. This they do not only by frequent reference to the works of nature as manifestations of the perfections of God, but by direct assertions. "The heavens declare the glory of God; and the firmament showeth his handywork. Day unto day uttereth speech, and night unto night showeth knowledge. There is no speech nor language, where their voice is not heard. Their line is gone out through all the earth, and their words to the end of the world" (Ps. 19:1-4)....

The sacred writers in contending with the heathen appeal to the evidence which the works of God bear to His perfections: "Understand, ye brutish among the people: and ye fools, when will ye be wise? He that planted the ear, shall he not hear? He that formed the eye, shall he not see? He that chastiseth the heathen, shall not he correct? He that teacheth man knowledge, shall not he know?" (Ps. 94:8-10). Paul said to the men of Lystra, "Sirs, why do ye these things? We also are men of like passions with you, and preach unto you that ye should turn from these vanities unto the living God, which made heaven and earth, and the sea, and all things that are therein: Who in times past suffered all nations to walk in their own ways. Nevertheless he left not himself without witness, in that he did good, and gave us rain from heaven, and fruitful seasons, filling our hearts with food and gladness" (Acts 14:15-17; see also Acts 17:24-29)....

Not only the fact of this revelation, but its clearness is distinctly asserted by the apostle: "That which may be known of God is manifest in them; for God hath showed it unto them. For the invisible things of him from the creation of the world are clearly seen, being understood by the things that are made, even his eternal power and Godhead; so that they are without excuse: because that when they knew God, they glorified him not as God, neither were thankful" (Rom. 1:19–21). It cannot, therefore, be reasonably doubted that not only the being of God, but also His eternal power and Godhead, are so revealed in His works as to lay a stable foundation for natural theology. . . .

§3. Insufficiency of Natural Theology

The second extreme opinion respecting natural theology is that it precludes the necessity of a supernatural revelation. The question whether the knowledge of God derived from His works be sufficient to lead fallen men to salvation is answered affirmatively by rationalists, but negatively by every historical branch of the Christian Church. . . .

The question as to the sufficiency of natural theology, or of the truths of reason, is to be answered on the authority of the Scriptures. No man can tell *a priori* what is necessary to salvation. Indeed, it is only by supernatural revelation that we know that any sinner can be saved. It is from the same source alone that we can know what are the conditions of salvation or who are to be its subjects.

A. *What the Scriptures Teach as to the Salvation of Men*

1. Salvation of infants

One of Scripture's teachings on the subject of salvation, according to the common doctrine of evangelical Protestants, is that all who die in infancy are saved. This is inferred from what the Bible teaches of the analogy between Adam and Christ. "As by the offence of one judgment came upon all men to condemnation; even so by the righteousness of one the free gift came upon all men unto justification of life. For as by one man's disobedience many were made sinners, so by the obedience of one shall many be made righteous" (Rom. 5:18–19). We have no right to put any limit on these general terms, except what the Bible itself places upon them. The Scriptures nowhere exclude any class of infants, baptized or unbaptized, born in Christian or in heathen lands, of believing or unbelieving parents, from the benefits of the redemption of Christ. All the descendants of Adam, except Christ, are under condemnation; all the descendants of Adam, except those of whom it is expressly revealed that they cannot inherit the kingdom of

God, are saved. This appears to be the clear meaning of the apostle, and therefore he does not hesitate to say that where sin abounded, grace has much more abounded; that the benefits of redemption far exceed the evils of the fall; that the number of the saved far exceeds the number of the lost.

This is not inconsistent with the declaration of our Lord, in Matthew 7:14, that only a few enter the gate which leadeth unto life. This is to be understood of adults. What the Bible says is intended for those in all ages to whom it is addressed. But it is addressed to those who can either read or hear. It tells them what they are to believe and do. It would be an entire perversion of its meaning to make it apply to those to whom and of whom it does not speak. When it is said, "He that believeth not the Son shall not see life; but the wrath of God abideth on him" (John 3:36), no one understands this to preclude the possibility of the salvation of infants. . . .

2. Rule of judgment for adults

Another general fact clearly revealed in Scripture is that men are to be judged according to their works and according to the light which they have severally enjoyed. God "will render to every man according to his deeds: to them who by patient continuance in well doing seek for glory and honour and immortality, eternal life; but unto them that are contentious, and do not obey the truth, but obey unrighteousness, indignation and wrath, tribulation and anguish, upon every soul of man that doeth evil, of the Jew first, and also of the Gentile; but glory, honour, and peace to every man that worketh good, to the Jew first, and also to the Gentile: for there is no respect of persons with God. For as many as have sinned without law shall also perish without law, and as many as have sinned in the law shall be judged by the law" (Rom. 2:6–12). Our Lord teaches that those who sinned with a knowledge of God's will shall be beaten with many stripes, and that those who sinned without such knowledge shall be beaten with few stripes, and that it will be more tolerable in the day of judgment for the heathen, even for Sodom and Gomorrah, than for those who perish under the light of the gospel (Matt. 10:15; 11:20–24). The Judge of all the earth will do right. No human being will suffer more than he deserves, or more than his own conscience shall recognize as just.

3. All men under condemnation

But the Bible tells us that, judged according to their works and according to the light which they have severally enjoyed, all men will be condemned. There is none righteous; no, not one. The whole world is guilty before God. This verdict is confirmed by every man's conscience. The consciousness of guilt and of moral pollution is absolutely universal.

Here it is that natural theology utterly fails. It cannot answer the question, How can man be just with God? or, How can God be just and yet justify the ungodly? Mankind have anxiously pondered this question for ages, and have gained no satisfaction. . . . Reason, conscience, tradition, history, unite in saying that sin is death; and, therefore, that so far as human wisdom and resources are concerned, the salvation of sinners is as impossible as raising the dead. Every conceivable method of expiation and purification has been tried without success.

The Scriptures, therefore, teach that the heathen are "without Christ, being aliens from the commonwealth of Israel, and strangers from the covenants of promise, having no hope, and without God" (Eph. 2:12). They are declared to be without excuse, "because that, when they knew God, they glorified him not as God, neither were thankful; but became vain in their imaginations, and their foolish heart was darkened. Professing themselves to be wise, they became fools, and changed the glory of the uncorruptible God into an image made like to corruptible man, and to birds, and fourfooted beasts, and creeping things. Wherefore God also gave them up to uncleanness, through the lusts of their own hearts, to dishonour their own bodies between themselves: who changed the truth of God into a lie, and worshipped and served the creature more than the Creator, who is blessed for ever" (Rom. 1:21–25). . . .

All men being sinners, justly chargeable with inexcusable impiety and immorality, they cannot be saved by any effort or resource of their own. For we are told that "the unrighteous shall not inherit the kingdom of God. Be not deceived; neither fornicators, nor idolaters, nor adulterers, nor effeminate, nor abusers of themselves with mankind, nor thieves, nor covetous, nor drunkards, nor revilers, nor extortioners, shall inherit the kingdom of God" (1 Cor. 6:9–10). "For this ye know, that no whoremonger, nor unclean person, nor covetous man, who is an idolater, hath any inheritance in the kingdom of Christ and of God" (Eph. 5:5). More than this, the Bible teaches us that a man may be outwardly righteous in the sight of men and yet be a whitened sepulchre, his heart being the seat of pride, envy, or malice. In other words, he may be moral in his conduct yet, by reason of inward evil passions, be in the sight of God the chief of sinners, as was the case with Paul himself. To go a step further, even freedom from outward sins and, were it possible, from the sins of the heart (what we might characterize as negative goodness) would not suffice. For without holiness "no man shall see the Lord" (Heb. 12:14). "Except a man be born

again, he cannot see the kingdom of God" (John 3:3). "He that loveth
not knoweth not God" (1 John 4:8; see also 1 John 2:15; Matt. 10:37).
Who then can be saved? If the Bible excludes from the kingdom of
heaven all the immoral; all whose hearts are corrupted by pride, envy,
malice, or covetousness; all who love the world; all who are not holy;
all in whom the love of God is not the supreme and controlling principle of action, it is evident that, so far as adults are concerned, salvation must be confined to very narrow limits. It is also evident that
mere natural religion, the mere objective power of general religious
truth, must be as inefficacious in preparing men for the presence of
God as were the waters of Syria to heal Naaman's leprosy.

4. The necessary conditions of salvation

Seeing then that the world by wisdom knows not God, seeing that
men when left to themselves inevitably die in their sins, it has "pleased
God by the foolishness of preaching to save them that believe" (1 Cor.
1:21). God has sent His Son into the world to save sinners. Had any
other method of salvation been possible, Christ is dead in vain (Gal.
2:21; 3:21). There is, therefore, no other name whereby men can be
saved (Acts 4:12). The knowledge of Christ and faith in Him are declared to be essential to salvation. This is proved: (1) Because men are
declared to be guilty before God. (2) Because no man can expiate his
own guilt and restore himself to the image of God. (3) Because it is
expressly declared that Christ is the only Saviour of men. (4) Because
Christ gave His Church the commission to preach the gospel to every
creature under heaven, as the appointed means of salvation. (5) Because the apostles in the execution of this commission went everywhere preaching the Word, testifying to all men, Jews and Gentiles,
to the wise and the unwise, that they must believe in Christ as the Son
of God in order to be saved. Our Lord Himself teaching through His
forerunner said, "He that believeth on the Son hath everlasting life:
and he that believeth not the Son shall not see life; but the wrath of
God abideth on him" (John 3:36). (6) Because faith without knowledge
is declared to be impossible. "Whosoever shall call upon the name of
the Lord shall be saved. How then shall they call on him in whom
they have not believed? and how shall they believe in him of whom
they have not heard? and how shall they hear without a preacher?
and how shall they preach, except they be sent?" (Rom. 10:13–15).

It is, therefore, as before stated, the common faith of the Christian
world that, so far as adults are concerned, there is no salvation without
the knowledge of Christ and faith in Him. This has ever been regarded
as the ground of the obligation which rests upon the Church to preach
the gospel to every creature.

B. *Responses to the Objection to the Scriptural Doctrine*

To the objection that this doctrine is inconsistent with the goodness and justice of God, it may be answered (1) that the doctrine assumes only what the objector, if a theist, must admit, namely, that God will deal with men according to their character and conduct, and that He will judge them according to the light which they have severally enjoyed. It is because the Judge of all the earth must do right that all sinners receive the wages of sin, by an inexorable law, unless saved by the miracle of redemption. In teaching, therefore, that there is no salvation for those ignorant of the gospel, the Bible teaches only that a just God will punish sin. (2) The doctrine of the Church on this subject does not go beyond the facts of the case. It teaches only that God will do what we see He actually does. He leaves mankind, in a large measure, to themselves. He allows them to make themselves sinful and miserable. It is no more difficult to reconcile the doctrine than the undeniable fact with the goodness of our God. (3) In the gift of His Son, the revelation of His Word, the mission of the Spirit, and the institution of the Church, God has made abundant provision for the salvation of the world. That the Church has been so remiss in making known the gospel is her guilt. We must not charge the ignorance and consequent perdition of the heathen upon God. The guilt rests on us. We have kept to ourselves the bread of life and allowed the nations to perish. . . .

Some, admitting the insufficiency of the light of nature, hold that God gives sufficient grace, or an inward supernatural light, which, if properly cherished and followed, will lead men to salvation. But this is merely an amiable hypothesis. For such universal and sufficient grace there is no promise in the Scripture and no evidence in experience. Besides, if admitted it does not help the matter. If this sufficient grace does not actually save, if it does not deliver the heathen from those sins upon which the judgment of God is pronounced, it only aggravates their condemnation. All we can do is to adhere closely to the teachings of the Bible, assured that the Judge of all the earth will do right, that although clouds and darkness are round about Him, and His ways past finding out, justice and judgment are the habitation of His throne.

§4. **Christian Theology**

As science, concerned with the facts of nature, has its several departments (mathematics, chemistry, astronomy, etc.), so theology, having the facts of Scripture for its subject, has its distinct and natural departments.

A. *Theology Proper*

Theology proper includes all the Bible teaches of the being and attributes of God; the threefold personality of the Godhead, or that the Father, Son, and Spirit are distinct persons, the same in substance and equal in power and glory; the relation of God to the world, or His decrees and His works of creation and providence.

B. *Anthropology*

Anthropology includes the origin and nature of man; his original state and probation; his fall; the nature of sin; the effect of Adam's first sin upon himself and upon his posterity.

C. *Soteriology*

Soteriology includes the purpose or plan of God in reference to the salvation of man; the person and work of the Redeemer; the application of the redemption of Christ to the people of God in their regeneration, justification, and sanctification; and the means of grace.

D. *Eschatology*

Eschatology is the doctrines which concern the state of the soul after death; the resurrection; the second advent of Christ; the general judgment and end of the world; heaven and hell.

E. *Ecclesiology*

Ecclesiology includes the idea or nature of the Church; its attributes; its prerogatives; its organization. . . .

The above classification, although convenient and generally received, is far from being exhaustive. It leaves out of view the law (or at least subordinates it unduly), or rule of moral duty. This is a department in itself, and under the title of moral theology is sometimes, as in the Latin Church, regarded as the most important. Among Protestants it is often regarded as a mere department of philosophy.

It has been assumed that theology has to do with the facts or truths of the Bible; in other words, that the Scriptures of the Old and New

Testaments are the only infallible rule of faith and practice. This, however, is not a conceded point. Some claim for reason a paramount or at least a coordinate authority in matters of religion. Others assume an internal supernatural light to which they attribute paramount or coordinate authority. Others rely on the authority of an infallible Church. With Protestants, the Bible is the only infallible source of knowledge of divine things. It is necessary, therefore, before entering on our work, briefly to examine these systems.

Rationalism

§1. Meaning and Usage of the Word

By rationalism is meant the system or theory which assigns undue authority to reason in matters of religion. . . . The word reason is here taken in its ordinary sense for the cognitive faculty, that which perceives, compares, judges, and infers.

Rationalism has appeared under different forms. (1) Deistical rationalism denies either the possibility or the fact of any supernatural revelation, and maintains that reason is both the source and ground of all religious knowledge and conviction. (2) Another form of rationalism admits the possibility and the fact of a supernatural revelation, and that such a revelation is contained in the Christian Scriptures, but nevertheless maintains that the truths revealed are the truths of reason; that is, truths which reason can comprehend and demonstrate. (3) The third form of rationalism has received the name of dogmatism, which admits that many of the truths of revelation are undiscoverable by human reason, and that they are to be received upon authority. Nevertheless, it maintains that those truths when revealed admit of being philosophically explained and established, and raised from the sphere of faith into that of knowledge. . . .

§2. Deistical Rationalism

A. Possibility of a Supernatural Revelation

The first point to be determined in the controversy with the deistical rationalists concerns the possibility of a supernatural revelation. This they commonly deny on either philosophical or moral grounds. It is said to be inconsistent with the nature of God, and with His relation to the world, to suppose that He interferes by His direct agency in the course of events. The true theory of the universe, according to their doctrine, is that God, having created the world and endowed His creatures with their attributes and properties, has done all that is consistent with His nature. He does not interfere by His immediate agency in the production of effects. These belong to the efficiency of second causes. Or if the metaphysical possibility of such intervention be admitted, it is nevertheless morally impossible because it would imply imperfection in God. If His work needs His constant interference, it must be imperfect, and if imperfect, it must be that God is deficient in either wisdom or power.

That this is a wrong theory of God's relation to the world is manifest. (1) It contradicts the testimony of our moral nature. The relation in which we stand to God, as that relation reveals itself in our consciousness, implies that we are constantly in the presence of a God who takes cognizance of our acts, orders our circumstances, and interferes for our correction or protection. He is not to us a God afar off with whom we have no immediate concern, but a God who is not far from any one of us, in whom we live, move, and have our being, who numbers the hairs of our head, and without whose notice a sparrow does not fall to the ground. (2) Reason itself teaches that the conception of God as a ruler of the world, having His creatures in His hands, able to control them at pleasure and to hold communion with them, is a far higher conception and more consistent with the idea of infinite perfection than is that on which this system of rationalism is founded. (3) The common consciousness of men is opposed to this doctrine, as is plain from the fact that all nations, the most cultivated and the most barbarous, have been forced to conceive of God as a Being able to take cognizance of human affairs and to reveal Himself to His creatures. (4) The argument from Scripture, although not admitted by rationalists, is for Christians conclusive. The Bible reveals a God who is constantly and everywhere present with His works, and who acts upon them not only mediately, but immediately, when, where, and how He sees fit.

B. Necessity of a Supernatural Revelation

Admitting, however, the metaphysical possibility of a supernatural revelation, the next question is whether such a revelation is necessary. There are a number of indications that this question must be answered in the affirmative: (1) Every man feels that he needs a supernatural revelation. He knows that there are questions concerning the origin, nature, and destiny of man, as well as concerning sin and the method by which it can be pardoned and conquered, which he cannot answer. They are questions, however, which must be answered. So long as these problems are unsolved, no man can be either good or happy. (2) He is equally certain that no man answers these questions for his fellow men. Every one sees intuitively that they relate to matters beyond the reach of human reason. What can reason decide as to the fate of the soul after death? Can he who has been unable to make himself holy or happy here, secure his own well-being in the eternal future? . . . (3) Even if philosophers could solve these great problems to their own satisfaction, what is to become of the mass of mankind? Are they to be left in darkness and despair? (4) The experience of ages proves that the world by wisdom knows not God. The heathen nations, ancient and modern, civilized and savage, have without exception failed by the light of nature to solve any of the great problems of humanity. This is the testimony of history as well as of Scripture. (5) Even where the light of revelation is enjoyed, it is found that those who reject its guidance are led not only to the most contradictory conclusions, but to the adoption of principles, in most cases, destructive of domestic virtue, social order, and individual worth and happiness. The reason of man has led the great body of those who know no other guide, into what has been well called "The Hell of Pantheism."

C. The Scriptures Contain Such a Revelation

But even if we grant the possibility and the necessity of a supernatural revelation, has such a revelation been actually made? This the deistical rationalist denies and the Christian affirms. He confidently refers to the Bible as containing such a revelation and maintains that its claims are authenticated by an amount of evidence which renders unbelief unreasonable and criminal.

(1) In the first place, its authors claim to be the messengers of God, to speak by His authority and in His name, so that what they teach is to be received not on the authority of the writers themselves, nor on the ground of the inherent evidence in the nature of the truths communicated, but on the authority of God. It is He who affirms what the sacred writers teach. This claim must be admitted, or the sacred writers must be regarded as fanatics or impostors. It is absolutely certain that they were neither. To pronounce Homer and Newton idiots would be no more irrational than to set down Isaiah and Paul as either impostors or fanatics. It is as certain as any self-evident truth that they were wise, good, sober-minded men. That such men would falsely claim to be the authoritative messengers of God and to be endowed with supernatural powers in confirmation of their mission is a contradiction.

(2) The Bible contains nothing inconsistent with the claim of its authors to divine authority as teachers. It contains nothing impossible, nothing absurd, nothing immoral, nothing inconsistent with any well-authenticated truth. This itself is well-nigh miraculous, considering the circumstances under which the different portions of the Scriptures were written.

(3) More than this, the Bible reveals truths of the highest order, not elsewhere made known—truths which meet the most urgent necessities of our nature, which solve the problems which reason has never been able to solve. . . . These truths are as essential to the soul as is

the atmosphere to our lungs, or the sun to the earth on which we live. . . .

(4) The several books of which the Scriptures are composed were written by many different authors living in the course of fifteen hundred years, and yet they are found to be an organic whole, the product of one mind. They are as clearly a development as the oak from the acorn. The Gospels and Epistles are but the expansion, fulfilment, the culmination of the protevangelium ("The seed of the woman shall bruise the serpent's head") as uttered to our first parents (Gen. 3:15). All that intervenes is to the New Testament what the roots, stem, branches, and foliage of the tree are to the fruit. No one book of Scripture can be understood by itself, any more than any one part of a tree or member of the body can be understood without reference to the whole of which it is a part. . . .

(5) God bears witness to the divine authority of the Scriptures by signs and wonders, divers miracles, and gifts of the Holy Ghost. The leading events recorded in the New Testament were predicted in the Old. Of this any man may satisfy himself by a comparison of the two. The coincidence between the prophecies and the fulfilment admits of no rational solution except that the Bible is the work of God, or that holy men of old spake as they were moved by the Holy Ghost. The miracles recorded in the Scriptures are historical events which are not only entitled to be received on the same testimony which authenticates other facts of history, but are so implicated with the whole structure of the New Testament that they cannot be denied without rejecting the whole gospel, which rejection involves the denial of the best-authenticated facts in the history of the world.

Besides this external supernatural testimony, the Bible is everywhere attended by "the demonstration of the Spirit," which gives to its doctrines the clearness of self-evident truths and the authority of the voice of God, which is analogous to the authority of the moral law for the natural conscience.

(6) The Bible ever has been and still is a power in the world. It has determined the course of history. It has overthrown false religion wherever it is known. It is the parent of modern civilization. It is the only guarantee of social order, of virtue, and of human rights and liberty. Its effects cannot be rationally accounted for upon any other hypothesis than that it is what it claims to be, "the Word of God."

(7) It makes known the person, work, the acts, and words of Christ, who is the clearest revelation of God ever made to man. He is the manifested God. His words were the words of God. His acts were the acts of God. . . .

§3. The Second Form of Rationalism

A. Its Nature

The more common form of rationalism admits that the Scriptures contain a supernatural revelation. It teaches, however, that the object of that revelation is to make more generally known and to authenticate for the masses the truths of reason (or doctrines of natural religion). These doctrines are received by cultivated minds not on the ground of authority, but of rational evidence. The fundamental principle of this class of rationalists is that nothing can be rationally believed which is not understood. . . . The rationalist does not feel bound to believe all that the sacred writers teach. The Bible, he admits, contains a divine revelation. But this revelation was made to fallible men, men under no supernatural guidance in communicating the truths revealed. They were men whose mode of thinking and manner of arguing and of presenting truth were modified by their culture and by the modes of thought prevailing during the age in which they lived. The Scriptures, therefore, abound with misapprehensions, inconclusive arguments, and accommodations to Jewish errors, superstitions, and popular beliefs. It is the office of reason to sift these incongruous materials and separate the wheat from the chaff. . . .

B. Refutation

(1) This form of rationalism is founded upon a false principle. It is not necessary to the rational exercise of faith that we should understand the truth believed. The unknown and the impossible cannot be believed, but every man does and must believe the incomprehensible. Assent to truth is founded on evidence. That evidence may be external or intrinsic. Some things we believe on the testimony of our senses; other things we believe on the testimony of men. Why, then, may we not believe on the testimony of God? A man may believe that paper thrown upon fire will burn, although he does not understand the process of combustion. All men believe that plants grow and that like begets like, but no man understands the mystery of reproduction. . . . If, therefore, the incomprehensible must be believed in every other department of knowledge, no rational ground can be given why it should be banished from religion.

(2) Rationalism assumes that the human intelligence is the measure of all truth. This is an insane presumption on the part of such a creature as man. If, on the testimony of a parent, a child believes with

implicit confidence what it cannot understand, surely, on the testimony of God, man may believe what he cannot understand.

(3) Rationalism destroys the distinction between faith and knowledge, which all men and all ages admit. Faith is assent to truth founded on testimony. Knowledge is assent founded on the direct or indirect apprehension of its object. If there can be no rational faith, if we are to receive as true only what we know and understand, the whole world is beggared. It loses all that sustains, beautifies, and ennobles life.

(4) ... If we must understand what we believe, ... only philosophers can be religious. They alone can comprehend the rational grounds on which the great truths of even natural religion are to be received. Widespread, therefore, as has been the influence of a rationalistic spirit, it has never taken hold of the people; it has never controlled the creed of any church, because all religion is founded on the incomprehensible and the infinite.

(5) The protest which our religious nature makes against the narrow, cold, and barren system of rationalism is a sufficient proof that it cannot be true, because it cannot meet our most urgent necessities. . . .

(6) Faith implies knowledge. And if we must understand in order to know, faith and knowledge become alike impossible. The principle, therefore, on which rationalism is founded leads to nihilism or universal negation. . . .

§4. Dogmatism, or the Third Form of Rationalism

A. Meaning of the Term

It was a common objection made in the early age of the Church against Christianity, by the philosophical Greeks, that its doctrines were received upon authority, and not upon rational evidence. Many of the fathers, especially those of the Alexandrian school, answered that this was true only of the common people. They could not be expected to understand philosophy. They could receive the high spiritual truths of religion only on the ground of authority. But the educated classes were able and were bound to search after the philosophical or rational evidence of the doctrines taught in the Bible, and to receive those doctrines on the ground of that evidence. They made a distinction, therefore, between faith and knowledge. The former is for the common people, the latter for the cultivated. The objects of faith are the doctrinal statements of the Bible in the form in which they are there presented. The ground of faith is simply the testimony of the Scriptures as the Word of God. The objects of knowledge are the speculative or philosophical ideas which underlie the doctrines of the Bible, and the ground on which those ideas or truths are received and incorporated in our system of knowledge is their own inherent evidence. They are seen to be true by the light of reason. Faith is thus elevated into knowledge, and Christianity exalted into a philosophy. . . .

B. Refutation

(1) Dogmatism is essentially rationalistic. The rationalist demands philosophical proof of the doctrines which he receives. He is not willing to believe on the simple authority of Scripture. He requires his reason to be satisfied by a demonstration of the truth independent of the Bible. This demand the dogmatist admits to be reasonable, and he undertakes to furnish the required proof. . . .

(2) In thus shifting faith from the foundation of divine testimony and making it rest on rational demonstration, it is removed from the Rock of Ages to a quicksand. There is as much difference between a conviction founded on the well-authenticated testimony of God and a conviction founded on so-called philosophical demonstration as there is between God and man, the divine and the human. Let any man read the pretended philosophical demonstrations of the Trinity, the incarnation, the resurrection of the body, or any other of the great truths of the Bible, and he will feel at liberty to receive or reject it at pleasure. Such demonstrations have no authority or certainty. They are products of a mind like his own and therefore can have no more power than belongs to the fallible human intellect.

(3) . . . In transmuting Christianity into a philosophy, its whole nature is changed and its power is lost. It takes its place as one of the numberless phases of human speculation which in the history of human thought succeed each other as the waves of the sea—no one ever abides.

(4) It proceeds on an essentially false principle. It assumes the competency of reason to judge of things entirely beyond its sphere. God has so constituted our nature that we are authorized and necessitated to confide in the well-authenticated testimony of our senses within their appropriate sphere. And in like manner, we are constrained to confide in the operation of our minds and in the conclusions to which they lead within the sphere which God has assigned to human reason. But the senses cannot sit in judgment on rational truths. We cannot study logic with the microscope or scalpel. It is no less irrational to depend upon reason or demand rational or philosophical demonstration for truths which become the objects of knowledge only as they are revealed. From the nature of the case the truths concerning crea-

tion, the probation and apostasy of man, the purpose and plan of redemption, the person of Christ, the state of the soul in the future world, the relation of God to His creatures, etc., since they depend not on general principles of reason, but in great measure on the purposes of an intelligent, personal Being, can be known only so far as He chooses to reveal them, and must be received simply on His authority.

(5) The testimony of the Scriptures is decisive on this subject. From the beginning to the end of the Bible the sacred writers present themselves in the character of witnesses. They demand faith in their teachings and obedience to their commands not on the ground of their own superiority in wisdom or excellence, not on the ground of rational demonstration of the truth of what they teach, but simply as the organs of God, as men appointed by Him to reveal His will. Their first and last and sufficient reason for faith is, "Thus saith the Lord." . . . Such being the nature of the gospel, if received at all it must be received on authority. It is to be believed or taken on trust, not demonstrated as a philosophical system. Nay, the Bible goes still further. It teaches that a man must become a fool in order to be wise; he must renounce dependence upon his own reason or wisdom in order to receive the wisdom of God. Our Lord told His disciples that unless they were converted and became as little children, they could not enter into the kingdom of God (Matt. 18:3). And the apostle Paul when writing to those imbued with Greek philosophy (e.g., the Corinthians) made it the indispensable condition of their becoming Christians that they renounce philosophy as a guide in matters of religion and receive the gospel on the testimony of God. Nothing, therefore, can be more opposed to the whole teaching and spirit of the Bible than this disposition to insist on philosophical proof of the articles of our faith. Our duty, privilege, and security are in believing, not in knowing; in trusting God and not our own understanding. They are to be pitied who have no more trustworthy teacher than themselves.

(6) The instructions of the Bible on this subject are abundantly confirmed by the lessons of experience. From the time of the Gnostics and of the Platonizing fathers, the attempt has been made in every age to exalt faith into knowledge, to transmute Christianity into philosophy, by demonstrating its doctrines on the principles of reason. These attempts have always failed. . . .

The natural tendency and the actual consequences of the indulgence of a disposition to demand philosophical demonstration for articles of faith are a state of mind which revolts at authority and refuses to admit as true what it cannot comprehend and prove. And this state of mind, as it is incompatible with faith, is the parent of unbelief and of all its consequences. There is no safety for us, therefore, but to remain within the limits which God has assigned us. Let us rely on our senses within the sphere of our sense perceptions, on our reason within the sphere of rational truths, and on God, and God alone, in all that relates to the things of God. Only he who consents with the docility of a child to be taught of God truly knows.

§5. Proper Office of Reason in Matters of Religion

A. *Reason Necessary for the Reception of a Revelation*

Christians, in repudiating rationalism in all its forms, do not reject the service of reason in matters of religion. They acknowledge its high prerogatives and the responsibility involved in their exercise.

In the first place, reason is necessarily presupposed in every revelation. Revelation is the communication of truth to the mind. But the communication of truth supposes the capacity to receive it. Revelations cannot be made to brutes or idiots. Truths, to be received as objects of faith, must be intellectually apprehended. A proposition to which we attach no meaning, however important the truth it may contain, cannot be an object of faith. If it be affirmed that the soul is immortal, or God is a Spirit, unless we know the meaning of the words nothing is communicated to the mind, and the mind can affirm or deny nothing on the subject. In other words, knowledge is essential to faith. . . . The first and indispensable office of reason, therefore, in matters of faith, is the cognition or intelligent apprehension of the truths proposed for our reception. . . .

It is important, however, to bear in mind the difference between knowing and understanding (or comprehending). A child knows what the words "God is a Spirit" mean, but no created being can comprehend the Almighty unto perfection. We must know the plan of salvation, but no one can comprehend its mysteries. This distinction is recognized in every department. Men know unspeakably more than they understand. We know that plants grow, that the will controls our voluntary muscles, that Jesus Christ is God and man in two distinct natures and one person forever; but here as everywhere we are surrounded by the incomprehensible. We can rationally believe that a thing is, without knowing how or why it is. It is enough for the true dignity of man as a rational creature that he is not called upon by his Creator to believe without knowledge, to receive as true propositions which convey no meaning to the mind. This would be not only irrational, but impossible.

B. Reason Must Judge of the Credibility of a Revelation

In the second place, it is the prerogative of reason to judge of the credibility of a revelation. . . . Nothing is incredible but the impossible. . . . A thing may be strange, unaccountable, unintelligible, and yet perfectly credible. . . .

1. The impossible cannot be believed

. . . Christians concede to reason the prerogative of deciding whether a thing is possible or impossible. If it is seen to be impossible, no authority and no amount or kind of evidence can impose the obligation to receive it as true. Whether or not a thing be possible, however, is not to be arbitrarily determined. Men are prone to pronounce everything impossible which contradicts their settled convictions, their preconceptions or prejudices, or which is repugnant to their feelings. Men in former times did not hesitate to say that it is impossible that the earth should turn round on its axis and move through space with incredible rapidity and yet we not perceive it. It was pronounced absolutely impossible that information should be transmitted thousands of miles in the fraction of a second. . . . It is no less unreasonable for men to reject the truths of revelation on the assumption that they involve the impossible when they merely contradict our previous convictions or when we cannot see how they can be. Men say that it is impossible that the same person can be both God and man, and yet they admit that man is at once material and immaterial, mortal and immortal, angel and animal. The impossible cannot be true, but reason in pronouncing a thing impossible must act rationally and not capriciously. Its judgments must be guided by principles which commend themselves to the common consciousness of men.

2. What is impossible

(1) That is impossible which involves a contradiction, as that a thing is and is not, or that right is wrong and wrong is right. (2) It is impossible that God should do, approve, or command what is morally wrong. (3) It is impossible that He should require us to believe what contradicts any of the laws of belief which He has impressed upon our nature. (4) It is impossible that one truth should contradict another. It is impossible, therefore, that God should reveal anything as true which contradicts any well-authenticated truth, whether of intuition, experience, or previous revelation.

3. Proof of this prerogative of reason

That reason has this prerogative is plain, in the first place, from the very nature of the case. Faith includes an affirmation of the mind that a thing is true. But it is a contradiction to say that the mind can affirm that to be true which it sees cannot by possibility be true. This would be to affirm and deny, to believe and disbelieve, at the same time. From the very constitution of our nature, therefore, we are forbidden to believe the impossible. We are consequently required to pronounce anathema any one, even an apostle or an angel from heaven, who calls upon us to receive as a revelation from God anything absurd, or wicked, or inconsistent with the intellectual or moral nature with which He has endowed us (Gal. 1:8). . . . As it is impossible that God should contradict Himself, so it is impossible that He should, by an external revelation, declare that to be true which by the laws of our nature He has rendered it impossible we should believe.

This prerogative of reason is constantly recognized in Scripture. . . . Moses taught that nothing was to be believed, no matter what amount of external evidence should be adduced in its support, which contradicted a previous, duly authenticated revelation from God. Paul does the same thing when he calls upon us to pronounce accursed even an angel who should teach another gospel. Recognizing the paramount authority of the intuitive judgments of the mind, he says that the damnation of any man is just who calls upon us to believe that right is wrong, or that men should do evil that good may come.

The ultimate ground of faith and knowledge is confidence in God. We can neither believe nor know anything unless we confide in those laws of belief which God has implanted in our nature. If we can be required to believe what contradicts those laws, then the foundations are broken up. All distinction between truth and falsehood, between right and wrong, would disappear. All our ideas of God and virtue would be confounded, and we would become the victims of every adroit deceiver, or minister of Satan, who, by lying wonders, calls upon us to believe a lie. We are to try the spirits. But how can we try them without a standard? And what other standard can there be, except the laws of our nature and the authenticated revelations of God?

C. Reason Must Judge of the Evidences of a Revelation

(1) As faith involves assent, and assent is conviction produced by evidence, it follows that faith without evidence is either irrational or impossible.

(2) This evidence must be appropriate to the nature of the truth believed. Historical truth requires historical evidence; empirical truths the testimony of experience; mathematical truth, mathematical evidence; moral truth, moral evidence; and "the things of the Spirit," the demonstration of the Spirit. . . .

(3) Evidence must be not only appropriate, but adequate. That is, such as to command assent in every well-constituted mind to which it is presented.

As we cannot believe without evidence, and as that evidence must be appropriate and adequate, it is clearly a prerogative of reason to judge of these several points. This is plain, first, from the nature of faith, which is not a blind, irrational assent, but an intelligent reception of truth on adequate grounds.

Second, the Scriptures never demand faith except on the ground of adequate evidence. "If I had not done among them," says our Lord, "the works which none other man did, they had not had sin" (John 15:24), clearly recognizing the principle that faith cannot be required without evidence. The apostle Paul proves that the heathen are justly liable to condemnation for their idolatry and immorality, because such a revelation of the true God and of the moral law has been made to them as to leave them without excuse.

Third, the Bible regards unbelief as sin, and the great sin for which men will be condemned at the bar of God. This presumes that unbelief cannot arise from the want of appropriate and adequate evidence, but is to be referred to the wicked rejection of the truth notwithstanding the proof by which it is attended. . . . The fact that unbelief is a great sin, and the special ground of the condemnation of men, of necessity supposes that it is inexcusable, that it does not arise from ignorance or want of evidence. "How shall they believe," asks the apostle, "in him of whom they have not heard?" (Rom. 10:14). And our Lord says, "This is the condemnation, that light is come into the world, and men loved darkness rather than light, because their deeds were evil" (John 3:19).

Fourth, another indication that the Scriptures recognize the necessity of evidence in order to come to faith, and the right of those to whom a revelation is addressed to judge of that evidence, is found in the frequent command to consider, to examine, to try the spirits, i.e., those who claim to be the organs of the Spirit of God. The duty of judging is enjoined, and the standard of judgment is given. And then men are held responsible for their decision.

Christians, therefore, concede to reason all the prerogatives it can rightfully claim. God requires nothing irrational of His rational creatures. He does not require faith without knowledge, or faith in the impossible, or faith without evidence. Christianity is equally opposed to superstition and rationalism. The one is faith without appropriate evidence; the other refuses to believe what it does not understand, in despite of evidence which should command belief. The Christian, conscious of his imbecility as a creature and his ignorance and blindness as a sinner, places himself before God, in the posture of a child, and receives as true everything which a God of infinite intelligence and goodness declares to be worthy of confidence. And in thus submitting to be taught, he acts on the highest principles of reason.

§6. Relation of Philosophy and Revelation

. . . Whether we take the word philosophy to mean the knowledge of God and nature attained by reason, or the principles which should guide all efforts for the attainment of knowledge, the word is intended to cover the whole domain of human intelligence. Popularly, we distinguish between philosophy and science, the former having for its sphere the spiritual, and the latter having the material. Commonly, philosophy is understood as comprising both departments. . . . Such being the compass of the domain which philosophers claim as their own, the proper relation between philosophy and theology becomes a question of vital importance. This is, indeed, the great question at issue in the rationalistic controversy; and therefore, at the conclusion of this chapter, all that remains to be done is to give a concise statement of familiar principles.

A. Philosophy and Theology Occupy Common Ground

Philosophy and theology occupy common ground. Both assume to teach what is true concerning God, man, the world, and the relation in which God stands to His creatures. While their objects are so far identical, both striving to attain a knowledge of the same truths, their methods are essentially different. Philosophy seeks to attain knowledge by speculation and induction, or by the exercise of our own intellectual faculties. Theology relies upon authority, receiving as truth whatever God in His Word has revealed. . . . God is the author of our nature and the maker of heaven and earth; therefore, nothing which the laws of our nature or the facts of the external world prove to be true can contradict the teaching of God's Word. Neither can the Scriptures contradict the truths of philosophy or science.

B. Philosophers and Theologians Should Strive After Unity

As these two great sources of knowledge must be consistent in their valid teachings, it is the duty of all parties to endeavor to exhibit that consistency. Philosophers should not ignore the teachings of the Bible, and theologians should not ignore the teachings of science. Much less should either class needlessly come into collision with the other. It is unreasonable and irreligious for philosophers to adopt and promulgate theories inconsistent with the facts of the Bible, when those theories are sustained by only plausible evidence which does not command the assent even of the body of scientific men themselves. On the other hand, it is unwise for theologians to insist on an interpretation of Scripture which brings it into collision with the facts of science. Both of these mistakes are often made.... Considering the overwhelming weight of evidence of the divine authority of the Scriptures and the unspeakable importance of that authority being maintained over the minds and hearts of men, those who wantonly impugn its teachings evince fearful recklessness. On the other hand, it is unwise in theologians to array themselves needlessly against the teachings of science. Romanists and Protestants vainly resisted the adoption of the Copernican theory of our solar system. They interpreted the Bible in a sense contradictory to that theory. So far as in them lay, they staked the authority of the Bible on the correctness of their interpretation. The theory proved to be true, and the received interpretation had to be given up. The Bible, however, has received no injury, although theologians have been taught an important lesson; that is, to let science take its course, assured that the Scriptures will accommodate themselves to all well-authenticated scientific facts in time to come, as they have in the past.

C. The Authority of Facts

The relation between revelation and philosophy (taking the word in its restricted sense) is different from that between revelation and science. Or, to express the same idea in different words, the relation between revelation and facts is one thing, and the relation between revelation and theories is another thing. Facts do not admit of denial. They are determined by the wisdom and will of God. To deny facts is to deny what God affirms to be true. This the Bible cannot do. It cannot contradict God. The theologian, therefore, acknowledges that the Scriptures must be interpreted in accordance with established facts. He has a right, however, to demand that those facts should be verified beyond the possibility of doubt....

While acknowledging their obligation to admit undeniable facts, theologians are at liberty to receive or reject the theories deduced from those facts. Such theories are human speculations and can have no higher authority than their own inherent probability.... Obvious as this distinction between facts and theories is, it is nevertheless often disregarded. Scientific men are disposed to demand for their theories the authority due only to established facts. And theologians, because at liberty to reject theories, are sometimes led to assert their independence of facts.

D. *The Authority of the Bible Higher than That of Philosophy*

Philosophy, in its widest sense, being the conclusions of the human intelligence as to what is true, and the Bible being the declaration of God as to what is true, it is plain that where the two contradict each other, philosophy must yield to revelation; man must yield to God. . . . If the Bible teaches that God is a person, the philosophy that teaches that an infinite being cannot be a person is false. If the Bible teaches that God creates, controls, regenerates, the philosophy that forbids the assumption that He acts in time is to be rejected. . . . In short, the Bible teaches certain doctrines concerning the nature of God and His relation to the world; concerning the origin, nature, and destiny of man; concerning the nature of virtue, the ground of moral obligation, human liberty and responsibility, the rule of duty, what is right and what is wrong in all our relations to God and to our fellow creatures. These are subjects on which philosophy undertakes to speculate and dogmatize; wherever these speculations come into conflict with what is taught or necessarily implied in the Bible, they are thereby refuted. The disposition which refuses to give up these speculations in obedience to the teachings of the Bible is inconsistent with Christianity. It is the indispensable condition of salvation through the gospel that we receive as true whatever God has revealed in His Word. We must make our choice between the wisdom of men and the wisdom of God. The wisdom of men is foolishness with God, and the wisdom of God is foolishness to the wise of this world.

The relation, therefore, between philosophy and revelation, as determined by the Scriptures themselves, is what every right-minded man must approve. To philosophy and science is conceded everything which they can rightfully demand. It is admitted that they have a large and important sphere of investigation. It is admitted that within that sphere they are entitled to the greatest deference. It is cheerfully conceded that they have accomplished much, not only as a means of mental discipline, but in the enlargement of the sphere of human knowledge and in promoting the refinement and well-being of men. It is admitted that theologians are not infallible in the interpretation of Scripture. It may, therefore, happen in the future, as it has in the past, that interpretations of the Bible, long confidently received, must be modified or abandoned to bring revelation into harmony with what God teaches in His works. This change of view as to the true meaning of the Bible may be a painful trial to the Church, but it does not in the least impair the authority of the Scriptures. They remain infallible; we are merely convicted of having mistaken their meaning.

§7. Office of the Senses in Matters of Faith

The question, What authority is due to the senses in matters of faith? arose out of the controversy between Romanists and Protestants. The doctrine of transubstantiation, as taught by the Church of Rome, contradicts the testimony of our senses of sight, taste, and touch. It was natural for Protestants to appeal to this contradiction as decisive evidence against the doctrine. . . .

Protestants maintain the validity of the testimony of the senses on the following grounds: (1) Confidence in the well-authenticated testimony of our senses is one of those laws of belief which God has impressed upon our nature; from the authority of those laws it is impossible that we should emanicipate ourselves. (2) Confidence in our senses is, therefore, one form of confidence in God. . . . (3) All ground of certainty in matters of either faith or knowledge is destroyed if confidence in the laws of our nature be abandoned. . . . (4) All external supernatural revelation is addressed to the senses. Those who heard Christ had to trust to their sense of hearing; those who read the Bible have to trust to their sense of sight; those who receive the testimony of the Church receive it through their senses. It is suicidal, therefore, in the Romanists to say that the senses are not to be trusted in matters of faith.

All the arguments derived from the false judgments of men when misled by the senses are answered by the simple statement of the proposition that the senses are to be trusted only within their legitimate sphere. The eye may indeed deceive us when the conditions of correct vision are not present, but this does not prove that it is not to be trusted within its appropriate limits.

Chapter IV

Mysticism

§1. Meaning of the Word Mysticism

A. Its Meaning in General and in Church History

... Few words indeed have been used in such a vague, indefinite sense as mysticism. Its etymology does not determine its meaning. A mystic was one initiated into the knowledge of the Greek mysteries, one to whom secret things had been revealed. Hence in the wide sense of the word, a mystic is one who claims to see or know what is hidden from other men, whether this knowledge be attained by immediate intuition or by inward revelation. In most cases these methods were assumed to be identical, as intuition was held to be the immediate vision of God and of divine things. Hence, in the wide sense of the word, mystics are those who claim to be under the immediate guidance of God or of His Spirit. . . .

There has been a religious theory, which has more or less extensively prevailed in the Church, which is distinguished from the Scriptural doctrine by unmistakable characteristics, and which is known in Church history as mysticism, and the word should be restricted to that theory. It is the theory, variously modified, that the knowledge, purity, and blessedness to be derived from communion with God are not to be attained from the Scriptures and the use of the ordinary means of grace, but by a supernatural and immediate divine influence, which influence (or communication of God to the soul) is to be secured by passivity, a simple yielding the soul without thought or effort to the divine influx.

A still wider use of the word mysticism has to some extent been adopted. Any system, whether in philosophy or religion, which assigns more importance to the feelings than to the intellect is called mystical. . . . The mystic assumes that the senses and reason are alike untrustworthy and inadequate as sources of knowledge, that nothing can be received with confidence as truth, at least in the higher departments of knowledge, in all that relates to our own nature, to God, and our relation to Him, except what is revealed either naturally or supernaturally in the feelings. . . .

B. Mysticism Distinguished from Various Doctrines

1. Mysticism not identical with the doctrine of spiritual illumination

Mysticism is not to be confounded with the doctrine of spiritual illumination as held by all evangelical Christians. The Scriptures clearly teach that the mere outward presentation of the truth in the Word does not suffice to the conversion or sanctification of men; that the natural or unrenewed man does not receive the things of the Spirit of God, for they are foolishness unto him; neither can he know them; that in order to come to any saving knowledge of the truth, i.e., such knowledge as produces holy affections and secures a holy life, there is need of an inward supernatural teaching of the Spirit, producing what the Scriptures call "spiritual discernment." This supernatural teaching our Lord promised to His disciples when He said that He would send them the Spirit of truth to dwell in them and to guide them into the knowledge of the truth. The sacred writers pray that this teaching may be granted not to themselves only, but to all who heard their words or read their writings. On this they depended exclusively for their success in preaching or teaching. . . .

God, therefore, does hold immediate intercourse with the souls of men. He reveals Himself unto His people, as He does not unto the world. He gives them the Spirit of revelation in the knowledge of Himself (Eph. 1:17). He unfolds to them His glory and fills them with a joy which passes understanding. All this is admitted, but this is very different from mysticism. The two things, namely, spiritual illumination and mysticism, differ, firstly, as to their object. The object of the inward teaching of the Spirit is to enable us to discern the truth and excellence of what is already objectively revealed in the Bible. The illumination claimed by the mystic communicates truth independently of its objective revelation. It is not intended to enable us to appreciate what we already know, but to communicate new knowledge. . . .

The doctrines of spiritual illumination and of mysticism differ not only in the object, but secondly, in the manner in which that object is to be attained. The inward teaching of the Spirit is to be sought by prayer and the diligent use of the appointed means; the intuitions of the mystic are sought in the neglect of all means, in the suppression of all activity inward and outward, and in a passive waiting for the influx of God into the soul. They differ, thirdly, in their effects. The effect of spiritual illumination is that the Word dwells in us "in all wisdom and spiritual understanding" (Col. 1:9). What dwell in the mind of the mystic are his own imaginings, the character of which depends on his own subjective state; and whatever they are, they are of man and not of God.

2. It differs from the doctrine of the "leading of the Spirit"

Neither is mysticism to be confounded with the doctrine of spiritual guidance. Evangelical Christians admit that the children of God are led by the Spirit of God, that their convictions as to truth and duty, their inward character and outward conduct, are moulded by His influence. They are children unable to guide themselves, who are led by an ever-present Father of infinite wisdom and love. This guidance is partly providential, ordering their external circumstances; partly through the Word, which is a lamp to their feet; and partly by the inward influence of the Spirit on the mind. This last, however, is also through the Word, making it intelligible and effectual, bringing it suitably to remembrance. God leads His people by the cords of a man, i.e., in accordance with the laws of his nature. This is very different from the doctrine that the soul, by yielding itself passively to God, is filled with all truth and goodness, or that in special emergencies it is controlled by blind, irrational impulses.

3. It differs from the doctrine of "common grace"

... All Christians believe that as God is everywhere present in the material world, guiding the operation of second causes so that they secure the results which He designs, so His Spirit is everywhere present with the minds of men, exciting to good and restraining from evil, effectually controlling human character and conduct consistently with the laws of rational beings. ... There is little analogy, however, between this doctrine of common (or sufficient) grace and mysticism as it has revealed itself in the history of the Church. The one assumes an influence of the Spirit on all men analogous to the providential efficiency of God in nature, the other an influence analogous to that granted to prophets and apostles, involving both revelation and inspiration.

§2. Mysticism in the Early Church
§3. Mysticism During the Middle Ages
§4. Mysticism at and after the Reformation

Such a great and general movement of the public mind as occurred during the sixteenth century, when the old foundations of doctrine and order in the Church were overturned, could hardly fail to be attended by irregularities and extravagancies in the inward and outward life of the people. There are two principles advanced, both Scriptural and both of the greatest importance, which are specially liable to abuse in times of popular excitement.

The first is the right of private judgment. This, as understood by the Reformers, is the right of every man to decide what a revelation made by God to him requires him to believe. It was a protest against the authority assumed by the Church (i.e., the bishops) of deciding for the people what they were to believe. It was very natural that the fanatical, in rejecting the authority of the Church, should reject all external authority in matters of religion. They understood by the right of private judgment the right of every man to determine what he should believe from the operations of his own mind and from his own inward experience, independently of the Scriptures. ... Private revelations, an inward light, the testimony of the Spirit, came to be exalted over the authority of the Bible.

Secondly, the Reformers taught that religion is a matter of the heart, that a man's acceptance with God does not depend on his membership in any external society, on obedience to its officers, and on sedulous observance of its rites and ordinances, but on the regeneration of his heart and his personal faith in the Son of God, manifesting itself in a holy life. This was a protest against the fundamental principle of Romanism that all within the external organization which Romanists call the Church are saved, and all out of it are lost. It is not a matter of surprise that evil men should wrest this principle, as they do all other truths, to their own destruction. Because religion does not consist in externals, many rushed to the conclusion that externals—the Church, its ordinances, its officers, its worship—were of no account. These principles were soon applied beyond the sphere of religion. Those who regarded themselves as the organs of God, emancipated from the authority of the Bible and exalted above the Church, came to claim exemption from the authority of the State. . . . These ideas Thomas Münzer and his followers applied to themselves. They were the true Church. They were inspired. They were entitled to determine what is true in matters of doctrine. They were entitled to rule with absolute authority in Church and State. All who opposed them opposed God and ought to be exterminated. Münzer died upon the scaffold; thus was fulfilled anew our Lord's declaration, "Those who take the sword shall perish by the sword."

§5. Quietism
§6. The Quakers or Friends
§7. Objections to the Mystical Theory

The idea on which mysticism is founded is Scriptural and true. It is true that God has access to the human soul. It is true that He can, consistently with His own nature and with the laws of our being, supernaturally and immediately reveal truth objectively to the mind and attend that revelation with evidence which produces an infallible assurance of its truth and of its divine origin. It is also true that such revelations have been made to the children of men. But these cases of immediate supernatural revelation belong to the category of miracles. They are rare and are to be duly authenticated.

The common doctrine of the Christian Church is that '. . . what eye hath not seen, or ear heard, what never could have entered into the heart of man, God has revealed by His Spirit to those whom He selected to be His spokesmen to their fellow men. . . . These holy men of old who spake as they were moved by the Holy Ghost communicated the revelations not only orally, but in writing, employing not the words which man's wisdom teacheth, but which the Holy Ghost teacheth; so that we have in the sacred Scriptures the things of the Spirit recorded in the words of the Spirit. These Scriptures, therefore, are the Word of God—i.e., what God says to man, what He declares to be true and obligatory—and constitute for His Church the only infallible rule of faith and practice.

Romanists, while admitting the infallibility of the written Word, still contend that it is not sufficient, and hold that God continues in a supernatural manner to guide the Church by rendering its bishops infallible teachers in all matters pertaining to truth and duty.

Mystics, making the same admission as to the infallibility of Scripture, claim that the Spirit is given to every man as an inward teacher and guide whose instructions and influence are the highest rule of faith and sufficient, even without the Scriptures, to secure the salvation of the soul.

A. Mysticism Has No Foundation in the Scriptures

The objections to the Romanist and mystical theory are substantially the same. There is no foundation for either in Scripture. As the Scriptures contain no promise of infallible guidance to bishops, so they contain no promise of the Spirit as the immediate revealer of truth to every man. Under the Old Testament dispensation the Spirit did indeed reveal the mind and purposes of God, but it was to selected persons chosen to be prophets, authenticated as divine messengers, whose instructions the people were bound to receive as coming from God. In like manner, under the new dispensation, our Lord selected twelve men, endowed them with plenary knowledge of the gospel, rendered them infallible as teachers, and required all men to receive their instructions as the words of God. It is true that during the apostolic age there were occasional communications made to a class of persons called prophets. But this "gift of prophecy," that is, the gift of speaking under the inspiration of the Spirit, was analogous to the gift of miracles. The one has as obviously ceased as the other.

It is true, also, that our Lord promised to send the Spirit, who was to abide with the Church, to dwell in His people, to be their teacher, and to guide them into the knowledge of all truth. But what truth? Not historical or scientific truth, but plainly revealed truth—truth which He Himself had taught or made known by His authorized messengers . . . the things revealed to the apostles and clearly made known in the Scriptures. . . .

In view of the fact that the Bible gives no support to the mystical doctrine of an inward, supernatural, objective revelation of truth made by the Spirit to every man, that doctrine is destitute of all foundation, for it is only by the testimony of God that any such doctrine can be established.

B. Mysticism Is Contrary to the Scriptures

The doctrine in question is not only destitute of support from Scripture, but it contradicts the Scriptures. It is opposed not only to isolated declarations of the Word of God, but to the whole revealed plan of God's dealing with His people. Everywhere and under all dispensations the rule of faith and duty has been the teaching of authenticated messengers of God. The appeal has always been "to the law and testimony." The prophets came saying, "Thus saith the Lord." Men were required to believe and obey what was communicated to them and not what the Spirit revealed to each individual. It was the outward and not the inward Word to which they were to attend. . . . This idea runs through the whole New Testament. Christ commissioned His disciples to preach the gospel. He declared that to be the way in which men were to be saved. Accordingly, the disciples went forth preaching everywhere. So that this preaching might continue to the end of the world, provision was made for continuing the ministry. Men called and qualified by the Spirit are selected and set apart to this work by divine command. It is in this way, so far, the world has been converted. In no case do we find the apostles calling upon the people, whether Jews or Gentiles, to look within themselves, to listen to the inner Word. They were to listen to the outward Word, to believe what they heard, and to pray for the Holy Spirit to enable them to understand, receive, and obey what was thus externally made known to them.

C. Contrary to the Facts of Experience

The doctrine in question is no less contrary to fact than it is to Scripture. The doctrine teaches that by the inward revelation of the Spirit saving knowledge of truth and duty is given to every man. But all experience shows that without the written Word men everywhere and in all ages are ignorant of divine things—without God, without Christ, and without hope in the world. . . . As right apprehensions of God and holiness of heart and life are nowhere found where the Scriptures are unknown, it is plain that the Scriptures, and not an inward

light common to all men, are, by the ordinance of God, the only source
to us of saving and sanctifying knowledge.

There is a sense in which, as all evangelical Christians believe, the
Spirit is given to every man. He is present with every human mind,
exciting to good and restraining from evil. To this the order and what
there is of morality in the world are due. . . . In like manner, there is
a general providential efficiency of God by which He cooperates with
second causes in the productions of the wonderful phenomena of the
external world. Without that cooperation—the continued guidance of
mind—the cosmos would become chaos. But the fact that this providential efficiency of God is universal is no proof that He everywhere
works miracles, that He constantly operates without the intervention
of second causes. So, also, the fact that the Spirit is present with every
human mind and constantly enforces the truth present to that mind
is no proof that He makes immediate, supernatural revelations to
every human being. . . .

D. No Criterion by Which to Judge of the Source
of Inward Suggestions

A fourth objection to the mystical doctrine is that there is no criterion by which a man can test these inward impulses or revelations
and determine which are from the Spirit of God and which are from
his own heart or from Satan, who often appears and acts as an angel
of light. . . . Many men who are under the influence of some evil spirit
honestly believe themselves to be inspired. The assurance or certainty
of conviction may be as strong in one case as in the other. In the one
it is well founded, in the other it is a delusion. Irresistible conviction
is not enough. It may satisfy the subject of it himself. But it cannot
either satisfy others or be a criterion of truth. Thousands have been
and still are fully convinced that the false is true and that what is
wrong is right. To tell men, therefore, to look within for an authoritative guide and to trust to their irresistible convictions is to give them
a guide which will lead them to destruction. When God really makes
revelations to the soul, He not only gives an infallible assurance that
the revelation is divine, but accompanies it with evidence satisfactory
to others as well as to the recipient that it is from God. All His revelations have had the seal of both internal and external evidence. . . .

E. The Doctrine Productive of Evil

Our Lord says of men, "By their fruits ye shall know them." The
same rule of judgment applies to doctrines. Mysticism has always been

productive of evil. It has led to the neglect or undervaluing of divine institutions—of the Church, of the ministry, of the sacraments, of the Sabbath, and of the Scriptures. History shows that it has also led to the greatest excesses and social evils. . . .

Roman Catholic Doctrine Concerning the Rule of Faith

The Protestant Rule of Faith

§1. Statement of the Doctrine
§2. The Scriptures Are Infallible, i.e., Given by Inspiration of God
    A. The Nature of Inspiration. Definition
        1. Inspiration Supernatural
        2. Distinction Between Revelation and Inspiration
        3. Inspired Men the Organs of God
    B. Proof of the Doctrine of Inspiration
        1. The Signification and Usage of the Word
        2. Argument from the Meaning of the Word Prophet
        3. What the Prophets Said, God Said
        4. Inspiration of the New Testament Writers
    C. The Extent of Inspiration
        1. Inspiration Extends Equally to All Parts of Scripture
        2. The Inspiration of the Scriptures Extends to the Words
    D. General Considerations in Support of the Doctrine
    E. Objections
        1. Objections Based on Denial of the Common Principles of Religion
        2. Allegations of Discrepancies
        3. Allegations of Historical and Scientific Error
§3. Adverse Theories
    [A. Naturalistic Doctrine]
    B. Gracious Inspiration
    C. Partial Inspiration
§4. The Completeness of the Scriptures

§1. Statement of the Doctrine

All Protestants agree in teaching that "the word of God, as contained in the Scriptures of the Old and New Testaments, is the only infallible rule of faith and practice." . . . Protestants hold (1) that the Scriptures of the Old and New Testaments are the Word of God written under the inspiration of the Holy Spirit, and are therefore infallible, and of divine authority in all things pertaining to faith and practice, and consequently free from all error whether of doctrine, fact, or precept; (2) that they contain all the extant supernatural revelations of God designed to be a rule of faith and practice to His Church; (3) that they are sufficiently perspicuous to be understood by the people, in the use of ordinary means and by the aid of the Holy Spirit, in all things necessary to faith or practice, without the need of any infallible interpreter.

Before entering on the considering of these points, it is necessary to answer the question, What books are entitled to a place in the canon or rule of faith and practice? Romanists answer this question by saying that all those which the Church has decided to be divine in their origin, and none others, are to be thus received. Protestants answer it by saying, so far as the Old Testament is concerned, that those books, and those only, which Christ and His apostles recognized as the written Word of God are entitled to be regarded as canonical. This recognition was afforded in a twofold manner: First, many of the books of the Old Testament are quoted as the Word of God, as being given by the Spirit; or the Spirit is said to have uttered what is therein recorded. Secondly, Christ and His apostles refer to the sacred writings of the Jews—the volume which they regarded as divine—as being what it claimed to be, the Word of God. . . . When Christ or His apostles quote the "Scriptures," or the "law and the prophets," and speak of the volume then so called, they give their sanction to the divine authority of all the books which that volume contained. All, therefore, that is necessary to determine for Christians the canon of the Old Testament is to ascertain what books were included in the "Scriptures" recognized by the Jews of that period. This is a point about which there is no reasonable doubt. The Jewish canon of the Old Testament included all the books, and no others, which Protestants now recognize as constituting the Old Testament Scriptures. On this ground Protestants reject the so-called apocryphal books. They were not ... included in the canon of the Jews. They were, therefore, not recognized by Christ as the Word of God. This reason is of itself sufficient. It is, however, confirmed by considerations drawn from the character of the books themselves. They abound in errors and in statements contrary to those found in the undoubtedly canonical books.

The principle on which the canon of the New Testament is determined is equally simple. Those books, and those only, which can be proved to have been written by the apostles, or to have received their sanction, are to be recognized as of divine authority. The reason of this rule is obvious. The apostles were the duly authenticated messengers of Christ, of whom He said, "He that heareth you heareth me."

§2. The Scriptures Are Infallible, i.e., Given by Inspiration of God

The infallibility and divine authority of the Scriptures are due to the fact that they are the Word of God, and they are the Word of God because they were given by the inspiration of the Holy Ghost.

A. The Nature of Inspiration. Definition

The nature of inspiration is to be learnt from the Scriptures: from their didactic statements and from their phenomena.... On this subject the common doctrine of the Church is, and ever has been, that inspiration was an influence of the Holy Spirit on the minds of certain select men which rendered them the organs of God for the infallible communication of His mind and will. They were in such a sense the organs of God that what they said God said.

1. Inspiration supernatural

This definition includes several distinct points. First, inspiration is a supernatural influence. It is thus distinguished, on the one hand, from the providential agency of God, which is everywhere and always in operation, and, on the other hand, from the gracious operations of the Spirit on the hearts of His people. According to the Scriptures and the common views of men, a marked distinction is to be made between those effects which are due to the efficiency of God operating regularly through second causes and those which are produced by His immediate efficiency without the intervention of such causes. The one class of effects is natural; the other, supernatural. Inspiration belongs to the latter class. It is not a natural effect due to the inward state of its subject or to the influence of external circumstances.

No less obvious is the distinction which the Bible makes between the gracious operations of the Spirit and those by which extraordinary gifts are bestowed upon particular persons. Inspiration, therefore, is not to be confounded with spiritual illumination. They differ, first, as to their subjects. The subjects of inspiration are a few selected persons; the subjects of spiritual illumination are all true believers. And, secondly, they differ as to their design. The design of the former is to render certain men infallible as teachers; the design of the latter is to render men holy. And of course they differ as to their effects. Inspiration in itself has no sanctifying influence. Balaam was inspired. Saul was among the prophets. Caiaphas uttered a prediction which "he spake not of himself" (John 11:51). In the last day many will be able to say to Christ, "Lord, Lord, have we not prophesied in thy name? and in thy name have cast out devils? and in thy name done many wonderful works?" to whom He will say, "I never knew you; depart from me, ye that work iniquity" (Matt. 7:22–23).

2. Distinction between revelation and inspiration

Second, the above definition assumes a difference between revelation and inspiration. They differ, first, as to their object. The object of revelation was the communication of knowledge. The object or design of inspiration was to secure infallibility in teaching. Consequently they differ, secondly, in their effects. The effect of revelation was to render its recipient wiser. The effect of inspiration was to preserve him from error in teaching. These two gifts were often enjoyed by the same person at the same time. That is, the Spirit often imparted knowledge and controlled its communication orally or in writing to others. This was no doubt the case with the psalmists, and often with the prophets and apostles. Often, however, the revelations were made at one time and were subsequently, under the guidance of the Spirit, committed to writing. Thus the apostle Paul tells us that he received his knowledge of the gospel not from man, but by revelation from Jesus Christ; and this knowledge he communicated from time to time in his discourses and epistles. In many cases these gifts were separated. Many of the sacred writers, although inspired, received no revelations. This was probably the fact with the authors of the historical books of the Old Testament. The evangelist Luke does not refer his knowledge of the events which he records to revelation, but says he derived it from those "which from the beginning were eyewitnesses, and ministers of the word" (Luke 1:2). It is immaterial to us where Moses obtained his knowledge of the events recorded in the book of Genesis—whether from early documents, from tradition, or from direct revelation. No more causes are to be assumed for any effect than are necessary. If the sacred writers had sufficient sources of knowledge in themselves, or in those about them, there is no need to assume any direct revelation. It is enough for us that they were rendered infallible as teachers. . . .

3. Inspired men the organs of God

A third point included in the Church doctrine of inspiration is that the sacred writers were the organs of God, so that what they taught, God taught. It is to be remembered, however, that when God uses any of His creatures as His instruments, He uses them according to their nature. He uses angels as angels, men as men, the elements as elements. Men are intelligent volitional agents, and as such were made the organs of God. The sacred writers were not made unconscious or irrational. The spirits of the prophets were subject to the prophets (1 Cor. 14:32). They were not like calculating machines which grind out logarithms with infallible correctness. The ancients, indeed, were accustomed to say, as some theologians have also said, that the sacred writers were as pens in the hand of the Spirit, or as harps from which He drew what sounds He pleased. These representations were, however, intended simply to illustrate one point, namely, that the words uttered or recorded by inspired men were the words of God. The Church has never held what has been stigmatized as the mechanical theory of inspiration. The sacred writers were not machines. Their self-consciousness was not suspended, nor were their intellectual powers superseded. Holy men spake as they were moved by the Holy Ghost. It was men, not machines; it was not unconscious instruments, but living, thinking, willing minds, whom the Spirit used as His organs. Moreover, as inspiration did not involve the suspension or suppression of the human faculties, so neither did it interfere with the free exercise of the distinctive mental characteristics of the individual. If a Hebrew was inspired, he spake Hebrew; if a Greek, he spake Greek; if an educated man, he spoke as a man of culture; if uneducated, he spoke as such a man is wont to speak. If his mind was logical, he reasoned, as Paul did; if emotional and contemplative, he wrote as John wrote. All this is involved in the fact that God uses His instruments according to their nature. The sacred writers impressed their peculiarities on their several productions as plainly as though they were the subjects of no extraordinary influence. . . . The inspired penmen wrote out of the fulness of their own thoughts and feelings, and employed the language and modes of expression which to them were the most natural and appropriate. Nevertheless, and none the less, they spoke as they were moved by the Holy Ghost, and their words were His words.

B. Proof of the Doctrine of Inspiration

1. The signification and usage of the word

It is, of course, admitted that words are to be understood in their historical sense. If it can be shown what idea the men living in the apostolic age attached to the word inspired (*theopneustos*) and its equivalents, that is the idea which the apostles intended to express by them. All nations have entertained the belief not only that God has access to the human mind and can control its operations, but that He at times did take such possession of particular persons as to make them the organs of His communications. [To describe such persons, the Greeks, the Septuagint, and Josephus use expressions very similar to what we find in Peter (2 Peter 1:21) and Paul (2 Tim. 3:16).] The idea of inspiration is therefore fixed. . . . According to all antiquity, an inspired man was one who was the organ of God in what he said, so that his words were the words of the god of which he was the organ. When, therefore, the sacred writers use the same words and forms of expression which the ancients used to convey that idea, they must in all honesty be assumed to mean the same thing.

2. Argument from the meaning of the word prophet

That this is the Scriptural idea of inspiration is further proved from the meaning of the word prophet. The sacred writers divide the Scriptures into the "law and the prophets." As the law was written by Moses, and as Moses was the greatest of the prophets, it follows that all the Old Testament was written by prophets. If, therefore, we can determine the Scriptural idea of a prophet, we shall thereby determine the character of their writings and the authority due to them. A prophet, in the Scriptural sense of the term, is a spokesman, one who speaks for another, in his name, and by his authority; so that it is not the spokesman, but the person for whom he acts, who is responsible for the truth of what is said. In Exodus 7:1 it is said, "See, I have made thee a god to Pharaoh; and Aaron thy brother shall be thy prophet," i.e., thy spokesman. This is explained by what is said in Exodus 4:14–16, "Is not Aaron the Levite thy brother? I know that he can speak well. . . . Thou shalt speak unto him, and put words in his mouth; and I will be with thy mouth, and with his mouth, and will teach you what ye shall do. And he shall be thy spokesman unto the people; and he shall be, even he shall be to thee instead of a mouth, and thou shalt be to him instead of God." (See Jer. 36:17–18.) This determines definitely what a prophet is. He is the mouth of God, one through whom God speaks to the people, so that what the prophet says God says. So when a prophet was consecrated, it was said, "Behold, I have put my words in thy mouth" (Jer. 1:9; Isa. 51:16). That this is the Scriptural idea of a prophet is moreover evident from the formulas, constantly recurring, which relate to his duties and mission. He was the messenger of God; he spoke in the name of God; the words, "Thus saith the Lord," were continually in his mouth. It is frequently said that the word of the Lord came to a prophet, or that the Spirit, power, or hand of God was upon him. All of this implies that the prophet was the organ of God, that his words were uttered in God's name and by His authority.

This is precisely what the apostle Peter teaches when he says (2 Peter 1:20–21), "No prophecy of the Scripture is of any private interpretation. For the prophecy came not in old time by the will of man: but holy men spake as they were moved (*borne along* as a ship by the wind) by the Holy Ghost." Prophecy, i.e., what a prophet said, was not human, but divine. It was not the prophet's own interpretation of the mind and will of God. He spoke as the organ of the Holy Ghost.

3. *What the prophets said, God said*

Another decisive proof that the sacred writers were the organs of God in the sense above stated is that whatever they said, the Spirit is declared to have said. Christ Himself said that David by the Spirit called the Messiah Lord (Matt. 22:43). David in the 95th Psalm (vv. 7–8) said, "Today if ye will hear his voice, harden not your heart"; but the apostle (Heb. 3:7–8) says that these were the words of the Holy Ghost. . . . In Acts 28:25 Paul said to the Jews, "Well spake the Holy Ghost by Esaias the prophet unto our fathers." It is in this way that Christ and His apostles constantly refer to the Scriptures, showing beyond doubt that they believed and taught that what the sacred writers said, the Holy Ghost said.

4. *Inspiration of the New Testament writers*

This proof bears specially, it is true, only on the writings of the Old Testament. But no Christian puts the inspiration of the Old Testament above that of the New. The tendency, and we may even say the evidence, is directly the other way. If the Scriptures of the old economy were given by inspiration of God, much more were those writings which were penned under the dispensation of the Spirit. Besides, the inspiration of the apostles is proved (1) from the fact that Christ promised them the Holy Spirit, who would bring all things to their remembrance and render them infallible in teaching. It is not you, He said, that speak, but the Spirit of my Father speaketh in you. He that heareth you heareth me. He forbade them to enter upon their office as teachers until they were endued with power from on high. (2) This promise was fulfilled on the day of Pentecost, when the Spirit descended upon the apostles as a mighty rushing wind, and they were filled with the Holy Ghost and began to speak as the Spirit gave them utterance. . . . From this moment they were new men, with new views, with new spirit, and with new power and authority. The change was sudden. It was not a development. It was something altogether supernatural, as when God said, "Let there be light," and there was light. Nothing can be more unreasonable than to ascribe to mere natural causes this sudden transformation of the apostles from narrow-minded, bigoted Jews into enlightened, large-minded, catholic Christians. Their Jewish prejudices had resisted all the instructions and influence of Christ for three years, but gave way in a moment when the Spirit came upon them from on high. (3) After the day of Pentecost the apostles claimed to be the infallible organs of God in all their teachings. They required men to receive what they taught not as the word of man but as the Word of God (1 Thess. 2:13); they declared, as Paul does (1 Cor. 14:37), that the things which they wrote were the commandments of the Lord. They made the salvation of men to depend on faith in the doctrines which they taught. Paul pronounces anathema even an angel from heaven who should preach any other gospel than that which he had taught (Gal. 1:8). John says, "He that knoweth God heareth us; he that is not of God heareth not us" (1 John 4:6). This assertion of infallibility, this claim for the divine authority of their teaching, is characteristic of the whole Bible. The sacred writers all, and everywhere, disclaim personal authority; they never rest the obligation to faith in their teachings, on their own knowledge or wisdom; they never rest it on the truth of what they taught as manifest to reason or as capable of being proved by argument. They speak as messengers, as witnesses, as organs. They declare that what they said, God said; and, therefore, on His authority it was to be received and obeyed.

The Corinthians objected that Paul did not attempt any rational or philosophical proof of the doctrines which he propounded, that his language and whole manner of discourse were not in accordance with rhetorical rules. He answers these objections, first, by saying that the doctrines which he taught were not the truths of reason, were not derived from the wisdom of men, but were matters of divine revelation; that he simply taught what God declared to be true; and secondly, that as to the manner of presenting these truths, he was the mere organ of the Spirit of God. In 1 Corinthians 2:7–13 he sets forth this whole subject in the clearest and most concise manner. The things which he taught, which he calls "the wisdom of God," "the things of the Spirit," i.e., the gospel, the system of doctrine taught in the Bible, he says had never entered into the mind of man. God had revealed those truths by His Spirit, for the Spirit is the only competent source of such knowledge. "For what man knoweth the things of a man, save the spirit of man which is in him? even so the things of God knoweth no man, but the Spirit of God." So much for the source of knowledge and the ground on which the doctrines he taught were to be received. As to the second objection, which concerned his language and mode of presentation, he says that these things of the Spirit, thus revealed, we teach "not in the words which man's wisdom teacheth, but which the Holy Ghost teacheth," *combining spiritual with spiritual*, i.e., clothing the truths of the Spirit in the words of the Spirit. There is neither in the Bible nor in the writings of men a simpler or clearer statement of the doctrines of revelation and inspiration. Revelation is the Spirit's act of communicating divine knowledge to the mind. Inspiration is the same Spirit's act of controlling those who make the truth known to others. The thoughts, the truths made known, and the words in which they are recorded, are declared to be equally from the Spirit. . . . This is the ground on which the sacred writers rested their claims. They were the mere organs of God. They were His messengers. Those who heard them heard God, and those who refused to hear them refused to hear God (Matt. 10:40; John 13:20).

This claim to infallibility on the part of the apostles was duly authenticated not only by the nature of the truths which they communicated, and by the power which those truths have ever exerted over the minds and hearts of men, but also by the inward witness of the Spirit of which John speaks when he says, "He that believeth on the Son of God hath the witness in himself" (1 John 5:10), "an unction from the Holy One" (1 John 2:20). It was confirmed also by miraculous gifts. As soon as the apostles were endued with power from on high, they spake in "other tongues"; they healed the sick, restored the lame and the blind—"God also," as the apostle says (Heb. 2:4), "bearing them witness, both with signs and wonders, and with divers miracles, and gifts of the Holy Ghost, according to his own will." . . .

The above considerations are sufficient to show that, according to the Scriptures, inspired men were the organs or mouth of God in the sense that what they said and taught has the sanction and authority of God.

C. *The Extent of Inspiration*

1. *Inspiration extends equally to all parts of Scripture*

This . . . means, first, that all the books of Scripture are equally inspired. All alike are infallible in what they teach. And secondly, that inspiration extends to all the contents of these several books. It is not confined to moral and religious truths, but extends to the statements of facts, whether scientific, historical, or geographical. It is not confined to those facts the importance of which is obvious, or which are involved in matters of doctrine. It extends to everything which any sacred writer asserts to be true.

This is proved (1) because it is involved in, or follows as a necessary consequence from, the proposition that the sacred writers were the organs of God. If what they assert, God asserts, which, as has been shown, is the Scriptural idea of inspiration, their assertions must be free from error. (2) Our Lord expressly says, "The Scripture cannot be broken" (John 10:35), i.e., it cannot err. (3) Christ and His apostles refer to all parts of the Scriptures, or to the whole volume, as the Word of God. They make no distinction as to the authority of the Law, the Prophets, or the Hagiographa (Writings). They quote the Pentateuch, the historical books, the Psalms, and the Prophets as all and equally the Word of God. (4) Christ and the writers of the New Testament refer to all classes of facts recorded in the Old Testament as infallibly true. Not only doctrinal facts, such as those of the creation and probation of man, his apostasy, the covenant with Abraham, the giving the law upon Mount Sinai; not only great historical facts, as the deluge, the deliverance of the people out of Egypt, the passage of the Red Sea, and the like; but incidental circumstances, or facts of apparently minor importance, as, e.g., that Satan in tempting our first parents took the form of a serpent, that Moses lifted up a serpent in the wilderness, that Elisha healed Naaman the Syrian, that David ate the shewbread, and even that great stumbling-block, that Jonah was three days in the whale's belly, are all referred to by our Lord and His apostles with the sublime simplicity and confidence with which they are received by little children. (5) It lies in the very idea of the Bible, that God chose some men to write history, some to indite psalms, some to unfold the future, some to teach doctrines. All were equally His organs, and each was infallible in his own sphere. As the principle of vegetable life pervades the whole plant, the root, stem, and flower; as the life of the body belongs as much to the feet as to the head, so the Spirit of God pervades the whole Scripture and is not more in one part than in another. Some members of the body are more important than others, and some books of the Bible could be far better spared than others. There may be as great a difference between John's Gospel and the Book of Chronicles as between a man's brain and his hair; nevertheless the life of the body is as truly in the hair as in the brain.

2. The inspiration of the Scriptures extends to the words

(1) This too is included in the infallibility which our Lord ascribes to the Scriptures. A mere human report or record of a divine revelation must of necessity be not only fallible, but more or less erroneous.

(2) The thoughts are in the words. The two are inseparable. If the words priest, sacrifice, ransom, expiation, propitiation, purification by blood, and the like, have no divine authority, then the doctrine which they embody has no such authority.

(3) Christ and His apostles argue from the very words of Scripture. Our Lord says that David by the Spirit called the Messiah Lord, i.e., David used that word. It was in regard to the use of a particular word that Christ said (John 10:35) that the Scriptures cannot be broken: "If he call them gods unto whom the word of God came, and the Scripture cannot be broken." The use of that word, therefore, according to Christ's view of the Scripture, was determined by the Spirit of God. Paul in Galatians 3:16 lays stress on the fact that in the promise made to Abraham a word used is singular and not plural, "seed," "as of one," and not "seeds, as of many." Constantly it is the very words of Scripture which are quoted as of divine authority.

(4) The very form in which the doctrine of inspiration is taught in the Bible assumes that the organs of God in the communication of His will were controlled by Him in the words which they used. "I have put my words in thy mouth" (Jer. 1:9). "It is not ye that speak, but the Spirit of your Father which speaketh in you" (Matt. 10:20). They spake "as the Spirit gave them utterance" (Acts 2:4). "Holy men of God spake as they were moved by the Holy Ghost" (2 Peter 1:21). All these and similar modes of expression with which the Scriptures abound imply that the words uttered were the words of God. This, moreover, is the very idea of inspiration as understood by the ancient world. The words of the oracle were assumed to be the words of the divinity, and not those selected by the organ of communication. And this, too, as has been shown, was the idea attached to the gift of prophecy. The words of the prophet were the words of God, or he could not be God's spokesman and mouth. It has also been shown that in the most formally didactic passage in the whole Bible on this subject (1 Cor. 2:10–13), the apostle expressly asserts that the truths revealed by the Spirit he communicated in words taught by the Spirit.

The view presented above is known as the doctrine of plenary inspiration. Plenary is opposed to partial. The Church doctrine denies that inspiration is confined to parts of the Bible, and affirms that it applies to all the books of the sacred canon. It denies that the sacred writers were merely partially inspired; it asserts that they were fully inspired as to all that they teach, whether of doctrine or fact. This of course does not imply that the sacred writers were infallible in areas other than the special purpose for which they were employed. They were not imbued with plenary knowledge. As to all matters of science, philosophy, and history, they stood on the same level with their contemporaries. They were infallible only as teachers and when acting as the spokesmen of God. . . . Nor does the Scriptural doctrine on this subject imply that the sacred writers were free from errors in conduct. Their infallibility did not arise from their holiness, nor did inspiration render them holy. Balaam was inspired, and Saul was among the prophets. David committed many crimes, although inspired to write psalms. Peter erred in conduct at Antioch, but this does not prove that he erred in teaching. The influence which preserved him from mistakes in teaching was not designed to preserve him from mistakes in conduct.

D. General Considerations in Support of the Doctrine

. . . The organic unity of the Scriptures proves them to be the product of one mind. Not only are they so united that we cannot believe one part without believing the whole, we cannot believe the New Testament without believing the Old, we cannot believe the Prophets without believing the Law, we cannot believe Christ without believing His apostles; but besides all this they present the regular development, carried on through centuries and millennia, of the great original promise, "The seed of the woman shall bruise the serpent's head." This development was conducted by a variety of independent writers, many of whom understood very little of the plan they were unfolding, but each contributed his part to the progress and completion of the whole.

If the Bible be the work of one mind, that mind must be the mind of God. Only He knows the end from the beginning. Only He could know what the Bible reveals. No one but the Spirit of God, says the apostle, knows the things of God. Only He could reveal the nature, the thoughts, and purposes of God. Only He could tell whether sin can be pardoned. No one but the Father knows the Son. The revelation of the person and work of Christ is as clearly the work of God as are the heavens in all their majesty and glory.

Besides, we have the witness in ourselves. We find that the truths revealed in the Bible have the same adaptation to our souls that the atmosphere has to our bodies. The body cannot live without air, which it receives and appropriates instinctively with full confidence in its adaptation to the end designed. In like manner the soul receives and appropriates the truths of Scripture as the only atmosphere in which it can breathe and live. Thus in receiving the Bible as true, we necessarily receive it as divine. In believing it a supernatural revelation, we believe its plenary inspiration.

This doctrine involves nothing out of analogy with the ordinary operations of God. We believe that He is everywhere present in the material world and controls the operations of natural causes. We know that He causes the grass to grow and gives rain and fruitful seasons. We believe that He exercises a like control over the minds of men, turning them as the rivers of water are turned. All religion, natural and revealed, is founded on the assumption of this providential government of God. Besides this, we believe in the gracious operations of His Spirit by which He works in the hearts of His people to will and to do; we believe that faith, repentance, and holy living are due to the ever-present influence of the Holy Spirit. If, then, this wonder-working God everywhere operates in nature and in grace, why should it be deemed incredible that holy men should speak as they were moved by the Holy Ghost, so that they should say just what He would have them say, so that their words should be His words.

Finally, Christ is the great object of the Christian's faith. We believe Him, and we believe everything else on His authority. He hands us the Old Testament and tells us that it is the Word of God, that its authors spoke by the Spirit, that the Scriptures cannot be broken. And we believe on His testimony. His testimony to His apostles is no less explicit, although given in a different way. He promised to give them a mouth and a wisdom which their adversaries could not gainsay or resist. He told them to take no thought what they should say, "for the Holy Ghost shall teach you in the same hour what ye ought to say" (Luke 12:12). "It is not ye that speak, but the Spirit of your Father which speaketh in you" (Matt. 10:20). He said to them, "He that receiveth you receiveth me" (Matt. 10:40); and He prayed for those who would believe on Him through their word. We believe the Scriptures, therefore, because Christ declares them to be the Word of God. Heaven and earth may pass away, but His Word cannot pass away.

E. Objections

1. Objections based on denial of the common principles of religion

A large class of the objections to the doctrine of inspiration, which for many minds are the most effective, arise from the rejection of one or another of the presuppositions assumed on the preceding pages. If a man denies the existence of a personal, extramundane God, he must deny the doctrine of inspiration, but it is not necessary in order to prove that doctrine that we should first prove the being of God. If he denies that God exerts any direct efficiency in the government of the world, and holds that everything is the product of fixed laws, he cannot believe what the Scriptures teach of inspiration. If the supernatural be impossible, inspiration is impossible. It will be found that most of the objections are based on unscriptural views of the relation of God to the world, or on the peculiar philosophical views of the objectors as to the nature of man or of his free agency. . . . But if God, without interfering with a man's free agency, can make it infallibly certain that he will repent and believe, He can render it certain that he will not err in teaching. It is in vain to profess to hold the common doctrine of theism and yet assert that God cannot control rational creatures without turning them into machines.

2. Allegations of discrepancies

But although the theologian may rightfully dismiss all objections founded on the denial of the common principles of natural and revealed religion, there are others which cannot be thus summarily disposed of. The most obvious of these is that the sacred writers contradict each other and that they teach error. . . .

As to the former of these objections, it would require not a volume, but volumes to discuss all the cases of alleged discrepancies. All that can be expected here is a few general remarks: (1) These apparent discrepancies, although numerous, are for the most part trivial, relating in most cases to numbers or dates. (2) The great majority of them are only apparent and yield to careful examination. (3) Many of them may fairly be ascribed to errors of transcribers. (4) The marvel and the miracle is that there are so few of any real importance. Considering that the different books of the Bible were written not only by different authors, but by men of all degrees of culture, living in the course of fifteen hundred or two thousand years, the only possible explanation for their perfect agreement is that the writers were under the guidance of the Spirit of God. In this respect, as in all others, the Bible stands alone. It is enough to impress any mind with awe when it contemplates the sacred Scriptures filled with the highest truths, speaking with authority in the name of God, and so miraculously free from the soiling touch of human fingers. The errors in matters of fact which skeptics search out bear no proportion to the whole. No sane man would deny that the Parthenon was built of marble, even if here and there a speck of sandstone should be detected in its structure. Not less unreasonable is it to deny the inspiration of such a book as the Bible because one sacred writer says that on a given occasion twenty-four thousand, and another says that twenty-three thousand, men were slain. Surely a Christian may be allowed to tread such objections under his feet.

Although the Scriptures do contain, in a few instances, discrepancies which, with our present means of knowledge, we are unable satisfactorily to explain, they furnish no rational ground for denying Scriptural infallibility. "The scripture cannot be broken" (John 10:35). This is the whole doctrine of plenary inspiration, taught by the lips of

Christ Himself. The universe teems with evidences of design so manifold, so diverse, so wonderful, as to overwhelm the mind with the conviction that it has had an intelligent author. Yet here and there isolated cases of monstrosity appear. It is irrational, because we cannot account for such cases, to deny that the universe is the product of intelligence. So the Christian need not renounce his faith in the plenary inspiration of the Bible, although there may be some things about it in its present state which he cannot account for.

3. Allegations of historical and scientific error

The second great objection to the plenary inspiration of the Scripture is that it teaches what is inconsistent with historical and scientific truth.

Here it is to be remarked (1) that we must distinguish between what the sacred writers themselves thought or believed, and what they teach. They may have believed that the sun moves round the earth, but they do not so teach. (2) The language of the Bible is the language of common life, and the language of common life is founded upon apparent and not upon scientific truth. It would be ridiculous to refuse to speak of the sun rising and setting, because we know that it is not a satellite of our planet. (3) There is a great distinction between theories and facts. Theories are of men. Facts are of God. The Bible often contradicts the former, never the latter. (4) There is also a distinction to be made between the Bible and our interpretation. The latter may come into competition with settled facts, and then it must yield. Science has in many things taught the Church how to understand the Scriptures. The Bible was for ages understood and explained according to the Ptolemaic system of the universe; it is now explained, without doing the least violence to its language, according to the Copernican system. Christians have commonly believed that the earth has existed only a few thousands of years. If geologists finally prove that it has existed for myriads of ages, it will be found that the first chapter of Genesis is in full accord with the facts and that the last results of science are embodied on the first page of the Bible. It may cost the Church a severe struggle to give up one interpretation and adopt another, as it did in the seventeenth century, but no real evil need be entailed. The Bible has stood and still stands in the presence of the scientific world with its claims unshaken. Men hostile or indifferent to its truths may, on insufficient grounds, or because of their personal opinions, reject its authority; but even in the judgment of the greatest authorities in science, its teachings cannot fairly be impeached.

It is impossible duly to estimate the importance of this subject. The Bible being the Word of God, all the great questions which for ages have agitated the minds of men are settled with infallible certainty. Human reason has never been able to answer to its own satisfaction, or to the assurance of others, the vital questions, What is God? What is man? What lies beyond the grave? If there is a future state of being, what is it? How may future blessedness be secured? Without the Bible we are, on all these subjects, in utter darkness. Without the Bible the answers to the greatest of all questions, What is God? have been completely unsatisfying. The whole Eastern world answers by saying, "God is the unconscious ground of being." The Greek philosophers gave the same answer, while the uneducated people thought of all nature as God. The moderns have reached no higher doctrine. . . . But a Christian child says, "God is a Spirit, infinite, eternal, and unchangeable, in his being, wisdom, power, holiness, justice, goodness, and truth" ("Westminster Catechism"). Men and angels veil their faces in the presence of that answer. It is the highest, greatest, and most fruitful truth ever embodied in human language. Without the Bible we are without God and without hope, the present is a burden, and the future a dread.

§3. Adverse Theories

[A. Naturalistic Doctrine]

B. Gracious Inspiration

. . . There are many theologians who . . . regard inspiration to be one of the ordinary fruits of the Spirit. Inspired and uninspired men are not distinguished by any specific difference. The sacred writers were merely holy men under the guidance of the ordinary influence of the Spirit. . . .

That this theory is anti-scriptural is obvious (1) because the Bible makes a marked distinction between those whom God chose to be His messengers, His prophets, His spokesmen, and other men. This theory ignores that distinction, so far as the people of God are concerned.

(2) It is inconsistent with the authority claimed by these special messengers of God. They spoke in His name. God spoke through them. They said, "Thus saith the Lord," in a sense and way in which no ordinary believer dare use those words. It is inconsistent with the authority not only claimed by the sacred writers, but attributed to them by our Lord Himself. He declared that the Scripture could not be broken, that it was infallible in all its teachings. The apostles declared those anathema who did not receive their doctrines. This claim

to divine authority in teaching was confirmed by God Himself in signs and wonders, and divers miracles, and gifts of the Holy Ghost.

(3) It is inconsistent with the whole nature of the Bible, which is and professes to be a revelation of truths which neither human reason nor any amount of holiness can enable the mind of man to perceive. This is true not only of the strictly prophetic revelations relating to the future, but also of all things concerning the mind and will of God. The doctrines of the Bible are called "mysteries," *things concealed,* unknown and unknowable, except as revealed to the holy apostles and prophets by the Spirit (Eph. 3:4–5).

(4) It is inconsistent with the faith of the Church universal, which has always made the broadest distinction between the writings of the inspired men and those of ordinary believers. Even Romanists, with all their reverence for the fathers, never presumed to place their writings on a level with the Scriptures. They do not attribute to them any authority but as witnesses of what the apostles taught. If the Bible has no more authority than is due to the writings of pious men, then our faith is vain and we are yet in our sins. We have no sure foundation for our hopes of salvation.

C. *Partial Inspiration*

Under the head of partial inspiration are included several different doctrines.

(1) Many hold that only some parts of Scripture are inspired, i.e., that the writers of some books were supernaturally guided by the Spirit, and the writers of others were not. . . .

(2) Others limit the inspiration of the sacred writers to their doctrinal teaching. . . . Beyond these limits they were as liable to error as were other men. That there should be scientific, historical, geographical mistakes; errors in the citation of passages or in other unessential matters; or discrepancies as to matters of fact between the sacred writers, leaves their inspiration as religious teachers untouched.

(3) Another form of the doctrine of partial inspiration limits it to the thoughts as distinguished from the words of Scripture. Verbal inspiration is denied. It is assumed that the sacred writers selected their words without any guidance of the Spirit to prevent their adopting improper or inadequate terms in which to express their thoughts. . . .

In attempting to prove the doctrine of plenary inspiration the arguments which bear against all these forms of partial inspiration were given or suggested. The question is not an open one. It is not what theory is in itself most reasonable or plausible, but simply, What does the Bible teach on the subject? If our Lord and His apostles declare that the Old Testament is the Word of God; that its authors spake as they were moved by the Holy Ghost; that what they said, the Spirit said; if they refer to the facts and to the very words of Scripture as of divine authority; and if the same infallible guidance was promised to the writers of the New Testament and claimed by themselves; and if their claim was authenticated by God Himself—then there is no room for, as there is no need of, these theories of partial inspiration. The whole Bible was written under such an influence as preserved its human authors from all error and makes it for the Church the infallible rule of faith and practice.

§4. The Completeness of the Scriptures

By the completeness of the Scriptures is meant that they contain all the extant revelations of God designed to be a rule of faith and practice for the Church. It is not denied that God reveals Himself, even His eternal power and Godhead, by His works, and has done so from the beginning of the world. But all the truths thus revealed are clearly made known in His written Word. Nor is it denied that there may have been, and probably were, books written by inspired men which are no longer in existence. Much less is it denied that Christ and His apostles delivered many discourses which were not recorded and which, could they now be known and authenticated, would be of equal authority with the books now regarded as canonical. All that Protestants insist upon is that the Bible contains all the extant revelations of God which He designed to be the rule of faith and practice for His Church, so that nothing can rightfully be imposed on the consciences of men as truth or duty which is not taught directly or by necessary implication in the Holy Scriptures. This excludes not only all unwritten traditions, but also all decrees of the visible Church and all resolutions of conventions or other public bodies declaring this or that to be right or wrong, true or false. The people of God are bound by nothing but the Word of God. . . .

§5. Perspicuity of the Scriptures.
The Right of Private Judgment

The Bible is a plain book. It is intelligible by the people. And they have the right and are bound to read and interpret it for themselves, so that their faith may rest on the testimony of the Scriptures and not on that of the Church. Such is the doctrine of Protestants on this subject.

It is not denied that the Scriptures contain many things hard to understand, that they require diligent study, that all men need the guidance of the Holy Spirit in order to come to right knowledge and true faith. But it is maintained that in all things necessary to salvation they are sufficiently plain to be understood even by the unlearned. . . .

If the Scriptures be a plain book, and the Spirit performs the functions of a teacher to all the children of God, it follows inevitably that they must agree in all essential matters in their interpretation of the Bible. And from that fact it follows that for an individual Christian to dissent from the faith of the universal Church (i.e., the body of true believers) is tantamount to dissenting from the Scriptures themselves.

What Protestants deny on this subject is that Christ has appointed any officer, or class of officers, in His Church to whose interpretations of the Scriptures the people are bound to submit as of final authority. What they affirm is that He has made it obligatory upon every man to search the Scriptures for himself and determine on his own discretion what they require him to believe and to do. . . .

The most obvious reasons in support of the right of private judgment are:

(1) The obligations to faith and obedience are personal. Every man is responsible for his religious faith and his moral conduct. He cannot transfer that responsibility to others, nor can others assume it in his stead. He must answer for himself; and if he must answer for himself, he must judge for himself. It will not avail him in the day of judgment to say that his parents or his Church taught him wrong. He should have listened to God and obeyed Him rather than men.

(2) The Scriptures are everywhere addressed to the people and not to the officers of the Church either exclusively or specially. The prophets were sent to the people and constantly said, "Hear, O Israel," "Hearken, O ye people." Thus, also, the discourses of Christ were addressed to the people, and the people heard Him gladly. All the Epistles of the New Testament are addressed to the congregation, to "the called of Jesus Christ," "to the beloved of God," "to those called to be saints." . . . It is the people who are addressed. . . . They are everywhere assumed to be competent to understand what is written and are everywhere required to believe and obey what thus came from the inspired messengers of Christ. They were not referred to any other authority from which they were to learn the true import of these inspired instructions. To forbid the people to read and interpret the Scriptures for themselves is, therefore, not only to deprive the people of a divine right, but to interpose between them and God, and to prevent their hearing His voice, that they may listen to the words of men.

(3) Not only are the Scriptures addressed to the people, but the

people were called upon to study them and to teach them unto their children. One of the most frequently recurring injunctions to parents under the old dispensation was to teach the law unto their children, that they again might teach it unto theirs. The "holy oracles" were committed to the people to be taught by the people, and taught immediately out of the Scriptures, that the truth might be retained in its purity. Thus our Lord commanded the people to search the Scriptures, saying, "They are they which testify of me" (John 5:39). He assumed that they were able to understand what the Old Testament said of the Messiah, although its teachings had been misunderstood by the scribes and elders and by the whole Sanhedrin. Paul rejoiced that Timothy had from his youth known the Holy Scriptures, which were able to make him wise unto salvation (2 Tim. 3:15). He said to the Galatians (1:8–9), "Though we, or an angel from heaven . . . if any *man* preach any other gospel unto you than that ye have received, let him be accursed." . . . The principle laid down by the apostle is precisely that long before given by Moses (Deut. 13:1–3), who tells the people that if a prophet should arise, although he worked wonders, they were not to believe or obey him, if he taught them anything contrary to the Word of God. This again assumes that the people had the ability and the right to judge, and that they had an infallible rule of judgment. It implies, moreover, that their salvation depended upon their judging rightly. For if they allowed these false teachers, robed in sacred vestments and surrounded by the insignia of authority, to lead them from the truth, they would inevitably perish.

(4) It need hardly be remarked that this right of private judgment is the great safeguard of civil and religious liberty. . . .

§6. Rules of Interpretation

If every man has the right and is bound to read the Scriptures and to judge for himself what they teach, he must have certain rules to guide him in the exercise of this privilege and duty. These rules are not arbitrary. They are not imposed by human authority. They have no binding force which does not flow from their own intrinsic truth and propriety. They are few and simple.

(1) The words of Scripture are to be taken in their plain historical sense. That is, they must be taken in the sense attached to them in the age and by the people to whom they were addressed. This assumes that the sacred writers were honest and meant to be understood.

(2) If the Scriptures be what they claim to be, the Word of God, they are the work of one mind, and that mind divine. From this it

follows that Scripture cannot contradict Scripture. God cannot teach in one place anything which is inconsistent with what He teaches in another. Hence Scripture must explain Scripture. If a passage admits of different interpretations, the true one will agree with what the Bible teaches elsewhere on the same subject. If the Scriptures teach that the Son is the same in substance and equal in power and glory with the Father, then when the Son says, "The Father is greater than I," the superiority must be understood in a manner consistent with this equality. Either it must refer to subordination as to the mode of subsistence and operation, or it must be official. A king's son may say, "My father is greater than I," although personally his father's equal. This rule of interpretation is sometimes called the analogy of Scripture and sometimes the analogy of faith.

(3) The Scriptures are to be interpreted under the guidance of the Holy Spirit, which guidance is to be humbly and earnestly sought. The ground of this rule is twofold: First, the Spirit is promised as a guide and teacher. He was to come to lead the people of God into the knowledge of the truth. And secondly, the Scriptures teach that "the natural man receiveth not the things of the Spirit of God: for they are foolishness unto him; neither can he know them, because they are spiritually discerned" (1 Cor. 2:14). The unrenewed mind is naturally blind to spiritual truth. His heart is in opposition to the things of God. Congeniality of mind is necessary to the proper apprehension of divine things. As only those who have a moral nature can discern moral truth, so only those who are spiritually minded can truly receive the things of the Spirit.

The fact that all the true people of God in every age and in every part of the Church, in the exercise of their private judgment, in accordance with the simple rules above stated, agree as to the meaning of Scripture in all things necessary either in faith or in practice, is a decisive proof of the perspicuity of the Bible and of the safety of allowing the people the enjoyment of the divine right of private judgment.

Theology Proper

Chapter I

Origin of the Idea of God

All men have some knowledge of God. That is, they have the conviction that there is a Being on whom they are dependent and to whom they are responsible. What is the source of this conviction? In other words, what is the origin of the idea of God? . . .

§1. The Knowledge of God Is Innate

A. What Is Meant by Innate Knowledge

By innate knowledge is meant that which is due to our constitution as sentient, rational, and moral beings. It is opposed to knowledge founded on experience, to that obtained by instruction, and to that acquired by a process of research and reasoning.

It cannot be doubted that there is such knowledge, i.e., that the soul is so constituted that it sees certain things to be true immediately in their own light. They need no proof. Men need not be told or taught that the things thus perceived are true. These immediate perceptions are called intuitions, primary truths, laws of belief, innate knowledge or ideas. . . . The word innate simply indicates the source of the knowledge. That source is our nature, that which is born with us. . . . All that is meant by innate knowledge is that the mind is so constituted that it perceives certain things to be true without proof and without instruction.

These intuitive truths belong to the several departments of the senses, the understanding, and our moral nature. In the first place, all our sense perceptions are intuitions. We apprehend their objects immediately and have an irresistible conviction of their reality and truth. . . . These are intuitions, because they are immediate perceptions of what is true. The conviction which attends our sensations is due not to instruction but to the constitution of our nature.

In the second place, there are intuitions of the intellect. That is, there are certain truths which the mind perceives to be true immediately, without proof or testimony. Such are the axioms of geometry. No man needs to have it proved to him that the part of a thing is less than the whole, or that a straight line is the shortest distance between two given points. It is an intuitive truth that "nothing" cannot be a cause, that every effect must have a cause. This conviction is not founded on experience, because experience is of necessity limited. And the conviction is not merely that every effect which we or other men have observed has had a cause, but that in the nature of things there can be no effect without an adequate cause. . . .

In the third place, there are moral truths which the mind intuitively recognizes as true. The essential distinction between right and wrong, the obligation of virtue, responsibility for character and conduct, and that sin deserves punishment are examples of this class of truths. No man needs to be taught them. No one seeks for further evidence of their being truths than that which is found in his nature. . . .

There is, then, a class of truths so plain that they never fail to reveal themselves to the human mind, and to them the mind cannot refuse its assent. Hence the criteria of those truths which are accepted as axioms, and which are assumed in all reasoning, and the denial of which renders all faith and all knowledge impossible, are universality and necessity. What all believe, and what all men must believe, is to be assumed as undeniably true. . . .

B. *Proof That the Knowledge of God Is Innate*

... Asking whether the existence of God is an intuitive truth is equivalent to asking whether the belief in His existence is universal and necessary. If it be true that all men do believe there is a God and that no man can possibly disbelieve His existence, then His existence is an intuitive truth. It is one of those which are given in the constitution of our nature or which, our nature being what it is, no man can fail to know and to acknowledge.

Such has been the common opinion in all ages. . . . The word God, however, is used in a very wide sense. . . . It is in the general sense of a Being on whom we are dependent, and to whom we are responsible, that the idea is asserted to exist universally and of necessity in every human mind. . . .

1. *The knowledge of God is universal*

(1) The first proof of this doctrine is the testimony of Scripture. The Bible asserts that the knowledge of God is universal. This it does both directly and by necessary implication. The apostle directly asserts that the heathen have the knowledge of God, and such knowledge as to render their impiety and immorality inexcusable: "Because that, when they knew God," he says, "they glorified him not as God, neither were thankful" (Rom. 1:19–21). He says that the most depraved of men know the righteous judgment of God, namely, that those who commit sin are worthy of death (Rom. 1:32). The Scripture everywhere addresses men as sinners; it calls upon them to repent; it threatens them with punishment in case of disobedience or promises pardon to those who turn from their sins. All this is done without any preliminary demonstration of the being of God. It assumes that men know that there is a God and that they are subject to His moral government. . . . In teaching the universal sinfulness and condemnation of men, their inexcusableness for idolatry and immorality, and in asserting that even the most degraded are conscious of guilt and just exposure to the divine judgment, the Bible takes for granted that the knowledge of God is universal, that it is written on the heart of every man.

This is still more apparent from what the Bible teaches of the law as written on the heart. The apostle tells us that those who have a written revelation shall be judged by that revelation, and that those who have no externally revealed law shall be judged by the law written on the heart. That the heathen have such a law he proves, first, from the fact that "they do by nature the things contained in the law," i.e., they do under the control of their nature the things which the law prescribes; and, secondly, from the operations of conscience. When it condemns, it pronounces some deed to be contrary to the moral law; and when it approves, it pronounces some deed to be conformed to that law (Rom. 2:12–16). The recognition of God, therefore, that is, of a Being to whom we are responsible, is involved in the very idea of accountability. Hence every man carries in the very constitution of his being as a moral agent the evidence of the existence of God. And as this sense of sin and responsibility is absolutely universal, so must also, according to the Bible, be the knowledge of God.

(2) The second argument in favor of the universality of this knowledge is the historical one. History shows that the religious element of our nature is just as universal as the rational or social one. Wherever men exist, in all ages and in all parts of the world, they have some form of religion. The idea of God is impressed on every human language. And as language is the product and revelation of human consciousness, the fact that all languages have some name for God proves that the idea of God, in some form, belongs to every human being.

2. The belief in God necessary

But if it be admitted that the knowledge of God is universal among men, is it also a necessary belief? Is it impossible for the mind to dispossess itself of the conviction that there is a God? . . .

The question then is, Is it possible for a sane man to disbelieve in the existence of God? This question is commonly answered in the negative. It is objected, however, that facts prove the contrary. No man who denies that two and two make four has ever been found, whereas atheists abound in every age and in every part of the world.

There are, however, . . . truths which cannot be denied without doing violence to the laws of our nature. In such cases the denial is forced and can only be temporary. The laws of our nature are sure sooner or later to assert themselves and constrain an opposite belief. A pendulum when at rest hangs perpendicularly to the horizon. It may by extraneous force be made to hang at any degree of inclination. But as soon as such force is removed, it is sure to swing back to its normal position. Under the control of a metaphysical theory, a man may deny the existence of the external world or the obligation of the moral law, and his disbelief may be sincere and for a time persistent; but the moment the speculative reasons for his disbelief are absent from his mind, it of necessity reverts to its original and natural convictions. It is also possible that a man's hand may be so hardened or cauterized as to lose the sense of touch. But that would not prove that the hand in man is not normally the great organ of touch. So it is possible that the moral nature of a man may be so disorganized by vice or by a false philosophy as to have its testimony for the existence of God effectually silenced. This, however, would prove nothing as to what that testimony really is. Besides this, insensibility and the consequent unbelief cannot last. Whatever rouses the moral nature, whether it be danger, or suffering, or the approach of death, banishes unbelief in a moment. Men pass from skepticism to faith, in many cases instantaneously, not of course by a process of argument, but by the existence of a state of consciousness with which skepticism is irreconcilable and in the presence of which it cannot exist. This fact is illustrated continually, not only in the case of the uneducated and superstitious, but even in the case of men of the highest culture. The simple fact of Scripture and experience is that the moral law as written upon the heart is indelible, and the moral law in its nature implies a lawgiver, one from whom that law emanates and by whom it will be enforced. And, therefore, so long as men are moral creatures, they will and must believe in the existence of a Being on whom they are dependent and to whom they are responsible for their character and conduct. To this extent and in this sense, therefore, it is to be admitted that the knowledge of God is innate and intuitive, and that men no more need to be taught that there is a God than they need to be taught that there is such a thing as sin. But as men are ignorant of the nature and extent of sin, while aware of its existence, until instructed by the Word of God and enlightened by His Spirit, so they greatly need the same sources of instruction to give them any adequate knowledge of the nature of God and of their relations to Him.

§2. The Knowledge of God Is Not Due to a Process of Reasoning
§3. Knowledge of God Not Due Exclusively to Tradition
§4. Can the Existence of God Be Proved?

. . . The existence of God is an objective fact. It may be shown that it is a fact which cannot be rationally denied. Although all men have feelings and convictions which necessitate the assumption that there is a God, it is, nevertheless, perfectly legitimate to show that there are other facts which necessarily lead to the same conclusion.

Besides, it is to be remembered that theistical arguments are designed not only to prove that there is a necessity for the assumption of an extramundane and eternal Being, but mainly to show what that Being is—that He is a personal Being, self-conscious, intelligent, moral. . . .

Most of the objections to the conclusiveness of the arguments in question arise from a misapprehension of what they are intended to prove. It is often assumed that each argument must prove the whole doctrine of theism, whereas one argument may prove one element of that doctrine, and other arguments different elements. The cosmological argument may prove the existence of a necessary and eternal Being; the teleological argument may prove that that Being is intelligent; the moral argument that He is a person possessing moral attributes. The arguments are not designed so much to prove the existence of an unknown being as to demonstrate that the Being who reveals Himself to man in the very constitution of his nature must be all that theism declares Him to be.

Chapter **II**

Theism

Theism is the doctrine of an extramundane, personal God, the creator, preserver, and governor of the world. The design of all arguments on this subject is to show that the facts around us and the facts of consciousness necessitate the assumption of the existence of such a Being. The arguments usually urged on this subject are the ontological, the cosmological, the teleological, and the moral.

§1. The Ontological Argument

This is a metaphysical *a priori* argument. It is designed to show that the real, objective existence of God is involved in the very idea of such a Being. . . .

105

We have the idea of an infinitely perfect Being. As we are finite, that idea could not have originated with us. As we are conversant only with the finite, it could not have originated from anything around us. It must, therefore, have come from God, whose existence is thus a necessary assumption. . . . It is true we have many ideas or conceptions to which there is no answering existence. But in such cases the ideas are arbitrary, or voluntary creations of our own minds. But the idea of God is necessary; we cannot help having it. And since we cannot help having it, there must be a Being who answers to it. . . . There are, doubtless, minds which are affected by this kind of reasoning, but it has no power over the generality of men.

§2. The Cosmological Argument

This is founded on the principle of a sufficient cause. Syllogistically stated, the argument stands thus: Every effect must have an adequate cause. The world is an effect. Therefore the world must have had a cause outside of itself and adequate to account for its existence.

The validity and the meaning of this argument depend on the sense given to the words effect and cause. If an effect be correctly defined to be an event or product not due to anything in itself, but produced by something outside itself, and if by cause be understood an antecedent to whose efficiency the effect is due, then the conclusion is inevitable that the existence of the world supposes the existence of a cause adequate to its production, provided it can be proved that the world is an effect, i.e., that it is not self-caused or eternal. . . .

We are reduced, therefore, to this alternative. The universe is. Either it has been from all eternity, or it owes its existence to a cause outside of itself and adequate to account for its being what it is. The theistical argument is that the world is an effect, that it has not the cause of existence in itself, that it is not eternal, and therefore we are necessitated to assume the existence of a great First Cause to whose efficiency the existence of the universe is to be referred.

The first argument to prove that the world as a whole is not self-existent and eternal is that all its parts, everything that enters into its composition, are dependent and mutable. A whole cannot be essentially different from its constituent parts. An infinite number of effects cannot be self-existent. If a chain of three links cannot support itself, much less can a chain of a million links. Nothing multiplied by infinity is nothing still. If we do not find the cause of our existence in ourselves, nor our parents in themselves, nor their progenitors in themselves, going back *ad infinitum* is only adding nothing to nothing. What the mind demands is a sufficient cause, and no approach to it is made by

going back indefinitely from one effect to another. We are forced, therefore, by the laws of our rational nature to assume the existence of a
self-existent cause, i.e., a Being endued with power adequate to produce this ever-changing phenomenal world. In all ages thinking men
have been forced to this conclusion. . . .

The second argument is the historical one. That is, we have historical evidence that the race of man, for example, has existed only a few
thousand years. That mankind has existed from eternity is absolutely
incredible. Even if we adopt the development theory, it affords no relief.
It only substitutes millions for thousands of years. Both are equally
insignificant when compared to eternity. Darwin's germ-cell as necessarily demands a self-existing cause outside itself as does a fully
developed man, or the whole race of man, or the universe itself. We
are forced to the conclusion that the universe sprang out of nothing
or that there is a self-existing, eternal, extramundane Being. . . .

It is universally admitted that we have no foundation for knowledge
or for faith but the veracity of consciousness. This principle must be
kept constantly in view and must be often reiterated. Any doctrine,
therefore, which contradicts the facts of consciousness or the laws of
belief which God has impressed on our nature must be false. If, therefore, it can be shown that there are certain truths which men are
constrained by the constitution of their nature to believe, those truths
are to be retained in despite of all the arts of sophistry. If, therefore,
it be a fact of consciousness that we ourselves are something, a substance, and that we have power, that we can produce effects, then it
is certain that there is such a thing as power and efficient cause. If,
moreover, it be an intuitive and necessary truth that every effect must
have a cause, then it is absolutely certain that if the world began to
be, it had an adequate cause outside itself. . . .

The cosmological argument is not intended to prove all that theists
hold to be true concerning God. It is enough that it proves that we
must admit the existence of an eternal and necessary Being. Other
arguments prove that that Being is self-conscious and intelligent. The
argument, moreover, fairly proves that this Being is extramundane,
for the principle of causation is that everything contingent must have
a cause outside itself.

§3. The Teleological Argument

A. *Its Nature*

This argument also admits of being stated in a syllogistic form.
Design supposes a designer. The world everywhere exhibits marks of
design. Therefore the world owes its existence to an intelligent author.

By design is intended (1) the selection of an end to be attained; (2) the choice of suitable means for its attainment; and (3) the actual application of those means for the accomplishment of the proposed end.

Such being the nature of design, it is a self-evident truth that design is indicative of intelligence, will, and power. This is saying simply that intelligence in the effect implies intelligence in the cause.

It is moreover true that the intelligence indicated by design is not in the thing designed. It must be in an external agent. The mind indicated in a book is not in the book itself, but in the author and printer. . . . The mind indicated in the structure of the bodies of plants and animals is not in them, but in Him who made them. And in like manner the mind indicated in the world at large must be in an extra-mundane Being. . . .

The argument is, Such is the nature of design that it of necessity implies an intelligent agent; and, therefore, wherever or whenever we see evidence of design we are convinced that it is to be referred to the operation of mind. On this ground we are not only authorized but compelled to apply the argument from design far beyond the limits of experience and to say that it is just as evident that the world had an intelligent creator as that a book had an author. If a man can believe that a book was written by chance or by blind, unconscious force, then, and not otherwise, can he rationally deny the validity of the argument from design in proof of the existence of a personal God.

B. Evidences of Design in the World

No work of human art can compare with the nicety and completeness of the separate organs of organized bodies for the purpose for which they are designed. In the eye, for example, there is the most perfect optical instrument constructed in accordance with the hidden laws of light. We find there the only nerve in the body susceptible of the impressions of light and color. That nerve is spread out on the retina. The light is admitted through an orifice which by the most delicate arrangement of muscles is enlarged or contracted according to the degree of light which falls on the retina. . . . The light is made to pass through lenses perfect in form which so refract the rays as to bring them to a proper focus on the retina. If the inner chamber of the eye were white, it would so reflect the rays entering the pupil at every angle as to render vision impossible. That chamber, and that alone, is lined with a black pigment. By a delicate muscular arrangement the eye is enabled to adapt itself to the distance of external objects so that the proper focus may be preserved. These are a small part of the wonders exhibited by this single organ of the body. This organ was fashioned in the darkness of the womb with a self-evident reference to the nature and properties of light, of which the creature for whose use it was fashioned had neither knowledge nor experience. If the eye, therefore, does not indicate the intelligent adaptation of means to an end, no such adaptation can be found in any work of human ingenuity. . . .

The body is a perfect marvel of mechanical contrivances. The several organs of the animal frame, viewed separately, present the most incontestable evidence of foresight, intelligence, and wisdom. This, however, is only a small part of the evidence of design furnished even by the body. . . .

There cannot be a more decisive proof of intelligence than prevision—preparation for an event in the future. The world is full of evidence of such prevision. It is seen not only in the preparation of the organs of sight, hearing, breathing, nutrition, etc., for necessities still future, but still more strikingly in the provision made for the support of young animals as soon as they are born. In the mammalia before the birth of the offspring, the breast or udder begins to swell; it commences the secretion of milk, so that the moment the young animal enters the world he finds prepared the most nutritious and suitable food the world contains. The egg furnishes a still more instructive illustration. It consists of albumen and the yolk. To the yolk is attached a minute germ or cell. When by heat the germ begins to develop, if nourishment were not provided and at hand, it would of necessity perish. But the yolk is there to supply the needed material out of which the future animal is fashioned. If this does not indicate a foreseeing mind and a providing power, then the most skilful productions of human craft and kindness do not prove the intelligence of man. Where then is this intelligence? Not in the parent bird, for it understands nothing about it. Not in mere blind forces of nature. There may possibly be room for question where to place it, but to deny that these provisions indicate an intelligent agency somewhere is altogether irrational. . . .

The evidences of design are . . . to be found just as abundantly in the adaptation of external nature to the necessities of animal and vegetable life. Neither plants nor animals could exist without light, air, heat, water, and soil to produce the common food of all living things. Who created the light and heat and diffuses them over the whole earth? Who made the sun from which they radiate? Who constituted the atmosphere with its chemical adjustments, precisely what is necessary for the support of life, everywhere and always the same, and poured it round our globe? How is it that water at a certain temper-

ature evaporates, rises in mist, is gathered into clouds, is carried everywhere by the winds, and falls in rain to fertilize the earth? . . . Surely
this is one great system. There is unity and mutual relation in all its
parts. It must have had one author, and He must be infinite in intelligence and goodness. . . .

If a father by providing a home for his children gives indisputable
evidence of intelligence and love, then are those attributes to be ascribed to Him who fitted up this world to be the home of His creatures.
This is seen, as already intimated, in the constitution of the atmosphere, in the distribution of light and heat, in the establishment of
those laws which secure the regular succession of the seasons, in the
preparation of soil by the disintegration of rocks, the falling of rain,
the deposition of dew which falls gently with life-giving power on the
thirsty earth, and in innumerable other provisions and dispositions of
the forces of nature without which neither vegetable nor animal life
could be sustained. There are many special provisions of this kind
which fill the mind with gratitude and wonder. . . .

The whole configuration of the earth, its position in relation to the
sun, and the inclination of its axis are obviously intended to render it
a suitable residence for the creatures by which it is inhabited. Their
well-being depends on the distribution of land and water over its surface, on the elevation of its mountain ranges and plateaus, and on the
ocean currents which are determined by the configuration of its
coasts. . . . When we see such benevolent arrangements among men,
we refer them instinctively and by a rational necessity to a benevolent
and intelligent agent. No rational ground exists for refusing to ascribe
like arrangements in nature to a similar source. Is it any more an
evidence of prudent or benevolent foresight that a man should store
away abundant fuel for himself or others, knowing that winter is approaching, than that God has laid up inexhaustible stores of coal in
the bowels of the earth for the use of His children? . . .

This argument from design is constantly urged in the Old Testament, which appeals to the heavens and the earth as revealing the
being and perfections of God. The apostle Paul says that the living
God, who made heaven and earth and the sea and all that is therein,
hath not left Himself without a witness (Acts 14:15–17). Paul also
demonstrated to the Athenians the nature of God from His works and
from our relation to Him as His offspring (Acts 17:23–31). To the Romans he said that the eternal power and Godhead of the Supreme
Being are clearly seen, being understood from the things that are made
(Rom. 1:20). The ancient philosophers drew the same conclusion from
the same premises. . . . Socrates constantly dwells on this as the great
proof of the being of God. Cicero (*De natura deorum* 2.37) says that it

is as impossible that an ordered world could be formed by the fortuitous concurrence of atoms as that a book should be composed by the throwing about letters at random. . . . Philo (*De monarchia* 1.4) presents the argument in its simplest syllogistic form. "No work of art is self-made. The world is the most perfect work of art. Therefore, the world was made by a good and most perfect Author. Thus we have the knowledge of the existence of God." All the Christian fathers and subsequent theologians have reasoned in the same way. . . .

[§4. Objections to the Argument from Design]

§5. The Moral or Anthropological Argument

A. Nature of the Argument

As the image of the sun reflected from a mirror or from the smooth surface of a lake reveals to us that the sun is and what it is, so the soul of man, just as clearly and just as certainly, reveals that God is and what He is. The reflection of the sun does not teach us everything that is true concerning that luminary; it does not reveal its internal constitution nor tell us how its light and heat are maintained from age to age. In like manner the soul, as the image of God, does not reveal all that God is. Yet in both cases, and equally in both cases, what is revealed is true, that is, trustworthy. . . .

It has been shown in the preceding chapter that every man has in his own nature the evidence of the existence of God, an evidence which never can be obliterated and which will force conviction on the most unwilling. It is no less true that every man has in himself the same irresistible evidence that God is an extramundane personal Being; that He is intelligent, volitional, and moral; that He knows; that He has the right to command; and that He can punish and can save.

It may naturally be asked, If every man has in his own nature a witness whose competency he cannot question and whose testimony he cannot ignore, what is the use of arguing about the matter? For three reasons, first, because even self-evident truths are often denied; and secondly, because men, in their present moral state, are under a strong temptation to deny the existence of a holy and just God; and thirdly, because efforts are constantly made to pervert or contradict the testimony of our nature to the existence and nature of God.

B. Argument from the Existence of the Mind

Every man has in his own consciousness the evidence of the existence of mind. He knows that he is an intelligent, personal being. He knows that his personality does not reside in his body, but in his soul. It is included in the facts of consciousness that the soul and body are distinct, that they are different substances having not only different but incompatible attributes. That such is the general conviction of men is plain from all languages recognizing the distinction, and from the fact that it is never denied except by speculative or theoretical writers. The common consciousness of men as revealed by their forms of speech, and by their avowals, and by the universal belief in a state of conscious existence after death, bears witness to the truth that the soul is something different from and far superior to the body. How is the existence of this immaterial, thinking, immortal substance which we call self to be accounted for? That it has not always existed is undeniable. If it began to be, it must have a cause outside itself. That cause cannot be the soul of the parent, for that also is an effect. It began to be. And it is universally admitted that an infinite series of effects is unthinkable. If the soul cannot be accounted for as a product of an unending series of steps from those who preceded us, neither can it be conceived of as a product of the body or of physical forces and combinations. It would seem to be a self-evident proposition that the effect cannot contain in it more than is in its cause, that intelligence cannot be the product of what is unintelligent. This also is confirmed by all experience. . . .

We have a right to appeal to the general conviction of mankind that mind cannot be the product of matter. If this be so, as our minds are not self-existent and eternal, it must be true, as even the heathen believed, that our spirits owe their existence to Him who is the Father of spirits.

C. *From the Nature of the Soul*

. . . Man's physical necessities are all met by the present circumstances of his being. In this stage of existence his body becomes all that it is capable of being. But these things are not true with regard to his soul. It has capacities which are not fully developed in this world and never can be. It has desires, aspirations, and necessities for which the world does not furnish the appropriate objects. It is, therefore, as evidently designed and adapted for a higher and spiritual state of existence as his body is adapted to the present order of things. The soul of man has, in the first place, intellectual powers capable of indefinite expansion, which in this world never reach their utmost limit. With these is connected a desire for knowledge which is never satisfied. In the second place, the soul of man has a capacity for happiness which nothing in the world, nor the whole world could it be attained, can by possibility fill. The animal is satisfied. Its capacity for happiness is here fully provided for. In the third place, the soul has aspirations to which nothing in this life corresponds. It longs for fellowship with what is far above itself, with what is boundless and eternal. In the fourth place, with all these powers, desires, and aspirations, it is conscious of its own weakness, insufficiency, and dependence. It must have an object to worship, to love, to trust; a Being who can satisfy all its necessities, and under whose guardianship it can be safe from those powers of evil to which it knows that it is on all sides and at all times exposed; a Being whose existence and whose relation to the soul can explain all the mysteries of its being and secure its felicity in the future, on which it knows it must soon enter. Just as certainly as hunger in the animal supposes that there is food adapted to still its cravings, so certainly does this hunger of the soul suppose that there is some Being in the universe to satisfy its necessities. In both cases the craving is natural, universal, and imperative. . . .

D. From the Moral Nature of Man

Among the familiar facts of consciousness on the subject of the moral nature of man is (1) that we have, by the constitution of our nature, a sense of right and wrong; we perceive or judge some things to be right and others to be wrong. This perception is immediate. As the reason perceives some things to be true and others false, and as the senses take immediate knowledge of their appropriate objects, so the soul takes immediate cognizance of the moral character of feelings and acts. The reason, the senses, and the conscience are alike infallible within certain limits and liable to error beyond those limits.

(2) Our moral perceptions or judgments have their peculiar, distinctive character, which belongs to no other of our states of consciousness. The right is as distinct from the true, the proper, the agreeable, or the expedient, as these latter are from our sensations. The right is that which we are bound to do and to approve; the wrong is that which we are bound to avoid and to disapprove. Moral obligation, as expressed by the word ought, is a simple and primary idea. It can be understood only by those who have felt it. And it can be confounded with nothing else.

(3) These moral judgments are independent. They are not under the control of the understanding or of the will. No man can will to regard an axiom as false, or to think that black is white or white black. Nor can any sophistry of the understanding lead him to such false judgment. In like manner, no man can will to believe that to be right which his conscience tells him to be wrong; nor can he argue himself

into the conviction that he has done right, when his conscience tells him he has done wrong.

(4) Our moral judgments or the conscience has an authority from which we cannot emancipate ourselves. We can neither deny nor ignore it. It has a lordship. It commands and it forbids. And we are bound to obey. It has power also to enforce its decisions. It can reward and punish. Its rewards are among the greatest blessings we can enjoy. Its punishments are the most intolerable agony the human soul can endure.

(5) Our moral judgments involve the idea of law, i.e., of a rule or standard to which we are bound to be conformed. . . .

(6) This law has an authority which it does not derive from us. It is essentially different from a sense of propriety or a perception of expediency. It is something which is imposed upon us and to which an authority outside ourselves requires us to be conformed.

(7) Our moral nature involves, therefore, a sense of responsibility. We must answer for what we are and for what we do. This responsibility is not to ourselves, not to society, nor to being in general. It must be to a person; that is, to a Being who knows what we are, what we do, and what we ought to be and do; who approves of the right and disapproves of the wrong; and who has the power and the purpose to reward and punish us according to our character and conduct. Sin, from its very nature, as it reveals itself in our consciousness, involves not only a sense of pollution or moral degradation, but also a sense of guilt; i.e., a conviction that we deserve punishment, that we ought to be punished, and, therefore, that punishment is inevitable.

If such be the facts of our moral nature, it is plain that we are under the necessity of assuming the existence of an extramundane, personal God on whom we are dependent and to whom we are responsible. This is undoubtedly the ground for the universal conviction of the being of God. Having the idea given in the constitution of their nature, or being under an inward necessity of believing in such a Being, cultivated men have sought and found evidence of His existence in the world outside themselves. But these external proofs have been neither as general nor as operative as those derived from what we ourselves are and from what we know that we deserve. . . .

Moral truths have a self-evidencing light. They can no more be denied than the intuitions of sense and reason. . . . All men are moral beings; all have this sense of moral obligation and of responsibility; and no man can free himself from these convictions. The apostle, therefore, speaking out of the common consciousness of men as well as under the guidance of the Holy Spirit, speaks of sinners as "knowing the judgment of God" (Rom. 1:32); that is, a sense of sin involves the knowledge of a righteous God.

We, then, are placed in the midst of a vast universe of which we constitute a part. We are forced not merely by the desire of knowledge, but from the necessities of our nature, to ask, How did this universe originate? How is it sustained? To what does it tend? What are we? Whence did we come? Whither are we going? These questions must be answered. This complicated problem must be solved. To refer everything to chance is no solution, but rather a frivolous denial that any solution is necessary, that such questions need any answer. To refer everything to necessity is to say that the existence of things as they are is the ultimate fact. The universe is and always has been and always must be. It is the evolution of necessary being by necessary laws. This is all we can know and all that need be known. This, however, is no solution. It is merely the denial that any solution is possible. Could this theory be accepted with regard to the outward world, it leaves all the phenomena of man's nature—intellectual, moral, and religious—unaccounted for. Theism is a solution. It assumes the existence of an eternal and necessary Being, a Spirit that is intelligent, volitional, self-conscious, and endowed with moral perfections. This hypothesis accounts for the origin of the universe. "In the beginning God created the heaven and the earth." This is a satisfactory answer to the first question. It accounts for all the universe is, its immensity, its variety, its order, its numberless organisms, the adaptation of external nature to the wants of all living things. It accounts for the nature of man. It gives what that nature demands—an infinite object of love, confidence, and adoration. It reveals to whom we are responsible and on whom we are dependent. We know that this solution is true, because it is a solution. It meets all the facts of the case. And it so meets them that it cannot fail to be accepted as true, either intelligently or blindly. The God whom all men ignorantly worship, the Scriptures reveal, not only in the certainty of His existence, but in the plentitude of His perfections.

Chapter III

Anti-theistic Theories

§1. What Is Meant by Anti-Theism

As theism is the doctrine of an extramundane, personal God, the creator, preserver, and governor of all things, any doctrine which denies the existence of such a Being is anti-theistic. Not only avowed atheism, therefore, but polytheism, hylozoism, materialism, and pantheism belong to the class of anti-theistic theories.

Atheism does not call for any separate discussion. It is in itself purely negative. It affirms nothing. It simply denies what theism asserts. The proof of theism is, therefore, the refutation of atheism. . . .

The question whether atheism is possible has often been discussed. The answer to the question depends on the meaning of the term. If the question be whether a man can emancipate himself from the conviction that there is a personal Being to whom he is responsible for his character and conduct, and who will punish him for his sins, it must be answered in the negative. For that would be to emancipate himself from the moral law, which is impossible. If, however, the question be whether a man may, by speculation or otherwise, bring himself into such a state as to lose the consciousness of the belief in God as written in his heart, and free himself, for a time, from its power, it must be answered affirmatively. A man may, in this sense, deny his individuality or identity; the real, objective existence of soul or body, mind or matter; the distinction between right and wrong. But this is unnatural and cannot last. It is like deflecting a spring by force. The moment the force is removed, the spring returns to its normal position. Men, therefore, often pass in a moment from a state of entire skepticism to a state of unquestioning faith, not of course by a process of argument, but by a change in their inward state. This transition from unbelief to faith, though sudden and not produced by an intellectual process, is perfectly rational. The feelings which rise in the mind contain evidence of the truth which the understanding cannot resist. . . . So the speculative atheist lives with the abiding conviction that there is a God to whom he must render an account.

§2. Polytheism

As the word implies, polytheism is the theory which assumes the existence of many gods. Monotheism was the original religion of our race. This is evident from the teachings of the Scriptures. . . .

The first departure from monotheism seems to have been nature worship. As men lost the knowledge of God as creator, they were led to reverence the physical elements with which they were in contact, whose power they witnessed, and whose beneficent influence they constantly experienced. Hence not only the sun, moon, and stars, the great representatives of nature, but fire, air, and water, became the objects of popular worship. . . .

These powers were personified, and soon it came to be generally believed that a personal being presided over each. And these imaginary beings were the objects of popular worship. . . .

In the Bible the gods of the heathen are declared to be "vanity" and "nothing," mere imaginary beings without power either to hurt or to save (Jer. 2:28; Isa. 41:29; 42:17; Ps. 106:28). . . . They are not what men take them to be. They have no divine power. . . . The prevalence and persistency of polytheism show that it must have a strong affinity with fallen human nature. Although it has no philosophical basis, it constitutes a formidable obstacle to the progress of true religion in the world.

[§3. Hylozoism]

§4. Materialism

Three general theories have been proposed to solve the great problem of the universe: the materialistic, the pantheistic, and the theistic. According to the first all the phenomena of the universe are due to matter and its forces; according to the second, in its most rational form, all power, activity, and life are the power, activity, and life of the one universal mind. The third, or theistic theory, assumes the existence of an infinite, extramundane God who created matter endowed with forces and finite minds gifted with intelligence and will; it also assumes that all the ordinary phenomena of the universe are proximately due to these physical and mental forces as constantly upheld and controlled by the omnipresent wisdom and power of God. It may be doubted whether any amount of argument can deepen the conviction that the theistic solution of this great problem is the true one. It is seen to be true because it is seen to be a solution. It satisfactorily accounts for all the facts of consciousness and observation. It satisfies the reason, the heart, and the conscience. It is in fact self-evidently true in the sense that no man to whom it has been once proposed can ever permanently shake off the conviction of its truth. The other theories are not solutions. They may account for some classes of facts, but not for others. Our present concern, however, is with materialism.

Materialism is that system which ignores the distinction between matter and mind, and refers all the phenomena of the world, whether physical, vital, or mental, to the functions of matter. . . . As materialism in its modern form, in all that is essential to the theory, is the same as it was a thousand years ago, the old arguments against it are as cogent now as they ever were. Its fundamental affirmation is that all the phenomena of the universe, physical, vital, and mental, are to be referred to unintelligent physical forces; and its fundamental negation is that there is no such objective entity as mind or spirit. If, therefore, it can be shown that unintelligent force cannot account for all the phenomena of the universe, and that there is such an objective entity or substance as mind, the theory is refuted. . . .

(1) *Materialism contradicts the facts of consciousness.* The primary principle of all knowledge is the knowledge of self. This must be assumed. Unless we *are* we cannot *know.* This knowledge of self is a knowledge that we are something, a real existence, not merely a state or mode of something else, but a substance, a real, objective entity. It is, moreover, a knowledge not only that we are a substance, but also that we are an individual subsistence which thinks, feels, and wills.

Here, then, is mind, i.e., an individual, intelligent, volitional agent, necessarily included in the first and the most essential of all truths. . . . It is, moreover, included in this knowledge of the self, that the body is not the Ego. Although the body is intimately and even vitally united to the substance in which our personality resides, it is nevertheless objective to it. It is the organ which the self uses and by which it holds communion with the external world. That these are really facts of consciousness and not merely arbitrary assumptions is clear because they are universally and of necessity recognized. They are imbedded in all human languages; they are involved in all expressions of human thought; they are of necessity assumed by those who theoretically deny them. The materialist cannot think or speak or write without assuming the existence of mind as distinct from matter. . . .

Another fact of consciousness which materialism denies, either avowedly or by necessary implication, is the fact of free agency. . . . It needs no proof that consciousness attests that men have the power of self-determination. Every man knows this to be true with regard to himself. Every man recognizes the fact with regard to his fellow men. This again is a conviction which no obduracy of the conscience and no sophistry of argument can permanently obliterate from the human mind. This, however, materialism denies. Physical forces act necessarily and uniformly. In referring all mental action to physical forces, materialism cannot but exclude all freedom of action. . . . Every man, therefore, who knows that he is a free agent knows that materialism cannot be true.

Materialism also contradicts the facts of our moral and religious consciousness. Our moral perceptions are the clearest, the most certain, and the most authoritative of all of our cognitions. If a man is compelled to deny either the testimony of his senses and the truths of reason on the one hand, or the testimony of his moral nature on the other, all experience shows that he will give up sense and reason, and bow to the authority of conscience. He cannot help it. No man can free himself from the sense of sin or of accountability. These moral convictions involve in them or at least necessitate the belief in a God to whom we must give an account. But materialism, in banishing all mind in man, leaves nothing to be accountable, and in banishing all mind from the universe, leaves no Being to whom an account can be rendered. To substitute for an intelligent, extramundane, personal God mere "inscrutable force" is a mockery, an insult. Our whole moral and religious nature declares any such theory to be false. It cannot be true unless our whole nature be a lie. . . .

(2) *Materialism contradicts the truths of reason.* . . . It is self-evident that an unintelligent cause cannot produce an intelligent effect; it

cannot purpose, foresee, organize, or choose.... If every man recognizes the absurdity of referring all the works of human ingenuity and intellect to unintelligent, physical force, how much greater is the absurdity of referring to blind force the immeasurably more stupendous, complicated, and ordered works of God, everywhere indicative of purpose, foresight, and choice. Of this absurdity materialism is guilty....

(3) *Materialism is inconsistent with the facts of experience.* It is generally admitted that ... all the resources of science are incompetent to raise matter from one plane to another. The plant contains ingredients derived from the mineral kingdom, with something specifically different. The animal contains all that is in the plant, with something specifically different. Man contains all that enters into the constitution of the plant and animal, with something specifically different.... There is something in the plant which is not in lifeless matter, something in the animal which is not in the plant, and something in man which is not in the animal. To assume, with the materialist, that the organizing life of the plant comes out of lifeless matter, that the sensitive and voluntary life of the animal comes out of the insensible and involuntary life of the plant, or that the rational, moral, and spiritual life of man comes out of the constituents of the animal, is to assume as a fact something which all experience contradicts....

§5. Pantheism

If the etymology of the word pantheism be allowed to determine its meaning, the answer to the question, What is pantheism? is easy. The universe is God, and God is the universe.... The essential distinction between matter and mind, between soul and body, between God and the world, between the Infinite and the finite is repudiated. There is but one substance, but one real Being....

Pantheism, therefore, merges everything into God. The universe is the existence-form of God; that is, the universe is His existence. All reason is His reason; all activity is His activity; the consciousness of creatures is all the consciousness God has of Himself; good and evil, pain and pleasure, are phenomena of God—modes in which God reveals Himself, the way in which He passes from Being to Existence. He is not, therefore, a person whom we can worship and in whom we can trust. He is only the substance of which the universe and all that it contains are the ever-changing manifestation. Pantheism admits of no freedom, no responsibility, no conscious life after death....

The fact that pantheism has extensively prevailed in every age and in every part of the world is a proof of its fascination and power. Apart from a divine revelation, it seems to have been regarded as the most probable solution of the great problem of the universe. Nevertheless it is so unsatisfactory and does such violence to the laws of our nature that it has never to any extent taken hold on the hearts of the people. India may be regarded as furnishing an exception to this remark. But even there, although pantheism was the ground form of the popular religion, it had to resolve itself into polytheism in order to meet the necessities of the people. Men must have a personal god whom they can worship and to whom they can pray.

The most obvious remark to be made of the whole system is that it is a hypothesis. From its very nature it is incapable of proof. It is a mere theory assumed to account for the phenomena of the universe. If it did satisfactorily account for them and did not contradict the teachings of the Bible, it might be safely admitted. But not only is it inconsistent with all that the Scriptures reveal concerning the nature of God and His relation to the world, it also contradicts the laws of belief which God has impressed on our nature. . . .

(1) We are conscious that we are free agents. This is a truth which no man can deny with regard to himself and which every man assumes with regard to others. This truth pantheism denies. It makes our activity only a form of the activity of God and assumes that His acts are determined by necessity as much as is the development of a plant or animal.

(2) It is intuitively certain that there is a real distinction between moral good and evil: that the one is that to which man is bound to be conformed, and the other that which he is bound to hate and to avoid; that the one deserves approbation, and that the other deserves disapprobation and merits punishment. These are convictions which belong to the rational nature of man, and they cannot be destroyed without destroying his rationality. Pantheism, however, pronounces that these convictions are delusions, that there is no such thing as sin, and that what we call sin is mere weakness, imperfect development as unavoidable as feebleness in an infant. It goes further: it pronounces evil good. It makes the sinful acts and passions of men as much the acts and states of God as are holy acts and holy feelings. . . .

(3) Pantheism not only destroys the foundation of morals, but renders all rational religion impossible. Rational religion supposes a personal Being endowed not only with intelligence and power, but with moral excellence; moreover, that Being must be infinite in all His perfections. Pantheism, however, denies that an infinite Being can be a person; that it can be intelligent, self-conscious, or possessed of moral attributes. It is just as impossible to worship such a Being as it is to

worship the atmosphere, or the law of gravitation, or the axioms of Euclid.

(4) It is no extravagance to say that pantheism is the worst form of atheism. For mere atheism is negative. It deifies neither man nor evil. But pantheism teaches that man, the human soul, is the highest form in which God exists, and that evil is as much a manifestation of God as is good; Satan is the ever-blessed and adorable Redeemer. Beyond this it is impossible for the insanity of wickedness to go.

(5) Man, according to this system, is no more immortal than the leaves of the forest or the waves of the sea. We are transient forms of universal Being.

Our nature is indestructible; as it is impossible that we should not believe in our own individual existence, in our free agency, in our moral obligations, in our dependence on and responsibility to a Being capable of knowing what we are and what we do, and of rewarding and punishing as He sees fit, so it is impossible that pantheism should be more than a philosophical speculation wherever the moral nature of man has once been developed by the knowledge of the living and true God.

The Knowledge of God

Having considered the arguments in favor of the doctrine that God is and also the various systems opposed to theism, we come now to consider the question, Can God be known? and if so, How? that is, How does the mind proceed in forming its idea of God, and How do we know that God really is what we believe Him to be?

§1. God Can Be Known

It is the clear doctrine of the Scriptures that God can be known. Our Lord teaches that eternal life consists in the knowledge of God and of Jesus Christ, whom He hath sent. The psalmist says, "In Judah is God known" (Ps. 76:1). Isaiah predicts that "the earth shall be full of the knowledge of the LORD" (Isa. 11:9). Paul says that even the heathen knew God, but they did not like to retain that knowledge (Rom. 1:19–21, 28).

A. State of the Question

It is, however, important to understand distinctly what is meant when it is said, God can be known. This does not mean that . . . He can be comprehended. To comprehend is to have a complete and exhaustive knowledge of an object. . . . God is past finding out. We cannot understand the Almighty unto perfection. . . .

It is included in what has been said that our knowledge of God is partial and inadequate. There is infinitely more in God than we have any idea of; and what we do know, we know imperfectly. We know that God knows, but in His mode of knowing and in its relation to its objects there is much we cannot understand. We know that He acts, but we do not know how He acts or the relation which His activity bears to time or to things outside Himself. We know that He feels: He loves, pities, is merciful, is gracious, and He hates sin. But this emotional element of the divine nature is covered with an obscurity as great as, but no greater than, that which rests over His thoughts or purposes. . . .

While, therefore, it is admitted not only that the infinite God is incomprehensible and that our knowledge of Him is both partial and imperfect, that there is much in God which we do not know at all, and that what we do know, we know very imperfectly, nevertheless our knowledge, as far as it goes, is true knowledge. God really is what we believe Him to be, so far as our idea of Him is determined by the revelation which He has made of Himself in His works, in the constitution of our nature, in His Word, and in the person of His Son. To know is simply to have such apprehensions of an object as conform to what that object really is. We know what the word Spirit means. We know what the words infinite, eternal, and immutable mean. And, therefore, the sublime proposition, pregnant with more truth than was ever compressed in any other sentence, "God is a Spirit, infinite, eternal, and immutable," conveys to the mind as distinct an idea and as true (i.e., trustworthy) knowledge as the proposition "The human soul is a finite spirit." In this sense God is an object of knowledge. . . .

B. How Do We Know God?

How does the mind proceed in forming its idea of God? The older theologians answered this question by saying that it is by the way of negation, by the way of eminence, and by the way of causality. That is, we deny to God any limitation; we ascribe to Him every excellence in the highest degree; and since He is the great First Cause, we refer to Him every attribute manifested in His works. We are the children of God, and, therefore, we are like Him. We are, therefore, authorized to ascribe to Him, without limitation and to an infinite degree, all the attributes of our own nature as rational creatures. If we are like God, God is like us. This is the fundamental principle of all religion. This is the principle which Paul assumed in his address to the Athenians (Acts 17:29): "Forasmuch then as we are the offspring of God, we ought not to think that the Godhead is like unto gold, or silver, or stone, graven by art and man's device." For the same reason we ought not to think that He is simple being, or a mere abstraction, a name for the moral order of the universe, or the unknown and unknowable cause of all things—mere inscrutable force. If we are His children, He is our Father, whose image we bear and of whose nature we partake. . . .

C. *Proof That This Method Is Trustworthy*

(1) This method of forming an idea of God is a law of nature. Even in the lowest form of animism the life of the worshipper is assumed to belong to the object which he worships. The power dreaded is assumed to possess attributes like our own. . . . The only question, therefore, is, Are we invincibly led to think of God as possessing the attributes of our rational nature? This cannot be denied, for universality proves invincibility of belief. And it is a historical fact that men have universally thus thought of God. . . . We are forced by the constitution of our nature thus to think of God. And by the fundamental principle of all true philosophy, what we are forced to believe must be true. It is true, therefore, that God really is what we take Him to be when we ascribe to Him, without limitation and to an infinite degree, the perfections of our own nature.

(2) We have already shown, when speaking of the moral argument for the existence of God, that all men are conscious of their accountability to a Being superior to themselves, a Being who knows what they are and what they do, and who has the will and purpose to reward or punish men according to their works. The God, therefore, who is revealed to us in our nature is a God who knows and wills and acts, who rewards and punishes. That is, He is a person—an intelligent, volitional agent endowed with moral attributes. This revelation of God must be true. It must make known to us what God really is, or our nature is a lie. . . . Now if our moral nature compels us to believe that God is a person, He must be a person; consequently, we arrive at a

true knowledge of God by attributing to Him the perfections of our own nature.

(3) The argument from our religious nature, as distinct from our moral nature, is essentially the same. Morality is not all of religion. The one is as much a law and necessity of our nature as the other. To worship, in the religious sense of the word, is to ascribe infinite perfection to its object. It is to express to that object our acknowledgments for the blessings we enjoy and to seek their continuance; it is to confess and praise and pray and to adore. We cannot worship the law of gravity, or unconscious force, or the mere order of the universe. Our religious nature, in demanding an object of supreme reverence, love, and confidence, demands a personal God, a God clothed with the attributes of a nature like our own; who can hear our confessions, praises, and prayers; who can love and be loved; who can supply our wants and fill all our capacities for good. Thus again it appears that unless our whole nature is a contradiction and a falsehood, we arrive at a true knowledge of God when we ascribe to Him the perfections of our own nature. . . .

(4) The fourth argument on this subject is that if we are not justified in referring to God the attributes of our own nature, then we have no God. . . . An unknown God, a God of whose nature and of whose relation to us we know nothing, to us is nothing. It is a historical fact that those who reject this method of forming our idea of God, who deny that we are to refer to Him the perfections of our own nature, have become atheists. . . .

(5) A fifth argument is from the fact that the works of God manifest a nature like our own. It is a sound principle that we must refer to a cause the attributes necessary to account for its effects. If the effects manifest intelligence, will, power, and moral excellence, these attributes must belong to the cause. As, therefore, the works of God are a revelation of all these attributes on a most stupendous scale, they must belong to God in an infinite degree. This is saying only that the revelation made of God in the external world agrees with the revelation which He has made of Himself in the constitution of our own nature. In other words, it proves that the image of Himself which He has enstamped on our nature is a true likeness.

(6) The Scriptures declare God to be just what we are led to think He is when we ascribe to Him the perfections of our own nature in an infinite degree. We are self-conscious; so is God. We are spirits; so is He. We are volitional agents; so is God. We have a moral nature, miserably defaced indeed; God has moral excellence in infinite perfection. We are persons; so is God. All this the Scriptures declare to be true. The great primal revelation of God is as the "I am," the personal

God. . . . [Moreover,] the relations in which, according to the Scriptures, we stand to God are such as we can sustain only to a Being who is like ourselves. He is our ruler and father, with whom we can commune. His favour is our life, his loving-kindness better than life. This sublime revelation of God in His own nature and in His relation to us is not a delusion. It is not mere regulative truth, or it would be a deceit and mockery. It makes God known to us as He really is. We therefore know God, although no creature can understand the Almighty unto perfection.

(7) Finally, God has revealed Himself in the person of His Son. No man knoweth the Father but the Son and he to whom the Son shall reveal Him. Jesus Christ is the true God. The revelation which He made of Himself was the manifestation of God. He and the Father are one. The words of Christ were the words of God. The works of Christ were the works of God. The love, mercy, tenderness, the forgiving grace, as well as the holiness, the severity, and power manifested by Christ, were all manifestations of what God truly is. We see, therefore, as with our own eyes, what God is. We know that although infinite and absolute, He can think, act, and will; that He can love and hate; that He can hear prayer and forgive sin; that we can have fellowship with Him, as one person can commune with another. Philosophy must veil her face in the presence of Jesus Christ as God manifest in the flesh. She may not presume in that presence to say that God is not, and is not known to be, what Christ Himself most clearly was. This doctrine that God is the object of certain and true knowledge lies at the foundation of all religion and therefore must never be given up.

[§2. God Cannot Be Fully Known]

§3. Hamilton's Doctrine

. . .

Necessity of a Supernatural Revelation

God has not so constituted our nature as to make it of necessity deceptive. The senses, reason, and conscience, within their appropriate spheres and in their normal exercise, are trustworthy guides. They teach us real and not merely apparent truth. Their combined spheres comprehend all the relations in which we, as rational creatures, stand to the external world, to our fellow men, and to God. Were it not for the disturbing element of sin, we know not that man, in full communion with his maker, whose favour is light and life, would have needed any other guides. But man is not in his original and normal state. In apostatizing from God, man fell into a state of darkness and confusion. Reason and conscience are no longer adequate guides as to "the things of God." Of fallen men the apostle says that "when they knew God, they glorified him not as God, neither were thankful; but became vain in their imaginations, and their foolish heart was darkened. Professing themselves to be wise, they became fools, and changed the glory of the uncorruptible God into an image made like to corruptible man, and to birds, and fourfooted beasts, and creeping things" (Rom. 1:21–23). . . . It is true, therefore, as the same apostle tells us, that the world by wisdom knows not God (1 Cor. 1:21). It is true in a still higher sense, as the Lord Himself says, that no man "knoweth the Father, save the Son, and he to whomsoever the Son will reveal him" (Matt. 11:27).

We need, therefore, a divine supernatural revelation. Of this revelation it is to be remarked, first, that it gives us real knowledge. It teaches us what God really is, what sin is, what the law is, what Christ and the plan of salvation through Him are, and what is to be the state of the soul after death. The knowledge thus communicated is real in the sense that the ideas which we are thus led to form of the things revealed conform to what those things really are. God and Christ, holiness and sin, heaven and hell, really are what the Bible declares them to be. . . . If the testimony of men can give us clear and certain knowledge of facts beyond our experience, surely the testimony of God is greater. What He reveals is made known. We apprehend it as it truly is. The conviction that what God reveals is made known in its true nature is the very essence of faith in the divine testimony. We are certain, therefore, that our ideas of God, founded on the testimony of His Word, correspond to what He really is and constitute true knowledge. It is also to be remembered that while the testimony of men is to the mind, the testimony of God is not only to but also within the mind. It illuminates and informs, so that the testimony of God is called the demonstration of the Spirit.

The second remark concerning the revelation contained in the Scriptures is that while it makes known truths far above the reach of sense or reason, it reveals nothing which contradicts either. It harmonizes with our whole nature. It supplements all our other knowledge and authenticates itself by harmonizing the testimony of enlightened consciousness with the testimony of God in His Word.

The conclusion, therefore, of the whole matter is that we know God in the same sense in which we know ourselves and things outside ourselves. We have the same conviction that God is and that He is, in Himself and independently of our thought of Him, what we take Him to be. Our subjective idea corresponds to the objective reality. This knowledge of God is the foundation of all religion; therefore, to deny that God can be known is really to deny that rational religion is possible. In other words, it makes religion a mere sentiment or blind feeling instead of its being what the apostle declares it to be, *a rational service* (Rom. 12:1)—the homage of the reason as well as of the heart and life.

Chapter V

Nature and Attributes of God

§1. Definition of God

. . . To define is simply to bound, to separate, or distinguish, so that the thing defined may be discriminated from all other things. . . . When we say we can define God, all that is meant is that we can analyze the idea of God as it lies in our mind, or that we can state the class of beings to which He belongs and the attributes by which He is distinguished from all other beings. . . . Probably the best definition of God ever penned by man is that given in the "Westminster Catechism": "God is a Spirit, infinite, eternal, and unchangeable, in his being, wisdom, power, holiness, justice, goodness, and truth." This is a true definition, for it states the class of beings to which God is to be referred. He is a Spirit, and He is distinguished from all other spirits in that He is infinite, eternal, and unchangeable in His being and perfections. It is also a complete definition insofar as it is an exhaustive statement of the contents of our idea of God.

By *being* is here meant that which has a real, substantive existence. It is equivalent to substance or essence. It is opposed to what is merely thought and to a mere force or power. . . . God is in His nature a substance or essence which is infinite, eternal, and unchangeable—the common subject of all divine perfections and the common agent of all divine acts. . . . In defining the divine essence as a Spirit we are denying of it, as we do of our own spiritual essence, what belongs to material substances. We also affirm that in itself and its attributes it is infinite, eternal, and unchangeable. . . .

§2. Divine Attributes

To the divine essence, which in itself is infinite, eternal, and unchangeable, belong certain perfections revealed to us in the constitution of our nature and in the Word of God. These divine perfections, which are called attributes, are essential to the nature of a divine Being and necessarily involved in our idea of God. The older theologians distinguished the attributes of God (1) from predicates which refer to God in the concrete and indicate His relation to His creatures (e.g., creator, preserver, ruler); (2) from properties which are technically the distinguishing characteristics of the several persons of the Trinity (there are certain acts or relations peculiar or proper to the Father, others to the Son, and others to the Spirit); and (3) from accidents or qualities which may or may not belong to a substance, which may be acquired or lost. Thus holiness was not an attribute of the nature of Adam, but an accident, something which he might lose and still remain a man, whereas intelligence was an attribute, because the loss of intelligence involves the loss of humanity. The perfections of God, therefore, are attributes without which He would cease to be God.

In attempting to explain the relation in which the attributes of God stand to His essence and to each other, there are two extremes to be avoided. First, we must not represent God as a composite being composed of different elements; and, secondly, we must not confound the attributes, making them all mean the same thing, which is equivalent to denying them altogether. . . .

It is evident that this question of the relation of the divine attributes to the divine essence merges itself into the general question of the relation between attributes and substance. . . . We are conscious of ourselves as a thinking substance. That is, we are conscious that that which is ourselves has identity, continuance, and power. We are further conscious that the substance self thinks, wills, and feels. Intelligence, will, and sensibility are its functions or attributes, and consequently the attributes of a spirit. These are the ways in which a spirit acts. Anything which does not thus act, which has not these functions or attributes, is not a spirit. If you take from a spirit its intelligence, will, and sensibility, nothing remains; its substance is gone; at least it ceases to be a spirit. Substance and attributes are inseparable. The one is known in the other. A substance without attributes is nothing, i.e., no real existence. . . .

Accordingly, no metaphysical speculations as to the difference between essence and attribute in an infinite Being should lead us to give up the conviction that God is really in Himself what He reveals Himself to be. The attributes of God, therefore, are not merely different conceptions in our minds, but different modes in which God reveals Himself to His creatures (or to Himself), just as our several faculties are different modes in which the inscrutable substance self reveals itself in our consciousness and acts. Clement of Alexandria says, "If any one knows himself, he will know God" (*Paedagogus* 3.1). And Leibnitz expresses the same great truth when he says, "The perfections of God are those of our own souls, but He possesses them without limit. He is an ocean of which we have received only a few drops. There is in us something of power, something of knowledge, something of goodness; but these attributes are in entireness in Him" (*Théodicée*, preface). . . .

§3. Classification of the Divine Attributes

The object of classification is order, and the object of order is clearness. . . . Some arrange the attributes of God according to the mode in which we arrive at the knowledge of them. We form our idea of God, it is said, (1) by the way of causation; that is, by referring to Him as the great First Cause every virtue manifested by the effects which He produces; (2) by the way of negation; that is, by denying to Him the limitations and imperfections which belong to His creatures; (3) by the way of eminence, in exalting to an infinite degree or without limit the perfections which belong to an infinite Being. . . . This principle of classification is perhaps the one most generally adopted. It gives rise, however, really but to two classes, namely, the positive and negative, the former affirming and the latter denying things concerning God. To the negative class are commonly referred simplicity, infinity, eternity, immutability; to the positive class, power, knowledge, holiness, justice, goodness, and truth. Instead of calling the one class negative and the other positive, they are often distinguished as absolute and relative. By an absolute attribute is meant one which belongs to God considered in Himself and which implies no relation to other beings; by a relative attribute is meant one which implies relation to an object. They are also distinguished as immanent and transitive, as communicable and incommunicable. These terms are used interchangeably. They do not express different modes of classification, but are different modes of designating the same classification. Negative, absolute, immanent, and incommunicable are designations of one class; and positive, relative, transitive, and communicable are designations of the other class. . . .

It is proposed in what follows, however, to accept the guidance of the answer given in the "Westminster Catechism" to the question, What is God? It is assumed in that answer that God is a self-existent and necessary Being; and it is affirmed of Him (1) that He is a Spirit; (2) that as such He is infinite, eternal, and immutable; and (3) that He is infinite, eternal, and immutable (a) in His being; (b) in all that belongs to His intelligence, namely, in His knowledge and wisdom; and (c) in all that belongs to His will, namely, His power, holiness, justice, goodness, and truth. Whatever speculative objections may be made to this plan, it has the advantage of being simple and familiar.

§4. Spirituality of God

A. The Meaning of the Word Spirit

The fundamental principle of interpretation of all writings, sacred or profane, is that words are to be understood in their historical sense, that is, in the sense in which they were used by their authors and intended to be understood by those to whom they were addressed. Unless words are taken in the sense in which those who employ them intend that they be understood, they fail of their design, which is communication of thought. The sacred writings being the words of God to man, we are bound to take them in the sense in which those to whom they were originally addressed must inevitably have taken them. What is the meaning of the word spirit? or rather, What is the *usus loquendi* of the Hebrew and Greek words to which our word spirit corresponds? In answering this question, we learn what our Lord meant when He said God is a Spirit. Originally the Hebrew and Greek words (*rûah* and *pneuma*) meant the moving air, especially the breath; then any invisible power; then the human soul. In saying, therefore, that God is a Spirit, our Lord authorizes us to believe that whatever is essential to the idea of a spirit, as learned from our own consciousness, is to be referred to God as determining His nature.

(1) On this subject consciousness teaches and has taught all men, first of all, that the soul is a substance, that our thoughts and feelings have a common ground of which they are the varying states or acts. Substance is that which has an objective existence and has permanence and power. Even Kant says that where operation and conse-

quently activity and power are, there is substance. . . . That there should be action without something acting is as unthinkable as that there should be motion without something moving.

(2) Consciousness teaches that the soul is an individual subsistence. This is included in the consciousness of the unity, identity, and permanence of the soul. . . . Individual subsistence is intuited in the consciousness of self, because in self-consciousness we distinguish ourselves from all that is not ourselves.

(3) As power of some kind belongs to every substance, the power which belongs to spirit, to the substance self, is that of thought, feeling, and volition. All this is given in the simplest form of consciousness. We are not more certain that we exist than that we think, feel, and will. We know ourselves only as thinking, feeling, and willing, and we are therefore sure that these powers or faculties are the essential attributes of a spirit and must belong to every spirit.

(4) Consciousness also informs us of the unity or simplicity of the soul. It is not compounded of different elements. It is composed of substance and form. It is a simple substance endowed with certain attributes. It is incapable of separation or division.

(5) In being conscious of our individual subsistence, we are conscious of personality. Not every individual subsistence is a person. But every individual subsistence that thinks, feels, and has the power of self-determination is a person; and, therefore, the consciousness of our subsistence and of the powers of thought and volition is the consciousness of personality.

(6) We are also conscious of being moral agents—susceptible of moral character and the subjects of moral obligation.

(7) It need not be added that every spirit must possess self-consciousness. This is involved in all that has been said. Without self-consciousness we would be a mere power in nature. This is the very ground of our being and is necessarily involved in the idea of self as a real existence.

It is impossible, therefore, to overestimate the importance of the truth contained in the simple proposition, God is a Spirit. It is involved in that proposition that God is immaterial. None of the properties of matter can be predicated of Him. He is not extended or divisible, or compounded, or visible, or tangible. He has neither bulk nor form. The Bible everywhere recognizes as true the intuitive convictions of men. One of those convictions is that spirit is not matter or matter spirit, and that different and incompatible attributes cannot belong to the same substance. In revealing, therefore, that God is a Spirit, the Bible reveals to us that no attribute of matter can be predicated of the divine essence. The realistic dualism which lies at the bottom of all human convictions underlies also all the revelations of the Bible.

B. *Consequences of the Spirituality of God*

If God be a Spirit, it follows of necessity that He is a person—a self-conscious, intelligent, volitional agent. As all this is involved in our consciousness of ourselves as spirit, it must all be true of God, or God is of a lower order of being than man.

It follows also that God is a simple Being, not only as not composed of different elements, but also as not admitting of the distinction between substance and accidents. Nothing can be added to or taken away from God. In this view the simplicity, as well as the other attributes of God, is of a higher order than are the corresponding attributes of our spiritual nature. The soul of man is a simple substance, but it is subject to change. It can gain and lose knowledge, holiness, and power. These are in this view accidents in our substance. But in God they are attributes, essential and immutable.

Finally, it follows from God's being a Spirit that He is a moral as well as an intelligent Being. It is involved in the very nature of rational, volitional being that it should be conformed to the rule of right, which in the case of God is His own infinite reason. These are primary truths which are not to be sacrificed to any speculative objections. It is vain to tell us that an infinite Spirit cannot be a person because personality implies self-consciousness, and self-consciousness implies the distinction between the self and the not-self, and this is a limitation. It is equally vain to say that God cannot have moral excellence because moral goodness implies conformity to law, and conformity to law again is inconsistent with the idea of an absolute Being. These are empty speculations, and even if incapable of a satisfactory solution, would afford no rational ground for rejecting the intuitive truths of reason and conscience. There are mysteries enough in our nature, and yet no sane man denies his own personal existence and moral accountability. And he is worse than insane who is beguiled by such sophistries into renouncing his faith in God as a personal Spirit and a loving Father.

It need hardly be remarked that the Scriptures everywhere represent God as possessing all the above-mentioned attributes of a spirit. On this foundation all religion rests: all intercourse with God, all worship, all prayer, all confidence in God as preserver, benefactor, and Redeemer. The God of the Bible is a person. He spoke to Adam. He revealed Himself to Noah. He entered into covenant with Abraham. He conversed with Moses, as a friend with a friend. He everywhere uses the personal pronouns: He calls Himself "I am"; I am the Lord your God; I am merciful and gracious; Call upon me, and I will answer you; Like as a father pitieth his children, so the Lord pitieth them that fear Him. In teaching us to pray, "Our Father who art in heaven, hallowed be thy name. Thy kingdom come. Thy will be done," our Lord has put on our lips words which reveal that God is a Spirit and all that being a spirit implies. Everywhere the God of the Bible is contrasted with the gods of the heathen as a God who sees, hears, and loves.... He thus presents Himself to us as a personal Being with whom we can have intercourse and who is everywhere present to help and save....

§5. Infinity

Although God reveals Himself as a personal Being capable of fellowship with man, a Being whom we can worship and love, and to whom we can pray with the assurance of being heard and answered, nevertheless He fills heaven and earth; He is exalted above all we can know or think. He is infinite in His being and perfections.... Regrettably, in all ages wrong views of what the infinite is have led to fatal errors in philosophy and religion. Without attempting to detail the speculations of philosophers on this subject, we shall simply endeavor to state what is meant when it is said that God is infinite in His being and perfections.

Being, in this connection, is that which is or exists. The being of God is His essence or substance, of which His perfections are the essential attributes or modes of manifestation. When it is said that God is infinite as to His being, what is meant is that no limitation can be assigned to His essence.

A. The Infinite Not the All

The infinite, although illimitable and incapable of increase, is not necessarily all.... A thing may be infinite in its own nature without precluding the possibility of the existence of things of a different nature. An infinite spirit does not forbid the assumption of the existence of matter. There may even be many infinites of the same kind, as we can imagine any number of infinite lines. The infinite, therefore, is not all. An infinite spirit is a spirit to whose attributes as a spirit no limits can be set. It no more precludes the existence of other spirits than infinite goodness precludes the existence of finite goodness, or infinite power the existence of finite power. God is infinite in being because no limit can be assigned to His perfections and because He is present in all portions of space. A being is said to be present wherever it perceives and acts. As God perceives and acts everywhere, He is everywhere present. This, however, does not preclude the presence of other beings. A multitude of men even may perceive and act at the same time and place. Besides, we have very little knowledge of the relation which spirit bears to space. We know that bodies occupy portions of space to the exclusion of other bodies, but we do not know that spirits may not coexist in the same portion of space. A legion of demons dwelt in one man.

B. Infinitude of God in Relation to Space

The infinitude of God, so far as space is concerned, includes His immensity and His omnipresence. These are not different attributes, but one and the same attribute viewed under different aspects. His immensity is the infinitude of His being viewed as belonging to His nature from eternity. He fills immensity with His presence. His omnipresence is the infinitude of His being viewed in relation to His creatures. He is equally present with all His creatures at all times and in all places. He is not far from any one of us. "The Lord is in this place," may be said with equal truth and confidence everywhere. Theologians are accustomed to distinguish three modes of presence in space. Bodies are in space circumscriptively. They are bounded by it. Spirits are in space definitively. They are not everywhere, but only somewhere. God is in space repletively. He fills all space. In other words, the limitations of space have no reference to Him. He is not absent from any portion of space, nor more present in one portion than in another. This of course is not to be understood of extension or diffusion. Extension is a property of matter and cannot be predicated of God. If extended, He would be capable of division and separation, and part of God would be here and part elsewhere. Nor is this omnipresence to be understood as a mere presence in knowledge and power. It is an omnipresence of the divine essence. Otherwise the essence of God would be limited. . . . As God acts everywhere, He is present everywhere; for, as the theologians say, a being can no more act where he is not than when he is not. . . .

The Bible teaches the infinitude of God, as involving His immensity and omnipresence, in the clearest terms. He is said to fill all in all, i.e., the universe in all its parts (Eph. 1:23). "Am I a God at hand, saith the Lord, and not a God afar off? Can any hide himself in secret places that I shall not see him? saith the Lord. Do not I fill heaven and earth? saith the Lord" (Jer. 23:23–24). "Whither shall I go from thy Spirit?

or whither shall I flee from thy presence? If I ascend up into heaven, thou art there: if I make my bed in hell, behold, thou art there. If I take the wings of the morning, and dwell in the uttermost parts of the sea; even there shall thy hand lead me, and thy right hand shall hold me" (Ps. 139:7–10). It is "in him we (i.e., all creatures) live, and move, and have our being" (Acts 17:28). Everywhere in the Old and New Testament, God is represented as a spiritual Being, without form, invisible, whom no man hath seen or can see; as dwelling in the light which no man can approach unto, and full of glory; as not only the creator and preserver, but as the governor of all things; as everywhere present and everywhere imparting life and securing order; as present in every blade of grass, yet guiding Arcturus in his course, marshalling the stars as a host, calling them by their names; as present also in every human soul, giving it understanding, endowing it with gifts, working in it both to will and to do. The human heart is in His hands, and He turneth it even as the rivers of water are turned. Wherever throughout the universe there is evidence of mind in material causes, there, according to the Scriptures, is God, controlling and guiding those causes to the accomplishment of His wise designs. He is in all and over all things, yet essentially different from all, being over all, independent, and infinitely exalted. This immensity and omnipresence of God, therefore, is the ubiquity of the divine essence and consequently of the divine power, wisdom, and goodness. As the birds in the air and the fish in the sea, so also are we always surrounded and sustained by God. It is thus that He is infinite in His being, without absorbing all created beings into His own essence, but sustaining all in their individual subsistence and in the exercise of their own powers.

§6. Eternity

The infinitude of God vis-à-vis space is His immensity or omnipresence; vis-à-vis duration, it is His eternity. As He is free from all limitations of space, so He is exalted above all the limitations of time. As He is not more in one place than in another, but is everywhere equally present, so He does not exist during one period of duration more than another. With Him there is no distinction between the present, past, and future; but all things are equally and always present to Him. With Him duration is an eternal now. This is the popular and the Scriptural view of God's eternity. "Before the mountains were brought forth, or ever thou hadst formed the earth and the world, even from everlasting to everlasting thou art God" (Ps. 90:2). "Of old hast thou laid the foundation of the earth: and the heavens are the work of thy hands.

They shall perish, but thou shalt endure: yea, all of them shall wax old like a garment; as a vesture shalt thou change them, and they shall be changed: but thou art the same, and thy years shall have no end" (Ps. 102:25–27). "I am the first, and I am the last; and beside me there is no God" (Isa. 44:6). "One day is with the Lord as a thousand years, and a thousand years as one day" (2 Peter 3:8). He is "the same yesterday, and today, and for ever" (Heb. 13:8). God's primal revelation of Himself to His covenant people was as the "I am."

What is taught in these and similar passages is, first, that God is without beginning of years or end of days—He is and always has been and always will be; and secondly, that to Him there is neither past nor future; the past and the future are always and equally present to Him. . . .

§7. Immutability

The immutability of God is intimately connected with His immensity and eternity, and is frequently included with them in the Scriptural statements concerning His nature. Thus when it is said, He is the First and the Last, the Alpha and Omega, the same yesterday, today, and forever; or when in contrast with the ever-changing and perishing world it is said, "They shall be changed, but thou art the same," His immutability is just as much in view as is His eternity. As an infinite and absolute Being, self-existent and absolutely independent, God is exalted above all the causes of and even above the possibility of change. Infinite space and infinite duration cannot change. They must ever be what they are. So God is absolutely immutable in His essence and attributes. He can neither increase nor decrease. He is subject to no process of development or of self-evolution. His knowledge and power can never be greater or less. He can never be wiser or holier or more righteous or more merciful than He ever has been and ever must be. He is no less immutable in His plans and purposes. Infinite in wisdom, there can be no error in their conception; infinite in power, there can be no failure in their accomplishment. He is "the Father of lights, with whom is no variableness, neither shadow of turning" (James 1:17). "God is not a man, that he should lie; neither the son of man, that he should repent: hath he said, and shall he not do it? or hath he spoken, and shall he not make it good?" (Num. 23:19). "I am the LORD, I change not" (Mal. 3:6). "The counsel of the LORD standeth for ever, the thoughts of his heart to all generations" (Ps. 33:11). . . .

When theologians attempt to state in philosophical language the doctrine of the Bible on the unchangeableness of God, they are apt to confound immutability with immobility. In denying that God can change, they seem to deny that He can act. . . . But we know that God is immutable in His being, His perfections, and His purposes; and we know that He is perpetually active. And, therefore, activity and immutability must be compatible; and no explanation of the latter inconsistent with the former ought to be admitted. . . .

§8. Knowledge

A. Its Nature

By knowledge is meant the intellectual apprehension of truth. It supposes a subject and object—an intelligent subject that apprehends and something true that is apprehended.

So far as we are concerned, knowledge is either intuitive or discursive. Our senses give us immediate knowledge of their appropriate objects; the understanding intuitively perceives primary truths; our moral and aesthetic nature gives us the immediate cognition of things right or wrong, and beautiful or deformed. Most of our knowledge, however, is derived by instruction, observation, comparison, deduction, etc. In all cases there is the distinction between the mind which perceives and the object which is perceived. . . .

The Scriptural view assumes that knowledge in God, in its essential nature, is what knowledge is in us. . . . We must, however, remove from our conception of the divine attribute all the limitations and imperfections which belong to the corresponding attribute in us, though we are not to destroy its nature. And in determining what is and what is not consistent with the nature of God as an infinitely perfect Being, we are to be controlled by the teachings of the Scriptures and by the necessities (or laws) of our moral and religious nature, and not by our speculative notions of the Infinite and Absolute. God, therefore, does and can know in the ordinary and proper sense of that word. He is an ever-present eye to which all things are perfectly revealed. "All things," says the apostle, "are naked and opened unto the eyes of him with whom we have to do" (Heb. 4:13). "O LORD, thou hast searched me, and known me. Thou knowest my downsitting and mine uprising, thou understandest my thought afar off" (Ps. 139:1–2). "The eyes of the LORD are in every place, beholding the evil and the good" (Prov. 15:3). "Great is our Lord, and of great power: his understanding is infinite" (Ps. 147:5). "O house of Israel: . . . I know the things that come into your mind, every one of them" (Ezek. 11:5). "Known unto God are all his works from the beginning of the world" (Acts 15:18). "The very hairs of your head are all numbered" (Matt. 10:30).

This knowledge of God is not only all-comprehending, but intuitive and immutable. He knows all things as they are, being as being, phenomena as phenomena, the possible as possible, the actual as actual, the necessary as necessary, the free as free, the past as past, the present as present, the future as future. Although all things are ever present in His view, yet He sees them as successive in time. The vast procession of events, thoughts, feelings, and acts stands open to His view.

This infinite knowledge of God is not only clearly and constantly asserted in Scripture, but is also obviously included in the idea of an absolutely perfect Being. Such a Being cannot be ignorant of anything; His knowledge can neither be increased nor diminished. The omniscience of God follows also from His omnipresence. As God fills heaven and earth, all things are transacted in His presence. He knows our thoughts far better than they are known to ourselves. This plenitude of divine knowledge is taken for granted in all acts of worship. We pray to a God who, we believe, knows our state and wants, who hears what we say, and who is able to meet all our necessities. Unless God were thus omniscient, He could not judge the world in righteousness. Faith in this attribute in its integrity is, therefore, essential even to natural religion. . . .

B. Foreknowledge

Among the objects of the divine knowledge are the free acts of men. The Scriptures abundantly teach that such acts are foreknown. Such knowledge is involved in the prediction of events which either concern the free acts of men or are dependent on them. If God be ignorant of how free agents will act, His knowledge must be limited and it must be constantly increasing, a notion which is altogether inconsistent with the true idea of His nature. His government of the world also, in that case, must be precarious, for it would be dependent on the unforeseen conduct of men. The Church, therefore, in obedience to the Scriptures has almost with one voice professed faith in God's foreknowledge of the free acts of His creatures.

The Socinians, however, and some of the Remonstrants, unable to reconcile this foreknowledge with human liberty, deny that free acts can be foreknown. As the omnipotence of God is His ability to do whatever is possible, so His omniscience is His knowledge of everything knowable. But as free acts are in their nature uncertain, as they may or may not be, they cannot be known before they occur. Such is the argument of Socinus. This whole difficulty arises out of the assumption that contingency is essential to free agency. If an act may be certain as to its occurrence and yet free as to the mode of its occurrence, the difficulty vanishes. That free acts may be absolutely certain is plain because they have in a multitude of cases been predicted. It was certain that the acts of Christ would be holy, yet they were free. The continued holiness of the saints in heaven is certain, and yet they are perfectly free. The foreknowledge of God is inconsistent with a false theory of free agency, but not with the true doctrine on that subject.

After Augustine the common way of meeting the difficulty of reconciling foreknowledge with liberty was to represent it as merely subjective. The distinction between knowledge and foreknowledge is only in us. There is no such difference in God. . . .

C. The Wisdom of God

Wisdom and knowledge are intimately related. The former is manifested in the selection of proper ends and of proper means for the accomplishment of those ends. As there is abundant evidence of design in the works of nature, so all the works of God declare His wisdom. They show, from the most minute to the greatest, the most wonderful adaptation of means to accomplish the high end of the good of His creatures and the manifestation of His own glory. So also, in the whole course of history, we see evidence of the controlling power of God making all things work together for the best interests of His people and the promotion of His kingdom upon earth. It is, however, in the work of redemption that this divine attribute is specially revealed. It is by the Church that God has determined to manifest, through all ages, to principalities and powers, His manifold wisdom. . . . "O LORD, how manifold are thy works! in wisdom hast thou made them all," is the devout exclamation of the psalmist (Ps. 104:24). And in contemplation of the work of redemption the apostle exclaims, "O the depth of the riches both of the wisdom and knowledge of God!" (Rom. 11:33).

§9. The Will of God

A. The Meaning of the Term

. . . In our day the word will is limited to the faculty of self-determination and the determinations themselves. That is, the power to will and volitions or purposes. God as a Spirit is a volitional agent. We are authorized to ascribe to Him the power of self-determination.

This the Bible does everywhere. From the beginning to the end it speaks of the will of God, of His decrees, purposes, counsels, and commands. The will is not only an essential attribute of our spiritual being, but the necessary condition of our personality. Without the power of rational self-determination we would be a mere force like electricity or magnetism or the principle of vegetable life. To deny to God the power of self-determination, of acting or not acting, according to His own good pleasure, is, therefore, to degrade Him below the sphere of being which we ourselves occupy as rational creatures.

B. The Freedom of the Divine Will

The will of God is free in the highest sense of the word. An agent is said to be free (1) when he is at liberty to act or not to act, according to his good pleasure—this is liberty in acting; and (2) when his volitions are determined by his own sense of what is wise, right, or desirable. . . .

God is free, then, in creating and preserving, because these acts do not arise from the necessity of His nature. He was free to create or not create, to continue the universe in existence or to cause it to cease to be. He is free also in keeping His promises, because His purpose so to do is determined by His own infinite goodness. It is indeed inconceivable that God should violate His word. But this proves only that moral certainty may be as inexorable as necessity.

C. The Decretive and Preceptive Will of God

The decretive will of God concerns His purposes and relates to the futurition of events. The preceptive will relates to the rule of duty for His rational creatures. He decrees whatever He purposes to effect or to permit. He prescribes, according to His own will, what His creatures should do or abstain from doing. The decretive and preceptive will of God can never be in conflict. God never decrees to do, or to cause others to do, what He forbids. He may, as we see He does, decree to permit what He forbids. He permits men to sin, although sin is forbidden. To put this in scholastic terms: A positive decretive will cannot consist with a negative preceptive will; i.e., God cannot decree to make men sin. But a negative decretive will may consist with an affirmative preceptive will; e.g., God may command men to repent and believe, and yet, for wise reasons, He may abstain from giving them repentance. . . .

By the secret will of God is meant His purposes as still hidden in

His own mind; by His revealed will, His precepts and His purposes as far as they are made known to His creatures. . . .

It should be noted here that both the Greek and English verbs to will sometime express feeling and sometimes a purpose. A correct rendering of Matthew 27:43 would be "let him deliver him, if he *delight in* him" (cf. Ps. 22:8). The word is also used in this sense when it is said that God wills all men to be saved (1 Tim. 2:4). He cannot be said to purpose or determine upon any event which is not to come to pass. A judge may will the happiness of a man whom he sentences to death. He may will him not to suffer when he in fact wills him to suffer. The infelicity in such forms of expression is that the word will is used in different senses. In one part of the sentence it means desire and in the other purpose. To say that God wills all men to be saved means that He as a benevolent Being desires the happiness of all men, even while He purposes to save only His own people.

D. The Will of God as the Ground of Moral Obligation

Are things right or wrong simply because God commands or forbids them? Or does He command or forbid them because they are right or wrong for some reason other than His will? . . . The common doctrine of Christians on this subject is that the will of God is the ultimate ground of moral obligation for all rational creatures. No higher reason can be assigned why anything is right than that God commands it. This means (1) that the divine will is the only rule for deciding what is right and what is wrong; and (2) that His will is that which binds us, or that to which we are bound to be conformed. By the word will is not meant any arbitrary purpose, so that it were conceivable that God should will right to be wrong or wrong right. The will of God is the expression or revelation of His nature, or is determined by it; so that His will, as revealed, makes known to us what infinite wisdom and goodness demand. Sometimes things are right simply because God has commanded them; e.g., circumcision and other ritual obligations of the Old Testament Jews. Other things are right because of the present constitution of things which God has ordained; e.g., the duties relating to property and the permanent relations of society. Others, again, are right because they are demanded by the immutable excellence of God. In all cases, however, so far as we are concerned, it is His will that binds us and constitutes the difference between right and wrong—His will, that is, as the expression of His infinite perfection. So that the ultimate foundation of moral obligation is the nature of God.

§10. The Power of God

A. The Nature of Power

We get the idea of power from our own consciousness. That is, we are conscious of the ability of producing effects. Power in man is confined within very narrow limits. We can change the current of our thoughts, or fix our attention on a particular object, and we can move the voluntary muscles of our body. Beyond this our direct power does not extend. It is from this small measure of efficiency that all the stores of human knowledge and all the wonders of human art are derived. It is only our thoughts, volitions, and purposes, together with certain acts of the body, that are immediately subject to the will. For all other effects we must avail ourselves of the use of means. We cannot will a book, a picture, or a house into existence. The production of such effects requires protracted labor and the use of diverse appliances.

B. Omnipotence

It is by removing all the limitations of power, as it exists in us, that we rise to the idea of the omnipotence of God. . . . We can do very little. God can do whatever He wills. We, beyond very narrow limits, must use means to accomplish our ends. With God means are unnecessary. He wills and it is done. He said, "Let there be light," and there was light. He by a volition created the heavens and the earth. At the volition of Christ, the winds ceased and there was a great calm. By an act of the will He healed the sick, opened the eyes of the blind, and raised the dead. This simple idea of the omnipotence of God, that He can do without effort and by a volition whatever He wills, is the highest conceivable idea of power and is that which is clearly presented in the Scriptures. In Genesis 17:1 it is said, "I am the Almighty God." The prophet Jeremiah exclaims, "Ah Lord God! behold, thou hast made the heaven and the earth by thy great power and stretched out arm, and there is nothing too hard for thee" (Jer. 32:17). God is said to have created all things by the breath of His mouth and to uphold the universe by a word. Our Lord says, "With God all things are possible" (Matt. 19:26). The psalmist long before had said, "Our God is in the heavens: he hath done whatsoever he hath pleased" (Ps. 115:3). That the Lord God omnipotent reigneth, and doeth His pleasure among the armies of heaven and the inhabitants of the earth, is the tribute of adoration which the Scriptures everywhere render unto God, and the truth which they everywhere present as the ground of confidence to

His people. This is all we know and all we need to know on this
subject. . . .

C. Absolute Power

By absolute power, as understood by the schoolmen and some of
the later philosophers, is meant power free from all the restraints of
reason and morality. According to this doctrine, contradictions, absurdities, and immoralities are all within the compass of the divine
power. Nay, it is said that God can annihilate Himself. . . .

Essential to the very idea of power, however, is that it has reference
to the production of possible effects. It is no more a limitation of power
that it cannot effect the impossible than it is of reason that it cannot
comprehend the absurd, or of infinite goodness that it cannot do wrong.
It is contrary to its nature. Instead of exalting, it degrades God, to
suppose that He can be other than He is, or that He can act contrary
to infinite wisdom and love. When, therefore, it is said that God is
omnipotent because He can do whatever He wills, it is to be remembered that His will is determined by His nature. It is certainly no
limitation to perfection to say that it cannot be imperfect. . . .

There is, however, a sense in which absolute power is generally
recognized among theologians. A distinction is commonly made between the *potentia absoluta* and the *potentia ordinata* of God. By the
latter is meant the efficiency of God as exercised uniformly in the
ordered operation of second causes; by the former, His efficiency as
exercised without the intervention of second causes. Creation, miracles, immediate revelation, inspiration, and regeneration are to be
referred to the *potentia absoluta* of God, and all His works of providence to His *potentia ordinata*. This distinction is important, as it
draws the line between the natural and supernatural, between what
is due to the operation of natural causes sustained and guided by the
providential efficiency of God, and what is due to the immediate exercise of His power. . . .

§11. Holiness of God

This is a general term for the moral excellence of God. In 1 Samuel
2:2 it is said, "There is none holy as the LORD"; no other being is
absolutely pure and free from all limitation in moral perfection. "Thou
Holy One of Israel" is the form of address which the Spirit puts on
the lips of the people of God. "Exalt the LORD our God, and worship
at his holy hill; for the LORD our God is holy" (Ps. 99:9). "Holy and

reverend is his name" (Ps. 111:9). "Thou art of purer eyes than to behold evil, and canst not look on iniquity" (Hab. 1:13). "Who shall not fear thee, O Lord, and glorify thy name? for thou only art holy" (Rev. 15:4). Holiness, on the one hand, implies entire freedom from moral evil and, on the other, absolute moral perfection. Freedom from impurity is the primary idea of the word. To sanctify is to cleanse; to be holy is to be clean. Infinite purity, even more than infinite knowledge or infinite power, is the object of reverence. "The Holy One of Israel" is He who is to be feared and adored. Seraphim round about the throne who cry day and night, "Holy, Holy, Holy is the Lord of hosts," give expression to the feelings of all unfallen rational creatures in view of the infinite purity of God. In offering this perpetual homage to the divine holiness they are the representatives of the whole universe. It is because of His holiness that God is a consuming fire. And it was a view of His holiness which led the prophet to exclaim, "Woe is me! for I am undone; because I am a man of unclean lips, and I dwell in the midst of a people of unclean lips: for mine eyes have seen the King, the LORD of hosts" (Isa. 6:5). . . .

If in answering the question, What is God? we allow ourselves to be determined by the teachings of His Word and the constitution of our own nature, and if we refer to Him, in an infinite degree, every good we find in ourselves, then we can have no hesitation in believing that He is holy, just, and good. But if we turn to philosophical speculations to decide every question concerning the divine nature, we must give up all confidence in our apprehensions of God as an object of knowledge. . . . It is surely most unreasonable to sacrifice to such speculations all religion and all confidence in the intuitive judgments of the human mind, as well as all faith in God and in the Bible.

§12. Justice

A. Meaning of the Word

The word justice or righteousness . . . means rightness, that which satisfies the demands of rectitude or law. . . . When we regard God as the author of our moral nature, we conceive of Him as holy; when we regard Him in His dealings with His rational creatures, we conceive of Him as righteous. He is a righteous ruler; all His laws are holy, just, and good. In His moral government He faithfully adheres to those laws. He is impartial and uniform in their execution. As a judge He renders unto every man according to his works. He neither condemns the innocent nor clears the guilty, neither does He ever punish with undue severity. Hence the justice of God is distinguished as *rectoral*, or that which is concerned in the imposition of righteous laws and in their impartial execution, and *distributive*, or that which is manifested in the righteous distribution of rewards and punishment. The Bible constantly represents God as a righteous ruler and a just judge. These two aspects of His character, or of our relation to Him, are not carefully distinguished. We have the assurance, which runs through the Scriptures, that "the Judge of all the earth" must "do right" (Gen. 18:25). "God is a righteous judge" (Ps. 7:11). "He shall judge the world with righteousness" (Ps. 96:13). "Clouds and darkness are round about him: righteousness and judgment are the habitation of his throne" (Ps. 97:2). Notwithstanding all the apparent inequalities in the distribution of His favours, notwithstanding the prosperity of the wicked and the afflictions of the righteous, the conviction is everywhere expressed that God is just, that somehow and somewhere He will vindicate His dealings with men and show that He is righteous in all His ways and holy in all His works.

B. Justice in Its Relation to Sin

As the sense of guilt is universal among men and as the manifestations of sin are so constant and pervading, it is mainly in its relation to sin that the justice of God is revealed. Hence many theologians define the justice of God as that attribute of His nature which is manifested in the punishment of sin. . . .

1. The reformation of the offender is not the primary object of punishment

As the justice of God is specially manifested in the punishment of sin, it is of primary importance to determine why sin is punished.

One prevalent theory on this subject is that the only legitimate end of punishment is the reformation of the offender.

It is of course to be admitted that the good of the offender is often the ground or reason why evil is inflicted. A father chastises a child in love and for its good. And God, our heavenly Father, brings suffering upon His children for their edification. But evil inflicted for the benefit of the sufferer is chastisement and not punishment. Punishment, by contrast, is evil inflicted in satisfaction of justice.

There are several indications that the good of the sufferer is not the primary end of the infliction of punishment:

(1) The punishment of the wicked is always, in the Scriptures, referred to the anger of God, and the chastisement of His people to His love. The cases, therefore, are not analogous. This difference of rep-

resentation is designed to teach us that the wicked and the good do not stand in the same relation to God as objects of benevolence, but that the one He punishes to testify His disapprobation and satisfy His justice, and the other He chastises to bring them nearer to Himself.

(2) In many cases the nature of the punishment precludes the possibility of the good of the offender being the ground of its infliction. The deluge, the destruction of the cities of the plain, and the overthrow of Jerusalem were certainly not designed for the benefit of the men who suffered from those desolating inflictions. Much less can it be assumed that the punishment of the fallen angels and of the finally impenitent is intended to be reformatory.

(3) Scripture and experience both teach that suffering, when of the nature of punishment, has no tendency to reform. When suffering is seen to come from a father's hand and to be a manifestation of love, it has a sanctifying power; but when it comes from the hand of God, as a judge and an avenger, and is the expression of displeasure and a proof of our alienation from God, its tendency is to harden and to exasperate. . . .

(4) On this subject, appeal may be fairly made to the common consciousness of men. . . . When any great crime is committed, there is an instinctive and universal demand for the punishment of the criminal. No man can pretend that the desire for his reformation is the feeling which prompts that demand. That is not so much as thought of. It is the instinctive judgment of the mind that he ought to suffer. It is not benevolence towards him which calls for the infliction of punishment.

2. The prevention of crime is not the primary end of punishment

The doctrine that the only legitimate end of punishment is the prevention of crime has had great prevalence in the Church and the world. It is the common doctrine of jurists. It is, of course, to be conceded that the good of society and of the moral government of God is one important end of punishment in all governments, human or divine. It is, however, an important collateral effect of the administration of justice rather than its immediate design. The doctrine in question merges justice into benevolence. According to this way of thinking, God visits sin with punishment only because He has a view to the happiness of His rational creatures. . . .

It is assumed that happiness is the greatest good, and hence that the purpose and desire to promote happiness is the sum of all virtue. From this it follows that this world, the work of a God of infinite benevolence, wisdom, and power, must be the best possible world for the production of happiness; and, therefore, both the permission of sin and its punishment must be referred to the benevolence of God. They are the necessary means for securing the greatest amount of happiness. However, if happiness be not the greatest good, if holiness be a higher end than happiness, if expediency be not the ground and measure of moral obligation, it is obvious that this whole structure collapses.

3. Proof of the Scriptural doctrine

It is admitted that happiness is promoted by justice and therefore that it is contrary to a wise benevolence that men should be allowed to sin with impunity. But justice cannot properly be merged into benevolence. And that the promotion of happiness by the prevention of crime is not the primary end of the infliction of punishment is evident on several counts:

(1) Every man knows that benevolence and justice, as revealed in his own consciousness, are different sentiments. The one prompts to the promotion of happiness, the other involves the instinctive judgment that a criminal ought to suffer for his crime. We do not stop to ask, or to think, what may be the collateral effect on others of the infliction of punishment. Anterior to such reflection and independent of it is the intuitive perception that sin should be punished for its own sake or on account of its inherent ill-desert. These instinctive moral judgments are as clear and as trustworthy revelations of the nature of God as can possibly be made. They force conviction in spite of all speculative sophistries. Every man knows the righteous judgment of God that those who sin are worthy of death. If justice and benevolence are distinct in us, they are distinct in God. If we, in obedience to the nature which He has given us, intuitively perceive or judge that sin ought to be punished for its own sake and irrespective of the good effect punishment may have on others, then such also is the judgment of God. This is the principle which underlies and determines all our ideas of the Supreme Being. If moral perfection be not in Him what it is in us, then He is to us an unknown something, and we use words without meaning when we speak of Him as holy, just, and good.

(2) This sense of justice, which is indestructible in the nature of man and which, in common with reason and conscience, has survived the fall, is revealed not only in the ordinary experience of men, but still more distinctly in their religious consciousness. What is commonly called "conviction of sin" is only a modification and higher form of those inward experiences which are common to all men. All men know that they are sinners. They all know that sin, as related to the justice of God, is guilt, that which ought to be punished; and that, as related to His holiness, it renders us polluted and offensive in His sight. They also know, intuitively, that God is just as well as holy and, therefore, that His moral perfection, by the same necessity by which He disapproves of and hates sin, calls for its punishment. Under the

pressure of these convictions and the consciousness of their utter inability either to satisfy divine justice or to free themselves from the defilement and power of sin, men either tremble, constantly anticipating judgment, or look outside themselves for help. When, under either the common or saving operations of the Spirit of God, these sentiments are deepened, then their nature is more clearly revealed. A man, when thus convinced of sin, sees not only that it would be right for him to be punished, but that the justice or moral excellence of God demands his punishment. It is not that he ought to suffer for the good of others or for the purpose of sustaining the moral government of God, but that he, as a sinner and for his sins, ought to suffer. . . . We have, therefore, an inward revelation, which can neither be suppressed nor perverted, that justice is not benevolence. . . .

(3) The truth of this doctrine may also be inferred from the holiness of God. If He is infinitely pure, His nature must be opposed to all sin; and as His acts are determined by His nature, His disapprobation of sin must manifest itself in His acts. But the disfavour of God, the manifestation of His disapprobation, is death, as His favour is life. . . .

(4) The inseparable connection between sin and misery is a revelation of the justice of God. That holiness promotes happiness is a revelation of the relation in which God stands to holiness, and that sin produces misery is no less a revelation of the relation in which He stands to moral evil. This constitution of things, depending on the nature and will of God, proves that sin is evil in its own nature and is punished for its own sake. The law of God, which includes a penalty as well as precepts, is in both a revelation of the nature of God. If the precepts manifest His holiness, the penalty as clearly manifests His justice. If the one is immutable, so also is the other. The wages of sin is death. Death is what is due to it in justice and what without injustice cannot be withheld from it. If the prevention of crime were the primary end of punishment, then if the punishment of the innocent, the execution, for example, of the wife and children of a murderer, would have a greater restraining influence than would the punishment of the guilty murderer, their execution would be just. But this would shock the moral sense of men.

(5) The Scriptural doctrines of satisfaction and justification rest on the principle that God is immutably just, i.e., that His moral excellence, in the case of sin, demands punishment or expiation. The Bible clearly teaches that satisfaction to justice is necessary if sin is to be forgiven. Christ was set forth as a propitiation in order that God might be just in justifying the ungodly. This assumes that it would be unjust, i.e., contrary to moral rectitude, to pardon the guilty without such a propitiation. This necessity for a satisfaction is never referred to expediency or to governmental considerations. If sin could have been

pardoned without a satisfaction, the apostle says, Christ is dead in vain (Gal. 2:21). If there could have been a law which could have given life, salvation would have been by the law (Gal. 3:21).

Moreover, if there is no such attribute in God as justice, as distinguished from benevolence, then there can be no such thing as justification. There may be pardon, as the act of a sovereign remitting a penalty and restoring an offender to favour, but no such thing as justification, as an act of a judge proceeding according to law and pronouncing the demands of justice satisfied. The Scriptures, however, according to the almost unanimous judgment of the Church, pronounce that justification is more than an act of executive clemency. Conscience is not satisfied with mere forgiveness. It is essential to peace with God that the soul should see that justice is satisfied. This is the reason why the death of Christ, why His blood, is so inexpressibly precious in the eyes of His people. All the experience of the saints is a protest against the principle that expiation is unnecessary, that sin can be pardoned without a satisfaction of justice.

The whole argument of the apostle in his Epistle to the Romans is founded on the principle that justice is a divine attribute distinct from benevolence. His argument is: God is just. All men are sinners. All, therefore, are guilty, i.e., under condemnation. Therefore no man can be justified, i.e., pronounced not guilty, on the ground of his character or conduct. Sinners cannot satisfy justice. But what they could not do, Christ, the eternal Son of God, clothed in our nature, has done for them. He has brought in everlasting righteousness, which meets all the demands of the law. All those who renounce their own righteousness and trust to the righteousness of Christ, God justifies and saves. This is the gospel preached by Paul. It all rests on the assumption that God is just.

The doctrine of vindicatory justice, the truth of which is clearly evidenced in the moral nature of man, in the religious experience of believers, and in the teaching and doctrines of the Scriptures, has ever been considered as a turning point in theology. . . .

§13. The Goodness of God

A. *The Scriptural Doctrine*

Goodness, in the Scriptural sense of the term, includes benevolence, love, mercy, and grace. By benevolence is meant the disposition to promote happiness; all sensitive creatures are its objects. Love includes complacency, desire, and delight, and has rational beings for its objects. Mercy is kindness exercised towards the miserable and includes pity, compassion, forbearance, and gentleness, which the Scriptures so abundantly ascribe to God. Grace is love exercised towards the unworthy. The love of a holy God to sinners is the most mysterious attribute of the divine nature. The manifestation of this attribute for the admiration and beatification of all intelligent creatures is declared to be the special design of redemption. God saves sinners, we are told, "that in the ages to come he might show the exceeding riches of his grace in his kindness toward us through Christ Jesus" (Eph. 2:7). This is the burden of that Epistle.

As all these elements of goodness are found even in our dilapidated nature and commend themselves to our moral approbation, we know they must exist in God without measure and without end. In Him they are infinite, eternal, and immutable.

1. Benevolence

The goodness of God in the form of benevolence is revealed in the whole constitution of nature. As the universe teems with life, it teems also with enjoyment. There are no devices in nature for the promotion of pain for its own sake, whereas the manifestations of design for the production of happiness are beyond computation. The manifestation of the goodness of God in the form of love, and specially of love to the undeserving, is, as just stated, the great end of the work of redemption. "God so loved the world, that he gave his only begotten Son, that whosoever believeth in him should not perish, but have everlasting life" (John 3:16). "Herein is love, not that we loved God, but that he loved us, and sent his Son to be the propitiation for our sins" (1 John 4:10). Paul prays that believers might be able to comprehend the height and depth, the length and breadth, of the love which passes knowledge (Eph. 3:18–19).

2. Love

Love in us includes complacency and delight in its object, with the desire of possession and communion. . . . We must believe that God is love in the sense in which that word comes home to every human heart. The Scriptures do not mock us when they say, "Like as a father pitieth his children, so the LORD pitieth them that fear him" (Ps. 103:13). He meant what He said when He proclaimed Himself "The LORD, the LORD God, merciful and gracious, long-suffering, and abundant in goodness and truth" (Exod. 34:6). "Beloved," says the apostle, "let us love one another: for love is of God; and every one that loveth is born of God, and knoweth God. He that loveth not knoweth not God; for God is love. In this was manifested the love of God toward us, because that God sent his only begotten Son into the world, that we might live through him. Herein is love, not that we loved God, but that he loved us, and sent his Son to be the propitiation for our sins. Beloved, if God so loved us, we ought also to love one another" (1 John 4:7–11). The word love has the same sense throughout this passage. God is love; and love in Him is, in all that is essential to its nature, what love is in us. Herein we do rejoice, yea, and will rejoice.

B.   The Existence of Evil

How can the existence of evil, physical and moral, be reconciled with the benevolence and holiness of a God infinite in His wisdom and power? This is the question which has exercised the reason and tried the faith of men in all ages of the world. Such is the distance between God and man, such the feebleness of our powers, and such the limited range of our vision, it might seem reasonable to leave this question to be answered by God Himself. If a child cannot rationally sit in judgment on the conduct of his parents, nor a peasant comprehend the affairs of an empire, we certainly are not competent to call God to account or to ask of Him the reason of His ways. We might rest satisfied with the assurance that the Judge of all the earth must do right. These considerations, however, have not availed to prevent speculation on this subject. The existence of evil is constantly brought forward by skeptics as an argument against religion, and it is constantly in the minds of believers as a difficulty and a doubt. While it is our duty to obey the injunction, "Be still and know that I am God," it is no less our duty to protest against those solutions of this great problem which destroy either the nature of sin or the nature of God.

1. Theories which involve the denial of sin as an evil

Most of the theories proposed to account for the existence of evil come under one or the other of the three following classes: First, those which really or virtually deny the existence of evil in the world. What we call evil is distinguished as physical and moral, pain and sin. There is some plausibility in the argument to prove that pain is not necessarily an evil. It is necessary to the safety of sentient creatures. But pain exists far beyond the bounds of this necessity. Such are the amount and variety of suffering in the world, of the just and of the unjust, of infants and adults, that no philosophy can smother the conviction that the misery which weighs so heavily on the children of men is an appalling evil. There is no such trial to our faith as to see an infant suffering excruciating pain. If, however, pain could be removed from the category of evil, sin is not so easily disposed of. The world lies in wickedness. The history of man is, to a large degree, the history of sin. If God be holy, wise, and omnipotent, how can we account for this widely extended and long-continued prevalence of sin?

One solution is sought in the denial that sin is an evil. In other words, it is denied that there is any such thing as sin. What we so regard is, as some maintain, nothing more than limitation of being. To be free from sin, we must be free from limitation, i.e., infinite. It is not an evil that one tree is smaller, less beautiful, or less valuable than others; or that a plant has not the sensitive life of an animal; or that all animals have not the rational powers of man. As in a forest we see trees of every shape and size, perfectly and imperfectly developed, and this diversity is itself a good, so among men there are some more and some less conformed to the ideal standard of reason and right, but this is not an evil. It is only diversity of development.

Others say that what we call sin is the necessary condition of virtue. There can be no action without reaction, no strength without obstacles to be overcome, no pleasure without pain, and no virtue without vice. Moral goodness is mastery over moral evil. There cannot be one without the other. All would be dead and motionless, a stagnant sea, were it not for this antagonism.

Others again say that sin has only a subjective reality. It is analogous to pain. Some things affect us agreeably, others disagreeably; some excite self-approbation, some disapprobation. But that is simply our own concern. God no more participates in our judgments than He does in our sensations. . . .

A much more plausible theory, belonging to the class of those which virtually, although not professedly, destroy the nature of sin, is that which regards it as the necessary means of the greatest good. Sin in itself is an evil; relatively, it is a good. The universe is better with it than without it. In itself it is an evil that the smaller animals should be devoured by the larger; but as this is necessary to prevent the undue development of animal life, and as it ministers to the higher forms thereof, it becomes a benevolent arrangement. The amputation of a limb is an evil, but if necessary to save life, it is a good. Wars are dreadful evils, yet the world is indebted to wars for the preservation of civil and religious liberty, for which they are a small price. Better have war than lose the liberty wherewith Christ has made us free. Thus, if sin be the necessary means of the greatest good, it ceases to be an evil on the whole, and it is perfectly consistent with the benevolence of God to permit its occurrence. . . .

Plausible though this theory be, [it makes happiness the end of creation.] It is unscriptural and contrary to our moral reason, however, to make happiness the end of creation. The Bible declares the glory of

God, an infinitely higher end, to be the final cause for which all things exist. It is the instinctive judgment of men that holiness or moral excellence is a greater good than happiness. But, according to the theory in question, holiness has no value except as a means of producing happiness. Consequently, this theory cannot be believed. . . .

2. The doctrine that God cannot prevent sin in a moral system

The second general method of reconciling the existence of sin with the benevolence and holiness of God is not to deny that sin, even all things considered, is an evil, but to affirm that God cannot prevent all sin, or even the present amount of sin, in a moral system. It assumes that certainty is inconsistent with free agency. Any kind or degree of influence which renders it certain how a free agent will act destroys his liberty in acting. He must always be able to act contrary to any degree of influence brought to bear upon him, or he ceases to be free. God, therefore, of necessity limits Himself when He creates free agents. They are beyond His absolute control. He may argue and persuade, but He cannot govern. . . .

If this theory be so, then God cannot secure the accomplishment of His purposes or the fulfilment of His promises. There is no security for the triumph of good in the universe. Angels and saints in heaven may all sin, and evil become dominant and universal. On this theory, all prayer that God would change our own hearts, or the hearts of others, becomes irrational. All this is so contrary to the teaching of the Bible, which everywhere asserts the sovereignty and supremacy of God, declaring that the hearts of men are in His hand, that He turns them as the rivers of water, and that He makes His people willing in the 'day of His power, working in them to will and to do according to His good pleasure; it is so inconsistent with the promise to give repentance and faith, with the assertion of His power to change the heart; it is so incompatible with the hopes and confidence of the believer that God can keep him from falling, and so subversive of the idea of God as presented in the Bible and revealed in our nature, that the Church has, almost with one accord, preferred to leave the mystery of evil unexplained rather than to seek its solution in a principle which undermines the foundation of all religion.

3. The Scriptural doctrine

The third method of dealing with this question is to rest satisfied with the simple statements of the Bible. The Scriptures teach (1) that the glory of God is the end to which the promotion of holiness and the production of happiness and all other ends are subordinate. (2) Therefore, the self-manifestation of God, the revelation of His infinite perfection, being the highest conceivable or possible good, is the ultimate end of all His works in creation, providence, and redemption. (3) As sentient creatures are necessary for the manifestation of God's benevolence, so there could be no manifestation of His mercy without misery, or of His grace and justice if there were no sin. As the heavens declare the glory of God, so He has devised the plan of redemption "to the intent that now unto the principalities and powers in heavenly places might be known by the church the manifold wisdom of God" (Eph. 3:10). The knowledge of God is eternal life. It is for creatures the highest good. And the promotion of that knowledge, the manifestation of the manifold perfections of the infinite God, is the highest end of all His works. This is declared by the apostle to be the end contemplated both in the punishment of sinners and in the salvation of believers. It is an end to which, he says, no man can rationally object—"What if God, willing to show his wrath (or justice), and to make his power known, endured with much longsuffering the vessels of wrath fitted to destruction: and that he might make known the riches of his glory on the vessels of mercy, which he had afore prepared unto glory" (Rom. 9:22–23). Sin, therefore, according to the Scriptures, is permitted so that the justice of God may be known in its punishment, and His grace in its forgiveness. And the universe, without the knowledge of these attributes, would be like the earth without the light of the sun.

The glory of God being the great end of all things, we are not obliged to assume that this is the best possible world for the production of happiness, or even for securing the greatest degree of holiness among rational creatures. It is wisely adapted to the end for which it was designed, namely, the manifestation of the manifold perfections of God. That God, in revealing Himself, does promote the highest good of His creatures in a manner consistent with the promotion of His own glory may be admitted. But to reverse this order, to make the good of the creature the highest end, is to pervert and subvert the whole scheme; it is to put the means for the end, to subordinate God to the universe, the Infinite to the finite. This putting the creature in the place of the creator disturbs our moral and religious sentiments and convictions, as well as our intellectual apprehensions of God and of His relation to the universe. . . .

There is a great difference whether the earth or the sun be assumed as the center of our solar system. If we make the earth the center, our astronomy will be in confusion. And if we make the creature and not God the end of all things, our theology and religion will in like manner be perverted. It may, in conclusion, be safely asserted that a universe constructed for the purpose of making God known is a far better universe than one designed for the production of happiness.

§14. The Truth of God

... In the Bible the primary idea of the word truth is that which sustains, which does not fail or disappoint our expectations. The true, therefore, is (1) that which is real, as opposed to that which is fictitious or imaginary. Jehovah is the true God because He is really God, while the gods of the heathen are vanity and nothing, mere imaginary beings having neither existence nor attributes. (2) The true is that which completely comes up to its idea or to what it purports to be.... The true God is He in whom is found all that Godhead imports. (3) The true is that in which the reality exactly corresponds to the manifestation. God is true because He really is what He declares Himself to be, because He is what He commands us to believe Him to be, and because all His declarations correspond to what really is. (4) The true is that which can be depended upon, which does not fail or change or disappoint. In this sense also God is true as He is immutable and faithful. His promise cannot fail; His Word never disappoints. His Word abideth forever. When our Lord says, "Thy word is truth," He says that all that God has revealed may be confided in as exactly corresponding to what really is or is to be. His Word can never fail, though heaven and earth pass away.

The truth of God, therefore, is the foundation of all religion. It is the ground of our assurance that what He has revealed of Himself and of His will, in His works and in the Scriptures, may be relied upon. He certainly is, wills, and will do whatever He has thus made known. It is no less the foundation of all knowledge. That our senses do not deceive us, that consciousness is trustworthy in what it teaches, that anything is what it appears to us to be, and that our existence is not a delusive dream have no other foundation than the truth of God. In this sense, all knowledge is founded on faith, i.e., the belief that God is true....

§15. Sovereignty

Sovereignty is not a property of the divine nature, but a prerogative arising out of the perfections of the Supreme Being. If God be a Spirit and therefore a person, infinite, eternal, and immutable in His being and perfections, the creator and preserver of the universe, He is of right its absolute sovereign. Infinite wisdom, goodness, and power, with the right of possession, which belongs to God in regard to all His creatures, are the immutable foundation of His dominion. "Our God is in the heavens; he hath done whatsoever he hath pleased" (Ps. 115:3). "All the inhabitants of the earth are reputed as nothing: and he doeth according to his will in the army of heaven, and among the inhabitants of the earth: and none can stay his hand, or say unto him, What doest thou?" (Dan. 4:35). "All that is in the heaven and in the earth is thine" (1 Chron. 29:11). "Behold, all souls are mine; as the soul of the father, so also the soul of the son is mine" (Ezek. 18:4). "Woe unto him that striveth with his Maker! Let the potsherd strive with the potsherds of the earth. Shall the clay say to him that fashioned it, What makest thou? or thy work, He hath no hands?" (Isa. 45:9). "Is it not lawful for me to do what I will with mine own?" (Matt. 20:15). He "worketh all things after the counsel of his own will" (Eph. 1:11). "Of him, and through him, and to him are all things: to whom be glory for ever" (Rom. 11:36).

From these and similar passages of Scripture it is plain (1) that the sovereignty of God is universal. It extends over all His creatures from the highest to the lowest. (2) It is absolute. There is no limit to be placed to His authority. He doeth His pleasure in the armies of heaven and among the inhabitants of the earth. (3) It is immutable. It can neither be ignored nor rejected. It binds all creatures as inexorably as physical laws bind the material universe.

This sovereignty is exercised (1) in establishing the laws, physical and moral, by which all creatures are to be governed; (2) in determining the nature and powers of the different orders of created beings, and in assigning each its appropriate sphere; (3) in appointing to each individual his position and lot. It is the Lord who fixes the bounds of our habitation. Our times are in His hands. He determines when, where, and under what circumstances each individual of our race is to be born, live, and die. Nations, no less than individuals, are thus in the hands of God, who assigns them their heritage in the earth and controls their destiny. (4) God is no less sovereign in the distribution of His favours. He does what He wills with His own. He gives to some riches, to others honour, to others health, while others are poor, unknown, or the victims of disease. To some the light of the gospel is sent; others are left in darkness. Some are brought through faith unto salvation; others perish in unbelief. To the question, Why is this? the only answer is that given by our Lord: "Even so, Father: for so it seemed good in thy sight" (Matt. 11:26).

Although this sovereignty is thus universal and absolute, it is the sovereignty of wisdom, holiness, and love. The authority of God is limited by nothing outside Himself, but it is controlled, in all its manifestations, by His infinite perfections. If a man is free and exalted in proportion as he is governed by enlightened reason and a pure conscience, so is he supremely blessed who cheerfully submits to be governed by the infinite reason and holiness of God. This sovereignty of God is the ground of peace and confidence for all His people. They rejoice that the Lord God omnipotent reigneth, and that neither necessity, nor chance, nor the folly of man, nor the malice of Satan controls the sequence of events and all their issues. Infinite wisdom, love, and power belong to Him, our great God and Saviour, into whose hands all power in heaven and earth has been committed.

Chapter **VI**

The Trinity

§1. Preliminary Remarks

. . . The design of all the revelations contained in the Word of God is the salvation of men. . . . God does not make known His being and attributes to teach men science, but to bring them to the saving knowledge of Himself. The doctrines of the Bible are, therefore, intimately connected with religion or the life of God in the soul. They determine the religious experience of believers and are presupposed in that experience. This is specially true of the doctrine of the Trinity. It is a great mistake to regard that doctrine as a mere speculative or abstract truth which is of no practical concern to us or which we are required

165

to believe simply because it is revealed. On the contrary, this doctrine concerning the constitution of the Godhead underlies the whole plan of salvation and determines the character of the religion (in the subjective sense of that word) of all true Christians. It is the unconscious or unformed faith even of those of God's people who are unable to understand the term by which it is expressed. They all believe in God, the creator and preserver against whom they have sinned, whose justice they know they cannot satisfy, and whose image they cannot restore to their apostate nature. They, therefore, as of necessity, believe in a divine Redeemer and a divine Sanctifier. They have, as it were, the factors of the doctrine of the Trinity in their own religious convictions. No mere speculative doctrine, especially none so mysterious and so out of analogy with all other objects of human knowledge as is the doctrine of the Trinity, could ever have held the abiding control over the faith of the Church which this doctrine has maintained. It is not, therefore, by any arbitrary decision, nor from any bigoted adherence to hereditary beliefs, that the Church has always refused to recognize as Christians those who reject this doctrine. This judgment is only the expression of the deep conviction that anti-Trinitarians must adopt a radically and practically different system of religion from that on which the Church builds her hopes. . . .

§2. Biblical Form of the Doctrine

A. What That Form Is

The form in which this doctrine lies in the Bible and in which it enters into the faith of the Church universal includes substantially the following particulars:

(1) There is only one living and true God or divine Being. The religion of the Bible stands opposed not only to atheism, but to all forms of polytheism. The Scriptures everywhere assert that Jehovah alone is God. "The LORD our God is one LORD" (Deut. 6:4). "I am the first, and I am the last; and beside me there is no God" (Isa. 44:6). "Thou believest that there is one God; thou doest well" (James 2:19). The Decalogue, which is the foundation of the moral and religious code of Christianity, as well as of Judaism, has as its first and greatest commandment, "Thou shalt have no other gods before me." No doctrine, therefore, can possibly be true which contradicts this primary truth of natural as well as of revealed religion.

(2) In the Bible all divine titles and attributes are ascribed equally to the Father, Son, and Spirit. The same divine worship is rendered to

them. The one is as much the object of adoration, love, confidence, and devotion as are the others. It is not more evident that the Father is God than that the Son is God, nor is the deity of the Father and Son more clearly revealed than that of the Spirit.

(3) The terms Father, Son, and Spirit do not express different relations of God to His creatures. They are not analogous to the terms creator, preserver, and benefactor, which do express such relations. The Scriptural facts are: (a) the Father says I, the Son says I, the Spirit says I; (b) the Father says Thou to the Son, and the Son says Thou to the Father, and in like manner the Father and the Son use the pronouns He and Him in reference to the Spirit; (c) the Father loves the Son, the Son loves the Father, the Spirit testifies of the Son. The Father, Son, and Spirit are severally subject and object. They act and are acted upon, or are the objects of action. Nothing is added to these facts when it is said that the Father, Son, and Spirit are distinct persons; for a person is an intelligent subject who can say I, who can be addressed as Thou, and who can act and can be the object of action. The above facts are summed up in the proposition, The one divine Being subsists in three persons, Father, Son, and Spirit. This proposition adds nothing to the facts themselves, for the facts are: (a) there is one divine Being; (b) the Father, Son, and Spirit are divine; (c) the Father, Son, and Spirit are, in the sense just stated, distinct persons; and (d) attributes being inseparable from substance, the Scriptures, in saying that the Father, Son, and Spirit possess the same attributes, say they are the same in substance; and if the same in substance, they are equal in power and glory.

(4) Notwithstanding that the Father, Son, and Spirit are the same in substance and equal in power and glory, it is no less true, according to the Scriptures, that (a) the Father is first, the Son second, and the Spirit third; (b) the Son is of the Father, and the Spirit is of the Father and of the Son; (c) the Father sends the Son, and the Father and Son send the Spirit; and (d) the Father operates through the Son, and the Father and Son operate through the Spirit. The converse of these statements is never found. The Son is never said to send the Father nor to operate through Him; nor is the Spirit ever said to send the Father or the Son, or to operate through them. The facts contained in this paragraph are summed up in the proposition, In the Holy Trinity there is a subordination of the persons as to the mode of subsistence and operation.

(5) According to the Scriptures, the Father created the world, the Son created the world, and the Spirit created the world. The Father preserves all things, the Son upholds all things, and the Spirit is the source of all life. These facts are expressed by saying that the persons

of the Trinity concur in all external acts. Nevertheless, there are some acts which are predominantly referred to the Father, others to the Son, and others to the Spirit. The Father creates, elects, and calls; the Son redeems; and the Spirit sanctifies. And, on the other hand, certain acts or conditions predicated of one person of the Trinity are never predicated of either of the others. Thus, generation belongs exclusively to the Father, filiation to the Son, and procession to the Spirit. This is the form in which the doctrine of the Trinity lies in the Bible. . . .

B. Scriptural Proof of the Doctrine

No such doctrine as that of the Trinity can be adequately proved by any citation of Scriptural passages. Some of its constituent elements are brought into view in one place, some in another. The unity of the divine Being; the true and equal divinity of the Father, Son, and Spirit; their distinct personality; and the relation in which they stand to one another, to the Church, and to the world, are not presented in a doctrinal formula in the Word of God; but the several constituent elements of the doctrine are asserted or assumed over and over from the beginning to the end of the Bible. It is, therefore, by proving these elements separately that the whole doctrine can be most satisfactorily established. All that is here necessary is a reference to the general teachings of Scripture on the subject and to a few passages in which everything essential to the doctrine is included.

(1) The progressive character of divine revelation is recognized in relation to all the great doctrines of the Bible. One of the strongest arguments for the divine origin of Scripture is the organic relation of its several parts. They comprise more than sixty books written by different men in different ages, and yet they form one whole. This unity is not a matter merely of external historical relations, nor of a general identity of subjects treated, but of internal organic development. All that is in the full-grown tree was potentially in the seed. All that we find unfolded in the fulness of the gospel lies in a rudimental form in the earliest books of the Bible. What at first is only obscurely intimated is gradually unfolded in subsequent parts of the sacred volume until the truth is revealed in its fulness. This is true of the doctrines of redemption, the person and work of the Messiah, the nature and office of the Holy Spirit, and a future state beyond the grave. And this is specially true of the doctrine of the Trinity. Even in the book of Genesis there are intimations of the doctrine which receive full explication in later revelations. That the names of God are in the plural form and that the personal pronouns are often in the first-person plural ("Let us make man in our image") may be explained in different ways.

But when it becomes plain, from the progress of the revelation, that there are three persons in the Godhead, then such forms of expression can hardly fail to be recognized as having their foundation in that great truth.

(2) Much more important, however, is the fact that not only in Genesis, but also in all the early books of Scripture, we find a distinction made between Jehovah and the angel of Jehovah, who, being Himself God, is given all divine titles and rendered divine worship. As the revelation is unfolded, such distinction becomes more and more manifest. This messenger of God is called the Word, the Wisdom, the Son of God. His personality and divinity are clearly revealed. He is of old, even from everlasting, the Mighty God, the Adonai, the Lord of David, Jehovah our Righteousness; He was to be born of a virgin and bear the sins of many.

(3) In like manner, even in the first chapter of Genesis, the Spirit of God is represented as the source of all intelligence, order, and life in the created universe; and in the following books of the Old Testament He is represented as inspiring the prophets and giving wisdom, strength, and goodness to statesmen, warriors, and the people of God. This Spirit is not an agency, but an agent who teaches and selects, who can be sinned against and grieved, and who, in the New Testament, is unmistakably revealed as a distinct person. When John the Baptist appeared, he spoke of the Holy Spirit as of a person with whom his countrymen were familiar as an object of divine worship and the giver of saving blessings. Our divine Lord also took this truth for granted and promised to send the Spirit, as a Paraclete, to take His place: the Spirit would instruct, comfort, and strengthen the disciples, and they in turn were to receive and obey Him. Thus, without any violent transition, the earliest revelations of this mystery were gradually unfolded until the Triune God, Father, Son, and Spirit, appears in the New Testament as the universally recognized God of all believers.

(4) In the formulas of baptism and of the apostolic benediction, provision was made to keep this doctrine constantly before the minds of the people. Every Christian is baptized in the name of the Father, of the Son, and of the Holy Ghost. The personality, the divinity, and consequently the equality of these three subjects are here taken for granted. The association of the Son and Spirit with the Father; the identity of relation, so far as dependence and obedience are concerned, which we sustain to the Father, Son, and Spirit respectively; the confession and profession involved in the ordinances—all forbid any other interpretation of this formula than that which it has always received in the Church. If the expression "in the name of the Father" implies the personality of the Father, a similar implication is involved

in the references to the Son and Spirit. If we acknowledge our subjection and allegiance to the one, we acknowledge the same subjection and allegiance to the other divine persons here named.

In the apostolic benediction a prayer is addressed to Christ for His grace, to the Father for His love, and to the Spirit for His fellowship (2 Cor. 13:14). The personality and divinity of each are solemnly recognized every time that this benediction is pronounced and received.

(5) In the record of our Lord's baptism, the Father addresses the Son, and the Spirit descends in the form of a dove. In the discourse recorded in John 14–16 our Lord speaks of the Father and their relationship, and promises to send the Spirit to teach, guide, and comfort His disciples. In that discourse the personality and divinity of the Father, Son, and Spirit are recognized with equal clearness. In 1 Corinthians 12:4–6 Paul speaks of diversity of gifts, but the same Spirit; of diversity of administration, but the same Lord; and of diversities of operations, but the same God.

It is not to be forgotten, however, that the faith of the Church in the doctrine of the Trinity does not rest exclusively or principally on such arguments as those mentioned above. The great foundation of that faith is what is taught everywhere in the Bible concerning the unity of the divine Being and the personality, divinity, and mutual relations of the Father, Son, and Spirit.

§3. The Transition Period

A. The Necessity for a More Definite Statement of the Doctrine

The Biblical form of the doctrine of the Trinity, as given above, includes everything that is essential to the integrity of the doctrine and all that is embraced in the faith of ordinary Christians. It is not all, however, that is included in the creeds of the Church. . . . A truth often lies in the mind of the Church as an object of faith long before it is wrought out in its doctrinal form; that is, before it is analyzed, its contents clearly ascertained, and its elements stated in due relation to each other. When a doctrine so complex as that of the Trinity is presented as an object of faith, the mind is forced to reflect upon what it includes and how its several parts are to be stated so as to avoid confusion or contradiction. Besides this internal necessity for a definite statement of the doctrine, such statement was forced upon the Church from without. Even among those who honestly intended to receive what the Scriptures taught upon the subject, it was inevitable that there should arise diversity in the mode of statement as well as confusion and contradiction in the use of terms. . . . There was, therefore, in the Church itself an inward and outward necessity for a clear, comprehensive, and consistent statement of the various elements of this complex doctrine of the Christian faith.

B. Conflict with Error

Besides this necessity for such a statement of the doctrine as would satisfy the minds of those who received it, there was a further necessity of guarding the truth from the evil influence of false or erroneous exhibitions of it. The conviction was deeply settled in the minds of all Christians that Christ is a divine person. The glory which He displayed, the authority which He assumed, the power which He exhibited, the benefits which He conferred, necessitated the recognition of Him as the true God. No less strong, however, was the conviction that there is only one God. The difficulty was to reconcile these two fundamental articles of the Christian faith. . . . In order to bring the Church to an agreement as to the manner in which this fundamental doctrine of Christianity should be stated, the Emperor Constantine summoned the First Ecumenical Council to meet at Nice in Nicomedia in A.D. 325.

§4. The Church Doctrine as Presented by the Council of Nice

. . . To harmonize the apparently incompatible convictions that there is only one God and yet that the Father is God, and the Son as a distinct person is God, the same in substance and equal in power and glory, the Council of Nice framed the following creed:

> We believe in one God, the Father almighty, the maker of all things visible and invisible; and in one Lord Jesus Christ, the Son of God, only begotten, begotten of the Father, that is, of the essence of the Father, God of God, Light of Light, very God of very God, begotten and not made, consubstantial with the Father, by whom all things were made whether in heaven or on earth; who for us men and our salvation came down from heaven, and was incarnate and became man, suffered, and rose again on the third day, ascended into heaven, and will come to judge the living and the dead. And we believe in the Holy Ghost. But those who say that there was a time when He (the Son) was not, that He was not before He was made, or was made out of nothing, or of another or different essence or substance, that He was a creature, or mutable, or susceptible of change, the Holy Catholic Church anathematizes.

The most obvious deficiency in the Nicene Creed is the omission of any definite statement concerning the Holy Spirit.... Athanasius, however, and other expounders and defenders of the Nicene Creed insisted that the Spirit is consubstantial with the Father and the Son.... It was opposition to this doctrine which led to the calling of the Second Ecumenical Council, which met at Constantinople in A.D. 381. In the modification of the Nicene Creed as issued by that council, the clause "we believe in the Holy Ghost" was augmented by the following words: "who is the Lord and giver of life, who proceedeth from the Father, who with the Father and the Son together is worshipped and glorified, who spoke by the prophets." Some of the Greek and the great body of the Latin fathers held that the Spirit proceeded from the Son as well as from the Father, and so the Synod of Toledo (A.D. 589) added the words "and from the Son" (*filioque*) to the creed....

After the Council of Constantinople, the controversies which agitated the Church had reference to the constitution of the person of Christ. Before the questions involved in those controversies were authoritatively decided, the so-called Athanasian Creed, an amplification of those of Nice and of Constantinople, came to be generally adopted, at least among the Western churches. That creed included these words:

> We worship one God in trinity, and trinity in unity, neither confounding the persons nor dividing the substance. For the person of the Father is one; of the Son, another; of the Holy Spirit, another. But the divinity of the Father and of the Son and of the Holy Spirit is one, the glory equal, the majesty equal. Such as is the Father, such also is the Son, and such the Holy Spirit. The Father is uncreated, the Son is uncreated, the Holy Spirit is uncreated. The Father is infinite, the Son is infinite, the Holy Spirit is infinite. The Father is eternal, the Son is eternal, the Holy Spirit is eternal. And yet there are not three eternal Beings, but one eternal Being. So also there are not three uncreated Beings, nor three infinite Beings, but one uncreated and one infinite Being. In like manner, the Father is omnipotent, the Son is omnipotent, and the Holy Spirit is omnipotent. And yet there are not three omnipotent Beings, but one omnipotent Being. Thus the Father is God, the Son is God, and the Holy Spirit is God. And yet there are not three Gods, but one God only. The Father is Lord, the Son is Lord, and the Holy Spirit is Lord. And yet there are not three Lords, but one Lord only. For as we are compelled by Christian truth to confess each person distinctively to be both God and Lord, we are prohibited by the Catholic religion to say that there are three Gods or Lords. The Father is made by none, nor created, nor begotten. The Son is from the Father alone, not made, not created, but begotten. The Holy Spirit is not created by the Father and the Son, nor begotten, but proceeds. Therefore, there is one Father, not three Fathers; one Son, not three Sons; one Holy Spirit, not three Holy Spirits. And in

this Trinity there is nothing prior or posterior, nothing greater or less, but all three persons are coeternal and coequal to themselves. So that through all, as was said above, both unity in trinity and trinity in unity is to be adored. Whoever would be saved, let him thus think concerning the Trinity.

. . . The doctrine of the Trinity as set forth in these three ancient creeds—the Nicene, the Constantinopolitan, and Athanasian—is the Church form of that fundamental article of the Christian faith. There is no difference, except as to amplification, between these several formulas.

§5. Points Decided by These Councils
§6. Examination of the Nicene Doctrine
§7. Philosophical Form of the Doctrine of the Trinity

Chapter VII

The Divinity of Christ

§1. Testimony of the Old Testament

The doctrine of redemption is the distinguishing doctrine of the Bible. The person and work of the Redeemer is therefore the great theme of the sacred writers. In view of the nature of the work which He was to accomplish, it was necessary that He should be at once God and man. He must participate in the nature of those whom He came to redeem; at the same time He must have both power to subdue all evil and dignity to give value to His obedience and sufferings. From the beginning to the end, therefore, of the sacred volume, from Genesis to Revelation, a God-man Redeemer is held up as the object of supreme reverence, love, and confidence to the perishing children of men. . . . This doctrine is to the Bible what the soul is to the body—its living and all-pervading principle, without which the Scriptures would be a cold, lifeless system of history and moral precepts. . . .

A. The Protevangelium

Immediately after the apostasy of our first parents it was announced that the seed of the woman should bruise the serpent's head. The meaning of this promise and prediction is to be determined by subsequent revelations. When interpreted in the light of the Scriptures themselves, it is manifest that the seed of the woman means the Redeemer and that bruising the serpent's head means His final triumph over the powers of darkness. In this protevangelium, as it has ever been called, we have the dawning revelation of the humanity and divinity of the great deliverer. As seed of the woman His humanity is distinctly asserted, and the nature of the triumph which He was to effect, in the subjugation of Satan, proves that He was to be a divine person. In the great conflict between good and evil, between the kingdom of light and the kingdom of darkness, between Christ and Belial, between God and Satan, He that triumphs over Satan is and can be nothing less than divine. In the earliest books of Scripture, even in Genesis, we have, therefore, clear intimations of two great truths: first, that there is a plurality of persons in the Godhead; and secondly, that one of those persons is specially concerned in the salvation of men— in their guidance, government, instruction, and ultimate deliverance from all the evils of their apostasy.

B. Jehovah and the Angel of Jehovah

The language employed in the record of the creation of man, "Let us make man in our image, after our likeness," admits of no satisfactory explanation other than that furnished by the doctrine of the Trinity. On this primary and fundamental revelation of this great truth all the subsequent revelations of Scripture are founded. As there is more than one person in the Godhead, we find at once the distinction between Jehovah as the messenger-mediator and Jehovah as He who sends; this distinction between the Father and the Son as coequal,

coeternal persons runs through the Bible with ever-increasing clearness. This is not an arbitrary or an unauthorized interpretation of the
Old Testament Scriptures. In Luke 24:27 it is said of our Lord that
"beginning at Moses and all the prophets, he expounded unto them in
all the scriptures the things concerning himself." Moses therefore did
testify of Christ, and we have a sure ground on which to rest in interpreting as references to Christ those passages of the Old Testament
which set forth the person and work of the great deliverer.

He who was promised to Adam as the seed of the woman, it was
next declared should be the seed of Abraham. That this does not refer
to his descendants collectively, but to Christ individually, we know
from the direct assertion of the apostle (Gal. 3:16) and from the fulfilment of the promise. It is not through the children of Abraham as a
nation, but through Christ, that all the nations of the earth are blessed.
And the blessing referred to, the promise to Abraham, which, as the
apostle says, has come upon us, is the promise of redemption. . . . This
proves that the person predicted as the seed of the woman and as the
seed of Abraham, through whom redemption was to be effected, was
to be both God and man. He could not be the seed of Abraham unless
a man, and He could not be the Saviour of men unless God.

We accordingly find throughout the Old Testament constant mention made of a person to whom, though distinct from Jehovah as a
person, the titles, attributes, and works of Jehovah are nevertheless
ascribed. This person is called the angel of God, the angel of Jehovah,
Adonai, Jehovah, and Elohim. He claims divine authority, exercises
divine prerogatives, and receives divine homage. . . . Since this is a
pervading representation of the Bible—since we find that these terms
are applied, not first to one and then to another angel indiscriminately,
but to one particular angel; that the person so designated is also called
the Son of God, the Mighty God; and that the work attributed to Him
is elsewhere attributed to God Himself—it is certain that by the angel
of Jehovah in the early books of Scripture we are to understand a
divine person distinct from the Father. . . .

Besides this we have the express testimony of the inspired writers
of the New Testament that the angel of the Lord, the manifested Jehovah who led the Israelites through the wilderness and who dwelt in
the temple, was Christ; that is, the angel was the Word or eternal Son
of God who became flesh and fulfilled the work which it was predicted
the Messiah should accomplish. The apostles do not hesitate to apply
to Christ the language of the Old Testament used to set forth the majesty, the works, or the kingdom of the Jehovah of the Hebrew Scriptures (John 12:41; Rom. 14:11; 1 Cor. 10:4; Heb. 1:10–13, etc.). The
New Testament, therefore, clearly identifies the Word or Son of God

with the angel of Jehovah or the messenger of the covenant of the Old Testament. . . . The angel who appeared to Hagar, to Abraham, to Moses, to Joshua, to Gideon, and to Manoah, the angel who was called Jehovah and worshipped as Adonai, who claimed divine homage and exercised divine power, whom the psalmists and prophets set forth as the Son of God, as the Counsellor, the Prince of Peace, the Mighty God, and who they predicted was to be born of a virgin, and to whom every knee should bow and every tongue confess . . . is none other than He whom we now recognize and worship as our God and Saviour Jesus Christ. . . .

C. The Psalms

In Psalm 2 the heathen are represented as combining against the Messiah (vv. 1-3). God derides their efforts (vv. 4-5). He declares His purpose to constitute the Messiah king in Zion. That this Messiah is a divine person is plain because (1) He is called the Son of God, which, as has been shown, implies equality with God; (2) He is invested with universal and absolute dominion; (3) He is the Jehovah whom the people are commanded in verse 11 to worship; (4) all are required to acknowledge His authority and do Him homage; and (5) those are pronounced blessed who put their trust in Him, whereas the Scriptures declare them to be cursed who put their trust in princes.

Psalm 22:1-18 describes a sufferer whose words our Lord upon the cross appropriated to Himself. This sufferer prays for deliverance (vv. 19-21). The consequences of that deliverance are such as prove that the subject of the psalm must be a divine person. His sufferings and deliverance render it certain that (1) all good men will fear and love God for having rescued this sufferer from His enemies; (2) provision will be made for the wants of all men; (3) all nations will be converted unto God; and (4) the blessings which He secures will last forever. . . .

Psalm 72 contains a description of an exalted king and of the blessings of his reign. These blessings are of such a nature as to prove that the subject of the psalm must be a divine person: (1) His kingdom is to be everlasting. (2) It is to be universal. (3) It secures perfect peace with God and good-will among men. (4) Through love all men are to be brought to submit to Him. (5) In Him all the nations of the earth are to be blessed; i.e., as we are distinctly taught in Galatians 3:13-14, it is in Him that all the blessings of redemption are to come upon the world. The subject of this psalm is, therefore, the Redeemer of the world.

Psalm 110 is repeatedly quoted and expounded in the New Testament and applied to Christ to set forth the dignity of His person and the nature of His work. (1) He is David's Lord. But if David's Lord, how can He be David's Son? Christ put this question to the Pharisees in order to convince them that their ideas of the Messiah fell far below the doctrine of their own Scriptures. He was indeed to be David's Son, as they expected, but at the same time He was to be possessed of a nature which made Him David's Lord. (2) In virtue of this divine nature He was to sit at God's right hand; that is, to be associated with Him on terms of equality as to glory and dominion. Such is the apostle's exposition of this passage in Hebrews 1:13. To no angel, i.e., to no creature, has God ever said, "Sit on my right hand." The subject of this psalm is no creature; and if not a creature, He is the creator. (3) This person, who is at once David's Son and David's Lord, is eternally both Priest and King. This again is referred to in Hebrews 7:17 to prove that He must be a divine person. It is only because He is possessed of "an endless life" or, as it is elsewhere said, because He has life in Himself even as the Father has life in Himself, that it is possible for Him to be a perpetual Priest and King. (4) In verse 5 He is declared to be the supreme Lord, for He is called Adonai, a title never given to any but the true God.

D. The Prophetical Books

Isaiah 4:2 predicts the appearance of the Branch of Jehovah. The effects of His advent—purification, the pardon of sin, and perfect security—prove Him to be a divine person.

Isaiah 6 contains an account of the prophet's vision of Jehovah in His holy temple, surrounded by hosts of angels who worship Him day and night. John 12:41 tells us that the person thus declared to be Jehovah, the object of angelic worship, is none other than Christ, whom all Christians and all angels now worship.

In Isaiah 7-9 the birth of a child to a virgin is predicted. That this child is the eternal Son of God, equal with the Father, is proved (1) from His name Immanuel, which means God with us, i.e., God in our nature. (2) The land of Israel is said to be His land. (3) He is called Wonderful, Counsellor, the Mighty God, Father of Eternity, and Prince of Peace. (4) His kingdom is everlasting and universal. (5) The consequences of His advent and dominion are such as flow only from the dominion of God. In Isaiah 11 we have another description of the perfection of His person and of His kingdom, a description which is applicable only to the person and kingdom of God. The peace, holiness, and blessedness which attend the coming of the predicted deliverer are found only where God reigns. The same argument may be drawn from the prophetic account of the Messiah and of His kingdom contained in Isaiah 40-66. This Messiah was to effect the redemption of His people not merely from the Babylonian captivity, but from all evil, and to secure for them the pardon of sin, reconciliation with God, the prevalence of true religion to the ends of the earth, and, finally, the complete triumph of the kingdom of light over the kingdom of darkness. This is a work which none other than a divine person could effect.

The prophet Micah (5:1-5) made several statements about one who was to be born in Bethlehem: (1) He shall be the ruler of Israel, i.e., of all the people of God. (2) Although to be born in time and made of a woman, His "goings forth have been from of old, from everlasting." (3) He shall rule in the strength and majesty of God, i.e., His government shall manifest divine attributes and glory. (4) His dominion shall be universal. And (5) its effects shall be peace; i.e., perfect harmony, order, and blessedness. . . .

In Jeremiah 23 the restoration or redemption of God's people is foretold. This redemption was to be effected by one who is declared to be (1) a descendant of David. (2) He is called the Branch, a designation which connects this prophecy with the Messianic prophecies of Isaiah 4 and 11. (3) He was to be a King. (4) His reign was to be prosperous—Judah and Israel were to be again united; i.e., perfect harmony and peace were to be secured. (5) This deliverer is called Jehovah our Righteousness. . . .

In Daniel 2:44 it is foretold that the kingdom of the Messiah is to be everlasting and is destined to supersede and absorb all other kingdoms. In Daniel 7:9-14 it is said that one like unto the Son of man was brought unto the Ancient of days; and a dominion, glory, and kingdom were given unto Him that all people, nations, and languages might serve Him. His dominion is to be an everlasting dominion which shall not pass away, and His kingdom shall not be destroyed. In Daniel 9:24-27 is recorded the prediction concerning the seventy weeks and the coming and work of the Messiah, which work is truly divine.

The prophecies of Zechariah foreshadow . . . the advent of the Messiah and the establishment of His kingdom. In chapter 9 Jerusalem is called upon to rejoice at the advent of her King. He is to be meek and lowly, unostentatious and peaceful, and His dominion universal. In chapter 11 He is presented as a shepherd who makes a last attempt to gather His flock. He is to be rejected and sold for thirty pieces of silver by those whom He came to save. For this outrage the people are to be given up to long desolation, but at last God will pour upon them the Spirit of grace and supplication, and they shall look upon me, saith Jehovah, whom they have pierced, and mourn. This shepherd is declared to be God's fellow, associate, or equal. His kingdom shall triumph and become universal, and holiness shall everywhere prevail.

In Malachi 3:1-4 it is predicted that (1) a messenger shall appear to prepare the way of the Lord; (2) the Lord, i.e., Jehovah, the messenger of the covenant, i.e., the Messiah, shall come to His temple; and (3) at His advent the wicked shall be destroyed and the Church saved.

It is plain, even from this cursory review, that the Old Testament clearly predicts the advent of a divine person clothed in our nature who was to be the Saviour of the world. He was to be the seed of the woman, the seed of Abraham, of the tribe of Judah, of the house of David; born of a virgin, He was to be a man of sorrows who would make "his soul an offering for sin." He is, however, no less clearly declared to be the angel of Jehovah, Jehovah, Elohim, Adonai, the Mighty God, exercising all divine prerogatives and entitled to divine worship from men and angels. Such is the doctrine of the Old Testament as to what the Messiah was to be, and this is the doctrine of the New Testament as to what Jesus of Nazareth in fact is.

§2. General Characteristics of the New Testament Teaching Concerning Christ

A. The Sense in Which Christ Is Called Lord

The first argument from the New Testament in proof of the divinity of Christ is derived from the fact that He is everywhere called Lord. . . . Christ is called Lord in the New Testament with as much constancy and preeminence as Jehovah is called Lord in the Old Testament. This was the word which all the readers, whether of the Hebrew or Greek Scriptures, under the old economy were accustomed to use to express their relation to God. They recognized Him as their owner, as their supreme sovereign, and as their protector. . . . The same feelings of reverence, adoration, and love, the same sense of dependence and desire of protection are expressed throughout the New Testament in calling Jesus Lord. . . .

Jesus Christ, therefore, is Lord to Christians in the same sense that Jehovah was Lord to the Hebrews. The usage referred to is altogether peculiar; no man—not Moses, nor Abraham, nor David, nor any of the prophets or apostles—is ever thus prevailingly addressed or invoked as Lord. We have but one Lord, and Jesus Christ is Lord. . . .

B. Christ Presented as the Object of Our Religious Affections

Another general feature of the New Testament, intimately connected with the one just mentioned and consequent upon it, is that Christ is

everywhere recognized as the proper object of all the religious affections. As He is our Lord, in the sense of being our absolute proprietor,
our maker, preserver, Redeemer, and sovereign, having the right to do
with us as seems good in His sight, we are called upon to make Him
the supreme object of our love, His will the highest rule of duty, and
His glory the great end of our being. We are to exercise the same faith
and confidence in Him that we do in God, and we are to yield Him
the same obedience, devotion, and homage. We find that such is the
theme from the beginning to the end of the New Testament writings.
Christ is the God of the apostles and early Christians in the sense that
He is the object of all their religious affections. . . . Accordingly, every
reader of the New Testament to whom Christ is a mere creature, however exalted, must feel himself to be out of communion with the apostles and early Christians, who avowed themselves and were universally
recognized by others as being worshippers of Christ. . . .

C. The Relations Which Christ Bears to His People and to the World

As the relation which believers bear to Christ is one that we can
sustain to God only, so the relation which He assumes to us, which
He claims as belonging to Him in virtue of His nature as well as His
work, is one that only God can sustain to rational creatures.

1. His authority as a teacher

This is plain as to the authority He assumes as a teacher of both
truth and duty. Everything which He declared to be true, all Christians
have ever felt bound to believe, without examination; and all that He
commanded them to do or to avoid, they have ever regarded as binding the conscience. His authority is the ultimate and highest ground
of faith and moral obligation. . . . He declared Himself to be the Truth,
and therefore to question what He said is to reject the truth; to disobey
Him is to disobey the truth. . . .

2. His control over all creatures

The divine authority of Christ is manifest in the control which He
claimed over all His people and over all creatures. All power was and
is in His hands. His ministers are under His direction; He sends one
here and another there. All Paul's labors and journeyings were performed under His continued guidance. This is but an illustration of
the universal and absolute control which He constantly exercises over
the whole universe. The angels in heaven are His messengers, and the
course of human history, as well as the circumstances of every indi-

vidual man, is determined by Him. So also is the eternal destiny of all men in His hands. I will reward every man, He says, according to his works (Matt. 16:27; Rev. 22:12). . . .

3. *The nature of His promises*

That Christ is divine is plain also from the nature of His promises. Christ promises to His people blessings which none but God has either the right or the power to bestow. He promises to forgive sin. It is intuitively certain that only God can forgive sin. He is our moral governor; it is against Him that all sin is committed, and only He has the right to remit its penalty. When therefore Christ says to the soul, Thy sins are forgiven, He exercises a divine prerogative. . . .

Again, Christ promises the Holy Spirit. . . . And accordingly it is recorded that He did send down on His disciples, especially on the day of Pentecost, power from on high. . . . All the sanctifying influences, as well as all the gifts of teaching and of miracles which the Church has ever enjoyed, come from the Lord Jesus Christ. He gives the Spirit to every one severally as He will. "Unto every one of us," says Paul, "is given grace according to the measure of the gift of Christ" (Eph. 4:7).

He also promises to hear and answer the prayers of His people in all ages and in all parts of the world. "Whatsoever ye shall ask in my name, I will do it." "Wherever two or three are gathered together in my name, there am I in the midst of them." "Lo, I am with you alway, even unto the end of the world." He thus promises His continued presence to His disciples wherever they may be.

He also promises eternal life to all who believe on Him. He has power to quicken or to give life to as many as He will. "My sheep follow me, and I give unto them eternal life." "I will raise them up at the last day." "To him that overcometh will I give to eat of the tree of life.". . . .

It is obvious that the infinite God Himself can neither promise nor give anything greater or higher than Christ gives His people. To Him they are taught to look as the source of all blessings, the giver of every good and perfect gift. There is no more comprehensive prayer in the New Testament than that with which Paul closes his Epistle to the Galatians: "The grace of our Lord Jesus Christ be with your spirit." His favour is our life; this could not be if He were not our God.

4. *His control over nature*

A fourth general feature of the New Testament teaching concerning Christ relates to the control attributed to Him over the external world. . . . When Moses, the prophets, or the apostles wrought miracles, they expressly disclaimed the idea that it was by their own efficiency. . . . Christ, however, wrought miracles by His own inherent power; and it was to His efficiency the apostles attributed the miracles wrought through them. It was His name, or faith in His name, as Peter taught the people, which effected the instantaneous healing of the lame man. Christ never referred this miraculous power to any source outside Himself. He claimed it as His own prerogative, and He conferred the power upon others. He said of Himself that He had power to lay down His life and power to take it again, and that He had life in Himself and could give life to as many as He pleased. "I give unto you," He said to His disciples, "power to tread on serpents and scorpions, and over all the power of the enemy" (Luke 10:19). Every miracle of Christ, therefore, was a visible manifestation of His divinity. By a mere word, an effortless exercise of His will, He healed the sick, opened the eyes of the blind, restored the lame, raised the dead, fed thousands with a few loaves of bread, and calmed the raging of the sea. He thus manifested forth His glory, giving visible demonstration that He was God in fashion as a man. Appealing directly to His works, He said, "Though ye believe not me, believe the works: that ye may know, and believe, that the Father is in me, and I in him" (John 10:38; see also 15:24).

It is only a small part of the evidence of the divinity of our Lord that can thus be gathered up from the general teaching of the New Testament. It is important to bear in mind that faith in this doctrine rests not on this or that passage, or on this or that mode of representation, but on the whole revelation of God concerning His Son. The divinity of the Lord Jesus Christ is wrought into the texture of the Scriptures and is everywhere asserted or assumed.

[§3. Particular Passages Which Teach the Divinity of Christ]

The Holy Spirit

§1. His Nature

... The Third Person of the Trinity is called "the Spirit," first, to indicate that He is the power or efficiency of God, i.e., the person through whom the efficiency of God is directly exercised; and secondly, to express His relation to the other persons of the Trinity. As Father and Son are terms expressive of relation, it is natural to infer that the word Spirit is to be understood in the same way. The Son, as the revealer or image of God, is called the Word; and the Third Person, as His breath or power, is called Spirit. He is also predominantly called the Holy Spirit to indicate both His nature and operations. He is absolutely holy in His own nature and the cause of holiness in all creatures. For the same reason He is called the Spirit of truth, the Spirit of wisdom, of peace, of love, and of glory. . . .

185

Terms denoting the Spirit occur in all parts of Scripture from Genesis to Revelation. These terms are evidently to be understood in the same sense throughout the Scriptures. The Spirit who moved on the face of the waters, strove with the antediluvians, came upon Moses, gave skill to artisans, and inspired the prophets is the same divine power who came upon the apostles, whom Christ promised to send as a comforter and advocate, and to whom the instruction, sanctification, and guidance of the people of God are referred. Though the earlier portions of Scripture are relatively obscure on the subject, we know that the Spirit is a person because He is clearly revealed as such in the later parts, and Scripture must interpret Scripture.

The Spirit of God is equally prominent in all parts of the Word of God. His intervention does not occur on rare occasions, as the appearance of angels or the theophanies of which mention is made here and there in the sacred volume; but He is represented as everywhere present and everywhere operative. We might as well strike from the Bible the name and doctrine of God as the name and office of the Holy Spirit. In the New Testament alone He is mentioned not far from three hundred times. It is not only, however, merely the frequency with which the Spirit is mentioned and the prominence given to His person and work, but the multiplied and interesting relations in which He is represented as standing to the people of God, the importance and number of His gifts, and the absolute dependence of the believer and of the Church upon Him for spiritual and eternal life, which render the doctrine of the Holy Ghost absolutely fundamental to the gospel. The work of the Spirit in applying the redemption of Christ is represented to be as essential as that redemption itself. It is therefore indispensable that we know what the Bible teaches concerning the Holy Ghost as to both His nature and office.

A. His Personality

The Scriptures clearly teach that the Holy Spirit is a person. Personality includes intelligence, will, and individual subsistence. If, therefore, it can be proved that all these are characteristic of the Spirit, it is thereby proved that He is a person. . . .

(1) The first argument for the personality of the Holy Spirit is derived from the use of the personal pronouns in relation to Him. . . . Thus in Acts 13:2, "The Holy Ghost said, Separate *me* Barnabas and Saul for the work whereunto *I* have called them." Our Lord says (John 15:26), "When the Comforter is come, whom I will send unto you from the Father, even the Spirit of truth, which proceedeth from the Father, *he* shall testify of me." The use of the masculine pronoun *he* instead

of *it* shows that the Spirit is a person. . . . In the following chapter (John 16:13–14) it is said, "When he, the Spirit of truth, is come, he will guide you into all truth; for he shall not speak of himself; but whatsover he shall hear, that shall he speak: and he will show you things to come. He shall glorify me: for he shall receive of mine, and shall show it unto you." Here there is no possibility of accounting for the use of the personal pronoun *he* on any other ground than the personality of the Spirit.

(2) We stand in relations to the Holy Spirit which we can sustain only to a person. He is the object of our faith. We believe on the Holy Ghost. This faith we profess in baptism. We are baptized in the name not only of the Father and of the Son, but also of the Holy Ghost. . . . We stand in the same relation to Him as to the Father and to the Son; we acknowledge Him to be a person as distinctly as we acknowledge the personality of the Son or of the Father. Christians not only profess to believe on the Holy Ghost, but are also the recipients of His gifts. He is to them an object of prayer. In the apostolic benediction (2 Cor. 13:14) the grace of Christ, the love of the Father, and the fellowship of the Holy Ghost are solemnly invoked. We pray to the Spirit for the communication of Himself to us that He may, according to the promise of our Lord, dwell in us, as we pray to Christ that we may be the objects of His unmerited love. Accordingly we are exhorted not "to sin against," "not to resist," not "to grieve" the Holy Spirit. He is represented, therefore, as a person who can be the object of our acts, whom we may please or offend, with whom we may have communion (i.e., personal intercourse), who can love and be loved, who can say "thou" to us, and whom we can invoke in every time of need.

(3) The Spirit also sustains relations to us and performs offices which none but a person can sustain or perform. He is our teacher, sanctifier, comforter, and guide. He governs both every believer who is led by the Spirit and the whole Church. He calls, as He called Barnabas and Saul, to the work of the ministry or to some special field of labour. Pastors or bishops are made overseers by the Holy Ghost.

(4) In the exercise of these and other functions, personal acts such as imply intelligence, will, and activity or power, are constantly performed by the Spirit. The Spirit searches, selects, reveals, and reproves. We often read that "the Spirit said" (Acts 13:2; 21:11; 1 Tim. 4:1, etc.). So constantly does the Spirit thus appear as a personal agent from one end of the Scriptures to the other that His personality is beyond dispute. . . .

(5) Not only are all the elements of personality, namely, intelligence, will, and individual subsistence, involved in all that is thus revealed concerning the relation in which the Spirit stands to us and

that which we sustain to Him, but they are all distinctly attributed to Him. The Spirit is said to know, to will, and to act. He searches or knows all things, even the deep things of God. The things of God are known by no man, but only by the Spirit of God (1 Cor. 2:10–11). He distributes "to every man severally as he will" (1 Cor. 12:11). His individual subsistence is involved in His being an agent and in His being the object on which the activity of others terminates. If He can be loved, reverenced, and obeyed, or offended and sinned against, He must be a person.

(6) The personal manifestations of the Spirit when He descended on Christ after His baptism and on the apostles at the day of Pentecost of necessity involve His personal subsistence. It was not any attribute of God, nor His mere efficiency, but God Himself that was manifested in the burning bush, in the fire and clouds on Mount Sinai, in the pillar which guided the Israelites through the wilderness, and in the glory which dwelt in the tabernacle and in the temple.

(7) The people of God have always regarded the Holy Spirit as a person. They have looked to Him for instruction, sanctification, direction, and comfort. This is part of their religion. Christianity (subjectively considered) would not be what it is without this sense of dependence on the Spirit and this love and reverence for His person. All the liturgies, prayers, and praises of the Church are filled with appeals and addresses to the Holy Ghost. This is a fact which admits of no rational solution if the Scriptures do not really teach that the Spirit is a distinct person. . . .

B. Divinity of the Holy Spirit

On this subject there has been little dispute in the Church. The Spirit is so prominently presented in the Bible as possessing divine attributes and exercising divine prerogatives that since the fourth century His true divinity has never been denied by those who admit His personality.

(1) In the Old Testament all that is said of Jehovah is said of the Spirit of Jehovah, and therefore the latter must of necessity be divine. The expressions "Jehovah said" and "the Spirit said" are constantly interchanged, and the acts of the Spirit are said to be acts of God.

(2) In the New Testament the language of Jehovah is quoted as the language of the Spirit. In Isaiah 6:9 it is written, "Jehovah said, Go, and tell this people. . . ." This passage is thus quoted by Paul (Acts 28:25–26): "Well spake the Holy Ghost by Esaias the prophet unto our fathers, saying, Go unto this people, and say. . . ." In Jeremiah 31:31–34 it is said, "Behold, the days come, saith Jehovah, that I will make a

new covenant with the house of Israel. . . ." This is quoted by the apostle in Hebrews 10:15–17: "Whereof the Holy Ghost also is a witness to us: for after that he had said before, This is the covenant that I will make with them after those days, saith the LORD. . . ." Thus constantly the language of God is quoted as the language of the Holy Ghost. The prophets were the messengers of God; they uttered His words, delivered His commands, pronounced His threatenings, and announced His promises because they spake as they were moved by the Holy Ghost. They were the organs of God because they were the organs of the Spirit. The Spirit, therefore, must be God.

(3) In the New Testament the same mode of representation is continued. Believers are the temple of God, because the Spirit dwells in them (Eph. 2:22; 1 Cor. 6:19). . . . In Acts 5:1–4 Ananias is said to have lied unto God because he lied against the Holy Ghost.

(4) Our Lord and His apostles constantly speak of the Holy Spirit as possessing all divine perfections. Christ says, "The blasphemy against the Holy Ghost shall not be forgiven unto men" (Matt. 12:31). The unpardonable sin, then, is speaking against the Holy Ghost. This could not be unless the Holy Ghost were God. The apostle in 1 Corinthians 2:10 says that the Spirit knows all things, even the deep things (the most secret purposes) of God. His knowledge is commensurate with the knowledge of God. . . . The psalmist teaches us that the Spirit is omnipresent and everywhere efficient. "Whither," he asks, "shall I go from thy Spirit? or whither shall I flee from thy presence?" (Ps. 139:7). The presence of the Spirit is the presence of God. . . .

(5) The works of the Spirit are the works of God. He fashioned the world (Gen. 1:2). He regenerates the soul: to be born of the Spirit is to be born of God. He is the source of all knowledge, the giver of inspiration, and the teacher, the guide, the sanctifier, and the comforter of the Church in all ages. He fashions our bodies, He formed the body of Christ as a fit habitation for the fulness of the Godhead, and He is to quicken our mortal bodies (Rom. 8:11).

(6) He is therefore presented in the Scriptures as the proper object of worship, not only in the formula of baptism and in the apostolic benediction, which bring the doctrine of the Trinity into constant remembrance as the fundamental truth of our religion, but also in the constant requirement that we look to Him and depend upon Him for all spiritual good, and reverence and obey Him as our divine teacher and sanctifier.

C. Relation of the Spirit to the Father and to the Son

The relation of the Spirit to the other persons of the Trinity has been stated before: (1) He is the same in substance and equal in power and glory. (2) As to mode of subsistence and operation He is subordinate to the Father and Son, for He is said to be of the Father and of the Son. He is sent by them, and they operate through Him. (3) He bears the same relation to the Father as to the Son; for He is said to be of the one as well as of the other, and He is given by the Son as well as by the Father. (4) His eternal relation to the other persons of the Trinity is indicated by the word Spirit and by the statement that He proceeds from God.

§2. The Office of the Holy Spirit

A. In Nature

The general doctrine of the Scriptures on this subject is that the Spirit is the executive of the Godhead. Whatever God does, He does by the Spirit. . . . He is the immediate source of all life. Even in the external world the Spirit is everywhere present and everywhere active. Matter is not intelligent. It has its peculiar properties which act blindly according to established laws. The intelligence, therefore, manifested in vegetable and animal structures is not to be referred to matter, but to the omnipresent Spirit of God. It was He who brooded over the waters and reduced chaos to order. It was He who garnished the heavens. It is He who causes the grass to grow and gives breath to all living creatures (Ps. 104:29–30). . . . And the psalmist, after describing the omnipresence of the Spirit, refers to His agency the wonderful mechanism of the human body (Ps. 139:14–16). . . .

The Spirit is also represented as the source of all intellectual life. When man was created, God "breathed into his nostrils the breath of life; and man became a living soul" (Gen. 2:7). Job 32:8 says, "The inspiration of the Almighty giveth understanding," i.e., a rational nature; He "teacheth us more than the beasts of the earth, and maketh us wiser than the fowls of heaven" (Job 35:11). The Scriptures ascribe in like manner to Him all special or extraordinary gifts. Thus the Lord said of Bezaleel, "I have filled him with the Spirit of God, in wisdom, in understanding, and in knowledge, and in all manner of workmanship, to devise cunning works, to work in gold, and in silver, and in brass" (Exod. 31:2–4). By His Spirit God gave Moses the wisdom requisite for his high duties, and when he was commanded to devolve part of his burden upon the seventy elders, God said, "I will take of the Spirit which is upon thee, and will put it upon them" (Num. 11:17). In like manner the judges, who from time to time were raised up as emergency demanded, were qualified by the Spirit for their peculiar work, whether as rulers or warriors. . . . Furthermore, "the Spirit of the LORD came upon David" from the day of his anointing by Samuel (1 Sam. 16:13). In like manner under the new dispensation the Spirit is represented as not only the author of miraculous gifts, but also as the giver of the qualifications to teach and rule in the Church. All these operations are independent of the sanctifying influences of the Spirit. When the Spirit came on Samson and Saul, for example, it was not to render them holy, but to endue them with extraordinary physical or intellectual power. His departure from them, accordingly, meant that those extraordinary endowments were withdrawn.

B. The Spirit's Office in the Work of Redemption

With regard to the office of the Spirit in the work of redemption the Scriptures teach:

(1) He fashioned the body and endued the human soul of Christ with every qualification for His work. To the Virgin Mary it was said, "The Holy Ghost shall come upon thee, and the power of the Highest shall overshadow thee; therefore also that holy thing which shall be born of thee shall be called the Son of God" (Luke 1:35). The prophet Isaiah predicted that the Messiah would be filled with all spiritual gifts: "There shall come forth a rod out of the stem of Jesse, and a Branch shall grow out of his roots: and the Spirit of the LORD shall rest upon him, the spirit of wisdom and understanding, the spirit of counsel and might, the spirit of knowledge and of the fear of the LORD" (Isa. 11:1–2). When our Lord appeared on earth, the Spirit without measure was given unto Him (John 3:34). "And John bare record, saying, I saw the Spirit descending from heaven like a dove, and it abode upon him" (John 1:32). He was, therefore, said to have been full of the Holy Ghost.

(2) The Spirit is the revealer of all divine truth. The doctrines of the Bible are called the things of the Spirit. And the writers of the Old Testament are said to have spoken as they were moved by the Holy Ghost. The language of Micah is applicable to all the prophets, "Truly I am full of power by the Spirit of the LORD, and of judgment, and of might, to declare unto Jacob his transgression, and to Israel his sin" (Mic. 3:8). What David said, the Holy Ghost is declared to have said. The New Testament writers were in like manner the organs of the Spirit. The doctrines which Paul preached he did not receive from men, "but God," he says, "hath revealed them unto us by his Spirit" (1 Cor. 2:10). The Spirit also guided the utterance of those truths, for Paul adds: "Which things also we speak, not in the words which man's wisdom teacheth, but which the Holy Ghost teacheth; communicating

the things of the Spirit in the words of the Spirit" (v. 13). The whole Bible, therefore, is to be referred to the Spirit as its author.

(3) Not only does the Spirit reveal divine truth, but He everywhere attends it by His power. All truth is enforced on the heart and conscience with more or less power by the Holy Spirit, wherever that truth is known. To this all-pervading influence we are indebted for all there is of morality and order in the world. But besides this general influence, which is usually called common grace, the Spirit especially illuminates the minds of the children of God that they may know the things freely given (or revealed to them) by God. The natural man does not receive them, neither can he know them, because they are spiritually discerned. All believers are therefore called spiritual, because they are thus enlightened and guided by the Spirit (1 Cor. 2:14–15).

(4) It is the special office of the Spirit to convince the world of sin; to reveal Christ, to regenerate the soul, to lead men to the exercise of faith and repentance; and, as a principle of a new and divine life, to dwell in those whom He thus renews. By this indwelling of the Spirit, believers are united to Christ and to another, so that they form one body. This is the foundation of the communion of saints, making them one in faith, one in love, one in their inward life, and one in their hopes and final destiny.

(5) The Spirit also calls men to office in the Church and endows them with the qualifications necessary for the successful discharge of its duties. The role of the Church in this matter is simply to ascertain and authenticate the call of the Spirit. Thus the Holy Ghost is the immediate author of all truth, of all holiness, of all consolation, of all authority, and of all efficiency in the children of God individually and in the Church collectively. . . .

[§3. History of the Doctrine Concerning the Holy Spirit]

Chapter IX

The Decrees of God

§1. The Nature of the Decrees

It must be remembered that theology is not philosophy. It does not assume to discover truth or to reconcile what it teaches as true with all other truths. Its province is simply to state what God has revealed in His Word and to vindicate those statements as far as possible from misconceptions and objections. This limited and humble office of theology it is especially necessary to bear in mind when we come to speak of the acts and purposes of God. "The things of God knoweth no man,

193

but the Spirit of God" (1 Cor. 2:11). In treating, therefore, of the decrees of God, all that is proposed is simply to state what the Spirit has seen fit to reveal on that subject.

Answer 7 in the "Westminster Shorter Catechism" states, "The decrees of God are his eternal purpose according to the counsel of his will, whereby, for his own glory, he hath foreordained whatsoever comes to pass." There are various affirmations in this statement: (1) the end or final cause contemplated in all of God's decrees is His own glory; (2) they are all reducible to one eternal purpose; (3) they are free and sovereign, determined by the counsel of His own will; and (4) they comprehend all events.

A. The Glory of God the Final Cause of All His Decrees

The final cause of all of God's purposes is His own glory. This is frequently declared to be the end of all things. "Thou art worthy," say the heavenly worshippers, "O Lord, to receive glory, and honour, and power: for thou hast created all things, and for thy pleasure they are and were created" (Rev. 4:11). All things are said to be not only of God and through Him, but for Him (Rom. 11:36). He is the beginning and the end. The heavens declare His glory; that is the purpose for which they were made. . . . This is also said to be the end of all the dispensations of His providence, whether beneficent or punitive. "For mine own sake, even for mine own sake, will I do it: for how should my name be polluted? and I will not give my glory unto another" (Isa. 48:11). In like manner the whole plan of redemption and the dispensations of His grace are declared to be designed to reveal the glory of God (1 Cor. 1:26-31; Eph. 2:8-10). This is the end which our Lord proposed to Himself. He did everything for the glory of God, and for this end all His followers are required to live and act. As God is infinite and all creatures are as nothing in comparison with Him, it is plain that the revelation of His nature and perfections must be the highest conceivable end of all things and the most conducive to securing all other good subordinate ends. We should also note here that order and truth depend on things being put in their right relations. If we make the good of the creature the ultimate object of all God's works, we subordinate God to the creature, and endless confusion and unavoidable error are the consequence. It is characteristic of the Bible that it places God first and the good of the creation second. This also is the characteristic feature of Augustinianism as distinguished from all other forms of doctrine. . . .

The Bible, Augustine, and Reformed theology give one answer to all such questions as the following: Why did God create the world? Why did He permit the occurrence of sin? Why was salvation provided for men and not for angels? Why was the knowledge of that salvation so long confined to one people? Why among those who hear the gospel do some receive and others reject it? To all these and similar questions the answer is, . . . Thus it seemed good in the eyes of God. Whatever He does or permits to be done is done or permitted for the more perfect revelation of His nature and perfections. . . .

B. The Decrees Reducible to One Purpose

The second point included in this doctrine is that the decrees of God are all reducible to one purpose. By this is meant that from the indefinite number of systems or series of possible events present to the divine mind, God determined on the futurition or actual occurrence of the existing order of things, with all its changes, minute as well as great, from the beginning of time to all eternity. The reason, therefore, why an event occurs, or passes from the category of the possible into that of the actual, is that God has so decreed. The decrees of God, therefore, are not many, but one purpose. They are not successively formed as the emergency arises, but are parts of one all-comprehending plan. This view of the subject is rendered necessary by the nature of an infinitely perfect Being. That the purposes of God are successive, or that He ever purposes what He did not originally intend, or that one part of His plan is independent of other parts is inconsistent with the idea of absolute perfection. It is one scheme and therefore one purpose. As, however, this one purpose includes an indefinite number of events, and as those events are mutually related, we therefore speak of the decrees of God as many and as having a certain order. The Scriptures consequently speak of God's judgments, counsels, or purposes in the plural number and also of His determining one event because of another. . . . Despite the infinite multiplicity of causes and effects, however, we must understand that the vast scheme of creation, providence, and redemption lies in the divine mind as one simple purpose.

C. The Decrees of God Are Eternal

That the decrees of God are eternal follows necessarily from the perfection of the divine Being. He cannot be supposed to have at one time plans or purposes which He had not at another. He sees the end from the beginning; the distinctions of time have no reference to Him who inhabits eternity. The Scriptures therefore always speak of events in time as revelations of a purpose formed in eternity. The salvation of men, for example, is said to be "according to the eternal purpose which he purposed in Christ Jesus" (Eph. 3:11). Believers were chosen in Christ before the foundation of the world (Eph. 1:4). Christ as a sacrifice was "foreordained before the foundation of the world, but was manifest in these last times for you, who by him do believe in God" (1 Peter 1:20-21). This is the constant representation of Scripture. History in all its details, even the most minute, is but the evolution of the eternal purposes of God. It is no objection to this doctrine that the Scriptures often represent one purpose of God as consequent upon another, or that they speak of His purposes as determined by the conduct of men. The language of Scripture, as is always true of the language of men, reflects how things appear rather than what they are known or believed to be. . . . Thus the Bible speaks of the decrees of God as they appear to us in their successive revelations and in their mutual relations, and not as they exist from eternity in the divine mind. . . .

D. The Decrees of God Are Immutable

Change of purpose arises either from the want of wisdom or from the want of power. As God is infinite in wisdom and power, there can be with Him no unforeseen emergency and no inadequacy of means, and nothing can resist the execution of His original intention. To Him, therefore, the causes of change have no existence. With God there is, as the Scriptures teach, "no variableness, neither shadow of turning" (James 1:17). "The counsel of the LORD standeth for ever, the thoughts of his heart to all generations" (Ps. 33:11). The uniformity of the laws of nature is a constant revelation of the immutability of God. They are now what they were at the beginning of time, and they are the same in every part of the universe. No less stable are the laws which regulate the operations of the reason and conscience. The whole government of God, as the God of nature and as moral governor, rests on the immutability of His counsels.

E. The Decrees of God Are Free

This includes three ideas:

(1) They are rational determinations founded on sufficient reasons. This is opposed to the doctrine of necessity, which assumes that God acts by a mere necessity of nature, and that all that occurs is due to the law of development or of self-manifestation of the divine Being. . . . The true doctrine is opposed also to the idea that the only cause of events is a force analogous to the instincts of irrational animals. The

acts performed under the guidance of instinct are not free acts, for
liberty is a spontaneity determined by reason. It is therefore involved
in the idea of God as a rational and personal Being that His decrees
are free. He was free to create or not to create, to create such a world
as now is or one entirely different. He is free to act or not to act, and
when He purposes, it is not from any blind necessity, but according
to the counsel of His own will.

(2) Our purposes are free even when formed under the influence of
other minds. We may be argued or persuaded into certain courses of
action, or induced to form our designs out of regard to the wishes or
interests of others. But God is infinitely exalted above all external
influence. "Who hath known the mind of the Lord? or who hath been
his counsellor?" (Rom. 11:34). "Behold, God exalteth by his power:
who teacheth like him? Who hath enjoined him his way?" (Job
36:22–23). God adopted the plan of the universe on the ground of His
own good pleasure, for His own glory, and every subordinate part of
it in reference to the whole. His decrees are free, therefore, in a far
higher sense than that in which the ordinary purposes of men are free.
His decrees were formed purely on the counsel of His own will. He
purposes and does what seemeth good in His sight.

(3) The decrees of God are free in the sense of being absolute or
sovereign. The meaning of this proposition is expressed negatively by
saying that the decrees of God are in no case conditional. . . . To assume
suspense or indecision on God's part is inconsistent with what we
know of His nature. If He has not absolutely determined on what is to
occur, but waits until an undetermined condition is or is not fulfilled,
then His decrees are neither eternal nor immutable. . . . The Scriptures
therefore teach that He doeth whatsoever He pleaseth (Ps. 115:3). He
doeth His pleasure in the army of heaven and among the inhabitants
of the earth (Dan. 4:35; Ps. 135:6). Of Him, and through Him, and to
Him are all things (Rom. 11:36). . . .

F. The Decrees of God Are Certainly Efficacious

The decrees of God are certainly efficacious, that is, they render
certain the occurrence of what He decrees. Whatever God foreordains,
must certainly come to pass. The distinction between the efficient (or
efficacious) and the permissive decrees of God, although important,
has no relation to the certainty of events. All events embraced in the
purpose of God are equally certain, whether He has determined to
bring them to pass by His own power, or simply to permit their occurrence through the agency of His creatures. It was no less certain
from eternity that Satan would tempt our first parents, and that they

would fall, than that God would send His Son to die for sinners. The distinction in question has reference only to the relation which events bear to the efficiency of God. Some things He purposes to do, others He decrees to permit to be done. He effects good, He permits evil. He is the author of the one, but not of the other.

That the decrees of God are certainly efficacious, or render certain all events to which they refer, is proved:

(1) From the perfection of God, which forbids the ascription to Him of purposes uncertain as to their accomplishment. No man fails to execute what he purposes, except through the want of wisdom or power to secure the end proposed, or through some vacillation in his own mind. To assume that what God decrees could fail to come to pass would be to reduce Him to the level of His creatures.

(2) From the unity of God's plan. If that plan comprehends all events, all events stand in mutual relation and dependence. If one part fails, the whole may fail or be thrown into confusion. . . .

(3) From the providential and moral government of God. There could be no certainty in either if the decrees of God were not efficacious. There could be no assurance that any divine prophecy, promise, or threat would be accomplished. All ground of confidence in God would thus be lost, and chance and not God would become the arbiter of all events. Various passages of Scripture teach the efficaciousness of God's decrees: (a) those passages which assert the immutability and sovereignty of the divine decrees; (b) those which affirm that He fixes the bounds of our habitations, that our days are all numbered, and that even a hair from our heads cannot perish without His notice; (c) those which declare that nothing can counteract His designs—"The Lord of hosts hath purposed, and who shall disannul it? And his hand is stretched out, and who shall turn it back?" (Isa. 14:27); and (d) those which teach doctrines that necessarily assume the certainty of all God's decrees. The whole plan of redemption rests on that foundation. It is inconceivable that God should devise such a scheme and not secure its execution, or that He should send His Son into the world and leave the consequences of that infinite condescension undetermined. It is, therefore, the doctrine of reason as well as of Scripture that God has a plan or end for which the universe was created, that the execution of that plan is not left contingent, and that whatever is embraced in the decrees of God must certainly come to pass.

G. *The Decrees of God Relate to All Events*

. . . The doctrine of the Bible is that all events, whether necessary or contingent, good or sinful, are included in the purpose of God, and that their futurition or actual occurrence is rendered absolutely certain.... The Scriptures in various ways teach that God foreordains whatever comes to pass:

(1) They teach that God works all things according to the counsel of His will (Eph. 1:11). There is nothing to limit the words "all things," and therefore they must be taken in the fullest extent.

(2) It is expressly declared that fortuitous events, that is, events which depend on causes so subtle and so rapid in their operation as to elude our observation, are predetermined; e.g., the casting of the lot, the flight of an arrow, the falling of a sparrow.

(3) The Bible especially declares that the free acts of men are decreed beforehand. This is involved in the doctrine of prophecy, which assumes that events involving the free acts of a multitude of men are foreseen and foreordained. God promises to give faith and a new heart, to write His law upon the minds of His people, to work in them to will and to do, to convert the Gentiles, to fill the world with the true worshippers of Christ, to whom every knee is gladly to bow. If God has promised these things, He must of course purpose them, but they all involve the free acts of men.

(4) The Scriptures teach that sinful acts, as well as such as are holy, are foreordained. In Acts 2:23 it is said, "Him, being delivered by the determinate counsel and foreknowledge of God, ye have taken, and by wicked hands have crucified and slain"; and in Acts 4:27, "For of a truth against thy holy child Jesus, whom thou hast anointed, both Herod, and Pontius Pilate, with the Gentiles, and the people of Israel, were gathered together, for to do whatsoever thy hand and thy counsel determined before to be done." And similarly in Luke 22:22, "Truly the Son of man goeth, as it was determined: but woe unto that man by whom he is betrayed!" Here foreordination and responsibility are by our Lord Himself declared to coexist and to be consistent.... The crucifixion of Christ, the greatest crime ever committed, was foreordained of God. It is therefore beyond all doubt the doctrine of the Bible that sin is foreordained.

(5) Besides this, the conquests of Nebuchadnezzar, the destruction of Jerusalem, and many other similar events were predicted and therefore predetermined; but they included the commission of innumerable sins without which the predictions, and consequently the revealed purposes of God, could not have been accomplished.

(6) The whole course of history is represented as the development of the plan and purposes of God, and yet human history is little else than the history of sin. No one can read the simple narrative concerning Joseph, as given in the book of Genesis, without seeing that everything in his history occurred in execution of a preconceived purpose

of God. The envy of his brethren, their selling him into Egypt, and his
unjust imprisonment were all embraced in God's plan. "God," as Joseph himself said to his brethren, "sent me before you to preserve you
a posterity in the earth, and to save your lives by a great deliverance.
So now it was not you that sent me hither, but God" (Gen. 45:7–8).
This is but an illustration. What is true of the history of Joseph is true
of all history. It is the development of the plan of God. God is in
history, and although we cannot trace His path step by step, yet it is
plain in the general survey of events, through long periods, that they
are ordered by God to the accomplishment of His divine purposes.
This is obvious enough in the history of the Jewish nation as recorded
in the Scripture, but it is no less true in regard to all history. The acts
of the wicked in persecuting the early Church were ordained of God
as the means for the wider and more speedy proclamation of the gospel. The sufferings of the martyrs were the means not only of extending
but of purifying the Church. . . . It would destroy the confidence of
God's people could they be persuaded that God does not foreordain
whatsoever comes to pass. It is because the Lord reigns and doeth His
pleasure in heaven and on earth that they repose in perfect security
under His guidance and protection.

§2. Objections to the Doctrine of Divine Decrees

A. Foreordination Inconsistent with Free Agency

It is urged that the foreordination of all events is inconsistent with
the free agency of man. . . . By foreordination is to be understood the
purpose of God rendering certain the occurrence of future events. By
a free act is meant an act of rational self-determination by an intelligent person. If such an act is from its very nature contingent or uncertain, then it is clear that foreordination is inconsistent with free
agency. This theory of liberty has been adopted by a large body of
philosophers and theologians and is for them an insuperable objection
to the doctrine of the divine decrees.

In answer to the objection it may be remarked that it bears with
equal force against foreknowledge. What is foreknown must be certain,
as much as what is foreordained. If the one, therefore, be inconsistent
with liberty, so also is the other. . . . We find, however, that the Scriptures are filled with predictions of future free actions. It is, therefore,
evident that the sacred writers fully believed that free acts are foreknown by the divine mind and therefore are certain as to their occurrence. Besides, if God cannot foreknow how free agents will act, He

must be ignorant of the future and be constantly increasing in knowledge. This is so incompatible with all proper ideas of the infinite mind that it has been almost universally rejected both by philosophers and by Christian theologians.

A still weaker evasion is the proposal of some Arminian writers that God's knowledge is not limited by anything outside Himself, but may be limited by His own will. In creating free agents, He willed not to foreknow how they would act; thus He left their freedom unimpaired. But this proposal assumes that God wills not to be God, that the Infinite wills to be finite. Furthermore, since God's knowledge is independent of His will, it cannot be limited by it. . . .

That an event may be free and yet certain may be easily proved. (1) It is a matter of consciousness. We are often absolutely certain how we shall act and yet conscious that we act freely. A parent may be certain that he will succor a child in distress and be conscious that his free agency is not thereby impaired. The more certain, in many cases, the more perfectly are we self-determined. (2) Free acts have been predicted, and therefore their occurrence was certain. (3) Nothing was more certain than that our Lord would continue holy, harmless, and undefiled, yet His acts were all free. (4) It is certain that the people of God will repent, believe, and persevere in holiness forever in heaven, yet they do not cease to be free agents. The decrees of God, therefore, in that they secure only the certainty of events, are not inconsistent with liberty as to the mode of their occurrence. Although God's purpose comprehends all things and is immutable, yet thereby "no violence is offered to the will of the creatures, nor is the liberty or contingency of second causes taken away, but rather established" (*Westminster Confession* 3.1).

B. *Foreordination of Sin Inconsistent with Holiness*

It is further objected that it is inconsistent with the holiness of God that He should foreordain sin. There are two methods of dealing with this and all similar objections. The one may be called the Scriptural method, as it is the one often adopted by the sacred writers. It consists in showing that the objection bears against the plain declarations of Scripture or against the facts of experience. In either case it is for us sufficiently answered. It is vain to argue that a holy and benevolent God cannot permit sin and misery, if sin and misery actually exist. It is vain to say that His impartiality forbids that there should be any diversity in the endowments, advantages, or happiness of His rational creatures. It is vain to insist that a holy God cannot permit children to suffer for the sins of their parents, when we constantly see that they do thus suffer. So it is utterly irrational to contend that God cannot foreordain sin, if He foreordained (as no Christian doubts) the crucifixion of Christ. The occurrence of sin in the plan adopted by God is a palpable fact; the consistency, therefore, of foreordination of sin with the holiness of God cannot rationally be denied.

The second method of dealing with such objections is to show that the principle on which they are founded is unsound. The principle on which the objection under consideration rests is that an agent is responsible for all the necessary or certain consequences of his acts. . . . That principle, however, is utterly untenable. A righteous judge, in pronouncing sentence on a criminal, may be sure that he will cause wicked and bitter feelings in the criminal's mind, or in the hearts of his friends, and yet the judge be guiltless. A father in excluding a reprobate son from his family may see that the inevitable consequence of such exclusion will be his greater wickedness, and yet the father may do right. It is the certain consequence of God's leaving the fallen angels and the finally impenitent to themselves that they will continue in sin, and yet the holiness of God remains untarnished. The Bible clearly teaches that God judicially abandons men to their sins, giving them up to a reprobate mind, and He therein is most just and holy. It is not true, therefore, that an agent is responsible for all the certain consequences of his acts. It may be, and doubtless is, infinitely wise and just in God to permit the occurrence of sin and to adopt a plan of which sin is a certain consequence or element; yet as He neither causes sin nor tempts men to its commission, He is neither its author nor its approver. He sees and knows that higher ends will be accomplished by its admission than by its exclusion, that a perfect exhibition of His infinite perfections will be thereby effected; and therefore for the highest reason He decrees that it shall occur through the free choice of responsible agents.

Our great ground of confidence, however, is the assurance that the Judge of all the earth must do right. Sin is and God is; therefore the occurrence of sin must be consistent with His nature; and as its occurrence cannot have been unforeseen or undesigned, God's purpose or decree that it should occur must be consistent with His holiness.

C. The Doctrine of Decrees Destroys All Motive to Exertion

A third objection is that the doctrine of foreordination, which supposes the certainty of all events, tends to the neglect of all use of means. If everything will happen just as God has predetermined, we need give ourselves no concern and need make no effort. This objection supposes that God has determined the end without reference to the means. The reverse, however, is true. The event is determined in connection with the means. If the latter fail, so will the former. God has decreed that men shall live by food. If any man refuses to eat, he will die. He has ordained that men shall be saved through faith. If a man refuses to believe, he will perish. . . .

There is another fallacy included in this objection. It supposes that the certainty that an event will happen acts as a motive to neglect the means of its attainment. This is not according to reason or experience. The stronger the hope of success, the greater the motive to exertion. . . .

The rational and Scriptural foundation for the use of means, and the proper motives to avail ourselves of them, are: (1) the command of God; (2) their adaptation to produce the effect; (3) the divine ordination which makes the means necessary to the attainment of the end; and (4) the promise of God to give His blessing to those who obediently avail themselves of the means of His appointment.

D. It Is Fatalism

It is objected, in the fourth place, that the doctrine of decrees amounts to the heathen doctrine of fate. There is only one point of agreement between these doctrines, however. They both assume absolute certainty in the sequence of all events. . . . On the other hand, there are significant differences between fatalism, the doctrine that all events come to pass under the operation of a blind necessity, and the Scriptural doctrine of foreordination: (1) Fatalism excludes the idea of final causes. There is no end to which all things tend and for the accomplishment of which they exist. According to the Scriptural doctrine, all things are ordained and controlled to accomplish the highest conceivable or possible good. (2) According to fatalism, the sequence of events is determined by an unintelligent concatenation of causes and effects. According to the doctrine of decrees, that sequence is determined by infinite wisdom and goodness. (3) Fatalism admits of no distinction between necessary and free causes. The acts of rational agents are as much determined by a necessity outside themselves as are the operations of nature. According to the Scriptures, the freedom and responsibility of man are fully preserved. The two systems differ, therefore, as much as a machine differs from a man, or as the actions of infinite intelligence, power, and love differ from the law of gravitation. (4) The one system, therefore, leads to the denial of all moral distinctions and to stolid insensibility or despair. The other leads to a sedulous regard of, filial confidence in, and submission to the will of an infinitely wise and good ruler, all of whose acts are determined by a sufficient reason.

Chapter X

Creation

§1. Different Theories Concerning the Origin of the Universe

The question concerning the origin of the universe has forced itself on the minds of men in all ages. That the mutable cannot be eternal would seem to be self-evident. As everything within the sphere of human observation is constantly changing, men have been constrained to believe that the world as it now is had a beginning. But if it began to be, whence did it come? Without the light of a divine revelation, this question is unanswerable. The data for the solution of the problem do not lie within the sphere either of experience or of reason. All human theories on this subject are nothing more than conjectures more or less ingenious. . . .

[*A. The Purely Physical Theory*]

B. Theories Which Assume Intelligence in Nature Itself

... It is enough to remark concerning these theories (1) that they leave the origin of things unaccounted for. ... To suppose that matter in a state of chaos is eternal, or that there has been an endless succession of living germs, or that there has been an eternal succession of cycles in the history of the universe, chaos unfolding itself into cosmos during immeasurable ages, is to make an assumption which shocks the reason and must of necessity be destitute of proof.

(2) These theories are atheistic. They deny the existence of a personal Being to whom we are related as creatures and children. The existence of such a Being is an innate, intuitive truth. It cannot be permanently disbelieved. And, therefore, any theory which denies the existence of God must be not only false but short-lived.

C. The Scriptural Doctrine

The Scriptural doctrine on this subject is expressed in the first words of the Bible: "In the beginning God created the heaven and the earth." The heaven and the earth include all things outside God. The Scriptures teach that these things owe their existence to the will and power of God. The Scriptural doctrine therefore is: (1) the universe is not eternal—it began to be; (2) it was not formed out of any preexistence or substance, but was created out of nothing; and (3) the creation was not necessary—God was free to create or not to create, to create the universe as it is, or any other order and system of things, according to the good pleasure of His will. ...

§2. Mediate and Immediate Creation

But while it has ever been the doctrine of the Church that God created the universe out of nothing by the word of His power, which creation was instantaneous and immediate, i.e., without the intervention of any second causes, yet it has generally been admitted that this is to be understood only of the original call of matter into existence. Theologians have, therefore, distinguished between a first and second creation, or between an immediate and mediate creation. The one was instantaneous, the other gradual; the one precludes the idea of any preexisting substance and of cooperation, the other admits and implies both. There is evident ground for this distinction in the Mosaic account of the creation. God, we are told, "created the heaven and the earth.

And the earth was without form, and void; and darkness was upon the face of the deep. And the Spirit of God moved upon the face of the waters." Here it is clearly intimated that the universe, when first created, was in a state of chaos, and that by the life-giving, organizing power of the Spirit of God, it was gradually moulded into the wonderful cosmos which we now behold. The whole of the first chapter of Genesis, after the first two verses, is an account of the progress of creation—the production of light, the formation of an atmosphere, the separation of land and water, the vegetable productions of the earth, the animals of the sea and air, then the living creatures of the earth, and, last of all, man. In Genesis 1:27 it is said that God created man male and female; in chapter 2:7 it is said that "the LORD God formed man out of the dust of the ground." It thus appears that forming out of preexisting material comes within the Scriptural idea of creating. . . . Moreover, the Bible constantly speaks of God as causing the grass to grow and as being the real author or maker of all that the earth, air, or water produces. There is, therefore, according to the Scriptures, not only an immediate, instantaneous creation out of nothing by the simple word of God, but a mediate, progressive creation; i.e., the power of God working in union with second causes. . . .

Thus far there is little room for diversity of opinion. But when the question is asked, How long was the universe in passing from its chaotic to its ordered state? such diversity is at once manifested. According to the more obvious interpretation of the first chapter of Genesis, this work was accomplished in six days. This therefore has been the common belief of Christians. It is a belief founded on a given interpretation of the Mosaic record; this interpretation, however, must be controlled not only by the laws of language, but by facts. This is at present an open question. The facts necessary for its decision have not yet been duly authenticated. The believer may calmly await the result. . . .

§3. Proof of the Doctrine

(1) There is no mention of any preexisting substance out of which the world was made. The original creation is never represented as a moulding of matter into form and imbuing it with life. Nor do the Scriptures ever represent the world as an emanation of God, proceeding from Him by a necessity of His nature. Much less does the Bible ever equate God and the world. In thus ignoring all other doctrines, the Scriptures leave us under the necessity of believing that God created the world out of nothing.

(2) The descriptions of the work of creation given in the Bible preclude the idea of emanation or mere formation. God said, "Let there be light: and there was light." In Psalm 33:6 it is said, "By the word of the LORD were the heavens made; and all the host of them by the breath of his mouth," and in verse 9, "He spake, and it was done; he commanded, and it stood fast." . . .

(3) The same doctrine is involved in the absolute dependence of all things on God and in His absolute sovereignty over them. "Thou, even thou, art Jehovah alone; thou hast made heaven, the heaven of heavens, with all their host, the earth, and all things that are therein, the seas, and all that is therein, and thou preservest them all" (Neh. 9:6; see also Col. 1:16–17; Rev. 4:11). The "all things" spoken of in these passage includes everything external to God. There can, therefore, have been no preexisting matter subsisting independently of His will. Everything external to God is said to owe its existence to His will. . . .

(4) The apostle in Hebrews 11:3 begins his illustration of the nature and power of faith by referring to the creation as the great fundamental truth of all religion. If there be no creation, there is no God. If the universe was called into being out of nothing, then there must be an extramundane Being to whom it owes its existence. The creation is a fact which we know only by revelation. What the sacred writer here asserts is, first, that the worlds were created, set in order, and established by the simple word or command of God. Secondly, this being the case, it follows that the universe was not formed out of any preexisting substance. Thirdly, God is not a mere former, but the creator of the ordered universe. . . .

(5) The Scriptural doctrine on this subject is confirmed by all those passages which ascribe a beginning to the world. . . . According to the Bible there is nothing eternal but God. He and He alone is the Eternal. . . . And so, inasmuch as the world began to be and includes everything outside God, there was nothing of which the world could be made. It was therefore created out of nothing. This is taught in the first chapter of Genesis, "In the beginning (before anything was) God created the heaven and the earth." In many other parts of Scripture a beginning is ascribed to the world, as in Psalm 90:2, "Before the mountains were brought forth, or ever thou hadst formed the earth and the world, even from everlasting to everlasting, thou art God" (see also Ps. 102:25; John 17:5). . . .

(6) The doctrine of creation flows from the infinite perfection of God. There can be but one infinite Being. If anything exists independent of His will, God is thereby limited. The idea of the absolute dependence of all things on God pervades the Scripture and is involved in our religious consciousness. The God of the Bible is an extra-

mundane God existing outside and before the world, absolutely independent of it, its creator, preserver, and governor. Thus the doctrine of creation is a necessary consequence of theism. . . .

[§4. Objections to the Doctrine]

§5. Design of the Creation

Men have long endeavored to find a satisfactory answer to the question, Why did God create the world? What end was it designed to accomplish? . . . The only satisfactory method of determining the answer is by appealing to the Scriptures. There it is explicitly taught that the glory of God, the manifestation of His perfections, is the last end of all His works. . . . This in the Bible is declared to be the end of the universe as a whole, of the external world or works of nature, of the plan of redemption, of the whole course of history, of the mode in which God administers His providence and dispenses His grace, and of particular events, such as the choice of the Israelites and all the dealings of God with them as a nation. It is the end which all rational creatures are commanded to keep constantly in view, and it comprehends and secures all other right ends. . . .

§6. The Mosaic Account of the Creation

There are three methods of interpreting this portion of the Bible: (1) the historical, (2) the allegorical, and (3) the mythical. The first assumes it to be a veritable history. The second . . . seeks for a hidden moral or spiritual sense. . . . [The third] regards the record of the creation as a mere fable . . . of no more value than the similar cosmogonies which are found in the early literature of all nations. In favour of the historical character of the record are the following considerations: (a) It purports to be a veritable history. (b) It is the appropriate and necessary introduction of an acknowledged history. (c) It is referred to and quoted in other parts of the Bible as the true account of the creation of the world; the fourth commandment, e.g., makes it the foundation of the institution of the Sabbath. (d) The facts here recorded, including as they do the creation and probation of man, lie at the foundation of the whole revealed plan of redemption. The whole Bible, therefore, rests upon the record here given of the work of creation, and consequently all the evidence which goes to support the divine authority of the Bible tends to sustain the historical verity of that record. . . .

The most serious objections to the Mosaic record are geological in nature. According to the commonly received chronology, our globe has existed only a few thousand years. According to geologists, it must have existed for countless ages. And again, according to the generally received interpretation of the first chapter of Genesis, the process of creation was completed in six days, whereas geology teaches that it must have been in progress through periods of time which cannot be computed.

Two methods of reconciling the Mosaic account with the facts as presented by geologists have been adopted. First, some understand the first verse of Genesis to refer to the original creation of the matter of the universe in the indefinite past, and what follows to refer to the last reorganizing change in the state of our earth to fit it for the habitation of man. Second, the word day as used throughout the chapter is understood to signify geological periods of indefinite duration.

In favour of this latter view it is urged that the Hebrew word translated "day" in Genesis 1 is used in Scripture in many different senses: sometimes for the time the sun is above the horizon, sometimes for a period of twenty-four hours, sometimes for a year (Lev. 25:29; Judg. 17:10), and sometimes for an indefinite period, as in the phrases "the day of your calamity," "the day of salvation," "the day of the Lord," "the day of judgment." And in this account of the creation it is used for the period of light in antithesis to night, for the separate periods in the progress of creation, and then, in Genesis 2:4, for the whole period ("in the day that the LORD God made the earth and the heavens").

It is of course admitted that, taking this account by itself, it would be most natural to understand the word in its ordinary sense; but if that sense brings the Mosaic account into conflict with facts, and another sense avoids such conflict, then it is obligatory on us to adopt that other. Now it is urged that if the word day be taken in the sense of an indefinite period of time, a sense which it undoubtedly has in other parts of Scripture, there is not only no discrepancy between the Mosaic account of the creation and the assumed facts of geology, but there is a most marvelous coincidence between them. . . .

As the Bible is of God, it is certain that there can be no conflict between the teachings of the Scriptures and the facts of science. It is not with facts, but with theories, believers have to contend. Many theories apparently or really inconsistent with the Bible have, from time to time, been presented. But these theories have proved either to be false or to harmonize with the Word of God, properly interpreted. The Church has been forced more than once to alter her interpretation of the Bible to accommodate the discoveries of science. But this has been done without doing any violence to the Scriptures or in any degree impairing their authority. Such change, however, cannot be effected without a struggle, for our mode of understanding the Bible is inevitably determined by our views of the subjects of which it treats. So long as men believed that the earth was the center of our system, the sun its satellite, and the stars its ornamentation, they of necessity understood the Bible in accordance with that hypothesis. But when it was discovered that the earth is only one of the smaller satellites of the sun and that the stars are worlds, then faith, although at first it staggered, soon grew strong enough to take all this in and rejoice to find that the Bible, and the Bible alone of all ancient books, is in full accord with these stupendous revelations of science. And so if it should be proved that the creation was a process continued through countless ages and that the Bible alone of all the books of antiquity recognizes that fact, then the idea of its being of human origin would be utterly refuted.

Providence

§1. Preservation

God's works of providence are His most holy, wise, and powerful preserving and governing all His creatures and all their actions. Providence, therefore, includes preservation and government. By preservation is meant that all things external to God owe the continuance of their existence, with all their properties and powers, to the will of God. This is clearly the doctrine of the Scriptures. The passages relating to this subject are very numerous. They are of different kinds. First, some assert in general terms that God does sustain all things by the word of His power. In Colossians 1:17 it is said, "By him all things consist," or continue to be; and in Nehemiah 9:6, "Thou, even thou, art LORD alone; thou hast made heaven, the heaven of heavens, with all their host, the earth, and all things that are therein, the seas, and all that is therein, and thou preservest them all." Secondly, some passages (e.g., Pss. 104 and 148) declare that the regular operations of nature are preserved in their efficiency by the power of God. Thirdly, some passages relate to irrational animals, while others relate to rational creatures, who are said to live, move, and have their being in God (Acts 17:28). These passages clearly teach (1) that the universe as a whole does not continue in being of itself—it would cease to exist if unsupported by His power; (2) that all creatures, whether plants or animals, are continued in existence not by any inherent principle of life, but by the will of God; and (3) that this preservation extends not only to the substance, but also to the form; not only to the essence, but also to the qualities, properties, and powers of all created things.

This doctrine, thus clearly taught in the Scriptures, is so consonant to reason and to the religious nature of man that it is not denied among Christians. The only question is as to the nature of the divine efficiency to which the continued existence of all things is to be referred. On this subject there are three general opinions.

First, there are those who assume that everything is to be referred to the original purpose of God. He created all things and determined that they should continue in being according to the laws which He impressed upon them at the beginning. There is no need, it is said, of supposing His continued intervention for their preservation. It is enough that He does not will that they should cease to be. This is the theory adopted by the deists. According to this view, God is seated on His throne in the heavens, a mere spectator of the world and of its operations, exerting no direct efficiency in sustaining the things which He has made. . . .

A second view of the nature of preservation goes to the opposite extreme of confounding creation and preservation. . . . [This view holds] that all efficiency is in God, that all effects are to be referred to His agency. As there was no cooperation in calling the world out of nothing, so there is no cooperation of second causes in its continuance and operations. At each instant God creates the universe anew, as it were. . . .

Between the two extremes of representing preservation as a mere negative act, a not willing to destroy, which denies any continued efficiency of God in the world, and the theory which resolves everything into the immediate agency of God, denying the reality of all second causes, is the plain doctrine of the Scriptures, which teaches that the continuance of the world in existence, the preservation of its substance, properties, and forms, is to be referred to the omnipresent power of God. He upholds as He created all things—by the word of His power. How He does this it is vain to inquire. So long as we cannot tell how we move our lips, or how mind can operate on matter, or in what way the soul is present and operative in the whole body, it requires little humility to suppress the craving curiosity to know how God sustains the universe with all its hosts in being and activity. . . . It is best, therefore, to rest satisfied with the simple statement that preservation is that omnipotent energy of God by which all created things, animate and inanimate, are upheld in existence with all the properties and powers with which He has endowed them.

§2. Government

Providence includes not only preservation, but government. The latter includes the ideas of design and control. It supposes an end to be attained and the disposition and direction of means for its accomplishment. If God governs the universe, He has some great end, including an indefinite number of subordinate ends, towards which it is directed, and He must control the sequence of all events so as to render certain the accomplishment of all His purposes. Of this providential government the Scriptures teach (1) that it is universal, including all the creatures of God and all their actions. The external world, rational and irrational creatures, things great and small, ordinary and extraordinary, are equally and always under the control of God. The doctrine of providence excludes both necessity and chance from the universe, substituting for them the intelligent and universal control of an infinite, omnipresent God. (2) The Scriptures also teach that this government of God is powerful. It is the universal sway of omnipotence which renders certain the accomplishment of His designs, which embrace in their compass everything that occurs. (3) It is wise; this means not only that the ends which God has in view are consistent with His infinite wisdom, and that the means employed are wisely adapted to their respective objects, but also that His control is suited to the nature of the creatures over which it is exercised. He governs the material world according to fixed laws which He Himself has established; this includes governing irrational animals by their instincts and rational creatures in keeping with their nature. (4) God's providence is holy. That is, there is nothing in the ends proposed, the means adopted, or the agency employed, which is inconsistent with His infinite holiness or which the highest moral excellence does not demand. . . .

A. Proof of the Doctrine

This doctrine necessarily flows from the Scriptural idea of God. He is declared to be a personal Being, infinite in wisdom, goodness, and power, and to be the Father of spirits. From this it follows not only that He acts intelligently, i.e., with a view to an end and on sufficient reasons, but that He must be concerned for the good of creatures rational and irrational, great and small. The idea that God would create this vast universe teeming with life in all its forms and exercise no control over it, to secure it from destruction or from working out nothing but evil, is utterly inconsistent with the nature of God. And to suppose that anything is too great to be comprehended in His control, or anything so minute as to escape His notice, or that the infinitude of particulars can distract His attentions, is to forget that God is infinite. It cannot require any effort in Him, the omnipresent and infinite intelligence, to comprehend and to direct all things however complicated, numerous, or minute. . . . God is as much present everywhere, and with everything, as though He were only in one place and had but one object of attention. . . .

1. Proof from the evidence of the operation of mind everywhere

The whole universe, so far as it can be subjected to our observation, exhibits evidence of God's omnipresent intelligence and control. Mind is everywhere active. There is everywhere manifest the intelligent adaptation of means to an end. . . . This mind is not in matter. It is and must be the intelligence of an infinite, omnipresent Being. It is just as much beyond the power of a creature to form an insect as it is to create the universe. And it is as unreasonable to assume that the organized forms of the vegetable and animal worlds are due to the laws of nature as it would be to assume that a printing press could be constructed to compose a poem. . . . Wherever there is the intelligent adaptation of means to an end, there is evidence of the presence of mind. And as such evidence of mental activity is found in every part of the universe, we see God ever active and everywhere present in all His works.

2. Argument from our religious nature

The Scriptural doctrine of a universal providence is demanded by the religious nature of man. It is therefore an instinctive and necessary belief. It is banished from the mind or overruled only by persistent effort. In the first place, we cannot but regard it as a limitation of God to suppose Him deficient in either knowledge or power with respect to any part of His creation. In the second place, our sense of dependence involves the conviction not only that we owe our existence to His will, but that it is in Him that we and all His creatures live, move, and have our being. In the third place, our sense of responsibility implies that God is cognizant of all our thoughts, words, and actions, and that He controls all our circumstances and our destiny both in this life and in the life to come. This conviction is instinctive and universal. It is found in men of all ages, and under all forms of religion, and in all states of civilization. Men universally believe in the moral government of God, and they universally believe that that moral government is administered, at least in part, in this world. They see, for example, that God often restrains or punishes the wicked. . . . In the fourth place, our religious nature demands intercourse with God. He must be to us the object of prayer and the ground of confidence. We must look to Him in trouble and danger; we cannot refrain from calling upon Him for help or thanking Him for our mercies. Unless the doctrine of a universal providence be true, all this is a delusion. Such, however, is the relation in which the Scriptures and the constitution of our nature assume that we stand to God and He stands to the world. He is ever present, all-controlling, the hearer and answerer of prayer, giving us our daily mercies and guiding us in all our ways. This doctrine of providence, therefore, is the foundation of all practical religion, and the denial of it is practically atheism, for we are then without God in the world. . . .

3. Argument from predictions and promises

Another general argument on this subject is derived from the predictions, promises, and threatenings recorded in the Word of God. Those predictions are not mere general declarations of the probable or natural consequences of certain courses of action, but specific revelations of events in the future, the occurrence of which cannot be secured except through the exercise of an absolutely certain control over causes and agents both natural and moral. God promises to give health, long life, and prosperous seasons; or He threatens to inflict severe judgments, the desolations of war, famine, drought, and pestilence. Such promises and threatenings suppose a universal providence, a control over all the creatures of God and over all their actions. As such promises and threatenings abound in the Word of God, and as His people and all nations recognize such benefits or calamities as divine dispensations, it is evident that the doctrine of providence underlies all religion, both natural and revealed.

4. Argument from experience

All experience confirms the doctrine of providence. Every man can see that his life has been ordered by an intelligence and will not his own. His whole history has been determined by events over which he had no control, events often in themselves apparently fortuitous, so that he must either assume that the most important events are determined by chance, or admit that the providence of God extends to all events, even the most minute. What is true of individuals is true of nations. The Old Testament is a record of God's providential dealings with the Hebrew people. The history of the patriarchs, of Abraham, of Joseph, of the sojourn of the Israelites in Egypt, of their deliverance and journey through the wilderness, of their conquest of the land of Canaan, and their whole subsequent experience, is a continuous record of the control of God over all their circumstances—a control which is represented as extending to all events. In like manner the history of the world reveals to an intelligent eye the all-pervading providence of God.

B. The Scriptures Teach God's Providence over Nature

We find that the Bible asserts that the providential agency of God is exercised over all the operations of nature. This is asserted with regard to the ordinary operations of physical laws: the motion of the heavenly bodies, the succession of the seasons, the growth and decay of the productions of the earth, and the falling of the rain, hail, and snow. It is He who guides Arcturus in his course, who makes the sun to rise and the grass to grow. These events are represented as due to the omnipresent agency of God and are determined not by chance, nor by necessity, but by His will. Paul says that God "left not himself without witness," even among the heathen, "in that he did good, and gave us rain from heaven, and fruitful seasons, filling our hearts with food and gladness" (Acts 14:17). Our Lord says that God "maketh his sun to rise on the evil and on the good, and sendeth rain on the just and on the unjust"; He clothes "the grass of the field, which today is, and tomorrow is cast into the oven" (Matt. 5:45; 6:30). In like manner the more unusual and striking operations of natural laws—earthquakes, tempests, and pestilences—are said to be sent, governed, and determined by Him, so that all the effects which they produce are referred to His purpose. He makes the winds His messengers, and the lightnings are His ministering spirits. Even apparently fortuitous events, such as are determined by causes so rapid or so inappreciable as to elude our notice—the falling of the lot, the flight of an arrow—are all controlled by the omnipresent God. "Are not two sparrows sold for a farthing? and one of them shall not fall on the ground without your Father" (Matt. 10:29).

1. Providence extends over the animal world

The Scriptures teach that irrational animals are the objects of God's providential care. He fashions their bodies; He calls them into the world, sustains them in being, and supplies their wants. In His hand is the life of every living thing (Job 12:10). The psalmist says (104:21), "The young lions roar after their prey, and seek their meat from God" (see also vv. 27–28; Matt. 6:26; Acts 17:25). . . . His creatures depend on the constant exercise of His care. He gives or withholds what they need according to His good pleasure. When our Lord put on the lips of His disciples the petition, "Give us this day our daily bread," He was recognizing the fact that all living creatures depend on the constant intervention of God for the supply of their daily wants.

2. Over nations

The Bible teaches that the providential government of God extends over nations and communities of men: "He ruleth by his power for ever; his eyes behold the nations: let not the rebellious exalt themselves" (Ps. 66:7); "he changeth the times and the seasons: he removeth kings, and setteth up kings" (Dan. 2:21; see also Dan. 4:25, 35; Isa. 10:5–7, 15). The Scriptures are full of this doctrine. God uses the nations with the absolute control that a man uses a rod or a staff. They are in His hands, and He employs them to accomplish His purposes. He breaks them in pieces like a potter's vessel, or He exalts them to greatness, according to His good pleasure.

3. Over individuals

The providence of God extends not only over nations, but also over individuals. The circumstances of every man's birth, life, and death are ordered by God. Whether we are born in a heathen or in a Christian land, in the Church or out of it; whether we are weak or strong, with many or with few talents, prosperous or afflicted; whether we live a longer or a shorter time, are not matters determined by chance, or by the unintelligent sequence of events, but by the will of God. "The LORD killeth, and maketh alive: he bringeth down to the grave, and bringeth up. The LORD maketh poor and maketh rich: he bringeth low and lifteth up" (1 Sam. 2:6–7). "My times (the vicissitudes of life) are in thy hands" (Ps. 31:15). God "hath made of one blood all nations of men for to dwell on all the face of the earth, and hath determined the times before appointed (i.e., the turning points in history), and the bounds of their habitation" (Acts 17:26; see also Ps. 75:6–7; Prov. 16:9; Isa. 45:5).

4. God's providence in relation to free acts

The Bible no less clearly teaches that God exercises a controlling power over the free acts of men as well as over their external circumstances. This is true of all their acts, good and evil. It is asserted in general terms that His dominion extends over their whole inward life and especially over their good acts: "The preparations of the heart in man, and the answer of the tongue, is from the LORD" (Prov. 16:1); "the king's heart is in the hand of the LORD, as the rivers of water: he turneth it whithersoever he will" (Prov. 21:1; see also Ezra 7:27; Exod. 3:21; Ps. 119:36). A large part of the predictions, promises, and threatenings of the Word of God are founded on the assumption of this absolute control over the free acts of His creatures. Without this there can be no government of the world and no certainty as to its issue. The Bible is filled with prayers founded on this same assumption. All Christians believe that the hearts of men are in the hand of God, that He works in them both to will and to do according to His good pleasure.

5. The relation of God's providence to sin

With regard to the sinful acts of men the Scriptures teach (1) that they are so under the control of God that they can occur only by His permission and in execution of His purposes. He so guides men in the exercise of their wickedness that the particular forms of its manifestation are determined by His will. . . . It is said that He hardened the heart of Pharaoh, that He turned the hearts of the heathen to hate His people, that He blinds the eyes of men and sends them strong delusion that they may believe a lie, and that He stirs up the nations to war. . . .

(2) The Scriptures teach that the wickedness of men is restrained within prescribed bounds: "Surely the wrath of man shall praise thee: the remainder of wrath shalt thou restrain" (Ps. 76:10); "Because thy rage against me and thy tumult is come up into mine ears, therefore I will put my hook in thy nose, and my bridle in thy lips, and I will turn thee back by the way by which thou camest" (2 Kings 19:28).

(3) Wicked actions are overruled for good. The wicked conduct of

Joseph's brethren, the obstinacy and disobedience of Pharaoh, and above all, the crucifixion of Christ, the persecutions of the Church, the revolutions and wars among the nations, have been all so overruled by God as to fulfil His wise and merciful designs.

(4) The Scriptures teach that God's providence in relation to the sins of men is such that the sinfulness thereof proceedeth only from the creature and not from God, who neither is nor can be the author or approver of sin. "All that is in the world, the lust of the flesh, and the lust of the eyes, and the pride of life, is not of the Father (not from Him as its source or author), but is of the world" (1 John 2:16). "Let no man say when he is tempted, I am tempted of God: for God cannot be tempted with evil, neither tempteth he any man" (James 1:13). . . .

Thus the fact that God does govern all His creatures and all their actions is clearly revealed in the Scriptures. And that fact is the foundation of all religion. It is the ground of the consolation of His people in all ages, and it may be said to be the intuitive conviction of all men, however inconsistent it may be with their philosophical theories or with their professions. . . .

[§3. Different Theories of the Divine Government]

§4. Principles Involved in the Scriptural Doctrine of Providence

As this doctrine of providence involves the question of God's relation to the world, it is confessedly the most comprehensive and difficult in the compass either of theology or of philosophy. As the world, meaning thereby the universe of created beings, includes the world of matter and the world of mind, the doctrine of providence concerns, first, the relation of God to the external or material universe and, secondly, His relation to the world of mind or to His rational creatures.

A. The Providence of God over the Material Universe

1. Laws of nature

. . . The phrase "laws of nature" . . . means uniformly acting forces in nature, e.g., the laws of gravitation, light, heat, electricity, etc. . . . The chief question here is, In what relation does God stand to these laws? The answer to that question, as drawn from the Bible, is, first, that He is their author. He endowed matter with these forces and ordained that they should be uniform. Secondly, He is independent of them. He can change, annihilate, or suspend them at pleasure. He can operate with them or without them. Thirdly, as the stability of the universe and the welfare and even the existence of organized creatures depend on the uniformity of the laws of nature, God never does disregard them except for the accomplishment of some high purpose. He, in the ordinary operations of His providence, operates with and through the laws which He has ordained. He governs the material as well as the moral world by law. . . .

It is by a natural law or physical force that vapour arises from the surface of the ocean, is formed into clouds, and condenses and falls in showers upon the earth, yet God so controls the operation of the laws producing these effects that He sends rain when and where He pleases. The same is true of all the operations of nature and of all events in the external world. They are due to the efficiency of physical forces; but those forces, which are combined, adjusted, and made to cooperate or to counteract each other in the greatest complexity, are all under the constant guidance of God and are made to accomplish His purpose. It is perfectly rational, therefore, in a world where blind, natural forces are the proximate cause of everything that occurs, to pray for health, for protection, for success, for fruitful seasons, and for the peace and prosperity of nations, since all those events are determined by the intelligent agency of God.

The providence of God is thus seen to be universal and to extend to all His creatures and all their actions. The distinction usually and properly made between the general and special providence of God has reference to the effects produced, and not to His agency in their production; for this is the same in all cases. But if the object to be accomplished be a general one, such as the orderly motion of the heavenly bodies, or the support and regular operation of the laws of nature, then the providence of God is spoken of as general. Many men are willing to admit of this general superintendence of the world on the part of God, but deny His intervention in the production of definite effects. The Bible, however, clearly teaches and all men instinctively believe in a special providence; that is, that God uses His control over the laws of nature to bring about special effects. Men in sickness, in danger, or in any distress pray to God for help. This is not irrational. It supposes God's relation to the world to be precisely what it is declared to be in the Bible. It does not suppose that God sets aside or counteracts the laws of nature, but simply that He controls them and causes them to produce whatever effects He sees fit. The Scriptures, the history of the world, and almost every man's experience bear abundant evidence to such divine interpositions. We should be as helpless orphans were it not for this constant oversight and protection of our heavenly Father. . . .

2. God's providence in relation to vital processes

. . . Certain processes go on where life is present and are never seen when it is absent. These processes are organization, growth, and reproduction. They imply the perception of an end, a purpose or will to secure that end, and the intelligent choice and application of means for its attainment. This is the work of mind. . . .

But if life be mind or, rather, if vital force be mental force, as indicated by the mode in which it acts, where does that mind reside? . . . [The best answer is that] the intelligence required to account for the processes of vegetable and animal life is in the everywhere present and everywhere active mind of God Himself. This does not imply that physical or second causes have no efficiency, or that those causes are merged into the efficiency of God. It simply means that God uses the chemical, electric, photic, and other forces of nature in carrying on organization and other vital processes in the vegetable and animal worlds. In such processes there is a combination of two specifically different forces—physical and mental. The physical are in the matter used; the mental are in God, who uses the matter and its forces. Examples of this combination of mental and physical force are familiar. All voluntary motion on the part of animals and all the works of men are due to such combination. Walking, speaking, and writing are possible only so far as mind controls our material organization. In writing, for example, the vital functions are going on in the hand . . . but the guiding power is in the mind. It is the mind that determines what letters and sentences the fingers shall form and what ideas shall be expressed. In like manner, it is the ever-present mind of God that guides the action of physical causes in the processes of animal and vegetable life. . . .

In support of the view that the intelligence displayed in all vital processes is the intelligence of the everywhere present and everywhere active mind of God, it may be urged, in the first place, that the principle involved in this doctrine is assumed in the simplest truths of natural religion. If God be not thus everywhere present and everywhere active in the control of secondary causes, there is no propriety or use in prayer and no ground of confidence in divine protection.

In the second place, it seems to be the only way to account for the facts of the case. That the processes of life in vegetables and animals do manifest intelligence cannot be denied. They manifest foresight, purpose, choice, and controlling power. This intelligence simply cannot be referred to matter or to physical forces. . . .

In the third place, the authority of Scripture may be claimed in support of the doctrine in question. The Bible teaches the omnipresence of God; i.e., the omnipresence of mind. The phrase "God fills heaven and earth" means that mind pervades heaven and earth, that there is no portion of space in which mind is not present and active. The Scriptures also teach that all things, even the most minute, as the number of the hairs of our head, the falling of a sparrow, the flight of an arrow, are under the control of God. He also is said to cause the grass to grow, which means not only that He so orders physical causes that vegetation is the result, but also, as appears from other representations, that the organization and growth of the plant are determined by His agency. This seems to be clearly taught in Psalm 139:15–16 with regard to the bodies of men: "My substance was not hid from thee, when I was made in secret, and curiously wrought in the lowest parts of the earth. Thine eyes did see my substance, yet being unperfect; and in thy book all my members were written, which in continuance were fashioned, when as yet there was none of them." . . . This teaches that the human body is fashioned in the womb by the intelligence of God and not by undirected physical causes acting blindly.

B.   *The Providence of God over Rational Creatures*

God's providence extends over the world of mind, i.e., over rational free agents, as well as over the material universe. The principles involved in the Scriptural doctrine concerning God's providential government of rational creatures are:

(1) The mind is essentially active. It originates its own acts. This is a matter of consciousness. It is essential to liberty and responsibility. We know that this is a Scriptural doctrine, for the Bible calls on men to act and regards them as the authors of their own acts. . . .

(2) Although free agents have the power to act and originate their own acts, God not only upholds them in being and efficiency, but controls the use which they make of their ability. . . . He determines their action to be in one way and not in another, so that it is rational to pray that God would incline the hearts of men to show us favour, that He would change the dispositions and purposes of wicked men, and that He would work in us to will as well as to do. No creature, therefore, is independent of God in the exercise of the powers with which He has endowed it. The hearts of men are in His hands, and He controls their action as effectually as He controls the operations of nature. But His agency in the world of spirits no more interferes with the laws of mind than His agency in the external world interferes with the efficiency of material causes.

(3) The providential agency of God in the government of free agents is not to be confounded with the operations of His grace. These two

things are constantly represented in the Bible as distinct. The one is natural, the other supernatural. In the one, God acts according to uniform laws, or by His *potentia ordinata;* in the other, according to the good pleasure of His will, or by His *potentia absoluta.* The control which God exercises over the ordinary acts of men, and especially over the wicked, is analogous to that which He exercises in the guidance of material causes, whereas His agency in the operations of His grace is more analogous to His mode of action in prophecy, inspiration, and miracles. In the former, or in His providential agency over minds, nothing is effected which transcends the efficiency of second causes. In the latter the effects are such as second causes are utterly inadequate to accomplish. There are obvious points of difference between the two cases: (a) The ability to perform ordinary operations or acts arises out of the free agent's nature as a rational creature and is inseparable from it, whereas the acts of faith, repentance, and other holy affections do not flow from the ability of men in the present condition of their nature, but from a new principle of life supernaturally communicated and maintained. (b) The ordinary acts of men, and especially their wicked acts, are determined by their own natural inclinations and feelings. God does not awaken or infuse those feelings or dispositions in order to determine sinners to act wickedly. On the other hand, all gracious or holy affections are thus infused or excited by the Spirit of God. (c) The providential government of God over free agents is exercised as much in accordance with the laws of mind as His providential government over the material world is in accordance with the established laws of matter. Both belong to the *potentia ordinata* or ordered efficiency of God. This is not the case in the operations of His grace. Holy affections and exercises are not due to the mere moral power of the truth, or its control over our natural affections, but to the indwelling of the Spirit of God. Thus it is not we that live, but Christ that liveth in us. It is indeed our life, but it is a life divine in its origin and sustained and guided in all its exercises by a higher influence than the laws of mind.... This distinction between nature and grace, between the providential efficiency of God and the workings of His Spirit in the hearts of His people, is one of the most important in all theology. It makes all the difference between Augustinianism and Pelagianism, between rationalism and supernatural, evangelical religion.

Such are the general principles involved in this most difficult doctrine of divine providence. We should be equally on our guard against the extreme which merges all efficiency in God and which, in denying all second causes, destroys human liberty and responsibility, and makes

God not only the author of sin, but in reality the only Being in the universe; and the opposite extreme, which banishes God from the world He has made and which, by denying that He governs all His creatures and all their actions, destroys the foundation of all religion and dries up the fountains of piety. If this latter view be correct, there is no God to whom we can look for the supply of our wants or for protection from evil, whose favour we can seek, or whose displeasure we need dread. We and all other things are in the hands of blindly operating causes. Between these equally fatal extremes lies the Scriptural doctrine that God governs all His creatures and all their actions. This doctrine admits the reality and efficiency of second causes, both material and mental, but denies that they are independent of the creator and preserver of the universe. It teaches that an infinitely wise, good, and powerful God is everywhere present, controlling all events great and small, necessary and free, in a way perfectly consistent with the nature of His creatures and with His own infinite excellence, so that everything is ordered by His will and is made to subserve His wise and benevolent designs.

Chapter XII

Miracles

§1. Their Nature. Meaning and Usage of the Word

[God's work in the world falls into a number of categories.] In the first place, there are events due to the ordinary operations of second causes as upheld and guided by God. To this class belong the common processes of nature—the growth of plants and animals, the orderly movements of the heavenly bodies—and the more unusual occurrences—earthquakes, volcanic eruptions, and violent agitations and revolutions in human societies. In the second place, there are events due to the influences of the Holy Spirit upon the hearts of men, such as regeneration, sanctification, spiritual illumination, etc. Thirdly, there are events which belong to neither of these classes and whose distinguishing characteristics are (1) that they take place in the external world, i.e., in the sphere of the observation of the senses, and (2) that they are produced or caused by the simple volition of God without the intervention of any subordinate cause. To this class belongs the original act of creation, in which all cooperation of second causes was

227

impossible. To the same class belong all events truly miraculous. A miracle, therefore, may be defined to be an event brought about in the external world by the immediate efficiency or simple volition of God.

An examination of any of the great miracles recorded in Scripture will establish the correctness of this definition. The raising of Lazarus from the dead may be taken as an example. This was an event which occurred in the outward world, one which could be seen and verified by the testimony of the senses. It was not brought about either in whole or in part by the efficiency of natural causes. It was due to the simple word, or volition, or immediate agency of God. The same may be said of ... Christ's walking upon the sea, multiplying the loaves and the fishes, and calming the winds and the waves by a command—any cooperation of physical causes is not only ignored but, by clearest intimation, denied. . . .

[§2. The Possibility of Miracles]

§3. Can a Miracle Be Known as Such?

. . . There are some events which so evidently transcend the power of nature that there can be no rational doubt as to their supernatural origin. No creature can create or originate life, or work without the intervention of means. A large class of the miracles recorded in Scripture imply the exercise of a power which can belong to God alone. The multiplying a few loaves and fishes so as to satisfy the hunger of thousands of men, raising the dead, and giving sight to the blind and hearing to the deaf, not by the appliances of art, but by a command, are clearly effects which imply the exercise of almighty power.

It is to be kept in mind, however, that the nature of the event is not the only criterion by which we are to determine its character. To prove an event in the external world to be miraculous, we have to prove not only that it is not the effect of any natural cause, but also that it is to be referred to the immediate agency of God. . . . An event may be, as far as we can see, supernatural either in its nature or in the mode of its occurrence, but that alone would not justify us in referring it to God. Much depends on the character of the agent and the design for which the wonder is wrought. If these be evidently bad, we cannot be convinced that God has wrought a miracle. But if both the character of the agent and the design of his work are good, then we are easily and rationally convinced that the wonder is really a miracle. . . .

Such is the latitude with which the words "signs and wonders" are used in the Scriptures that they apply not only to works due to God's immediate agency, but to those effected by the power of evil spirits. . . .

It is admitted that the signs performed by the Egyptian magicians and the predicted wonders of Antichrist are not to be regarded as mere tricks and juggleries, but are the works of Satan and his angels. The question is, Are they to be regarded as true miracles? The answer to this question depends on the meaning of the word. If by a miracle we mean any event transcending the efficiency of physical causes and the power of man, then they are miracles. But if we adhere to the definition given above, which requires that the event be produced by the immediate power of God, they of course are not miracles. They are "lying wonders," not only because they are intended to sustain the kingdom of lies, but because they falsely profess to be what they are not. They are wonders only in the sight of men.

The difficulty of discriminating between miracles and these lying wonders, i.e., between the works of God and the works of Satan, has been anticipated and provided for by the sacred writers themselves. In Deuteronomy 13:1-3 Moses says, "If there arise among you a prophet . . . and giveth thee a sign or a wonder, and the sign or the wonder come to pass, whereof he spake unto thee, saying, Let us go after other gods . . . ; thou shalt not hearken unto the words of that prophet." In Matthew 7:22-23 our Lord says, "Many will say to me in that day, Lord, Lord, have we not prophesied in thy name? and in thy name have cast out devils? and in thy name done many wonderful works? And then will I profess unto them, I never knew you: depart from me, ye that work iniquity" (see also Matt. 24:24; 2 Thess. 2:9). These passages teach that supernatural events, i.e., events transcending the power of material causes and the ability of man, may be brought about by the agency of higher intelligences, and that no such supernatural events are to be regarded as of any authority if produced by wicked agents or for a wicked purpose. It was on this principle our Lord answered the Pharisees who accused Him of casting out devils by Beelzebub the prince of devils. He appealed to the design for which His miracles were wrought to prove that they could not be referred to a Satanic influence. Satan will not cooperate to confirm the truth or to promote good. God cannot cooperate to confirm what is false or to promote evil. Thus the character of the agent and the design for which a supernatural event is brought about determine whether it is truly a miracle or one of the lying wonders of the devil. . . .

§4. The Value of Miracles as a Proof of a Divine Revelation

On this subject extreme opinions have been held. On the one hand, it has been maintained that miracles are the only satisfactory evidence of a divine revelation; on the other, that they are neither necessary nor available.... What the Bible teaches on this subject is (1) that the evidence of miracles is important and decisive, and (2) that it is, nevertheless, subordinate and inferior to that of the truth itself. Both of these points are abundantly evident from the language of the Bible and from the facts contained therein: (a) That God has confirmed His revelations, whether made through prophets or apostles, by these manifestations of His power is of itself a sufficient proof of their validity and importance as seals of a divine mission. (b) The sacred writers under both dispensations appealed to these wonders as proofs that they were the messengers of God. In the New Testament it is said that God confirmed the testimony of His apostles by signs, wonders, divers miracles, and gifts of the Holy Ghost. (c) Even Christ, in whom the fulness of the Godhead dwelt bodily, constantly appealed to His miracles as a decisive proof of His divine mission: "The works which the Father hath given me to finish, the same works that I do, bear witness of me" (John 5:36; see also 10:25, 38). Undoubtedly the highest evidence of the truth is the truth itself, as the highest evidence of goodness is goodness itself. Christ is His own witness. His glory reveals Him as the Son of God to all whose eyes the god of this world has not blinded. The point which miracles are designed to prove is not so much the truth of the doctrines taught as the divine mission of the teacher.... What a man teaches may be true, although not divine as to its origin. But when a man presents himself as a messenger of God, whether he is to be received as such or not depends first on the doctrines which he teaches and, secondly, upon the works which he performs. If he not only teaches doctrines conformed to the nature of God and consistent with the laws of our own constitution, but also performs works which evince divine power, then we know not only that the doctrines are true, but also that the teacher is sent of God.

Chapter XIII

Angels

§1. Their Nature

So much is said in the Scriptures of angels, and such important functions in the providence of God over the world, and especially in the experience of His people and of His Church, are ascribed to them that the doctrine of the Bible concerning them should not be overlooked. . . . They are described as pure spirits, i.e., immaterial and incorporeal beings. The Scriptures do not attribute bodies of any kind to them. . . . They are invisible, incorruptible, and immortal, but not omnipresent. They are always somewhere and not everywhere at any given moment, but they are not confined to space circumscriptively as bodies are, and can move from one portion of space to another. As spirits they are possessed of intelligence, will, and power. With regard to their knowledge, whether as to its modes or objects, nothing special is revealed. All that is clear is that in their intellectual faculties and in the extent of their knowledge they are far superior to man. Their power also is very great and extends over mind and matter. They have

231

the power to communicate with one another and with other minds and to produce effects in the natural world. The greatness of their power is manifest (1) from the names and titles given to them, e.g., principalities, powers, dominions, and world rulers; (2) from the direct assertions of Scripture, as they are said to "excel in strength"; and (3) from the effects attributed to their agency. However great their power may be, it is nevertheless subject to all the limitations which characterize creatures. Angels, therefore, cannot create, they cannot change substances, they cannot alter the laws of nature, they cannot perform miracles, they cannot act without means, and they cannot search the heart; for all these are, in Scripture, declared to be prerogatives peculiar to God. The power of angels is, therefore, dependent and derived. It must be exercised in accordance with the laws of the material and spiritual world. Moreover, their intervention is not optional, but permitted or commanded by God at His pleasure; and, so far as the external world is concerned, it would seem to be only occasional and exceptional. These limitations are of the greatest practical importance. We are not to regard angels as intervening between us and God, or to attribute to them the effects which the Bible everywhere refers to the providential agency of God. . . .

§2. Their State

As to the state of the angels, it is clearly taught that they were all originally holy. It is also plainly to be inferred from the statements of the Bible that they were subjected to a period of probation and that some kept and some did not keep their first estate. Those who maintained their integrity are represented as confirmed in a state of holiness and glory. This condition, although one of complete security, is one of perfect liberty; for the most absolute freedom in action is, according to the Bible, consistent with absolute certainty as to the character of that action. These holy angels are evidently not all of the same rank. This appears from the terms by which they are designated, terms which imply diversity of order and authority. Some are princes, others potentates, others rulers of the world. Beyond this the Scriptures reveal nothing, so the speculations of schoolmen and theologians as to the hierarchy of the angelic hosts have neither authority nor value.

§3. Their Employments

The Scriptures teach that the holy angels are employed (1) in the worship of God, (2) in executing the will of God, and (3) especially in

ministering to the heirs of salvation. They are represented as surround-
ing Christ and as ever ready to perform any service in the advancement of His kingdom that may be assigned to them. In the Old
Testament they repeatedly appear to the servants of God to reveal to
them His will. They smote the Egyptians, were employed in the giving
of the law at Mount Sinai, attended the Israelites during their journey,
destroyed their enemies, and encamped around the people of God as
a defence in hours of danger. They predicted and celebrated the birth
of Christ (Luke 1:26–33; 2:9–14), they ministered to Him after His
temptation and in His sufferings (Matt. 4:11; Luke 22:43), and they
announced His resurrection and ascension (Matt. 28:2–6; Acts 1:10–11).
They delivered Peter from prison, they are still ministering spirits to
believers (Heb. 1:14), they watch over children (Matt. 18:10), they bear
the souls of the departed to Abraham's bosom (Luke 16:22), they are
to attend Christ at His second coming and gather His people into His
kingdom (Matt. 13:39; 16:27; 24:31). Such are the general statements
of the Scriptures on this subject, and with these we should be
content. . . .

With regard to the work of the good angels several points are clear:

(1) They can and do produce effects in the natural or external world.
The Scriptures everywhere assume that matter and mind are two distinct substances, and that the one can act upon the other. We know
that our minds act upon our bodies and that our minds are acted upon
by material causes. Therefore, the doctrine that spirits may act on the
material world in no way contradicts our experience. The extent of
their agency is limited by the principles stated above, and yet from
their exalted nature the effects which they are able to produce may
far exceed our comprehension. An angel slew all the first-born of the
Egyptians in a single night; the thunder and lightning attending the
giving of the law on Mount Sinai were produced by angelic agency. . . .

(2) The angels not only execute the will of God in the natural world,
but also act on the minds of men. They have access to our minds and
can influence them for good in accordance with the laws of our nature.
They do not act by that direct operation which is the peculiar prerogative of God and His Spirit, but by the suggestion of truth and guidance of thought and feeling, much as one man may act upon another.
If the angels may communicate one with another, there is no reason
why they may not, in like manner, communicate with our spirits. In
the Scriptures, therefore, the angels are represented as not only af-
fording general guidance and protection, but also as giving inward
strength and consolation. If an angel strengthened our Lord Himself
after His agony in the garden, His people also may experience the
support of angels; and if evil angels tempt to sin, good angels may

allure to holiness. Certain it is that Scripture attributes a wide influence and operation to them in furthering the welfare of the children of God and in protecting them from evil and defending them from their enemies. The use which our Lord makes of the promise, "He shall give his angels charge over thee, to keep thee in all thy ways. They shall bear thee up in their hands, lest thou dash thy foot against a stone" (Ps. 91:11–12), shows that it is not to be taken as a mere poetic form of promising divine protection. Angels watch over infants (Matt. 18:10); they aid those of mature age (Ps. 34:7) and are present with the dying (Luke 16:22).

(3) A special agency is also attributed to them as the servants of Christ in the advancement of His Church. As the law was given through their ministry, as they had charge of the theocratic people under the old economy, so they are spoken of as being still present in the assembly of the saints (1 Cor. 11:10) and as constantly warring against the dragon and his angels.

This Scriptural doctrine of the ministry of angels is full of consolation for the people of God. They may rejoice in the assurance that these holy beings encamp round about them, defending them day and night from unseen enemies and unapprehended dangers. At the same time they must not come between us and God. We are not to look to them nor to invoke their aid. They are in the hands of God and exercise His will; He uses them as He does the winds and the lightning (Heb. 1:7), and we are not to look to the instruments in the one case more than in the other.

§4. Evil Angels

The Scriptures inform us that certain of the angels kept not their first estate. They are spoken of as the angels that sinned. They are called evil or unclean spirits, principalities, powers, rulers of this world, and spiritual wickednesses (i.e., wicked spirits) in high places. . . . These evil spirits are represented as belonging to the same order of beings as the good angels. All the names and titles expressive of the nature and powers of the one group are also given to the other group. Their original condition was holy. When the evil angels fell or what was the nature of their sin is not revealed. The general opinion is that it was pride, for 1 Timothy 3:6 stipulates that a bishop must not be "a novice, lest being lifted up with pride he fall into the condemnation of the devil." This is commonly understood to mean the condemnation which the devil incurred for the same sin. Some have conjectured that a desire to rule over our globe and the race of man moved Satan to rebel against God and to seduce our race from its allegiance. Of this, however, there is no intimation in Scripture.

That there is one fallen angel exalted in rank and power above all his associates is clearly taught in the Bible. He is called Satan (the adversary), the traducer, the evil one, the prince of the power of the air, the prince of darkness, the god of this world, Beelzebub, Belial, the tempter, the old serpent, and the dragon. These and similar titles set him forth as the great enemy of God and man, the opposer of all that is good and the promoter of all that is evil. He is so constantly represented as a personal being that the rationalistic notion that he is only a personification of evil is irreconcilable with the authority of Scripture and inconsistent with the faith of the Church. The opinion that the doctrine of Satan was introduced among the Hebrews after the exile and from a heathen source is no less contrary to the plain teachings of the Bible. He is represented as the tempter of our first parents and is distinctly mentioned in the book of Job, which was written long before the Babylonian captivity. Besides this representation of Satan in general terms as the enemy of God, he is specially set forth in Scripture as the head of the kingdom of darkness, which embraces all evil beings. Man by his apostasy fell under the dominion of Satan, and his salvation consists in his being translated from Satan's kingdom into the kingdom of God's dear Son. . . .

As to the power and agency of these evil spirits, they are represented as being exceedingly numerous, as everywhere efficient, as having access to our world, and as operating in nature and in the minds of men. The same limitations, of course, belong to their agency as belong to that of the holy angels: (1) they are dependent on God and can act only under His control and by His permission; (2) their operations must be according to the laws of nature; and (3) they cannot interfere with the freedom and responsibility of men. Nevertheless, their power is very great. Men are said to be led captive by Satan; evil spirits are said to work in the hearts of the disobedient. Christians are warned against their devices and called upon to resist them, not in their own strength, but in the strength of the Lord. . . .

The most marked exhibition of the power of evil spirits over the bodies and minds of men is afforded by the demoniacs so often mentioned in the evangelical history. These demoniacal possessions were of two kinds: (1) those in which the soul alone was the subject of the diabolic influence, as in the case of the "damsel possessed with a spirit of divination" (Acts 16:16)—perhaps in some instances false prophets and magicians were examples of this kind of possession; and (2) those in which the bodies alone or, as was more frequently the case, both the body and mind were the subject of diabolical influence. By possession is meant an evil spirit's inhabiting the body and soul in such a way as to exert a controlling influence, producing violent agitations and great suffering, both mental and corporeal. That the demoniacs mentioned in the New Testament were not mere lunatics or the subjects of epilepsy or other analogous diseases, but cases of real possession, is plain, first, because this was the prevailing belief of the Jews at that time and, secondly, because Christ and His apostles evidently adopted and sanctioned that belief. They not only called those thus affected demoniacs, but addressed the spirits as persons, commanded them, disposed of them, and in every way spoke and acted as they would have done had the popular belief been well founded. It is certain that all who heard Christ thus speak would and did conclude that He regarded the demoniacs as really possessed by evil spirits. This conclusion He nowhere contradicted but, on the contrary, in His most private conferences with the disciples abundantly confirmed. He promised to give them power to cast out demons, and referred to His possession of this power and His ability to delegate its exercise to His disciples as one of the most convincing proofs of His Messiahship and divinity. He came to destroy the works of the devil; and that He did thus triumph over him and his angels proved that He was what He claimed to be, the promised almighty King and conqueror who was to found that kingdom of God of which there is to be no end. To explain all this on the principle of accommodation would destroy the authority of Scripture. . . . We must take the Scriptures in their plain historical sense—in that sense in which they were designed to be understood by those to whom they were addressed—or we do thereby reject them as a rule of faith. . . .

We are not to deny what is plainly recorded in the Scriptures as facts on this subject, nor have we any right to assert that Satan and his angels do not now in any cases produce similar effects. On the other hand, we should abstain from reading Satanic or demoniacal influence or possession into any case where the phenomena can be otherwise accounted for. The difference between believing whatever is possible and believing only what is certain is strikingly illustrated in the case of Luther and Calvin. The former was disposed to refer all evil to the spirits of darkness; the latter referred to their agency only what could be proved to be actually their work.

Anthropology

Chapter I
_____

Origin of Man

§1. Scriptural Doctrine

The Scriptural account of the origin of man is contained in Genesis 1:26–27, "And God said, Let us make man in our image, after our likeness: and let them have dominion over the fish of the sea, and over the fowl of the air, and over the cattle, and over all the earth, and over every creeping thing that creepeth upon the earth. So God created man in his own image, in the image of God created he him; male and female created he them"; and in Genesis 2:7, "And the Lord God formed man of the dust of the ground, and breathed into his nostrils the breath of life; and man became a living soul." Two things are included in this account. First, man's body was formed by the immediate intervention of God. It did not grow, nor was it produced by any process of development. Secondly, the soul was derived from God.

He breathed into man "the breath of life," that is, that life which constituted him a man, a living creature bearing the image of God. . . .

§2. Anti-Scriptural Theories

[A. *The Doctrine of Spontaneous Generation*]

B. *Theories of Development*

[In contrast to the Scriptural doctrine] Charles Darwin accounts for the origin of all the varieties of plants and animals by the gradual operation of natural causes. . . . His theory includes the following principles:

First, like begets like; this is the law of heredity, according to which the offspring is like the parent throughout the vegetable and animal world.

Second, while in all that is essential the offspring is like the parent, it always differs more or less from its progenitor; this is the law of variation. The variations are sometimes deteriorations, sometimes indifferent, sometimes improvements, that is, such as enable the plant or animal more advantageously to exercise its functions.

Third, as plants and animals increase in a geometrical ratio, they tend to outrun enormously the means of support, and this of necessity gives rise to a continued and universal struggle for life.

Fourth, in this struggle the fittest survive; that is, those individuals which have an accidental variation of structure which renders them superior to their fellows in the struggle for existence survive and transmit that peculiarity to their offspring. This is "natural selection"; i.e., nature, without intelligence or purpose, selects the individuals best adapted to continue and to improve the race. It is by the operation of these few principles that in the course of countless ages all the diversified forms of vegetables and animals have been produced.

With regard to the Darwinian theory it should be noted, first, that it shocks the common sense of unsophisticated men to be told that the whale and the hummingbird, man and the mosquito, are derived from the same source. Not that the whale was developed out of the hummingbird, or man out of the mosquito, but that both derived by a slow process of variations continued through countless millions of years. Such is the theory with its scientific feathers plucked off. No wonder that at its first promulgation it was received by the scientific world not only with surprise, but also with indignation. . . .

A second remark is that the theory in question cannot be true, because it is founded on the assumption of an impossibility. It assumes that matter does the work of mind.... The doctrine of Darwin is that a primordial germ, with no inherent intelligence, has developed, under purely natural influences, into all the infinite variety of vegetable and animal organisms with all their complicated relations to each other and to the world around them. Not only does he assert that all this is due to natural causes and that the lower impulses of vegetable life pass by insensible gradations into the instinct of animals and the higher intelligence of man, but he also argues against the intervention of mind anywhere in the process. God, says Darwin, created the unintelligent living cell; after that first step, all else has followed by natural law, without purpose and without design. Whoever believes this can also believe that all the works of art, literature, and science in the world are the products of carbonic acid, water, and ammonia.

Thirdly, the system is thoroughly atheistic and therefore cannot possibly stand. God has revealed His existence and His government of the world so clearly and so authoritatively that any philosophical or scientific speculations inconsistent with those truths are like cobwebs in the track of a tornado. They offer no sensible resistance. The mere naturalist, the man devoted so exclusively to the study of nature as to believe in nothing but natural causes, is not able to understand the strength with which moral and religious convictions take hold of the minds of men. These convictions, however, are the strongest, the most ennobling, and the most dangerous for any class of men to disregard or ignore.

To say that this system is atheistic is not to say that Darwin is an atheist. He expressly acknowledges the existence of God and seems to feel the necessity of His existence to account for the origin of life. Nor does every one who adopts the theory do so in an atheistic sense.... Darwin's doctrine is that hundreds or thousands of millions of years ago God called a living germ, or living germs, into existence, and that since that time God has had no more to do with the universe than if He did not exist. This is atheism to all intents and purposes, because it leaves the soul entirely without God, without a Father, helper, or ruler. Darwin, moreover, obliterates all the evidences of the being of God in the world. He refers to physical causes what all theists believe to be due to the operations of the divine mind....

A fourth remark on this theory is that it is a mere hypothesis incapable of proof.... From the nature of the case, what concerns the origin of things cannot be known except by a supernatural revelation. All else must be speculation and conjecture. And no man under the guidance of reason will, in obedience to human speculation however ingenious, renounce the teachings of a well-authenticated revelation. The uncertainty attending all philosophical or scientific theories as to the origin of things is sufficiently apparent from their number and inconsistencies. Science as soon as she gets past the actual and the extant is in the region of speculation; and merging into philosophy, she becomes subject to all its hallucinations.

C. Theories of the Universe

... It is Darwin's view that all the orders, classes, genera, species, and varieties of plants and animals, from the lowest to the highest, man included, have been formed from one or a few primordial germs. This process has occurred by the slow operation of unintelligent natural causes and accidental variations during untold ages. Teleology and therefore mind, or God, are expressly banished from the world....

[Darwin's view clashes sharply with] what may be called the Scriptural doctrine: (1) The universe and all it contains owe their existence to the will and power of God. Matter is not eternal, nor is life self-originating. (2) God endowed matter with properties or forces which He upholds and in accordance with which He works in all the ordinary operations of His providence. That is, He uses them everywhere and constantly, as we use them in our narrow sphere. (3) In the beginning He created, or caused to be, every distinct kind of plant and animal: "And God said, Let the earth bring forth grass, the herb yielding seed, and the fruit tree yielding fruit after his kind, whose seed is in itself, upon the earth: and it was so.... And God said, Let the earth bring forth the living creature after his kind, cattle, and creeping thing, and beast of the earth after his kind: and it was so" (Gen. 1:11, 24). This is the Scriptural account of the origin of species. According to this account each species was specially created, not out of nothing, nor without the intervention of secondary causes, but nevertheless originally, i.e., not by derivation, evolution, or development from preexisting species. These distinct species or kinds of plants and animals thus separately originated are permanent. They never pass from one into the other. It is, however, to be remembered that species are of two kinds: *natural* and *artificial*. The former are those which have their foundation in nature—they had a distinct origin and are capable of indefinite propagation.... It is only of such species that originality and permanence are asserted. Artificial species, as they are called, are simply varieties distinguished, for example, by the accidental shape of a leaf or colour of a feather....

[Comparison of the Scriptural doctrine and the Darwinian theory clearly reveals the inadequacy of the latter. Darwin himself] acknowledges that there are grave objections against the doctrine which he endeavors to establish. He admits that if one species is derived by slow gradations from another, it would be natural to expect the intermediate steps, or connecting links, to be everywhere visible. But he acknowledges that such are not to be found, that during the whole of the historical period, species have remained unchanged. They are now precisely what they were thousands of years ago. There is not the slightest indication of any one passing into another or of a lower advancing towards a higher. This is admitted. The only answer to the difficulty thus presented is that the change of species is so slow a process that no indications can be reasonably expected in the few thousand years embraced within the limits of history. To the further objection that geology presents the same difficulty, that the genera and species of fossil animals are just as distinct as those now living ... the answer is that the records of geology are too imperfect to give us full knowledge on this subject, and that innumerable intermediate and transitional forms *may have* passed away and left no trace of their existence. All this amounts to an admission that all history and all geology are against the theory. . . .

With regard to the more serious objection that the theory assumes that matter does the work of mind, that design is accomplished without any designer, Darwin is equally candid: "Nothing at first," he says, "can appear more difficult to believe than that the more complex organs and instincts have been perfected, not by means superior to, though analogous with, human reason, but by the accumulation of innumerable slight variations, each good for the individual possessor" (*Origin of Species*, ch. 15). . . . Again he says, "Although the belief that an organ so perfect as the eye could have been formed by natural selection, is more than enough to stagger any one; yet in the case of any organ, if we know of a long series of gradations in complexity, each good for its possessor, then, under changing conditions of life, there is no logical impossibility in the acquirement of any conceivable degree of perfection through natural selection" (*Origin of Species*, ch. 6). Darwin refuses to be staggered by that which he says is enough to stagger any one. Give him a sufficient number of millions of years, and fortuitous complications may accomplish anything. If a rude piece of flint be found in deposits, it is declared to be the work of man, because it indicates design, while such an organ as the eye may be formed by natural selection acting blindly. . . . Ordinary men reject this Darwinian theory with indignation as well as with decision not only because it calls upon them to accept the possible as demonstrably true, but because it ascribes to blind, unintelligent causes the wonders of purpose and design which the world everywhere exhibits, and because it effectually banishes God from His works. . . .

§3. Antiquity of Man

[Many scientists now agree that the antiquity of man is very great, indeed, that it is much greater than the chronology of the Bible would seem to allow.] On this it may be remarked, first, that it is a historical fact that nothing is less reliable than the naturalists' calculations of time. A volume might be filled with examples of their mistakes in this matter. . . . Second, the reasons assigned for the alleged great antiquity of the human race are, in the judgment of the most eminent men of science, unsatisfactory. . . .

It is also to be noted that the chronology of the Bible is very uncertain. The data are for the most part facts incidentally stated; that is, they are not stated for the purposes of chronology. The views most generally adopted rest mainly on the authority of Archbishop Ussher, who adopted the Hebrew text for his guide and assumed that in the genealogical tables each name marked one generation. A large part, however, of Biblical scholars adopt the Septuagint chronology in preference to the Hebrew; this yields a figure of nearly six thousand instead of four thousand years from the creation to the birth of Christ. Besides, it is admitted that the usual method of calculation founded on the genealogical tables is very uncertain. The design of those tables is not to give a strict succession of births in a given line, but simply to mark the descent. This is just as well done if three, four, or more generations be omitted. That this is the plan on which these genealogical tables are constructed is an admitted fact. According to Matthew 1:11, for instance, Josias begat his grandson Jechonias; and according to verse 8, Joram begat his great-great-grandson Ozias. And in Genesis 10:15–18 Canaan, the grandson of Noah, is said to have begotten several whole nations including the Jebusite, the Amorite, the Girgasite, and the Hivite. Nothing can be plainer, therefore, than that in the usage of the Bible, "to beget" is not restricted to immediate offspring but is used in a wide sense to indicate descent.

The extreme uncertainty attending all attempts to determine the chronology of the Bible is sufficiently evinced by the fact that Jewish and Christian authors have made 180 different calculations of the length of the period between Adam and Christ. The longest of these make it 6,984 and the shortest 3,483 years. Under these circumstances it is very clear that the friends of the Bible have no occasion for uneasiness. If the facts of science or of history should ultimately make it necessary to admit that eight or ten thousand years have elapsed since the creation of man, there is nothing in the Bible to prohibit such a concession. The Scriptures do not teach us how long men have existed on the earth. Their tables of genealogy were intended to prove that Christ was the Son of David and of the seed of Abraham, and not how many years had elapsed between the creation and the advent.

Nature of Man

§1. Scriptural Doctrine

The Scriptures teach that God formed the body of man out of the dust of the earth and breathed into him the breath of life, and he became *a living soul* (Gen. 2:7). According to this account, man consists of two distinct principles, a body and a soul: the one material, the other immaterial; the one corporeal, the other spiritual. It is involved in this statement, first, that the soul of man is a substance and, secondly, that it is a substance distinct from the body. In the constitution of man, then, two distinct substances are included.

The idea of substance is one of the primary truths of the reason. It is given in the consciousness of every man and is therefore a part of the universal faith of men. We are conscious of our thoughts, feelings, and volitions. We know that these exercises or phenomena are constantly changing, but that there is something of which they are the manifestation. That something is the self which remains unchanged, which is the same identical something yesterday, today, and tomor-

247

row. The soul is, therefore, not a mere series of acts, nor is it a form of the life of God, nor is it a mere unsubstantial force, but a real subsistence. Whatever acts *is*, and what *is* is an entity. . . . The soul of man, therefore, is an essence or entity or substance, the abiding subject of its varying states and exercises.

The second point just mentioned is no less plain. As we can know nothing of substance but from its phenomena, and as we are forced by a law of our nature to believe in the existence of a substance of which the phenomena are the manifestation, so by an equally stringent necessity we are forced to believe that where the phenomena are not only different but incompatible, there the substances are also different. As, therefore, the phenomena or properties of matter are essentially different from those of mind, we are forced to conclude that matter and mind are two distinct substances, that the soul is not material nor the body spiritual. . . .

The Scriptures do not formally teach any system of psychology, but there are certain truths relating to both our physical and mental constitution which they constantly assume. They assume, as we have seen, that the soul is a substance, that it is a substance distinct from the body, and that there are two, and not more than two, essential elements in the constitution of man. This is evident (1) from the distinction everywhere made between soul and body. Thus, in the original account of the creation a clear distinction is made between the body as formed from the dust of the earth, and the soul or principle of life which was breathed into it from God. And in Genesis 3:19 it is said, "Dust thou art, and unto dust shalt thou return." As it was only the body that was formed out of the dust, it is only the body that is to return to dust. In Ecclesiastes 12:7 it is said, "Then shall the dust return to the earth as it was: and the spirit shall return unto God who gave it." Our Lord (Matt. 10:28) commands His disciples, "Fear not them which kill the body, but are not able to kill the soul: but rather fear him which is able to destroy both soul and body in hell." . . . (2) A second class of passages equally decisive as to this point represents the body as a garment which is to be laid aside, a tabernacle or house in which the soul dwells, but which it may leave and return to. . . . Peter says he thought it meet, as long as he was in this tabernacle, to put his brethren in remembrance of the truth, "knowing," as he adds, "that shortly I must put off this my tabernacle" (2 Peter 1:13–14). Paul in 2 Corinthians 5:1 says, "If our earthly house of this tabernacle were dissolved, we have a building of God." In the same chapter he speaks of . . . being absent from the body and present with the Lord, recognizing that while we are at home in the body, we are absent from the Lord. (3) It is the common belief of mankind, the clearly revealed doctrine of the Bible, and part of the faith of the Church universal that the soul can and does exist and act after death. If this be so, then the body and soul are two distinct substances. The former may be disorganized, reduced to dust, dispersed, or even annihilated, and the latter retain its conscious life and activity. This doctrine is taught in the Old Testament, where the dead are represented as dwelling in Sheol. . . . Our Lord says that as God is not the God of the dead but of the living, His declaring Himself to be the God of Abraham, Isaac, and Jacob proves that Abraham, Isaac, and Jacob are now alive. Moses and Elijah conversed with Christ on the mount. To the dying thief our Lord said, "Today shalt thou (that in which his personality resided) be with me in paradise." . . .

Man, then, according to the Scriptures, is a created spirit in vital union with a material organized body. The relation between these two constituents of our nature is admitted to be mysterious. That is, it is incomprehensible. We do not know how the body acts on the mind, or how the mind acts on the body. These facts, however, are plain: (1) The relation between the two is a vital union of such a nature that the soul is the source of life to the body. When the soul leaves the body, the latter ceases to live. It loses its sensibility and activity; becoming at once subject to the chemical laws which govern unorganized matter, it is by their operation soon reduced to dust, undistinguishable from the earth whence it was originally taken. (2) It is a fact of consciousness that certain states of the body produce certain corresponding states of the mind. . . . The mind sees, the mind hears, and the mind feels, not directly or immediately (at least in our present and normal state), but through or by means of the corresponding organs of the body. It is also a matter of daily experience that a healthful condition of the body is necessary to a healthful state of the mind, and that certain diseases or disorders of the one produce derangement in the operations of the other. . . . (3) It is also a fact of consciousness that while certain operations of the body are independent of the conscious volitional action of the mind, as the processes of respiration and digestion, there are certain actions dependent on the will. We can will to move, and we can exert a greater or lesser degree of muscular force. These simple facts of consciousness and of experience prove an intimate and vital union between the mind and body. . . .

The Scriptural doctrine of the nature of man as a created spirit in vital union with an organized body . . . is one of great importance. It is intimately connected with some of the most crucial teachings of the Bible: the constitution of the person of Christ, the nature of His redeeming work, and His relation to the children of men; the fall, original sin, and regeneration; and the future state and resurrection. It is because of this connection, and not because of its interest as a question in psychology, that the nature of man demands the careful investigation of the theologian.

The doctrine of the Scriptures and of the Church, as we have stated it, is properly designated realistic dualism, for it asserts the existence of two distinct entities or substances: the one extended and divisible, the object of the senses; the other unextended and indivisible, the thinking, feeling, and willing subject in man. . . .

§2. Trichotomy

It is of consequence to remark that the Scriptural doctrine is opposed to trichotomy, which is the idea that man consists of three distinct substances, body, soul, and spirit. This view of the nature of man is of importance to the theologian not only because it has been held to a greater or lesser extent in the Church, but also because it has greatly influenced the form in which other doctrines have been presented, and because it has some semblance of support from the Scriptures themselves. The doctrine has been held in different forms. The simplest, the most intelligible, and the one most commonly adopted is that the body is the material part of our constitution, the soul is the principle of animal life, and the spirit is the principle of our rational and immortal life. . . .

In opposition to trichotomy it may be remarked (1) that it is opposed to the account of the creation of man as given in Genesis 2:7. According to that account God formed man out of the dust of the earth and breathed into him the breath of life, and he became a being in whom is a living soul. There is in this account no intimation of anything more than the material body formed of the earth and the living principle derived from God. (2) Trichotomy is opposed to the uniform usage of Scripture. The soul is not distinguished from the spirit as either originally different or as derived from it; rather, the words soul and spirit designate one and the same thing: breath, life, the living principle. They are constantly interchanged. The one is substituted for the other, and all that is, or can be, predicated of the one is predicated of the other. . . . Moreover, the soul is the man himself, that in which his identity and personality reside. It is the *Ego*. Higher than the soul there is nothing in man. Therefore it is often used as a synonym for self. "What shall a man give in exchange for his soul?" (Matt. 16:26). The end of our faith is said to be the salvation of our souls (1 Peter 1:9), and John saw in heaven the souls of them that were slain for the Word of God (Rev. 6:9; 20:4). From all this it is evident that the word soul does not designate merely the principle of animal life and is not a substance different from the spirit. (3) A third remark on this subject is that the words soul and spirit are used in the Scriptures indiscriminately of men and of irrational animals. . . . The living principle in the brute is called both soul and spirit. That principle in the brute creation is irrational and mortal; in man it is rational and immortal: "Who knoweth the spirit of man that goeth upward, and the spirit of the beast that goeth downward to the earth?" (Eccles. 3:21). The soul of the brute is the immaterial principle which constitutes its life, and which is endowed with sensibility and that measure of intelligence which experience shows the lower animals to possess. The soul in man is a created spirit of a higher order which has not only the attributes of sensibility, memory, and instinct, but also the higher powers which pertain to our intellectual, moral, and religious life. . . . (4) It is fair to appeal to the testimony of consciousness on this subject. We are conscious of our bodies and we are conscious of our souls, i.e., of the exercises and states of each; but no man is conscious of the soul as different from the spirit. In other words consciousness reveals the existence of two substances in the constitution of our nature, but it does not reveal the existence of three substances; therefore, the existence of more than two cannot rationally be assumed. . . .

§3. Realism

. . . Every man believes his soul to be a distinct, individual substance as much as he believes his body to be distinct and separate from every other human body. Such is the common judgment of men. And nothing short of the direct assertion of the Bible, or arguments which amount to demonstration, can rationally be admitted to invalidate that judgment. It is inconceivable that so crucial a truth concerning the constitution of our nature would not in some way reveal itself in the common consciousness of men. There is nothing more characteristic of the Scripture, and there are few things which more clearly prove its divine origin, than that it takes for granted and authenticates all the facts of consciousness. It declares us to be what the very constitution and present condition of our nature reveal us to be. It recognizes the soul as rational, free, and responsible. It assumes that it is distinct from the body. All this we know from consciousness. . . .

[§4. Another Form of the Realistic Theory]

Chapter III

The Origin of the Soul

§1. Theory of Preexistence
§2. Traducianism
§3. Creationism
§4. Concluding Remarks

Three theories have been advanced as to the origin of the soul: first, that of the preexistence of the soul; secondly, that of traducianism, or the doctrine that the soul of the child is derived from the soul of the parent; thirdly, that of immediate creation, or the doctrine that the soul is not derived as the body is, but owes its existence to the creative power of God.

§1. Theory of Preexistence

. . . Preexistence, as taught by Origen and as adopted here and there by some few philosophers and theologians, supposes that the souls of men had a separate, conscious, personal existence in a previous state, and that having sinned in that preexistent state, they are condemned to be born into this world in a state of sin and in connection with a material body. This doctrine was connected by Origen with his theory of an eternal creation. The present state of being is only one epoch in the existence of the human soul. It has passed through innumerable other epochs and forms of existence in the past, and is to go through other innumerable such epochs in the future. . . . But the Bible never speaks of a creation of men before Adam or of any apostasy anterior to his fall, and it never refers the sinfulness of our present condition to any earlier source than the sin of our first parent. The assumption that all human souls were created at the same time that the soul of Adam was created, and remain in a dormant, unconscious state until united to the bodies for which they were designed, has been adopted by so few as hardly to merit a place in the history of theological opinion.

§2. Traducianism

A far more important question is whether the soul of each man is immediately created or whether it is generated by the parents. The former is known as creationism, the latter as traducianism. . . . Traducianists on the one hand deny that the soul is created, and on the other hand they affirm that it is produced by the law of generation, being as truly derived from the parents as is the body. The whole man, soul and body, is begotten. The whole man is derived from the substance of his progenitors. . . . There is, then, a numerical identity of essence in Adam and all his posterity both as to soul and as to body [i.e., the essence of Adam and that of his posterity are not merely qualitatively similar, but numerically one]. . . .

Stress is laid on certain facts of Scripture which are assumed to favour traducianism. That in the account of the creation of the woman no mention is made of God's having breathed into her the breath of life is said to imply that her soul as well as her body was derived from Adam. Silence, however, proves nothing. In Genesis 1:27 it is simply said, "God created man in his own image," just as it is said that He created "every creeping thing that creepeth upon the earth." Nothing is there said of His breathing into man the breath of life, i.e., a principle of rational life. Yet we know that it was done. Its not being expressly mentioned in the case of Eve, therefore, is no proof that it did not occur.

It is also argued that God's resting on the Sabbath implies that His creating energy was not afterwards exerted. This is understood to draw the line between the immediate creation and the production of effects in nature by second causes under the providential control of God. (The doctrine of creationism, on the other hand, assumes that God constantly, now as well as at the beginning, exercises His immediate agency in producing something out of nothing.) But, in the first place, we do not know how the agency of God is connected with the operation of second causes, nor how far that agency is mediate and how far it is immediate; and in the second place, we do know that God has not bound Himself to mere providential direction, and that His omnipresent power is ever operating through means and without means in the whole sphere of history and of nature.

Of all arguments in favour of traducianism the most effective is that derived from the transmission of a sinful nature from Adam to his posterity. It is insisted that this can neither be explained nor justified unless we assume that Adam's sin was our sin and our guilt, and that the identical active, intelligent, volitional substance which transgressed in him has been transmitted to us. . . . Now the fact is admitted that the sin of Adam in a true and important sense is our sin, and that we derive from him a corrupt nature; but that this necessitates the adoption of the traducianist doctrine as to the origin of the soul is not so clear. In all ages of the Church it has been denied by the vast majority of the most strenuous defenders of the doctrine of original sin. . . .

Again, it is urged that the doctrine of the incarnation necessarily proves the traducianist theory. Christ was born of a woman. He was the seed of the woman. It is argued that unless both His soul and body derived from His human mother, He cannot truly be of the same race with us. This, however, is a simple *non sequitur*. All that is necessary is that Christ should be a man, a son of David, in the same sense as any other of the posterity of David, save only His miraculous conception. He was formed from the substance of His mother in the same sense in which every child born of a woman is born of her substance; but what that sense is, His birth does not determine.

The most plausible argument in favour of traducianism is the undeniable fact of the transmission of the ethnical, national, family, and even parental peculiarities of mind and temper. These peculiarities seem to evince that there is a derivation not only of the body but also of the soul. But even this argument is not conclusive, because it is impossible for us to determine to what proximate cause these peculiarities are due. They may all be referred, as far as we know, to something peculiar in the physical constitution. . . .

§3. Creationism

The common doctrine of the Church and especially of the Reformed theologians has ever been that the soul of the child is not generated or derived from the parents, but that it is created by the immediate agency of God. Various arguments are generally urged in favour of this view:

(1) Creationism is more consistent with the prevailing representations of the Scriptures. In the original account of the creation there is a marked distinction made between the body and the soul. The one is from the earth, the other from God. This distinction is kept up throughout the Bible. The body and soul are represented not only as being different substances, but also as having different origins. The body shall return to dust, says the wise man, and the spirit to God who gave it. Here the origin of the soul is represented as different from and higher than that of the body. The former is from God in a sense in which the latter is not. In like manner God is said to form "the spirit of man within him" (Zech. 12:1), and to give "breath unto the people upon [the earth], and spirit to them that walk therein" (Isa. 42:5). This language nearly agrees with the account of the original creation, in which God is said to have breathed into man the breath of life—an indication that the soul is not earthy or material, but had its origin immediately from God. Hence He is called "God of the spirits of all flesh" (Num. 16:22). It could not well be said that He is God of the bodies of all men. The relation in which the soul stands to God as its God and creator is very different from that in which the body stands to Him. And hence in Hebrews 12:9 it is said, "We have had fathers of our flesh which corrected us, and we gave them reverence: shall we not much rather be in subjection unto the Father of spirits, and live?" The obvious antithesis here presented is between those who are the fathers of our bodies and Him who is the Father of our spirits. Our bodies are derived from our earthly parents, our souls are derived from God. . . .

(2) Creationism, also, is clearly most consistent with the nature of the soul. The soul is admitted, among Christians, to be immaterial and spiritual. It is indivisible. The traducian doctrine denies this universally acknowledged truth. It asserts that the soul admits of "separation or division of essence." . . .

(3) A third argument in favour of creationism and against traducianism is derived from the Scriptural doctrine as to the person of Christ. He was very man; He had a true human nature, i.e., a true body and a rational soul. He was born of a woman; He was descended from the fathers. He was in all points made like us, yet without sin. But on the theory of traducianism, His being made like us necessitates the conclusion that Christ's human nature was guilty and sinful. We are partakers of Adam's sin as to both guilt and pollution, because the same numerical essence which sinned in him is communicated to us. . . . Now what is true of other men must be true of Christ. He must,

therefore, be as much involved in the guilt and corruption of the apostasy as are other men. . . . It is a contradiction to say that we are guilty of Adam's sin because we are partakers of his essence, and that Christ is not guilty of Adam's sin nor involved in its pollution, although He is a partaker of his essence. If participation of essence involve community of guilt and depravity in the one case, it must also in the other. As this seems a legitimate conclusion from the traducian doctrine and as this conclusion is anti-Christian and false, the doctrine itself cannot be true.

§4. Concluding Remarks

(1) While it is incumbent on us strenuously to resist any doctrine which assumes the divisibility and consequently the materiality of the human soul, or which leads to the conclusion that the human nature of our blessed Lord was contaminated with sin, yet it does not become us to be wise above that which is written. We should confess that generation, the production of a new individual of the human race, is an inscrutable mystery. . . .

(2) It is obviously most unreasonable and presumptuous, as well as dangerous, to make a theory as to the origin of the soul the ground of a doctrine so fundamental to the Christian system as that of original sin. Yet we see theologians, ancient and modern, boldly asserting that if their doctrine of derivation and the consequent numerical sameness of substance in all men be not admitted, then original sin is impossible. This is equivalent to saying that whatever they cannot explain cannot be true, no matter how plainly taught in the Word of God. . . . They will not believe in hereditary depravity unless they can explain the mode of its transmission. There can be no such thing, they say, as hereditary depravity unless the soul of the child is the same numerical substance as the soul of the parent. That is, the plain assertions of the Scriptures cannot be true unless the most obscure, unintelligible, and self-contradictory, and the least generally received philosophical theory as to the constitution of man and the propagation of the race be adopted. No man has a right to hang the millstone of his philosophy around the neck of the truth of God.

(3) There is a third cautionary remark which must not be omitted. The whole theory of traducianism is founded on the assumption that God, since the original creation, operates only through means. Since the sixth day the creator has rested and thus has exerted no strictly creative energy. . . . He now produces only mediately, i.e., through the operation of second causes. This is a near approach to the mechanical

theory of the universe, which supposes that God, having created the world and endowed His creatures with certain faculties and properties, leaves it to the operation of these second causes. . . . But what, then, becomes of the doctrine of regeneration? The new birth is not the effect of second causes. It is not a natural effect produced by the influence of the truth or the energy of the human will. It is due to the immediate exercise of the almighty power of God. God's relation to the world is not such as to limit Him to operating only through second causes. He is immanent in the world. He sustains and guides all causes. He works constantly through them, with them, and without them. . . . [With regard to the origination of life, then, it is reasonable to believe that] the organization of a seed, or of the embryo of an animal, so far as it consists of matter, may be due to the operation of material causes guided by the providential agency of God, while the vital principle itself is due to His creative power. . . .

The object of this discussion is not to arrive at certainty regarding a topic which is not clearly elucidated in Scripture, nor to explain what is, on all sides, admitted to be inscrutable, but to guard against the adoption of principles which are in opposition to plain and important doctrines of the Word of God. If traducianism teaches that the soul admits of abscission or division, or that the human race are constituted of numerically the same substance, or that the Son of God assumed into personal union with Himself the same numerical substance which sinned and fell in Adam, then it is to be rejected as both false and dangerous. But if, without pretending to explain everything, it simply asserts that the human race is propagated in accordance with the general law which secures that like begets like, that the child derives its nature from its parents through the operation of physical laws attended and controlled by the agency of God, whether directive or creative, as in all other cases of the propagation of living creatures, it may be regarded as an open question or matter of indifference. Creationism does not necessarily suppose that there is any other exercise of the immediate power of God in the production of the human soul than such as takes place in the production of life in other cases. It denies only that the soul is capable of division, that all mankind are composed of numerically the same essence, and that Christ assumed numerically the same essence that sinned in Adam.

Unity of the Human Race

Chapter V

Original State of Man

§1. The Scriptural Doctrine

The Scriptural doctrine on this subject is that man was originally created in a state of maturity and perfection. By this, however, is not meant that humanity in Adam before the fall existed in the highest state of excellence of which it is susceptible. It is altogether probable that our nature, in virtue of its union with the divine nature in the person of Christ, and in virtue of the union of the redeemed with their exalted Redeemer, shall hereafter be elevated to a dignity and glory far greater than that in which Adam was created or to which he ever could have attained. By the maturity of man as at first created is meant that he was not created in a state of infancy. It is a favourite assumption of skeptics that man at first as to both soul and body was imbecile and unfurnished; accordingly, he had to slowly form for himself an articulate language, and his moral powers were only gradually

261

awakened. This, however, is inconsistent not only with the Scriptural account of his creation, but also with the part he was designed to act and in fact did act. By the perfection of his original state is meant that he was perfectly adapted to the end for which he was made and to the sphere in which he was designed to move. This perfection as to his body consisted not only in the integrity and due proportion of all its parts, but also in its perfect adaptation to the nature of the soul with which it was united. It is commonly said by theologians that the body was created immortal and impassible. With regard to immortality, it is certain that if man had not sinned he would not have died. . . . By impassibility is not necessarily meant entire freedom from suscepti-bility to pain, for such susceptibility in our present earthly state, and perhaps in any conceivable earthly state, is a necessary condition of safety. It is a good and not an evil, a perfection and not a defect. All that need be meant by the term is that the body of Adam was free from the seeds of disease and death. There was nothing in its consti-tution inconsistent with the highest happiness and well-being of man in the state in which he was created and the conditions under which he was to live. . . .

§2. Man Created in the Image of God

Other animals besides man were created in maturity and perfection, each according to its kind. It was the distinguishing characteristic of man, however, that he was created in the image and likeness of God. . . . The simple declaration of the Scripture is that man at his creation was like God. . . .

According to the Reformed theologians and the majority of the theo-logians of other divisions of the Church, man's likeness to God included his intellectual and moral nature. God is a Spirit, the human soul is a spirit. The essential attributes of a spirit are reason, conscience, and will. A spirit is a rational, moral, and also a free agent. In making man after His own image, therefore, God endowed him with those attri-butes which belong to His own nature as a Spirit. Man is thereby distinguished from all other inhabitants of this world and raised im-measurably above them. He belongs to the same order of being as God Himself and is therefore capable of communion with his maker. This conformity of nature between man and God is not only the distin-guishing prerogative of humanity so far as earthly creatures are con-cerned, but it is also the necessary condition of our capacity to know God, and therefore the foundation of our religious nature. If we were not like God, we could not know Him. We should be like the beasts which perish. The Scriptures in declaring that God is the Father of spirits and that we are His offspring teach us that we are partakers of His nature as a spiritual being, and that an essential element of that likeness to God in which man was originally created consists in our rational or spiritual nature. . . .

While the Scriptures make the original moral perfection of man the most prominent element of that likeness to God in which he was created, it is no less true that they recognize man as a child of God in virtue of his rational nature. He is the image of God, and bears and reflects the divine likeness among the inhabitants of the earth, because he is a spirit, i.e., an intelligent, volitional agent; and as such he is rightfully invested with universal dominion. . . .

§3. Original Righteousness

In the moral image of God, or original righteousness, are included the perfect harmony and due subordination of all that constituted man. His reason was subject to God, his will was subject to his reason, his affections and appetites to his will, and the body was the obedient organ of the soul. . . . Besides this equilibrium and harmony in the original constitution of man, the moral perfection in which he resembled God included knowledge, righteousness, and holiness. . . . In Colossians 3:10 it is said, "[Ye] have put on the new man, which is renewed in knowledge after the image of him that created him." . . . The knowledge here intended is not mere cognition. It is full, accurate, living, or practical knowledge, such knowledge as is eternal life, so that this word here includes what in Ephesians 4:24 is expressed by righteousness and holiness: "Put on the new man, which after God is created in righteousness and true holiness." . . . These words when used in combination include all moral excellence. . . . It is plain from these passages that knowledge, righteousness, and holiness are elements of the image of God in which man was originally created. . . .

All that has been said with regard to the original state of man is involved in the account of the creation, which declares that he was made like God and that he was pronounced to be good, good exceedingly. What the goodness is which belongs to man as a rational, immortal, and religious being, and which was necessary to fit him for the sphere in which he was to move and the destiny for which he was created, we learn partly from the express declarations of the Scriptures, partly from the nature of the case, and partly from what is involved in humanity as restored by Christ. From all these sources it is plain that the Protestant doctrine concerning the image of God and the original righteousness in which and with which Adam was created includes not only his rational nature, but also knowledge, righteousness, and holiness.

§4. Dominion over the Creatures

The third particular which entered into the dignity of man's original state, and into the image of God with which he was invested, was his dominion over the creatures. This arose from the powers with which he was invested and from the express appointment of God. God constituted him ruler over the earth. He placed, as Psalm 8:6 says, all things under his feet. . . . To determine the extent of the dominion granted to man, however, is not easy. Judging from the account given in Genesis, or even from the stronger language used in Psalm 8, we should conclude that his authority was to extend only over the inferior animals belonging to this earth. But the apostle, in his exposition of the words of the psalmist, teaches us that far more was intended. In 1 Corinthians 15:27 Paul explains, "When he saith all things are put under him, it is manifest that he is excepted, which did put all things under him." And in Hebrews 2:8 it is said, "In that he put all in subjection under him, he left nothing that is not put under him." It was therefore an absolutely universal dominion, so far as creatures are concerned, with which man was to be invested. This universal dominion, as we learn from the Scriptures, has been realized and attained only by the incarnation and exaltation of the Son of God. But as God sees the end from the beginning, as His plan is immutable and all-comprehending, this supreme exaltation of humanity was designed from the beginning and included in the dominion with which man was invested.

§5. The Doctrine of the Roman Church
§6. Pelagian and Rationalistic Doctrine

Chapter VI

Covenant of Works

§1. God Entered into Covenant with Adam
§2. The Promise
§3. Condition of the Covenant
§4. The Penalty
§5. The Parties to the Covenant of Works
§6. Perpetuity of the Covenant of Works

God, having created man after His own image in knowledge, righteousness, and holiness, entered into a covenant of life with him upon condition of perfect obedience, forbidding him to eat of the tree of knowledge of good and evil upon the pain of death. . . .

§1. God Entered into Covenant with Adam

This statement does not rest upon any express declaration of the Scriptures. It is, however, a concise and correct mode of asserting a plain Scriptural fact, namely, that God made to Adam a promise which depended on man's satisfying a condition, and He also attached to disobedience a certain penalty. This is what in Scriptural language is meant by a covenant, and this is all that is meant by the term as here used. Although the word covenant does not occur in the Biblical account of this transaction, yet inasmuch as the plan of salvation is

265

constantly represented as a new covenant, new not merely in antithesis to that made at Sinai, but new in reference to all legal covenants whatever, it is plain that the Bible does represent the arrangement made with Adam as a truly covenantal transaction. The Scriptures know of only two methods of attaining eternal life: the one demands perfect obedience, and the other demands faith. If the latter is called a covenant, the former is of the same nature.

(It is of great importance that the Scriptural form of presenting truth be retained. Rationalism was introduced into the Church under the guise of a philosophical statement of the truths of the Bible free from the outward form in which the sacred writers, trained in Judaism, had presented them. On this ground the federal system, as the covenantal arrangement was called, was discarded. On the same ground the prophetic, priestly, and kingly offices of Christ were pronounced a cumbrous and unsatisfactory form under which to set forth His work as our Redeemer. And then the sacrificial character of His death and all idea of atonement were rejected as mere Jewish drapery. Thus, by the theory of accommodation, every distinctive doctrine of the Scriptures was set aside and Christianity reduced to deism. It is, therefore, far more than a mere matter of method that is involved in adhering to the Scriptural form of presenting Scriptural truths.)

God then did enter into a covenant with Adam. That covenant is sometimes called a covenant of life, because life was promised as the reward of obedience. Sometimes it is called the covenant of works, because works were the condition on which the fulfilment of that promise depended, and because it is thus distinguished from the new covenant, which promises life on condition of faith.

§2. The Promise

There are various evidences that the reward promised to Adam on condition of his obedience was life. (1) The threat, "In the day that thou eatest thereof thou shalt surely die," plainly involved the assurance that man would not die if he did not eat. (2) This is confirmed by innumerable passages and by the general drift of Scripture, in which it is so plainly and so variously taught that life was, by the ordinance of God, connected with obedience: "This do, and thou shalt live"; "The man that doeth [the works of the law] shall live by them." This is the uniform mode in which the Bible speaks of that law or covenant under which man by the constitution of his nature and by the ordinance of God was placed. (3) As the Scriptures everywhere present God as a judge or moral ruler, it follows of necessity that His rational creatures will be dealt with according to the principles of justice. If there be no transgression, there will be no punishment. And those who continue holy thereby continue in the favour and fellowship of Him whose favour is life and whose loving-kindness is better than life. (4) And finally, holiness or, as the apostle expresses it, to be spiritually minded is life. There can therefore be no doubt that had Adam continued in holiness, he would have enjoyed that life which flows from the favour of God.

The life thus promised included happy, holy, and immortal existence of the soul and body. This is plain (1) because the life promised was suited to the being to whom the promise was made, and the life suited to man as a moral and intelligent being composed of soul and body includes the happy, holy, and immortal existence of his whole nature. (2) The Scriptures everywhere connect obedience with the life which flows from the favour and fellowship of God, and includes glory, honour, and immortality, as the apostle teaches us in Romans 2:7. (3) The life secured by Christ for His people was the life forfeited by sin, and that life which the believer derives from Christ is spiritual and eternal life, the exaltation and complete blessedness of his whole nature, both soul and body.

§3. Condition of the Covenant

The condition of the covenant made with Adam is said in the symbols of our Church to be perfect obedience. That that statement is correct may be inferred (1) from the nature of the case and from the general principles clearly revealed in the Word of God. Such is the nature of God, and such the relation which He sustains to His moral creatures, that sin, the transgression of the divine law, must involve the destruction of the fellowship between man and his creator, and the manifestation of the divine displeasure. The apostle therefore says that he who offends in one point, who breaks one precept of the law of God, is guilty of the whole. (2) It is everywhere assumed in the Bible that the condition of acceptance under the law is perfect obedience: "Cursed is every one that continueth not in all things written in the book of the law to do them" (Gal. 3:10). This is not a peculiarity of the Mosaic economy, but a declaration of a principle which applies to all divine laws. (3) The whole argument of the apostle in his epistles to the Romans and to the Galatians is founded on the assumption that the law demands perfect obedience. If that be not granted, his whole argument falls to the ground.

The specific command to Adam not to eat of a certain tree was therefore not the only command he was required to obey. It was given simply to be the outward and visible test to determine whether he was willing to obey God in all things. Since Adam was created holy, with all his affections pure, there was the more reason that the test of his obedience should be an outward and positive command, and that something should be wrong simply because it was forbidden rather than because it was evil in its own nature. It would thus be seen that Adam obeyed for the sake of obeying. His obedience was more directly to God and not to his own reason. . . .

§4. The Penalty

The penalty attached to the covenant is expressed by the comprehensive term death: "In the day that thou eatest thereof thou shalt surely die" (Gen. 2:17). That this does not refer merely to the dissolution of the body is plain (1) because the word death, as used in Scripture in reference to the consequences of transgression, includes all penal evil. The wages of sin is death. The soul that sinneth, it shall die. Any and every form of evil, therefore, which is inflicted as the punishment of sin is comprehended under the word death. (2) The death threatened was the opposite of the life promised. Inasmuch as the life promised, as we have seen, included all that is involved in the happy, holy, and immortal existence of the soul and body, death must include not only all the miseries of this life and the dissolution of the body, but also all that is meant by spiritual and eternal death. (3) God is the life of the soul. His favour and fellowship with Him are essential to its holiness and happiness. If His favour be forfeited, the inevitable consequences are the death of the soul, i.e., loss of spiritual life, and unending sinfulness and misery. (4) The nature of the penalty threatened is learned from its infliction. The consequences of Adam's sin were the loss of the image and favour of God and all the evils which flowed from that loss. (5) Finally, the death which was incurred by the sin of our first parents is that from which we are redeemed by Christ. Christ, however, does not merely deliver the body from the grave, He saves the soul from spiritual and eternal death; and therefore spiritual and eternal death, together with the dissolution of the body and all the miseries of this life, were included in the penalty originally attached to the covenant of works. In the day in which Adam ate the forbidden fruit he did die. The penalty threatened was not a momentary infliction but permanent subjection to all the evils which flow from the righteous displeasure of God.

§5. The Parties to the Covenant of Works

It lies in the nature of a covenant that there must be two or more parties. A covenant is not of one. The parties to the original covenant were God and Adam. Adam, however, acted not in his individual capacity but as the head and representative of his whole race. This is plain (1) because everything said to him had as much reference to his posterity as to Adam himself. Everything granted to him was granted to them. Everything promised to him was promised to them. And everything threatened against him, in case of transgression, was threatened against them. God did not give the earth to Adam for him alone, but as the heritage of his race. The dominion over the lower animals with which he was invested belonged equally to his descendants. The promise of life embraced them as well as him, and the threat of death concerned them as well as him. (2) It is an undeniable fact that the penalty which Adam incurred has fallen upon his whole race. The earth is cursed for them as it was for him. They must earn their bread by the sweat of their brows. The pains of childbirth are the common heritage of all the daughters of Eve. All men are subject to disease and death. All are born in sin, destitute of the moral image of God. There is not an evil consequent on the sin of Adam which does not affect his race as much as it affected him. (3) Not only did the ancient Jews infer the representative character of Adam from the record given in Genesis, but the inspired writers of the New Testament give this doctrine the sanction of divine authority. In Adam, says the apostle, all died. The sentence of condemnation, he teaches us, passed on all men for one offence. By the offence of one all were made sinners. (4) This great fact is made the ground on which the whole plan of redemption is founded. As we fell in Adam, we are saved in Christ. To deny the principle in the one case is to deny it in the other, for the two are inseparably united in the representations of Scripture. (5) The principle involved in the headship of Adam underlies all the religious institutions ever ordained by God for men, all His providential dealings with our race, and even the distributions of the saving influences of His Spirit. . . . (6) What is thus clearly revealed in the Word and providence of God finds a response in the very constitution of our nature. All men are led as it were instinctively to recognize the validity of this principle of representation. Rulers represent their people, parents their children, guardians their wards. All these considerations are in place when the nature of the covenant of works and the parties to that covenant are under discussion. . . . Men may dispute as to the grounds of the headship of Adam, but the fact itself can hardly be questioned by those who recognize the authority of the Scriptures. . . .

§6. Perpetuity of the Covenant of Works

That Adam acted not only for himself but also for his posterity answers the question whether the covenant of works be still in force. In the obvious sense of the terms, to say that men are still under the covenant is to say that they are still on probation and that the race did not fall when Adam fell. But inasmuch as Adam acted as the head of the whole race, all men were on probation and fell with him in his first transgression. The Scriptures therefore teach that we come into the world under condemnation. We are by nature, i.e., we were born, the children of wrath. This fact is assumed in all the provisions of the gospel and in all the institutions of our religion. Children are required to be baptized for the remission of sin. But while the Pelagian doctrine which teaches that each man comes into the world free from sin and free from condemnation and is on probation in his own person is to be rejected, it is nevertheless true that where there is no sin there is no condemnation. Hence our Lord said to the young man, "This do, and thou shalt live." And hence the apostle in Romans 2:6–8 says that God will reward every man according to his works. To those who are good, He will give eternal life; to those who are evil, indignation and wrath. This is saying only that the eternal principles of justice are still in force. If any man can present himself before the bar of God and prove that he is free from sin, imputed and personal, original and actual, he will not be condemned. But the fact is that the whole world lies in wickedness. Man is an apostate race. Men are all involved in the penal and natural consequences of Adam's transgression. They were on probation in him, and thus are not tested each man for himself.

Chapter **VII**

The Fall

A. *The Scriptural Account*

The Scriptural account of the probation and fall of man is found in Genesis 2:15–17 and 3:1–6. The consequences of the disobedience of Adam and Eve were (1) an immediate sense of guilt and shame; (2) a desire and effort to hide themselves from the face of God; (3) denunciation and immediate execution of the righteous judgment of God upon the serpent, upon the man, and upon the woman; and (4) expulsion from the garden of Eden and prohibition of access to the tree of life.

That the Genesis account of the probation and fall of man is neither an allegory nor a myth, but a true history, is evident (1) from internal evidence. When contrasted with the mythological accounts of the creation and origin of man as found in the records of early heathen nations, whether Oriental, Grecian, or Etruscan, the difference is at once apparent. The latter are evidently the product of crude speculation;

271

the Scriptural account is simple, intelligible, and pregnant with the highest truths. (2) Not only is Adam's fall presented as a matter of history in a book which all Christians recognize as of divine authority, but it also forms an integral part of the book of Genesis, which is confessedly historical. . . . (3) It is an essential part not only of the book of Genesis, but also of Scriptural history as a whole, which treats of the origin, apostasy, and development of the human race as connected with the plan of redemption. (4) We accordingly find that in both the Old and New Testaments the facts recorded in Genesis are assumed and referred to as matters of history. (5) And finally, these facts underlie the whole doctrinal system revealed in the Scriptures. Our Lord and His apostles refer to them not only as true, but as furnishing the ground of all the subsequent revelations and dispensations of God. It was because of tempting man and leading him into disobedience that Satan became the head of the kingdom of darkness, whose power Christ came to destroy and from whose dominion He redeemed His people. It was because we died in Adam that we must be made alive in Christ. Accordingly, the Church universal has felt bound to receive the record of Adam's temptation and fall as a true historical account.

There are many who, while admitting the historical character of this account, still regard it as in a great measure figurative. They understand it as a statement not so much of external events as of an internal process of thought explaining how it was that Eve came to eat of the forbidden tree and to induce Adam to join in her transgression. They do not admit that a serpent was the tempter or that he spoke to Eve, but assume that she was attracted by the beauty of the forbidden object and began to question in her own mind either the fact or the justice of the prohibition. But not only is there no valid reason for departing from the literal interpretation of the passage, but that interpretation is supported by the authority of the writers of the New Testament. They recognize the serpent as present and as the agent in the temptation and fall of our first parents.

[B. *The Tree of Life*
C. *The Tree of Knowledge*]

D. *The Serpent*

It may be inferred from the narrative that Adam was present with Eve during the temptation. In Genesis 3:6 it is said the woman gave of the fruit of the tree to her husband, who was "with her." He was therefore a party to the whole transaction. We are bound to take literally the statement that a serpent addressed Eve. The serpent is not a figurative designation of Satan, nor did Satan assume the form of a serpent. That a real serpent was the agent of the temptation is plain from what is said of the natural characteristics of the serpent in the first verse of the chapter, from the curse pronounced upon the animal itself, and from the enmity which was declared should subsist between it and man through all time. But that Satan was the real tempter and that he used the serpent merely as his organ or instrument is evident (1) from the nature of the transaction. What is here attributed to the serpent far transcends the power of any irrational creature. The serpent may be the most subtile of all the beasts of the field, but he has not the high intellectual faculties which the tempter here displays. (2) In the New Testament it is both directly asserted and in various forms assumed that Satan seduced our first parents into sin. In Revelation 12:9 it is said, "The great dragon was cast out, that old serpent, called the Devil, and Satan, which deceiveth the whole world." And in 2 Corinthians 11:3 Paul says, "I fear lest . . . as the serpent beguiled Eve through his subtilty, so your minds should be corrupted from the simplicity that is in Christ." That by "the serpent" Paul understood Satan is plain from verse 14, where he depicts Satan as the great deceiver. Moreover, what is said in Romans 16:20, "The God of peace shall bruise Satan under your feet," is in obvious allusion to Genesis 3:15. In John 8:44 our Lord calls the devil a murderer from the beginning and the father of lies, because through him sin and death were introduced into the world. . . .

As to the serpent's speaking there is no more difficulty than in the utterance of articulate words from Sinai, or the sounding of a voice from heaven at the baptism of our Lord, or the speaking of Balaam's ass. The words uttered were produced by the power of Satan. In the Bible there are numerous other instances of such effects produced by angelic beings good and evil.

E. The Nature of the Temptation

The first address of the tempter to Eve was designed to awaken distrust in the goodness of God and doubt as to the truth of the prohibition: "Hath God said, Ye shall not eat of every tree of the garden?" . . . The next address was a direct assault upon her faith: "Ye shall not surely die" but, on the contrary, become as God Himself in knowledge. To this temptation she yielded, and Adam joined in the transgression. From this account it appears that doubt, unbelief, and pride were the factors which led to this fatal act of disobedience. Eve doubted God's goodness; she disbelieved His threatening; she aspired after forbidden knowledge.

F.   The Effects of the First Sin

The effects of sin upon our first parents themselves were (1) shame, a sense of degradation and pollution, and (2) dread of the displeasure of God, or a sense of guilt and a consequent desire to hide from His presence. These effects were unavoidable. They prove the loss not only of innocence but of original righteousness, and with it of the favour and fellowship of God. The state therefore to which Adam was reduced by his disobedience, so far as his subjective condition was concerned, was analogous to that of the fallen angels. He was entirely and absolutely ruined. It is said that no man becomes thoroughly depraved by one transgression. In one sense this is true. But one transgression, by incurring the wrath and curse of God and the loss of fellowship with Him, as effectually involves spiritual death as one perforation of the heart causes the death of the body, or one puncture of the eyes involves us in perpetual darkness. The other evil effects of Adam's disobedience were merely subordinate. They were but the expressions of the divine displeasure and the consequences of that spiritual death in which the threatened penalty essentially consisted.

Chapter VIII

Sin

§1. The Nature of the Question to Be Considered

By sinning against God our first parents, we are told, fell from the estate wherein they were created. This presents one of the most difficult and comprehensive questions in morals and in theology: What is sin? The existence of sin is an undeniable fact. No man can examine his own nature, or observe the conduct of his fellow men, without having the conviction forced upon him that there is such an evil as sin.... In approaching the great question of the definition of sin the Christian theologian has certain presuppositions. He assumes the existence of a personal God of infinite perfection, and he assumes the responsibility of man. No theory of the nature or origin of sin which conflicts with either of these fundamental principles can for him be true.... [The Christian theologian then proceeds to define sin on the basis of] the declarations of the Word of God and the facts of our own moral nature. Ignoring either wholly or in part these two sources of knowledge ... is unreasonable and is sure to lead to false conclusions.... The facts of our moral nature must be assumed as true and trustworthy.... Thus the man who ignores the facts of our moral nature in his theories of the origin and essence of sin will labour in vain....

[§2. Philosophical Theories of the Nature of Sin]

§3. The Doctrine of the Early Church

... So far as the early Church is concerned, the doctrine respecting sin was stated only in general terms. In almost all cases the explicit and discriminating doctrinal affirmations received their form as counterstatements to erroneous views. So long as the truth was not denied, the Church was content to hold and state it in the simple form in which it is presented in the Bible. But when positions were assumed which were inconsistent with the revealed doctrine, or when one truth was so stated as to contradict some other truth, it became necessary to be more explicit and to frame such an expression of the doctrine as should comprehend all that God had revealed on the subject. This process in the definition of doctrines was of necessity a gradual one. It was only as one error after another arose in the Church that the truth came to be distinguished from them severally by more explicit and guarded statements. As the earliest heresies were those of Gnosticism and Manicheism, in which, in different forms, sin was represented as a necessary evil having its origin in a cause independent of God and beyond the control of the creature, the Church was called upon to deny those errors and to assert that sin was neither necessary nor eternal, but had its origin in the free will of rational creatures. In the struggle with the early heresies ... the following points were constantly insisted upon: (1) all men in their present state are sinners; (2) this universal sinfulness of men had its historical and causal origin in the voluntary apostasy of Adam; (3) such is the present state of human nature that salvation can be attained in no other way than through Christ and by the assistance of His Spirit; and (4) even infants as soon as born need regeneration and redemption and can be saved only through the merit of Christ. These great truths, which lie at the foundation of the gospel, entered into the general faith of the Church before they were so strenuously asserted by Augustine in his controversy with Pelagius....

§4. Pelagian Theory

In the early part of the fifth century, Pelagius, Coelestius, and Julian introduced a new theory as to the nature of sin, the state of man since the fall, and our relation to Adam. That their doctrine was an innovation is proved by the fact that it was universally rejected and condemned as soon as it was fully understood. . . . The radical principle of the Pelagian theory is that lack of ability limits obligation. "If I ought, I can," is the aphorism on which the whole system rests. . . . Pelagius laid down the principle that man must have plenary ability to do and to be whatever can be righteously required of him. . . .

A. Fundamentals of Pelagianism

(1) The intimate conviction that men are not responsible for what is not in their power led to the Pelagian doctrine of the freedom of the will. It was not enough to constitute free agency that the agent should be self-determined or that all his volitions should be determined by his own inward states. It was required that he should have power over those states. Liberty of the will, according to the Pelagians, is plenary power, at all times and at every moment, of choosing between good and evil, and of being either holy or unholy. Whatever does not thus fall within the imperative power of the will can have no moral character. . . .

(2) Sin, therefore, consists only in the deliberate choice of evil. It presupposes knowledge of what is evil as well as the full power of choosing or rejecting it.

(3) It follows that there can be no such thing as original sin or inherent hereditary corruption. . . . Since the fall men are born into the world in the same state in which Adam was created. This was the point on which the Pelagians principally insisted, that it is contrary to the nature of sin that it should be transmitted or inherited. If nature is sinful, then God as the author of nature must be the author of sin.

(4) Consequently Adam's sin injured only himself. . . . Pelagius maintained that the sin of Adam exerted merely the influence of a bad example and in that sense and to that degree injured his posterity. But Pelagius denied that there is any causal relation between the sin of Adam and the sinfulness of his race, or that death is a penal evil. Adam would have died from the constitution of his nature whether he had sinned or not; and his posterity, whether infant or adult, die from like necessity of nature. As Adam was in no sense the representative of his race, as they did not stand their probation in him, each

man stands a probation for himself and is justified or condemned solely on the ground of his own individual personal acts.

(5) As men come into the world without the contamination of original sin, and as they have plenary power to do all that God requires, they may and in many cases do live without sin. If at any time they transgress, they may turn unto God and perfectly obey all His commandments. Hence Pelagius taught that some men have no need for themselves to repeat the petition in the Lord's Prayer, "Forgive us our trespasses." ...

(6) Another consequence which Pelagius unavoidably drew from his principles was that men can be saved without the gospel. As free will in the sense of plenary ability belongs essentially to man as much as does reason, men whether heathen, Jews, or Christians may fully obey the law of God and attain eternal life. The only difference is that under the light of the gospel, this perfect obedience is rendered more easy. ...

(7) The Pelagian system denies the necessity of grace in the sense of the supernatural influence of the Holy Spirit. When the Scriptures speak of the grace of God in the salvation of men, [they mean] everything which we derive from the goodness of God. Our natural faculties of reason and free will, the revelation of the truth whether in His works or His Word, all the providential blessings and advantages which men enjoy, fall under the Pelagian idea of grace. ...

(8) As infants are destitute of moral character, baptism in their case cannot either symbolize or effect the remission of sin. It is, according to Pelagius, only a sign of their consecration to God. ...

B. Arguments Against the Pelagian Doctrine

(1) The fundamental principle on which the whole system is founded contradicts the common consciousness of men. It is not true, as our own conscience teaches us, that our obligation is limited by our lack of ability. Every man knows that he is bound to be better than he is and better than he can make himself by any exertion of his will. We are bound to love God perfectly, but we know that such perfect love is beyond our power. We recognize the obligation to be free from all sin and absolutely conformed to the perfect law of God. Yet no man is so infatuated or so blinded to his actual character as really to believe that he either is thus perfect or has the power to make himself so. It is the daily and hourly prayer or aspiration of every saint and of every sinner to be delivered from the bondage of evil. The proud and malignant would gladly be humble and benevolent, the covetous would rejoice to be liberal, the infidel longs for faith, and the hardened sinner

for repentance. Sin is a burden and a torment; although it is loved and cherished as the cups of the drunkard are cherished, it would cease to reign in any rational creature if emancipation could be effected by an act of the will. There is no truth, then, of which men are more intimately convinced than that they are the slaves of sin, that they cannot do the good they would, and that they cannot alter their character at will. There is no principle, therefore, more at variance with the common consciousness of men than the fundamental principle of Pelagianism that our lack of ability limits our obligation, that we are not bound to be better than we can make ourselves by a volition.

(2) It is no less revolting to the moral nature of man to assert, as Pelagianism teaches, that nothing is sinful but the deliberate transgression of known law; that there is no moral character in feelings and emotions; that love and hatred, malice and benevolence, considered as affections of the mind, are alike indifferent; that the command to love God is an absurdity, because love is not under the control of the will. All our moral judgments must be perverted before we can assent to a system involving such consequences.

(3) The Pelagian doctrine, which confounds freedom with ability, or which makes the liberty of a free agent to consist in the power to determine his character by a volition, is contrary to every man's consciousness. We feel, and cannot but acknowledge, that we are free when we are self-determined, while at the same time we are conscious that the controlling states of the mind are not under the power of the will or, in other words, are not under our power. A theory which is founded on equating things which are essentially different, as liberty and ability, must be false.

(4) The Pelagian system leaves the universal sinfulness of men, a fact which cannot be denied, altogether unaccounted for. To refer it to the mere free agency of man is to say that simply because a thing may be, it always is.

(5) This system fails to satisfy the deepest and most universal necessities of our nature. In making man independent of God by assuming that God cannot control free agents without destroying their liberty, it makes all prayer for the controlling grace of God over ourselves and others a mockery, and throws man back completely on his own resources to grapple with sin and the powers of darkness without hope of deliverance.

(6) It makes redemption (in the sense of a deliverance from sin) unnecessary or impossible. It is unnecessary that there should be a Redeemer for a race which has not fallen and which has full ability to avoid all sin or to recover itself from its power. And it is impossible if free agents are independent of the control of God.

(7) It need hardly be said that a system which asserts that Adam's sin injured only himself, that men are born into the world in the state in which Adam was created, that men may and often do live without sin, that we have no need of divine assistance in order to be holy, and that Christianity has no essential superiority over heathenism or natural religion, is altogether at variance with the Word of God. The opposition indeed between Pelagianism and the gospel is so open and so radical that the former has never been regarded as a form of Christianity at all. It has, in other words, never been the faith of any organized Christian Church. It is little more than a form of rationalism.

§5. Augustinian Doctrine

Augustine drew his doctrine of sin from his own religious experience as guided and determined by the Spirit of God. He was (1) conscious of sin. He recognized himself as guilty and polluted, as liable to the justice of God and offensive to His holiness. (2) He felt himself to be thus guilty and polluted not only because of deliberate acts of transgression, but also because of his affections, feelings, and emotions. This sense of sin attached not only to these positive and consciously active states of mind, but also to the mere absence of right affections, to hardness of heart, to the want of love, humility, faith, and other Christian virtues, or to their feebleness and inconstancy. (3) He recognized the fact that he had always been a sinner. His earliest memories included the presence of sin. (4) He was deeply convinced that he had no power to change his moral nature or to make himself holy. Whatever liberty he possessed, however free he was in sinning, or (after regeneration) in holy acting, he had not the liberty of ability which Pelagians claimed as an essential prerogative of humanity. (5) It was involved in this consciousness of sin as including guilt or just liability to punishment, as well as pollution, that it could not be a necessary evil, but must have its origin in the free act of man and be therefore voluntary. . . . (6) What consciousness taught him to be true with regard to himself he saw to be true with regard to others. All men showed themselves to be sinners. They all gave evidence of sinfulness as soon as they gave evidence of reason. They all appeared not only as transgressors of the law of God, but as spiritually dead, devoid of all evidence of spiritual life. They were the willing slaves of sin, entirely unable to deliver themselves from their bondage to corruption. No man had ever given proof of possessing the power of self-regeneration. All who gave evidence of being regenerated ascribed the work not to themselves, but to the grace of God.

From these facts of consciousness and experience Augustine drew several inevitable conclusions: (1) If men are saved, it cannot be by their own merit, but solely through the undeserved love of God. (2) The regeneration of the soul must be the exclusive and supernatural work of the Holy Ghost; the sinner can neither effect the work nor cooperate in its production. In other words, that grace is certainly efficacious or irresistible. (3) Salvation is of grace or of the sovereign mercy of God in that (a) God might justly have left men to perish in their apostasy without any provision for their redemption; (b) men, being destitute of the power of doing anything holy or meritorious, cannot be justified by works, but only as a matter of favour; and (c) partaking of the redemption of Christ depends not on the will of the persons saved, but on the good pleasure of God. In other words, election to eternal life is founded on the sovereign pleasure of God and not on the foresight of good works. (4) A fourth inference from the principles of Augustine is the perseverance of the saints. If God of His own good pleasure elects some to eternal life, they cannot fail of salvation. It thus appears that as all the distinguishing doctrines of the Pelagians are the logical consequences of their principle of plenary ability as the ground and limit of obligation, so the distinguishing doctrines of Augustine are the logical consequences of his principle of the entire inability of fallen man to do anything spiritually good.

Taught by his own experience that he was from his birth guilty and polluted, and that he had no power to change his own nature, and seeing that all men are involved in the same sinfulness and helplessness, Augustine accepted the Scriptural solution of these facts of consciousness and observation. His systematized doctrine of sin therefore included the following elements: (1) God created man originally in His own image and likeness. This entailed knowledge, righteousness, holiness, immortality, and dominion over the creatures. Augustine held also that Adam was endowed with perfect liberty of the will, not only with spontaneity and the power of self-determination, but with the power of choosing good or evil, and thus of determining his own character. (2) Being left to the freedom of his own will, Adam, under the temptation of the devil, voluntarily sinned against God and thus fell from the estate in which he was created. (3) The consequences of this sin upon Adam were the loss of the divine image and the corruption of his whole nature, so that he became spiritually dead and thus indisposed, disabled, and made opposite to all spiritual good. Besides this spiritual death, he became mortal, liable to all the miseries of this life and to eternal death. (4) Such was the union between Adam and his descendants that the consequences of his transgression came on them as well. They are born the children of wrath, i.e., in a state of condemnation, destitute of the image of God, and morally depraved. (5) This inherent, hereditary depravity is truly and properly of the nature of sin, involving both guilt and corruption. Formally it consists in the privation of original righteousness and disorder of the whole nature.... It is voluntary in that it did not arise from necessity of nature, or from the efficiency of God, but from the free agency of Adam. (6) The loss of original righteousness and the corruption of nature consequent on the fall of Adam are penal inflictions, being the punishment of his first sin. (7) Regeneration, or effectual calling, is a supernatural act of the Holy Spirit in which the soul is the subject and not the agent. A sovereign act of God, it is granted or withheld according to His good pleasure; consequently, salvation is entirely of grace. This is the Augustinian system in all that is essential.

§6. Doctrine of the Church of Rome

A. The Semi-Pelagians

... The doctrine of Augustine, as exhibited above, was sanctioned by the Latin Church and pronounced to be the true orthodox faith. But even during the lifetime of Augustine, and to a greater extent in the following century, serious departures from his system began to prevail.... This opposition to Augustinianism arose with the monks and prevailed principally among them. This was very natural. Augustine taught that man could do nothing good of himself and could acquire no merit in the sight of God. The monks believed that they could do not only all, but more than all that God required of them. Else why submit to their vows of celibacy, poverty, and obedience? The party thus formed against the orthodox or established doctrine was called Semi-Pelagian, because it held a middle ground between Pelagius and Augustine....

Semi-Pelagians rejected the Pelagian doctrine that Adam's sin injured only himself; they admitted that the effects of that sin passed on all men, affecting both the soul and body. It rendered the body mortal and liable to disease and suffering; and the soul it weakened, so that it became prone to evil and incapable, without divine assistance, of doing anything spiritually good. But against Augustine they held that (1) the beginning of salvation is with man—man begins to seek God, and then God aids him; (2) this incipient turning of the soul towards God is something good and in one sense meritorious; and (3) the soul, in virtue of its liberty of will or ability for good, cooperates with the grace of God in regeneration as well as in sanctification....

[The councils of Orange and Valence (A.D. 529) decided] the two great points in dispute between the Augustinians and Semi-Pelagians in favour of the former. They decided (1) that original sin, or the corruption of nature derived from Adam, is not simply a weakening of our power for good, but is spiritual death—it is real sin, incapacitating the soul for any spiritual good; and (2) that in the work of conversion it is not man that begins, but the Spirit of God. The sinner has no power to turn himself unto God, but is turned or renewed by divine grace before he can do anything spiritually good. . . .

B.   *The Doctrine of Anselm*
C.   *Doctrine of Abelard*
D.   *Doctrine of Thomas Aquinas*
E.   *Doctrine of the Scotists*
F.   *Tridentine Doctrine on Original Sin*
G.   *The True Doctrine of the Church of Rome*

§7. Protestant Doctrine of Sin

. . . Founding their doctrine on their moral and religious consciousness and on the Word of God, the Protestant churches at the time of the Reformation declared sin to be the transgression of, or want of conformity to, the divine law. In this definition all classes of theologians, Lutheran and Reformed, agree. . . .

A.   *Sin Is a Specific Evil*

The first element in the Protestant definition is that sin is a specific evil. This we know from our own consciousness. . . . Every man in virtue of his being a moral creature and a sinner has in his own consciousness the knowledge of sin. He knows that when he is not what he *ought* to be, when he does what he *ought not* to do, or omits what he *ought* to do, he is chargeable with sin. He knows that sin is not simply limitation of his nature, nor merely a subjective state of his own mind, having no character in the sight of God. Moreover, he knows not only that it is something which is unwise, or derogatory to his own dignity, or inexpedient because hurtful to his own interests, or injurious to the welfare of others, but that it has a specific character of its own and includes both guilt and pollution.

B. Sin Has Relation to Law

A second truth included in our consciousness of sin is that it has relation to law. As moral and rational beings we are of necessity subject to the law of right. This is included in the consciousness of obligation. The word ought would otherwise have no meaning. To say we ought is to say that we are bound, that we are under authority of some kind. The word law, in relation to moral and religious subjects, . . . means that which binds, a command of one in authority. This is the usual sense of the term in the New Testament. As the rule which binds the conscience of men, and prescribes what they are to do and not to do, has been variously revealed in the constitution of our nature, in the Decalogue, in the Mosaic institutions, and in the whole Scriptures, the word is sometimes used in a sense to include all these forms of revelation, sometimes in reference exclusively to one of them, and sometimes exclusively in reference to another. In all cases the general idea is retained. The law is that which binds the conscience.

C. Sin Is Related to the Law of God

The great question is, What is that law which prescribes to man what he ought to be and to do? . . . It is clear from the very constitution of our nature that we are subject to the authority of a rational and moral Being, a Spirit whom we know to be infinite, eternal, and immutable in His being and perfections. All men, in every age and in every part of the world, under all forms of religion and of every degree of culture, have felt and acknowledged that they are subject to a personal Being higher than themselves. No forms of speculative philosophy, however plausible or however widely diffused or confidently held in the schools or in the closet, have ever availed to invalidate this instinctive or intuitive judgment of the mind. Men ignorant of the true God have fashioned for themselves imaginary gods (Rom. 1:23) whose wrath they have endeavored to appease and whose favour they have endeavored to win. But once the Scriptural idea of God as an infinitely perfect personal Being has been presented to the mind, it can never be discarded. It commends itself to the reason and the conscience. It solves all the enigmas of our nature. It satisfies all our desires and aspirations; and to this Being, to Him and to His will, we feel ourselves bound to be conformed and know ourselves to be responsible for our character and conduct. This allegiance we cannot possibly throw off. The law of gravitation no more inexorably binds the earth to its orbit than our moral nature binds us to our allegiance and responsibility to God. It would be as unreasonable to deny the one as the other and as useless to argue against the one as against the other. This is clearly the doctrine of Paul in the passage just referred to. He is speaking of the most debased and vicious of the heathen world, men whom God had given up to a reprobate mind (Rom. 1:28). And yet the apostle asserts that they not only knew God, but knew His righteous judgment (v. 32), and that in committing sin they were worthy of death, that is, they were rightfully subject to the authority and inevitably exposed to the wrath and indignation of a moral ruler. This is a fact given in the universal consciousness of men. Sin is related to law, and that law is not one of our own enacting. It is not a mere idea or abstraction, it is not mere truth or reason, or the moral order of the universe, but the nature and will of God. Law as it reveals itself in the conscience implies a lawgiver, a Being of whose will it is the expression, and who has the power and the purpose to enforce all its demands—and not only this, but one who, from the very perfection of His nature, must enforce them. He can no more pass by transgression than He can love evil. It is in vain to argue against these convictions. It is in vain to say there is no God, no Being on whom we are dependent and to whom we are responsible for our character and conduct.

1. The extent of the law's demands

The next question is, What does this law demand? This is the point on which there has been most diversity of opinion, and systems of theology as well as of morals are founded on the different answers which it has received. The answer given by the unsophisticated and enlightened conscience of men and by the Word of God is that the law demands complete perfection, or the entire conformity of the moral nature and conduct of a rational creature with the nature and will of God. We are commanded to love God with all the heart, with all the soul, with all the strength, and with all the mind, and our neighbour as ourselves. This implies entire congeniality with God, the unreserved consecration of all our powers to His service, and absolute submission to His will. Nothing more than this can be required of any creature. No angel or glorified saint can be or do more than this, and this is what the law demands of every rational creature at all times and in every state of his being. . . . The absolute moral perfection which the law demands includes the entire absence of all sin and the entire conformity of nature to the image and will of God. As this is the doctrine of the Bible, so also it is the teaching of conscience. Every man, at least every Christian, feels that he sins or is sinful whenever and howsoever he comes short of full conformity to the image of God. He feels that languor, coldness of affection, defect of zeal, and the want of due humility, gratitude, meekness, forbearance, and benevolence are in him of the nature of sin. The old maxim "everything less than good entails evil" authenticates itself in the conscience of every unsophisticated believer.... If this principle is correct, if the law demands entire conformity to the nature and will of God, several conclusions inevitably follow:

(1) There can be no perfection in this life. Every form of perfectionism which has ever prevailed in the Church is founded on one of two assumptions: either the law does not demand entire freedom from moral evil or sin is restricted to acts of the will. But if the law is so extensive in its demands as to pronounce sinful all defect in any duty, all coming short in the purity, ardour, or constancy of holy affections, then there is an end to the presumption that any mere man since the fall has ever attained perfection.

(2) No man can ever achieve merit through good works; that is, no man can lay just claim to reward on the basis of complete satisfaction of the demands of the law. For since those demands have never been perfectly fulfilled by any fallen man, no such man can either be justified by his own works or have, as the apostle expresses it, any claim founded on merit in the sight of God. He must always depend on mercy and expect eternal life as a free gift of God....

2. Sin not confined to acts of the will

(3) Another conclusion drawn from the Scriptural doctrine as to the extent of the divine law is that sin is not confined to acts of the will.... Since that law demands perfect conformity to the image of God, impulses of evil are clearly sinful.... The Protestant doctrine which pronounces these impulsive acts to be of the nature of sin is confirmed by the consciousness of the believer. He recognizes as evil in their own nature the first risings of malice, envy, pride, or cupidity. He knows that they spring from an evil or imperfectly sanctified nature. They constitute part of the burden of corruption which he hopes to lay down in the grave....

(4) From the principle that the law condemns all want of conformity to the nature of God it follows that the law condemns evil dispositions or habits as well as all voluntary sins, whether deliberate or impulsive. According to the Bible and the dictates of conscience there is a sinfulness as well as sins; there is such a thing as character as distinguished from transient acts by which it is revealed; that is, a sinful state—abiding, inherent, immanent forms of evil which are truly and properly of the nature of sin. Some sin, therefore, is not an agency, activity, or act, but a condition or state of the mind. This distinction between habitual and actual sin has been recognized and admitted in the Church from the beginning. Our Lord teaches us this distinction

when He speaks of an evil heart as distinguished from evil exercises, which are as distinct as a tree and its fruits. The apostle speaks of sin as a controlling principle regulating or determining his acts despite his better nature. He says sin dwells in him. He complains of it as a burden too heavy to be borne, from which he groans to be delivered. And his experience in this matter is the experience of all the people of God. They know there is more in them of the nature of sin than mere acts and exercises, that their heart is not right in the sight of God, that the fountain from which the waters flow is itself bitter, that the tree is known by its fruits.

D. Sin Is Want of Conformity to the Law of God

Protestants teach not only that sin is a specific evil, that it has relation to law, and that that law is the nature and will of God and takes cognizance of and condemns all forms and degrees of moral evil or want of moral excellence, but also that the formal nature of sin is the want of conformity to the divine law or standard of excellence. This want of conformity is not a mere negation such as may be predicated of a stone or of a brute which may be said not to be conformed to the image of God. The want of conformity to the divine law which constitutes sin is the want of congeniality of one moral nature with another, of the dependent and created nature with the infinitely holy nature, which of necessity is not only the sum but the standard of all excellence. Herein is sin: that we are not like God. As the opposite of reason is unreason, the opposite of wisdom is folly, and the opposite of good is evil, so the opposite of the divine holiness is sin.... The want of congeniality with God is alienation from God and, as the Scriptures say, enmity towards Him. The Protestant symbols and theologians in defining sin not merely as selfishness or the love of the creature or the love of the world, which are only modes of its manifestation, but as the want of conformity of an act, habit, or state of a man with the divine law, which is the revelation of the divine nature, have in their support both reason and conscience. This doctrine of the nature of sin is fully sustained by the authority of Scripture. The apostle John says that all want of conformity to law is sin (1 John 3:4). The two ideas are coextensive.... With this agree also all the representations of Scripture. The words there used for sin in all its forms express the idea of nonconformity to a standard. And besides this the Bible everywhere teaches that God is the source and standard of all good. His favour is the life of the soul. Congeniality with Him, conformity to His will and nature, is the sum and essence of all excellence; and the opposite state, the want of this congeniality and conformity, is the sum and essence of all evil.

E. Sin Includes Guilt and Pollution

Sin includes guilt and pollution; the one expresses its relation to the justice, the other to the holiness of God. These two elements of sin are revealed in the conscience of every sinner. He knows himself to be liable to the justice of God and offensive in His holy eyes. Even to himself he is hateful and degraded and self-condemned. . . .

§8. The Effects of Adam's Sin upon His Posterity

That the sin of Adam injured not himself only, but also all descending from him by ordinary generation, is part of the faith of the whole Christian world. The nature and extent of the evil thus entailed upon his race, and the ground or reason why the descendants of Adam are involved in the evil consequences of his transgression, have ever been matters of diversity and discussion. As to both of these points the common Augustinian doctrine is briefly stated in the symbols of our Church. According to our standards, "the sinfulness of that estate whereinto man fell consists in the guilt of Adam's first sin, the want of original righteousness, and the corruption of his whole nature, which is commonly called original sin, together with all actual transgressions which proceed from it." This corruption of nature is in the *Westminster Confession* declared to be "both in itself and in all motions thereof, truly and properly sin." And in virtue of this original corruption men are "utterly indisposed, disabled, and made opposite to all good, and wholly inclined to all evil." As to the ground of these evils, we are taught that "the covenant being made with Adam not only for himself, but for his posterity, all mankind descending from him by ordinary generation, sinned in him, and fell with him in his first transgression." Or, as it is expressed in the *Westminster Confession*, "Our first parents being the root of all mankind, the guilt of their sin was imputed, and the same death in sin and corrupted nature were conveyed to all their posterity, descending from them by ordinary generation."

In this view of the relation of mankind to Adam and of the consequences of his apostasy, the three leading subjects are the imputation of Adam's first sin, the corruption of nature derived from him, and the inability of fallen man to any spiritual good.

§9. Immediate Imputation

... Protestants generally, Lutherans as well as Reformed, and also the great body of the Latin Church adopt the position that in virtue of the union, federal and natural, between Adam and his posterity, his sin, although not their act, is so imputed to them that the penalty threatened against him comes also upon them. This is the doctrine of immediate imputation. ...

To impute is simply to attribute to, as we are said to impute good or bad motives to someone. In the juridical and theological sense of the word, *to impute* is to attribute something to a person or persons, upon adequate grounds, as the judicial or meritorious reason for reward or punishment, i.e., for the bestowment of good or the infliction of evil. ...

To impute is to reckon or to lay to one's account. So far as the meaning of the word is concerned, it makes no difference whether the thing imputed be sin or righteousness, nor whether it is our own personally or the sin or righteousness of another. ... By all Reformed and Lutheran theologians it is admitted that in the imputation of Adam's sin to us, of our sins to Christ, and of Christ's righteousness to believers, the nature of imputation is the same, so that the one case illustrates the others. When it is said that our sins were imputed to Christ, or that He bore our sins, it is not meant that He actually committed our sins, or that He was morally criminal on account of them, or that the demerit of them rested upon Him. All that is meant is that He assumed, in the language of the older theologians, "our law-place." He undertook to answer the demands of justice for the sins of men or, as it is expressed by the apostle, to be made a curse for them (Gal. 3:13). In like manner, when it is said that the righteousness of Christ is imputed to believers, it does not mean that they wrought out that righteousness, that they were the agents of the acts of Christ in obeying the law, nor that the merit of His righteousness is their personal merit, nor that it constitutes their moral character. It simply means that His righteousness, having been wrought out by Christ serving as representative for His people, is laid to their account, so that God can be just in justifying the ungodly. ... When, therefore, God pronounces the unrighteous to be righteous, He does not declare them to be what they are not. He simply declares that their debt to justice has been paid by another. And when it is said that the sin of Adam is imputed to his posterity, it is not meant that they committed his sin or were the agents of his act, nor is it meant that they are morally criminal for his transgression, that it is for them the ground of remorse and self-reproach; but simply that in virtue of the union between him and his descendants, his sin is the judicial ground of the condemnation of his race, precisely as the righteousness of Christ is the judicial ground of the justification of His people.

It is both a doctrine of Scripture and a fact of experience that mankind are a fallen race. Men universally, under all the circumstances of their being in this world, are sinful and exposed to innumerable evils. Many of these evils, and in many instances the most appalling, come upon the children of men in early infancy anterior to any possible transgressions of their own. This is a fact which cannot be denied and for which the human mind has tortured itself to find a solution. The Scriptural solution of this fearful problem is that God constituted our first parent the federal head and representative of his race and placed him on probation not only for himself, but also for all his posterity. Had he retained his integrity, he and all his descendants would have been confirmed in a state of holiness and happiness forever. But as he fell from the estate in which he was created, they fell with him in his first transgression, so that the penalty of that sin came upon them as well as upon him. Men therefore stood their probation in Adam. As he sinned, his posterity come into the world in a state of sin and condemnation. They are by nature the children of wrath. The evils which they suffer are not arbitrary impositions, nor simply the natural consequences of his apostasy, but judicial inflictions. The loss of original righteousness, and the death spiritual and temporal under which men commence their existence, are the penalty of Adam's first sin. . . .

A. *The Ground of the Imputation of Adam's Sin*

The ground of the imputation of Adam's sin, or the reason why the penalty of his sin has come upon all his posterity, according to the doctrine above stated, is the union between us and Adam. There could of course be no propriety in imputing the sin of one man to another unless there were some connection between them to explain and justify such imputation. The Scriptures never speak of the imputation of the sins of angels either to men or to Christ, or of the imputation of His righteousness to angels; for there is no such relation between men and angels, or between angels and Christ, as to involve the one in the judicial consequences of the sin or righteousness of the other. The union between Adam and his descendants which is the ground of the imputation of his sin to them is both natural and federal. He was their natural head. Such is the relation between parent and child, not only in the case of Adam and his descendants, but in all other cases, that the character and conduct of the one of necessity to a greater or lesser degree affect the other. No fact in history is plainer than that children bear the iniquities of their fathers. Children suffer for their fathers' sins. There must be a reason for this—a reason founded in the very constitution of our nature. But there was something peculiar in the case of Adam. Over and beyond this natural relation which exists between a man and his posterity there was a special divine constitution by which Adam was appointed the head and representative of his whole race.

B. *Adam the Federal Head of His Race*

The chief argument in favour of the doctrine of imputation is that the Scriptures present Adam as not only the natural, but also the federal head of his posterity. This is plain, as already remarked, from the narrative given in Genesis. Everything there said to Adam was said to him in his representative capacity. The promise of life was for him and for his seed after him. The dominion with which he was invested belonged to his posterity as well as to himself. All the evils threatened against him in case of transgression included them, and have in fact come upon them. They are mortal; they have to earn their bread by the sweat of their brows; they are subject to all the inconveniences and sufferings which originated with the banishment of our first parents from paradise and the curse pronounced upon the earth. They no less obviously are born destitute of original righteousness and subject to spiritual death. The full penalty, therefore, threatened against Adam has been inflicted upon them. . . . Besides the plain assumption of the truth of this federal relation, it is expressly asserted in the Word of God. The parallel drawn by the apostle between Adam and Christ relates precisely to this point. Adam was the type of Him who was to come, because as the one was the representative of his race, so the other is the representative of His people. And the consequences of the relation are shown to be in like manner analogous. Because Adam was the representative of his race, his sin is the judicial ground of their condemnation; and because Christ is the representative of His people, His righteousness is the judicial ground of the justification of believers.

C. *The Representative Principle in the Scriptures*

This representative principle pervades the whole Scriptures. The imputation of Adam's sin to his posterity is not an isolated fact. It is only an illustration of a general principle which characterizes the dispensations of God from the beginning of the world. To Moses God declared Himself to be, "The LORD, The LORD God, merciful and gracious, longsuffering, and abundant in goodness and truth, keeping mercy for thousands, forgiving iniquity and transgression and sin, and that will by no means clear the guilty; visiting the iniquity of the fathers upon the children, and upon the children's children, unto the third and to the fourth generation" (Exod. 34:6–7). Jeremiah says: "Thou showest lovingkindness unto thousands, and recompensest the iniquities of the fathers into the bosom of their children after them: the Great, the Mighty God, the LORD of hosts, is his name" (Jer. 32:18). The curse pronounced on Canaan fell upon his posterity. Esau's selling his birthright shut out his descendants from the covenant of promise. The children of Moab and Ammon were excluded from the congregation of the Lord forever, because their ancestors opposed the Israelites when they came out of Egypt. . . . This principle runs through the whole Scriptures. When God entered into covenant with Abraham, it was not for himself only, but also for his posterity. They were bound by all the stipulations of that covenant. They shared its promises and its threatenings, and in hundreds of cases the penalty of disobedience came upon those who had no personal part in the transgressions. Children suffered equally with adults in the judgments, whether famine, pestilence, or war, which came upon the people for their sins. In like manner, when God renewed and enlarged the Abrahamic covenant at Mount Sinai, it was made with the adults of that generation as representing their descendants to the remotest generations. And the Jews to this day are suffering the penalty of the sins of their fathers for their rejection of Him of whom Moses and the prophets spoke. The whole plan of redemption rests on this same principle. Christ is the representative of His people, and on this ground their sins are imputed to Him and His righteousness to them. In like manner, in the baptismal covenant the parent acts for the child and binds him without the child's consent, and the child's destiny is, as a general rule, suspended on the fidelity of the parent. No man who believes the Bible can shut his eyes to the fact that it everywhere recognizes the representative character of parents and that the dispensations of God have from the beginning been founded on the principle that children bear the iniquities of their fathers. . . .

D. The Same Principle Involved in Other Doctrines

That the sin of Adam is imputed to his posterity is proved not only (1) from the fact that he was their natural head and representative, (2) from the fact that this principle of representation pervades the Scriptures, (3) from the fact that it is the ground on which the providence of God is administered, and (4) from the fact that evils consequent on the apostasy of Adam are expressly declared in Scripture to be penal inflictions, but also (5) from the fact that the principle of imputation is involved in other great doctrines of the Bible. The assumption that one man cannot righteously, under the government of God, be punished for the sins of another is not only contrary, as we have seen, to the express declarations of Scripture and to the administration of the divine government from the beginning, but also subversive of the doctrines of atonement and justification.

The idea of the transfer of guilt or of vicarious punishment lies at the foundation of all the expiatory offerings in the Old Testament and of the great atonement under the new dispensation. To bear sin is, in Scriptural language, to bear the penalty of sin. The victim bore the sin of the offerer. To express the transfer of guilt, hands were imposed upon the head of the animal about to be slaughtered. That animal had to be free from all defect or blemish to make it the more apparent that its blood was shed not for its own deficiencies but for the sin of another. All this was symbolical and typical. There could be no real transfer of guilt to an irrational animal, and no real atonement by its blood. But these services were significant. They were intended to teach these great truths: (1) the penalty of sin is death; (2) sin cannot be pardoned without an atonement; and (3) atonement consists in vicarious punishment. The innocent takes the place of the guilty and bears the penalty in his stead. This is the idea attached to expiatory offerings in all ages and among all nations. This is the idea inculcated in every part of the Bible. And this is what the Scriptures teach concerning the atonement of Christ. He bore our sins; He was made a curse for us; He suffered the penalty of the law in our stead. All this proceeds on the ground that the sins of one man can be justly imputed to another.

In justification the same radical idea is included. Justification is not a subjective change in the moral state of the sinner; it is not mere pardon; it is not simply pardon and restoration to favour, as when a rebel is forgiven and restored to the enjoyment of his civil rights. It is a declaration that the demands of justice have been satisfied. It proceeds on the assumption that the righteousness which the law requires belongs either personally and inherently, or by imputation, to the person who is justified, or declared to be just. There is a logical connection, therefore, between the denial of the imputation of Adam's sin and the denial of the Scriptural doctrines of atonement and justification. The objections urged against the former bear equally against the latter doctrines. And it is a matter of history that those who reject the one reject also the others.

E. The Argument from Romans 5:12–21

The apostle in Romans 5:12–21 teaches this doctrine in the most formal and explicit manner. The design of that passage is to illustrate the method of salvation. The apostle had taught that all men are sinners and the whole world guilty before God. All men being under the condemnation of the law, it is impossible that they should be justified by the law. The same law cannot both justify and condemn the same persons. As therefore no flesh can be justified by the works of the law, God sent His Son for our salvation. He assumed our nature, took our place, and obeyed and suffered in our stead, and thus wrought out for us a perfect and infinitely meritorious righteousness. On the ground of that righteousness God can now be just in justifying the ungodly if, renouncing their own righteousness, they receive and trust in this righteousness of God which is freely offered to them in the gospel. The fundamental doctrine of the Epistle to the Romans, as it is the fundamental doctrine of the gospel, is, therefore, that the righteousness of one man, even Christ, can be and is so imputed to believers as to be the meritorious ground of their justification at the bar of God.

To make this doctrine the more plain to his readers, the apostle refers to the analogous case of the condemnation of the human race for the sin of Adam, and shows that as the sin of Adam is the judicial ground of the condemnation of all who were in him, i.e., of all represented by him, so the obedience of Christ is the judicial ground of the justification of all who are in Him. . . . The doctrine that Adam's sin is imputed to his posterity is asserted in the twelfth verse of this chapter. It was by one man, Paul says, that sin and death passed upon all men; all sinned through, or in, that one man. His sin was the sin of all in virtue of the union between them and him. The proof of this doctrine is contained in verses 13 and 14. The apostle argues thus: Punishment supposes sin, and sin supposes law, for sin is not imputed where there is no law. All men are punished; they are all subject to penal evils. They are, therefore, all chargeable with sin and consequently are all guilty of violation of law. That law cannot be the law of Moses, for men died (i.e., were subject to the penalty of the law) before that law was given. It cannot be the law as written on the heart, for those die who have never committed any personal sin. There are penal evils, therefore, which come upon all mankind prior to anything in their state or conduct to merit such infliction. The ground of that infliction must therefore be sought outside themselves, i.e., in the sin of their first parent. Hence Adam is a type of Christ. As the one is the head and representative of his race, so the other is the head and representative of His people. As the sin of the one is the ground of the condemnation of his posterity, so the righteousness of the other is the ground of the justification of all who are in Him.

But although there is this grand analogy between the fall and the redemption of man, there are nevertheless certain points of difference, all in favour of the scheme of redemption. If we die for the offence of one man, *much more* shall grace abound unto many through one man. If for *one* offence the sentence of condemnation passed on all, the free justification is from *many* offences. If condemned for a sin in which we had no personal and voluntary participation, how much more shall we live on account of a righteousness which we cordially receive. Therefore, continues the apostle, in the application of his illustration, if all men (in union with Adam) are condemned by the offence of one man, so also all (in union with Christ) shall be justified on the ground of the righteousness of one man. As one man's disobedience constituted us sinners, so the obedience of one man constitutes us righteous (vv. 18–19). . . .

Few can doubt, and few ever have doubted, that the apostle does here clearly teach that the sin of Adam is the judicial ground of the condemnation of his race. With this agrees not only, as we have already seen, the Scriptural account of the fall, but also what the apostle teaches in 1 Corinthians 15:21–22: "For since by man came death, by man came also the resurrection of the dead. For as in Adam all die, even so in Christ shall all be made alive." Union with Adam is the cause of death; union with Christ is the cause of life. . . .

⎡ **§10. Mediate Imputation** ⎤
| **§11. Preexistence** |
⎣ **§12. Realistic Theory** ⎦

§13. Original Sin

A. Statement of the Protestant Doctrine

The effects of Adam's sin upon his posterity are declared in our standards to be the guilt of his first sin, the loss of original righteousness, and the corruption of our whole nature. . . . This inherent corruption in which all men since the fall are born is properly called original sin because it is truly of the nature of sin, it flows from our first parents as the origin of our race, it is the origin of all other sins, and it is in its nature distinguished from actual sins.

The affirmative elements of the Protestant doctrine of original sin are: (1) corruption of nature affects the whole soul; (2) it consists in the loss or absence of original righteousness and consequent entire moral depravity of our nature, including or manifesting itself in an aversion from all spiritual good and from God as well as an inclination to all evil; (3) it is truly and properly of the nature of sin, involving both guilt and pollution; (4) it retains its character as sin even in the regenerated; and (5) it renders the soul spiritually dead, so that the natural or unrenewed man is entirely unable of himself to do anything good in the sight of God.

This doctrine therefore stands opposed to (1) the teaching that the race of man is uninjured by the fall of Adam; (2) the teaching that the evils consequent on the fall are merely physical; (3) the doctrine which makes original sin entirely negative, consisting in the want of original righteousness; (4) the doctrine which admits a hereditary depravity of nature and makes it consist in an inclination to sin, but denies that it is itself sinful; . . . (5) the teaching of those who, while admitting a moral deterioration which deserves the displeasure of God and which is therefore truly sin, yet deny that the evil is so great as to amount to spiritual death and to involve the entire inability of the natural man to what is spiritually good; and (6) the teachings of those who deny that original sin affects the whole man and assert that it has its seat exclusively in the affections or the heart, while the understanding and reason are uninjured or uninfluenced.

In order to sustain the Augustinian (or Protestant) doctrine of original sin, therefore, three points are to be established: (1) all mankind descending from Adam by ordinary generation are born destitute of original righteousness and infected with a corruption of nature which is truly and properly sin; (2) this original corruption affects the whole man—not the body only to the exclusion of the soul, not the lower faculties of the soul to the exclusion of the higher, and not the heart to the exclusion of the intellectual powers; and (3) this corruption is of such a nature that before regeneration fallen men are "utterly indisposed, disabled, and opposed to all good."

B. Proof of the Doctrine of Original Sin

1. Argument from the universality of sin

The first argument in proof of this doctrine is drawn from the universal sinfulness of men. All men are sinners. This is undeniably the doctrine of the Scriptures. It is asserted, assumed, and proved. The assertions of this fact are too numerous to be quoted: "There is no man that sinneth not" (1 Kings 8:46); "There is not a just man upon earth, that doeth good, and sinneth not" (Eccles. 7:20); "If we say that we have no sin, we deceive ourselves, and the truth is not in us" (1 John 1:8). Such are only a few of the Scriptural assertions of the universal sinfulness of men.

But in the second place, this melancholy fact is constantly assumed in the Word of God. The Bible everywhere addresses men as sinners. The religion which it reveals is a religion for sinners. All the institutions of the Old Testament and all the doctrines of the New take it for granted that men universally are under the power and condemnation of sin. "The world," as used in Scripture, designates the mass of mankind as distinguished from the Church or the regenerated people of God, and always involves in its application the idea of sin; e.g., "I have chosen you out of the world; therefore the world hateth you" (John 15:19). All the exhortations of the Scriptures addressed to men indiscriminately, calling them to repentance, of necessity assume the universality of sin. The same is true of the general threatenings and promises of the Word of God. In short, if all men are not sinners, the Bible is not adapted to their real character and state.

But the Scriptures not only directly assert and everywhere assume the universality of sin among men, but this is a point which perhaps more than any other is made the subject of a formal and protracted argument. Paul in his Epistle to the Romans begins with a regular process of proof that all, whether Jews or Gentiles, are under sin. Until this fact is admitted and acknowledged, there is no place for and no need of the gospel, which is God's method of saving sinners. . . .

What the Scriptures so clearly teach is taught no less clearly by experience and history. Every man knows that he himself is a sinner. He knows that every human being whom he has ever seen is in the same state of apostasy from God. History contains the record of no sinless man, save Christ Jesus, who, by being sinless, is distinguished from all other men. We have no account of any family, tribe, or nation free from the contamination of sin. The universality of sin among men is therefore one of the most undeniable doctrines of Scripture and one of the most certain facts of experience.

2. Argument from the entire sinfulness of men

This universal depravity of men is no slight evil. The whole human race, by their apostasy from God, are totally depraved. By total depravity is not meant that all men are equally wicked, nor that any man is as thoroughly corrupt as it is possible for a man to be, nor that men are destitute of all moral virtues. The Scriptures recognize the fact, which experience abundantly confirms, that men, to a greater or lesser degree, are honest in dealings, kind in their feelings, and beneficent in their conduct. Even the heathen, the apostle teaches us, do by nature the things of the law. They are more or less under the dominion of conscience, which approves or disapproves their moral conduct. All this is perfectly consistent with the Scriptural doctrine of total depravity, which includes the entire absence of holiness as well as the want of due apprehensions of the divine perfections and of our relation to God as our creator, preserver, benefactor, governor, and redeemer. There is common to all men a total alienation of the soul from God so that no unrenewed man either understands or seeks after God; no such man ever makes God his portion, or God's glory the end of his being. The apostasy from God is total or complete. All men worship and serve the creature rather than the creator. They are all therefore declared in Scripture to be spiritually dead. They are destitute of any principle of spiritual life. . . .

A proof of the dreadful evil of this hereditary corruption is seen in the universal rejection of Christ by those whom He came to save. He is in Himself the chief among ten thousand and altogether lovely, uniting in His own person all the perfections of the Godhead and all the excellences of humanity. His mission was one of love, of a love utterly incomprehensible, unmerited, immutable, and infinite. Through love He not only humbled Himself to be born of a woman and to be made under the law, but to live a life of poverty, sorrow, and persecution, to endure inconceivably great sufferings for our sakes, and finally to bear our sins in His own body on the tree. He has rendered it possible for God to be just and yet justify the ungodly. He therefore offers blessings of infinite value, without price, to all who will accept them. He has secured and offers to us wisdom, righteousness, sanctification, and redemption; He offers to make us kings and priests unto God and to exalt us to an unending state of inconceivable glory and blessedness. Notwithstanding all this—notwithstanding the divine excellence of His person, the greatness of His love, the depth of His sufferings, and the value of the blessings which He has provided and without which we must perish eternally—men universally, when left to themselves, reject Him. He came to His own, and His own received Him not. The world hated and still hates Him, will not recognize Him as their God and Saviour, will not accept of His offers, will neither love nor serve Him. The conduct of men towards Christ is the clearest proof of the apostasy of our race and of the depth of the depravity into which they are sunk; it is, so far as the hearers of the gospel are concerned, the great ground of their condemnation. All other grounds seem merged into this, for our Lord says that men are condemned because they do not believe in the only begotten Son of God (John 3:18). And the Holy Spirit by the mouth of Paul says, "If any man love not the Lord Jesus Christ, let him be Anathema Maranatha" (1 Cor. 16:22), a sentence which will be ratified in the day of judgment by every rational creature, fallen and unfallen, in the universe. . . .

On the subject of the entire sinfulness of men we may appeal to the experience of God's people in every age and in every part of the world. In no respect has that experience been more uniform than in the conviction of their depravity in the sight of an infinitely Holy God. The patriarch Job, represented as the best man of his generation, declared,

"I abhor myself, and repent in dust and ashes" (Job 42:6). David's penitential Psalms are filled not only with the confessions of sin, but also with the avowals of his deep depravity in the sight of God. Isaiah cried out, "Woe is me! for I am undone; because I am a man of unclean lips, and I dwell in the midst of a people of unclean lips" (Isa. 6:5). The ancient prophets, even when sanctified from the womb, pronounced their own righteousnesses to be filthy rags. What is said of the body politic is everywhere represented as true of the individual man. The whole head is sick and the whole heart faint. From the sole of the foot even unto the head there are wounds and bruises and putrefying sores. In the New Testament the sacred writers evince the same deep sense of their own sinfulness and strong conviction of the sinfulness of the race to which they belong. Paul speaks of himself as the chief of sinners. He groans under the burden of an evil nature, saying, "O wretched man that I am! who shall deliver me from the body of this death?" (Rom. 7:24). From the days of the apostles to the present time there has been no diversity as to this point in the experience of Christians. There is no disposition ever evinced by them to palliate or excuse their sinfulness before God. They uniformly humble and abhor themselves under a sense of their guilt and pollution. This is not an irrational nor exaggerated experience. It is the natural effect of the apprehension of the truth, of even a partial discernment of the holiness of God, the spirituality of the law, and the lack of conformity to that divine standard. There is always connected with this consciousness of sin the conviction that our sense of its evil and its power over us, and consequently of our guilt and pollution, is altogether inadequate. It is always a part of the believer's burden that he feels less than his reason and conscience, enlightened by the Scriptures, teach him he ought to feel of his moral corruption and degradation.

It need scarcely be added that what the Scriptures so manifestly teach indirectly of the depth of the corruption of our fallen nature, they teach also by direct assertion. The human heart is pronounced deceitful above all things and desperately wicked (Jer. 17:9). Even in the beginning it was said, "God saw that the wickedness of man was great in the earth, and that every imagination of the thoughts of his heart was only evil continually" (Gen. 6:5). With such passages the Word of God is filled. It in the most explicit terms pronounces the degradation and moral corruption of man consequent on the fall to be a total apostasy from God, a state of spiritual death implying the entire absence of any true holiness.

3. Argument from the early manifestation of sin

A third great fact of Scripture and experience on this subject is the early manifestation of sin. As soon as a child is capable of moral action, it gives evidence of a perverted moral character. Not only do we see the manifestations of anger, malice, selfishness, envy, pride, and other evil dispositions, but the whole development of the soul is toward the world. The soul of a child turns by an inward law from God to the creature, from the things that are unseen and eternal to the things that are seen and temporal. In its earliest manifestations it is worldly, of the earth, earthy. As this is the testimony of universal experience, so also it is the doctrine of the Bible: "Man [is] born like a wild ass's colt" (Job 11:12); "The wicked are estranged from the womb: they go astray as soon as they be born, speaking lies" (Ps. 58:3); "Foolishness (moral evil) is bound in the heart of a child" (Prov. 22:15). . . .

As the fact that all men perform moral actions is proof that they have a moral nature, so the fact that such moral action is always evil, or that all men sin from the earliest development of their powers, is a proof that their moral nature is depraved. It is utterly inconsistent with all just ideas of God that He created man with a nature which with absolute uniformity leads him to sin and destruction, or that He placed him in circumstances which inevitably secure his ruin. The present state of human nature cannot therefore be its normal and original condition. We are a fallen race. Our nature has become corrupted by our apostasy from God, and therefore every imagination (i.e., every exercise) of the thoughts of man's heart is only evil continually (see also Gen. 8:21). This is the Scriptural and the only rational solution of the undeniable fact of the deep, universal, and early manifested sinfulness of men in all ages, of every class, and in every part of the world. . . .

4. The Scriptures expressly teach the doctrine

The Scriptures not only indirectly teach, but also directly assert the doctrine of original sin or of the hereditary, sinful corruption of our nature as derived from Adam. Not only do they expressly teach that men sin universally from the first dawn of their being, but they also assert that the heart of man is evil; e.g., "The heart of the sons of men is fully set in them to do evil" (Eccles. 8:11; see also Gen. 6:5; 8:21; Jer. 17:9). By heart in Scriptural language is meant the man himself, the soul, the seat and source of life. It is that which thinks, feels, desires, and wills. It is that out of which good or evil thoughts, desires, and purposes proceed. It never signifies a mere act or a transient state of the soul. It is that which is abiding, which determines character. It bears the same relation to acts that the soil does to its productions. As a good soil brings forth herbs suited for man and beast, and an evil soil brings forth briars and thorns, so we are told that the human heart (human nature in its present state) is proved to be evil by the prolific crop of sins which it everywhere and always produces. Still more distinctly is this doctrine taught in Matthew 7:16–19, where our Lord says that men are known by their fruits (see also 12:33). . . .

The psalmist also directly asserts this doctrine when he says, "Behold, I was shapen in iniquity; and in sin did my mother conceive me" (Ps. 51:5). In the preceding verses he has confessed his actual sins, and he here humbles himself still more completely before God by acknowledging his innate, hereditary depravity—a depravity which he does not regard as a mere weakness or inclination to evil, but which he pronounces iniquity and sin. . . . What David says of himself as born in sin is confirmed by other representations of Scripture which show that what was true of him is no less true of all mankind. Thus Job asks, "Who can bring a clean thing out of an unclean?" and "What is man, that he should be clean? and he which is born of a woman, that he should be righteous?" (14:4; 15:14). Thus also our Lord says, "That which is born of the flesh is flesh" (John 3:6). This clearly means that whatever is born of corrupt parents is itself corrupt in virtue of its descent or derivation. . . .

Another way in which the Scriptures clearly teach the doctrine of original sin is to be found in the passages which describe the natural state of man since the fall. Men, all men, men of every nation, of every age, and of every condition, are represented as spiritually dead. The natural man, man as he is by nature, is destitute of the life of God, i.e., of spiritual life. His understanding is darkness, so that he does not know or receive the things of God (1 Cor. 2:14; Eph. 4:17–18). He is not susceptible of impression from the realities of the spiritual world. He is as insensible to them as a dead man to the things of this world. He is alienated from God and utterly unable to deliver himself from this state of corruption and misery. Only those who are renewed by the Holy Ghost, who are quickened or made alive by the power of God, and who are therefore called spiritual as governed and actuated by a higher principle than any which belongs to our fallen nature, are represented as delivered from this state in which men are born. . . .

Another argument in support of the doctrine of original sin is that the Bible everywhere teaches that all men need redemption through the blood of Christ. The Scriptures know of no salvation other than through the redemption which is in Christ Jesus. This is so plainly the doctrine of the Bible that it never has been questioned in the Christian Church. Infants need redemption as surely as adults do, for they also are included in the covenant of grace. But redemption, in the Christian sense of the term, is deliverance through the blood of Christ from the power and consequences of sin. Christ came to save sinners. He saves none but sinners. If He saves infants, infants must be in a state of sin. . . . The Bible clearly teaches that the death of Christ is absolutely necessary; had there been any other way in which men could be saved, Christ is dead in vain (Gal. 2:21; 3:21). The question rises, If men were an unfallen, uncorrupted race, and if they could be preserved from sin by a mere change of their circumstances, why should there be the costly array of remedial means, the incarnation, the sufferings and death of the eternal Son of God, for their salvation? It is perfectly plain that the whole Scriptural plan of redemption is founded on the apostasy of the whole human race from God. It assumes that men, all men, infants as well as adults, are in a state of sin and misery from which none but a divine Saviour can deliver them. . . .

5. *Argument from the universality of death*

Another decisive argument on this subject is drawn from the universality of death. Death, according to the Scriptures, is a penal evil. It presupposes sin. No rational moral creature is subject to death except on account of sin. Infants die, therefore infants are the subjects of sin. . . . The physical death of infants is a patent proof that they are subject to the penalty which came on men (which entered the world and passed on all men) on account of one man or by one man's disobedience. And as that penalty was death spiritual as well as the dissolution of the body, the death of infants is a Scriptural and decisive proof of their being born destitute of original righteousness and infected with a sinful corruption of nature. . . .

C. *Objections*

The objections to this doctrine, it must be admitted, are many and serious. But this is true of all the great doctrines of religion, whether natural or revealed. . . . For example, we know that God is and that He governs all His creatures, but we do not know how His effectual controlling agency is consistent with the free agency of rational beings. We know that sin and misery exist in the world, and we know that God is infinite in power, holiness, and benevolence. But how to reconcile the prevalence of sin with the character of God we know not. Nevertheless, a statement or doctrine against which there are seemingly unanswerable objections may be and often certainly is true. There are two important practical principles which follow from the fact just mentioned. First, our inability to free any well-authenticated truth from objections or difficulties is not a sufficient or a rational ground for rejecting it. And, secondly, any objection against a religious doctrine is to be regarded as sufficiently answered if it can be shown to bear with equal force against an undeniable fact. If the objection is not a rational reason for denying the fact, it is not a rational reason for rejecting the doctrine. This is the method which the sacred writers adopt in vindicating truth.

Almost all the objections against the doctrine of original sin are in conflict with one or the other of the principles just mentioned. Either they are addressed not to the Scriptural and experiential evidences of the truth of the doctrine, but to the difficulty of reconciling it with other truths; or it is insisted that these objections are fatal to the doctrine even though they obviously are just as valid against certain undeniable facts as they are against the teachings of Scripture.

1. The objection that men are responsible only for their voluntary acts

The most obvious objection to the doctrine of original sin is founded on the assumption that nothing can have moral character except voluntary acts and the states of mind which result from or are produced by our voluntary agency, and which are subject to the power of the will. This objection rests on a principle which has already been considered. It reaches very far. If it be sound, then there can be no such thing as concreated holiness, or habitual grace, or innate, inherent, or indwelling sin. But the moral character of dispositions depends on their nature and not on their origin. Adam was holy, although so created. Saints are holy, although regenerated and sanctified by the almighty power of God. And therefore the soul as the subject of sinful dispositions is truly sinful, although those dispositions are innate and entirely beyond the control of the will. . . .

2. Objection founded on the justice of God

It is objected that it is inconsistent with the justice of God that men should come into the world in a state of sin. In answer to this objection it may be remarked (1) that whatever God does must be right. If He permits men to be born in sin, that fact must be consistent with His divine perfection. (2) It is a fact of experience no less than a doctrine of Scripture that men are either, as the Church teaches, born in a state of sin and condemnation or, as all men must admit, in a state which inevitably leads to their becoming sinful and miserable. The objection, therefore, bears against an undeniable fact as much as against a Scriptural doctrine. We must either deny God or admit that the universality of sin among men is compatible with His nature and with His government of the world. (3) The Bible, as often before remarked, accounts for and vindicates the corruption of our race on the ground that mankind had a full and fair probation in Adam and that the spiritual death in which they are born is part of the judicial penalty of his transgression. If we reject this solution of the fact, we cannot deny the fact itself, which, being a fact, must be consistent with the character of God.

3. The doctrine represents God as the author of sin

A third objection often and confidently urged is that the Church doctrine on this subject makes God the author of sin. God is the author of our nature. If our nature be sinful, God must be the author of sin. The obvious fallacy of this syllogism is that the word nature is used in one sense in the major proposition and in a different sense in the minor. In the one it means substance or essence; in the other, natural disposition. It is true that God is the author of our essence. . . . But He is not the author of the evil dispositions with which that essence is infected at birth. The doctrine of original sin in no way attributes to God the production of evil. It simply supposes that He judicially abandons our apostate race and withholds from the descendants of Adam the manifestations of His favour and love, which are the life of the soul. That the inevitable consequence of this judicial abandonment is spiritual death no more makes God the author of sin than the immorality and desperate and unchanging wickedness of the reprobate, from whom God withholds His Spirit, are to be referred to the infinitely Holy One as their author. . . .

4. It is said to destroy the free agency of men

It is further objected to this doctrine that it destroys the free agency of man. If we are born with a corrupt nature by which we are inevitably determined to sinful acts, we cease to be free in performing those acts and consequently are not responsible for them. This objection is founded on a particular theory of liberty and must stand or fall with it. The same objection is urged against the doctrines of decrees, of efficacious grace, of the perseverance of the saints, and all other doctrines which assume that a free act can be absolutely certain as to its occurrence. It is enough here to remark that the doctrine of original sin supposes that men, in sinning under the influence of a corrupt nature, have the same kind and degree of liberty that saints and angels have in acting rightly under the influence of a holy nature. To act according to its nature is the only liberty which belongs to any created being.

§14. The Seat of Original Sin

Now that we have considered the nature of original sin, the next question concerns its seat. According to one theory, the seat of original sin is the body. Some theologians maintain that the only evil effect of Adam's sin upon his posterity is the disorder of our physical nature, whereby undue influence is secured to bodily appetites and passions. . . . Another position is that the heart, considered as the seat of the affections as distinguished from the understanding, is the seat of natural depravity. This position is connected with the idea that all sin and holiness are forms of feeling or states of the affections. It is also made the ground on which the nature of regeneration and conversion, the relation between repentance and faith, and other points of practical theology are explained. Everything is made to depend on the inclinations or state of the feelings. Instead of the affections following the understanding, the understanding, it is said, follows the affections. A man understands and receives the truth only when he loves it. Regeneration is simply a change in the state of the affections, and the only inability under which sinners labour as to the things of God is disinclination. In opposition to all these positions Augustinianism teaches that the whole man, soul and body, the higher as well as the lower, the intellectual as well as the emotional faculties of the soul, is affected by the corruption our nature derived from our first parents.

The Scriptures . . . clearly represent the body as affected by the apostasy of our race. Not only is it employed in the service of sin or as an instrument to unrighteousness, but it is in every respect deteriorated. It is inordinate in its cravings, rebellious, and hard to restrain. It is, as the apostle says, the opposite of the glorious, spiritual body with which the believer is hereafter to be invested.

In addition to the body the soul—the whole soul—is the seat of original sin. The theory that the affections (or the heart in the limited sense of that word), to the exclusion of the rational faculties, are alone affected by original sin is unscriptural. Indeed, there are several evidences that the Bible represents the whole soul as the subject of inherent corruption:

(1) Unlike philosophy the Scriptures do not make a broad distinction between the understanding and the heart. They speak of "the thoughts and intents of the heart" (Heb. 4:12) as well as of its emotions and affections. The whole immaterial principle is in the Bible designated as the soul, the spirit, the mind, the heart. And therefore when the Bible speaks of the heart, it means the man, the self, that in which personal individuality resides. If the heart be corrupt, the whole soul in all its powers is corrupt.

(2) The opposite position assumes that there is nothing moral in our cognitions or judgments, that all knowledge is purely speculative. According to the Scripture, however, the chief sins of men consist in their wrong judgments, in thinking and believing evil to be good and good to be evil. This in its highest form, as our Lord teaches us, is the

unpardonable sin or blasphemy against the Holy Ghost. It was because the Pharisees thought that Christ was evil, that His works were the works of Satan, that He declared that they could never be forgiven. . . . It is, as the Bible clearly reveals, because men are ignorant of God, and blind to the manifestation of His glory in the person of His Son, that they are lost. On the other hand, the highest form of moral excellence consists in knowledge. To know God is eternal life. To know Christ is to be like Christ. . . . Nothing can be more repugnant to the philosophy of the Bible than the dissociation of moral character from knowledge, and nothing can be more at variance with our own consciousness. We know that every affection in a rational creature includes an exercise of the cognitive faculties, and every exercise of our cognitive faculties, in relation to moral and religious subjects, includes the exercise of our moral nature.

(3) A third argument on this subject is drawn from the fact that the Bible represents the natural or unrenewed man as blind or ignorant as to the things of the Spirit. It declares that he cannot know them. And the fallen condition of human nature is represented as consisting primarily in this mental blindness. Men are corrupt, says the apostle, through the ignorance that is in them.

(4) Conversion is said to consist in a translation from darkness to light. God is said to open the eyes. The eyes of the understanding (or heart) are said to be enlightened (Eph. 1:18). All believers are declared to be the subjects of a spiritual illumination. Paul describes his own conversion as the revelation of Jesus Christ to him. God opened his eyes to enable him to see that Jesus is the Son of God, God manifest in the flesh. Paul thereby became a new creature, and his whole life was thenceforth devoted to the service of Him whom before he hated and persecuted.

(5) Knowledge is said to be the effect of regeneration. Men are renewed so as to know. They are brought to the knowledge of the truth, and they are sanctified by the truth. From all these considerations it is evident that the whole man is the subject of original sin, that our cognitive as well as our emotional nature is involved in the depravity consequent on our apostasy from God, and that in knowing as well as in loving or in willing, we are under the influence and dominion of sin.

§15. Inability

A. The Protestant Doctrine

. . . In the Church there have been three general views as to the ability of fallen man. The first, the Pelagian doctrine, asserts the plenary ability of sinners to do all that God requires of them. The second is the Semi-Pelagian doctrine (taking the word Semi-Pelagian in its wide and popular sense), which admits the powers of man to have been weakened by the fall of the race, but denies that he lost all ability to perform what is spiritually good. The third is the Augustinian or Protestant doctrine, which teaches that such is the nature of inherent, hereditary depravity that men since the fall are utterly unable to turn themselves unto God or to do anything truly good in His sight. With these three views of the ability of fallen men are connected corresponding views of grace, i.e., of the influence and operations of the Holy Spirit in man's regeneration and conversion. Pelagians deny the necessity of any supernatural influence of the Spirit in the regeneration and sanctification of men. Semi-Pelagians admit the necessity of such divine influence to assist the enfeebled powers of man in the work of turning unto God, but claim that the sinner cooperates in that work and that upon his voluntary cooperation the issue depends. Augustinians and Protestants ascribe the whole work of regeneration to the Spirit of God, the soul being passive therein, the subject and not the agent of the change. . . .

B. The Nature of the Sinner's Inability

The inability under which man is said to labour since the fall does not arise from the loss of any faculty of his mind or of any original, essential attribute of his nature. He retains his reason, will, and conscience. He has the intellectual power of cognition, the power of self-determination, and the faculty of discerning between moral good and evil. His conscience, as the apostle says, approves or disapproves of his moral acts.

The doctrine of man's inability, therefore, does not assume that man has ceased to be a free moral agent. He is free because he determines his own acts. Every volition is an act of free self-determination. . . . Whenever he sins, he acts freely against the convictions of conscience or the precepts of the moral law. That a man is in such a state that he uniformly prefers and chooses evil instead of good, as do the fallen angels, is not inconsistent with his free moral agency. . . .

According to the Scriptures, man's inability consists in the want of power rightly to discern spiritual things, and the consequent want of all right affections toward them. This want of power of spiritual discernment arises from the corruption of our whole nature, by which the reason or understanding is blinded, and the taste and feelings are perverted. As this state of mind is innate, as it is a state or condition of our nature, it lies below the will and is beyond its power, controlling both our affections and our volitions. . . . Everywhere in the Scriptures it is asserted or assumed that the feelings follow the understanding, that the illumination of the mind in the due apprehension of spiritual objects is the necessary preliminary condition of all right feeling and conduct. We must know God in order to love Him. This is distinctly asserted by the apostle in 1 Corinthians 2:14. He there says that the natural or unrenewed man does not receive the things of the Spirit, for they must be spiritually discerned. It is ignorance, the want of discernment of the beauty, excellence, and suitableness of the things of the Spirit (i.e., of the truths which the Spirit has revealed), that is the reason or cause of unbelief (see also Eph. 4:18). . . . Hence true conversion is said to be effected by a revelation. . . . In accordance with this principle that knowledge is essential to holiness, true religion and life everlasting are said to consist in the knowledge of God (John 17:3), and men are said to be saved and sanctified by the truth. . . .

It should be noted that man's inability since the fall relates only to "the things of the Spirit." He has retained not only the liberty of choice or power of self-determination, but also the ability to perform moral acts, good as well as evil. He can be kind and just and fulfil his social duties in a manner to secure the approbation of his fellow men. This is not to say that the state of mind in which these acts are performed, or the motives by which they are determined, are such as to meet the approbation of an infinitely holy God, but simply that these acts, as to the matter of them, are prescribed by the moral law. Those areas where fallen man retains his ability are designated "things external"; those areas where he has lost his ability are designated "the things of God," "the things of the Spirit," "things connected with salvation." Although it may not be easy to state in words the difference between these two classes of acts, it is universally recognized. There is an obvious difference between morality and religion, and between those affections of reverence and of gratitude which all men more or less experience and true piety. The difference lies in the state of mind, the motives, and the apprehension of the objects of these affections. It is the difference between holiness and mere natural feeling. What the Bible and all the confessions of the churches of the Reformation assert is that man, since the fall, cannot change his own heart; he cannot regenerate his soul; he cannot repent with godly sorrow or exercise that faith which is unto salvation. He cannot, in short, put forth any holy exercise or perform any act in such a way as to merit the approbation of God. Sin cleaves to all he does, and from the dominion of sin he cannot free himself. . . .

C. Proof of the Doctrine

The first and most obvious argument in support of the Augustinian or orthodox argument on this subject is the negative one; that is, the fact that the Scriptures nowhere attribute to fallen men ability to change their own hearts or to turn themselves unto God. As their salvation depends on their regeneration, if that work is within the compass of their own powers, it is incredible that the Bible never rests the obligation of effecting it upon the sinner's ability. If he has the power to regenerate himself, we should expect to find the Scriptures affirming his possession of this ability and calling upon him to exercise it. . . .

Besides this negative testimony of the Scriptures, we have the repeated and explicit declarations of the Word of God on this subject. Our Lord compares the relation between Himself and His people to that which exists between the vine and its branches. The point of analogy is the absolute dependence common to both relations: "As the branch cannot bear fruit of itself, except it abide in the vine; no more can ye, except ye abide in me. . . . Without me ye can do nothing" (John 15:4–5). We are here taught that Christ is the only source of spiritual life, that those who do not abide in Him are destitute of that life and of all ability to produce its appropriate fruits, and that even those who are in Him do not possess this ability of themselves, but derive it entirely from Him. In like manner the apostle asserts his insufficiency (or inability) to do anything of himself. Our "sufficiency," he says, "is of God" (2 Cor. 3:5). Christ tells the Jews, "No man can come to me, except the Father which hath sent me draw him" (John 6:44). . . . In 1 Corinthians 2:14 it is said, "The natural man receiveth not the things of the Spirit of God: for they are foolishness unto him: neither can he know them, because they are spiritually discerned. . . ." This passage not only asserts the fact of the sinner's inability, but teaches the ground or source of it. It is no mere aversion or disinclination, but the lack of true knowledge. No man can see the beauty of a work of art without aesthetic discernment; and no man, according to the apostle, can see the truth and beauty of spiritual things without spiritual discernment. Such is the constant representation of Scripture. Men are everywhere spoken of and regarded not only as guilty and polluted, but also as helpless. . . .

D. Objections

The most obvious and plausible objection to this doctrine is the old one so often considered already, namely, that it is inconsistent with moral obligation. A man, it is said, cannot be justly required to do anything for which he has not the requisite ability. The fallacy of this objection lies in the way in which it has been applied. It is self-evidently true in one sphere, but utterly untrue in another. It is true that the blind cannot justly be required to see, or the deaf to hear. A child cannot be required to understand the calculus, or an uneducated man to read the classics. These things belong to the sphere of nature. The inability which thus limits obligation arises out of the limitations which God has imposed on our nature. On the other hand, when the inability arises not out of the limitation, but out of the moral corruption of our nature, the principle in question does not apply in the sphere of morals and religion. . . . There is an obligation when one's inability arises from sin and can be removed by the removal of sin. And as it has been shown from Scripture that the inability of the sinner to repent and believe, to love God and to lead a holy life, does not arise from the limitation of his nature as a creature (as is the case with idiots or brutes), nor from the want of the requisite faculties or capacity, but simply from the corruption of our nature, it follows that it does not exonerate him from the obligation to be and to do all that God requires. . . .

Another popular objection to the Scriptural doctrine on this subject is that it destroys all rational grounds on which rests the use of the means of grace. If we cannot accomplish a given end, why should we use the means for its accomplishment? So the farmer might say, If I cannot secure a harvest, why should I cultivate my fields? But in every department of human activity the result depends on the cooperation of causes over which man has no control. He is expected to use the means adapted to the desired end and trust for the cooperation of other agencies without which his own efforts are of no avail. The Scriptural grounds on which we are bound to use the means of grace are (1) the command of God. This of itself is enough. Even if there is no apparent adaptation of the means to the end and no connection which we can discover between them, the command of God is still a sufficient reason and motive for their diligent use. There was no natural adaptation in the waters of the Jordan to heal the leprosy, or in those of the pool of Siloam to restore sight to the blind. It would, however, have been fatal folly on the part of Naaman to refuse on that account to obey the command to bathe himself seven times, and on the part of the blind man to refuse to wash in the pool as Jesus directed. (2) If the command of God is enough even when there is no apparent connection between the means and the end, much more is it enough when the means have a natural adaptation to the end. We can see such adaptation in the department of nature, and it is no less apparent in that of grace. There is an intimate connection between truth and holiness, as between sowing the grain and reaping the harvest. Man sows but God gives the increase in the one case as well as in the other. (3) Not only is there this natural adaptation of the means of grace to the end to be accomplished, but in all ordinary cases the end cannot be attained without the use of those means. Men are not saved without the truth. Those who do not seek fail to find. Those who refuse to ask do not receive. This is as much the ordinary course of the divine administration in the kingdom of grace as in the kingdom of nature. (4) We have not only the experience of this visible connection between the means of grace and the salvation of the soul, but also the express promise of God that those who seek shall find, that those who ask shall receive, and that to those who knock it shall be opened. More than this cannot be rationally demanded. It is more than is given to the men of the world to stimulate them in their exertions to secure wealth or knowledge. The doctrine of inability, therefore, does not impair the force of any of the motives which should determine sinners to exercise all diligence in seeking their own salvation in the way which God has appointed. . . .

Chapter IX

Free Agency

In all discussions concerning sin and grace, the question concerning the nature of free agency is of necessity involved. . . . There is a theory of free agency with which the doctrines of original sin and of efficacious grace are utterly irreconcilable, and there is another theory with which those doctrines are perfectly consistent. In all ages of the Church, therefore, those who have adopted the former of these theories reject those doctrines; and, on the other hand, those who are constrained to believe those doctrines are no less constrained to adopt the other and congenial theory of free agency. . . . This is a question which every theologian finds in his path and which he must dispose of. . . . On this matter there is but one sure guide and but one path to either truth or unity, the Spirit and Word of God; happy are those who submit to be led by that guide and to walk in that path.

§1. Different Theories of the Will

A. Necessity

The doctrine of fatalism teaches that all events are determined by a blind necessity. This necessity does not arise from the will of an intelligent Being governing all creatures and all their acts according to their nature and for purposes of wisdom and goodness, but from a law of sequence to which God (or rather the gods) as well as men is subject. It precludes the idea of foresight or plan, the voluntary selection of an end, and the adoption of means for its accomplishment. Things are as they are, and must be as they are, and are to be, without any rational cause. This theory ignores any distinction between physical laws and free agency. The acts of men and the operations of nature are determined by a necessity of the same kind. Events are like a mighty stream borne onward by a resistless force—an external force which cannot be controlled or modified. . . .

B. Contingency (Uncertainty)

Directly opposed to necessity is the doctrine of contingency, which has been held under different names and variously modified. Sometimes it is called the liberty of indifference, by which is meant that the will, at the moment of decision, is self-poised among conflicting motives and decides one way or the other, not because it is influenced by one motive more than the others, but because it is indifferent or undetermined, able to act in accordance with the weaker against the stronger motive, or even without any motive at all. Sometimes this doctrine is expressed by the phrase self-determining power of the will. This phrase is intended to deny that the will is determined by motives and to affirm that the reason of its decisions is to be sought in itself. It is a cause and not an effect and therefore requires nothing outside itself to account for its acts. Sometimes this doctrine is called the power of contrary choice; that is to say, in every volition there is and must be power to do the contrary. Thus in a situation where all antecedents external and internal are precisely the same, the decision might well be the reverse of the one actually made. Contingence is therefore necessary to liberty. This is the essential idea of this theory in all its forms. A contingent event is one which may or may not happen. Contingence, therefore, is opposed not merely to necessity, but also to certainty. If a man may act in opposition to all motives external and internal, and in despite of all influence which can be exerted on him short of destroying his liberty, then it must forever remain uncertain how he will act. The advocates of this theory of liberty therefore maintain that the will is independent of reason, of feeling, and of God. There is no middle ground, they say, between contingency (i.e., uncertainty) and fatalism, between the independence of the will and of the agent and the denial of all free agency....

C. Certainty

The third general theory on this subject is separated by an equal distance from the doctrine of necessity on the one hand and that of contingency on the other. It teaches that a man is free when his outward acts and volitions are truly and properly his own, determined by nothing outside himself but proceeding from his own views, feelings, and immanent dispositions, so that they are the real, intelligent, and conscious expression of his character or of what is in his mind....

By the old Latin writers the theory of moral certainty is commonly designated rational spontaneity. This implies that in every volition there are the elements of rationality and spontaneous action. In brutes there is a spontaneity but no reason, and therefore they are not free agents in such a sense as to be the objects of approbation or disapprobation. In maniacs also there is self-determination, but it is irrational and therefore not free. But wherever reason and the power of self-determination or spontaneity are combined in an agent, he is free and responsible for his outward acts and for his volitions....

To sum up the general theory of certainty: The will is not determined by any law of necessity, nor is it independent, indifferent, and self-determined, but it is always determined by the preceding state of mind, so that a man is free so long as his volitions are the conscious expression of his own mind, or so long as his activity is determined and controlled by his reason and feelings.

§2. Definitions of Terms

... No little ambiguity arises from confounding liberty of the will with liberty of the agent. These forms of expression are ... not really equivalent. The man may be free when his will is in bondage. It is a correct and established usage of language, expressive of a real fact of consciousness, to speak of an enslaved will in a free agent. This is not a mere metaphor but a philosophical truth. He that commits sin is the servant of sin. Long-continued mental or bodily habits may bring the will into bondage, while the man continues a free agent. The will of a man who has been for years a miser is in a state of slavery, yet the man himself is perfectly free. He is self-determined. His avarice is himself. It is his own darling, cherished feeling. . . . We maintain that the man is free, but we deny that the will is free in the sense of being independent of reason, conscience, and feeling. In other words, a man cannot be independent of himself, nor can any one of his faculties be independent of all the rest.

Another source of confusion on this subject is the failure to distinguish between liberty and ability. The usage which attaches the same meaning to these terms is very ancient. Augustine denied free will to man since the fall. Pelagius affirmed freedom of will to be essential to our nature. The former intended simply to deny to fallen man the ability to turn himself unto God. The latter defined liberty to be the ability at any moment to determine oneself either for good or for evil. The controversy between Luther and Erasmus was really about ability; nominally it was about free will. . . . This usage pervades all the symbols of the Reformation and was followed by the theologians of the sixteenth century. They all ascribe free agency to man in the true sense of the words, but deny to him freedom of will. To a great extent this confusion is still kept up. Many of the prevalent definitions of liberty are definitions of ability, and much that is commonly advanced to prove the liberty of the will is really intended to support the doctrine of ability. . . .

But liberty and ability are distinct and should not be confounded. We are conscious of liberty. We know ourselves to be free in all our volitions. They reveal themselves to our inmost consciousness as acts of self-determination. We cannot disown them or escape responsibility for them even if we try, and yet no man is conscious of ability to change his own heart. Free agency belongs to God, to angels, to saints in glory, to fallen men, and to Satan; and it is the same in all. Yet in the strictest sense of the words, God cannot do evil; neither can Satan recover, by a volition, his lost inheritance of holiness. It is a great evil thus to confound things essentially distinct. It produces endless confusion. . . .

Confusion of thought and language, however, is not the principal evil which arises from making liberty and ability identical. It necessarily brings us into conflict with the truth and with the moral judgments of men. There are three truths of which every man is convinced from the very constitution of his nature: (1) he is a free agent; (2) none but free agents can be accountable for their character or conduct; and (3) he does not possess ability to change his moral state by an act of the will. . . . Free agency is the power to decide according to our character; ability is the power to change our character by a volition. The former, the Bible and consciousness affirm belongs to man in every condition of his being; the latter, the Bible and consciousness teach with equal explicitness does not belong to fallen man. The two things, therefore, ought not to be confounded. . . .

§3. Certainty Consistent with Liberty

Although the doctrine of necessity subverts the foundation of all morality and religion, our present concern is with the doctrine of contingency. We wish simply to state the case as between certainty and uncertainty. The doctrine of necessity, in the proper sense of the word, is anti-Christian, but the Christian world is and ever has been divided between the advocates and opponents of the doctrine of contingency. All Augustinians maintain that a free act may be inevitably certain as to its occurrence. All anti-Augustinians, whether Pelagians, Semi-Pelagians, or Arminians, and most moral philosophers and metaphysicians take the opposite ground. They teach that as the will has a self-determining power, it may decide against all motives internal or external, against all influences divine or human, so that its decisions cannot be rendered inevitable without destroying its liberty. The very essence of liberty, they say, is power to do the contrary. In other words, a free act is one performed with the consciousness that under precisely the same circumstances, that is, in the same internal as well as external state of the mind, the act performed might have been the opposite. . . . According to the one doctrine, our acts are or may be inevitably certain and yet be free; according to the other, in order to be free, they must be uncertain. . . . The point at issue, then, is, May the acts of free agents be rendered inevitably certain without destroying their liberty? . . .

It is a strong argument in favour of that view which makes free agency consistent with certainty, or which supposes that an agent may be determined with inevitable certainty as to his acts and yet those acts remain free, that it suits all classes or conditions of free agents. To deny free agency to God would be to deny Him personality and to reduce Him to a mere power or principle. And yet, in all the universe, is there anything so certain as that God will do right? . . . The saints in heaven beyond doubt continue to be free agents, and yet their acts are and to everlasting will be determined with absolute and inevitable certainty to good. . . . Moreover, when we look on a newborn infant, we know that whatever may be uncertain in its future, it is absolutely, inevitably certain that, should it live, it will sin. In every aspect, therefore, in which we can contemplate free agency, whether in God, in the redeemed in heaven, or in man here on earth, we find that it is compatible with absolute certainty.

A second argument on this subject is derived from those doctrines of Scripture which necessarily suppose that free acts may be certain as to their occurrence.

(1) The first and most obvious of these doctrines is the foreknowledge of God. . . . To deny foreknowledge to God, to say that free acts, because necessarily uncertain as to their occurrence, are not the objects of foreknowledge, . . . is to destroy the very idea of God. The future must be as dark to Him as to us, and He must every moment be receiving vast accessions of knowledge. He cannot be an eternal Being pervading all duration with a simultaneous existence, much less an omniscient Being to whom there is nothing new. It is impossible, therefore, to believe in God as He is revealed in the Bible unless we believe that all things are known unto Him from the beginning. But if all things are known, all things, whether fortuitous or free, are certain; consequently, certainty must be consistent with freedom. . . .

(2) Another doctrine which of necessity precludes the doctrine of contingency is that of the foreordination of future events. Those who believe that God foreordains whatever comes to pass must believe that the occurrence of all events is determined with unalterable certainty. . . . Whereas foreknowledge supposes the certainty of free acts, foreordination secures their certainty. If their being certain is consistent with liberty, their being rendered certain cannot be incompatible with it. All that foreordination does is to render it certain that specific free acts shall occur. The whole difficulty lies in their being certain— a point which must be admitted by every consistent theist. Our object here is not to prove foreknowledge or foreordination, but simply to note that those who believe that the Bible teaches the doctrine of foreordination must conclude that an event may be free and yet certain, and that the theory of contingency, which supposes that if an act is to be free it must be uncertain, is unscriptural and false.

(3) The doctrine of divine providence involves the same conclusion. That doctrine teaches that God so governs all His creatures and all their actions as to accomplish all His purposes. . . . Foreknowledge supposes certainty, foreordination determines it, and providence effects it. . . . Is there any one who because of a metaphysical difficulty— e.g., his inability to comprehend how God can effectually govern free agents without destroying their nature—would give up the doctrine of providence? Who would wish to see the reins of universal empire fall from the hands of infinite wisdom and love to be seized by chance or fate? Who would not rather be governed by a Father than by a tornado? But if God were unable to effectually control the acts of free

agents, there could be no prophecy, no prayer, no thanksgiving, no promises, no security of salvation, no certainty whether in the end God or Satan is to be triumphant, whether heaven or hell is to be the consummation. Give us certainty—the secure conviction that a sparrow cannot fall, or a sinner move a finger, but as God permits and ordains. . . . And if God has a providence, He must be able to render the free acts of His creatures certain; therefore, certainty must be consistent with liberty. Was it not certain that Christ would, according to the Scriptures, be by wicked hands crucified and slain, and yet were not His murderers free in all they did? . . .

(4) The whole Christian world believes that God can convert men. They believe that He can effectually lead them to repentance and faith, and that He can secure them in heaven from ever falling into sin. That is, they believe that He can render their free acts absolutely certain. . . . Since this is just as much a part of the established faith of Christians as is the divinity of our Redeemer, the idea that contingency is necessary to liberty cannot be reconciled with Christian doctrine. Although this idea has been extensively held by Christians, it is in obvious conflict with doctrines which they themselves as Christians must admit. If God can fulfil His promise to give men a new heart, if He can translate them from the kingdom of darkness into the kingdom of His dear Son, if He can give them repentance unto life, if there be no impropriety in praying that He would preserve them from falling and give them the secure possession of eternal life, then He can control their free acts. He can, by His grace, without violating their freedom, make it absolutely certain that they will repent and believe and persevere in holiness. If these things are so, then it is evident that any theory which makes contingency or uncertainty essential to liberty must be irreconcilable with some of the plainest and most precious doctrines of the Scriptures. . . .

The doctrine of free agency, therefore, which underlies the Bible, is at an equal remove, on the one hand, from the doctrine of physical or mechanical necessity, which precludes the possibility of liberty and responsibility; and, on the other, from the doctrine of contingency, which assumes that an act in order to be free must be uncertain, or that the will is self-determined, acting independently of the reason, conscience, inclinations, and feelings. It teaches that a man is a free and responsible agent in that he is author of his own acts, being led to them not by anything external to himself, but by his own views, convictions, inclinations, feelings, and dispositions, so that his acts are the true products of the man and really represent or reveal what he is. . . .

Soteriology

The Plan of Salvation

§1. God Has Such a Plan

The Scriptures speak of an economy of redemption—the plan or purpose of God in relation to the salvation of men.... Paul, for example, makes mention of God's plan to gather all the objects of redemption into one harmonious body in Christ (Eph. 1:10). It was the great design of the gospel to reveal this mysterious purpose or plan which had been hidden for ages in God. Thus is made known to principalities and powers the manifold wisdom of God (Eph. 3:9–11).

A plan supposes (1) the selection of some definite end or object to be accomplished, (2) the choice of appropriate means, and (3) effectual application and control of those means to the accomplishment of the contemplated end. As God works according to a definite plan in the external world, it is fair to infer that the same is true in reference to the moral and spiritual world. To the eye of an uneducated man the heavens are a chaos of stars. The astronomer, however, sees order and system in this confusion. . . . Similarly, the innumerable forms of vegetable life are not a confused mass, but to the eye of science arrange themselves into regular classes, orders, genera, and species exhibiting a unity of design pervading the whole. . . . As in all these lower departments of His works God acts according to a preconceived plan, it is not to be supposed that in the higher sphere of His operations, which concerns the destiny of men, everything is left to chance and allowed to take its undirected course to an undetermined end. We accordingly find that the Scriptures distinctly assert in reference to the dispensations of grace not only that God sees the end from the beginning, but that He works all things according to His eternal purpose.

A. The Importance of a Knowledge of This Plan

It is obviously of the greatest importance that God's plan concerning the redemption of man be known and correctly apprehended. . . . If we are ignorant of the great end aimed at in the scheme of redemption, or of the relation of the several parts of that scheme, or if we misconceive that end and that relation, all our views will necessarily be confused or erroneous. We shall be unable either to exhibit God's plan to others or to apply it to ourselves. If the end of redemption as well as of creation and of providence is the production of the greatest amount of happiness, then Christianity is one thing; if the end is the glory of God, then Christianity is another thing. The whole character of our theology and religion depends on the answer to that question. In like manner, if the special and proximate design of redemption is to render certain the salvation of the people of God, then the whole Augustinian system follows by a logical necessity; if its design is simply to render the salvation of all men possible, the Arminian system must be received as true. The order of the divine decrees or, in other words, the relation in which the several parts of the divine plan stand to each other is therefore very far from being a matter of idle speculation. It determines our theology, and our theology determines our religion!

B. *How the Plan of God Can Be Known*

Here the question arises, How can we ascertain the preconceived divine scheme relating to the salvation of men? The first answer to this question is that the interrelationships in every system of facts are revealed in the very nature of the facts. The astronomer, the geologist, and the zoologist very soon discover that the facts of their several sciences stand in a certain relation to each other and admit of no other. If this relation is not recognized, the facts themselves will be denied or distorted. The only source of mistake is either an incomplete induction of the facts or a failure to allow them their due relative importance. One system of astronomy has given place to another only because the earlier astronomers were not acquainted with facts which their successors discovered. . . . The same, to a greater or lesser extent, is true in all departments of natural science. It must be no less true in theology. What the facts of nature are to the naturalist, the facts of the Bible and of our moral and religious consciousness are to the theologian. If, for example, the Bible and experience teach the fact of the entire inability of fallen men to anything spiritually good, we cannot accept any system which denies efficacious grace or sovereign election. That fact of itself determines the relation in which the eternal purpose of God stands to the salvation of the individual sinner. So of all other great Scriptural facts. They arrange themselves in a certain order by an inward law, just as certainly and as clearly as the particles of matter in the process of crystallization or in the organic unity of the body of an animal. It is true here, as in natural science, that it is only by an imperfect induction of facts, or by denying or perverting them, that their relative position in the scheme of salvation can be a matter of doubt or of diversity of opinion.

But secondly, we have in theology a guide which the man of science does not possess. The Scriptures not only declare God's own glory to be His grand design in all His works of creation, providence, and redemption, but in many cases expressly state the relation which one part of this scheme bears to other parts. Thus, for example, it is said that Christ died *in order that* He might save His people from their sins. We are elected to holiness. Therefore election precedes sanctification. We are chosen to be made holy, and not because we are holy. These revelations concerning the relation of the subordinate parts of the scheme of redemption make plain the nature of the whole plan.

§2. Supralapsarianism

As men differ in their understanding of the facts of Scripture, and as some are more careful than others to gather all the facts which are to be considered, or more faithful in submitting to their authority, so they differ in their views of the plan which God has devised for the salvation of men. Our discussion of the more important views begins with the supralapsarian scheme. According to this view, God in order to manifest His grace and justice selected from "creatable" men (i.e., from merely possible men whom He had not yet purposed to create) a certain number to be vessels of mercy and certain others to be vessels of wrath. In the order of thought, election and reprobation precede the purposes to create and to permit the fall. Creation is a means to the end of redemption. God creates some to be saved and others to be lost.

This scheme is called supralapsarian because it supposes that men before the fall were the objects of election to eternal life and foreordination to eternal death. . . . [On the other hand,] those who adopt the Augustinian system are infralapsarians. That is, they hold that it was from the mass of fallen men that some were elected to eternal life and others, in just punishment for their sins, were foreordained to eternal death. . . .

There are obvious objections to the supralapsarian theory: (1) It seems to involve a contradiction. The purpose to save or condemn must of necessity, in the order of thought, follow the purpose to create. The latter is presupposed in the former. (2) It is a clearly revealed Scriptural principle that where there is no sin there is no condemnation. Therefore, any one who has been foreordained to death must have been regarded as already sinful. (3) It seems plain from the whole argument of the apostle in Romans 9:9–21 that the "mass" out of which some are chosen and others left is the mass of fallen men. . . . Since all are equally unworthy and guilty, God has mercy on one but not on another according to His own good pleasure. . . . Moreover, in texts like Romans 1:24, 26, and 28, reprobation is declared to be judicial, founded upon the sinfulness of its objects. Otherwise it could not be a manifestation of the justice of God. . . . (4) A further objection to the supralapsarian scheme is that it is not consistent with the Scriptural exhibition of the character of God. He is declared to be a God of mercy and justice. But it is not compatible with these divine attributes that men should be foreordained to misery and eternal death before they apostatized from God. If they are passed by and foreordained to death *for* their sins, it must be that in predestination they are contemplated as guilty and fallen creatures.

§3. Infralapsarianism

According to the infralapsarian doctrine, God, with the design to reveal His own glory, that is, the perfections of His own nature, determined, first, to create the world; secondly, to permit the fall of man; thirdly, to elect from the mass of fallen men a multitude as "vessels of mercy"; fourthly, to send His Son for their redemption; and fifthly, to leave the residue of mankind, as He left the fallen angels, to suffer the just punishment of their sins. . . .

§4. Hypothetical Redemption
§5. The Lutheran Doctrine as to the Plan of Salvation

§6. The Remonstrant Doctrine (Arminianism)

In the early part of the seventeenth century Arminius introduced a new system of doctrine in the Reformed churches of Holland. . . . Because the advocates of the new doctrine presented a "Remonstrance" which reflected their divergence from the established belief, they were at first called Remonstrants, but in later years their more common designation has been Arminians. . . . A serious departure from the system of Augustinianism, which in all ages had been the life of the Church, the tenets of Arminianism include:

(1) While all men derive from Adam a corrupt nature by which they are inclined to sin, this corruption is not itself of the nature of sin. Men are responsible only for their own voluntary acts and the consequences of such acts.

(2) Man by his fall has not lost his ability to good. Such ability, or liberty as the Arminians call it, is essential to our nature and cannot be lost without the loss of humanity.

(3) This ability, however, is not of itself sufficient to secure the return of the soul to God. For their conversion and holy living men need the prevenient, exciting, and assisting grace of God.

(4) This divine grace is afforded to all men in sufficient measure to enable them to repent, believe, and keep all the commandments of God.

(5) Those who of their own free will, and in the exercise of that ability which belongs to them since the fall, cooperate with this divine grace, are converted and saved.

(6) Those who thus believe have been predestinated to eternal life, not however as individuals, but as a class. The decree of election does

not concern specific persons, but is simply the general purpose of God to save believers.

[§7. Wesleyan Arminianism]

§8. The Augustinian Scheme

A. Preliminary Remarks

It is plain that the main point of difference between the Arminian scheme and Augustinianism is that according to the latter, God determines who are to be saved; according to the former, man makes the determination. Augustine taught that out of the fallen family of men, all of whom might have been justly left to perish in their apostasy, God in mercy selected some to everlasting life, sent His Son for their redemption, and gives to them the Holy Spirit to secure their repentance, faith, and holy living unto the end. . . . It is God, therefore, and not man, who determines who are to be saved. . . .

[In weighing Augustinianism against Arminianism] it is to be remembered that the question is not which view of the plan of God is the freest from difficulties, the most agreeable to our natural feelings, and therefore the most plausible to the human mind. It may be admitted that it would appear to us more consistent with the character of God that provision should be made for the salvation of all men, and that sufficient knowledge and grace should be granted to every human being to secure his salvation. . . . But we are constrained by facts: the facts of providence, of the Bible, and of religious experience. These facts must determine our theory. We cannot say that the goodness of God forbids the permission of sin and misery if sin and misery actually exist. We cannot say that justice requires that all rational creatures should be treated alike, enjoy the same advantages, and have the same opportunity to secure knowledge, holiness, and happiness, if, under the government of a God of infinite justice, the greatest disparity actually exists. A reasonable theory must accord with certain basic facts admitted by all Christians:

(1) It is admitted that God reigns and that His providence extends to all events great and small, so that nothing can occur which is contrary to His will, or which He does not either effect by His own power or permit to be done by other agents. . . . The prayers and thanksgivings which men by a law of their nature address to God assume that He controls all events. . . .

(2) No less clear and universally admitted is the principle that God can control the free acts of rational creatures without destroying either

their liberty or their responsibility. Men universally pray that the wrath of their enemies may be turned aside or that the state of their minds may be changed. All Christians pray that God would change the hearts of men, give them repentance and faith, and so control their acts that His glory and the good of others may be promoted. This is one of those simple, profound, and far-reaching truths which men take for granted and on which they cannot avoid acting, whatever may be the doubts of philosophers or the speculative difficulties with which such truths are attended.

(3) All Christians admit that God has a plan or purpose in the government of the world. There is an end to be accomplished. It is inconceivable that an infinitely wise Being would create, sustain, and control the universe without contemplating an end to be attained by this wonderful manifestation of His power and resources. The Bible therefore teaches us that God works all things after the counsel of His own will. This truth is incorporated in all the systems of faith adopted among Christians and is assumed in all religious worship and experience.

(4) It is a necessary corollary from the foregoing principles that the facts of history are the fulfilment of the eternal purposes of God. Whatever actually occurs entered into His purpose. We can, therefore, learn the design or intention of God from the evolution or development of His plan in the history of the world and of every individual man. Whatever occurs, He for wise reasons permits to occur. He can prevent whatever He sees fit to prevent. If, therefore, sin occurs, it was God's design that it should occur. If misery follows in the train of sin, such was God's purpose. If some men are saved while others perish, such must have entered into the all-comprehending purpose of God. It is not possible for any finite mind to comprehend the designs of God or to see the reasons of His dispensations. But we cannot, on that account, deny that He governs all things, or that He rules according to the counsel of His own will.

The Augustinian system of doctrine is nothing more than the application of these general and almost universally recognized principles to the special case of the salvation of man.

B. Statement of the Doctrine

The Augustinian scheme includes the following points: (1) The glory of God, or the manifestation of His perfections, is the highest and ultimate end of all things. (2) For that end God purposed the creation of the universe and the whole plan of providence and redemption. (3) He placed mankind in a state of probation, making Adam, their first parent, their head and representative. (4) The fall of Adam brought all his posterity into a state of condemnation, sin, and misery from which they are utterly unable to deliver themselves. (5) From the mass of fallen men God elected a multitude to eternal life and left the rest of mankind to the just recompense of their sins. (6) The ground of this election is not the foresight of anything in the one class to distinguish them favourably from the members of the other class, but the good pleasure of God. (7) For the salvation of those thus chosen to eternal life, God gave His own Son to become man and to suffer for His people, thus making a full satisfaction for sin, bringing in everlasting righteousness, and rendering the ultimate salvation of the elect absolutely certain. (8) While the Holy Spirit in His common operations of restraining evil and exciting good is present with every man so long as he lives, His efficacious and saving power is exercised only in behalf of the elect. (9) All those whom God has thus chosen to life, and for whom Christ specially gave Himself in the covenant of redemption, shall certainly (unless they die in infancy) be brought to the knowledge of the truth, to the exercise of faith, and to perseverance in holy living unto the end. Such is the great scheme of doctrine known in history as the Pauline, Augustinian, or Calvinistic. . . .

C. Proof of the Doctrine

1. Argument from self-consistency

In the first place, Augustinianism is a simple, harmonious, self-consistent scheme. It supposes no conflicting purposes in the divine mind (no willing first one thing and then another), no purposing ends which are never accomplished, and no assertion of principles in conflict with others which cannot be denied. All the parts of this vast plan admit of being reduced to one comprehensive purpose hidden for ages in the divine mind. God's purposes to create, to permit the fall, to elect some to everlasting life while others are left, to send His Son to redeem His people, and to give the Spirit to apply that redemption, harmonize with one another and form one consistent plan. The parts of this scheme are not only harmonious, but also connected in such a way that each one involves the others, so that if one be proved, the truth of all the rest is proved. . . . Admit that the death of Christ renders certain the salvation of His people, and all the rest follows. Admit that election is not of works, and the whole plan must be admitted as true. Admit that nothing happens contrary to God's purposes; then again the whole Augustinian scheme must be admitted. . . .

2. Argument from the facts of providence

In the second place, only Augustinianism is consistent with the facts of God's providence. . . . It is a fact that God created man; it is a fact that the fall of Adam involved our whole race in sin and misery; it is a fact that some of this fallen family are saved and others perish; it is a fact that the salvation of those who actually attain eternal life is secured by the mediation of Christ and the work of the Holy Spirit. These providential facts admitted by all Christians are consistent with Augustinianism, the essence of which is that these facts were not unexpected by the divine mind, but that God foreknew they would occur and intended that they should come to pass. This is all. What actually does happen, God intended should happen. Although His purposes or intentions cannot fail, to secure their accomplishment He uses no influence which is incompatible with the perfect liberty and entire responsibility of rational creatures. . . . The Augustinian system is nothing but the assumption that God intended in eternity what He actually does in time. That system, therefore, is in accordance with all the facts of divine providence and thus is founded on an immovable basis.

There is, however, another view which must be taken of this subject. Augustinianism is founded on the assumption of the sovereignty of God. It supposes that it belongs to Him, in virtue of His own perfection, His relation to the universe as its creator and preserver, and His relation to the world of sinners as their ruler and judge, to deal with them according to His own good pleasure. He can rightfully pardon some and condemn others, or can rightfully give His saving grace to one and not to another; therefore, it is of Him, and not of man, that one is made a partaker of eternal life while another is not. On the other hand, all anti-Augustinian systems assume that God is bound to provide salvation for all, to give sufficient grace to all, and to leave the question of salvation and perdition to be determined by each man for himself. Anti-Augustinians maintain that we are not condemned criminals of whom the sovereign may rightfully pardon some and not others, but rather we are rational creatures all of whom have an equal and valid claim on our maker to receive whatever is necessary for our salvation. Now the question is not which of these theories is the more agreeable, but which is true. One method of deciding that question is to ascertain which accords better with providential facts. Does God in His providential dealings with men act on the principles of sovereignty, distributing His favours according to the good pleasure of His will, or on the principle of impartial justice, dealing with all men alike? This question admits of but one answer. . . . The fact is patent that the greatest inequalities do exist among men, that God deals far more favourably with some than with others, and that He distributes His providential blessings, which include not only temporal good but also religious advantages and opportunities, as an absolute sovereign according to His own good pleasure, and not as an impartial judge. The time for judgment is not yet.

This sovereignty of God in the dispensation of His providence is evinced in His dealings both with nations and with individuals.... Some individuals are happy, others are miserable. Some have uninterrupted health, others are the victims of disease and suffering. Some have all their faculties, others are born blind or deaf. Some are rich, others sunk in the misery and degradation of abject poverty. Some are born in the midst of civilized society and in the bosom of virtuous families, others are from the beginning of their being surrounded by vice and wretchedness. These are facts which cannot be denied. Nor can it be denied that the lot of each individual is determined by the sovereign pleasure of God.

The same principle is carried out with regard to the communication of religious knowledge and advantages. God chose the Jews from among the families of the earth to be the recipients of His oracles and of the divinely instituted ordinances of religion. The rest of the world was left for centuries in utter darkness.... In like manner, the position of the inhabitants of Christendom is unspeakably more desirable than that of pagans. No American Christian can persuade himself that it would have been as well had he been born in Africa; nor can he give any answer to the question, Why was I born here and not there? other than, "Even so, Father, for so it seemed good in thy sight."

It is vain to adopt a theory which does not accord with these facts. Since it is undeniable that God acts as a sovereign in His providence, it is vain for us to deny that He is sovereign in the distribution of His favours. Augustinianism accords with these facts of providence and therefore must be true. It alone assumes that God acts in the dispensation of His grace precisely as He acts in the distribution of His other favours. On the other hand, all anti-Augustinian systems, which are founded on the principle that this sovereignty of God is inconsistent with His justice and His parental relation to the children of men, are in obvious conflict with the facts of His providence.

3. Argument from the facts of Scripture

The third source of proof on this subject is found in the facts of the Bible or in the truths plainly revealed therein. Augustinianism is the only system consistent with those facts or truths.

(1) This appears first from Scripture's clear revelation that God is infinitely exalted above all His creatures.... His glory is the end of all things, and His good pleasure the highest reason for whatever comes to pass.... Augustinianism is the only system which accords

with this depiction of the character of God and His relation to His creatures.

(2) It is a fact that men are a fallen race, that by their alienation from God they are involved in a state of guilt and pollution from which they cannot deliver themselves. They have by their guilt forfeited all claim on God's justice; they might in justice be left to perish; and by their depravity they have rendered themselves unable to turn unto God or to do anything spiritually good. These are facts already proved. The sense of guilt is universal and indestructible. All sinners know the righteous judgment of God that they are worthy of death. And the inability of sinners is clearly and repeatedly asserted in the Scriptures. . . . Now if men are unable to change their own hearts, to prepare themselves for that change, or to cooperate in its production, then all those systems which assume the ability of the sinner and attribute the distinction between one man's being saved and another's being lost to whether or not that ability has been used, must be false. They are contrary to facts. They are inconsistent with what every man, in the depth of his own heart, knows to be true. The point illustrated when the Scriptures compare sinners to dead men and even to dry bones is their entire hopelessness. In this respect they are all alike. Should Christ pass through a graveyard and bid one here and another there to come forth, the reason why one is restored to life and another left in his grave can be sought only in His good pleasure. From the nature of the case it cannot be found in the dead themselves. Likewise, since the Scriptures, observation, and consciousness teach that men are unable to restore themselves to spiritual life, their being quickened must be referred to the good pleasure of God.

(3) This is confirmed by another obvious fact or truth of Scripture. The regeneration of the human heart, the conversion of a sinner to God, is the work not of the subject of that change, but of the Spirit of God. This is plain because the Bible always attributes it to the Holy Ghost. We are said to be born not of the will of man, but of God. We are the subjects of the renewing of the Holy Ghost and are quickened or raised from the dead by the Spirit of the Lord; the dry bones live only when the Spirit blows upon them. Such is the representation which pervades the Scriptures from beginning to end. . . . Accordingly, the intimate conviction of the people of God in all ages has been and is that regeneration, or the infusion of spiritual life, is an act of God's power exercised according to His good pleasure, and therefore it is the gift for which the Church specially prays. This fact involves the truth of Augustinianism, which simply teaches that the reason why one man is regenerated and another not, and consequently one is saved and another not, is the good pleasure of God. . . .

(4) Another plainly revealed fact is that we are chosen to holiness; we are created unto good works. In other words, all good in us is the fruit and therefore cannot by any possibility be the ground of election. In Ephesians 1:3–6 the apostle says: "Blessed be the God and Father of our Lord Jesus Christ, who hath blessed us with all spiritual blessings in heavenly places in Christ: according as he hath chosen us in him before the foundation of the world, that we should be holy and without blame before him in love: having predestinated us unto the adoption of children by Jesus Christ to himself, according to the good pleasure of his will, to the praise of the glory of his grace, wherein he hath made us accepted in the beloved." In this passage the Augustinian doctrine of election is stated clearly and comprehensively: (a) The end or design of the whole scheme of redemption is the praise of the glory of the grace of God, i.e., its purpose is to exhibit to the admiration of intelligent creatures the glorious attribute of divine grace, or the love of an infinitely holy and just God towards guilty and polluted sinners. (b) To this end God of His mere good pleasure predestinated those who were the objects of this love to the high dignity of being the children of God. (c) To prepare them for this exalted state He chose them, before the foundation of the world, to be holy and without blame in love. (d) In consequence of His choice, or in execution of this purpose, He confers upon them all spiritual blessings, regeneration, faith, repentance, and the indwelling of the Spirit. That foresight of faith and of repentance should be the ground of election is utterly incompatible with this fact. Men, according to the apostle, repent and believe because they are elected; God has chosen them to be holy, and therefore their holiness or their goodness in any form or measure cannot be the reason why He chose them. In like manner the apostle Peter says that believers are elect "unto obedience and sprinkling of the blood of Jesus Christ" (1 Peter 1:2). It is, then, the clear doctrine of the Bible that men are chosen to be holy. The fact that God has predestinated them to salvation is the reason why they are brought to repentance and a holy life. . . .

(5) Another decisive fact is that salvation is of grace. The two ideas of grace and works, of gift and debt, of undeserved favour and what is merited, of what is to be referred to the good pleasure of the giver and what to the character or state of the receiver, are antithetical. The one excludes the other: "If by grace, then is it no more of works: otherwise grace is no more grace. But if it be of works, then is it no more grace: otherwise work is no more work" (Rom. 11:6). Nothing concerning the plan of salvation is more plainly revealed or more strenuously insisted upon than its gratuitousness from beginning to end. "Ye are saved by grace" is engraved upon almost every page of

the Bible and in the hearts of all believers. (a) It was a matter of grace that a plan of salvation was devised for fallen man but not for fallen angels. (b) It was a matter of grace that that plan was revealed to some portions of our race and not to others. (c) The acceptance or justification of every individual heir of salvation is a matter of grace. (d) The work of sanctification is a work of grace, i.e., a work carried on by the unmerited, supernatural power of the Holy Spirit. (e) It is a matter of grace that some of those who hear the gospel accept the offered mercy, while others reject it. All these points are so clearly taught in the Bible that they are practically acknowledged by all Christians. Although beyond our understanding, they are conceded by the heart, as is evident from the prayers and praises of the Church in all ages and in all its divisions. . . .

(6) The Scriptures clearly assert that God has mercy on whom He will have mercy, and compassion on whom He will have compassion (Rom. 9:15). . . . In the same chapter it is said that election is "not of works, but of him that calleth. . . . So then it is not of him that willeth, nor of him that runneth, but of God that showeth mercy" (Rom. 9:11, 16). . . . Paul said of himself, "It pleased God, who separated me from my mother's womb, and called me by his grace, to reveal his Son in me" (Gal. 1:15–16). To the Ephesians he says that those obtain the inheritance who were "predestinated according to the purpose of him who worketh all things after the counsel of his own will" (Eph. 1:11). And in 2 Timothy 1:9 Paul says that we are saved "not according to our works, but according to [God's] own purpose and grace, which was given us in Christ Jesus before the world began." . . .

Of all the teachers sent by God to reveal His will, no one more frequently asserts the divine sovereignty than does our blessed Lord Himself. He speaks of those whom the Father has given Him; to these He gives eternal life (John 17:2, 24). . . . "My sheep hear my voice, and I know them, and they follow me: and I give unto them eternal life; and they shall never perish, neither shall any man pluck them out of my hand. My Father, which gave them me, is greater than all; and no man is able to pluck them out of my Father's hand" (John 10:27–29). As the sheep of Christ are chosen out of the world and given to Him, God is the chooser. They do not choose Him, but He chooses them. . . . "No man can come to me, except the Father which hath sent me draw him: and I will raise him up at the last day" (John 6:44). Who shall be brought to the saving knowledge of the truth rests entirely with God. . . . The Scriptures therefore say that repentance, faith, and the renewing of the Holy Ghost are gifts of God. If gifts of God, they must be the fruits of election. They cannot possibly be its ground.

If the office of the theologian, as is so generally admitted, be to take the facts of Scripture as the man of science does those of nature, and found upon them his doctrines, instead of deducing his doctrines from the principles or primary truths of his philosophy, it seems impossible to resist the conclusion that the doctrine of Augustine is the doctrine of the Bible. According to that doctrine God is an absolute sovereign. He does what seems good in His sight. He sends the truth to one nation but not to another. He gives that truth saving power in one mind but not in another. It is of Him, and not of us, that any man is in Christ Jesus and is an heir of eternal life. . . .

With these facts of Scripture the experience of Christians agrees. It is the intimate conviction of every believer, on the basis of the testimony of his own consciousness as well as the Scriptures, that his salvation is of God; that he has been brought to the exercise of faith and repentance is of God and not of himself. So long as he looks within, the believer is satisfied of the truth of these doctrines. It is only when he looks outward, and attempts to reconcile these truths with the dictates of his own understanding, that he becomes confused and skeptical. But as our faith is not founded on the wisdom of men, but on the power of God, and as the foolishness of God is wiser than men, the part of wisdom, as well as the path of duty and safety, is to receive as true what God has revealed, even though we cannot comprehend His ways unto perfection.

[§9. Objections to the Augustinian Scheme]

Chapter II

The Covenant of Grace

§1. The Plan of Salvation Is a Covenant

The plan of salvation is presented in the form of a covenant. This is evident, first, from the frequent use of the word covenant in reference to the divine scheme of redemption. There can be no doubt that according to its prevailing usage in the Old Testament the word covenant means a mutual contract between two or more parties. It is very often used of compacts between individuals, especially between rulers. Abraham and Abimelech made a covenant (Gen. 21:27). Joshua made a covenant with the people (Josh. 24:25). Jonathan and David made a covenant (1 Sam. 18:3). . . . We have no right to interpret the word in any other sense when it is used of transactions between God and man. Repeated mention is made of the covenant of God with Abraham (e.g., Gen. 15:18; 17:13), and afterwards with Isaac and Jacob, and then with the Israelites at Mount Sinai. The Old Testament centers on the idea of a covenant relation between God and the theocratic people.

In the Greek Scriptures the meaning of the word covenant is just as certain and uniform. . . . It is used in the New Testament to designate the mutual contract God made with Abraham, with the Israelites, and with believers. . . . Since the word has this meaning when applied to the transaction with Abraham and with the Hebrews, it must have the same meaning when applied to the plan of salvation revealed in the gospel.

Secondly, that the Bible presents the plan of salvation in the form of a covenant is proved not only from the signification and usage of the word covenant, but also and more decisively from the fact that the elements of a covenant are included in this plan. There are parties, mutual promises or stipulations, and conditions. Thus it is in fact a covenant, whatever it may be called. As this is the Scriptural mode of representation, it is of great importance that it be retained in theology. . . .

§2. Different Views of the Nature of This Covenant

It is assumed by many that the parties to the covenant of grace are God and fallen man. Man by his apostasy having forfeited the favour of God, having lost the divine image, and having involved himself in sin and misery, would have perished in this state had not God provided a plan of salvation. Moved by compassion for His fallen creatures, God sent His Son into the world to assume their nature and to do and suffer whatever was requisite for their salvation. On the ground of this redeeming work of Christ, God promises salvation to all who will comply with the terms on which it is offered, i.e., with the demands of the gospel. This general statement embraces forms of opinion which differ very much one from the others. . . .

Our present object, however, is simply to state what Augustinians mean by the covenant of grace. The essential distinctions of their view are (1) that the provisions of the covenant of grace do not have equal reference to all mankind, but refer specially to that portion of our race who are actually saved, and (2) that it is God and not man who determines who are to be saved.

The word grace is used in Scripture and in ordinary religious writings in three senses: (1) unmerited love, i.e., love exercised towards the undeserving; (2) any unmerited favour, especially spiritual blessings—hence all the fruits of the Spirit in believers are called graces or unmerited gifts of God; and (3) the supernatural influence of the Holy Ghost. This is preeminently grace, being the great gift which was secured by the work of Christ and without which His redemption would not avail to our salvation. In all these senses of the word the plan of salvation is properly called a covenant of grace. It is of grace (1) because it originated in the mysterious love of God for sinners who deserved only His wrath and curse; (2) because it promises salvation not on the condition of works or anything meritorious on our part, but as an unmerited gift; and (3) because its benefits are secured and applied not in the course of nature, nor in the exercise of the natural powers of the sinner, but by the supernatural influence of the Holy Spirit, granted as an unmerited gift.

§3. Parties to the Covenant

At first view there appears to be some confusion in the statements of the Scriptures as to the parties to this covenant. Sometimes Christ is presented as one of the parties. At other times He is represented not as a party, but as the mediator and surety of the covenant; in such cases the parties are represented to be God and His people. As the old covenant was made between God and the Hebrews, Moses acting as mediator, so the new covenant is commonly represented in the Bible as formed between God and His people, Christ acting as mediator. He is, therefore, called the mediator of a better covenant founded on better promises. . . .

To remove the incongruity of Christ's being represented as at once a party and a mediator of the same covenant, it is essential to recognize that there are in fact two covenants relating to the salvation of fallen man, the one between God and Christ, the other between God and His people. These covenants differ not only in their parties, but also in their promises and conditions. Both are so clearly presented in the Bible that they should not be confounded. The latter, the covenant of grace, is founded on the former, the covenant of redemption. Of the one Christ is the mediator and surety; of the other He is one of the contracting parties. . . .

§4. Covenant of Redemption

The covenant of redemption is a mutual compact between the Father and the Son in reference to the salvation of man. This is a subject which, from its nature, is entirely beyond our comprehension. We must receive the teachings of the Scriptures in relation to it without presuming to penetrate the mystery which naturally belongs to it. . . .

The covenant between the Father and the Son was formed in eternity and revealed in time. . . . Christ speaks of promises made to Him before His advent and of His coming into the world in execution of a commission which He had received from the Father. The parallel so distinctly drawn between Adam and Christ is also a proof of the point in question. As Adam was the head and representative of his posterity, so Christ is the head and representative of His people. And as God entered into covenant with Adam, so He entered into covenant with Christ. This, in Romans 5:12–21, is set forth as the fundamental idea of all God's dealings with men, both in their fall and in their redemption.

The proof of the doctrine has, however, a much wider foundation. When one person assigns a stipulated work to another person with the promise of a reward upon the condition of the performance of that work, there is a covenant. Nothing can be plainer than that all this is true in relation to the Father and the Son. The Father gave the Son a work to do, sent Him into the world to perform it, and promised Him a great reward when the work was accomplished. Such is the constant representation of the Scriptures. We have, therefore, the contracting parties, the promise, and the condition. These are the essential elements of a covenant. . . . In Psalm 40:7–8, which the writer of Hebrews interprets as a reference to the Messiah, it is said, "Lo, I come: in the volume of the book it is written of me, I delight to do thy will," i.e., to execute thy purpose, to carry out thy plan. "By the which will," says the New Testament expositor, "we are sanctified (i.e., cleansed from the guilt of sin) through the offering of the body of Jesus Christ once for all" (Heb. 10:10). Christ came, therefore, in execution of a purpose of God, to fulfil a work which had been assigned Him. In John 17:4 He says, "I have finished the work which thou gavest me to do." This statement was made at the close of His earthly course. At its beginning, when yet a child, He had said to His parents, "Wist ye not that I must be about my Father's business?" (Luke 2:49). Our Lord is also spoken of as sent into the world: "When the fulness of the time was come, God sent forth his Son, made of a woman" (Gal. 4:4); "God sent his only begotten Son into the world . . . to be the propitiation for our sins" (1 John 4:9–10).

It is plain, therefore, that Christ came to execute a work, that He was sent of the Father to fulfil a plan or preconceived design. It is no less plain that special promises were made by the Father to the Son and that their realization depended upon the accomplishment of the work assigned Him. . . . The transaction was, therefore, of the nature of a covenant. An obligation was assumed by the Son to accomplish the work assigned Him, and an obligation was assumed by the Father to grant Him the stipulated reward. . . .

A. The Work Assigned to the Redeemer

(1) Christ was to assume our nature, humbling Himself to be born of a woman and to be found in fashion as a man. This was to be a real incarnation, not a mere theophany such as occurred repeatedly under the old dispensation. He was to become flesh, to be bone of our bone and flesh of our flesh, made in all things like unto His brethren, yet without sin, that He might be touched with a sense of our infirmities and able to sympathize with those who are tempted, being Himself also tempted. (2) He was to be made under the law, voluntarily undertaking to fulfil all righteousness by obeying the law of God perfectly in all the forms in which it had been made obligatory on man. (3) He was to bear our sins, to be a curse for us, offering Himself as a sacrifice or propitiation to God in expiation of the sins of men. This involved His whole life of humiliation, sorrow, and suffering, and His ignominious death upon the cross. . . .

B. The Promises Made to the Redeemer

(1) The Father would prepare a body for the Son, fit up a tabernacle for Him, formed as was the body of Adam by the immediate agency of God, uncontaminated and without spot or blemish. (2) The Father would give the Spirit to the Son without measure, that His whole human nature might be replenished with grace and strength and so adorned with the beauty of holiness that He would be altogether lovely. (3) The Father would be ever at the Son's right hand to support and comfort Him in the darkest hours of His conflict with the powers of evil; ultimately the Son would bruise Satan under His feet. (4) The Father would deliver the Son from the power of death and exalt Him to His own right hand in heaven, where all power in heaven and earth

would be committed to Him. (5) As the Theanthropos and head of the Church Christ would have the Holy Spirit to send to whom He willed, to renew their hearts, to satisfy and comfort them, and to qualify them for His service and kingdom. (6) All given by the Father to the Son would come to Him and be kept by Him, so that none of them would be lost. (7) A multitude whom no man can number would thus be made partakers of His redemption, and ultimately the kingdom of the Messiah would embrace all the nations of the earth. (8) In Christ and His ransomed Church there would be made the highest manifestation of the divine perfections to all orders of holy intelligences throughout eternity.

§5. The Covenant of Grace

In virtue of what the Son of God covenanted to perform, and what in the fulness of time He actually accomplished, in accordance with the stipulations of the compact with the Father, two things follow. First, salvation is offered to all men on the condition of faith in Christ. Our Lord commanded His disciples to go into all the world and preach the gospel to every creature. . . . In this sense, the covenant of grace is formed with all mankind. . . . But as it is no less true that the whole scheme of redemption has special reference to those who are given by the Father to the Son (John 6:37), it follows, secondly, from the nature of the covenant between the Father and Son, that the covenant of grace has also special reference to the elect. To them God has promised to give His Spirit in order that they may believe, and to them alone all the promises made to believers belong. . . . What is important here is that we adopt a mode of representation that will comprehend the various facts recognized in the Scriptures. One of those facts is that salvation is offered to all men on the condition of faith in Christ. To that extent the covenant of grace is made with all men. Another crucial fact is that those who, having heard the gospel, refuse to accept that covenant place themselves without its pale.

A. Christ as Mediator of the Covenant

Christ is the mediator of the covenant of grace not only in the sense that He like Moses served as a messenger between God and His people, but also in the sense that it was through Christ's intervention and solely on the ground of what He had done, or promised to do, that God entered into this new covenant with fallen men. Christ is also mediator in the sense of a surety (Heb. 7:22). He guarantees the fulfilment of all the promises and conditions of the covenant. His death not only bound the parties to the contract, but also secured the fulfilment of all its provisions. By His fulfilling the conditions on which the promises of the covenant of redemption depended, the veracity and justice of God are pledged to secure the salvation of His people, and this secures the fidelity of His people. Thus Christ's work renders certain the gifts of God's grace and the perseverance of His people in faith and obedience. He is therefore, in every sense, our salvation.

B. The Condition of the Covenant

The condition of the covenant of grace, so far as adults are concerned, is faith in Christ. That is, in order to partake of the benefits of this covenant we must receive the Lord Jesus Christ as the Son of God in whom and for whose sake its blessings are vouchsafed to the children of men. Until we thus believe, we are aliens and strangers from the covenant of promise, without God and without Christ. We must acquiesce in this covenant, renouncing all other methods of salvation, and consenting to be saved on the terms which it proposes, before we are made partakers of its benefits. . . .

C. The Promises of the Covenant

The promises of this covenant are all included in the comprehensive formula so often occurring in the Scriptures, "I will be your God, and ye shall be my people." This involves the complete restoration of our normal relation to God. All ground of alienation, every bar to fellowship is removed. He communicates Himself in His fulness to His people, and they become His by entire conformity to His will and devotion to His service, and are the special objects of His favour. . . . As our God He is our infinite portion; His perfections are revealed to us as the highest knowledge and are pledged for our protection, blessedness, and glory. His being our God implies also that He assures us of His love and admits us to communion with Himself. As His favour is life and His loving-kindness better than life, and as the vision of God, the enjoyment of His love, and fellowship with Him secure the highest possible exaltation and beatification of His creatures, it is plain that the promise to be our God includes all conceivable and all possible good.

That we are to be His people means that we are His peculiar possession. His delights are with the children of men. From the various orders of His creatures He has chosen man to be the special object of His favour and the special medium through which and by which to manifest His glory. And from the mass of fallen men He has, of His own good pleasure, chosen an innumerable multitude to be His portion, as He condescends to call them, on whom He lavishes the plenitude of His grace and in whom He reveals His glory to the admiration of all holy intelligences. Being thus selected for the special love of God and for the highest manifestation of His glory, they are in all things fitted for this high destiny. They are justified, sanctified, and glorified. They are rendered perfectly conformed to His image, devoted to His service, and obedient to His will.

§6. The Oneness of the Covenant of Grace Under All Dispensations

The plan of salvation has, under all dispensations, the patriarchal, the Mosaic, and the Christian, been the same. . . . There are the same promise of deliverance from the evils of the apostasy, the same Redeemer, the same condition required for participation in the blessings of redemption, and the same complete salvation for all who embrace the offers of divine mercy.

In determining the degree of knowledge possessed by the ancient people of God, we are not to be governed by our own capacity of discovering from the Old Testament Scriptures the doctrines of grace. We cannot tell what amount of supplementary instruction the people received from the prophets, or what degree of divine illumination was granted to them. It is, however, clear from the writings of the New Testament that the knowledge of the plan of salvation current among the Jews at the time of the advent was much greater than we would deem possible from a mere perusal of the Old Testament. Not only did the Jews confidently expect the Messiah, who was to be a teacher as well as a deliverer, but the devout among them waited for the salvation of Israel. They spoke as familiarly of the Holy Spirit and of His baptism as Christians now do. It is principally from the assertions of the New Testament writers and from their expositions of the ancient Scriptures that we learn the amount of truth revealed to those who lived before the coming of Christ.

From the Scriptures, therefore, as a whole—from the New Testament and from the Old as interpreted by infallible authority in the New—we learn that the plan of salvation has always been one and the same; it has always had the same promise, the same Saviour, and the same condition.

A. The Pre-Advent Promise of Eternal Life

That the same promise was made to those who lived before the advent as is made to us is plain. Immediately after the fall God gave to Adam the promise of redemption. That promise was contained in the prediction that the seed of the woman would bruise the serpent's head (Gen. 3:15). . . . The prince of darkness who had triumphed over our first parents was to be cast down and despoiled of his victory. This overthrow was to be accomplished by the seed of the woman. This phrase might mean the posterity of the woman and in this sense would convey an important truth: man was to triumph over Satan. But it evidently has a more specific reference. It refers to one individual who, in a sense peculiar to Himself, was to be the seed of the woman. This is clear from the analogy of prophecy. We know from Galatians 3:16 that the promise to Abraham that in his seed all the nations of the earth would be blessed had one individual in view, namely, Christ. So, too, when Isaiah predicts that the "servant of the Lord" would suffer, triumph, and be the source of blessings to all people, the servant is to be understood to be the Messiah, even though many understood and many still understand the prophet to be speaking of the Jewish nation. In all these and similar cases we have two guides as to the real meaning of the Spirit. The one is found in subsequent explanatory declarations of the Scriptures, the other in the fulfilment of the predictions. . . .

We have, then, the promise of redemption made to our first parents immediately after the fall. . . . This promise was repeated and amplified from time to time until the Redeemer actually came. In these additional and fuller predictions the nature of this redemption was set forth with ever increasing clearness. This general promise included many specific promises. Thus we find God promising to His faithful people the forgiveness of their sins, restoration to His favour, the renewing of their hearts, and the gift of His Spirit. No higher blessings than these are offered under the Christian dispensation. And for these blessings the ancient people of God earnestly longed and prayed. The Old Testament, especially the Psalms and other devotional parts of the early Scriptures, are filled with the record of such prayers and longings. Nothing can be plainer than that pardon and the favour of God were promised to holy men before the coming of Christ, and these are the blessings which are now promised to us.

Hebrews 11 teaches that the hopes of the patriarchs were not confined to the present life, but were fixed on a future state of existence. Such a state, therefore, must have been revealed to them, and eternal life must have been promised to them. Thus we read in verse 10 that

Abraham "looked for a city which hath foundations, whose builder and maker is God." That this was heaven is plain from verse 16, where it is said, "They desire a better country, that is, an heavenly: wherefore God is not ashamed to be called their God: for he hath prepared for them a city." Ancient worthies gladly sacrificed all earthly good and even life itself, "not accepting deliverance; that they might obtain a better resurrection" (v. 35). That this was the common faith of the Jews long before the coming of Christ appears from 2 Maccabees 7:9, where the dying martyr says to his tormentor, "Thou like a fury takest us out of this present life, but the King of the world shall raise us up, who have died for his laws, unto everlasting life." Furthermore, our Lord teaches us that Abraham, Isaac, and Jacob are still alive; and that where Abraham is, is heaven. His bosom is the resting place of the faithful.

B. Christ the Redeemer Under All Dispensations

It is clear as well that the Redeemer is the same under all dispensations. He who was predicted as the seed of the woman, the seed of Abraham, the Son of David, the Branch, the Servant of the Lord, the Prince of Peace, is our Lord Jesus Christ, the Son of God, God manifest in the flesh. He, therefore, from the beginning has been held up as the hope of the world. He was set forth in all His offices—Prophet, Priest, and King. His work was described as a sacrifice as well as a redemption. All this is so obvious and so generally admitted as to render the citation of proof texts unnecessary. It is enough to refer to the general declarations of the New Testament on this subject. Our Lord commanded the Jews to search their Scriptures, because they testified of Him. He said that Moses and all the prophets wrote of Him. Beginning at Moses, He expounded to the disciples all the Scriptures concerning Himself. The apostles, when they began to preach the gospel, not only everywhere proved from the Scriptures that Jesus was the Christ, but also referred to them continually in support of everything which they taught concerning His person and His work. It is from the Old Testament they proved His divinity, His incarnation, and the sacrificial nature of His death. From the Old Testament they proved that He was truly a Priest who made reconciliation for the people, and that He was to die, to rise again on the third day, to ascend into heaven, and to be invested with absolute authority over all the earth and over all orders of created beings. There is no New Testament doctrine concerning Christ which the apostles do not affirm to have been revealed under former dispensations. They therefore distinctly assert that it was through Him and the efficacy of His death that men were saved before as well as after His advent. Paul says that Christ was set forth as a propitiation "for the remission of sins that are past" (Rom. 3:25). And in Hebrews 9:15 it is still more explicitly asserted that He died for the forgiveness of sins under the first covenant. He was, therefore, as said in Revelation 13:8, "the Lamb slain from the foundation of the world. . . ."

Such a revelation of the Messiah was undoubtedly made in the Old Testament to turn the eyes of the whole Jewish nation in hope and faith. What the two disciples on the way to Emmaus said, "We trusted that it had been he which should have redeemed Israel" (Luke 24:21), reveals the general expectation and desire of the people. Paul speaks of the Messiah as the hope of Israel. He declares the promise of redemption through Christ to be the great object of the people's hope. When arraigned before Agrippa, the apostle declared that in preaching Christ and the resurrection he had not departed from the religion of the fathers, but adhered to it, while his enemies had deserted it: "Now I stand and am judged for the hope of the promise made of God unto our fathers" (Acts 26:6). Later he said to the Jews in Rome, "For the hope of Israel I am bound with this chain" (Acts 28:20). . . . It is needless to dwell upon this point, because the doctrine of a personal Messiah who was to redeem the people of God not only pervades the Old Testament, but is everywhere in the New Testament declared to be the great promise which is fulfilled in the advent and work of our Lord Jesus Christ.

C. Faith the Condition of Salvation from the Beginning

As the same promise was made to those who lived before the advent as is now made to us in the gospel, and as the same Redeemer was revealed to them who is presented as the object of faith to us, it of necessity follows that the condition (or terms) of salvation was the same then as now. It was not mere faith or trust in God, or simply piety, which was required, but faith in the promised Redeemer or faith in the promise of redemption through the Messiah.

In addition to the considerations just mentioned, there are various evidences that faith in the promised Redeemer was from the beginning the condition of salvation: (1) Paul teaches that faith, not works, was before as well as after Christ the condition of salvation. This, in his Epistle to the Romans, he not only asserts but proves. He argues that from the nature of the case the justification of sinners by works is a contradiction. If sinners, they are under condemnation for their works and therefore cannot be justified by them. Moreover, he proves that the Old Testament everywhere speaks of gratuitous forgiveness and acceptance of men with God—if gratuitous, it cannot be meritorious! He further argues from the case of Abraham, who, according to the express declaration of the Scriptures, was justified by faith (Gen. 15:6; Rom. 4:3); and he quotes from the old prophets the great principle, true then as now, that "the just shall live by faith" (Rom. 1:17). (2) Paul proves that the faith intended was faith in a promise and not merely general piety or confidence toward God. Abraham, he says, "staggered not at the promise of God through unbelief; but was strong in faith, giving glory to God; and being fully persuaded that, what he had promised, he was able also to perform" (Rom. 4:20–21). (3) Paul proves that the specific promise which was the object of the faith of the patriarch was the promise of redemption through Christ. . . . In Galatians 3:14 the apostle says that the blessing promised to Abraham has now come on the Gentiles through faith. Since it is now offered to all men through the gospel, the blessing to Abraham must have been redemption through Christ from the guilt and power of sin and from the consequent alienation from God.

Not only from these explicit declarations that faith in the promised Redeemer was required from the beginning, but from the admitted fact that the Old Testament is full of the doctrine of redemption by the Messiah, it follows that those who received the religion of the Old Testament received that doctrine and exercised faith in the promise of God concerning His Son. Furthermore, the Epistle to the Hebrews is designed in great part to show that the whole of the old dispensation was an adumbration of the new, and that it loses all its value and import if its reference to Christ be ignored. Therefore, to deny that the faith of the Old Testament saints was a faith in the Messiah and His redemption is to deny that they had any knowledge of the import of the revelations and promises of which they were the recipients.

Paul in Romans 3:21 says that the method of salvation revealed in the gospel had been already revealed in the law and the prophets; and his definite object in Galatians 3:13–29 is to prove that the covenant under which we live and are to be saved is identical with the covenant made with Abraham, in which the promise of redemption was made on the condition of faith in Him in whom all the nations of the earth were to be blessed. . . . The covenant of grace or plan of salvation, then, has been the same in all its elements from the beginning. . . . It has always had the same promise, the same Redeemer, and the same condition, namely, faith in the Son of God as the Saviour of the world.

§7. Different Dispensations

A. The First Dispensation

Although the covenant of grace has always been the same, the dispensations of that covenant have changed. The first dispensation extended from Adam to Abraham. Of this period we have so few records that we cannot determine how far the truth was revealed, or what measures were adopted for its preservation. All we know is that the original promises concerning the seed of the woman as the Redeemer of our race had been given, and that the worship of God by sacrifices had been divinely instituted to teach the method of salvation. . . .

B. The Second Dispensation

The second dispensation extended from Abraham to Moses. It had several distinguishing characteristics: (1) The descendants of Abraham were selected to be the peculiar people of God. They were chosen to preserve the knowledge of the true religion in the midst of the general apostasy of mankind. To this end special revelations were made to them, and God entered into a covenant with them, promising that He would be their God and that they would be His people. (2) Besides thus gathering His Church out of the world and making its members a peculiar people distinguished by circumcision from the Gentiles around them, the promise of redemption was made more definite. The Redeemer was to be of the seed of Abraham. He was to be one person. The salvation He was to effect was to pertain to all nations. (3) Subsequently it was made known that the deliverer was to be of the tribe of Judah.

C. The Third Dispensation

The third dispensation of this covenant was from Moses to Christ. All that belonged to the previous periods was taken up and included in it. A multitude of new ordinances of polity, worship, and religion were enjoined. A priesthood and a complicated system of sacrifices were introduced. The prophets rendered more definite the promises concerning the person and work of the coming Redeemer as the Prophet, Priest, and King of His people. The nature of the redemption He was to effect and the nature of the kingdom He was to establish were thus more and more clearly revealed. The New Testament indicates that the covenant of grace, or plan of salvation, underlay the whole of the institutions of the Mosaic period, and that their principal design was to teach through types and symbols what is now taught in explicit terms in the gospel. Moses, we are told (Heb. 3:5), faithfully testified concerning the things which were to be spoken after. . . .

D. The Gospel Dispensation

The gospel dispensation is called new in contrast to the Mosaic economy, which was old and about to vanish away. There are several distinguishing marks of the gospel dispensation:

(1) It is catholic, i.e., it is not confined to one people, but is designed for and adapted to all nations and all classes of men.

(2) It is more spiritual, not only in that the types and ceremonies of the Old Testament are done away, but also in that the revelation itself is more inward. What was formerly made known objectively is now, to a greater extent, written on the heart (Heb. 8:8–11). It is incomparably more clear and explicit in its teachings.

(3) It is more purely evangelical. . . . In the New Testament the gospel greatly predominates over the law, whereas in the Old Testament the law predominated over the gospel.

(4) The Christian economy is specially the dispensation of the Spirit. It had been promised of old that the coming of Christ would be followed by the effusion of the Spirit on all flesh, i.e., on all nations and on all classes of men. . . . And indeed, after His death and ascension our Lord sent the Comforter, the Spirit of truth, to abide with His people, to guide them into the knowledge of the truth, and to convince the world of sin, of righteousness, and of judgment to come. . . .

(5) The old dispensation was temporary and preparatory; the new is permanent and final. In sending forth the disciples to preach the gospel and in promising them the gift of the Spirit, Jesus assured them that He would be with them in that work unto the end of the world. This dispensation is, therefore, the last before the restoration of all things—the last, that is, in which men will be converted and the elect ingathered. . . . There is no indication in Scripture that the dispensation of the Spirit is to give way to a new and better dispensation for the conversion of the nations. When the gospel is fully preached, then comes the end.

The Person of Christ

§1. Preliminary Remarks

The most mysterious and the most familiar fact of consciousness and experience is the union of soul and body in the constitution of our nature. According to the common faith of mankind and of the Church, man consists of two distinct substances, soul and body. . . . The substance which we designate the soul is immaterial, that is, it has none of the properties of matter. It is spiritual, i.e., it has all the properties of a spirit. It is a self-conscious, intelligent, volitional agent. The substance which we call the body, on the other hand, is material. That is, it has all the properties of matter and none of the properties of mind or spirit. This is the first fact universally admitted concerning the constitution of our nature.

The second fact concerns the nature of the union between the soul and body: (1) It is a personal union. Soul and body constitute one individual man or human person. There is but one consciousness. It is the man or person who is conscious of sensations and of thoughts, of affections of the body and of the acts of the mind. (2) It is a union without mixture or confusion. The soul remains spirit, and the body remains matter. Copper and zinc combined form brass. The constituent elements lose their distinctive characteristics and produce a third substance. There is no such mixture in the union of the soul and body, however. The two remain distinct. Neither is there a transfer of any of the properties of the one to the other. No property of the mind is transferred to the body, and no property of the body is transferred to the mind. (3) Nevertheless, the union is not a mere inhabitation, a union of contact or in space. The soul does not dwell in the body as a man dwells in a house or in his garments. The body is part of himself and is necessary to his completeness as a man. He is in every part of it and is conscious of the slightest change in the state of even the least important of its members.

Thirdly, a consequence of this union of the soul and body is a communion of attributes. That is, the person is the possessor of all the attributes both of the soul and of the body. We may predicate of the man whatever may be predicated of his body, and we may predicate of him whatever may be predicated of his soul. We say of the man that he is tall or short, that he is sick or well, that he is handsome or deformed. In like manner, we may say that he is judicious, wise, good, benevolent, or learned. Whatever is true of either element of his constitution is true of the man. What is true of the one, however, is not true of the other. When the body is wounded or burnt, it is not the soul that is the subject of these accidents; and when the soul is penitent or believing, or enlightened and informed, the body is not the subject spoken of. Each has its properties and changes, but the person or man is the subject of them all. Hence, inconsistent or apparently contradictory affirmations may be made of the same person. We may say that he is weak and that he is strong, that he is mortal and immortal, that he is a spirit and that he is dust and ashes. Or we may designate the man by one element of his nature and at the same time predicate of him something which is true only of the other element. We may call him a spirit and yet say that he hungers and thirsts. We may call him a worm of the dust when we speak of him as the subject of regeneration. . . .

Just as in virtue of the personal union of the soul and body all the properties of either are properties of the man, so all the acts of either are the acts of the man. Some of our acts are purely mental, like thinking, repenting, and believing; some are purely bodily, like the processes of digestion, assimilation, and the circulation of the blood; some are mixed, like walking, speaking, and writing. In these there is a direct concurrence or cooperation of the mind and body. All of these several classes of acts are acts of the man. It is the man who thinks, it is the man who speaks and writes, and it is the man who digests and assimilates his food. . . .

The union of soul and body in the constitution of man is an analogue of the union of the divine and human nature in the person of Christ. While no analogy is expected to answer in all points, there is in this case enough of resemblance to sustain faith and rebuke unbelief. There is nothing in the one more mysterious or inscrutable than in the other. And just as difficulties in understanding the union of two distinct substances, matter and mind, in the person of man have induced many to deny the plainest facts of consciousness, even so difficulties of the same kind attending the doctrine of the union of two natures, the one human and the other divine, in the person of Christ have led many to reject the plainest facts of Scripture.

§2. The Scriptural Facts Concerning the Person of Christ

The facts which the Bible teaches concerning the person of Christ are, first, that He was truly man, i.e., He had a perfect or complete human nature. Hence everything that can be predicated of man (that is, of man as man, and not of man as fallen) can be predicated of Christ. Secondly, He was truly God, i.e., He had a perfect divine nature. Hence everything that can be predicated of God can be predicated of Christ. Thirdly, He was one person. The same person, self, or ego who said, "I thirst," said, "Before Abraham was, I am." This is the whole doctrine of the incarnation. . . .

A. Proofs of the Individual Elements of the Doctrine

1. Christ is truly man

The Scriptures teach that Christ had a complete human nature. That is, He had a true body and a rational soul. By a true body is meant a material body which in everything essential was like the bodies of ordinary men. . . . This is plain from His being born of a woman. He was conceived in the womb of the Virgin Mary and was nourished of her substance so as to be consubstantial with her. His body increased in stature, passing through the ordinary process of development from infancy to manhood. It was subject to all the affections of a human body. It was subject to pain, pleasure, hunger, thirst, fatigue, suffering, and death. It could be seen, felt, and handled. The Scriptures declare it to have been flesh and blood: "Forasmuch then as the children are partakers of flesh and blood, he also himself likewise took part of the same" (Heb. 2:14). He was predicted in the Old Testament as the seed of the woman, the seed of Abraham, the Son of David. He was declared to be a man, a man of sorrows, the man Christ Jesus, and He called Himself the Son of man. This designation occurs some eighty times in the Gospels. Nothing, therefore, is revealed concerning Christ more distinctly than that He had a true body.

It is no less plain that Christ had a rational soul. He thought, reasoned, and felt; He was joyful and sorrowful; He increased in wisdom; He was ignorant of the time when the day of judgment would come. He must, therefore, have had a finite human intelligence. These two elements, a true body and a rational soul, prove that Christ had a perfect or complete human nature.

2. Christ is truly God

The Scriptures with equal clearness declare that Christ is truly God. All divine names and titles are applied to Him. He is called God, the Mighty God, the great God, God over all, Jehovah, Lord, the Lord of lords and the King of kings. All divine attributes are ascribed to Him. He is declared to be omnipresent, omniscient, almighty, and immutable, the same yesterday, today, and forever. He is set forth as the creator and upholder and ruler of the universe. All things were created by Him and for Him, and by Him all things consist. All intelligent creatures, even the angels, are commanded to prostrate themselves before Him. . . . To Him men and angels are responsible for their character and conduct. He requires that men should honour Him as they honour the Father, that they should exercise the same faith in Him that they do in God. He declares that He and the Father are one, that those who have seen Him have seen the Father also. He calls all men unto Him and promises to forgive their sins, to send them the Holy Spirit, to give them rest and peace, to raise them up at the last day, and to give them eternal life. God is not more, and cannot promise more, or do more than Christ is said to be, to promise, and to do. . . .

3. *Christ is one person*

Although perfect man and perfect God, Christ was, nevertheless, but one person. There is, in the first place, no evidence of a twofold personality in Christ. The Scriptures reveal the Father, Son, and Spirit as distinct persons in the Godhead: they use the personal pronouns in reference to each other. The Father says Thou to the Son, and the Son says Thou to the Father. . . . There is nothing analogous to this in the case of the two natures of Christ, however. The one nature is never distinguished from the other as a distinct person. The Son of God never addresses the Son of man as a person different from Himself. The Scriptures reveal but one Christ. In the second place, besides this negative proof the Bible affords abundant evidence of the individual personality of our Lord. He says I, me, mine; He is addressed as Thou; He is spoken of as He. "Thou art not yet fifty years old" (John 8:57) and "Thou, Lord, in the beginning hast laid the foundation of the earth; and the heavens are the works of thine hands" (Heb. 1:10), were addressed to the same person. . . . In teaching that Christ had a perfect human and a perfect divine nature and is one person, the Bible teaches the whole doctrine of the incarnation as it entered into the faith of the Church from the beginning. . . .

The conflicting representations, the constant setting forth the same person as man and also as God, admit of no solution but in the doctrine of the incarnation. This is the key to the whole Bible. If this doctrine be denied, all is confusion and contradiction. If it be admitted, all is light, harmony, and power. Christ is both God and man in two distinct natures and one person forever. This is the great mystery. God manifest in the flesh is the distinguishing doctrine of the religion of the Bible; without the incarnation Christianity would be a cold and lifeless corpse.

B. *Proofs of the Doctrine in Its Entirety*

In addition to Scriptural revelations of the individual elements of the doctrine of the incarnation, there are some passages in which this doctrine is so clearly stated in its entirety that they cannot be properly overlooked in treating of this subject. In John 1:1–14 numerous assertions are made concerning the Logos: (1) He existed in eternity; (2) He was in intimate relation to God; (3) He was God; (4) He was the creator of all things; (5) In Him was life—having life in Himself, He is the source of all natural, intellectual, and spiritual life; (6) therefore, He is the true light, that is, the fountain of all knowledge and all holiness; (7) He came into the world which He had made, but the world did not recognize Him; (8) He came to His own people, and even they did not receive Him; (9) He became flesh, i.e., He assumed our nature, dwelling among us as a man; and (10) we saw His glory, a glory which revealed Him to be the only begotten of the Father. It is here taught that a truly divine person, the eternal Word, the creator of the world, became man, dwelt among men, and revealed Himself as the eternal Son of God to those who had eyes to see. Here is the whole doctrine of the incarnation taught in the most explicit terms.

A second passage to the same effect is 1 John 1:1–3. It is there taught that what was in the beginning, what was with God, what was eternal, what was essentially life, appeared on earth so as to be seen, heard, and handled. Here again a divine, invisible, eternal person is said to have assumed our nature, a real body and a rational soul. He could be seen and touched as well as heard. This is the main idea of this epistle. The incarnation is declared to be the essential doctrine of the gospel: "Every spirit that confesseth that Jesus Christ is come in the flesh is of God: and every spirit that confesseth not that Jesus Christ is come in the flesh is not of God: and this is that spirit of antichrist, whereof ye have heard that it should come; and even now already is it in the world" (1 John 4:2–3; see also Rom. 1:1–5; 9:5; 1 Tim. 3:16; Heb. 2:14). . . .

No passage, however, is more full and explicit on this subject than is Philippians 2:5–11. It is here taught that Jesus Christ existed in the form of God. . . . Now, of course, only someone who is God can exist in the form of God, i.e., can manifest all divine perfections. Hence it is here asserted that Jesus Christ was God. But He became a man like other men. He assumed the form of a servant and even submitted to die upon the cross. For that reason He has been exalted above all created beings and invested with universal and absolute authority. Christ, therefore, has a divine nature and a human nature and is one person. . . .

Nothing can be plainer than that the Scriptures teach that Christ is truly God, that He is truly man, and that He is one person. They assert of Him whatever may be said of God and everything that can be said of a sinless man. They enter into no explanations. They assume it as a certain fact that Christ is God and man in one person, just as they assume that a man is a soul and body in one person.

We could conceivably end the present discussion with this simple statement of the doctrine concerning Christ's person as it is presented in the Scriptures. False explanations, however, create the necessity for a correct one. Errorists in all ages have so explained the facts recorded concerning Christ as to deny the truth concerning His divinity, or the integrity of His human nature, or the unity of His person. Hence the Church has been constrained to teach what the Bible doctrine involves as to (1) the nature of the union of the divine and human elements in Christ and (2) the consequences of that union.

§3. The Hypostatical Union

A. Two Natures in Christ

... In setting forth His Son as clothed in all the attributes of humanity—i.e., (1) a body which was born of a woman, which increased in stature, which was seen, felt, and handled, and (2) a soul which was troubled, joyful, and sorrowful, which increased in wisdom and was ignorant of certain things—God intends and requires that we should believe that Jesus Christ was a true man. He was not a phantom, not an abstraction, not a complex of properties without the substance of humanity, but a true or real man like other men, yet without sin. In like manner when He is declared to be God over all, to be omniscient, almighty, and eternal, it is no less evident that He has a truly divine nature, that the substance of God in Him is the subject in which these divine attributes inhere. This being so, we are taught that the elements combined in the constitution of His person, namely, humanity and divinity, are two distinct natures or substances. Such has been the faith of the Church universal. . . .

B. The Two Natures Are United but Not Mingled or Confounded

We have seen that the elements united or combined in the person of Christ are two distinct substances, humanity and divinity; He has in His constitution both the same essence or substance which constitutes us men and the same substance which makes God infinite, eternal, and immutable in all His perfections. Our second point is that this union is not by mixture so that a third substance is produced which is neither humanity nor divinity but possesses the properties of both. This is an impossibility, because the properties in question are incompatible. We cannot mingle mind and matter so as to make a substance which is neither mind nor matter but spiritual matter, for that would be a contradiction. . . . Neither is it possible that the divine and human natures should be so mingled as to result in a third, which is neither purely human nor purely divine. . . . Christ would then be neither God nor man—a direct contradiction of the Scriptures' constant declaration that He is both God and man. In all Christian creeds, therefore, it is declared that each of the two natures in Christ retains its own properties and attributes. They all teach that the natures are not confounded.

Just as the human body retains all its material properties and the soul all its spiritual attributes in their union in our persons, so humanity and divinity retain each its peculiar properties in their union in the person of Christ. And since intelligence, sensibility, and will are the properties of the human soul, without which it ceases to be a soul, it follows that the human soul of Christ retained its intelligence, sensibility, and will. But intelligence and will are no less the essential properties of the divine nature and thus were retained after its union with the human nature in Christ. Therefore, in teaching that Christ was truly man and truly God, the Scriptures teach that He had a finite intelligence and an infinite intelligence. Moreover, in Him there were and are two wills or operations. His human intellect increased; His divine intelligence was and is infinite. His human will had only human power; His divine will was and is almighty. Mysterious and inscrutable as all this is, it is not more so than the union of the discordant elements of mind and matter in our own constitution.

C. There Is No Transfer of the Attributes of One Nature to the Other

The third point in relation to the person of Christ is that no attribute of either nature is transferred to the other. This is virtually included in what has already been said. There are those, however, who while admitting that the two natures in Christ are not mixed or confounded, yet maintain that the attributes of the one are transferred to the other. But the properties or attributes of a substance constitute its essence, so that if they be removed or if others of a different nature be added to them, the substance itself is changed. If rationality be taken from mind, it ceases to be mind. If rationality be added to matter, it ceases to be matter. . . . If infinity be conferred on the finite, it ceases to be finite. If divine attributes be conferred on man, he ceases to be man; and if human attributes be transferred to God, He ceases to be God.

The Scriptures teach that the human nature of Christ remained in its integrity after the incarnation and that the divine nature remained divine. . . .

D. *The Union Is a Personal Union*

The union of the two natures in Christ is a personal or hypostatic union. By this is meant, in the first place, that it is not a mere indwelling of the divine nature analogous to the indwelling of the Spirit of God in His people. Much less is it a mere moral or sympathetic union, or a temporary and mutable relation between the two. In the second place, hypostatic union means that Christ is but one person. As the union of the soul and body constitutes a man one person, so the union of the Son of God with our nature constitutes Him one person. And as in man the personality is in the soul and not in the body, so the personality of Christ is in the divine nature. . . . This is proved by the fact that the Son was from all eternity a distinct person in the Godhead. It was a divine person, not merely a divine nature, that assumed humanity or became incarnate. Hence it follows that the human nature of Christ, separately considered, is impersonal. . . . The human nature never possessed distinct subsistence, which, along with rationality, is essential to personality. The Son of God, then, did not unite Himself with a human person, but with a human nature. The proof of this is that Christ is but one person. . . .

§4. Consequences of the Hypostatical Union

A. *Communion of Attributes*

The first and most obvious of the consequences of the hypostatical union is the communion of attributes. By this is not meant that the one nature participates in the attributes of the other, but simply that the person is the partaker of the attributes of both natures, so that whatever may be affirmed of either nature may be affirmed of the person. . . . Thus we may say that Christ is finite and infinite, that He is ignorant and omniscient, that He is less than God and equal with God, that He existed from eternity and was born in time, that He created all things and was a man of sorrows. Accordingly, the sacred writers easily and naturally predicate of our Lord the attributes of humanity and those of divinity, however His person may be denominated. They call Him Lord or Son of man and attribute to Him, often in the same sentence, what is true of Him only as God, what is true only of His humanity, and what is true of Him only as the God-man. . . .

B. The Acts of Christ

The second consequence of the hypostatical union relates to the acts of Christ. As a man is one person and all his acts are the acts of that one person, so all the acts of Christ are the acts of His whole person. We earlier remarked that the acts of a man are of three classes: such as are purely mental, like thought; such as belong exclusively to the body, like digestion and assimilation; and such as are mixed, i.e., both mental and corporeal, like speaking and writing. Yet all are equally the acts of the man. It is the man who thinks, who digests his food, and who speaks. So of the acts of Christ. Some are purely divine, like creation and preservation; some are purely human, like eating, drinking, and sleeping; some are theanthropic (i.e., acts in which both natures concur), like the work of redemption. Yet all these acts are the acts of Christ, of one and the same person. It was Christ who created the world. It was Christ who ate and drank. And it is Christ who redeems us from the power of darkness. . . .

Such being the Scriptural doctrine concerning the person of Christ, it follows that although the divine nature is immutable and impassible, and therefore neither the obedience nor the suffering of Christ is to be ascribed to His divine nature, they were none the less the obedience and suffering of a divine person. The soul of man cannot be wounded or burnt, but when the body is injured it is the man who suffers. In like manner the obedience of Christ was the righteousness of God, and the blood of Christ was the blood of God. It is to this fact that the infinite merit and efficiency of His work are due. . . . It was because Christ was possessed of an eternal Spirit that He by the one offering of Himself has perfected forever them who are sanctified. . . .

C. Christ Can Sympathize with His People

A third inference which the apostles drew from this doctrine is that Christ is a merciful and faithful High Priest. He is just the Saviour we need. God as God, the eternal Logos, could neither be nor do what our necessities demand. Much less could any mere man, however wise, holy, or benevolent, meet the wants of our souls. Only a Saviour who is both God and man in two distinct natures and one person forever could be all we need and all we might desire. As God He is ever present, almighty, and infinite in all His resources to save and bless; and as man He can be touched with a sense of our infirmities. Being a man, He was tempted as we are, was subject to the law which we violated, and endured the penalty which we had incurred. In Him all the fulness of the Godhead dwells in a bodily form. Thus He is accessible to us, and we can all partake of His fulness. We are therefore complete in Him, wanting nothing. . . .

§5. **Erroneous and Heretical Doctrines on the Person of Christ**
§6. **Doctrine of the Reformed Churches**
§7. **Lutheran Doctrine**
§8. **Later Forms of the Doctrine**
§9. **Modern Forms of the Doctrine**

Chapter IV

The Mediatorial Work of Christ

§1. Christ the Only Mediator

According to the Scriptures the incarnation of the eternal Son of God was not a necessary event arising out of the nature of God. It was not the culminating point in the development of humanity. It was an act of voluntary humiliation. God gave His Son for the redemption of man. He came into the world to save His people from their sins, to seek and save those who are lost. He took part in flesh and blood in order, by death, to destroy him who had the power of death, that is, the devil, and to deliver those who through fear of death (i.e., through apprehension of the wrath of God) were all their lifetime subject to bondage. He died the just for the unjust that He might bring us near to God. . . . There was no other way by which that end could be accomplished. This is clearly taught in the Scriptures. The name of Christ is the only name whereby men can be saved. If righteousness could have been attained in any other way, Christ, says the apostle, is dead in vain (Gal. 2:21). If the law (any institution or device) could have given life, verily righteousness should have been by the law (Gal. 3:21).

363

As the design of the incarnation of the Son of God was to reconcile us unto God, and as reconciliation of parties at variance is a work of mediation, Christ is called our mediator. . . . Furthermore, as reconciliation between God and man necessarily involves satisfaction for the sin committed against God, the mediator in this case must make an atonement for sin. As this was done and could be done only by Christ, it follows that He is the only mediator between God and man. He is our peacemaker, who reconciles Jews and Gentiles unto God in one body by the cross (Eph. 2:16). To us, therefore, there is but one mediator between God and man, the man Christ Jesus (1 Tim. 2:5). . . .

§2. Qualifications for the Work

Only Jesus Christ has the personal qualifications which the Scriptures clearly teach are necessary for the mediator between God and man:

(1) The mediator must be a man. The reason why Christ assumed our nature and not the nature of angels is that He came to redeem us (Heb. 2:14–16). It was necessary that He should be made under the law which we had broken, that He should fulfil all righteousness, that He should suffer and die, that He should be able to sympathize in all the infirmities of His people, and that He should be united to them in a common nature. He who sanctifies (purifies from sin both as guilt and as pollution) and those who are sanctified are and must be of one nature. Therefore as the children were partakers of flesh and blood, He also took part of the same (Heb. 2:11–14).

(2) The mediator between God and man must be sinless. Under the law the victim offered on the altar must be without blemish. Christ, in offering Himself unto God as a sacrifice for the sins of the world, had to be Himself free from sin. The High Priest, therefore, who became human, He whom our necessities demanded, had to be holy, harmless, undefiled, and separate from sinners (Heb. 7:26). Christ was, therefore, "without sin" (Heb 4:15; 1 Peter 2:22). A sinful saviour from sin is an impossibility. He would not have access to God. He could not be a sacrifice for sins, and he could not be the source of holiness and eternal life to his people.

The sinlessness of our Lord does not amount to absolute impeccability. As a true man, He must have been capable of sinning. That He did not sin under the greatest provocation, that when He was reviled He blessed, that when He suffered He threatened not, that He was dumb, as a sheep before its shearers, is held up to us as an example. Temptation implies the possibility of sin. If from the constitution of His person it had been impossible for Christ to sin, His temptation was unreal and without effect, and He cannot sympathize with His people.

(3) It was no less necessary that our mediator should be a divine person. The blood of no mere creature could take away sin. It was only because our Lord was possessed of an eternal Spirit that the one offering of Himself has forever perfected them that believe. None but a divine person could destroy the power of Satan and deliver those who were led captive by him at his will. None but He who had life in Himself could be the source of life, spiritual and eternal, to His people. None but an almighty person could control all events to the final consummation of the plan of redemption and could raise the dead; furthermore, infinite wisdom and knowledge are requisite in Him who is to be judge of all men and the head over all to His Church. None but one in whom dwelt all the fulness of the Godhead could be the object as well as the source of the religious life of all the redeemed. . . .

As it was necessary that Christ should be both God and man in two distinct natures and one person in order to effect our redemption, it follows that His mediatorial work, which includes all He did and is still doing for the salvation of men, is not the work of His human to the exclusion of His divine nature, nor of the latter to the exclusion of the former. It is the work of the God-man. . . .

All Christ's acts and sufferings in the execution of His mediatorial work were, therefore, the acts and sufferings of a divine person. And indeed there are several evidences that it was the Lord of glory who was crucified and the Son of God who poured out His soul unto death: (1) The Scriptures attribute the efficacy and power of His acts, the truth and wisdom of His words, and the value of His sufferings to the fact that they were the acts, words, and sufferings of God manifested in the flesh. They are predicated of one and the same person who from the beginning was with God and was God, who created all things and for whom all things were made and by whom all things consist. (2) If the mediatorial work of Christ belongs to His human nature exclusively or, in other words, if He is our mediator only as man, then we have only a human saviour, and all the glory, power, and sufficiency of the gospel are departed. (3) The redemption of fallen men is a work for which only a divine person is competent. . . . Only the eternal Son could deliver us from the bondage of Satan and from the death of sin, or raise the dead, or give eternal life, or conquer all His and our enemies. . . .

§3. The Threefold Office of Christ

It has long been customary with theologians to exhibit the mediatorial work of Christ under the heads of His prophetic, sacerdotal, and kingly offices. . . . This division has not only the sanction of established usage and obvious convenience, but a firm Scriptural basis as well. (1) In the Old Testament the several offices were distinct. The prophet as such was not a priest, and the king was neither priest nor prophet. Two of these offices were at times united in the same person under the theocracy, as Moses was both priest and prophet, and David prophet and king. Nevertheless the offices were distinct. (2) During the theocracy the Messiah was predicted as Prophet, Priest, and King. Moses, speaking of Christ, said, "The LORD thy God will raise up unto thee a Prophet from the midst of thee, of thy brethren, like unto me" (Deut. 18:15). It was abundantly taught that the coming deliverer was to discharge all the duties of a prophet as a revealer of the will of God. He was to be the great teacher of righteousness, a light to lighten the Gentiles as well as the glory of His people Israel. No less clearly and frequently was it declared that He should be a priest. "Thou art a priest for ever after the order of Melchizedek" (Ps. 110:4). He was to be a priest upon His throne (Zech. 6:13). He was to bear the sins of the people and make intercession for transgressors. His royal office is rendered so prominent in the Messianic prophecies that the Jews looked for Him only as a king. He was to reign over all nations. Of His kingdom there was to be no end. He was to be the Lord of lords and King of kings. (3) In the New Testament the Redeemer, in assuming the office of the promised Messiah, presented Himself to the people as their Prophet, Priest, and King; and those who received Him at all received Him in all these offices. He applied to Himself all the prophecies relating to the Messiah. He referred to Moses as predicting the Messiah as a prophet, to David as setting Him forth as a priest, and to Daniel's prophecies of the kingdom which He came to establish. . . . Moreover, nothing can be plainer than that as the Old Testament prophets predicted that the Messiah should be Prophet, Priest, and King, so the New Testament writers represent the Lord Jesus as filling all these offices. (4) That this is not a merely figurative representation is plain from the fact that Christ exercised all the functions of a prophet, of a priest, and of a king. He was not simply so called, but the work which He actually performed included in perfection all that the ancient prophets, priests, and kings performed in a lower sphere and as an adumbration of Christ's more perfect work. (5) We as fallen men, ignorant, guilty, polluted, and helpless, need a Saviour who is a prophet to instruct us, a priest to atone and to make intercession for us, and a king to rule over and protect us. . . . This is not, therefore, simply a convenient classification of the contents of His mission and work, but it enters into its very nature and must be retained in our theology if we would take the truth as it is revealed in the Word of God. . . .

Chapter V

Prophetic Office

§1. Nature of the Prophetic Office

According to Scriptural usage a prophet is one who speaks for another. In Exodus 7:1 the Lord says to Moses, "See, I have made thee a god to Pharaoh: and Aaron thy brother shall be thy prophet." Moses was to be the authoritative source of the communication, Aaron the organ of communication. This is the relation of the prophet to God. God communicates, the prophet announces the message which he has received. In Exodus 4:16 it is said of Aaron in relation to Moses, "He shall be to thee instead of a mouth." . . . Similarly, with regard to the Prophet who is to be raised up, the Lord says: "I will put my words in his mouth; and he shall speak unto them all that I shall command him. And it shall come to pass, that whosoever will not hearken unto my words which he shall speak in my name, I will require it of him" (Deut. 18:18–19). A prophet, therefore, is one who speaks in the name of God. He must, however, be the immediate organ of God. In one sense, of course, every one who reads or preaches the Word of God may be said "to speak in his name." The truths which he utters rest upon the authority of God; the words which the preacher is the organ of announcing to the people are God's words. Ministers, however, are not prophets. A broad distinction is made in both the Old and New Testaments between prophets and teachers (or ministers). The former were inspired, the latter were not.

Any man receiving a revelation from God, or inspired in the communication of it, is, in the Scriptures, called a prophet. . . . When, therefore, the Messiah was predicted as a prophet, it was predicted that He should be the great organ of God in communicating His mind and will to men. And, indeed, when our Lord did appear on earth, it was to speak the words of God: "The word which ye hear is not mine, but the Father's which sent me" (John 14:24); "Jesus of Nazareth, which was a prophet mighty in deed and word" (Luke 24:19).

§2. How Christ Executes the Office of a Prophet

Christ has executed His prophetic office in several ways: (1) As the eternal Word, the Logos, the manifested and manifesting Jehovah, He is the source of all knowledge to the intelligent universe and especially to the children of men. He was and is the light of the world. He is the truth. In Him dwell all the treasures of wisdom and knowledge, and from Him radiates all the light that men receive or attain. . . . (2) Under the old dispensation, or before His advent in the flesh, He made known God and His purposes and will not only by personal manifestations of Himself to the patriarchs and prophets, but also by His Spirit, who revealed the truth and will of God, inspired those appointed to record these revelations, and illuminated the minds of His people, thus bringing them to the saving knowledge of the truth. (3) While on earth Christ continued the exercise of His prophetic office by the instruction He gave in His discourses, parables, and expositions of the law and of the prophets, and in all that He taught concerning His own person and work, and concerning the progress and consummation of His kingdom. (4) Since His ascension He performs the same office not only in the fuller revelation of the gospel made to the apostles and in their inspiration as infallible teachers, but also in the institution of the ministry, the constant calling of men to that office, and the influences of the Holy Ghost, who cooperates with the truth in every human heart, rendering the truth effectual to the sanctification and salvation of His own people. Thus from the beginning, both in His state of humiliation and in His state of exaltation, both before and after His advent in the flesh, does Christ execute the office of a prophet in revealing to us by His Word and Spirit the will of God for our salvation.

Chapter VI

Priestly Office

§1. Christ Is Truly, Not Figuratively, a Priest

The meaning of the word priest and the nature of the office are to be determined from general usage and consent, the express declarations of the Scriptures, and the nature of the functions peculiar to the office. From these sources it is clear (1) that a priest is a man duly appointed to act for other men in things pertaining to God. The idea which lies at the foundation of the office is that men, being sinners, do not have liberty of access to God. Therefore, one who has that right in himself, or to whom it is conceded, must be appointed to draw near to God in their behalf. A priest, consequently, from the nature of his office, is a mediator. (2) A priest is appointed to offer gifts and sacrifices for sins. His function is to reconcile men to God, to make expiation for their sins, and to present their persons, acknowledgments, and offerings to God. (3) A priest makes intercession for the people. He not only prays as one man may pray for another, but also urges the efficacy of his sacrifice and the authority of his office as grounds on which his prayers should be answered. . . .

There are a number of evidences that this definition of a priest is correct and that Christ is a priest in the true sense of the term:

(1) Men have everywhere and at all times been conscious of sin. In that consciousness is included a sense of guilt (or of just exposure to the displeasure of God), of pollution, and of consequent unworthiness to approach God. Men's consciences, or the laws of their moral nature, have ever taught them both the necessity of the expiation of guilt by a satisfaction of divine justice and their own inability and unworthiness to make any adequate atonement or to secure by their own efforts the favour of God. They have, therefore, ever sought for some one or some class of men to act in their behalf, and to do for them what they know must be done and what they are convinced they cannot do for themselves. Hence the appointment of priests, who have always been regarded as men whose business it is to propitiate God by expiatory sacrifices, by oblations, and by prayers. . . .

(2) In the Old Testament a priest was a man selected from the people and appointed to act as their mediator, drawing nigh to God in their behalf; it was his business to offer expiatory sacrifices and to make intercession for offenders. The people were not allowed to draw near to God. The high priest alone could enter within the veil, and he was permitted to do so only with blood which he offered for himself and for the sins of the people. All this was both symbolical and typical. What the Aaronic priests were symbolically, Christ was really. What they in their office and services typified was fulfilled in Him. They were the shadow, He the substance. They taught how sin was to be taken away, He actually removed it. To deny that Christ is a priest in the Old Testament sense of the term, then, would be to set the Scriptures at naught, or to adopt principles of interpretation which would invalidate all their teaching.

(3) We have in the New Testament an authoritative definition of the word and an exhibition of the nature of the office. In Hebrews 5:1 it is said, "Every high priest. . . . is ordained for men (for their benefit and in their place) in things pertaining to God, that he may offer both gifts and sacrifices for sins." Here all the ideas earlier insisted upon are distinctly recognized. A priest is a man appointed to draw near to God and to offer sacrifices for others. Such a priest Christ is declared to have been.

(4) Not only is Christ called a priest in Hebrews, but the apostle throughout that epistle proves that (a) He had all the qualifications

for the office, (b) He was appointed by God, (c) He was a priest of a higher order than Aaron, (d) His priesthood superseded all others, (e) He performed all the functions of the office—mediation, sacrifice, and intercession, and (f) His sacrifice was so efficacious that it need not be repeated. By the one offering of Himself He hath obtained eternal redemption for us.

(5) The effects or benefits secured by the work of Christ flow from the exercise of the priestly office in our behalf. Those benefits are (a) expiation of our guilt, (b) the propitiation of God, and (c) our consequent reconciliation with Him, whence flow all the subjective blessings of spiritual and eternal life. These are benefits which are not secured by teaching, by moral influence, by example, or by any inward change wrought in us. Christ, therefore, is truly a priest in the full Scriptural sense of the term.

§2. Christ Our Only Priest

That Christ is our only Priest follows from the nature and design of the office: (1) No man, save the Lord Jesus Christ, has liberty of access unto God. All other men, being sinners, need some one to approach God on their behalf. (2) No other sacrifice than His could take away sin. (3) It is only through Him that God is propitious to sinful men, and (4) it is only through Him that the benefits which flow from the favour of God are conveyed to His people.

The priests of the Old Testament were, as before remarked, only symbols and types of the true priesthood of Christ. Their sacrifices could not purify the conscience from the sense of sin. . . . They secured reconciliation with God only so far as they were regarded as representing the real sacrifice of Christ as the object of faith and ground of confidence. Hence, as the apostle teaches, they were offered continually because the people needed to be constantly reminded of their guilt and of their need of the more effectual sacrifice predicted in their Scriptures.

If the Old Testament priests were not really priests, except typically, much less so are ministers of the gospel. . . . This is clear from the fact that the word priest is never once applied to them in the New Testament. Every appropriate title of honour is lavished upon them. They are called the bishops of souls, pastors, teachers, rulers, governors, the servants or ministers of God, stewards of the divine mysteries, watchmen, heralds, but never priests. As the sacred writers were Jews to whom nothing was more familiar than the word priest, the fact that they never once use the word, or any of its cognates, in reference to

the ministers of the gospel, whether apostles, presbyters, or evange-
lists, is little less than miraculous. It is one of those cases in which the
silence of Scripture speaks volumes.

Moreover, no priestly function is ever attributed to Christian ministers. They do not mediate between God and man. They are never
said to offer sacrifices for sins, and they have no power as intercessors
which does not belong to every believer. Rather, all believers are priests
in the only sense in which men under the gospel can be priests; that
is, all have liberty of access to God through Christ. . . . Since, then, the
ministry is not a class distinct from the people, Christ is the only
mediator between God and man, the only and all-sufficient High Priest
of our profession.

§3. Definition of Terms

Christ, it is said, by His once offering up Himself a sacrifice to satisfy
divine justice and reconcile us to God, and by His making continual
intercession for us, executes the office of a priest. Expiation, propitiation, reconciliation, and intercession are the several aspects under
which the work of Christ as a priest is presented in the Word of God.
Before attempting to state what the Scriptures teach in reference to
these points, it will be well to define a few terms which are of constant
occurrence in theological discussions of this subject. . . .

A. Satisfaction

The word satisfaction has for ages been generally used to designate
the special work of Christ in the salvation of men. . . . By the satisfaction of Christ is meant all that He, acting in the place and in behalf
of sinners, has done to meet the demands of the law and justice of
God. . . . Now there are two kinds of satisfaction, which, as they differ
essentially in their nature and effects, should not be confounded. The
one is pecuniary or commercial, the other penal or forensic. When a
debtor pays the demand of his creditor in full, he satisfies the claims
and is entirely free from any further demands. In this case the thing
paid is the precise sum due, neither more nor less. It is a simple matter
of an exact exchange, so much for so much. There can be no condescension, mercy, or grace on the part of a creditor receiving the payment of a debt. It matters not to him by whom the debt is paid,
whether by the debtor himself or by some one in his stead, for the
claim of the creditor is simply upon the amount due and not upon the
person of the debtor. In the case of crimes the matter is different. The

demand is then upon the offender. He himself is liable to justice. In human courts substitution is out of the question. The essential point in matters of crime is not the nature of the penalty, but who shall suffer. The soul that sins, it shall die. . . . Provision of a substitute to bear the penalty in the place of the criminal would be to the offender a matter of pure grace enhanced in proportion to the dignity of the substitute and the greatness of the evil from which the criminal is delivered. Moreover, in the case of crimes the penalty need not be (and very rarely is) of the nature of the injury inflicted. All that is required is that it should be a just equivalent. . . . Another important difference between pecuniary and penal satisfaction is that in the former case the very act serves to liberate; that is, the moment the debt is paid, the debtor is completely free. There is no delay, nor are any conditions attached to his deliverance. But in the case of a criminal, as he has no claim to have a substitute take his place, if one be provided, the terms on which the benefits of his substitution shall accrue to the offender are matters of agreement or covenant between the substitute and the magistrate who represents justice. The deliverance of the offender may be immediate, unconditional, and complete; or it may be deferred, suspended on certain conditions, and only gradually bestowed.

The fact that the satisfaction of Christ was not pecuniary, but penal or forensic, that is, a satisfaction for sinners and not for those who owed a certain amount of money, has certain implications:

(1) The satisfaction of Christ does not consist in an exact exchange, so much for so much. . . . All that justice demands in penal satisfaction is that it should be a real satisfaction and not merely something graciously accepted as such. It must bear an adequate proportion to the crime committed. It may be different in kind, but it must have inherent value. To fine a man a few pence for wanton homicide would be a mockery, but death or imprisonment for life would be a real satisfaction to justice. Therefore, when the Church says that Christ satisfied divine justice for the sins of men, it is teaching that what He did and suffered was a real and adequate compensation for the penalty remitted and the benefits conferred. His sufferings and death were adequate to accomplish all the ends which would have been accomplished by the punishment of the sins of men. He satisfied justice. He rendered it consistent with the justice of God that the sinner should be justified. But He did not suffer in either kind or degree what sinners would have suffered. In value, His sufferings infinitely transcended theirs. The death of an eminently good man would outweigh the annihilation of a universe of insects. So the humiliation, sufferings, and death of the eternal Son of God immeasurably transcended in worth and power the penalty which a world of sinners would have endured.

(2) The satisfaction of Christ was a matter of grace. The Father was not bound to provide a substitute for fallen men, nor was the Son bound to assume that office. It was an act of pure grace that God arrested the execution of the penalty of the law and consented to accept the vicarious sufferings and death of His only begotten Son. And it was an act of unparalleled love that the Son consented to assume our nature, bear our sins, and die, the just for the unjust, to bring us near to God. All the benefits, therefore, which accrue to sinners in consequence of the satisfaction of Christ are to them pure gratuities. Such blessings, to which sinners in themselves have no claim, call for gratitude and exclude boasting.

(3) Nevertheless, it is a matter of justice that the blessings which Christ intended to secure for His people should be actually bestowed upon them. They were promised to Him as the reward of His obedience and sufferings. God covenanted with Christ that if He fulfilled the conditions imposed, if He made satisfaction for the sins of His people, they would be saved. . . . Furthermore, the Scriptures teach that Christ gave Himself for a ransom. When a ransom is paid and accepted, the deliverance of the captive is a matter of justice. . . . So in the case of the satisfaction of Christ. Justice demands the salvation of His people. That is His reward. He has acquired this claim on the justice of God.

(4) The satisfaction of Christ being a matter of covenant between the Father and the Son, the distribution of its benefits is determined by the terms of that covenant. The very act of satisfaction does not of itself liberate. The people of God are not justified from eternity. They do not come into the world in a justified state. They remain (if adults) in a state of condemnation until they believe. And even then, the benefits of redemption are granted gradually. The believer receives more and more of them in this life, but the full plentitude of blessings is reserved for the life to come. All these are facts of Scripture and of experience, and they are all explained by the nature of the satisfaction rendered. It is not the payment of a debt, but a matter of agreement or covenant. It seemed good to the parties to the covenant of redemption that matters should be so arranged. . . .

B. Vicarious

By vicarious suffering or punishment is not meant merely sufferings endured for the benefit of others. The sufferings of martyrs, patriots, and philanthropists, although endured for the good of the Church, the country, and mankind, are not vicarious. That word, according to its signification and usage, includes the idea of substitution. Vicarious suffering is suffering endured by one person in the stead of another, i.e., in his place. It necessarily supposes the exemption of the party in whose place the suffering is endured. . . . When, therefore, it is said that the sufferings of Christ were vicarious, the meaning is that He suffered in the place of sinners. He was their substitute. He assumed their obligation to satisfy justice. What He did and suffered precluded the necessity of their fulfilling the demands of the law in their own persons. . . .

C. Guilt

The word guilt expresses the relation which sin bears to justice or, as the older theologians said, to the penalty of the law. This relation is twofold. First, there is that which is expressed by the words criminality, ill-desert, and demerit. This is inseparable from sin. It can belong to no one who is not personally a sinner, and it permanently attaches to all who have sinned. It is not removed by justification, much less by pardon. It cannot be transferred from one person to another. But secondly, guilt means the obligation to satisfy justice. This may be removed by the satisfaction of justice personally or vicariously. It may be transferred from one person to another, or assumed by one person for another. When a man steals or commits any other offence to which a specific penalty is attached by the law of the land, if he submit to the penalty, his guilt in this latter sense is removed. Not only is it proper that he should remain without further molestation by the State for that offence, but justice demands his exemption from any further punishment. It is in this sense that it is said that the guilt of Adam's sin is imputed to us, that Christ assumed the guilt of our sins, and that His blood cleanses from guilt. This is very different from demerit or personal ill-desert. . . .

D. Redemption

In its application to the work of Christ the word redemption means deliverance by purchase. This is plain because it is a deliverance not by authority, or power, or teaching, or moral influence, but by blood, by the payment of a ransom. . . .

E. Expiation and Propitiation

Expiation and propitiation are correlative terms. The sinner (or his guilt) is expiated; God (or justice) is propitiated. Guilt must, from the nature of God, be visited with punishment, which is the expression of God's disapprobation of sin. Scripture tells us that guilt can be expiated, or covered, by satisfaction, i.e., by vicarious punishment. God is thereby rendered propitious, i.e., it is now consistent with His nature to pardon and bless the sinner. Propitious and loving are not convertible terms. God is love. He loved us while we were yet sinners and before satisfaction was rendered. Satisfaction or expiation does not awaken love in the divine mind. It only renders it consistent with His justice that God should exercise His love towards transgressors of His law. . . .

In the Old Testament and in the New, God is declared to be just in the sense that His nature demands the punishment of sin; there can be no remission without such punishment, which can be either vicarious or personal. Now the plan of salvation symbolically and typically exhibited in the Mosaic institution, expounded in the prophets, and clearly and variously taught in the New Testament, involves the substitution of the incarnate Son of God in the place of sinners. Taking upon Himself their obligation to satisfy divine justice, He in fact made a full and perfect satisfaction for sin, bearing the penalty of the law in their stead. All this is so plain and undeniable that it has always been the faith of the Church. . . .

Chapter **VII**

Satisfaction of Christ

[§1. Statement of the Doctrine]

§2. The Intrinsic Worth of Christ's Satisfaction

The doctrine of the satisfaction of Christ is an essential part of the faith of the Church universal. Its first point is that Christ's work is of the nature of a satisfaction in that it meets and answers all the demands of God's law and justice against the sinner. The law no longer

377

condemns the sinner who believes in Christ. . . . For the work of Christ
. . . has an inherent worth which renders it a perfect satisfaction, so
that justice has no further demands. It is here as in the case of state
criminals. If such an offender suffers the penalty which the law prescribes as the punishment of his offence, he is no longer liable to condemnation. No further punishment can justly be demanded for that
offence. In a similar manner we speak of the perfection of Christ's
satisfaction. It perfectly, from its own intrinsic worth, meets the demands of justice. This is what is meant when the Scriptures compare
the work of Christ to the payment of a debt. The creditor has no further
claims when the debt due to him is fully paid.

This perfection of the satisfaction of Christ is not due to His having
suffered either in kind or in degree what the sinner would have been
required to endure, but principally to the infinite dignity of His person.
He was not a mere man, but God and man in one person. His obedience and sufferings were therefore the obedience and sufferings of a
divine person. (This does not imply, as the Patripassians in the ancient
Church assumed and as some writers in modern times assume, that
the divine nature itself suffered.) . . . The satisfaction of Christ has all
the value which belongs to the obedience and sufferings of the eternal
Son of God, and His righteousness, active as well as passive, is infinitely meritorious. This the apostle clearly teaches in Hebrews
9:13–14. . . .

[§3. Doctrine of the Scotists and Remonstrants]

§4. Satisfaction Rendered to Justice

The second point involved in the Scriptural doctrine concerning the
satisfaction of Christ is that it was a satisfaction to the justice of
God. . . . [We are speaking here of what is referred to as distributive,
retributive, or vindicatory justice:] that perfection of the divine nature
which renders it necessary that the righteous be rewarded and the
wicked punished. . . .

The Scriptures constantly and variously teach that God is just. . . .
Almost the first words which God spoke to Adam were, "In the day
that thou eatest thereof thou shalt surely die" (Gen. 2:17). The angels
who sinned are reserved in chains unto the judgment of the great day.
Death is declared to be the wages, i.e., the proper recompense, of sin.
God is declared to be a consuming fire. . . . The penalty of the law is
as much a revelation of the nature of God as its precept is. As His
perfections prevent Him from exonerating men from the obligation of

obedience, so He cannot allow them to sin with impunity. It is therefore declared that He will reward every man according to his works.

In addition, all the divinely ordained institutions of religion, whether patriarchal, Mosaic, or Christian, were founded on the assumption of the justice of God and were designed to impress that great truth on the minds of men. These institutions presuppose that men are sinners and that, being sinners, they need expiation for their guilt, as well as moral purification, if they are to experience salvation. Sacrifices, therefore, were instituted from the beginning to teach the necessity of expiation and to serve as prophetic types of the only effectual expiation, which, in the fulness of time, was to be offered for the sins of men. . . . It is not, then, simply this or that declaration of Scripture, or this or that institution which must be explained away if the justice of God be denied, but the whole form and structure of the religion of the Bible. That religion as the religion for sinners rests on the assumption of the necessity of expiation. This is its cornerstone; the whole fabric falls into ruin if that stone be removed.

That God cannot pardon sin without a satisfaction to justice and that He cannot have fellowship with the unholy are two great truths which are revealed in the constitution of our nature as well as in the Scriptures. . . . It is because the demands of justice are met by the work of Christ that His gospel is the power of God unto salvation, and that it is so unspeakably precious to those whom the Spirit of God has convinced of sin. . . . Through faith in Christ's blood we sinners can be pardoned and restored to the favour of God because Christ was set forth as an expiation for our sins, because He was made a curse for us, because He being just died for the unjust, because He bore our sins in His own body on the tree, and because the penalty due to us was laid on Him. It is clear, therefore, that the Scriptures recognize the truth that God is just in the sense that He is determined by His moral excellence to punish all sin, and thus the satisfaction of Christ which secures the pardon of sinners is rendered to the justice of God. The primary and principal design of the satisfaction of Christ is to meet the demands of justice, so that God can be just in justifying the ungodly.

§5. The Work of Christ Satisfies the Demands of the Law

A third point involved in the Church doctrine on the work of Christ is that it is a satisfaction to the divine law. . . . To satisfy justice is, as we have just seen, to satisfy the demand which justice makes for the punishment of sin. But the law demands far more than the punishment of sin, and therefore satisfaction to the law includes more than the satisfaction of vindicatory justice.

The Scriptural doctrine concerning Christ's satisfaction of the law of God includes the following points:

(1) The law of God is immutable. It can neither be abrogated nor dispensed with. This is true as respects both its precepts and penalty. Such is the nature of God as holy that He cannot cease to require His rational creatures to be holy. It can never cease to be obligatory on them to love and obey God. And such is the nature of God as just that He cannot cease to condemn sin and all those who are guilty of sin.

(2) Our relation to the law is twofold, federal and moral. The law is, in effect, a covenant prescribing the conditions of life. It says, "Ye shall keep my statutes and my judgments: which if a man do, he shall live in them" (Lev. 18:5); and "Cursed is every one that continueth not in all things which are written in the book of the law to do them" (Gal. 3:10; cf. Deut. 27:26).

(3) From this federal relation to the law we are, under the gospel, delivered. No longer is the condition of salvation that we be free from all sin and render perfect obedience to the law. If this were not the case, no flesh living could be saved. We are not under the law but under grace.

(4) This deliverance from the law is not effected by its abrogation, or by lowering its demands, but by the work of Christ. He was made under the law that He might redeem those who were under the law.

(5) The work of Christ was therefore of the nature of a satisfaction to the demands of the law. By His obedience and sufferings, by His whole righteousness, active and passive, He, as our representative and substitute, did and endured all that the law demands.

(6) Those who by faith receive this righteousness and trust upon it for justification are saved and receive the renewing of their whole nature into the image of God. Those who refuse to submit to this righteousness of God and go about to establish their own righteousness are left under the demands of the law; they are required to be free from all sin or, having sinned, to bear the penalty. . . .

These principles—the immutability of the divine law, the necessity of its demands being satisfied, the impossibility of sinners making that satisfaction for themselves, the possibility of its being rendered by substitution, and the accomplishment of this work in our behalf by a wonderfully constituted person—are the great constituent principles of the religion of the Bible. As the revelation contained in the Scriptures has been made in a progressive form, we find all these principles culminating in their full development in the late writings of the New Testament. In the Epistle to the Romans, for example, the following positions are assumed and established: (1) The law must be fulfilled. (2) It demands perfect obedience; in case of transgression, it prescribes the penalty of death. (3) No fallen man can fulfil those conditions or satisfy the demands of the law. (4) Christ, the eternal Son of God, clothed in our nature, has made this satisfaction to the law for us. (5) We are thus freed from the law. We are not under law, but under grace. (6) All that is now required of us is faith in Christ. To those who are in Him there is no condemnation. (7) By His obedience we are constituted righteous; and being thus reconciled to God, we become partakers of the holy and immortal life of Christ and are delivered not only from the penalty, but from the power of sin, and made the sons and heirs of God. (8) The great condemning sin of men under the gospel is rejection of the righteousness and Spirit of Christ and insistence either that they need no Saviour or that they can in some way save themselves, that they can satisfy all God's just demands and deliver themselves from the power of sin. If these principles are eliminated from the Pauline Epistles, their whole life and power are gone. Paul assures us that he received his doctrines not from men, but by the revelation of Jesus Christ. It is against this rock—the substitution of Christ in the place of sinners and His making a full satisfaction to the justice and law of God, thus working out for us a perfect righteousness by which we may be justified—that the assaults of philosophy, falsely so called, and of heresy in all its forms have been directed from the beginning. . . . But it remains what it ever has been—the foundation of the faith, hope, and life of the Church.

§6. Proof of the Doctrine

A. Christ Saves Us as Our Priest

Christ is said to save men as a priest. He does not save them by the mere exercise of power, nor by instruction and mental illumination, nor by any objective moral influence, nor by any subjective operation, whether natural or supernatural, whether intelligible or mystical, but by acting for them the part of a representative, substitute, propitiator, and intercessor. It was in the Old Testament foretold that the Messiah was to be both Priest and King, that He was to be a priest after the order of Melchizedek. In the New Testament, and especially in the Epistle to the Hebrews, it is taught that . . . Christ, the eternal Son of God, assumed our nature in order that He might be a merciful and faithful High Priest to make expiation for the sins of the people. The sacrifice which this great High Priest offered in our behalf was not the blood of irrational animals, but His own most precious blood. This one sacrifice has perfected forever (made a perfect expiation for) them that are sanctified (Heb. 10:14). It has superseded all others—no other is needed, and no other is possible. Those who reject this method of salvation certainly perish. To them there remaineth no more sacrifice for sins (Heb. 10:26). . . .

If we adhere to the doctrine of the Bible, we must believe that Christ saves us not by power, nor by moral influence, but by the priestly service of offering Himself as an expiatory sacrifice for our sins. To deny this express teaching of the Scriptures—whether by explaining it away as an accommodation to the mode of thought prevalent in the age of the apostles, or by substituting modern ideas of the nature of sacrifices for those of the Bible and of the whole ancient world, or by attempting to get at the truth inclosed in these Scriptural forms while we reject the forms themselves—is to substitute our thoughts for God's thoughts, our way of salvation for God's way. If we adhere to the ordinary authoritative rules of interpretation, we cannot deny that the Scriptures teach that Christ saves us as a priest by making a full expiation for our sins, bearing their penalty in His own person in our behalf.

B. *Christ Saves Us as a Sacrifice*

Intimately connected with the argument from the priestly office of Christ, and inseparable from it, is the argument derived from those numerous passages in which He is set forth as a sacrifice for sin. . . . He was a sacrifice in the same sense in which the sin offerings of the Old Testament were sacrifices. . . . Now the Scriptural idea of these sin offerings is that (1) they were designed to propitiate God—to satisfy His justice and to render it consistent and proper that the offence for which they were offered be forgiven; (2) this propitiation of God was secured by the expiation of guilt—by an offering which so covered sin that it did not appear before Him as demanding punishment; (3) this expiation was effected by vicarious punishment, the victim being substituted for the offender, bearing his guilt, and suffering the penalty which he had incurred; and (4) the effect of such sin offerings was the pardon of the offender and his restoration to favour and to the enjoyment of the privileges which he had forfeited. This being the Scriptural idea of a sacrifice for sin, the Scriptures in declaring that Christ was a sacrifice intend to teach that He was the substitute for sinners, that He bore their guilt, suffered the penalty of the law in their stead, and thereby reconciled them unto God, i.e., rendered it consistent with His perfections that they should be pardoned and restored to the divine fellowship and favour. . . .

The passages in which Christ is represented as a sacrifice for sin are too numerous to be here specially considered (see Isa. 53; Rom. 3:25; Eph. 5:2; 2 Cor. 5:21; Heb. 9:14; 10:10–14; 1 Peter 2:24; and 1 John 2:2). The New Testament, and particularly the Epistle to the Hebrews, as before remarked, declares and teaches that the priesthood of the old economy was a type of the priesthood of Christ; that the sacrifices of that dispensation were types of His sacrifice; that as the blood of bulls and goats purified the flesh, so the blood of Christ cleanses the soul from guilt; and that as they in their sphere were expiations effected by vicarious punishment, so was the sacrifice of Christ in the infinitely higher sphere to which His work belongs. Such being the relation between the old economy and the new, the whole sacrificial service of the Mosaic institutions becomes to the Christian an extended and irresistible proof and exhibition of the work of Christ as an expiation for the sins of the world and a satisfaction to the justice of God.

C. Christ Our Redeemer

There is a third class of passages equally numerous and equally important. Christ is set forth not only as a priest and as a sacrifice, but also as a Redeemer, and His work as a redemption. Redemption is deliverance from evil by the payment of a ransom. . . . The price or ransom paid for our redemption is always said to be Christ Himself, His blood, His death. As the evils consequent on our apostasy from God are manifold, Christ's work as a Redeemer is presented in manifold relations in the Word of God.

1. Redemption from the penalty of the law

The first and most obvious consequence of sin is subjection to the penalty of the law. The wages of sin is death. Every sin of necessity subjects the sinner to the wrath and curse of God. The first step, therefore, in the salvation of sinners is their redemption from that curse. Until this is done, they are of necessity separated from God. Alienation from Him involves both misery and subjection to the power of sin. So long as men are under the curse, they are cut off from the only source of holiness and life. Such is the doctrine taught throughout the Bible and elaborately in Romans 6 and 7. In effecting the salvation of His people, Christ "redeemed them from the curse of the law," not by a mere act of sovereignty or power, not by moral influence restoring them to virtue, but by being "made a curse for them." No language can be plainer than this. The curse is the penalty of the law. We were subject to that penalty. Christ has redeemed us from that subjection by being made a curse for us and paying the penalty of the law in our stead (Gal. 3:13). . . .

2. Redemption from the law

Nearly allied to this mode of representation are those passages in which Christ is said to have delivered us from the law. Redemption from bondage to the law includes deliverance not only from its penalty, but also from the obligation to satisfy its demands. This is the fundamental idea of Paul's doctrine of justification. The law demands perfect obedience. It says, Do this and live; and "Cursed is every one that continueth not in all things which are written in the book of the law to do them" (Gal. 3:10; cf. Deut. 27:26). No man since the fall is able to fulfil these demands, yet we must fulfil them or perish. The only possible method, according to the Scriptures, by which men can be saved is that they be delivered from this obligation of perfect obedience. This, the apostle teaches, has been effected by Christ. He was "made under the law, to redeem them that were under the law" (Gal. 4:4–5). Therefore Paul can say to believers, "Ye are not under the law, but under grace" (Rom. 6:14). This redemption from the law is said in Romans 7:4 to be "by the body of Christ." Hence we are justified not by our own obedience, but by the obedience of Christ (Rom. 5:18–19). Redemption in this case is not mere deliverance, but a true redemption, i.e., a deliverance effected by satisfying all the just claims which are against us. . . .

3. Redemption from the power of sin

In redeeming us from the curse of the law, Christ redeems us also from the power of sin. "Whosoever committeth sin," saith our Lord, "is the servant (the slave) of sin" (John 8:34). This is a bondage from which no man can deliver himself. To deliver us from this bondage was the great object of the mission of Christ (Gal. 1:4; Titus 2:14; 1 Peter 1:18–19). . . . This deliverance from sin is a true redemption in that it could have been effected only by payment of a ransom or a satisfaction of justice. . . .

4. Redemption from the power of Satan

The Scriptures teach that Christ redeems us from the power of Satan, the prince and god of this world. His kingdom is the kingdom of darkness, in which all men since Adam are born and in which they remain until translated into the kingdom of God's dear Son. They are Satan's subjects "taken captive by him at his will" (2 Tim. 2:26). The first promise was that the seed of the woman would bruise the serpent's head. Christ came to destroy the works of the devil, to cast him down from his place of usurped power, to deliver those who are subject to his dominion. The fact of Christ's redemption of His people from the power of Satan and the mode of its accomplishment are clearly stated in Hebrews 2:14–15. . . .

5. *Final redemption from all evil*

Christ redeems us not only from the curse of the law, from the law itself as a covenant of works, from the power of sin, and from the dominion of Satan, but also from all evil. Since evil is the consequence of the curse of the law, we are delivered from all evil when we are redeemed from the curse of the law. Hence the word redemption is often used for the sum of all the benefits of Christ's work, or for the consummation of the great scheme of salvation. Thus our Lord says that when the Son of man shall appear in His glory, His disciples may be sure that their "redemption draweth nigh" (Luke 21:28). They are sealed unto the day of redemption (Eph. 1:13–14). Christ has "obtained eternal redemption for us" (Heb. 9:12).

It is therefore the plain doctrine of Scripture that, as before said, Christ saves us neither by the mere exercise of power, nor by His doctrine, nor by His example, nor by the moral influence which He exerts, nor by any subjective influence on His people, whether natural or mystical, but by rendering satisfaction to divine justice, by expiating sin, and by giving Himself as a ransom for our deliverance from the curse and authority of the law. Thus He reconciles us to God by making it consistent with His perfections to exercise mercy toward sinners and then renewing them after His own image. . . .

[§7. Objections]

For Whom Did Christ Die?

§1. State of the Question

For whom did Christ die? This is a question disputed by Augustinians and anti-Augustinians. The former believe that God from all eternity elected some to everlasting life and that, accordingly, the mission and work of His Son had a special reference to their salvation. The latter, denying that there has been any such election of a part of the human family to salvation, maintain that the mission and work of Christ had an equal reference to all mankind.

This question does not, in the first place, concern the nature of Christ's work. . . . Both Augustinians and anti-Augustinians admit the work of Christ to have been a true satisfaction for sin. But while Lutherans and Reformed agree entirely as to the nature of the atonement, they differ as to its design. The former maintain that it had an equal reference to all mankind, the latter that it had special reference to the elect.

In the second place, the question does not concern the value of Christ's satisfaction. Augustinians admit the value to be infinite, for it is determined by the dignity of the sacrifice. As no limit can be placed on the dignity of the eternal Son of God who offered Himself for our sins, so no limit can be assigned to the meritorious value of His work. It is a gross misrepresentation of the Augustinian doctrine to say that it teaches that Christ suffered so much for so many, and that He would have suffered more had a greater number of people been included in the purpose of salvation. This is not the doctrine of any Church on earth and never has been. What was sufficient for one was sufficient for all. Nothing less than the light and heat of the sun is sufficient for any one plant or animal. But what is absolutely necessary for each is abundantly sufficient for the infinite number and variety of plants and animals which fill the earth. All that Christ did and suffered would have been necessary had only one human soul been the object of re-demption, and nothing different and nothing more would have been required had every child of Adam been saved through His blood.

In the third place, the question does not concern the suitableness of the atonement. What is suitable for one is suitable for all. The right-eousness of Christ, the merit of His obedience and death, is needed for justification by each individual of our race and therefore is needed by all. It is no more appropriate to one man than to another. Christ ful-filled the conditions of the covenant under which all men were placed. He rendered the obedience required of all and suffered the penalty which all had incurred; therefore, His work is equally suited to all.

In the fourth place, the question does not concern the actual appli-cation of the redemption purchased by Christ. The parties to this con-troversy are agreed that only some rather than all of mankind are to be actually saved.

The whole issue concerns simply the purpose of God in the mission of His Son. What was the design of Christ's coming into the world and doing and suffering all He actually did and suffered? Was it merely to make the salvation of all men possible, to remove the obstacles which stood in the way of the offer of pardon and acceptance to sinners? Or was it specially to render certain the salvation of His own people, i.e., of those given to Him by the Father? Augustinians answer the latter question in the affirmative.... Augustinians readily admit, however, that the death of Christ had a relation to the whole human family as well. It is the ground on which salvation is offered to every creature under heaven who hears the gospel.... Moreover, it secures to the whole race at large, and to all classes of men, innumerable blessings both providential and religious.... In view of the effects which the death of Christ produces on the relation of all mankind to God, it has in all ages been customary with Augustinians to say that Christ died sufficiently for all, but efficaciously only for the elect. There is a sense, therefore, in which He died for all, and there is a sense in which He died for the elect alone. The simple question is, Did the death of Christ have a reference to the elect which it did not have to other men? Did He come into the world to secure the salvation of those given to Him by the Father, so that the other effects of His work are merely incidental to what was done for the attainment of that object? Augustinians answer these questions in the affirmative.

§2. Proof of the Augustinian Doctrine

A. *Argument from the Nature of the Covenant of Redemption*

We earlier discussed the covenant between the Father and the Son in relation to the salvation of men (pp. 340–42). Christ came into the world in execution of that covenant. The nature of the covenant, therefore, determines the object of His death.... According to the Augustinians, men by their fall sank into a state of sin and misery in which they might justly have been left. But God, having in His infinite mercy determined to save a multitude whom no man could number, gave them to His Son as His inheritance, provided He would assume their nature and fulfil all righteousness in their stead. Christ came into the world to accomplish this plan. He obeyed and suffered in the place and for the salvation of those thus given to Him. This was the definite object of His mission, and therefore His death had a reference to them which it could not possibly have had to those whom God determined to leave to the just recompense of their sins.... Such being God's plan respecting the salvation of men, it of necessity follows that election preceded redemption, that God had determined whom He would save before He sent His Son to save them. Therefore our Lord said that those given to Him by His Father would certainly come to Him, and that He would raise them up at the last day. These Scriptural facts cannot be admitted without its being also admitted that the death of Christ had a reference to His people, whose salvation it rendered certain, which it did not have to others whom, for infinitely wise reasons, God determined to leave to themselves. It follows, therefore, from the nature of the covenant of redemption, as presented in the Bible, that

Christ did not die equally for all mankind, but that He gave Himself for His people and for their redemption.

B. *Argument from the Doctrine of Election*

This follows also from the doctrine of election. Indeed, that Christ died specially for the elect was never denied until the doctrine of election itself was rejected. Augustine, the follower and expounder of Paul, taught that God out of His mere good pleasure had elected some to everlasting life and that Christ came into the world to suffer and die for their salvation.... Not until the Remonstrants in Holland, under the teaching of Arminius, rejected the Church doctrine of the sovereignty of God in election was the doctrine that the atonement had a special reference to the people of God rejected. It is therefore a matter of history that the doctrine of election and the Augustinian doctrine as to the design of the work of Christ have been inseparably united. As this connection is historical, so also is it logical. The one doctrine necessarily involves the other. If God from eternity determined to save one portion of the human race and not another, it is a contradiction to say that the plan of salvation had equal reference to both portions, or that the Father as truly sent His Son to die for those whom He had predetermined not to save as for those whom He had chosen to make the heirs of salvation.

C. *Express Declarations of Scripture*

We find numerous passages which declare that Christ died to save His people from their sins. He did not come merely to render their salvation possible, but actually to deliver them from the curse of the law and from the power of sin. This is included in all the Scriptural representations of the nature and design of His work. No man pays a ransom without being certain that those for whom it is paid will be delivered. It is not a ransom unless it actually redeems. And an offering is not sacrifice unless it actually expiates and propitiates. The effect of a ransom and sacrifice may indeed be conditional, but the occurrence of the condition will be rendered certain before the costly sacrifice is offered.

There are numerous passages in which it is expressly declared that Christ gave Himself for His Church (Eph. 5:25), that He laid down His life for His sheep (John 10:15), that He laid down His life for His friends (John 15:13), that He died that He might gather together in one the children of God that are scattered abroad (John 11:52), that it was the Church which He purchased with His blood (Acts 20:28).

When mankind are divided into two classes, the Church and the world, the friends and the enemies of God, the sheep and the goats, whatever is affirmed distinctively of the one class is implicitly denied of the other. When it is said that Christ loved His Church and gave Himself for it, that He laid down His life for His sheep, it is clear that what is being said of the Church and of the sheep is not true of those who belong to the world. . . . Every assertion that Christ died for a people is a denial of the doctrine that He died equally for all men.

D. *Argument from the Special Love of God*

By the love of God is sometimes meant His . . . peculiar, mysterious, sovereign, immeasurable love of which His own people, the Church of the first-born whose names are written in heaven, are the objects. This love is (1) infinitely great; (2) discriminating, i.e., fixed on some and not on others of the children of men; (3) perfectly gratuitous and sovereign, i.e., not founded on the special attractiveness of its objects but, like parental affection, on the mere fact that they are His children; (4) immutable; and (5) all-providing, i.e., it secures all saving blessings and even all good. Now to this peculiar and infinite love the gift of Christ is uniformly referred: "Herein is love, not that we loved God, but that he loved us, and sent his Son to be the propitiation for our sins" (1 John 4:10); "Hereby perceive we the love of God (or hereby we know what love is), because he (Christ) laid down his life for us" (1 John 3:16); "He that spared not his own Son, but delivered him up for us all, how shall he not with him also freely give us all things?" (Rom. 8:32; see also vv. 35–39; 5:8; John 15:13). . . . This representation that the peculiar love of God to His people, to His Church, to the elect, is the source of the gift of Christ is so predominant in the Scriptures that it cannot be ignored in any view of the plan of salvation. With this representation every other statement of the Scriptures must be consistent; therefore, the theory which assumes that the love which secured the gift of God's eternal Son was mere benevolence which had all men for its object, many of whom are allowed to perish, must be unscriptural.

E. *Argument from the Believer's Union with Christ*

Another argument is derived from the nature of the union between Christ and His people. The Bible teaches that a certain portion of the human race were given to Christ before the foundation of the world, and that all thus given to Him will certainly come to Him and be saved. This union, so far as it was from eternity, was not a union of nature, nor by faith, nor by the indwelling of the Holy Spirit, but a federal union. Thus Christ came into the world as the federal head and representative not of the human race, but of those given to Him by the Father. And, therefore, His work, so far as its main design is concerned, was for them alone. Whatever reference it had to others was subordinate and incidental. All this is illustrated and proved by Paul in the parallel which he draws between Adam and Christ (Rom. 5:12–21). . . . As all in Adam died, so all in Christ are made alive. Such is the nature of the union in both cases that the sin of the one rendered certain and rendered just the death of all united to Adam, and the righteousness of the other rendered certain and just the salvation of all who are in Him. The sin of Adam did not make the condemnation of all men merely possible; it was the ground of their actual condemnation. So the righteousness of Christ did not make the salvation of men merely possible, but it secured the actual salvation of those for whom He wrought. . . .

F. *The Augustinian Doctrine Embraces All the Facts of the Case*

The final test of any theory is whether it agrees with the facts to be explained. The difficulty with all the anti-Augustinian views as to the design of Christ's death is that while they are consistent with some of the Scriptural facts connected with the subject, they are utterly irreconcilable with others not less clearly revealed and equally important. . . . On the other hand, the Augustinian doctrine recognizes and reconciles all the Scriptural assertions connected with the subject. The facts which are clearly revealed concerning the death or work of Christ are: (1) God from eternity gave a people to His Son; (2) the peculiar and infinite love of God to His people is declared to be the motive for the gift of His Son, and their salvation the design of His mission; (3) it was as their representative, head, and substitute He came into the world, assumed our nature, fulfilled all righteousness, and bore the curse of the law; and (4) the salvation of all given to Him by the Father is thus rendered absolutely certain. That the Augustinian scheme agrees with these great Scriptural facts is readily admitted. . . .

G. *Certain Passages of Scripture Considered*

How is the Augustinian doctrine to be reconciled with those passages which, in one form or another, teach that Christ died for all men? In answer to this question it may be remarked in the first place that Augustinians do not deny that Christ died for all men. What they deny is that He died equally and with the same design for all men. He died for all that He might arrest the immediate execution of the penalty of the law upon the whole of our apostate race; that He might secure for men the innumerable blessings attending their state on earth, which, in one important sense, is a state of probation; and that He might lay the foundation for the offer of pardon and reconciliation with God on condition of faith and repentance. . . . By this dispensation it is rendered manifest . . . that the perdition of those that perish is their own fault. They will not come to Christ that they may have life. . . . Every human being who does come, however, is saved. This is what is meant when it is said, or implied in Scripture, that Christ gave Himself as a propitiation not for our sins only, but for the sins of the whole world. He was a propitiation effectually for the sins of His people, and sufficiently for the sins of the whole world. Augustinians have no need to wrest the Scriptures. They are under no necessity of departing from their fundamental principle that it is the duty of the theologian to subordinate his theories to the Bible and teach not what seems to him to be true or reasonable, but simply what the Bible teaches.

But, in the second place, it is to be remarked that general terms are often used indefinitely and not comprehensively. They mean all kinds or classes, and not each and every individual. When Christ said, "I, if I be lifted up from the earth, will draw all men unto me" (John 12:32), He meant men of all ages, classes, and conditions, and not every individual man. . . . And while He is often called the Saviour of mankind, no one means by this that He actually saves all mankind. What is meant is that He is our Saviour, the Saviour of men rather than of angels, not of Jews exclusively nor of the Gentiles only, not of the rich or of the poor alone, not of the righteous only, but also of publicans and sinners. He is the Saviour of all men who come unto Him. . . .

On the same page we may find both declarations that God wills that all men should come unto Him and explicit assertions that He has determined to leave multitudes to perish in their sins. In like manner, the express declarations that the incomprehensible and peculiar love of God for His own people induced Him to send His Son for their redemption, that Christ came into the world for that specific object, that He died for His sheep, that He gave Himself for His Church, and that the salvation of all for whom He thus offered Himself is rendered certain by the gift of the Spirit to bring them to faith and repentance, are intermingled with declarations of good-will to all mankind and with offers of salvation to every one who will believe in the Son of God. . . . We must not ignore nor deny either of these modes of representation, but open our minds wide enough to receive them both and reconcile them as best we can. Both are true, whether we can see their consistency or not.

In review of this subject, it is plain that the doctrine that Christ died equally for all men with the purpose of rendering the salvation of all possible has no advantage over the doctrine that He died specially for His own people and with the purpose of rendering their salvation certain. It presents no higher view of the love of God or of the value of Christ's work. It affords no better ground for the offer of salvation "to every creature," nor does it render more obvious the justice of the condemnation of those who reject the gospel. They are condemned by God, angels, and men, and by their own consciences, because they refuse to believe that Jesus is the Son of God, God manifest in the flesh, and to love, worship, trust, and obey Him accordingly. Furthermore, the anti-Augustinian doctrine is founded on a partial view of the facts of the case. It leaves out of account the clearly revealed special love of God to His peculiar people, the union between Christ and His chosen, the representative character which He assumed as their substitute, and the certain efficacy of His sacrifice in virtue of the covenant of redemption. The anti-Augustinian position therefore is the limited and meager scheme whereas the orthodox doctrine is catholic and comprehensive, full of consolation and spiritual power as well as of justice to all mankind.

Chapter **IX**

Theories of the Atonement

Chapter X

Intercession of Christ

§1. Christ Our Intercessor

On the day of atonement the high priest under the old dispensation, after having offered sacrifices for sin in the outer court, took the blood of the victims and a censer with burning incense, entered within the veil, and there presented the blood before God, sprinkling it upon the mercy seat. In like manner, as we are taught by the apostle, Christ, having offered Himself on the cross as a sacrifice for our sins, has passed through the heavens, there to appear before God in our behalf. He is, therefore, said to be the minister of the true tabernacle, which the Lord pitched and not man. His priestly office is now exercised in heaven, where He ever lives to intercede for us.

This intercessory work of Christ is expressed in Scripture in various ways:

(1) Christ appears before God for us (Heb. 9:24). Christ presents Himself before God as our representative. His perfect manhood, His official character, and His finished work plead for us before the throne

of God. All that the Son of God as incarnate is, and all that He did on earth, He is and did for us, so that God can regard us with all the favour which is due to Him. His presence, therefore, is a perpetual and prevailing intercession with God in behalf of His people and secures for them all the benefits of His redemption.

(2) Christ draws near to God on our behalf (Rom. 8:34; Heb. 7:25). That is, Christ speaks to God in our behalf or, as it is expressed in John 17:9, He prays for us.

(3) Christ is called our Paraclete. This word is translated advocate in 1 John 2:1, and comforter in John 14:16; 15:26; and 16:7. Neither translation expresses its full meaning. A paraclete is, in the comprehensive sense of the word, a helper, some one who is called upon for help. As, however, the guilty, the ignorant, the friendless, when arraigned before a tribunal of justice, need above all things an advocate, one who will undertake their cause, present a plea in their behalf, and use all his influence to secure their acquittal, it is in this sense especially that Christ is set forth as our Paraclete. He is our advocate. He appears at the bar of God for us. He pleads our cause. He presents His work of obedience and suffering as the ground of our justification. He exerts His influence, the influence of His character as the Son of God in whom the Father is ever well pleased, and whom He heareth always, as well as the influence due to Him in virtue of the covenant of redemption and the perfect fulfilment of its conditions, to secure for His people all the good they need. It is, therefore, especially in passages which speak of justification and of judicial process that Christ's intercession is brought into view (see Rom. 8:34; 1 John 2:1).

§2. Its Nature

. . . The intercession of Christ involves a number of activities: (1) He appears before God as the sacrifice for our sins and as our High Priest, on the ground of whose work we receive the remission of our sins, the gift of the Holy Spirit, and all needed good. (2) He defends us against the sentence of the law and the charges of Satan, who is the great accuser. (3) He offers Himself as our surety, not only that the demands of justice shall be shown to be satisfied, but that His people shall be obedient and faithful. (4) He sanctifies the prayers and all the services of the redeemed, rendering them acceptable to God through the savour of His own merits.

§3. Its Objects

. . . Christ intercedes generally for all men and specially for the elect. The former is assumed on the authority of Luke 23:34, where

Christ is represented as praying for His murderers, saying, "Father, forgive them; for they know not what they do." It is said to be due to the intercession of Christ that the wicked are not immediately cut off, that they have the gospel preached to them and every opportunity afforded them of returning unto God. There is, however, an intercession of which only the people of Christ are objects. Our Lord Himself says: "I pray not for the world, but for them which thou hast given me" (John 17:9). So far as the intercession of Christ is part of His official work as the High Priest of our profession, He intercedes only for those who accept Him as their Priest and whom He represents in the covenant of redemption. This follows from the nature of His office as Priest, from His own express declaration, and from the fact that His intercession is certainly efficacious. Him the Father heareth always. If He interceded for all, all would certainly be saved.

[§4. Intercession of Saints]

Chapter XI

Kingly Office of Christ

§1. The Church God's Kingdom

As the creator and preserver of the universe, infinite in His being and perfections, God is the absolute sovereign of all His creatures. This sovereignty He exercises over the material world by His wisdom and power, and over rational beings as a moral ruler. From this rightful authority of God our race revolted and thereby became a part of the kingdom of darkness of which Satan is the head. To this kingdom the mass of mankind has ever since belonged. But God in His grace and mercy determined to deliver men from the consequences of their apostasy. He not only announced the coming of a Redeemer who would destroy the power of Satan, but He at once inaugurated an antagonistic kingdom consisting of men chosen out of the world and restored to their allegiance through the renewing of the Holy Ghost.

Until the time of Abraham this kingdom does not appear to have had any visible organization apart from the families of the people of God. Every pious household was a church of which the parent was the priest. To prevent the universal spread of idolatry, to preserve the knowledge of the truth, to gather in His elect, and to prepare the way for the coming of the promised Redeemer, God entered into covenant with the father of the faithful and with his descendants through Isaac, constituting them His visible kingdom and making them the depositaries and guardians of His supernatural revelations. In this covenant He promised eternal life upon condition of faith in Him that was to come.

When Moses led the Israelites out of Egypt, they were made a theocracy so constituted in its officers, in its institutions, and in its services as not only to preserve alive the knowledge of God's purpose and plan of salvation, but also to set forth the character, offices, and work of the promised seed of Abraham in whom all the nations of the earth were to be blessed.

The kingdom of God, then, has existed in our world ever since the fall of Adam. Consisting of those who acknowledge, worship, love, and obey Jehovah as the only living and true God, it has ever been the light and life of the world. It is the salt by which it is preserved. It is the leaven by which it is ultimately to be pervaded. To gather His people into this kingdom, and to carry it on to its consummation, is the end of all God's dispensations and the purpose for which His eternal Son assumed our nature. He was born to be a king. To this end He lived and died and rose again, that He might be Lord of all those given to Him by the Father.

§2. Christ Is Truly a King

. . . The Scriptures constantly speak of the Messiah as a king who was to set up a kingdom into which in the end all other kingdoms were to be merged. In addition, the Scriptures frequently designate Him as Lord, a term which, when used of God or Christ, means absolute proprietor and sovereign ruler. . . .

Already in the book of Genesis the Messiah is set forth as the Shiloh whom the people shall obey (Gen. 49:10). In reference to Him it is said in Numbers 24:17, "There shall come a Star out of Jacob, and a Sceptre shall rise out of Israel." Isaiah predicted that a virgin would bear a Son and call His name Immanuel; the government would be upon His shoulder, and His name would be called "Wonderful, Counsellor, The mighty God, The everlasting Father, The Prince of Peace. Of the increase of his government and peace there shall be no end, upon the throne of David, and upon his kingdom, to order it, and to establish it with judgment and with justice from henceforth even for ever. The zeal of the LORD of hosts will perform this" (Isa. 9:6–7). In the second psalm God declares in reference to the Messiah, "[I have] set my king upon my holy hill of Zion.... Ask of me, and I shall give thee the heathen for thine inheritance, and the uttermost parts of the earth for thy possession. Thou shalt break them with a rod of iron; thou shalt dash them in pieces like a potter's vessel" (Ps. 2:6–9). Psalms 45, 72, and 110 also show forth the Messiah in His office as King. In Daniel 7:13–14 it is said, "One like the Son of man came with the clouds of heaven, and came to the Ancient of days, and they brought him near before him. And there was given him dominion, and glory, and a kingdom, that all people, nations, and languages, should serve him: his dominion is an everlasting dominion, which shall not pass away, and his kingdom that which shall not be destroyed." ... This mode of representation pervades the Old Testament Scriptures (see also 2 Sam. 7:16; Mic. 5:2; Zech. 9:9). . . .

The New Testament likewise sets Christ forth as a king. In announcing to the Virgin Mary the approaching birth of the Messiah, the angel Gabriel said, "Thou shalt conceive in thy womb, and bring forth a son, and shalt call his name JESUS. He shall be great, and shall be called the Son of the Highest: and the Lord God shall give unto him the throne of his father David: and he shall reign over the house of Jacob for ever; and of his kingdom there shall be no end" (Luke 1:31–33). John the Baptist, the forerunner of Christ, prepared the people for His coming, saying, "Repent ye: for the kingdom of heaven is at hand" (Matt. 3:2). And our Lord Himself, when He entered upon His personal ministry, went everywhere "preaching the gospel of the kingdom of God" (Mark 1:14). Much of His teaching was devoted to setting forth the nature of the kingdom which He came to establish. Nothing, therefore, is more certain, according to the Scriptures, than that Christ is a king. . . .

§3. Nature of Christ's Kingdom

Although the kingdom of God on earth was set up immediately after the fall, yet as the Messiah was to come to make all things new and to take into His hands the administration of this kingdom, the Old Testament predicted and the New Testament announces the establishment of a new kingdom as consequent on His advent.

The word kingdom is used in Scripture in three senses: (1) royal

authority or such dominion as it is the prerogative of a king to exercise;
(2) those who are subject to that authority—among men any community, commonwealth, or territory subject to a king constitutes his
kingdom, and in the New Testament those who acknowledge Christ as
their King constitute His kingdom; and (3) the effects of the exercise
of royal authority. The word is to be understood in the first of these
senses when a kingdom or dominion is said to be given to Christ, or
when we pray, "Thy kingdom come," or when it is said, "Of his kingdom there shall be no end." It is used in the second sense when men
are said to enter into or to be cast out of the kingdom of Christ, or
when the character of those who are to constitute that kingdom is
described. And it is used in the third sense when men are said to
inherit, to see (or enjoy), to seek, and to value the kingdom of God
more than hid treasure. Hence the kingdom of God is said to consist
of righteousness, peace, and joy in the Holy Ghost. Such are the effects
of the reign of Christ.

The kingdom of God on earth is called the kingdom of Christ, or of
the Son of God, because it is administered by Him. The royal authority
is vested in Him. It is called the kingdom of God because Christ is
God, and because it is the kingdom which God was to establish on
earth in distinction from the kingdoms of men. It is called the kingdom
of heaven because its King dwells in heaven, because it is spiritual
and heavenly, and because it is to be consummated in heaven. All of
these designations are used to refer to the kingdom which the Messiah
came into the world to establish. In addition to these various designations that kingdom is also presented in different aspects; in other
words, Christ exercises His royal authority, so to speak, in different
spheres.

A. Christ's Dominion over the Universe

Christ has what theologians are accustomed to call His kingdom of
power. As God-man and as mediator, all power in heaven and earth
has been committed to His hands (Matt. 28:18). . . . In 1 Corinthians
15:27 it is said that the Father "hath put all things under his feet" (see
also Eph. 1:20–22). And the apostle says to the Philippians, "God hath
highly exalted [Christ Jesus] and given him a name which is above
every name: that at the name of Jesus every knee should bow, of things
in heaven, and things in earth, and things under the earth" (Phil.
2:9–10). . . . It is in this sense also that the writer of Hebrews says that
God hath appointed the Son heir of all things (Heb. 1:2). It is in virtue
of this dominion over the universe that Christ is called Lord of lords

and King of kings, i.e., the Sovereign over all other sovereigns in heaven and on earth.

This universal authority is exercised in a providential control and for the benefit of the Church. Christ employs the angels to minister to the heirs of salvation. He controls and restrains the principalities, powers, world rulers, and spirits of wickedness (Eph. 6:12). He over-rules all the affairs of nations and of individuals to the same end. He directs all events concerning His people severally and His Church collectively. Paul constantly recognized this providential control of Christ as directing all his steps. Under the present dispensation, therefore, Christ is the God of providence. It is in and through and by Him that the universe is governed. This dominion or kingdom is to last until its object is accomplished, i.e., until all His enemies, all forms of evil and even death itself, are subdued. Then this kingdom, this mediatorial government of the universe, is to be given up (1 Cor. 15:24).

B. Christ's Spiritual Kingdom

But besides this kingdom of power, Christ has a kingdom of grace. This kingdom of grace has two aspects: the relation in which He stands to His true people individually and collectively (the invisible Church), and the relation He sustains to the visible Church or the body of His professing people.

Christ is the King of every believing soul. He translates it from the kingdom of darkness. He brings it into subjection to Himself. He rules in and reigns over it. Every believer recognizes Christ as his absolute sovereign, as Lord of his inward as well as of his outward life. Every believer completely yields to Him reason, conscience, and heart, making Him the object of reverence, love, and obedience. . . .

The terms of admission into this spiritual kingdom are faith, repentance, and conversion: "Except a man be born of water and of the Spirit, he cannot enter into the kingdom of God" (John 3:5); "Except ye be converted, and become as little children, ye shall not enter into the kingdom of heaven" (Matt. 18:3). . . . On the other hand, we are taught that no external profession secures admission into this kingdom: "Not every one that saith unto me, Lord, Lord, shall enter into the kingdom of heaven" (Matt. 7:21). Nor will punctiliousness in the performance of rites and ceremonies avail: "Except your righteousness shall exceed the righteousness of the scribes and Pharisees, ye shall in no case enter into the kingdom of heaven" (Matt. 5:20); "He is not a Jew, which is one outwardly; neither is that circumcision, which is outward in the flesh" (Rom. 2:28). Nor will membership in any external community: "Think not to say within yourselves, We have Abraham to our father" (Matt. 3:9); "They are not all Israel, which are of Israel" (Rom. 9:6). The kingdom of Christ, in this aspect of it, is a purely spiritual community consisting of those truly and inwardly His people.

The laws of this kingdom require, first and above all, faith in Jesus Christ—the sincere belief that He is the Son of God and the Saviour of the world—and cordial submission to Him and trust in Him as our Prophet, Priest, and King. With this faith is united supreme love: "He that loveth father or mother more than me is not worthy of me: and he that loveth son or daughter more than me is not worthy of me" (Matt. 10:37); "If any man love not the Lord Jesus Christ, let him be Anathema Maranatha" (1 Cor. 16:22). With this supreme love . . . we are also bound to worship and obey Him. We stand to Him in the same relation that a slave does to his master, except that our subjection to Him is voluntary and joyful. We belong to Him not only because we are His creatures, but also because we have been purchased by His blood (1 Cor. 6:19–20). His will, and not our own, must govern our conduct and determine the use we make of our powers. All we gain, whether of knowledge, wealth, or influence, is His. He is the object or end of our living. His glory and the advancement of His kingdom are the only legitimate objects to which believers can devote their powers or resources. . . .

The laws of the kingdom moreover require not only these duties to Christ, but holiness in heart and life. His people must be poor in spirit, meek, merciful, peacemakers, long-suffering, ready to forgive, disinterested in self, bearing all things, believing all things, and hoping all things. They are forbidden to be avaricious, or covetous, or proud, or worldly-minded. In one word, they are required to be like Christ in disposition, character, and conduct.

The special law of Christ's kingdom is that its members should love one another with brotherly love—a love which leads to the recognition of all Christians as brethren belonging to the same family and entitled to the same privileges and blessings, and a love which ministers to their necessities so that there be no lack. This law is laid down at length in 2 Corinthians 8. The law of the kingdom is that every man should labour to the extent of his ability to supply the wants of those dependent on him: "Whoso hath this world's good, and seeth his brother have need, and shutteth up his bowels of compassion from him, how dwelleth the love of God in him?" (1 John 3:17). . . .

This kingdom of Christ over all His people is exercised not only by His power in their protection and direction, but especially by His Word and Spirit, through which and by whom He reigns in and rules over them. His kingdom is also everlasting. That is, the relation which believers sustain to Christ while they are on earth they will sustain to Him forever.

C. Christ's Visible Kingdom

As religion is essentially spiritual, an inward state, that aspect of the kingdom of Christ which consists of the truly regenerated is not a visible body, except so far as goodness renders itself visible by its outward manifestations. Nevertheless, as Christ has enjoined upon His people duties which render it necessary that they should organize themselves in an external society, it follows that there is and must be a visible kingdom of Christ in the world. Christians are required to associate for public worship, for the administration of the sacraments, for the maintenance and propagation of the truth. They therefore form themselves into churches and collectively constitute the visible kingdom of Christ on earth, consisting of all who profess the true religion, together with their children.

This visible kingdom is, first, spiritual in nature. That is, it is not of this world. It is not analogous to the other kingdoms which existed or do still exist among men. It has a different origin and a different end. Human kingdoms are organized among men for the temporal well-being of society. The kingdom of Christ was organized immediately by God for the promotion of religious objects. It is spiritual, or not of this world, moreover, because it has no power over the lives, liberty, or property of its members, and because all secular matters lie beyond its jurisdiction. Its prerogative is simply to declare the truth of God as revealed in His Word and to require that the truth be professed and obeyed by all under its jurisdiction. It can decide no question of politics or science which is not decided in the Bible. . . . Being designed to embrace all other kingdoms, the kingdom of Christ can exist under all forms of civil government without interfering with any. This is what Christ had in view when He declared that His kingdom was not of this world; His claim to be a king was not incompatible with the legitimate authority of the civil magistrate or of the Roman emperor. . . . His kingdom belonged to a different sphere. It took cognizance of things which lie beyond the province of secular power, and it left untouched all that belongs peculiarly to civil rulers. . . . Therefore, every form or claim of the Church which is incompatible with the legitimate authority of the State is inconsistent with the nature of Christ's kingdom as declared by Himself.

Secondly, this kingdom of Christ is catholic or universal. It embraces all who profess the true religion. It is confined to no one organization but includes them all, for all are under the authority of

Christ and subject to the laws which He has laid down in His Word. As all Christians are included in the kingdom of Christ, it is their duty to recognize each other as members of one great commonwealth and as subjects of the same sovereign.

Thirdly, this form of Christ's kingdom is temporary. It is to be merged into a higher form when He shall come the second time. As an external organization it is designed to answer certain ends and will cease when those ends are accomplished.

Fourthly, the kingdom of Christ is not a democracy, nor an aristocracy, but truly a kingdom of which Christ is absolute sovereign. Accordingly, the State has no authority to make laws to determine the faith, to regulate the worship, or to administer the discipline of the Church. It can neither appoint nor depose its officers. Nor does any civil officer in virtue of his office have any authority in the kingdom of Christ. Nor is Church power vested ultimately in the people or in the clergy. Rather, it is derived from Christ and is to be exercised by others in His name and according to the rules laid down in His Word. . . .

As Christ is the only head of the Church, it follows that its allegiance is to Him, and that whenever those outside the Church undertake to regulate its affairs or to curtail its liberties, its members are bound to obey Him rather than men. They are bound to resist by all legitimate means such usurpations and to stand fast in the liberty wherewith Christ has made them free. They are under equal obligation to resist all undue assumption of authority by those within the Church, whether it be by the brotherhood, or by individual officers, or by Church councils or courts. The allegiance of the people terminates on Christ. They are bound to obey others only so far as obedience to them is obedience to Him. . . .

As Christ is the head of His earthly kingdom, so is He its only lawgiver. He prescribes the terms of admission into His kingdom. . . . We are to receive all those whom Christ receives. No degree of knowledge nor confession beyond that which is necessary to salvation can be demanded as a condition of our recognizing any one as a Christian brother and treating him as such. Philip baptized the eunuch on the confession, "I believe that Jesus Christ is the Son of God" (Acts 8:37–38), for "whosoever believeth that Jesus is the Christ is born of God" (1 John 5:1). For men to reject from their fellowship those whom God has received into His is an intolerable presumption. All those terms of Church communion which have been set up beyond a credible profession of faith in Christ are usurpations of an authority which belongs to Him alone. . . .

§4. The Kingdom of Glory

The Scriptures teach that when Christ shall come again, He will gather His people into the kingdom prepared for them from the foundation of the world. That kingdom shall consist only of the redeemed. None but the regenerate or converted can enter it. The tares are to be separated from the wheat. The evil, we are told, "shall not inherit the kingdom of God" (Gal. 5:21). Those counted worthy of that kingdom, however, shall not only be elevated to the perfection of their nature, but shall also be exalted to great dignity, power, and glory. They shall be kings and priests unto God. They are to sit on thrones. They are to judge angels. They are to reign with Christ, sharing His dominion and glory in His everlasting kingdom. . . .

Chapter XII

Humiliation of Christ

§1. Includes His Incarnation

The apostle Paul tells us that Christ humbled Himself (Phil. 2:8). Recapitulating the simple statements of the Scriptures on this topic, the "Westminster Shorter Catechism" states that "Christ's humiliation consisted in his being born, and that in a low condition, made under the law, undergoing the miseries of this life, the wrath of God, and the cursed death of the cross; in being buried, and continuing under the power of death for a time." . . .

The person of whom all these particulars are predicated is the eternal Son of God. It was He who was born, who suffered, and who died. Though equal with God, He was made in the likeness of men and found in fashion as a man (Phil. 2:6–8). The very Son of God was born of a woman and made under the law (Gal. 4:4). . . . By the immediate or supernatural power of the Holy Ghost, the material and immaterial elements of Jesus' humanity (body and soul) were from the beginning of their existence united personally with the Logos, so that the child born of the Virgin Mary was in a true and exclusive sense the Son of God. . . .

The incarnation of the Son of God, His stooping to take into personal and perpetual union with Himself a nature infinitely lower than His own, was an act of unspeakable condescension and therefore is properly included among the particulars in which He humbled Himself. . . . Yet not only the assumption of human nature, but also all the circumstances by which it was attended enter into the Scriptural view of the humiliation of our Lord. Had He when He came into the world so manifested His glory, and so exercised His power, as to have coerced all nations to acknowledge Him as their Lord and God, and all kings to bow at His feet and bring Him their tributes, enthroning Him as the rightful and absolute sovereign of the whole earth, it would still have been an act of unspeakable condescension for God to become man. But to be a servant, to be born in a stable and cradled in a manger, to be so poor as not to have a place where to lay His head, to appear without form or comeliness so as to be despised and rejected of men—these circumstances make the condescension of our Lord to pass all comprehension. . . .

§2. He Was Made Under the Law

The humiliation of Christ included also His being made under the law. The law to which Christ subjected Himself was (1) the law given to Adam as a covenant of works, that is, as prescribing perfect obedience as the condition of life; (2) the Mosaic law which bound the chosen people; and (3) the moral law as a rule of duty. Christ was subject to the law in all these aspects in that He assumed the obligation to fulfil all righteousness, i.e., to do everything which the law in all its forms demanded. This subjection to the law was voluntary not only in that His incarnation was a voluntary act and therefore all its consequences were assumed of His own free will, but also in that even after He assumed our nature He was free from obligation to the law until He voluntarily subjected Himself to its demands. The law is made for men, i.e., for human persons. But Christ was not a human person. He remained after the incarnation, as He had been from eternity, a divine person. All His relations to the law, therefore, except as voluntarily assumed, were those which God Himself sustains to it. And God being the source of all law cannot be subject to it, except by an act of humiliation. . . . That Christ should assume the obligation to fulfil the conditions of the covenant made with Adam, to observe all the injunctions of the Mosaic law, and to submit to the moral law with its promises and penalty was, therefore, an act of voluntary humiliation.

Christ's subjection to the law was not only voluntary, but vicarious. He fulfilled it in our stead, as our representative, and for our benefit. He was made under the law that He might redeem those who were under the law (Gal. 4:4–5). It was in His role of Redeemer that He submitted. . . . He obeyed that we might be constituted righteous (Rom. 5:19). The whole course of Christ on earth was one of voluntary obedience. He came to do the will of His Father. The Old Testament prophets spoke of Him as a servant. He says of Himself, "I came down from heaven, not to do mine own will, but the will of him that sent me" (John 6:38). "Though he were a Son, yet learned he obedience" (Heb. 5:8). "Being found in fashion as a man, he humbled himself, and became obedient unto death, even the death of the cross" (Phil. 2:8). All this was for us. His subjection to the law and to the will of the Father was voluntary and vicarious for us men and for our salvation.

§3. His Sufferings and Death

The sufferings of Christ, and especially His ignominious death on the cross, are an important element in His humiliation. These sufferings continued from the beginning to the end of His earthly life. They arose partly from the natural infirmities and sensibilities of the nature which He assumed, partly from the condition of poverty in which He lived, partly from constant contact with sinners, partly from the cruel buffetings and scorning to which He submitted, and especially from the agonies of the crucifixion (the most painful as well as the most ignominious mode of death), partly from the anguish caused by the foresight of the dreadful doom that awaited the whole Jewish nation, and especially no doubt from the mysterious sorrow arising from the load of His people's sins and the hiding of His Father's face, which forced from His brow the sweat of blood in the garden, and from His lips the cry of anguish which He uttered on the cross. These are wonders not only of love, but of self-abnegation and of humiliation, which no human mind can understand or estimate. There was never sorrow like unto His sorrow.

§4. He Endured the Wrath of God

The wrath of God is a distinct particular of the burden of sorrow which Christ, for our sakes, humbled Himself to bear. The word wrath

414   Soteriology

is used in Scripture to express any manifestation of the displeasure of
God against sin. Christ, although in Himself perfectly holy, bore our
sins. He was "made sin" (2 Cor. 5:21), i.e., treated as a sinner. He was
"numbered with the transgressors" (Isa. 53:12) not only in the judgment of men, but in the dealing of God with His soul when He stood
in the place of sinners. Such Psalms as the sixteenth, fortieth, and
especially the twenty-second, which treat of the sufferings of the Messiah, represent Him as passing through all the experiences entailed in
the punishment of sin, save those which have their source in the sinfulness of the sufferer. . . . The words uttered by our Lord upon the
cross, "My God, my God, why hast thou forsaken me?" show that He
was suffering the hiding of His Father's face. What that experience
was it is impossible for us to understand. . . .

§5. His Death and Burial

Christ humbled Himself even unto death and continued under the
power of death until the third day. The reality of Christ's death has
always been an undisputed article of faith among Christians. . . .

Chapter XIII

The Exaltation of Christ

§1. Resurrection of Christ

Not only is the resurrection of Christ asserted in the Scriptures, but it is also declared to be the fundamental truth of the gospel. "If Christ be not risen," says the apostle, "then is our preaching vain, and your faith is also vain . . . ye are yet in your sins" (1 Cor. 15:14, 17). Indeed, it may be safely asserted that the resurrection of Christ is the most important fact in the history of the world:

(1) All of Christ's claims and the success of His work rest on the fact that He rose from the dead. If He rose, the gospel is true and He is the Son of God, equal with the Father, God manifest in the flesh, the Saviour of men, the Messiah predicted by the prophets, and the Prophet, Priest, and King of His people. If He rose, His sacrifice has been accepted as a satisfaction to divine justice, and His blood as a ransom for many.

(2) On His resurrection depended the mission of the Spirit, without which Christ's work would have been in vain.

415

(3) As Christ died as the head and representative of His people, His resurrection secures and illustrates theirs. As He lives, they shall live also. If He had remained under the power of death, there would be no source of spiritual life to men, for He is the vine and we are the branches. If the vine be dead, the branches must be dead also.

(4) If Christ did not rise, the whole scheme of redemption is a failure, and all the predictions and anticipations of its glorious results for time and for eternity are proved to be chimeras. "But now is Christ risen from the dead, and become the firstfruits of them that slept" (1 Cor. 15:20). . . . The kingdom of darkness has been overthrown. Satan has fallen like lightning from heaven, and the triumph of truth over error, of good over evil, of happiness over misery, is forever secured.

In addition to being the most important, the resurrection of Christ is the best-authenticated fact in the history of the world: (1) It was predicted in the Old Testament. (2) It was foretold by Christ Himself. (3) It was a fact admitting of easy verification. (4) Abundant, suitable, and frequently repeated evidence was afforded of its actual occurrence. (5) The witnesses to the fact that Christ was seen alive after His death upon the cross were numerous, competent, and on every account worthy of confidence. (6) Their sincerity of conviction was proved by the sacrifices, even that of life, which their testimony entailed upon them. (7) Their testimony was confirmed by God bearing witness together with them in signs and wonders, and divers miracles, and gifts of the Holy Ghost (Heb. 2:4). (8) That testimony of the Spirit is continued to the present time and granted to all the true children of God, for the Spirit bears witness to the truth in the heart and conscience. (9) Christ's resurrection has from its occurrence to the present time been commemorated by a religious observance of the first day of the week. (10) The effects which His gospel has produced in the state of the world admit of no other rational solution than the truth of His death and subsequent resurrection. The Christian Church is His monument. All believers are His witnesses. . . .

With regard to the nature of Christ's resurrection body there is indubitable evidence that it was identical with the body which expired upon the cross. It retained even the print of the nails which had pierced His hands and His feet. Nevertheless it was changed. To what extent is not clearly made known. . . . We do know, however, that the risen body of Christ as it now exists in heaven, although retaining its identity with His body while here on earth, is glorious, incorruptible, immortal, and spiritual. It still occupies a definite portion of space and retains all the essential properties of a body. . . .

§2. Ascension of Christ

The next step in the exaltation of Christ was His ascension to heaven (Mark 16:19; Luke 24:50–51). The most detailed account of our Lord's ascension is found in the first chapter of the Acts. There the last words of Christ to the apostles are recorded, and it is added, "When he had spoken these things, while they beheld, he was taken up; and a cloud received him out of their sight. And while they looked stedfastly toward heaven as he went up, behold, two men stood by them in white apparel; which also said, Ye men of Galilee, why stand ye gazing up into heaven? this same Jesus, which is taken up from you into heaven, shall so come in like manner as ye have seen him go into heaven" (Acts 1:9–11). From the Scriptural accounts it is apparent (1) that the ascension of Christ was of His whole person. It was the God-man, the Son of God clothed in our nature, having a true body and a rational soul, who ascended. (2) The ascension was visible. The disciples witnessed the whole transaction. They saw the person of Christ gradually rise from the earth until a cloud hid Him from their view. (3) It was a local transfer of His person from one place to another, from earth to heaven. Heaven, then, must be a definite portion of space where God specially manifests His presence, and where He is surrounded by His angels and by the spirits of the just made perfect. . . .

According to the teaching of Scripture there are a number of reasons why the ascension of Christ was necessary:

(1) Heaven was the home from which Christ came. It was the appropriate sphere of His existence. . . . Until this earth is purified from all evil and has undergone its great process of regeneration, it is not suited for the Redeemer's abode in His state of exaltation.

(2) It was necessary that as our High Priest Christ should, after offering Himself as a sacrifice, pass through the heavens to appear before God in our behalf. An essential part, and that a permanent one, of His priestly office was to be exercised in heaven. He there makes constant intercession for His people. . . .

(3) It was expedient, our Lord said, that He should go away, "for if I go not away, the Comforter will not come unto you; but if I depart, I will send him unto you" (John 16:7). It was necessary that redemption should not only be acquired but applied. Men if left to themselves would have remained in their sins, and Christ would have died in vain. One of the great blessings which the prophets predicted of the Messianic period was the effusion of the Holy Spirit. To secure that blessing for the Church Christ's ascension was necessary. . . .

(4) Our Lord told His sorrowing disciples, "I go to prepare a place

for you. And if I go and prepare a place for you, I will come again, and receive you unto myself; that where I am, there ye may be also" (John 14:2–3). His ascension, therefore, was necessary for the completion of His work.

§3. Sitting at the Right Hand of God

Having risen from the dead and ascended into heaven, the God-man sat down at the right hand of God the Father, that is, was associated with Him in glory and dominion. This is the third step in the exaltation of our Lord. . . .

The ground of Christ's exaltation is twofold: (1) the possession of divine attributes by which He was entitled to divine honour and was qualified to exercise absolute and universal dominion, and (2) His mediatorial work. Both of these are united in Hebrews 1:3. It is there said that Christ "sat down on the right hand of the Majesty on high"; He was entitled to do so, first, because He is the brightness of the Father's glory and His express image, and sustains the universe by the word of His power; and secondly, because by the sacrifice of Himself He made purification for our sins. So also in Philippians 2:6–11, where we are taught that because Christ existed in the form of God and was equal with God, and because He humbled Himself to be obedient unto death, even the death of the cross, "God also hath highly exalted him, and given him a name which is above every name: that at the name of Jesus every knee should bow, of things in heaven, and things in earth, and things under the earth." . . . The universal dominion of the risen Saviour was also taught by our Lord Himself: "All power is given unto me in heaven and in earth" (Matt. 28:18). . . .

This universal dominion is exercised by the God-man. It is vain for us to speculate on the relation of the divine and human natures in the acts of this supreme ruler. . . . It is enough for us to know that this supreme ruler of the universe is a perfect man as well as a perfect God. He still has all of the human sympathies and affections and can be touched with a sense of our infirmities. It is also an unspeakable delight to all His people that a person in whom dwells all the fulness of the Godhead bodily, and who is filled with all the love, tenderness, compassion, meekness, and forbearance which Christ manifested while here on earth, has all power in heaven and earth committed to His hands and is not far from any one of us. . . .

This absolute dominion has been committed to Christ as mediator. He who is over all is the head of the Church; it is for the Church, for the consummation of the work of redemption, that as the God-man

He has been thus exalted over all created beings (Eph. 1:22; Col. 1:17–18; 1 Cor. 15:25–28). Having been committed to Him for a special purpose, this universal dominion as mediator will be relinquished when that purpose is accomplished. He will reign until all His enemies are put under His feet. And when the last enemy is subdued, He will deliver up this kingdom unto the Father and reign forever as King over the redeemed.

§4. Christ's Coming to Judge the World

... The Scriptures teach that, as the last step in His exaltation, Christ is to come again. The object of this second advent, which is to be personal, visible, and glorious, is to judge the world. Before Him are to be gathered all nations and all the generations of men. They will receive their final sentence from the lips of Him who was arraigned at the bar of Pilate, unrighteously condemned, and crucified with malefactors amid cruel mockings. The persons to be judged are the quick and the dead, i.e., those then alive and those who will have died before His appearing. The rule of judgment will be the law of God, either as written on the heart or as revealed in His Word. Those having the written revelation will be judged by it; those who have had no such external revelation will be judged according to the light they have actually enjoyed. The ground of judgment will be the deeds done in the body. The sentence to be pronounced will be final, fixing the eternal destiny of every individual. . . .

Chapter XIV

Vocation

§1. Scriptural Usage of the Word

The Scriptures clearly teach that the several persons of the Trinity are engaged in the work of man's redemption. To the Father are referred the plan itself, the selection of its objects, and the mission of the Son to carry the gracious purpose into effect. To the Son, the accomplishment of all that is requisite to render the salvation of sinful men consistent with the perfections and law of God, and to secure the final redemption of those given to Him by the Father. The special work of the Spirit is the application of the redemption purchased by Christ. Such is the condition of men since the fall that if left to themselves, they would continue in their rebellion and refuse the offers of reconciliation with God. Christ would then have died in vain. To secure the accomplishment of the promise that He would "see of the travail of his soul, and . . . be satisfied," the Holy Spirit so operates on the chosen people of God that they are brought to repentance and faith and thus made heirs of eternal life through Jesus their Lord. . . .

This act of the Spirit by which men are brought into saving union with Christ is expressed by the word vocation (or calling): "partakers of the heavenly calling" (Heb. 3:1); "walk worthy of the vocation wherewith ye are called" (Eph. 4:1); "[God hath] called us with an holy calling" (2 Tim. 1:9). The verb used to express this act of the Spirit is to call: "whom he did predestinate, them he also called: and whom he called, them he also justified" (Rom. 8:30); "ye see your calling, brethren, how that not many wise men after the flesh, not many mighty, not many noble, are called" (1 Cor. 1:26); "it pleased God, who separated me from my mother's womb, and called me by his grace" (Gal. 1:15). . . .

Such then is the established usage of Scripture. It is by a divine call that sinners are made partakers of the benefits of redemption. And the influence of the Spirit by which they are translated from the kingdom of darkness into the kingdom of God's dear Son is a vocation or effectual calling. The ground of this usage is to be found in the Scriptural idea of God and of His relation to the world. He speaks and it is done. He said, "Let there be light," and light was. He calls the things that are not, and they are. All effects of His power are produced by a word. As in the external world He created all things by the power of His word, so all effects in the moral or spiritual world are accomplished by a volition or a command. . . . God spoke (or willed), and the universe was. Our Lord said, "Lazarus, come forth," and Lazarus lived. He said to the leper, "I will; be thou clean." When He put clay on the eyes of the blind man and bade him wash in the pool of Siloam, the restoration of sight was in no degree due to the properties of the clay or of the water. It was as truly the effect of the immediate divine efficiency as was the raising of the dead by a word. When, therefore, the Scriptures ascribe to the call of God that subjective change in the sinner by which he becomes a new creature, they teach that the effect is due not to natural or moral causes, nor to the man's own agency, but simply to the power of God. Hence, to call is frequently, in the Bible, to effect or to cause to be. A people or an individual becomes by the call of God that which the people or person is called to be. When God called the Hebrews to be His people, they became His people. . . . When Paul was called to be an apostle, he became an apostle. And those called to be saints become saints.

§2. The External Call

The Scriptures, however, distinguish between this effectual call and the external call which the Word of God addresses to all to whom it is made known. In this sense "many are called, but few are chosen" (Matt. 22:14). God said by His prophet, "When I called, ye did not answer" (Isa. 65:12). This external call includes (1) a declaration of the plan of salvation; (2) the promise of God to save all who accede to the terms of that plan; (3) a command, exhortation, and invitation to all to accept of the offered mercy; and (4) an exhibition of the reasons which should constrain men to repent and believe and thus escape from the wrath to come. All this is included in the gospel. . . .

This external call is universal in the sense that it is addressed to all men indiscriminately to whom the gospel is sent. It is confined to no age, nation, or class of men. It is made to the Jew and Gentile, to bond and free, to the learned and to the ignorant, to the righteous and to the wicked, to the elect and to the nonelect. . . . The Scriptures, therefore, in the most explicit terms teach that the external call of the gospel is addressed to all men. The command of Christ to His Church was to preach the gospel . . . to every human being on the face of the earth. We have no right to exclude any man, and no man has any right to exclude himself. God so loved the world, that He gave His only begotten Son, that whosoever believeth in Him should not perish, but have everlasting life. . . . Our Lord's call is unrestricted, "Come unto me, all ye that labour and are heavy laden, and I will give you rest" (Matt. 11:28). And the sacred canon closes with the same gracious words, "The Spirit and the bride say, Come. And let him that heareth say, Come. And let him that is athirst come. And whosoever will, let him take the water of life freely" (Rev. 22:17). The apostles, therefore, when they went forth in the execution of the commission which they had received, preached the gospel to every class of men and assured every man whom they addressed that if he would repent and believe in the Lord Jesus Christ, he would be saved. . . .

This general call of the gospel is not inconsistent with the doctrine of predestination. For predestination concerns the purpose of God to render effectual, in particular cases, the call which is addressed to every one. . . .

This universal external call is made only through the Word of God, as heard or read. That is, the revelation of the plan of salvation is not made by the works or by the providence of God, nor by the moral constitution of our nature, nor by the intuitions or deductions of reason, nor by direct revelation to all men everywhere and at all times, but only in the written Word of God. It is not denied that God may, and in past ages certainly did, convey this saving knowledge by direct revelation without the intervention of any external means of instruction. Consider, for example, the case of the apostle Paul. And such cases, for all we know, may even now occur. But these are miracles. This is not the ordinary method. We have no Scriptural promise and no experiential evidence of such supernatural revelations of truth once it was set forth in the written Word and committed to the Church with the command to teach all nations. . . .

There are a number of Scriptural evidences that saving knowledge is contained only in the Bible and consequently that those ignorant of its contents are ignorant of the way of salvation:

(1) The Old and the New Testament constantly represent the heathen as in a state of fatal ignorance. They are declared by the ancient prophets to be afar off from God, to be the worshippers of idols, to be sunk in sin. . . . In the New Testament the same representation is given of their condition. It is said that they know not God. Paul proves at length in the first chapter of his Epistle to the Romans that they are universally and justly in a state of condemnation. He exhorts the Ephesians to call to mind their condition before they received the gospel. They were "without Christ, being aliens from the commonwealth of Israel, and strangers from the covenants of promise, having no hope, and without God in the world" (Eph. 2:12). Such is the uniform teaching of the Word of God. It is utterly inconsistent with these representations to assume that the heathen either by tradition or by inward revelation have such knowledge of God as is sufficient to lead them to holiness and God.

(2) The gospel claims to be the only method of salvation. It takes for granted that men are in a state of sin and condemnation from which they are unable to deliver themselves. It teaches that . . . acceptance of Christ as God and Saviour is the one indispensable condition of salvation, that there is no other name under heaven whereby men can be saved. It provides, therefore, for a Church and a ministry whose great duty it is to make known to men this great salvation. All this takes for granted that without this knowledge men will perish in their sins.

(3) Ministers of the gospel are commissioned to go into all the world and say to every creature, "Believe on the Lord Jesus Christ, and thou shalt be saved." "He that believeth on the Son hath everlasting life: and he that believeth not the Son shall not see life; but the wrath of God abideth on him" (John 3:36). Where is the propriety of such a message if men can be saved without the knowledge of Christ and consequently without faith in Him? . . .

This is indeed a fearsome doctrine. But are not the words of our Lord also fearsome, "Wide is the gate, and broad is the way, that leadeth to destruction, and many there be which go in thereat: because strait is the gate, and narrow is the way, which leadeth unto life, and few there be that find it" (Matt. 7:13–14)? That the great majority even of those who hear the gospel reject its offers of mercy is a fact staring every man in the face. Facts are as mysterious as doctrines. If we must submit to the one, we may as well submit to the other. Our Lord has taught us, when we face facts or doctrines which try our faith, to remember the infinite wisdom and rectitude of God and say, "Even so, Father; for so it seemed good in thy sight." Accordingly, the proper response to the doctrine that the knowledge of the gospel is essential to the salvation of adults is submission and greatly increased exertion to send the gospel to those who are perishing for lack of knowledge.

But inasmuch as some men are not saved, the question arises, Why should the call be addressed to every one? or, What is the design of God in making the call of the gospel universal and indiscriminate? . . . [There are a number of answers to this question.] (1) The most obvious answer is found in the nature of the call itself. The call of the gospel is simply (a) the command of God to men to repent and believe on the Lord Jesus Christ together with (b) the promise that those who believe shall be saved. It is the revelation of a duty binding upon all men. . . . (2) The general call of the gospel is the means ordained by God to gather in His chosen people. . . . That only these particular people are made willing to perform the duty binding upon all men does not in any way conflict with the propriety of the universal proclamation. (3) This general call of the gospel with the promise that whoever believes shall be saved serves to show the unreasonable wickedness and perverseness of those who deliberately reject it. The justice of their condemnation is thus rendered the more obvious. . . .

§3. Common Grace

The word grace means a favourable disposition or kind feeling, and especially love as exercised towards the inferior, dependent, or unworthy. This is represented as the crowning attribute of the divine nature. Its manifestation is declared to be the grand end of the whole scheme of redemption. Paul teaches that predestination, election, and salvation are all intended for the praise of the glory of the grace of God which He exercises towards us in Christ Jesus (Eph. 1:3-6). He raises men from spiritual death and makes them "sit together in heavenly places in Christ Jesus: that in the ages to come he might show the exceeding riches of his grace" (Eph. 2:6-7). Therefore it is often asserted that salvation is of grace. The gospel is a system of grace. All its blessings are gratuitously bestowed; all is so ordered that in every step of the progress of redemption and in its consummation the grace or undeserved love of God is conspicuously displayed. Nothing is given or promised on the ground of merit. Everything is an undeserved favour. . . .

In addition to the grace of salvation to the elect, the Bible speaks of a divine grace to every man. Whatever God does in nature, in the material world, and in the minds of men He does through the Spirit. . . . The Holy Spirit as the Spirit of truth, of holiness, and of life in all its forms is present with every human mind, enforcing truth, restraining from evil, exciting to good, and imparting wisdom or strength when, where, and in what measure seemeth to Him good. In this sphere also He divides "to every man severally as he will" (1 Cor. 12:11). This is what in theology is called common grace.

That there is a divine influence of the Spirit granted to all men is plain both from Scripture and from experience. Already in Genesis 6:3 it is said, "My spirit shall not always strive with man." . . . And the martyr Stephen tells the Jews, "Ye do always resist the Holy Ghost: as your fathers did, so do ye" (Acts 7:51). The Spirit, then, is represented as striving with the wicked and with all men. They are charged with resisting, grieving, vexing, and quenching His operations. This is a familiar mode of Scriptural representation. As God is everywhere present in the material world, guiding its operations according to the laws of nature, so He is everywhere present with the minds of men, as the Spirit of truth and goodness, operating on them according to the laws of their free moral agency, inclining them to good and restraining them from evil. . . .

What is thus taught in Scripture is confirmed by the experience of every man. God leaves no man without a witness. Every one can recall times when he was led to serious thoughts, to anxious inquiries, to desires and efforts which he could not rationally refer to the operation of natural causes. . . . There is something in the nature of these experiences which proves that they are due to the operation of the Spirit of God.

The effects produced by common grace, or this influence of the Spirit common to all men, are most important to the individual and to the world. What the external world would be if left to the blind operation of physical causes without the restraining and guiding influence of God's providential efficiency, that would the world of mind be, in all its moral and religious manifestations, without the restraints and guidance of the Holy Spirit. There are two ways in which we may learn what the effect would be of the withholding the Spirit from the minds of men. The first is the Scriptural consideration of the effects of reprobation in the case of individual men. Such men have a seared conscience. They are reckless and indifferent and entirely under the control of the evil passions of their nature. . . . These effects of reprobation are depicted in a fearful manner by the apostle in the first chapter of his Epistle to the Romans. Not only individuals, but peoples and churches may be thus abandoned by the Spirit of God, and then unbroken spiritual death is the inevitable consequence. In the second place, the Scriptural account of the state of the lost reveals the effect of the Holy Spirit's withdrawal from His control of rational creatures. Heaven is a place and state in which the Spirit reigns with absolute control. Hell is a place and state in which the Spirit no longer restrains and controls. The presence or absence of the Spirit makes all the difference between heaven and hell.

To the general influence of the Spirit (or to common grace) we owe (1) all the decorum, order, refinement, and virtue existing among men. Mere fear of future punishment, the natural sense of right, and the restraints of human laws would prove feeble barriers to evil were it not for the repressing power of the Spirit, which, like the pressure of the atmosphere, is universal and powerful, although unfelt. (2) To the same divine agent are due specially that general fear of God and that religious feeling which secure for the rites and services of religion in all its forms the decorous or more serious attention which they receive. (3) The Scriptures refer to this general influence of the Spirit varied religious experiences which are not attended by genuine conversion or regeneration. . . .

We must speak with caution of the work which the Spirit exercises, in a greater or lesser degree, on the minds of all men. . . . For the mode of the Spirit's operation is inscrutable. . . . There are certain statements of the Bible, however, which throw some light on this subject. In the first place, the Scriptures speak of God's reasoning with men, of His teaching them inwardly by His Spirit, of His guiding or leading them, and of His convincing, reproving, and persuading them. These modes of representation indicate an operation which, consisting in the presentation of truth and urging of motives, accords with the ordinary laws of mind. In the second place, so far as appears, this common influence of the Spirit is never exercised except through the truth. In the third place, the moral and religious effects ascribed to it never rise above, so to speak, the natural operations of the mind. The knowledge, the faith, the conviction, the remorse, the sorrow, and the joy which the Spirit is said to produce by these common operations are all natural affections or exercises such as one man may measurably awaken in the minds of other men. In the fourth place, these common influences of the Spirit are all capable of being effectually resisted. In all these respects this common grace is distinguished from the efficacious operation of the Spirit to which the Scriptures ascribe the regeneration of the soul. The great truth, however, that concerns us here is that the Spirit of God is present with every human mind, restraining from evil and exciting to good, and that to His presence and influence we are indebted for all the order, decorum, and virtue, as well as the regard for religion and its ordinances, which exist in the world. Consequently, the greatest calamity that can befall an individual, a church, or a people is that God should take His Holy Spirit from them. And as this is a judgment which, according to the Scriptures, does often come upon individuals, churches, and people, we should above all things avoid grieving the Spirit or quenching His influences. We grieve the Spirit by resistance, by indulgence in sin, and especially by denying His agency and speaking evil of His work: "Whosoever speaketh a word against the Son of man, it shall be forgiven him: but whosoever speaketh against the Holy Ghost, it shall not be forgiven him, neither in this world, neither in the world to come" (Matt. 12:32).

§4. Efficacious Grace

Besides those operations of the Spirit which in a greater or lesser degree are common to all men, the Scriptures teach that the covenant of redemption secures the Spirit's certainly efficacious influence for all those who have been given to the Son as His inheritance. . . . According to the Augustinian doctrine this efficacy of divine grace in regeneration depends neither upon active cooperation nor upon passive nonresistance by its subject. Rather, it is wholly the exercise of "the mighty power of God": He speaks and it is done. This point is clearly affirmed in the *Westminster Confession* (10.1–2):

> All those whom God hath predestinated unto life, and those only, he is pleased, in his appointed and accepted time, effectually to call, by his Word and Spirit, out of that state of sin and death, in which they are by nature, to grace and salvation by Jesus Christ; enlightening their minds, spiritually and savingly, to understand the things of God, taking away their heart of stone, and giving unto them a heart of flesh; renewing their wills, and by his almighty power determining them to that which is good, and effectually drawing them to Jesus Christ; yet so as they come most freely, being made willing by his grace.
>
> This effectual call is of God's free and special grace alone, not from any thing at all foreseen in man, who is altogether passive therein, until, being quickened and renewed by the Holy Spirit, he is thereby enabled to answer this call, and to embrace the grace offered and conveyed in it.

. . . A corollary of the doctrine that efficacious grace is the almighty power of God is that this influence of the Holy Spirit acts immediately on the soul. All effects in the ordinary dealings of God with His creatures are produced through the agency of second causes. But in miracles and in the work of regeneration all second causes are excluded. When Christ said to the leper, "I will; be thou clean," nothing intervened between His volition and the effect. . . . In like manner nothing intervenes between the volition of the Spirit and the regeneration of the soul. Even truth, though it may accompany or attend the work of the Spirit, does not cooperate in the production of the effect. . . .

Another corollary of the doctrine that efficacious grace is the exercise of almighty power is that it is irresistible. Common grace, or that influence of the Spirit which is granted more or less to all men, is often effectually resisted. . . . But since the special work of regeneration is the effect of almighty power, it can no more be resisted than the act of creation. The effect follows immediately on the will of God, as when He said, "Let there be light," and light was.

It follows, further, from the same premises, that the soul is passive in regeneration. It is the subject and not the agent of the change. The soul cooperates or is active in what precedes and in what follows the change, but the change itself is something experienced and not something done. The blind and the lame who came to Christ may have undergone much labour in getting into His presence, and they joyfully exerted the new power imparted to them, but they were entirely passive in the moment of healing. They in no way cooperated in the production of that effect. The same must be true in regeneration. . . .

Regeneration, according to this view of the case, must also be instantaneous. There is no middle state between life and death. Since regeneration is a making alive those before dead, it must be as instantaneous as the quickening of Lazarus. . . . Since it is the work of omnipotence, an effect of a mere volition on the part of God, it is of necessity instantaneous. God bids the sinner live, and he is alive!

It follows, also, that regeneration is an act of sovereign grace. Since a tree must be made good before the fruit is good, the goodness of the fruit cannot be the reason which determines him who has the power to change the tree from bad to good. Similarly, since works spiritually good are the fruits of regeneration, they cannot be the ground on which God exerts His life-giving power. Regeneration is, then, a sovereign gift. It is not granted because of sight or foresight of anything good in the subjects of this saving change. None of those whom Christ healed pretended to seek the exercise of His almighty power in their behalf on the ground of their peculiar goodness; much less did they dream of referring the restoration of their sight or health to any cooperation of their own with His omnipotence.

§5. Proof of the Doctrine

. . . The Scriptural account of the nature of regeneration leads inevitably to the conclusion that it is the work of the immediate omnipotent agency of the Spirit. It is a kind of work which nothing but almighty power can accomplish. It is a making alive. Originating life is by its nature an act of God, for He alone can give life. It precludes the intervention of second causes as much as creation does. Christ was raised from the dead by the power of God. So was Lazarus. So are the regenerated. . . . In teaching that regeneration is a quickening, the Scriptures reveal to us its nature as a work not of man, nor of divine efficiency operating through second causes, but of the immediate and therefore the almighty power of God.

The Bible teaches the same truth when it declares believers to be new creatures and says that they are created anew in Christ Jesus. Creation is the work of God, and it is an immediate work. It precludes the intervention of means. It is of necessity the work of almighty power, and therefore the Scriptures often speak of it as the peculiar prerogative of God. . . .

Another common Scriptural representation leads to the same conclusion. Believers are the children of God, not merely as His rational creatures, but as the subjects of a new birth. They are born of God; they are born of the Spirit; they are begotten of God (1 John 5). The essential idea in such representations is that . . . God originates the life which He gives. As it is utterly incongruous to think of a creature's begetting itself, so is it utterly inconsistent with the Scriptures to regard regeneration as a man's own work, or as due to his cooperation, or as produced by the influences of truth. . . .

The fact, then, that the Bible represents regeneration as a spiritual resurrection, as a new creation, and as a new birth, proves it to be the work of God's immediate agency. Another familiar mode of speaking on this subject leads to the same conclusion. In Deuteronomy 30:6 Moses says, "The LORD thy God will circumcise thine heart, and the heart of thy seed, to love the LORD thy God with all thine heart, and with all thy soul, that thou mayest live." In Ezekiel 11:19 God says, "I will give them one heart, and I will put a new spirit within you; and I will take the stony heart out of their flesh, and will give them an heart of flesh" (see also 36:26–27; Jer. 24:7; Ps. 51:10). . . . All those passages in which God promises to give a new heart are proofs that regeneration is a supernatural work of the Holy Spirit, a creating and imparting a new form of life. . . .

Appeal on this subject may safely be made to the experience of the individual believer and to the history of the Church. All the phenom-

ena of the Christian life are in accordance with the Augustinian doctrine of efficacious grace. No believer ever ascribes his regeneration to
himself. He does not regard himself as the author of the work, or his
own relative goodness, his greater susceptibility to good impression,
or his greater readiness of persuasion, as the reason why he rather
than others is the subject of this change. He knows that it is a work
of God, and that it is a work of God's free grace. His heart responds
to Paul's words in Titus 3:5: "Not by works of righteousness which we
have done, but according to his mercy he saved us, by the washing of
regeneration, and the renewing of the Holy Ghost." Paul says of himself, "God . . . separated me from my mother's womb, and called me
by his grace" (Gal. 1:15). There was nothing in him, who was injurious
and a persecutor, to merit the special intervention of God in his behalf.
Far from referring his vocation to himself, to his greater readiness to
yield to the influence of the truth, he constantly represents himself as
a monument of the wonderful condescension and grace of God. . . .
Similarly, the instantaneous conversion of the three thousand on the
day of Pentecost . . . was produced by the immediate agency or volition
of the Spirit of God. . . . This scene of the day of Pentecost does not
stand alone in the history of the Church. Similar manifestations of the
power of the Spirit have occurred, and are still occurring, in every
part of the world. . . . We are justified, therefore, in saying that all the
phenomena of Christian experience in the individual believer and in
the Church collectively bear out the Augustinian doctrine of efficacious
grace. . . .

§6. **Objections**
§7. **History of the Doctrine of Grace**

Chapter XV

Regeneration

§1. Usage of the Word

The subjective change wrought in the soul by the grace of God is variously designated in Scripture. It is called a new birth, a resurrection, a new life, a renewing of the mind, a dying to sin and living to righteousness, a translation from darkness to light. In theological language it is called regeneration. . . .

§2. Nature of Regeneration

By a consent almost universal the word regeneration is used to designate, not the whole work of sanctification, nor the first stages of that work comprehended in conversion, much less justification or any mere external change of state, but the instantaneous change from spiritual death to spiritual life. Regeneration, therefore, is a spiritual resurrection, the beginning of a new life. Sometimes the word expresses the act of God. God regenerates. Sometimes it designates the subjective effect of His act. The sinner is regenerated. He becomes a new creature. He is born again. And this is his regeneration. These two applications of the word are so allied as not to produce confusion. The nature of regeneration is not explained in the Bible further than that its author is God, its subject is the whole soul, and its effects are spiritual life and all consequent holy acts and states. . . .

§3. The Evangelical Doctrine

The evangelical doctrine of regeneration is clearly set forth in the *Westminster Confession* (10.1–2):

> All those whom God hath predestinated unto life, and those only, he is pleased, in his appointed and accepted time, effectually to call, by his Word and Spirit, out of that state of sin and death, in which they are by nature, to grace and salvation by Jesus Christ; enlightening their minds, spiritually and savingly, to understand the things of God; taking away their heart of stone, and giving unto them a heart of flesh; renewing their wills, and by his almighty power determining them to that which is good, and effectually drawing them to Jesus Christ; yet so as they come most freely, being made willing by his grace.
>
> This effectual call is of God's free and special grace alone, not from any thing at all foreseen in man, who is altogether passive therein, until, being quickened and renewed by the Holy Spirit, he is thereby enabled to answer this call, and to embrace the grace offered and conveyed in it.

A. Regeneration an Act of God

Regeneration is an act of God. He is not simply its giver and author in the sense that He is the giver of faith and of repentance. Nor is it an act which by argument, persuasion, or moral power He induces the sinner to perform. But it is an act of which God is Himself the agent. It is God who regenerates. The soul is regenerated. The soul is passive in regeneration, which is a change wrought in us and not an act performed by us.

B. Regeneration an Act of God's Power

Regeneration is not only an act of God, but also an act of His almighty power. . . . An act of omnipotence, it is infallibly efficacious, for nothing can resist almighty power.... The assertion that regeneration is an act of God's omnipotence is, and is intended to be, a denial that it is an act of moral suasion. It is an affirmation that it is ... immediate as opposed to mediate.... The restoration of sight to the blind by the command of Christ was an act of omnipotence. It was immediate. Nothing in the way of instrumentary or secondary cooperating influence intervened between the divine volition and the effect.... Similarly, raising Lazarus from the dead was an act of omnipotence. Nothing intervened between the volition and the effect. The act of quickening was an act of God. In that matter Lazarus was passive.... According to the evangelical system it is in this sense that regeneration is an act of God's almighty power. Nothing intervenes between His volition that the soul which is spiritually dead should live and the desired effect. Note that this is not to deny that in all which precedes or follows the imparting of this new life the soul is active and is influenced by the truth acting according to the laws of our mental constitution....

C. Regeneration Is a New Life

... Evangelical Christians declare regeneration to be, in the language of Scripture, "a quickening," a communication of a new principle of life.... We know that when a man is dead as to the body, he neither sees, feels, nor acts. The objects which impress the senses of the living make no impression upon him. They awaken no corresponding feeling, and they call forth no activity. The dead are insensible and powerless. Now when the Scriptures declare that men are spiritually dead, they do not deny to them physical, intellectual, social, or moral life. They admit that the objects of sense, the truths of reason, our social relations, and moral obligations are more or less adequately apprehended; these do not fail to awaken feeling and to excite to action. But there is a higher class of objects which the Bible calls "the things of God," "the things of the Spirit," "the things pertaining to salvation." These things, although intellectually apprehended as presented to our cognitive faculties, are not spiritually discerned by the unrenewed man. A beautiful object in nature or art may be duly apprehended as an object of vision by an uncultivated man, who has no perception of its aesthetic excellence and no corresponding feeling of delight in its contemplation. So it is with the unrenewed man. He may have an intellectual knowledge of the facts and doctrines of the Bible, but no spiritual discernment of their excellence and no delight in them. The same Christ, as portrayed in the Scriptures, is by one man regarded as being without form or comeliness that we should desire

Him; by another He is regarded as the chief among ten thousand and the one altogether lovely, "God manifest in the flesh," whom it is impossible not to adore, love, and obey.

The new life communicated in regeneration manifests itself in new views of God, of Christ, of sin, of holiness, of the world, of the gospel, and of the life to come; in short, of all those truths which God has revealed as necessary to salvation. . . . Accordingly, the whole process of salvation is described as a translation from the kingdom of darkness into the kingdom of light. There is no wonder, therefore, that the ancients called regeneration an illumination. If a man born blind were suddenly given sight, such a flood of knowledge and delight would flow in upon him through the organ of vision that he might well think that all living consists in seeing. In like manner the New Testament writers represent the change consequent on regeneration, the opening the eyes on the certainty, glory, and excellence of divine things, and especially of the revelation of God in the person of His Son, as comprehending almost everything which pertains to spiritual life. . . .

In addition to being described as a raising of the soul dead in sin to spiritual life, regeneration is declared to be a new birth. At birth the child enters upon a new state of existence. All his faculties are awakened: he sees, feels, and hears. Gradually all his faculties as a rational, moral, and physical being are unfolded. The Scriptures teach that it is thus in regeneration. The soul enters upon a new state. It is introduced into a new world. A whole class of objects before unknown or unappreciated are revealed to it and exercise upon it their influence. The "things of the Spirit" become the chief objects of desire and pursuit, and all the energies of the newborn soul are directed towards the spiritual as distinguished from the seen and temporal. It should be noted that this representation is not consistent with any of the false theories of regeneration, which regard regeneration as the sinner's own act, as a mere change of purpose, or as a gradual process of moral culture.

Another mode in which this doctrine is set forth is found in those passages in which God is represented as giving His people a new heart. In Scripture the heart is that which thinks, feels, wills, and acts. It is the soul, the self. A new heart is, therefore, a new self, a new man. It implies a change of the whole character. It is a new nature. Out of the heart proceed all conscious, volitional, moral exercises. A change of heart, then, is a change which precedes these exercises and determines their character. . . .

To sum up: In regeneration a new life is communicated to the soul; man is the subject of a new birth; he receives a new nature or new heart and becomes a new creature. This change is neither in the substance nor in the mere exercises of the soul, but in those immanent dispositions, principles, tastes, or habits which underlie all conscious exercises and determine the character of the man and of all his acts. . . .

[§4. Objections]

Chapter **XVI**

Faith

§1. Preliminary Remarks

The first conscious exercise of the renewed soul is faith. An apt analogy is the case of a man born blind whose eyes have been opened.

439

His first conscious act is seeing. The exercise of vision in such a man is attended by so many new sensations and emotions that he cannot determine how much of this new experience comes through the eye and how much from other sources. It is so with the believer. As soon as his eyes are opened by the renewing of the Holy Ghost, he is in a new world. Old things have passed away; all things are become new. Apprehension of "the things of God" as true lies at the foundation of all the exercises of the renewed soul.... As the Scriptures assign so much prominence to faith, as all the promises of God are addressed to believers, and as all the conscious exercises of spiritual life are impossible without the exercise of faith, ... it is indispensable that clear and correct ideas be entertained on the subject....

§2. The Psychological Nature of Faith

Faith, in the widest sense of the word, is assent to the truth, or the persuasion of the mind that a thing is true.... The primary idea of truth is that which is trustworthy, that which sustains our expectations, which does not disappoint, because it really is what it is assumed or declared to be. It is opposed to the deceitful, the false, the unreal, the empty, and the worthless. To regard a thing as true is to regard it as worthy of trust, as being what it purports to be. Faith, in the comprehensive sense of the word, therefore, is trust.... In this wide sense of the word, it matters not what may be the objects or what the grounds of this trust.

But in the strict and special sense of the word, faith means a belief in things not seen which is based on testimony. "Testimony" here is not limited to the affirmation of an intelligent witness. There are other methods by which testimony may be given. A seal is a form of testimony; so is a sign. So is everything which pledges the authority of the attester to the truth to be established. When Elijah declared that Jehovah was God, and Baal a lie, he said, "The God that answereth by fire, let him be God" (1 Kings 18:24). The ensuing descent of fire was the testimony of God to the truth of the prophet's declaration. So in the New Testament, God is said to have borne witness to the truth of the gospel by signs and wonders, and divers miracles, and gifts of the Holy Ghost (Heb. 2:4); and the Spirit of God is said to witness with our spirits that we are the children of God (Rom. 8:16).... When, therefore, it is said that faith is founded on testimony, it is meant that it is founded not on sense, reason, or feeling, but on the authority of Him by whom it is authenticated....

The first proof that faith is founded on the testimony or authority of God is the fact that the Scriptures take the form of a revelation of things we could not otherwise know. The prophets of the Old Testament were messengers, the mouth of God, to declare what the people were to believe and what they were to do. The New Testament is called "the testimony of Jesus." Christ came, not as a philosopher, but as a witness. He said to Nicodemus, "We speak that we do know, and testify that we have seen; and ye receive not our witness" (John 3:11; see also vv. 31–33). In like manner the apostles were witnesses. As such they were ordained (Luke 24:48). After His resurrection and immediately before His ascension our Lord said to them, "Ye shall receive power, after that the Holy Ghost is come upon you: and ye shall be witnesses unto me both in Jerusalem, and in all Judaea, and in Samaria, and unto the uttermost part of the earth" (Acts 1:8). When they declared the death and resurrection of Christ as facts to be believed, they said, "Whereof we are witnesses" (Acts 2:32; 3:15; 5:32). . . .

The great complaint against the apostles, especially in the Grecian cities, was that they did not present their doctrines as propositions to be proved; they did not even state the philosophical grounds on which they rested or attempt to sustain them at the bar of reason. Paul gave a twofold answer to this complaint: (1) Philosophy, the wisdom of men, had proved itself utterly incompetent to solve the great problems of God and the universe, of sin and redemption. It was in fact neither more nor less than foolishness, so far as all its speculations as to the things of God were concerned. (2) The doctrines which the apostles taught were not the truths of reason, but matters of revelation to be received not on rational or philosophical grounds, but on the authority of God. The apostles were not philosophers, but witnesses; they did not argue using the words of man's wisdom, but simply declared the counsels of God. Faith in their doctrines, then, was to rest not on the wisdom of men, but on the powerful testimony of God.

The second proof that the Scriptures teach that faith is the reception of truth on the ground of the testimony or on the authority of God is that we are commanded to receive the record which God has given of His Son. This is faith—receiving as true what God has testified, and doing so because He has testified it. "He that believeth on the Son of God hath the witness in himself; he that believeth not God hath made him a liar; because he believeth not the record that God gave of his Son. And this is the record [testimony], that God hath given to us eternal life, and this life is in his Son" (1 John 5:10–11). There could hardly be a more distinct statement of the Scriptural doctrine as to the nature of faith. Its object is what God has revealed. Its ground is the testimony of God. To receive that testimony is to set to our seal that God is true (John 3:33). To reject it is to make God a liar. "If we receive the witness of men, the witness of God is greater: for this is the witness of God which he hath testified of his Son" (1 John 5:9).

Such is the constant teaching of Scripture. The ground on which we are authorized and commanded to believe is not the conformity between the truth revealed and our reason, nor the effect of this truth upon our feelings, nor its meeting the necessities of our nature and condition, but simply, "Thus saith the Lord." The truths of revelation do commend themselves to the reason; they do powerfully and rightfully affect our feelings; they do meet all the necessities of our nature as creatures and as sinners; and these considerations may incline us to believe, may strengthen our faith, lead us to cherish it, and render it joyful and effective. But they are not its ground! We believe on the testimony or authority of God. . . .

The third proof that the Scriptures teach that faith is a reception of truth on the ground of testimony is found in the examples and illustrations of faith given in the Scriptures. Immediately after the fall the promise was made to our first parents that the seed of the woman would bruise the serpent's head. On what possible ground could faith in this promise rest except on the authority of God? . . . When God promised to Abraham that he, a childless old man, would become the father of many nations, that through his seed all the nations of the earth would be blessed, his faith could have no other foundation than the authority of God. So of every illustration of faith given by the apostle in the eleventh chapter of his Epistle to the Hebrews. The same is true of the whole Bible. We have no foundation for our faith in a spiritual world, in the doctrine of redemption, in the security and ultimate triumph of the Church, other than the testimony of God. Similarly, our assurance that Christ rose on the third day rests solely upon the testimony which God has in various ways given to that fact, which Paul tells us is the foundation of the gospel—"If Christ be not risen, then is our preaching vain, and your faith is also vain" (1 Cor. 15:14). So then, if faith does not rest on testimony, it has nothing on which to rest.

This is a point of great practical importance. If faith, or our persuasion of the truths of the Bible, rests on philosophical grounds, then the door is opened for rationalism; if it rests on feeling, then it is open to mysticism. The only sure and satisfying foundation is the testimony of God, who cannot err and who will not deceive. . . .

§3. Different Kinds of Faith

Though the definition of faith as persuasion of the truth on the basis of God's testimony be accepted, it is to be admitted that there are different kinds of faith. In other words, the state of mind which the word designates is very different in one case from what it is in others. This difference arises partly from the nature of its objects, and partly from the nature or form of the testimony on which it is founded. Faith in a historical fact or speculative truth is one thing; faith in aesthetic truth is another thing; faith in moral truth another thing; faith in spiritual truth, especially faith in the promise of salvation made to ourselves, is yet another thing. . . . Also, the testimony which God bears to the truth is of different kinds. In one instance it is directed especially to the understanding, in another to the conscience, in another to our regenerated nature. This is the cause of the difference between speculative, temporary, and saving faith.

A. Speculative or Dead Faith

There are many men who believe the Bible to be the Word of God, who receive all that it teaches, and who are perfectly orthodox in their doctrinal belief. If asked why they believe, they may be at a loss for an answer. Reflection might enable them to say they believe because others believe. They receive their faith by inheritance. They were taught from their earliest years thus to believe. The Church to which they belong inculcates this faith, and it is enjoined upon them as true and necessary. Others of greater culture may say that the evidence of the divine origin of the Bible, both external and internal, satisfies their minds and produces a rational conviction that the Scriptures are a revelation from God, and they receive its contents on His authority. Such a faith as this, experience teaches, is perfectly compatible with a worldly or wicked life. This is what the Bible calls a dead faith.

B. Temporary Faith

Again, nothing is more common than for the gospel to produce a temporary impression, more or less deep and lasting. Those thus impressed believe. But, having no root in themselves, sooner or later they fall away. It is also a common experience that in times of danger, or on the near approach of death, men utterly indifferent or even skeptical are deeply convinced of the certainty of those religious truths previously known, but hitherto disregarded or rejected. This temporary faith is due to common grace; that is, to those influences of the Spirit which in a greater or lesser measure reveal the truth to the consciences of all men and operate on their souls without renewing them.

C. Saving Faith

That faith which secures eternal life, which unites us to Christ as living members of His body, which makes us the sons of God, which interests us in all the benefits of redemption, which works by love and is fruitful in good works, is founded, not on the external or the moral evidence of the truth, but on the testimony of the Spirit with and by the truth to the renewed soul. This testimony of the Spirit, which is said to be the ground of saving faith, . . . is within the mind itself. . . . The effects of this inward testimony are (1) a "spiritual discernment" not only of the truth, but also of the holiness, excellence, and glory of the things discerned; (2) flowing necessarily from this spiritual discernment, a delight and complacency (or love); (3) the apprehension that the truths revealed in Scripture are suited to our nature and necessities; (4) the firm conviction that these things are not only true, but divine; and (5) the fruits of this conviction (i.e., of the faith thus produced)—good works and holiness of heart and life.

When, therefore, a Christian is asked why he believes the Scriptures and the doctrines therein contained, his simple answer is that he believes the Scriptures on the basis of the testimony or authority of God. How else could he know that the worlds were created by God, that our race apostatized from God, that He sent His Son for our redemption, that faith in Him will secure salvation? Faith in such truths can have no other foundation than the testimony of God. If asked, further, how God testifies to the truth of the Bible, an educated man whose attention has been called to the subject will answer that God testifies in every conceivable way: by signs, wonders, and miracles, and by the divine knowledge, excellence, authority, and power exhibited in the Bible. In contrast an uneducated man may simply say, "Whereas I was blind, now I see." Such a man, and indeed every true Christian, passes from a state of unbelief to one of saving faith, not by any process of research or argument, but of inward experience. The change may, and often does, take place in a moment. The resultant faith which a Christian has in the truths of the Bible is analogous to that which all men have in the moral law, which they recognize not only as truth, but as having the authority of God. What the natural man perceives with regard to the moral law, the renewed man, by the testimony of the Spirit with and by the truth to his heart, is enabled to perceive with regard to "the things of the Spirit."

That this is the Scriptural doctrine on the subject is plain from the express declarations of the Scriptures. Our Lord promised to send the Spirit for this very purpose: "He will reprove the world [1] of sin," especially of the sin of not believing in Christ; "and [2] of righteousness," that is, of Christ's righteousness—the rightfulness of His claims to be regarded and received as the Son of God, God manifest in the flesh, and the Saviour of the world; "and [3] of judgment," that is, of the final overthrow of the kingdom of darkness and the triumph of the kingdom of light (John 16:8). Faith, therefore, is always represented in Scripture as one of the fruits of the Spirit, as a gift of God, as a product of His energy. . . . The apostle John tells his readers, "Ye have an unction from the Holy One, and ye know all things. . . . The anointing which ye have received of him abideth in you, and ye need not that any man teach you: but as the same anointing teacheth you of all things, and is truth, and is no lie, and even as it hath taught you, ye shall abide in him" (1 John 2:20, 27). This passage teaches that (1) true believers receive from Christ (the Holy One) an unction; (2) this unction is the Holy Ghost; (3) it secures the knowledge and conviction of the truth; and (4) this inward teaching which makes them believers is abiding and secures them from apostasy. (For an equally explicit passage see 1 Cor. 2:14–15.)

When Peter confessed that Jesus was the Christ, the Son of the living God, our Lord said, "Blessed art thou, Simon Bar-jona: for flesh and blood hath not revealed it unto thee, but my Father which is in heaven" (Matt. 16:17). Other men had the same external evidence of the divinity of Christ. Peter's faith, however, was due not to that evidence alone, but to the inward testimony of God. Our Lord rendered thanks that God had hidden the mysteries of His kingdom from the wise and prudent and revealed them unto babes (Matt. 11:25). The external revelation was made to both classes. Besides this external revelation, those called babes received an inward testimony which made them believers. Hence our Lord said that only those who are drawn or taught by God can come unto Him (John 6:44–45). . . .

Faith in the Scriptures is, then, founded on the testimony of God. By testimony, as before stated, is meant attestation, anything which pledges the authority of the attester in support of the truth to be established. As this testimony is of different kinds, different types of faith are produced. So far as the testimony is merely external, the faith it produces is simply historical or speculative. So far as the testimony is moral, consisting in the power which the Spirit gives to the truth over the natural conscience, the faith is temporary, being dependent on the state of mind which is its proximate cause. Besides these, there is the inward testimony of the Spirit, which is of such a nature and of such power as to produce a perfect revolution in the soul, a revolution Scripture compares to that effected by opening the eyes of the blind to the reality, the wonders, and glories of creation. There is, therefore, as much difference between a faith resting on this inward testimony of the Spirit and mere speculative faith as there is between the conviction a blind man has of the beauties of nature before and after the opening of his eyes. As this testimony is informing, enabling the soul to see the truth and excellence of the "things of the Spirit," faith is a form of knowledge. The believer sees to be true what the Spirit reveals and authenticates.

§4. Faith and Knowledge

The relation of faith to knowledge is a wide field. The discussions of the subject have been varied and endless. . . . The question which concerns us here is whether knowledge is essential to faith; that is, whether a truth must be known in order to be believed.

Now we of course admit that mysteries, or truths which we are unable to comprehend, may be and are proper objects of faith. We repudiate the rationalistic doctrine that we can believe only what we understand and what we can prove, or at least elucidate so that it appears to be true in its own light. On the other hand, we also maintain that knowledge, i.e., the cognition of the import of the proposition to be believed, is essential to faith and, consequently, that faith is limited by knowledge. We can believe only what we know, i.e., what we intelligently apprehend. If a proposition be announced to us in an unknown language, we can affirm nothing about it. We can neither believe nor disbelieve it. . . . This obvious truth is recognized in 1 Corinthians 14:9–16. According to the apostle, knowledge, or the intelligent apprehension of the meaning of what is proposed, is essential to faith. When the proposition "God is a Spirit" is announced, those who hear will be able to assent to its truth only if they understand the language and know what the words God and Spirit mean. Then they may receive or reject the truth which that proposition affirms. . . . When it is said God set forth Christ to be a propitiation for our sins, if we do not understand what the word propitiation means, the proposition to us means nothing and therefore cannot be an object of faith.

Being essential to faith, knowledge must be the measure of it as well. What lies beyond the sphere of knowledge lies beyond the sphere of faith. Of the unseen and eternal we can believe only what God has revealed; and of what God has revealed, we can believe only what we know. It has been said that he who believes the Bible to be the Word of God may properly be said to believe all it teaches, although much of its instruction may be to him unknown. But this is not a correct representation. The man who believes the Bible is prepared to believe on its authority whatever it declares to be true. But he cannot properly be said to believe any more of its contents than he knows. If asked if he believes that men bitten by poisonous serpents were ever healed by merely looking at a brazen serpent, he might, if ignorant of the Pentateuch, honestly answer no. But should he come to read and understand the record of the healing of the dying Israelites, as found in the Bible, he would rationally and sincerely answer yes. This disposition to believe whatever the Bible teaches, as soon as we know what is taught, may be called an implicit faith, but it is no real faith. It has none of its characteristics and none of its power.

That knowledge is essential to faith is obvious (1) from the very nature of faith. For faith is an affirmation of the mind that a thing is true or trustworthy, and it goes without saying that the mind cannot affirm the truth of an object about which it knows nothing.

(2) The Bible everywhere teaches that without knowledge there can be no faith. This, as just stated, is the doctrine of the apostle Paul. He condemned speaking in an unknown tongue, because the hearers could not understand what was said; and if they did not know the meaning of the words uttered, they could neither assent to them nor be profited by them. In another place (Rom. 10:14) he asks, "How shall they believe in him of whom they have not heard?" "Faith," he says, "cometh by hearing" (v. 17). The command of Christ was to preach the gospel to every creature. Those who accepted it would, He assured His disciples, be saved; those who rejected it would be damned. This takes for granted that without knowledge of the gospel there can be no faith. On this principle the apostles acted everywhere. They went abroad preaching Christ, proving from the Scriptures that He is the Son of God and Saviour of the world. The communication of knowledge always preceded the demand for faith.

(3) The connection between faith and knowledge is so intimate that in the Scriptures the one term is often used for the other. To know Christ is to believe upon Him. To know the truth is intelligently and believingly to apprehend and appropriate it. Conversion is effected by knowledge. Paul says he was made a believer by the revelation of Christ within him. . . . Men are said to perish for lack of knowledge. Nothing is more characteristic of the Bible than the importance which it attaches to the knowledge of the truth. We are said to be begotten and sanctified by the truth, and the whole duty of ministers and teachers is said to be to hold forth the word of life. Indeed, it is because knowledge is essential to faith that we insist so strenuously on the circulation of the Scriptures and the instruction of the people. . . .

§5. Faith and Feeling

. . . We also maintain that the faith which is connected with salvation is not merely an intellectual exercise, but an exercise of the affections as well. . . . To believe that Christ is "God manifest in the flesh" is not merely the intellectual conviction that only someone truly divine could be and do what Christ was and did, for this conviction demoniacs avowed; but it is to receive Him as our God. This includes the apprehension and conviction of His divine glory, and the adoring reverence, love, confidence, and submission which are due to God alone. When we are commanded to believe in Christ as the Saviour of men, we are not required merely to assent to the proposition that He does save sinners, but also to receive and rest upon Him alone for our salvation. What, therefore, the Scriptures mean by the faith which is required for salvation is an act of the whole soul, an act of the understanding, of the heart, and of the will.

That saving faith includes knowledge, assent, and trust, and is not merely assent, is proved, in the first place, from the nature of the object of saving faith. That object is not merely the general truth of Scripture, not the fact that the gospel reveals God's plan of saving sinners; but it is Christ Himself, His person and work, and the offer of salvation to us personally and individually. From the nature of the case we cannot believe in Christ on the inward testimony of the Spirit, which reveals His glory and His love, without our experiencing feelings of reverence, love, and trust mingling with the act and constituting its character. Nor is it possible that a man can receive the promise of deliverance from the guilt and power of sin without his feeling gratitude and confidence. The act of faith in such a promise is in its nature an act of appropriation and confidence. . . .

In the second place, various Biblical expressions explanatory of the act of faith show that it includes trust as an essential element of its nature. We are commanded to look to Christ as the dying Israelites looked up to the brazen serpent. This act of looking up, which is declared to be belief, involves trust. Sinners are exhorted to flee to Christ as a refuge. The manslayer fled to the city of refuge because he relied upon it as a place of safety. We are said to receive Christ, to rest upon Him, to lay hold of Him. All these modes of expression show that trust is an essential element in the act of saving faith. . . .

In the third place, every believer knows from his own experience that when he believes, he receives and rests on Jesus Christ for salvation. . . . Moreover, since all those who are to be saved must receive the record which God has given of His Son and must believe that He is God manifest in the flesh, the propitiation for our sins, the Prophet,

Priest, and King of His people, it must be admitted that faith involves trust in Christ as our source of wisdom, righteousness, sanctification, and redemption. . . .

[§6. Faith and Love]
§7. The Object of Saving Faith

A. *General Faith*

All Christians are bound to believe and do believe everything taught in the Word of God, so far as the contents of the Scriptures are known to them. It is correct, therefore, to say that the object of faith is the whole revelation of God as contained in His Word. As the Bible is with Protestants the only infallible rule of faith and practice, nothing not expressly taught in Scripture, or deduced therefrom by necessary inference, can be imposed on the people of God as an article of faith. This is "the liberty wherewith Christ hath made us free" (Gal. 5:1). . . . Against all undue assumptions of authority, Protestants hold fast to two great principles: (1) the right of private judgment and (2) the exclusivity of the Scriptures as the infallible rule of faith and practice. The object of faith, then, is all the truths revealed in the Word of God. All that God in the Bible declares to be true, we are bound to believe. This is what theologians call general faith.

B. *Special Faith*

But, besides this, there is a special faith necessary to salvation. In the general contents of the Scriptures there are certain doctrines concerning Christ and His work, and certain promises of salvation made through Him to sinful men, which we are bound to receive and required to trust. The special object of faith, therefore, is Christ and the promise of salvation through Him. And the special definite act of faith which secures our salvation is the act of receiving and resting on Him as He is offered to us in the gospel. This is so clearly and so variously taught in the Scriptures as hardly to admit of being questioned.

In the first place, our Lord repeatedly declares that men must believe on Him. He was lifted up "that whosoever believeth in him should not perish, but have eternal life. . . . He that believeth on him is not condemned: but he that believeth not is condemned already, because he hath not believed in the name of the only begotten Son of God" (John 3:15, 18; see also v. 36; 6:40, 47–51). In another place our Lord says, "This is the work of God, that ye believe on him whom he hath sent" (John 6:29). . . .

That Christ is the immediate object of saving faith is also taught in all those passages in which the act of receiving Christ, or the testimony of God concerning Christ, is said to secure our salvation. For example, "As many as received him, to them gave he power to become the sons of God" (John 1:12); "He that hath the Son hath life; and he that hath not the Son of God hath not life" (1 John 5:12); "Whosoever believeth that Jesus is the Christ is born of God" (v. 1). . . .

In like manner Paul teaches we are justified "by the faith of Christ." The faith by which we are justified, then, is not merely a pious disposition of the mind, nor a general confidence in God, nor a faith in the truth of divine revelation, much less faith in eternal verities or the general principles of truth and duty, but that faith of which Christ is the object: "The righteousness of God . . . is by faith of Jesus Christ unto all and upon all them that believe" (Rom. 3:22); "Knowing that a man is not justified by the works of the law, but by the faith of Jesus Christ, even we have believed in Jesus Christ, that we might be justified by the faith of Christ, and not by the works of the law" (Gal. 2:16); "I live by the faith of the Son of God" (v. 20). . . .

§8. Effects of Faith

A. Union with Christ

The first effect of faith, according to the Scriptures, is union with Christ. We are in Him by faith. There is indeed a federal union between Christ and His people which is founded on the covenant of redemption between the Father and the Son in the counsels of eternity. We are, therefore, said to be in Him before the foundation of the world. It is one of the promises of that covenant that all whom the Father has given the Son will come to Him. . . . Another stipulation of that covenant is that His people, so far as adults are concerned, will not receive the saving benefits of that covenant until they are united to Him by a voluntary act of faith. They are "by nature the children of wrath, even as others" (Eph. 2:3). They remain in this state of condemnation until they believe. Their union is consummated by faith. To be in Christ and to believe in Christ are, therefore, in the Scriptures convertible forms of expression. . . .

B. Justification

The proximate effect of this union (and, consequently, the second effect of faith) is justification. We are "justified by the faith of Christ"

(Gal. 2:16). "There is therefore now no condemnation to them which are in Christ Jesus" (Rom. 8:1). "He that believeth on him is not condemned" (John 3:18). Faith is the condition on which God promises in the covenant of redemption to impute unto men the righteousness of Christ. As soon, therefore, as they believe, they cannot be condemned. They are clothed with a righteousness which answers all the demands of justice. . . .

C. Participation of Christ's Life

The third effect of faith, or of union with Christ, is a participation of His life. Those united with Christ, the apostle teaches (Rom. 6:4–10), so as to be partakers of His death, are partakers also of His life. "Because I live, ye shall live also" (John 14:19). Christ dwells in our hearts by faith (Eph. 3:17). Christ is in us (Rom. 8:10). It is not we that live, but Christ liveth in us (Gal. 2:20). Our Lord illustrates this vital union in terms of a vine and its branches (John 15:1–6). As the life of the vine is diffused through the branches, and as they live only as connected with the vine, so the life of Christ is diffused through His people, and they are partakers of spiritual and eternal life only in virtue of their union with Him. . . .

D. Peace

The fourth effect of faith is peace. "Being justified by faith, we have peace with God through our Lord Jesus Christ" (Rom. 5:1). This peace arises from a sense of reconciliation. God promises to pardon, to receive into His favour, and finally to save all who believe the record which He has given of His Son. . . .

E. Sanctification

The fifth effect of faith is sanctification. Men "are sanctified," says our Lord, "by faith that is in me" (Acts 26:18). . . . Faith sanctifies because it is the indispensable condition of the indwelling of the Spirit, which is the source of all spiritual life. . . . Faith also sanctifies because it is the necessary condition of the efficacy of the means of grace. It is through the Word, sacraments, and prayer that God communicates constant supplies of grace. They are the means of calling the activities of spiritual life into exercise. But these means of grace are inoperative unless they are received and used by faith. Faith does not, indeed, give them their power, but it is the condition on which the Spirit of God renders them efficacious.

That good works are the certain effects of faith is included in the doctrine that we are sanctified by faith. For it is impossible that there should be inward holiness, love, spirituality, brotherly kindness, and zeal without an external manifestation of these graces in the whole outward life. Faith, therefore, without works is dead. . . .

F. Certainty of Salvation

A sixth effect which the Scriptures attribute to faith is security or certainty of salvation. "God so loved the world, that he gave his only begotten Son, that whosoever believeth in him should not perish, but have everlasting life" (John 3:16). "He that heareth my word, and believeth on him that sent me, hath everlasting life, and shall not come into condemnation; but is passed from death unto life" (John 5:24). "All that the Father giveth me shall come to me; and him that cometh to me I will in no wise cast out. . . . And this is the will of him that sent me, that every one which seeth the Son, and believeth on him, may have everlasting life: and I will raise him up at the last day" (John 6:37, 40). "My sheep hear my voice, and I know them, and they follow me: and I give unto them eternal life; and they shall never perish, neither shall any man pluck them out of my hand" (John 10:27–28).

Chapter **XVII**

Justification

§1. Symbolical Statement of the Doctrine

Justification is defined in the "Westminster Catechism" as "an act of God's free grace, wherein he pardoneth all our sins, and accepteth us as righteous in his sight, only for the righteousness of Christ imputed to us, and received by faith alone." . . . A number of points are entailed in this definition:

453

(1) Justification is an instantaneous act and not, like sanctification, a continued and progressive work.

(2) Justification is an act of grace to the sinner, who in himself deserves condemnation.

(3) As to the nature of the act, it is, in the first place, not an efficient act or an act of power. It does not produce any subjective change in the person justified. It does not effect a change of character, making those good who were bad, those holy who were unholy. That is done in regeneration and sanctification. In the second place, it is not a mere executive act, as when a sovereign pardons a criminal and thereby restores him to his civil rights or to his former status in the commonwealth. In the third place, it is a forensic or judicial act, the act of a judge, not of a sovereign. . . . It is a declarative act in which God pronounces the sinner just or righteous, that is, declares that the claims of justice, so far as the sinner is concerned, are satisfied, so that he cannot be justly condemned, but is in justice entitled to the reward promised or due to perfect righteousness.

(4) The meritorious ground of justification is not faith; we are not justified on account of our faith, considered as a virtuous or holy act or state of mind. Nor are our works of any kind the ground of justification. Nothing done by us or wrought in us satisfies the demands of justice, or can be the ground or reason of the declaration that justice as far as it concerns us is satisfied. The ground of justification is the righteousness of Christ, active and passive, i.e., including His perfect obedience to the law as a covenant and His enduring the penalty of the law in our stead and on our behalf.

(5) The righteousness of Christ is in justification imputed to the believer. That is, it is set to his account, so that he is entitled to plead it at the bar of God, as though it were personally and inherently his own.

(6) Faith is the condition of justification. That is, so far as adults are concerned, God does not impute the righteousness of Christ to the sinner until he (through grace) receives and rests on Christ alone for his salvation. . . .

§2. Justification Is a Forensic Act

. . . [It was the position of the Protestant Reformers] that by justification the Scriptures mean, in the first place, something different from sanctification. The two gifts, although inseparable, are distinct; justification, instead of being an efficient act changing the inward character of the sinner, is a declarative act announcing and determining his relation to the law and justice of God.

In the second place, the symbols of the Reformation no less explicitly teach that justification is not simply pardon and restoration. It includes pardon, but it also includes a declaration that the believer is just or righteous in the sight of the law. He has a right to plead a righteousness which completely satisfies its demands.

And, therefore, in the third place, affirmatively, the symbols of the Reformation teach that justification is a judicial or forensic act, i.e., an act of God as judge proceeding according to law, declaring that the sinner is just, i.e., that the law no longer condemns him, but acquits and pronounces him to be entitled to eternal life. . . .

A. Proof from the Usage of Scripture

The first of the proofs that to justify means neither simply to pardon nor to make inherently righteous or good is the uniform usage of the word to justify in Scripture. It is never used in either of those senses, but always in the sense of declaring or pronouncing just: "If there be a controversy between men, and they come unto judgment, that the judges may judge them; then they shall justify the righteous, and condemn the wicked" (Deut. 25:1); "He that justifieth the wicked, and he that condemneth the just, even they both are abomination to the LORD" (Prov. 17:15); "Ye are they which justify yourselves before men" (Luke 16:15); "All the people that heard him, and the publicans, justified God" (Luke 7:29). . . .

The usage of common life as to this word is just as uniform as that of the Bible. . . . The word always expresses a judgment, whether of the mind, as when one man justifies another for his conduct, or officially of a judge. . . . Therefore, when the Bible says that God justifies the believer, we are not at liberty to say that it means that He pardons or that He sanctifies him. It means and can mean only that He pronounces him just.

B. Justification the Opposite of Condemnation

Another evidence is the antithesis between condemnation and justification. Condemnation is not the opposite either of pardon or of reformation. To condemn is to pronounce guilty or worthy of punishment. To justify is to declare that some one is not guilty, or that justice does not demand punishment, or that the person concerned cannot justly be condemned. When the apostle says, "There is therefore now no condemnation to them which are in Christ Jesus" (Rom. 8:1), he declares that they are absolved from guilt, that the penalty of the law cannot justly be inflicted upon them. . . . God pronounces them just. . . .

As condemnation is a judicial act, so is justification. In condemnation a judge pronounces sentence on the guilty. In justification a judge declares that the person arraigned is free from guilt and entitled to be treated as righteous.

C. Argument from Equivalent Forms of Expression

The forms of expression which are used as equivalents of the word justify clearly indicate the nature of the act. Paul speaks of "the blessedness of the man, unto whom God imputeth righteousness without works" (Rom. 4:6). To impute righteousness is not to pardon; neither is it to sanctify. It means to justify, i.e., to attribute righteousness. The negative form in which justification is described is equally significant: "Blessed are they whose iniquities are forgiven, and whose sins are covered. Blessed is the man to whom the Lord will not impute sin" (Rom. 4:7–8). As "to impute sin" never means and cannot mean to make wicked, so the negative phrase "not to impute sin" cannot mean to sanctify. And as "to impute sin" does mean to lay sin to one's account and to treat him accordingly, so to justify means to lay righteousness to one's account and treat him accordingly. . . .

D. Argument from the Statement of the Doctrine

The judicial character of justification is evident from the mode in which the doctrine is presented in the Bible. The Scriptures speak of law, of its demands, of its penalty, of sinners as arraigned at the bar of God, of the day of judgment. The question is, How shall man be just with God? The answer to this question entails the whole method of salvation. The question is not, How can a man become holy? but, How can he become just? How can he satisfy the claims which justice has against him? . . . The human soul knows intuitively that it cannot be saved unless it be justified, and it knows that it cannot be declared just unless the demands of justice are fully satisfied. . . .

In the Epistle to the Romans Paul teaches that God is just, i.e., that He demands the satisfaction of justice, and that men are sinners and can render no such satisfaction themselves. Such a righteousness, however, has been provided and is revealed in the gospel. It is not our own righteousness, which is of the law, but the righteousness of Christ, and, therefore, the righteousness of God, in virtue of which, and on the ground of which, God can be just and yet justify the sinner who believes in Christ. This is what Paul teaches as to the method of salvation. . . .

E. Argument from the Ground of Justification

The nature of justification is determined by its ground. . . . If the Bible teaches that the ground of justification, the reason why God releases us from the penalty of the law and accepts us as righteous in His sight, is something outside ourselves, something done for us, and not what we do or experience, then it of necessity follows that justification is not subjective. . . . And in fact the Bible does teach that no man living can be justified for what he is. He is condemned for what he is and for what he does. He is justified for what Christ has done for him.

For the same reason justification cannot be mere pardon. Pardon does not proceed on the ground of a satisfaction. A prisoner delivered by a ransom is not pardoned. . . . When a sovereign pardons a criminal, it is not an act of justice. It is not on the ground of satisfaction to the law. The Bible, therefore, in teaching that justification is on the ground of an atonement or satisfaction, that the sinner's guilt is expiated, that he is redeemed by the precious blood of Christ, and that judgment is pronounced upon him as righteous, does thereby teach that justification is neither pardon nor infusion of righteousness.

F. Argument from the Immutability of the Law

The doctrine that justification consists simply in pardon and consequent restoration assumes that the divine law is imperfect and mutable. In human governments, of course, it is often expedient and right that men justly condemned to suffer the penalty of the law be pardoned. . . . But the law of the Lord is perfect. And being perfect it cannot be disregarded. It demands nothing which ought not to be demanded. It threatens nothing which ought not to be inflicted. . . . The penalty of the law is immutable and as little capable of being set aside as the precept. Accordingly, the Scriptures everywhere teach that in the justification of the sinner there is no relaxation of the penalty. There is no setting aside or disregarding the demands of the law. We are delivered from the law, not by its abrogation, but by its execution (Gal. 2:19). We are freed from the law by the body of Christ (Rom. 7:4). Christ, having taken our place, bore our sins in His own body on the tree (1 Peter 2:24). The handwriting which was against us, He took out of the way, nailing it to His cross (Col. 2:14). Such representations are inconsistent with the theory which supposes that the law may be dispensed with, that the restoration of sinners to the favour and fellowship of God requires no satisfaction to its demands, that the believer is pardoned and restored to fellowship with God just as a thief or forger is pardoned and restored to his civil rights by the executive in human governments. This is against the Scriptures. God is just in justifying the sinner. He acts according to justice. . . .

§3. Works Not the Ground of Justification

In reference to men since the fall the assertion that justification is not of works is so explicit and so often repeated that that proposition has never been called in question by any one professing to receive the Scriptures as the Word of God. . . . There are several Biblical evidences that the works excluded from the ground of our justification take in everything done by us or wrought in us:

(1) The language of Scripture is unlimited. The declaration is that we are not justified "by works." No specific kind of works is designated to the exclusion of all others. But it is "works"—anything and everything we do. . . .

(2) The word law is used in a comprehensive sense. It includes all revelations of the will of God as the rule of man's obedience, and, therefore, by "works of the law" must be intended all kinds of works. . . .

(3) The same is evident from what is taught of the gratuitous nature of our justification. Grace and works are antithetical. "To him that worketh is the reward not reckoned of grace, but of debt" (Rom. 4:4). "If by grace, then is it no more of works: otherwise grace is no more grace" (Rom. 11:6). Grace of necessity excludes works of every kind, and more especially those of the highest kind, which might have some show of merit. But merit of any degree is of necessity excluded if our salvation be by grace.

(4) When the positive ground of justification is stated, it is always declared to be not anything done by us or wrought in us, but what was done for us. It is ever represented as something external to ourselves. We are justified by the blood of Christ (Rom. 5:9), by His obedience (Rom. 5:19), by His righteousness (v. 18). This is involved in the whole method of salvation. Christ saves us as a priest, but a priest does not save by making those who come to him good. He does not work in them, but for them. Christ saves us by a sacrifice, but a sacrifice is effectual not because of its subjective effect upon the offerer, but as an expiation or satisfaction to justice. Christ is our Redeemer; He gave Himself as a ransom for many. But a ransom does not infuse righteousness. It is the payment of a price. It is the satisfaction of the

claims of the captor upon the captive. The whole plan of salvation, therefore, as presented in the Bible and as it is the life of the Church, is changed if the ground of our acceptance with God be transferred from what Christ has done for us to what is wrought in us or done by us. . . .

§4. The Righteousness of Christ the Ground of Justification

The imperative question remains, How shall a man be just with God? If our moral excellence be not the ground on which God pronounces us just, what is that ground? . . . The Bible and the people of God with one voice answer, "The righteousness of Christ." . . . Every believer relies for his acceptance with God, not on himself but on Christ, not on what he is or has done, but on what Christ is and has done for him.

By the righteousness of Christ is meant all He became, did, and suffered to satisfy the demands of divine justice and to merit for His people the forgiveness of sin and the gift of eternal life. . . . The Bible teaches that Christ obeyed the law in all its precepts and endured its penalty, and that this was done in such a sense for His people that they are said to have done it. They died in Him. They were crucified with Him. They were delivered from the curse of the law by His being made a curse for them. . . .

The righteousness of Christ on the ground of which the believer is justified is the righteousness of God. It is so designated in Scripture because it was provided and is accepted by Him; it is not only the righteousness which avails before God, but it is the righteousness of a divine person, of God manifest in the flesh. God purchased the Church with His own blood (Acts 20:28). It was the Lord of glory who was crucified (1 Cor. 2:8). He who was in the form of God and thought it not robbery to be equal with God became obedient unto death, even the death of the cross (Phil. 2:6–8). . . .

§5. Imputation of Righteousness

The righteousness of Christ is imputed to the believer for his justification. The word impute is familiar and unambiguous. To impute is to ascribe to, to reckon to, to lay to one's charge. . . . Philemon had no doubt what was meant when Paul asked that the debt of Onesimus be imputed to him instead. "Blood shall be imputed unto that man; he hath shed blood" (Lev. 17:4). "Blessed is the man unto whom the LORD imputeth not iniquity" (Ps. 32:2). "[Blessed is] the man, unto whom God imputeth righteousness without works" (Rom. 4:6). God is "in Christ, reconciling the world unto himself, not imputing their trespasses unto them" (2 Cor. 5:19).

The meaning of these and similar passages of Scripture has never been disputed. Every one understands them. We use the word impute in its simple admitted sense when we say that the righteousness of Christ is imputed to the believer for his justification.

It seems unnecessary to remark that this does not and cannot mean that the righteousness of Christ is infused into the believer, or in any way so imparted to him as to change or constitute his moral character. Imputation never changes the inward, subjective state of the person to whom the imputation is made.... So when righteousness is imputed to the believer, he does not thereby become subjectively righteous. If the righteousness be adequate, and if the imputation be made on adequate grounds and by competent authority, the person to whom the imputation is made has the right to be treated as righteous. And, therefore, in the forensic, although not in the moral or subjective sense, the imputation of the righteousness of Christ does make the sinner righteous. That is, it gives him a right to the full pardon of all his sins and a claim in justice to eternal life....

§6. Proof of the Doctrine

...As the question, What is the method of justification? is a Biblical question, it must be decided exegetically, and not by arguments drawn from assumed principles of reason.... What we must do is determine (1) What is the meaning of the word to justify as used in Scripture? and (2) On what ground does the Bible affirm that God pronounces the ungodly to be just? If the answer to these questions be what the Church in all ages and especially the Church of the Reformation has given, then we should rest satisfied. Paul in express terms says that God imputes righteousness to the sinner (Rom. 4:6, 24). By righteousness every one admits is meant that which makes a man righteous, that which the law demands. It does not consist in the sinner's own obedience or moral excellence, for it is said to be "without works," and it is declared that no man can be justified on the ground of his own character or conduct.... Rather, the righteousness imputed is declared to be the righteousness of Christ, His obedience (Rom. 5:19). It is, therefore, the righteousness of Christ, His perfect obedience in doing and suffering the will of God, which is imputed to the believer and on the ground of which the believer, although in himself ungodly, is pronounced righteous and therefore free from the curse of the law and entitled to eternal life (see Rom. 3:25; 4:6–8; 5:16–19; 10:3–4; 1 Cor. 1:30; 2 Cor. 5:21; Gal. 3:13; 4:4–5; Phil. 3:8–9). . . .

§7. The Consequences of the Imputation of Righteousness

. . . Because the perfect righteousness of Christ is therein imputed to the believing sinner, justification entails the pardon of sins. . . . The sins which are pardoned in justification include all sins, past, present, and future. . . . The righteousness of Christ is a perpetual donation. It is a robe which hides or, as the Bible expresses it, covers from the eye of justice the sins of the believer. Although they are sins deserving the wrath and curse of God, the necessity for the infliction of that curse no longer exists. . . . For in justification the believer receives the promise that God will not deal with him according to his transgressions.

This subject is thus presented by the apostle: believers "are not under the law, but under grace" (Rom. 6:14). They are not under a legal system administered according to the principles of retributive justice, a system which requires perfect obedience as the condition of acceptance with God, and which says, "Cursed is every one that continueth not in all things which are written in the book of the law to do them" (Gal. 3:10; cf. Deut. 27:26). They are under grace, that is, under a system in which believers are not dealt with according to the principles of justice, but according to the principles of undeserved mercy, and in which God does not impute "their trespasses unto them" (2 Cor. 5:19). There is therefore to them no condemnation. They are not condemned for their sins, not because they do not deserve condemnation, but because Christ has already made expiation for their guilt and makes continual intercession for them.

The second consequence attributed to the imputation of Christ's righteousness is a title to eternal life. This in the older writers is often expressed by the words "adoption and heirship." Being made the children of God by faith in Christ Jesus (Gal. 3:26), believers are heirs of God and joint heirs with Jesus Christ of a heavenly inheritance (Rom. 8:17). The mere expiation of guilt confers no title to eternal life. The condition of the covenant under which man was placed was perfect obedience. This, from all that appears in Scripture, the perfection of God requires. As He never pardons sins unless the demands of justice be satisfied, so He never grants eternal life unless perfect obedience be rendered. Heaven is always represented as a purchased possession. In the covenant between the Father and the Son the salvation of His people was promised as the reward of His humiliation, obedience, and

death. Having performed the stipulated conditions, He has a claim to
the promised recompense. And this claim inures to the benefit of His
people. But besides this, as the work of Christ consisted in His doing
all that the law of God or covenant of works requires for the salvation
of men, and as that righteousness is freely offered to every one that
believes, every such believer has as valid a claim to eternal life as he
would have if he had personally done all that the law demands. . . .

§8. Relation of Faith to Justification

. . . Faith is merely the instrumental cause of justification. It is the
act of receiving and resting upon Christ and has no other relation to
the end than does any other act by which a proffered good is accepted.
This is clearly the doctrine of Scripture: (1) We are constantly said to
be justified by or through faith. (2) The faith which justifies is described as a looking, as a receiving, as a coming, as a fleeing for refuge,
as a laying hold of, and as a calling upon. (3) The ground to which our
justification is referred and on which the sinner's trust is placed is
declared to be the blood, the death, the righteousness, the obedience
of Christ. (4) The fact that Christ is a ransom, a sacrifice, and as such
effects our salvation, of necessity supposes that the faith which interests us in the merit of His work is a simple act of trust. (5) Any other
view of the case is inconsistent with the gratuitous nature of justification, with the honour of Christ, and with the comfort and confidence
of the believer.

§9. Objections to the Protestant Doctrine of Justification
§10. Departures from the Protestant Doctrine
§11. Modern Views on Justification

Chapter **XVIII**

Sanctification

§1. Its Nature

Sanctification is defined in the "Westminster Catechism" as "the work of God's free grace, whereby we are renewed in the whole man after the image of God, and are enabled more and more to die unto sin, and live unto righteousness."

463

There are a number of ways, then, in which justification differs from sanctification: (1) The former is a transient act, the latter a progressive work. (2) Justification is a forensic act, God acting as judge, declaring justice satisfied so far as the believing sinner is concerned, whereas sanctification is an effect due to divine operation. (3) Justification changes, or declares to be changed, the relation of the sinner to the justice of God; sanctification involves a change of character. (4) The former, therefore, is objective, the latter subjective. (5) The former is founded on what Christ has done for us; the latter is the effect of what He does in us. (6) Justification is complete and the same in all, while sanctification is progressive and is more complete in some than in others.

Sanctification is declared to be a work of God's free grace. Two things are included in this. First, the power or influence by which sanctification is carried on is supernatural. Secondly, the granting of this influence to any sinner, to one sinner rather than another, and to one more than to another, is a matter of favour. No one has personally or in himself, on the ground of anything he has done, the right to claim this divine influence as a just recompense or as a matter of justice.

A. It Is a Supernatural Work

In representing, in accordance with Scripture, sanctification as a supernatural work, or as a work of grace, the Church intends to deny the Pelagian or rationalistic doctrine which confounds it with mere moral reformation. . . . Nor is sanctification to be confounded with the effects of moral culture or discipline. It is very possible, as experience proves, by careful moral training, by keeping the young from all contaminating influences, and by bringing them under the forming influences of right principles and good associates, to preserve them from much of the evil of the world and to render them like the young man in the Gospel whom Jesus loved. Such training cannot, however, change the nature. It cannot impart life. . . .

By contrast the effects of grace or fruits of the Spirit, which entail sanctification, are above the sphere of the natural; they belong to the supernatural. The mere power of truth, argument, motive, persuasion, or eloquence cannot produce repentance, faith, or holiness of heart and life. Nor can these effects be produced by the power of the will or by all the resources of man, however protracted or skilful in their application. They are the gifts of God, the fruits of the Spirit. Paul may plant and Apollos water, but it is God who gives the increase.

The cooperation of second causes is not excluded from the process of sanctification. When Christ opened the eyes of the blind, no second cause interposed between His volition and the effect. But men work out their own salvation, while God works in them to will and to do according to His own good pleasure. In the work of regeneration, the soul is passive. It cannot cooperate in the communication of spiritual life. But in conversion, repentance, faith, and growth in grace, all its powers are called into exercise. At the same time sanctification is supernatural or a work of grace, for the effects produced transcend the efficiency of our fallen nature and are due to the agency of the Spirit.

B. Proof of Its Supernatural Character

(1) Sanctification is constantly referred to God as its author. It is referred to God absolutely, or to the Father, as in 1 Thessalonians 5:23, "The very God of peace sanctify you wholly" (see also Heb. 13:20–21). It is also referred to the Son, as in Titus 2:14, "[Jesus Christ] gave himself for us, that he might . . . purify unto himself a peculiar people, zealous of good works" (see also Eph. 5:25–27). Predominantly sanctification is referred to the Holy Spirit as His peculiar work in the economy of redemption. Hence He is called the Spirit of all grace, the Spirit of joy, of peace, of love, of faith, and of adoption. All Christian graces are set forth as fruits of the Spirit. We are said to be born of the Spirit, and by Him to be enlightened, taught, led, and cleansed. We are said to be in the Spirit, to live, to walk, and to rejoice in the Spirit. The Spirit dwells in the people of God and is the abiding source of all the manifestations of that spiritual life which He implants in the soul. . . .

(2) All that the Scriptures teach concerning the union between the believer and Christ, and concerning the indwelling of the Holy Spirit, proves the supernatural character of our sanctification. Men do not make themselves holy; their holiness and their growth in grace are not due to their own fidelity, or firmness of purpose, or watchfulness and diligence, although all these are required, but to the divine influence by which they are rendered thus faithful, watchful, and diligent, and which produces in them the fruits of righteousness. "Without me," says our Lord, "ye can do nothing" (John 15:5). "As the branch cannot bear fruit of itself, except it abide in the vine; no more can ye, except ye abide in me" (v. 4). The hand is not more dependent on the head for the continuance of its vitality than is the believer on Christ for the continuance of spiritual life in the soul.

(3) The supernatural character of sanctification is one of those doctrines which pervade the whole Scriptures. It follows of necessity from what the Bible teaches of the natural state of man since the fall; it is assumed, asserted, and implied in all that is revealed of the plan of

salvation. By their apostasy men lost the image of God; they are born in a state of alienation and condemnation. They are by nature destitute of spiritual life. From this state it is as impossible that they should deliver themselves as that those in the grave should restore life to their wasted bodies and, when restored, continue to invigorate it by their own power. Our whole salvation is of Christ. Those who are in the grave hear His voice. They are raised by His power. And when they live, it is He who lives in them. This doctrine our Lord Himself clearly and frequently teaches. In addition, the main object of Romans 6–7 is to prove that as we are not justified on the grounds of our own righteousness, so we are not sanctified by our own power or by the mere objective power of the truth. . . .

§2. Wherein Sanctification Consists

Admitting sanctification to be a supernatural work, we are still faced with the question, What does it consist in? What is the nature of the effect produced? The truth which lies at the foundation of all the Scriptural representations of this subject is that while regeneration, the quickening of which believers are the subject, involves the implanting or communication of a new principle or form of life, it does not effect immediate and entire deliverance of the soul from all sin. A man raised from the dead may long continue to be in a very feeble, diseased, and suffering state. In like manner a soul by nature dead in sin may be quickened together with Christ but not thereby rendered perfect. The principle of life may be very feeble, much in the soul may be uncongenial with its nature, and the conflict between the old and the new life may be protracted and painful. Such is the case in all the ordinary experience of the people of God. . . . According to the Scriptures, the universal experience of Christians, and the undeniable evidence of history, regeneration does not remove all sin. The Bible is filled with the record of the inward conflicts of the most eminent of the servants of God, with their falls, their backslidings, their repentings, and their lamentations over their continued shortcomings. And not only this, but the nature of the conflict between good and evil in the heart of the renewed is fully described. . . . In the seventh chapter of the Epistle to the Romans Paul elaborately describes his own inward conflicts. And the same theme occurs in Galatians 5:16–17: "This I say then, Walk in the Spirit, and ye shall not fulfil the lust of the flesh. For the flesh lusteth against the Spirit, and the Spirit against the flesh: and these are contrary the one to the other: so that ye cannot do the things that ye would."

Such being the foundation of the Scriptural representations concerning sanctification, its nature is thereby determined. As all men since the fall are in a state of sin, not only guilty of specific acts of transgression, but also depraved, regeneration is the infusion of a new principle of life into their corrupt and perverse nature. It is leaven introduced to diffuse its influence gradually through the whole mass. Sanctification, therefore, consists in two things: first, gradual removal and destruction of the power of the principles of evil still infecting our nature; and secondly, the growth of the principle of spiritual life until it controls the thoughts, feelings, and acts, and brings the soul into conformity to the image of Christ (Eph. 4:22–24). . . .

§3. The Method of Sanctification

It has already been shown that although sanctification does not exclude all cooperation on the part of its subjects, but, on the contrary, calls for their unremitting and strenuous exertion, it is nevertheless the work of God. It is not carried on as a mere process of moral culture by moral means; it is as truly supernatural in its method as in its nature. The Biblical teaching as to how a soul by nature spiritually dead, being quickened by the mighty power of God, is gradually transformed into the image of Christ, is substantially as follows:

A. The Soul Is Led to Exercise Faith

The soul is led to exercise faith in the Lord Jesus Christ, to receive Him as its Saviour, committing itself to Him to be by His merit and grace delivered from the guilt and power of sin. This is the first step and secures all the rest, not because it has inherent virtue or efficacy, but because, according to the covenant of grace or plan of salvation which God has revealed and which He has pledged Himself to carry out, He is bound by His promise to accomplish the full salvation from sin of every one who believes.

B. The Effect of Union with Christ

The soul by this act of faith becomes united to Christ. We are in Him by faith. One of the consequences of this union is participation in His merits. In accordance with the stipulations of the covenant of redemption, His perfect righteousness is imputed to the believer, who is thereby justified. He is also introduced into a state of favour or grace and rejoices in hope of the glory of God (Rom. 5:1–2). This is, as the

Bible teaches, the essential preliminary condition of sanctification. . . .
Another consequence of the union with Christ which is effected by
faith is the indwelling of the Spirit. . . . The Spirit was given to the
people of God from the beginning. But as our Lord says that He came
into the world not only that men might have life, but that they might
have it more abundantly (John 10:10), the effusion of the Spirit is
always represented as the great characteristic of the Messiah's advent
(Joel 2:28–29; Acts 2:16–21; John 7:38–39). Our Lord, therefore, in
His last discourse to His disciples said it was expedient for them that
He go away, for "if I go not away, the Comforter (the helper) will not
come unto you; but if I depart, I will send him unto you" (John 16:7).
He was to fill the place of Christ as to His visible presence, carry on
His work, gather in His people, transform them into the likeness of
Christ, and communicate to them all the benefits of His redemption.
Where the Spirit is, there Christ is; so that, the Spirit being with us,
Christ is with us; and if the Spirit dwells in us, Christ dwells in us
(Rom. 8:9–11). . . .

C. The Inward Work of the Spirit

The indwelling of the Holy Spirit thus secured by union with Christ
becomes the source of a new spiritual life, which constantly increases
in power until everything uncongenial with it is expelled, and the soul
is perfectly transformed into the image of Christ. . . . The Spirit, we
are taught, especially opens the eyes to see the glory of Christ, to see
that He is God manifest in the flesh, to discern not only His divine
perfections, but His love to us, and His suitableness in all respects as
our Saviour, so that those who have not seen Him can yet believe on
Him, and rejoice in Him. This apprehension of Christ is transforming;
the soul is thereby changed into His image from glory to glory by the
Spirit of the Lord. . . .

It is not, however, only one object which the opened eye of the
believer is able to discern. The Spirit enables him to see the glory of
God as revealed in His works and in His Word; the holiness and spirituality of the law; the exceeding sinfulness of sin; his own guilt, pollution, and helplessness; the length and breadth, the height and depth
of the economy of redemption; and the reality, glory, and infinite importance of the things unseen and eternal. The soul is thus raised
above the world. It lives in a higher sphere. It becomes more and more
heavenly in its character and desires. All the great doctrines of the
Bible concerning God, Christ, and things spiritual and eternal are so
revealed by this inward teaching of the Spirit as to be not only rightly
discerned, but to exert, in a measure, their proper influence on the

heart and life. Thus the prayer of Christ, "Sanctify them through thy truth" (John 17:17), is answered in the experience of His people.

D. God Calls the Graces of His People into Exercise

The work of sanctification is carried on by God's giving constant occasion for the exercise of all the graces of the Spirit. Submission, confidence, self-denial, patience, and meekness, as well as faith, hope, and love, are called forth, or put to the test, more or less effectually every day the believer passes on earth. And by this constant exercise he grows in grace and in the knowledge of our Lord and Saviour Jesus Christ. It is, however, principally by calling His people to labour and suffer for the advancement of the Redeemer's kingdom, and for the good of their fellow men, that this salutary discipline is carried on. The best Christians are in general those who not merely from restless activity of natural disposition, but from love to Christ and zeal for His glory, labour most and suffer most in His service.

E. The Church and Sacraments as Means of Grace

One great end of the establishment of the Church on earth as the communion of saints is the edification of the people of God. The intellectual and social life of man is not developed in isolation and solitude. It is only in contact with his fellow men that his powers are called into exercise and his social virtues are cultivated. Thus also it is by the Church life of believers, by their communion in the worship and service of God, and by their mutual good offices and fellowship, that the spiritual life of the soul is developed (Heb. 10:24–25).

The Spirit renders the ordinances of God, the Word, sacraments, and prayer effectual means of promoting the sanctification of His people and of securing their ultimate salvation. . . .

F. The Kingly Office of Christ

In this connection, we are not to overlook or undervalue the constant exercise of the kingly office of Christ. He not only reigns over His people, but subdues them to Himself, rules and defends them, and restrains and conquers all His and their enemies. These enemies are both inward and outward, both seen and unseen; they are the world, the flesh, and the devil. The strength of the believer in contending with these enemies is not His own. He is strong only in the Lord and in the power of His might (Eph. 6:10). The weapons, both offensive and defensive, are supplied by Him, and the disposition and the skill to use them are His gifts to be sought by praying without ceasing. He is an ever-present helper. Whenever the Christian feels his weakness either in resisting temptation or in the discharge of duty, he looks to Christ and seeks aid from Him. And all who seek find. . . . The Christian runs his race "looking unto Jesus"; the life he lives, he lives by faith in the Son of God. It is by the constant worship of Christ, by the constant exercise of love toward Him, by constant endeavors to do His will, and by constantly looking to Him for the supply of grace and for protection and aid, that he overcomes sin and finally attains the prize of the high calling of God.

§4. The Fruits of Sanctification, or Good Works

The fruits of sanctification are good works. Our Lord says, "A good tree bringeth not forth corrupt fruit; neither doth a corrupt tree bring forth good fruit. For every tree is known by his own fruit. For of thorns men do not gather figs, nor of a bramble bush gather they grapes" (Luke 6:43–44). By good works, in this connection, are meant not only the inward exercises of the religious life, but also outward acts such as can be seen and appreciated by others.

There are three senses in which works may be called good:

(1) Works may be called good when their matter is what the law prescribes. In this sense even the heathen perform good works; as the apostle says in Romans 2:14, "The Gentiles . . . do by nature the things contained in the law." That is, they perform acts of justice and mercy. No man on earth is so wicked as never, in this sense of the term, to be the author of some good works. This is what the theologians call civil goodness, whose sphere is the social relations of men.

(2) Works may be called good when, in addition to their matter, the design and motives of the agent are what the law requires. In other words, a work is good when there is nothing either in the agent or in the act which the law condemns. In this sense not even the works of the holiest of God's people are good. Since the fall no man has ever been in such an inward state that he can stand before God and be accepted on the ground of what he is or of what he does. All our righteousnesses are as filthy rags (Isa. 64:6). Paul found to the last a law of sin in his members. He groaned under a body of death. . . . What the Scriptures teach of the imperfection of the best works of the believer is confirmed by the irrepressible testimony of consciousness. It matters not what the lips may say—every man's conscience tells him that he is always a sinner, that he never is free from moral defilement in the sight of an infinitely holy God. . . .

(3) Although no work even of the true people of God, while they continue in this world, is absolutely perfect, nevertheless those inward exercises and outward acts which are the fruits of the Spirit are properly designated good. It was said of Dorcas that she "was full of good works" (Acts 9:36). Believers are said to be "created in Christ Jesus unto good works" (Eph. 2:10). Christ "gave himself for us that he might . . . purify unto himself a peculiar people, zealous of good works" (Titus 2:14). There is no contradiction in pronouncing the same work good and bad, because these terms are relative, and the relations intended may be different. Feeding the poor, viewed in relation to the nature of the act, is a good work. Viewed in relation to the motive which prompts it, it may be good or bad. If done to be seen of men, it is offensive in the sight of God. If done from natural benevolence, it is an act of ordinary morality. If done to a disciple in the name of a disciple, it is an act of Christian virtue. The works of the children of God, therefore, although stained by sin, are truly and properly good because (a) they are, as to their nature or the thing done, commanded by God; (b) they are, as to the motive, the fruits not merely of right moral feeling, but of religious feeling, i.e., of love to God; and (c) they are performed with the purpose of complying with His will, of honouring Christ, and of promoting the interest of His kingdom. . . .

§5. Necessity of Good Works

On the subject of the necessity of good works there has never been any real difference of opinion among Protestants. First, it is universally admitted that good works are not necessary to our justification; they are consequences and indirectly the fruits of justification and, therefore, cannot be its ground. Secondly, it is also agreed that the faith by which the sinner is justified is not as a work the reason why God pronounces the sinner just. It is the act by which the sinner receives and rests upon the righteousness of Christ, the imputation of which renders him righteous in the sight of God. Thirdly, it is similarly agreed that it is not as the root or principle of good works that faith is said to justify. Fourthly, it is agreed that it is only a living faith, i.e., a faith which works by love and purifies the heart, that unites the soul to Christ and secures our reconciliation with God. Fifthly, it is universally admitted that an immoral life is inconsistent with a state of grace, that those who willfully continue in the practice of sin shall not inherit the kingdom of God. . . . For sanctification is inseparable from justification, and the one is just as essential as the other.

§6. Relation of Good Works to Reward

. . . Although Protestants deny the merit of good works and teach
that salvation is entirely gratuitous—that the remission of sins, adoption into the family of God, the gift of the Holy Spirit, and admission
to heaven are granted to the believer solely on the ground of the merits
of the Lord Jesus Christ—they nevertheless teach that God does reward His people for their works. They have both the gracious promise
that for Christ's sake the imperfection of their best services shall be
overlooked and the assurance founded on that promise that he who
gives to a disciple even a cup of cold water in the name of a disciple
shall in no wise lose his reward (Matt. 10:42). The Scriptures also
teach that the happiness or blessedness which believers will experience in a future life will be greater or less in proportion to their devotion to the service of Christ in this life. . . . The general drift of
Scripture is in favour of the doctrine that a man shall reap what he
sows, that God will reward every one according to (although not on
account of) his works.

§7. Perfectionism

The doctrine of Lutherans and Reformed, the two great branches
of the Protestant Church, is that sanctification is never perfected in
this life; sin is not in any case entirely subdued. Even the most advanced believer has need, as long as he continues in the flesh, to pray
daily for the forgiveness of sins. . . .

(1) The first proof that perfection is unattainable in this life is the
spirituality of the divine law and the immutability of its demands. It
condemns as sinful any want of conformity to the standard of absolute
perfection as exhibited in the Bible. Anything less than loving God
constantly with all the heart, all the soul, all the mind, and all the
strength, and our neighbour as ourselves, is sin.

(2) The second proof is the express declaration of Scripture that all
men are sinners. This does not mean simply that all men have sinned
and that all are guilty, but that all have sin cleaving to them. "If,"
declares the apostle John, "we say that we have no sin, we deceive
ourselves, and the truth is not in us" (1 John 1:8). The wise man had
said before him, "There is not a just man upon earth, that doeth good,
and sinneth not" (Eccles. 7:20). And the apostle James says, "In many
things we offend all" (James 3:2). . . .

(3) More definitely is this truth taught in those passages which de-

scribe the conflict in the believer between the flesh and the Spirit. The seventh chapter of Paul's Epistle to the Romans is an account of his own inward life at the time of writing. . . . It proves that even Paul was not free from sin, that he had to contend with a law in his members warring against the law of his mind, that he groaned constantly under the burden of indwelling sin. At a still later period of his life he writes: "Not as though I had already attained, either were already perfect: but I follow after, if that I may apprehend that for which also I am apprehended of Christ Jesus. Brethren, I count not myself to have apprehended: but this one thing I do, forgetting those things which are behind, and reaching forth unto those things which are before, I press toward the mark for the prize of the high calling of God in Christ Jesus" (Phil. 3:12–14). This is an unmistakable declaration on the part of the apostle that even at this late period of his life he was not yet perfect; he had not attained the end of perfect conformity to Christ, but was pressing forward, like one in a race, with all earnestness that he might reach the end of his calling. . . .

Similarly, Galatians 5:16–26 recognizes the fact that Christians are imperfectly sanctified and that in them the renewing principle, the Spirit as the source of spiritual life, is in conflict with the flesh, the remains of their corrupt nature. It exhorts them to mortify the flesh (not the body, but their corrupt nature) and to strive constantly to walk under the controlling influence of the Spirit. . . .

(4) Appeal may be made on this subject to the testimony of the Church universal. There are no forms of worship, no formulas for private devotion, in any age or part of the Church, which do not contain confession of sin and prayer for forgiveness. The whole Christian Church with all its members prostrates itself before God, saying, "Have mercy upon us miserable sinners." . . . We may also appeal to the conscience of every believer. He knows that he is a sinner. He never is in a state which satisfies his own conviction as to what he ought to be. . . .

[§8. Theories of Perfectionism]

Chapter **XIX**

The Law

By means of grace is not meant every instrumentality which God may please to make a means of spiritual edification to His children. The phrase is intended to indicate those institutions which God has ordained to be the ordinary channels of grace, i.e., of the supernatural influences of the Holy Spirit, to the souls of men. The means of grace, according to the standards of our Church, are the Word, sacraments, and prayer.

§1. The Word

(1) The Word of God, as here understood, is the Bible, the collection of the canonical books of the Old and New Testaments.

(2) These books are the Word of God because they were written by men who were His prophets, organs, or spokesmen in such a sense that whatever they declare to be true or obligatory, God declares to be true and binding.

(3) The Word of God, so far as adults are concerned, is an indispensable means of salvation. True religion never has existed and never can exist where the truths revealed in the Bible are unknown.

(4) The Word of God is not only necessary to salvation, but it is also divinely efficacious to the accomplishment of that end. One evidence of this power of the Word is the commission given to the Church. After His resurrection our Lord said to His disciples: "Go ye therefore, and teach all nations, baptizing them in the name of the Father, and of the Son, and of the Holy Ghost: teaching them to observe all things whatsoever I have commanded you: and, lo, I am with you alway, even unto the end of the world" (Matt. 28:19-20). The reading in Mark 16:15-16 is: "Go ye into all the world, and preach the gospel to every creature. He that believeth and is baptized shall be saved; but he that believeth not shall be damned." The end to be accomplished was the salvation of men. The means of its accomplishment was teaching. The disciples were to teach what Christ had taught them. That is, they were to teach the gospel to every creature under heaven. All means derive their efficiency from the ordinance of God; as He has ordained

the gospel to be the means of salvation, it must be efficacious to that end. A second evidence of this power of the Word is the manner in which the apostles executed the commission which they had received. They went everywhere, preaching Christ. They were sent to teach, and teaching was their whole work. "I determined," said Paul, "not to know any thing among you, save Jesus Christ and him crucified" (1 Cor. 2:2). The power of the Word is also proved from many direct assertions in the Bible. Paul tells the Romans that he is not ashamed of the gospel of Christ, because "it is the power of God unto salvation" (Rom. 1:16). To the Corinthians he says that in view of the utter impotence of the wisdom of the world, "it pleased God by the foolishness of preaching to save them that believe" (1 Cor. 1:21). The preaching of Christ crucified was "unto the Jews a stumblingblock, and unto the Greeks foolishness; but unto them which are called, both Jews and Greeks, Christ the power of God, and the wisdom of God" (vv. 23–24). In the Epistle to the Hebrews it is said: "The word of God is quick, and powerful, and sharper than any two-edged sword, piercing even to the dividing asunder of soul and spirit, and of the joints and marrow, and is a discerner of the thoughts and intents of the heart" (Heb. 4:12; see also Ps. 19:7–10; 119:105; Jer. 23:29; John 17:17; 2 Tim. 3:15–16; 1 Peter 1:23). . . .

A. To What Is the Power of the Word to Be Attributed?

. . . Although the truths of the Bible have this transforming and saving power, the minds of men because of the fall are not in a condition to receive it. Therefore it is necessary, in order to render the Word of God an effectual means of salvation, that it be attended by the supernatural power of the Holy Spirit. Paul says expressly, "The natural man receiveth not the things of the Spirit of God: for they are foolishness unto him: neither can he know them, because they are spiritually discerned" (1 Cor. 2:14). In the preceding chapter He has said that the same gospel which to the called is the power and wisdom of God is to the Jews a stumbling block and to the Greeks foolishness. Our Lord said to the Jews: "Why do ye not understand my speech? even because ye cannot hear my word. . . . He that is of God heareth God's words: ye therefore hear them not, because ye are not of God" (John 8:43, 47). Everything that the Scriptures teach of the state of men since the fall proves that until enlightened by the Holy Ghost they are spiritually blind, unable to discern the true nature of the things of the Spirit, and therefore incapable of receiving a due impression from them. . . .

[That the Spirit must quicken those who are spiritually dead if the

Word of God is to have effect] is felt and recognized by every parent, by every pastor, and by every missionary. The Spirit's sovereignty in this area must be acknowledged. God has chosen not the wise, nor the great, but the foolish, those who are of no account, in order "that no flesh should glory in his presence" (1 Cor. 1:26–29). No man is to be allowed to attribute his conversion or salvation to himself, to the law, or to the efficiency of the truths in the Word. It is in the hands of God. It is of Him that any man is in Christ Jesus (1 Cor. 1:30). Accordingly, every minister of the gospel, as the apostles themselves did, should feel and acknowledge that his success does not depend on his official dignity, or his fidelity, or his skill in argument, or his power of persuasion, but simply and solely on the demonstration of the Spirit, given or withheld as He sees fit. Why was it that so few were converted under the ministry of Christ and so many thousands under that of the apostles? Why is it that a like experience has marked the whole history of the Church? The only Scriptural or rational answer that can be given to that question is, "Even so, Father: for so it seemed good in thy sight." We know indeed that the Spirit's sovereignty is determined in its action by infinitely wise and good reasons; and we know that His withholding His cooperation is often judicial and punitive, that He abandons individuals, churches, communities, and nations that have sinned away their day of grace. It is important to remember that in living under the dispensation of the Spirit we are absolutely dependent on a divine person who gives or withholds His influence as He will; that He can be grieved and offended; that He must be acknowledged, feared, and obeyed; that His presence and gifts must be humbly and earnestly sought and assiduously cherished; and that to Him all right thoughts and right purposes, all grace and goodness, all strength and comfort, and all success in winning souls to Christ are to be ascribed.

B. The Office of the Word as a Means of Grace

Christians then do not refer the saving and the sanctifying power of the Scriptures to the moral power of the truths which they contain, but to the power of the Spirit as a divine person acting with and by the truth as in His sovereign pleasure He sees fit. This is not to deny the essentiality of the Word. Although light cannot restore sight to the blind or heal the diseases of the organs of sight, it is nevertheless essential to every exercise of the power of vision. So the Word is essential to all holy exercises in the human soul. . . .

Besides its general sanctifying power when it is spiritually discerned, the Word of God is the means of calling forth all holy thoughts, feelings, purposes, and acts. Even a regenerated soul without any truth before it would be in blank darkness. It would be in the state of a regenerated infant or in the state of an unborn infant in relation to the external world—having eyes and ears, but nothing to call its faculties of sight and hearing into exercise. It is obvious that we can have no rational feelings of gratitude, love, adoration, and fear toward God except in view of the truths revealed concerning Him in His Word. We can have no love or devotion to Christ except so far as the manifestation of His character and work is accepted by us as true. We can have no faith except as founded on some revealed promise of God, no resignation or submission except in view of the wisdom and love of God and of His universal providence as revealed in the Scriptures, no joyful anticipation of future blessedness except as rooted in what the gospel makes known of a future state of existence. The Bible, therefore, is essential to the conscious existence of the divine life in the soul and to all its rational exercises. The Christian can no more live without the Bible than his body can live without food. The Word of God is milk and strong meat; it is water to the thirsty; it is honey and the honeycomb. . . .

§2. The Sacraments. Their Nature

. . . The best method of arriving at the idea of a sacrament, in the Christian sense of the word, is to take those ordinances which by common consent are admitted to be sacraments and to determine their essential elements or characteristics. We should then exclude from the category all other ordinances, human or divine, in which those characteristics are not found. Baptism and the Lord's Supper are admitted to be sacraments. Analysis shows that (1) they are ordinances instituted by Christ. (2) They are signs—baptism of cleansing and the Lord's Supper of spiritual nourishment. (3) They were designed to be perpetual. (4) They were appointed to signify and to instruct, to seal and thus to confirm and strengthen, and to convey or apply the benefits of redemption and thus to sanctify those who by faith receive the sacraments. On this principle the definition of a sacrament is founded. "A sacrament," it is said in the "Westminster Catechism," is a "holy ordinance instituted by Christ; wherein, by sensible signs, Christ and the benefits of the new covenant are represented, sealed, and applied to believers." . . .

§3. Number of the Sacraments

If the word sacrament be taken in the wide sense in which it was used in the early Church for any significant religious rite, it is obvious that no definite limit can be set to the number. If the word be confined to such divine ordinances as answer the conditions which characterize baptism and the Lord's Supper, then it is evident that they are the only sacraments under the Christian dispensation; and such is the view taken by all Protestants. . . .

§4. The Efficacy of the Sacraments

. . .The first point which the symbols of the Reformed Church teach on the subject of the efficacy of the sacraments is that they are real means of grace, that is, means appointed and employed by Christ for conveying the benefits of His redemption to His people. They are not, as Roman Catholics teach, the exclusive channels; but they are channels. A promise is made to those who rightly receive the sacraments that they shall thereby and therein be made partakers of the blessings of which the sacraments are the divinely appointed signs and seals. The word grace, when we speak of the means of grace, includes three things: (1) an unmerited gift, such as the remission of sin; (2) the supernatural influence of the Holy Spirit; and (3) the subjective effects of that influence on the soul. Faith, hope, and charity, for example, are graces.

The second point in the Reformed doctrine on the sacraments concerns the source of their power. On this subject it is taught negatively that the virtue is not in them. . . . That is to say, the power or efficiency of the sacraments does not reside in the elements, in the water used in baptism or in the bread and wine used in the Lord's Supper. It is not in the sacramental actions, either in giving or in receiving the consecrated elements. Neither does the virtue or efficiency reside in or flow from the person by whom the sacraments are administered. It does not reside in his office. There is no supernatural power in the man, by virtue of his office, to render the sacraments effectual. Nor does their efficiency depend on the character of the administrator in the sight of God, nor upon his intention, that is, his purpose to render them effectual. . . . The affirmative statement on this subject is that the efficacy of the sacraments is due solely to the blessing of Christ and the working of His Spirit. The Spirit, it is to be ever remembered, is a personal agent who works when and how He will. God has promised that His Spirit shall attend His Word, and He thus renders it an effectual means for the sanctification of His people. So He has promised, through the attending operation of His Spirit, to render the sacraments effectual to the same end.

The third point included in the Reformed doctrine is that, so far as adults are concerned, the sacraments are effectual as means of grace only to those who by faith receive them. They may have a natural power on other than believers by presenting truth and exciting feeling, but their saving or sanctifying influence is experienced only by believers.

All these points are clearly presented in the standards of the Reformed Church. The sacraments are declared to be means of grace, that is, means for signifying, sealing, and applying the benefits of redemption. It is denied that this virtue is in them or in him by whom they are administered. It is affirmed that their efficiency in conveying grace is due solely to the blessing of Christ and the cooperation of His Spirit, and such efficiency is experienced only by believers. . . .

§5. The Necessity of the Sacraments
§6. Validity of the Sacraments

§7. Baptism

The "Westminster Catechism" defines baptism as "a sacrament, wherein the washing with water, in the name of the Father, and of the Son, and of the Holy Ghost, doth signify and seal our ingrafting into Christ and partaking of the benefits of the covenant of grace, and our engagement to be the Lord's." By washing is meant any such application of water to the body as effects its purification. This may be done by immersion, affusion, or sprinkling. The command, therefore, to baptize is simply a command to wash with water. It is not specifically a command to immerse, to affuse, or to sprinkle. The mode of applying water as the purifying medium is unessential. The only necessary thing is to make such an application of water to the person as shall render the act a sign of the purification of the soul. . . .

§8. The Formula of Baptism

The formula of baptism is authoritatively prescribed in Matthew 28:19. Christ gave a command perpetually binding on His Church to baptize men "in the name of the Father, and of the Son, and of the Holy Ghost." . . . According to this formula, he who receives baptism as a Christian rite thereby professes to stand in that relation to the Father, Son, and Spirit which those who receive the religion of Christ sustain. That is, he professes to receive God the Father as his Father, God the Son as his Saviour, and God the Holy Ghost as his teacher and sanctifier; this involves accepting the Word, of which the Spirit is the author, as the rule of faith and practice. . . .

§9. The Subjects of Baptism

After defining baptism the "Westminster Catechism" continues, "Baptism is not to be administered to any that are out of the visible Church, till they profess their faith in Christ, and obedience to Him; but the infants of such as are members of the visible Church are to be baptized." . . . With regard to the qualifications for adult baptism there has ever been a general agreement: (1) There must be a knowledge of at least the fundamental doctrines of the gospel. Some may unduly enlarge and some unduly restrict the number of such doctrines, but no Church advocates the baptism of the absolutely ignorant. Since baptism involves a profession of faith, it must involve a profession of faith in certain doctrines; and those doctrines must be known in order to be professed. In the early Church, therefore, there was a class of catechumens or candidates for baptism who were under a regular course of instruction. This course continued, according to circumstances, from a few months to three years. These catechumens were not only young men, but often persons in mature life and of all degrees of mental culture. . . . (2) All churches are agreed in demanding of adults who are candidates for baptism a profession of their faith in Christ and the gospel of His salvation. (3) They agree in requiring of those who are baptized the renunciation of the world, the flesh, and the devil. This involves a turning from sin and a turning to God. . . .

§10. Infant Baptism

The difficulty on the subject of infant baptism is that baptism from its very nature involves a profession of faith. It is the way in which Christ is to be confessed before men. But infants are incapable of making such confession; therefore they are not proper subjects of baptism. To state the difficulty in another form: The sacraments belong to the members of the Church, i.e., the company of believers. Since infants cannot exercise faith, they are not members of the Church and consequently ought not to be baptized.

In order to justify the baptism of infants, we must attain and authenticate such an idea of the Church as to include the children of believing parents. . . . With such an aim in view, the following propositions are maintained:

(1) *The visible Church is a divine institution.* It is clearly taught in Scripture that it is the will of God that such a Church should exist on earth. This no Christian denies. God has imposed duties upon His people which render it necessary for them thus to associate in a visible organized body. They are to unite in His worship, in teaching and propagating His truth, in testifying for God in all ages and in all parts of the world. He has prescribed the conditions of membership in this body and taught who are to be excluded from its communion. . . .

(2) *The visible Church does not consist exclusively of the regenerate.* There are several indications that it is not the purpose of God that the visible Church on earth should consist exclusively of true believers: (a) The attainment of such a result in any society or government administered by men is an impossibility. It would require that the officers of the Church or the Church itself have the power to read the heart and be infallible in judgments of character. (b) The conditions which, under both dispensations, God has prescribed for admission into this visible society of His professed worshippers are such as men not truly regenerated may possess. Those qualifications, as we have seen, are competent knowledge and a credible profession of faith and obedience. (c) Our Lord expressly forbids any attempt to restrict the visible Church to the regenerate. He compares His external kingdom, or the visible Church, to a field in which tares and wheat grow together. He charges His disciples not to undertake to separate them, because they cannot, in all cases, distinguish the one from the other. Both are to be allowed to grow together until the harvest. . . .

(3) *The commonwealth of Israel was the Church.* It is so called in Scripture (Acts 7:38). The Hebrews were called out from all the nations of the earth to be the peculiar people of God. They constituted His kingdom, and to them were committed His oracles. To the Israelites pertained "the adoption, and the glory, and the covenants, and the giving of the law, and the service of God, and the promises" (Rom. 9:4). Nothing more can be said of the Church under the new dispensation. Like the Church the Israelites were selected to be witnesses for God in the world in behalf of the true religion, to celebrate His worship, and to observe His ordinances. Their religious officers, prophets, and priests were appointed by God and were His ministers. No man could become a member of the commonwealth of Israel who did not profess the true religion, promise obedience to the law of God as revealed in His Word, and submit to the rite of circumcision as the seal of the covenant. Furthermore, every authorized definition of the Church includes the people of God under the Mosaic law.

(4) *The Church under the new dispensation is identical with that under the old.* It is not a new Church, but one and the same. It is the

same olive tree (Rom. 11:16-17). It is founded on the same covenant, the covenant made with Abraham. . . . In that covenant God promised that Abraham, although nearly a hundred years old, would have a son. He promised that his descendants, through Isaac, would be as numerous as the stars in heaven, that He would give them the land of Canaan for a possession, that He would be their national God, and that the Hebrews as a nation would be His peculiar people; and above all He promised the patriarch that in his seed all the nations of the earth would be blessed. By seed was not meant his descendants collectively, but one person, that is, Christ (Gal. 3:16). The blessing promised, therefore, was the blessing of redemption through Christ. This promise to Abraham, which was a repetition of the promise made to our first parents after the fall, was the gospel—the announcement of the plan of salvation through Christ, and the offer of that salvation to every one that believes. This gospel, Paul says, was preached before unto Abraham. The pious Hebrews are, therefore, described as those who hoped in Christ before His advent (Eph. 1:12). This promise of redemption made to Abraham was that "unto which," Paul says, "our twelve tribes, instantly serving God day and night, hope to come" (Acts 26:7). The condition of all these Abrahamic promises was faith. This the apostle abundantly teaches, especially in the fourth chapter of Romans and the third chapter of Galatians. . . .

Such being the nature of the covenant made with Abraham, it is plain that so far as its main element is concerned, it is still in force. It is the covenant of grace under which we now live and upon which the Church is now founded. This cannot be doubted by any who admit the account just given of the Abrahamic covenant. This is clear because the promise is the same. Paul says (Gal. 3:14) that the blessing promised to Abraham has come upon us. In his speech before Agrippa he said: "I stand and am judged for the hope of the promise made of God unto our fathers. . . . For which hope's sake, King Agrippa, I am accused of the Jews" (Acts 26:6-7). As the promise is the same, so also the condition is the same. The apostle argues that men now must be justified by faith, because Abraham was thus justified. Christians, therefore, are said to be the sons or heirs of Abraham, because faith in the promise of redemption secures their redemption just as faith in the same promise secured his. And Paul tells the Galatians, "If ye be Christ's, then are ye Abraham's seed, and heirs according to the promise" (Gal. 3:29). This doctrine that the Church now rests on the Abrahamic covenant, in other words, that the plan of salvation revealed in the gospel was revealed to Abraham and to the other Old Testament saints, and that they were saved just as men since the advent of Christ are saved, by faith in the promised seed, is not a matter incidentally revealed. It is wrought into the very substance of the gospel. It is involved in all the teachings of our Lord, who said that He came not to destroy, but to fulfil, and who commanded inquirers to search the Old Testament Scriptures for verification of what He taught. The apostles did the same thing. The Bereans were commended because they searched the Scriptures daily to see whether the doctrines taught by the apostles accorded with that infallible standard (Acts 17:11). The messengers of Christ constantly quoted the Old Testament in support of their teachings. Paul says that the gospel which he preaches has been taught already in the law and the prophets (Rom. 3:21). He tells the Gentiles that they are grafted into the old olive tree and made partakers of its root and fatness.

The conclusion is that God has ever had but one Church in the world. The Jehovah of the Old Testament is our Lord; the God of Abraham, Isaac, and Jacob is our covenant God and Father; our Saviour was the Saviour of the saints who lived before His advent in the flesh. The divine person who delivered the Israelites out of Egypt, who led them through the wilderness, who appeared in His glory to Isaiah in the temple, and towards whose coming the eyes of the people of God were turned in faith and hope from the beginning, is He whom we recognize as God manifest in the flesh, our Lord and Saviour Jesus Christ. He, therefore, who was the head of the theocracy is the head of the Church. The very blood which He shed for us was shed from the foundation of the world "for the redemption of the transgressions that were under the first testament" (Heb. 9:15). The promise unto which the twelve tribes, instantly serving God day and night, hoped to come (Acts 26:7) is the promise on which we rely. The faith which saved Abraham is, both as to its nature and as to its object, the condition of salvation under the gospel. The city for which Abraham looked, the "city which hath foundations, whose builder and maker is God" (Heb. 11:10), is "Jerusalem the golden," the heaven to which we aspire.

(5) *The terms of admission into the Church before the advent were the same that are required for admission into the Christian Church.* Those terms were a credible profession of faith in the true religion, a promise of obedience, and submission to the appointed rite of initiation. Every sincere Israelite received Jehovah as his God and relied upon all His promises, especially the promise of redemption through the seed of Abraham. He not only bound himself to obey the law of God as then revealed, but sincerely endeavored to keep all His commandments. . . . If any from among the heathen assayed to enter the congregation of the Lord, they were received upon the terms above specified and to a place equal to, and in some cases better than, that of sons and of daughters. If any Israelite renounced the religion of his father, he was

cut off from among the people. All this is true in reference to the Church that now exists. Of those whom it receives to membership in visible communion the Christian Church requires nothing more than a credible profession of faith, the promise of obedience to Christ, and submission to baptism as the rite of initiation. The introduction of the gospel has, then, effected no change in the terms of admission to the Church.

(6) *Infants were members of the Church under the Old Testament economy.* This is conclusively proved by the fact that infants, by the command of God, were circumcised on the eighth day after their birth. . . . Circumcision was enjoined upon Abraham and continued in practice hundreds of years before the giving of the law on Mount Sinai, when the people were inaugurated as a nation. It was instituted as the sign of the covenant (that is the Scriptural and proper word) made with Abraham. The essential features of that covenant we learn from such passages as Genesis 12:3, "in thee shall all families of the earth be blessed," and 17:7, "I will establish my covenant between me and thee and thy seed after thee in their generations for an everlasting covenant, to be a God to thee, and to thy seed after thee." These passages are shown in the New Testament to refer not to temporal or national blessings, but to the blessings of redemption. Thus in Romans 15:8 it is said, "Jesus Christ was a minister of the circumcision for the truth of God, to confirm the promises made unto the fathers." Christ has redeemed us from the curse of the law, that the blessing of Abraham might come on us (Gal. 3:14). This covenant, Paul goes on to argue, "that was confirmed before of God in Christ, the law, which was four hundred and thirty years after, cannot disannul, that it should make the promise of none effect" (v. 17). In short, the whole New Testament is designed to show that the covenant made with Abraham and the promises therein contained were executed and fulfilled in Jesus Christ. Of that covenant, circumcision was the sign and seal.

This is directly asserted by the apostle in Romans 4:9–12, where he proves that circumcision cannot be the ground of justification, because Abraham was justified before he was circumcised and "received the sign of circumcision, a seal of the righteousness of the faith which he had yet being uncircumcised." This is saying that circumcision is the seal of the covenant which promises salvation on the condition of faith. That is, it is the seal of the covenant of grace or of the plan of salvation which has been the only ground of hope for man since his apostasy. If, therefore, children were circumcised by the command of God, it was because they were included in the covenant made with their fathers.

Circumcision signifies cleansing from sin, just as baptism now does.

Thus we read even in the Old Testament of the circumcision of the heart (Deut. 10:16; Jer. 4:4; Ezek. 44:7). Uncircumcised lips are impure lips, and an uncircumcised heart is an unclean heart (Exod. 6:12; Lev. 26:41; see also Acts 7:51). Paul says the true circumcision is not that which is outward in the flesh, but that which is inward, of the heart, by the Spirit (Rom. 2:28–29). Therefore the apostle speaking of himself and of other believers says, "We are the circumcision, which worship God in the spirit, and rejoice in Christ Jesus, and have no confidence in the flesh" (Phil. 3:3). Such being the spiritual import of circumcision, . . . its main design was to signify and seal the promise of deliverance from sin through the redemption to be effected by the promised seed of Abraham.

Children, therefore, were included in the covenant of grace as revealed under the old dispensation and consequently were members of the Church as it was then constituted. In the sight of God parents and children are one. The former are the authorized representatives of the latter; they act for them; they contract obligations in their name. In all cases, therefore, where parents enter into covenant with God, they bring their children with them. The covenant made with Adam included all his posterity; the promise made to Abraham was to him and to his seed after him; and when the Mosaic covenant was solemnly ratified in the land of Moab, it was said, "Ye stand this day all of you before the LORD your God; your captains of your tribes, your elders, and your officers, with all the men of Israel, your little ones, your wives, and thy stranger that is in thy camp, from the hewer of thy wood unto the drawer of thy water: that thou shouldest enter into covenant with the LORD thy God, and into his oath, which the LORD thy God maketh with thee this day" (Deut. 29:10–12). It is vain to say that children cannot make contracts or take an oath. Their parents can act for them, not only bringing them under obligation, but securing for them the benefits of the covenants into which they thus vicariously enter. When a man joined the commonwealth of Israel, he secured for his children the benefits of the theocracy, unless they willingly renounced them. And so when a believer adopts the covenant of grace, he brings his children within that covenant in the sense that God promises to give them, in His own good time, all the benefits of redemption, provided they do not willingly renounce their baptismal commitments.

This is really the turning point in the controversy concerning the Church membership of infants. Since the Church is one under both dispensations, and infants were members of the Church under the theocracy, they are members of the Church now, unless the contrary can be proved.

(7) *Nothing in the New Testament justifies the exclusion of the children of believers from membership in the Church.* The burden of proof rests on those who take the negative on this subject. If children are to be deprived of a birthright which they have enjoyed ever since there was a Church on earth, there must be some positive command for their exclusion or some clearly revealed change in the conditions of membership. It need hardly be said that Christ gave no command excluding the children of believers, neither has there been any change in the conditions of Church membership. Those conditions are now what they were from the beginning. It was inevitable, therefore, when Christ commanded His apostles to disciple all nations, baptizing them in the name of the Father, of the Son, and of the Holy Spirit, that they should act on the principle to which they had always been accustomed. When under the Old Testament a parent joined the congregation of the Lord, he brought his minor children with him. When, therefore, the apostles baptized a head of a family, it was a matter of course that they should baptize his infant children. We accordingly find several cases of such household baptisms recorded in the New Testament. Lydia "was baptized, and her household" (Acts 16:15); the jailer at Philippi "was baptized, he and all his straightway" (v. 33); and in 1 Corinthians 1:16 Paul says that he baptized the household of Stephanas. The apostles, therefore, acted on the principle which had always been acted on under the old economy. . . .

The conduct of our Lord in its bearing on this subject must not be overlooked. Far from excluding children from the Church in whose bosom they had always been cherished, He called them the lambs of His flock, took them into His arms, and blessed them, and said, "Suffer little children, and forbid them not, to come unto me: for of such is the kingdom of heaven" (Matt. 19:14). If members of His kingdom in heaven, why should they be excluded from His kingdom on earth?

(8) *Children need and are capable of receiving the benefits of redemption.* On this point all Christians are agreed. All churches unite in the belief that if infants are to be saved, they need "the sprinkling of the blood of Jesus Christ" and the renewing of the Holy Ghost. The Reformed, at least, do not believe that those blessings are so tied to the ordinance of baptism that the reception of baptism is necessary to a participation in the spiritual benefits which it symbolizes; but all agree that infants are saved by Christ, that they are purchased by His blood, and that they need expiation and regeneration. All are united, also, in believing that those who seek the benefits of the work of Christ are bound to be baptized in acknowledgment of its necessity and of their faith, and that those who need, but cannot seek, are, by the ordinance of God, entitled to receive the appointed sign and seal of

redemption whenever and wherever they are presented by those who have the right to represent them.

[§11. Whose Children Are Entitled to Baptism?]

§12. Efficacy of Baptism

The Reformed doctrine on the efficacy of baptism is aptly summarized in the *Westminster Confession* (28.5-6): "Although it be a great sin to contemn or neglect this ordinance [baptism], yet grace and salvation are not so inseparably annexed unto it, as that no person can be regenerated or saved without it, or that all that are baptized are undoubtedly regenerated. The efficacy of baptism is not tied to that moment of time wherein it is administered; yet, notwithstanding, by the right use of this ordinance the grace promised is not only offered, but really exhibited and conferred by the Holy Ghost, to such (whether of age or infants) as that grace belongeth unto, according to the counsel of God's own will, in his appointed time." . . .

The doctrine of the Reformed Church, then, on the efficacy of baptism includes in the first place the rejection or denial of certain false doctrines on the subject: (1) It denies that baptism conveys grace *ex opere operato*, that is, by any objective supernatural power belonging to the ordinance itself or in virtue of the divine efficiency inherent in the word or promise of God connected with the sacrament. (2) The Reformed doctrine also denies that the cooperation of the Spirit, to which the efficacy of the ordinance is due, always attends its administration, so that those who are baptized, in all cases, if unresisting, experience the remission of sins and the renewing of the Holy Ghost. (3) Also rejected is the position that baptism was appointed to be the ordinary means or channel of conveying, in the first instance, the merits of Christ's death and the saving influences of the Spirit, so that those benefits may not, except in extraordinary cases, be obtained before or without baptism.

In the second place the Reformed doctrine makes several affirmations regarding the efficacy of baptism: (1) Baptism is a divine ordinance. (2) It is a means of grace to believers. (3) It is a sign and seal of the covenant of grace. (4) The ordinance was intended to be of perpetual obligation in the sense that all not baptized in infancy are required to submit to baptism as the divinely appointed way of publicly professing their faith in Christ and their allegiance to Him as their God and Saviour, and that all such professors of the true religion are bound to present their children for baptism as the divinely appointed way of consecrating them to God. (5) God, on His part, promises to grant the benefits signified in baptism to all adults who receive that sacrament in the exercise of faith and to all infants who, when they arrive at maturity, remain faithful to the vows made in their name when they were baptized. . . .

The question arises, What is meant by the Reformed doctrine that baptism is a sign, a seal, and a means of grace?

(1) As a sign, baptism signifies the great truths that the soul is cleansed from the guilt of sin by the sprinkling of the blood of Christ and purified from the pollution of sin by the renewing of the Holy Ghost. The Bible teaches that God sanctifies and saves men through the truth; the Spirit works with and by the truth in conveying to men the benefits of redemption. It matters not whether that truth be brought before the mind by hearing or reading the Word or through the use of significant divinely appointed emblems. The fact and the method of the deliverance of the children of Israel from their bondage in Egypt were as clearly taught in the sacrament of the Passover as in the written words of Moses. So the fundamental truths just mentioned are as clearly and impressively taught in the sacrament of baptism as in the discourses of our blessed Lord Himself. The Spirit can make either the truth signified in baptism or that same truth as read or heard the means of sanctification. It should be remembered, however, that the Spirit does not always cooperate with the truth as heard to make it a means of grace, neither does He always attend the administration of baptism with His sanctifying and saving power.

(2) Baptism is a seal or pledge. When God promised to Noah that He would never again drown the world in a deluge, He set the rainbow in the heavens as a pledge of the promise which He had made. When He promised Abraham to be a God to him and to his seed after him, He appointed circumcision as the seal and pledge of that promise. So when He promised to save men by the blood of Christ and by the renewing of the Holy Ghost, He appointed baptism to be not only the sign, but also the seal and pledge of those exceeding great and precious promises. No believer in the Bible can look on the rainbow without having his faith strengthened in the promise that a deluge shall never again destroy the earth. No pious Jew could witness the rite of circumcision, or advert to that sign in his own person, without an increased confidence that Jehovah was his God. And no Christian can recall his own baptism, or witness the baptism of others, without having his faith strengthened in the great promises of redemption. Every time the ordinance of baptism is administered in our presence, we hear anew the voice from heaven proclaiming that the blood of Jesus Christ cleanses us from all sin and that He saves us by the washing of regeneration and renewing of the Holy Ghost.

(3) Baptism, however, is not only a sign and seal; it is also a means of grace because in it the blessings which it signifies are conveyed, and the promises of which it is the seal are assured to or fulfilled in those who are baptized, provided they believe. We have already seen that as a means of grace the Word of God is the wisdom and power of God to salvation; it is the means used by the Holy Spirit in conferring on men the benefits of redemption. Of course all who merely hear or read the Word of God are not saved, neither do all who receive the baptism of water experience the baptism of the Holy Ghost; but this is not inconsistent with the Word's being the means of salvation, or with baptism's being the washing of regeneration. Our Lord says we are sanctified by the truth. Paul says we put on Christ in baptism (Gal. 3:27). When a man receives the gospel with a true faith, he receives the blessings which the gospel promises; when he receives baptism in the exercise of faith, he receives the benefits of which baptism is the sign and seal. Unless the recipient of this sacrament be insincere, baptism is an act of faith in which and by which he receives and appropriates the offered benefits of the redemption of Christ. And, therefore, to baptism may be properly attributed all that in the Scriptures is attributed to faith. Baptism washes away sin (Acts 22:16); it unites to Christ and makes us the sons of God (Gal. 3:26–27); we are therein buried with Christ (Rom. 6:3); it is (according to one interpretation of Titus 3:5) the washing of regeneration. . . . Such being the case, it is plain that baptism is as truly a means of grace as is the Word. It conveys truth to the mind, it confirms the promise of God, and it is the Spirit's means of conveying to believers the benefits of redemption. Hence it is a grievous mistake and a great sin to neglect or undervalue it.

All this is plain so far as adults are concerned. But if the saving benefits of baptism are suspended on the condition of faith on the part of the recipient, what benefit can there be in the baptism of infants? To this it may be answered:

(1) The baptism of infants is the commandment of God. This should be enough. It might as well be asked what benefit could there be in the circumcision of infants under the law. Paul tells us that the benefit to them as well as to others was "much every way" (Rom. 3:2). It secured their membership in the commonwealth of Israel, which was a greater honour and privilege than the highest peerage on earth. So baptism secures the membership of infants in the visible Church of God, which is a still greater distinction and blessing.

(2) Infants are the objects of Christ's redemption. They are capable of receiving all its benefits. Those benefits are promised to them on the same conditions as to their parents. Of course, not every baptized

adult is saved, nor are all those who are baptized in infancy made partakers of salvation. But baptism signs, seals, and actually conveys its benefits to all its subjects, whether infants or adults, who keep the covenant of which it is the sign. As a believer who recalls some promise of the Scriptures which he has read or heard receives the full benefit of that promise, so the infant when arrived at maturity receives the full benefit of baptism if he believes in the promises signified and sealed to him in that ordinance. . . .

§13. **Lutheran Doctrine of Baptism**
§14. **Doctrine of the Church of Rome**

§15. The Lord's Supper

The passages of Scripture directly referring to the sacrament of the Lord's Supper are Matthew 26:26–28; Mark 14:22–24; Luke 22:19–20; 1 Cor. 10:15–17; and 11:23–29. These passages plainly teach (1) that the Lord's Supper is a divine institution of perpetual obligation. (2) The material elements to be used in the celebration are bread and wine. (3) The important constituent parts of the service are (a) the consecration of the elements, (b) the breaking of the bread and pouring out of the wine, and (c) the distribution and the reception of the bread and wine. (4) The design of the ordinance is (a) to commemorate the death of Christ; (b) to represent, to effect, and to avow our participation in the body and blood of Christ; (c) to represent, effect, and avow the union of believers with Christ and with each other; and (d) to signify and seal our acceptance of the new covenant as ratified by the blood of Christ. (5) The conditions for profitable communion are (a) knowledge to discern the Lord's body, (b) faith to feed upon Him, and (c) love to Christ and to His people. . . .

A. The Design of the Lord's Supper

As the death of the incarnate Son of God for us men and for our salvation is of all events the most important, it should be held in perpetual remembrance. It was to this end that our blessed Lord instituted this sacrament and accompanied the institution with the command, "This do in remembrance of me." And Paul in 1 Corinthians 11:26 tells his readers, "As often as ye eat this bread, and drink this cup, ye do show the Lord's death till he come." This itself is of great importance. The fact that the Lord's Supper has been celebrated without interruption in the Church from the day of the crucifixion to the present time is an irresistible proof of the actual occurrence of the event which it is intended to commemorate. . . . This sacrament, however, authenticates not only the fact of Christ's death, but also its design. Our Lord declared that He died as a substitute and sacrifice: "This is my body which is given for you" (Luke 22:19), or, as the apostle reports it, "broken for you" (1 Cor. 11:24); "This is my blood of the new testament, which is shed for many for the remission of sins" (Matt. 26:28). Redemption, therefore, is not by power, or by teaching, or by moral influence, but by expiation. It is this truth which the Lord's Supper exhibits and authenticates. Still further, Christ's affirmation that His body was to be broken and His blood shed for the remission of sin involves on His part the promise and pledge that the sins of those who receive and trust Him shall certainly be forgiven. The sacrament thus becomes not only a sign but also a seal. It is the handwriting and signet of the Son of God attached to the promise of redemption. Thus the natural effect of the truths symbolized and authenticated in the Lord's Supper is to confirm the faith of the believer. But just as the natural or objective power of the truth as revealed in the Word is insufficient for conversion or sanctification without the supernatural influences of the Spirit, so the truths set forth in the Eucharist avail nothing towards our salvation unless the Spirit of all grace gives them effect. On the other hand, as the Word when attended by the demonstration of the Spirit becomes the wisdom and power of God unto salvation, so does the sacrament of the Lord's Supper, when thus attended, become a real means of grace, not only signifying and sealing, but also conveying to believing recipients Christ and all the benefits of His redemption. . . .

B. Qualifications for the Lord's Supper

It is plain from the preceding account of the nature and design of this sacrament that it is intended for believers, and that those who come to the table of the Lord do thereby profess to be His disciples. If sincere in this profession, they receive the inestimable gifts which the sacrament is intended to convey. If insincere, they eat and drink judgment to themselves. . . . Now the faith required of those who would acceptably partake of the Lord's Supper is faith not only in Christ, but also in the sacrament itself, that is, faith in its divine appointment and in its being what in the New Testament it is declared to be. We must not look upon it as a mere human device, as a mere ritual observance or ceremony, but as a means ordained by God of signifying, sealing, and conveying to believers Christ and the benefits of His redemption. The reason why believers receive so little by their attendance on this ordinance is that they expect so little. They expect to

have their affections somewhat stirred and their faith somewhat
strengthened, but they only rarely expect so to receive Christ as to be
filled with all the fulness of God. Yet Christ in offering Himself to us
in this ordinance offers us all of God we are capable of receiving. For
in Christ we are complete, that is, filled with the fulness of God (Col.
2:10).

The faith which this sacrament demands cannot exist in the heart
without producing supreme love and gratitude to Christ as well as the
fixed purpose to forsake all sin and to live devoted to His service.
Therefore, it is required of them who would worthily partake of the
Lord's Supper that they examine themselves for knowledge to discern
the Lord's body, for faith to feed upon Him, for repentance, love, and
new obedience.... "[The Church invites] to this holy table, such as,
sensible of their lost and helpless state of sin, depend upon the atonement of Christ for pardon and acceptance with God; such as, being
instructed in the Gospel doctrine, have a competent knowledge to discern the Lord's body; and such as desire to renounce their sins, and
are determined to lead a holy and godly life" (*Westminster Directory*
8.4)....

§16. Doctrine of the Reformed Church on the Lord's Supper

A. The Sense in Which Christ Is Present
in the Lord's Supper

... The Reformed Church affirms that Christ's presence in the Lord's
Supper is not His body and blood absolutely, but His body as broken
and His blood as shed. It is the sacrifice He offered which is present
and of which the believer partakes. It is present to the mind, not to
our bodies. It is perceived and received by faith and not otherwise. He
is not present to unbelievers. By presence is meant not local nearness,
but intellectual cognition and apprehension, believing appropriation,
and spiritual operation. The body and blood are present to us when
they fill our thoughts, are apprehended by faith as broken and shed
for our salvation, and exert upon us their proper effect. "The body of
Christ is in heaven at the right hand of God," says the *Helvetic Confession* (21.10). "Yet the Lord is not absent from his Church when cele-
brating his supper. The sun is absent from us in heaven; nevertheless,
it is efficaciously present with us. How much more is Christ, the sun
of righteousness, though absent as to the body, present with us, not
corporally in deed, but spiritually by his vivifying influence!" Calvin
says: "Every imagination of local presence is to be entirely removed.

For while the signs upon earth are seen by the eyes and handled by the hands, Christ, so far as He is a man, is nowhere else than in heaven; and is to be sought only by the mind and by faith. It is, therefore, an irrational and impious superstition to include Him in the earthly elements" (*Consensus Tigurinus* 21). He likewise teaches that Christ is present in the promise added to the bread and wine, and not in the signs themselves. . . .

The presence of Christ's body in the Lord's Supper is, then, not local, but spiritual; not to the senses, but to the mind and to faith; and not of nearness, but of efficacy. His presence being in the promise, the body of Christ is present, offered to, and received by the believer whenever and wherever he embraces and appropriates the promise. So far the doctrine of the Reformed Church is clear. . . .

B. The Efficacy of the Lord's Supper as a Sacrament

The subject of the efficacy of the Lord's Supper includes two points: (1) the effect produced, and (2) the agency or influence to which the effect is due. In the Lord's Supper we are said to receive Christ and the benefits of His redemption to our spiritual nourishment and growth in grace. As our natural food imparts life and strength to our bodies, so this sacrament is one of the divinely appointed means to strengthen the principle of life in the soul of the believer and to confirm his faith in the promises of the gospel. By partaking of the bread and wine, the symbols of Christ's body and blood given for us, we are united to Him as our head. . . . [As the principle of] our life, He then works in us to will and to do according to His own good pleasure. . . . He works in us according to the laws of our nature in the production of everything that is good, so that it is from Him that all holy desires, all good counsels, and all just works proceed. It is not, therefore, we that live, but Christ that liveth in us.

What our Lord said to the apostles He says in the most impressive manner in this ordinance to every believing communicant: "This is my body broken for you. . . . This is my blood shed for you." These words when received by faith fill the heart with joy, confidence, gratitude, love, and devotion, so that the believer rises from the Lord's table refreshed by the infusion of a new life.

The efficacy of this sacrament, according to the Reformed doctrine, is not to be referred to any virtue in the ordinance itself, whether in its elements or actions; much less to any virtue in the administrator; nor to the mere power of the truths which it signifies; nor to the inherent divine power in the word or promise by which it is attended; nor to the real presence of the material body and blood of Christ (i.e., of the body born of the Virgin), whether by the way of transubstantiation, consubstantiation, or impanation; but only to the blessing of Christ and the working of His Spirit in them that receive the sacrament of His body and blood. . . .

To summarize the Reformed position: The Lord's Supper is a holy ordinance instituted by Christ as a memorial of His death wherein, under the symbols of bread and wine, His body as broken and His blood as shed for the remission of sins are signified and, by the power of the Holy Ghost, sealed and applied to believers. Thereby their union with Christ and their mutual fellowship are set forth and confirmed, their faith strengthened, and their souls nourished unto eternal life.

In this sacrament Christ is present not bodily, but spiritually—not in the sense of local nearness, but of efficacious operation. His people receive Him not with the mouth, but by faith; they do not receive His flesh and blood as material particles, but His body as broken and His blood as shed. The union thus signified and effected is not a corporeal union, not a mixture of substances, but a spiritual and mystical union due to the indwelling of the Holy Spirit. The efficacy of this sacrament as a means of grace is not in the signs, nor in the service, nor in the minister, nor in the word, but in the attending influence of the Holy Ghost. . . .

§17. Modern Views Concerning the Lord's Supper
§18. The Lutheran Doctrine Concerning the Lord's Supper
§19. Doctrine of the Church of Rome on the Lord's Supper

§20. Prayer

Prayer is the soul's conversation with God. Therein we manifest or express to Him our reverence and love for His divine perfection, our gratitude for all His mercies, our penitence for our sins, our hope in His forgiving love, our submission to His authority, our confidence in His care, our desires for His favour and for the providential and spiritual blessings needed for ourselves and others. As religion, in the subjective sense of the word, is the state of mind induced by due apprehension of the character of God and of our relation to Him as our creator, preserver, and Redeemer, so prayer is the expression, uttered or unuttered, of all the feelings and desires which that state of mind produces or excites. A prayerless man, by contrast, is thoroughly irreligious and spiritually dead.

A. Presuppositions

The practice of prayer rests on a number of presuppositions. It assumes, in the first place, the personality of God. Only a person can say

I or be addressed as Thou; only a person can be the subject and object of intelligent action, can apprehend and answer, can love and be loved, or hold converse with other persons. If God be only a name for an unknown force or for the moral order of the universe, prayer is irrational and impossible. Secondly, prayer assumes that God is near us; that He is not only able, but also willing to hold intercourse with us, to hear and answer; that He knows our thoughts afar off; and that unuttered aspirations are intelligible to Him. Thirdly, prayer assumes that God has personal control of all nature, i.e., of all things outside Himself—that He governs all His creatures and all their actions. It assumes not only that He has created all things and endowed matter and mind with forces and powers, but that He is everywhere present controlling the operation of such forces and powers so that nothing happens without His direction or permission. Rain occurs because He wills it and controls the laws of nature to produce that effect. When the earth produces fruit in abundance, or when the hopes of the husbandman are disappointed, these effects are not to be referred to the blind operation of natural laws, but to God's intelligent and personal control. . . . He reigns and orders all the operations of nature so as to accomplish His own purposes. . . . Prayer also supposes that the government of God extends over the minds of men—over their thoughts, feelings, and volitions—that the heart is in His hands, and that He can turn it even as the rivers of water are turned. . . .

B. The Object of Prayer

As prayer involves the ascription of divine attributes to its object, it can be properly addressed to God alone. . . . The prayers recorded in the Old Testament are uniformly addressed to God, to the one divine Being, because the distinction of the persons in the Godhead was then but imperfectly revealed. In the New Testament, prayer is addressed either to the Triune God, or to the Father, to the Son, and to the Holy Spirit as distinct persons. . . . Examples of prayer addressed to Christ are very numerous in the New Testament. As prayer, in the Scriptural sense of the term, includes all converse with God whether in the form of praise, thanksgiving, confession, or petition, all the ascriptions of glory to Christ, as well as all direct supplications addressed to Him, come under this head. While He was yet on earth, the apostles asked of Him blessings which only God could bestow, as when they said, "Lord, increase our faith" (Luke 17:5). The dying thief, taught by the Spirit of God, said, "Lord, remember me when thou comest into thy kingdom" (Luke 23:42). In Revelation 1:5-6 it is said, "Unto him that loved us, and washed us from our sins in his own blood, and hath made us kings and priests unto God and his Father; to him be glory and dominion for ever and ever. Amen." As the Bible so clearly teaches that Christ is God manifest in the flesh, that all power in heaven and earth is committed to His hands, that He is exalted to give repentance and the remission of sins, that He gives the Holy Ghost, and that He dwells in us and is our life, it does thereby teach us that He is the proper object of prayer. Accordingly, as all Christians are worshippers of Christ, He has ever been the object of their adoration, thanksgiving, praises, confessions, and supplications.

C. Requisites of Acceptable Prayer

(1) *Sincerity.* The first and most obviously necessary requisite of acceptable prayer is sincerity. God is a Spirit. He searches the heart. He is not satisfied with words or with external homage. He cannot be deceived and will not be mocked. It is a great offence, therefore, to utter words before Him in which our hearts do not join. We sin against Him when we use the formulas of praise without a corresponding feeling of reverence, or those of thanksgiving without gratitude, or those of humility and confession without any due sense of our unworthiness, or those of petition without desire for the blessings we ask. Every one must acknowledge that this is an evil often attending the prayers of sincere Christians. And for the multitudes who without any corresponding feeling repeat the solemn forms of devotion in places of worship or profess to unite with those who utter them, the service is little more than mockery.

(2) *Reverence.* God is an infinitely exalted Being—infinite in His holiness as well as in knowledge and power. He is to be held in reverence by all who are round about Him. This holy fear is declared to be the first element of all true religion. . . . We offend God, therefore, when we address Him as we would a fellow creature or use forms of expression of undue familiarity. Nothing is more characteristic of the prayers recorded in the Bible than the spirit of reverence by which they are pervaded. The Psalms especially may be regarded as a prayer book. Every psalm is a prayer, whether of worship, of thanksgiving, of confession, or of supplication. In many cases all these elements are intermingled. They relate to all circumstances in the inward and outward life of those by whom they were indited. They recognize the control of God over all events and over the hearts of men. They assume that He is ever near and ever watchful, sustaining to His people the relation of a loving Father. But with all this, there is never any forgetfulness of His infinite majesty. . . .

(3) *Humility.* We must have both a due sense of our insignificance

as creatures and a proper apprehension of our ill-desert and uncleanness in the sight of God as sinners. This is the opposite of self-righteousness, of self-complacency, and self-confidence. It is the spirit manifested by Job when he said, "I abhor myself, and repent in dust and ashes" (Job 42:6); by Isaiah when he said, "Woe is me! for I am undone; because I am a man of unclean lips, and I dwell in the midst of a people of unclean lips" (Isa. 6:5); and by the publican, who was afraid to lift up so much as his eyes unto heaven, but smote upon his breast and said, "God be merciful to me a sinner" (Luke 18:13). Such language . . . reflects a proper apprehension of our character as sinners in the sight of a just and holy God.

(4) *Importunity.* Persistence in prayer is so important that on three different occasions our Lord impressed its necessity upon His disciples. This is one evident design of the history of the Syro-phoenician woman, who could not be prevented from crying, "Have mercy on me, O Lord, thou son of David" (Matt. 15:22). Thus also in the parable of the unjust judge, who said, "Because this widow troubleth me, I will avenge her, lest by her continual coming she weary me. And the Lord said, Hear what the unjust judge saith. And shall not God avenge his own elect, which cry day and night unto him, though he bear long with them? I tell you that he will avenge them speedily" (Luke 18:5–8). And in Luke 11:8 Christ says of the man who refused to give his friend bread, "Though he will not rise and give him, because he is his friend, yet because of his importunity he will rise and give him as many [loaves] as he needeth." God deals with us as a wise benefactor. He requires that we appreciate the value of the blessings for which we ask, and that we manifest a proper earnestness of desire. . . .

(5) *Submission.* Every man who duly appreciates his relation to God will, no matter what his request, be disposed to say, "Lord, not my will, but thine, be done." Even a child feels the propriety of subjecting his will in all his requests to his earthly father. How much more should we submit to the will of our Father in heaven! He alone knows what is best; granting our request might, in many cases, be our destruction. Our Lord in the garden of Gethsemane set us an example that should never be forgotten.

(6) *Faith.* We must believe (a) that God exists, (b) that He is able to hear and answer our prayers, (c) that He is disposed to answer them, and (d) that He certainly will answer them, if consistent with His own wise purposes and with our best good. For this faith we have the most express assurances in the Bible. Not only is it said, "Ask, and it shall be given you; seek, and ye shall find" (Matt. 7:7), but our Lord says explicitly, "Whatsoever ye shall ask in my name, that will I do" (John 14:13). And again, "If two of you shall agree on earth as touching any

thing that they shall ask, it shall be done for them of my Father which is in heaven" (Matt. 18:19). All the promises of God are conditional, however. The condition, if not expressed, is implied. It cannot be supposed that God in governing the world or dispensing His gifts has subjected Himself to the shortsighted wisdom of men by promising without condition to do whatever they ask. No rational man could wish this to be so. He would of his own accord supply the condition which, from the nature of the case and from the Scriptures themselves, must be understood. In 1 John 5:14 the condition elsewhere implied is expressed: "This is the confidence that we have in him, that, if we ask any thing according to his will, he heareth us." We have here the assurance that all prayers offered in faith for God's will to be done will be answered. Of course, the answer may be given, as in the case of Paul when he prayed to be delivered from the thorn in the flesh, in a way we do not expect. But the answer will be such as we, if duly enlightened, would ourselves desire. More than this we need not wish. Want of confidence in these precious promises of God, want of faith in His disposition and readiness to hear us, is one of the greatest and most common defects in the prayers of Christians. Every father desires the confidence of his children and is grieved by any evidence of distrust; God as our Father demands from us the feelings which children ought to have towards their earthly parents.

(7) *Reliance on the name of Christ.* The prayers of Christians must be offered in His name. Our Lord said to His disciples: "Hitherto have ye asked nothing in my name: ask, and ye shall receive" (John 16:24); "I have chosen you . . . that whatsoever ye shall ask of the Father in my name, he may give it you" (15:16); "Whatsoever ye shall ask in my name, that will I do" (14:13). . . . When one asks a favour in the name of another, the simple meaning is, for his sake. Regard for the person in whose name the favour is requested is relied on as the ground on which it is to be granted. Therefore, when we are told to pray in the name of Christ, we are required to urge that we be heard on the basis of who Christ is and what He has done. We are not to trust to our own merits, or our own character, nor even simply to God's mercy; we are to plead the merits and worth of Christ. It is only in Him, in virtue of His mediation and worth, that, according to the gospel, any blessing is conferred on the apostate children of men.

D. Different Kinds of Prayer

As prayer is converse with God, it includes those spiritual exercises, those goings forth of the soul towards God in thought and feeling, which reveal themselves in the forms of reverence, gratitude, sorrow for sin, an awareness of dependence, and obligation. In this sense, the man who lives and walks with God prays always. He fulfils to the letter the injunction, "Pray without ceasing." It is our duty and high privilege to have this constant converse with God. The heart should be like the altar of incense on which the fire never went out.

It is, however, a law of our nature that we clothe our thoughts and feelings in words. Therefore, prayer is in one form speech. Even when no audible utterance is given, words as the clothing or expression of inward states are present to the mind. There is power, however, in articulated words. When audibly expressed, the thought or feeling is more distinct and vivid even to ourselves. Prayer, in this sense, is usually distinguished as secret, social, and public. . . . The believer needs, in order to maintain his spiritual health and vigour, regular and stated seasons of prayer, as the body needs its daily meals. "When thou prayest," is the direction given by our Lord, "enter into thy closet, and when thou hast shut thy door, pray to thy Father which is in secret; and thy Father which seeth in secret shall reward thee openly" (Matt. 6:6). The Bible presents to us the example of our blessed Lord Himself as a rule of conduct on this subject. We read that Christ often retired for the purpose of prayer and not unfrequently spent whole nights in that exercise. If the spotless soul of Jesus needed these seasons of converse with God, none of His followers should venture to neglect this important means of grace. Let each day at least begin and end with God.

. . . As man's nature is social, he must have fellowship with his fellow men in all that concerns his inward and outward life. That no man lives or can live for himself is as true in the area of religion as in any other. Since the family is the most intimate bond of fellowship among men, it is of the utmost importance that it be hallowed by religion. Parents and children are purified and strengthened when the whole household is statedly assembled, morning and evening, for the worship of God. There is no substitute for this divinely appointed means of promoting family religion. . . . All persons subject to the watch or care of the Church should be required to maintain in their households this stated worship of God. The character of the Church and of the State depends on the character of the family. If religion dies out in the family, it cannot elsewhere be maintained. A man's responsibility to his children, as well as to God, binds him to make his house a Bethel; if not a Bethel, it will be a dwelling place of evil spirits. . . .

The public services of the sanctuary are designed for worship and instruction. The former includes prayer and singing; the latter, the reading of the Word of God and preaching. These elements should be preserved in due proportion. In some churches, instruction is made entirely subordinate to worship, twice as much time being devoted to the latter as is allotted to the former. This is contrary to the Scriptural rule. Knowledge in the Bible is represented as the essential element of religion. There can be no true worship of God without adequate knowledge of God; there can be no repentance, faith, or holy living unless the truths on which these exercises are dependent are understood and are present to the mind. Religion is a reasonable, that is, a rational service, with which ignorance is incompatible. Christian ministers, therefore, are always in the New Testament called teachers. Their Great Commission received from Christ was to "teach all nations." The apostles, therefore, went everywhere preaching. . . .

While teaching should be, as it clearly was during the apostolic age, the prominent object in the services of the Lord's Day, the importance of public prayer can hardly be overestimated. This, it is often said, is the weak point in the worship service. It is probably true that there are more good preachers than good prayers. The main reason for this is that the minister devotes a great part of the labour of the week to the preparation of his sermon and not a thought to his prayers. It is no wonder, therefore, that the one should be better than the other.

This situation can be remedied by keeping the requisites of edifying public prayer in view: (1) The officiating minister should have a truly devout spirit; the feelings and desires of which the prayers are the utterance should be in exercise in his own heart. (2) His mind and memory should be well stored with the thoughts and language of Scripture. Holy men of old spake as they were moved by the Holy Ghost. Their utterances, whether in adoration, thanksgiving, confession, or supplication, were controlled by the Spirit of God. Hence they express the mind of the Spirit; they are the most appropriate vehicles for the expression of those feelings and desires which the Spirit awakens in the minds of God's people. No prayers, therefore, are more edifying, other things being equal, than those which abound in appropriate use of Scriptural language. (3) The prayer should be well ordered so as to embrace all the proper parts and topics of prayer in due proportion. This will prevent its being rambling, diffuse, or repetitious. (4) It should also be suited to the occasion, whether that be the ordinary service on the Lord's Day, or the administration of the sacraments, or the special service on days of thanksgiving or of fasting and humiliation. (5) It is hardly necessary to say that the language employed should be simple, solemn, and correct. (6) The prayers should be short. Undue length in this service is generally due to useless repetitions.

E. *Prayer as a Means of Grace*

Means of grace, as before stated, are those institutions which God has ordained for the end of communicating the life-giving and sanctifying influences of the Spirit to the souls of men. Such are the Word and sacraments, and such is prayer. Not only does it lead to the end for which it was appointed—bestowal of the blessings of God—but it brings us near to God, who is the source of all good. Fellowship with Him, converse with Him, calls into exercise all gracious affections, reverence, love, gratitude, submission, faith, joy, and devotion. When the soul thus draws near to God, God draws near to it, manifests His glory, sheds abroad His love, and imparts that peace which passes all understanding. . . .

F. *The Power of Prayer*

The course of human events is not controlled by physical force alone. There are other powers at work in the government of the world. There are the power of ideas, the power of truth, the power of love and human sympathy, the power of conscience, and above all, the Supreme Power, which is an intelligent, volitional, personal power cooperating with and controlling the operations of all creatures without violating their nature. This Supreme Power is roused into action by prayer in a way analogous to that in which the energies of a man are called into action by the entreaties of his fellow men. This is the doctrine of the Bible; it is perfectly consistent with reason and is confirmed by the whole history of the world, and especially of the Church. Moses by his prayer saved the Israelites from destruction; at the prayer of Samuel the army of the Philistines was dispersed; "Elias was a man subject to like passions as we are, and he prayed earnestly that it might not rain: and it rained not on the earth by the space of three years and six months. And he prayed again, and the heaven gave rain, and the earth brought forth her fruit" (James 5:17–18). These facts prove that the prayer of a righteous man availeth much. Paul constantly begged his Christian brethren to pray for him and directed that prayer "be made for all men; for kings, and for all that are in authority; that we may lead a quiet and peaceable life in all godliness and honesty" (1 Tim. 2:1–2). This of course supposes that prayer is a power. . . . Once we admit the existence of a personal God and His constant control over all things outside Himself, all ground for doubt as to the efficacy of prayer is removed; and it becomes for us, as it has been for the people of God in all ages, the great source of spiritual joy and strength, of security for the present, and confidence for the future. The Forty-sixth Psalm still stands: "The LORD of hosts is with us; the God of Jacob is our refuge" (v. 7).

Eschatology

Chapter I

State of the Soul After Death

§1. Protestant Doctrine

. . . As all Christians believe in the resurrection of the body and a future judgment, they all believe in an intermediate state. That is, they believe that there is a state of existence which intervenes between death and the resurrection, and that the condition of the departed during that interval is, in some respects, different from that which it is to be subsequent to the resurrection. It is not, therefore, as to the fact of an intermediate state, but as to its nature, that diversity of opinion exists among Christians. . . .

The Protestant doctrine on the state of the soul after death includes the continued conscious existence of the soul after the dissolution of the body. This is opposed not only to the doctrine that the soul is merely a function of the body and perishes with it, but also to the doctrine that the soul sleeps during the interval between death and the resurrection. . . . Rather, "the souls of believers are at their death made perfect in holiness, and do immediately pass into glory; and

509

their bodies, being still united to Christ, do rest in their graves till the resurrection." According to this view, the intermediate state, so far as believers are concerned, is one of great exaltation and blessedness as well as of perfect freedom from sin and suffering. . . . Various arguments can be adduced in support of this position:

(1) . . . The Bible teaches the fact of the continued personal, individual existence of the soul after the death and dissolution of the body. . . . It assumes that soul and body in man are two distinct substances joined in a vital union so as to constitute the man, in the present state of existence, one individual person. It assumes that the seat of this personality is the soul. The soul is the self, the Ego, of which the body is the organ. It assumes that after being separated from the body the soul continues its conscious existence and its power of acting and of being acted upon. The dead, according to the Scriptures, do not cease to be; they do not cease to be conscious and active. . . .

(2) According to the Scriptures and the faith of the Church, the probation of man ends at death. As the tree falls, so it lies. He that is unjust remains unjust, and he that is righteous remains righteous. When the bridegroom comes, they that are ready enter in and the door is shut. According to the parable of the rich man and Lazarus, there is no passing after death from one state to another; there is a great gulf between the righteous and the wicked from that time forth. It is appointed unto all men once to die, and after that the judgment (Heb. 9:27). The destiny of the soul is decided at death.

(3) There is no satisfaction to be rendered in the future life for the sins done in the body. The Roman Catholic doctrine of satisfactions renders necessary the assumption of a purgatorial state after death for those who have not in this life made full expiation for their sins. But if the one offering of Christ forever perfects them that believe, and if His sacrifice is a perfect satisfaction for our sins, there is no reason why believers should be kept out of blessedness until they have expiated their sins by their own sufferings.

(4) There is nothing contrary to Scripture in the assumption of a sudden and immediate change from imperfect to perfect holiness. The Protestant doctrine is that the souls of believers are at death made perfect in holiness. But it is asked, What sanctifying power is there in death? Progress in moral excellence is gradual; as no one becomes thoroughly evil by one act or in a moment, so, it is said, it is unreasonable to suppose that a sudden change from imperfect to perfect moral excellence takes place at the moment of death. This objection supposes that the salvation of men is a natural process; if it be a supernatural work, however, the objection has no force. Curing a man

of leprosy by natural means was a slow process; but when Christ said to the leper, "I will; be thou clean," he was healed in a moment. The change which takes place in a believer at death can hardly be much greater than that instantaneously produced in Paul on his journey to Damascus. Paul in Galatians 1:16 attributes that change to the revelation of the Son of God to him. If the momentary vision of the divine glory of Christ produced such an effect upon the apostle, is it strange that the Scriptures teach that the souls of believers when separated from the world and the flesh, and redeemed from the power of the devil, and bathed in the full brightness of the glory of the blessed Redeemer, shall in a moment be purified from all sin?

Since there is nothing in the nature of the soul inconsistent with its separate existence, since the body is not a necessary condition of its consciousness or activity, since its probation terminates at death, since the perfection of Christ's work precludes all necessity of future satisfaction for sin, and since an immediate change from imperfect to perfect holiness is consistent with the analogy of faith, there is no *a priori* objection to the doctrine that the souls of believers at death do immediately pass into glory.

(5) That such is the doctrine of Scripture may be argued from the general drift of the sacred volume. The Bible constantly speaks of the present life as a state of conflict, of labour, and of suffering; and of death as the entrance into rest. There remains a rest for the people of God. That rest follows the state of labour and trial. Believers then cease from their works. The rest on which they enter is not merely a rest from conflict and sin, but a rest which arises from the attainment of the end of their being, from restoration to a proper relation to God, and from the full realization of their capacities.

(6) Besides these general considerations the doctrine in question is taught in many passages of Scripture with more or less distinctness. In Revelation 14:13 the apostle says, "I heard a voice from heaven saying unto me, Write, Blessed are the dead which die in the Lord from henceforth: Yea, saith the Spirit, that they may rest from their labours; and their works do follow them." The simple meaning of this passage is that those who die in the Lord are, from that moment onward, in a state of blessedness because they cease from their labours and enter into the reward of the righteous. Death is for them emancipation from evil and introduction into a state of happiness.

Our Lord constantly teaches that those who believe in Him are not condemned (i.e., they are no longer under the sentence of the law) but, to the contrary, experience eternal life. The effect of the union between Himself and them, which is consummated by faith, is that they partake of His life in a sense analogous to that in which the branch partakes of the life of the vine. As He lives eternally, those who partake of His life can never perish. And as He lives unto God, so the life of His people is a holy and divine life. That life, from its nature, is an unfailing source of blessedness. It purifies, exalts, and glorifies. It is impossible that the souls in which Christ thus lives should remain either in a state of misery and degradation or in that dreamy state of existence which so many of the fathers imagined to be the abode of the departed spirits of believers awaiting the second coming of Christ.

Furthermore, it would seem to be a corollary of the redemption of Christ, and of the union between Him and His people, that when absent from the body they are present with the Lord (2 Cor. 5:8). Now it is inconceivable that with the Spirit of God dwelling in them, the Spirit of holiness and of glory, they would sink at death into a lower state of existence than that which they enjoyed in this world. Accordingly, we read in the parable of the rich man and Lazarus that "the beggar died, and was carried by the angels into Abraham's bosom" (Luke 16:22). It is undeniable that in his case the transition from earth to heaven was immediate. Still more explicit is the declaration of our Lord to the penitent thief, "Today shalt thou be with me in paradise" (Luke 23:43). . . . There can be no doubt that "paradise" here is heaven (cf. 2 Cor. 12:2–4; Rev. 2:7); consequently, when Christ promised the dying thief that he would that day be in paradise, He promised that he would be in heaven. . . .

In Philippians 1:23–24 Paul says, "I am in a strait betwixt two, having a desire to depart, and to be with Christ; which is far better: nevertheless to abide in the flesh is more needful for you." Two things are here perfectly plain. First, Paul regards the state of the soul after death as more exalted than its condition while in the flesh. This he distinctly asserts. Secondly, this change for the better takes place immediately after death. He is confident that as soon as he departs he will be with Christ (see also 2 Cor. 5:1, 8). . . .

The Scriptures represent Abraham, Isaac, and Jacob as being in heaven. Moses and Elijah appeared in glory on the mount of transfiguration and conversed with Christ. In Hebrews 12:22–24 it is said, "Ye are come unto mount Sion, and unto the city of the living God, the heavenly Jerusalem, and to an innumerable company of angels, to the general assembly and church of the firstborn, which are written in heaven, and to God the Judge of all, and to the spirits of just men made perfect, and to Jesus the mediator of the new covenant, and to the blood of sprinkling, that speaketh better things than that of Abel." Nothing can be more utterly inconsistent with the nature of the gospel than the idea that the fire of divine life as it glows in the hearts of

God's elect is at death to be quenched in the damp darkness of an underground prison until the time of the resurrection.

§2. **The Sleep of the Soul**
§3. **Patristic Doctrine of the Intermediate State**
§4. **Doctrine of the Church of Rome**

Chapter II

The Resurrection

§1. The Scriptural Doctrine
    A. The Bodies of Men Are to Rise Again
    B. Nature of the Resurrection Body
[§2. History of the Doctrine]

§1. The Scriptural Doctrine

A. *The Bodies of Men Are to Rise Again*

... There are several indications that when the Scriptures speak of resurrection, they mean a literal resurrection of the body:

(1) The word resurrection signifies a rising again, a rising of that which was buried, or a restoration of life to that which was dead. The soul cannot be in view, for the soul, according to the Scriptures, does not die when the body is dissolved. It, therefore, cannot be the subject of a resurrection, except in the sense antithetical to spiritual death, which is not now in question. ...

(2) Those who are in the dust of the earth, that is, in the grave, are said to rise. But only the body can be said to be in the grave; therefore, the resurrection in view must be of the body.

(3) It is "our mortal bodies" which are to rise again. This form of expression is decisive of the Scriptural meaning: "he that raised up

Christ from the dead shall also quicken your mortal bodies by his Spirit that dwelleth in you" (Rom. 8:11); it is "our vile body" which is to be fashioned like unto Christ's glorious body (Phil. 3:21).

(4) This also is clearly the doctrine taught in the fifteenth chapter of First Corinthians. There were certain people in Corinth who denied the fact of the resurrection, arguing as well that our bodies would be unsuited to any future state of existence. Paul's argument is directed to both those points. To prove that the dead can rise, he refers to what no Christian can deny, the rising of Christ from the dead. This fact he supports by historical evidence. He then shows that denial of the resurrection of Christ is denial of the whole gospel: "If Christ be not risen, then is our preaching vain, and your faith is also vain" (v. 14). But if Christ did rise from the dead, all His people will also. Christ rose as the firstfruits of them that sleep (v. 20). There is in Paul's view the same divinely appointed and therefore necessary connection between the resurrection of Christ and that of His people as there is between the death of Adam and that of his descendants. As surely as all in Adam die, so surely shall all in Christ be made alive (v. 22). And finally, on this point, the apostle argues from the faith and practice of the Church. What is the use, he asks, of being baptized for the dead if the dead rise not (v. 29)? The whole daily life of the Christian is founded on the hope of the resurrection; this is not merely the continued existence of the soul, but a glorious existence of the whole man, soul and body, with Christ in heaven.

As to the second point, the argument that our body would be unsuited to any future state of existence is founded on the assumption that the future body is to be like the present body. Paul says that the man who makes that objection is a fool. The two are no more alike than a seed and a flower, a clod of earth and a star, the earthly and the heavenly: "It [the body] is sown in corruption; it is raised in incorruption: it is sown in dishonour; it is raised in glory: it is sown in weakness; it is raised in power: it is sown a natural body; it is raised a spiritual body" (vv. 42–44). This whole discourse, then, is about the body. To the objection that our present bodies are not suited to our future state of existence, he answers that while flesh and blood cannot inherit the kingdom of God, the corruptible will put on incorruption, and the mortal will put on immortality. . . .

(5) Another argument on this subject is drawn from the frequently presented analogy between the resurrection of Christ and that of His people. The sacred writers argue the possibility and the certainty of the resurrection of our bodies from the fact of Christ's resurrection, and the nature of our future bodies from the nature of His body in

heaven. There would be no force in this argument if it were not the body which is to rise again.

(6) Finally, the whole Christian world, in all ages, has understood the Bible to teach the literal rising from the dead of the body deposited in the grave. . . .

B. Nature of the Resurrection Body

It is obvious that we can know nothing about the nature of the resurrection body except from divine revelation. . . . Two negative statements in the Bible imply a great deal. One is the declaration of Christ that in the resurrection we will neither marry nor be given in marriage, but will be as the angels of God (Matt. 22:30). The other is the words of Paul in 1 Corinthians 15:50: "Flesh and blood cannot inherit the kingdom of God." Three things are plainly implied in these passages: (1) the bodies of men must be specially suited to the state of existence in which they are to live and act; (2) our present bodies, that is, our bodies as now organized, consisting as they do of flesh and blood, are not suited to our future state of being; and (3) everything in the organization or constitution of our bodies which is designed to meet our present necessities will cease with the life that now is. Nothing of that kind will belong to the resurrection body. With blood no longer our life, we shall have no need of organs of respiration and nutrition. So long as we are ignorant of the conditions of existence which await us after the resurrection, it is vain to speculate on the constitution of our future bodies. It is enough to know that the glorified people of God will not be cumbered with useless organs or trammeled by the limitations which are imposed by our present state of existence.

A number of particulars, however, may be inferred with more or less confidence from what the Bible has revealed on the subject:

(1) Our bodies after the resurrection will retain the human form. God, we are told, gave to each of His creatures on earth its own body suitable to its nature and necessary to attain the end of its creation. Any essential change in the nature of the body would involve a corresponding change in internal constitution. A bee in the form of a horse would cease to be a bee, and a man in any form other than human would cease to be a man. His body is an essential element in his constitution. Every intimation given in Scripture on this subject tends to sustain this conclusion. Every time Christ appeared to His disciples not only before, but also after His ascension, as to Stephen, Paul, and John, He did so in human form. . . .

(2) It is probable that the future body will not only retain the human form, but will also be a glorified likeness of what it was on earth.

We know that every man has here his individual character—peculiarities mental and emotional which distinguish him from every other man. We know that his body by its expression, air, and carriage more or less clearly reveals his character. This revelation of the inward by the outward will probably be far more exact and informing in heaven than it can be here on earth. How should we know Peter or John in heaven if there were not something in their appearance and bearing corresponding to the image of themselves impressed by their writings on the minds of all their readers?

(3) This leads to the further remark that we shall not only recognize our friends in heaven, but also know, without introduction, the prophets, apostles, confessors, and martyrs of whom we have read or heard while here on earth. Consider as evidence (a) the very nature of the case. If the future body is to be the same as the present, why should not that sameness, whatever else it may include, entail a certain sameness of appearance? (b) When Moses and Elias appeared on the mount with Christ, they were at once known by the disciples. Their appearance corresponded so exactly with the conceptions formed from the Old Testament account of their character and conduct that no doubt was entertained on the subject. (c) It is said that we are to sit down with Abraham, Isaac, and Jacob in the kingdom of heaven (Matt. 8:11). This implies that Abraham, Isaac, and Jacob will be known; and if they are known, surely others will be known also. (d) It is promised that our cup of happiness will then be full, but it cannot be full unless we meet in heaven those whom we loved on earth. Man is a social being with a soul full of social affections. Inasmuch as he is to be a man in heaven, is it not likely that he will retain all his social affections there? God would hardly have put this pure yearning in the hearts of His people if it were never to be gratified. Weeping over his dead son, David said, "I shall go to him, but he shall not return to me" (2 Sam. 12:23). This has been the language of every bereaved heart from that day to this. (e) The Bible clearly teaches that in his future life man will retain all his faculties. One of the most important of those faculties is memory. If it were not retained, there would be a chasm in our existence. The past for us would cease to exist. We could hardly, if at all, be conscious of our identity. We would enter heaven as newly created beings who have no history. Then all the songs of heaven would cease. There would be no thanksgiving for redemption, no recognition of all God's dealings with us in this world. Memory, however, is not only to continue, but will doubtless with all our faculties be greatly exalted, so that the records of the past will be as legible to us as are the events of the present. Since men are to retain in heaven the

knowledge of their earthly life, they will recollect all social relations and all the ties of respect, love, and gratitude which bind them in the family and in society. (f) The doctrine that in a future life we shall recognize those whom we knew and loved on earth has entered into the faith of all mankind. It is taken for granted both in the Old Testament and in the New. The patriarchs at their death always spoke of going to their fathers. And by his exhortation not to mourn for the departed after the manner of those who have no hope (1 Thess. 4:13), Paul assures believers that they shall be reunited with all those who die in the Lord.

(4) We know certainly that the future bodies of believers will be unlike the bodies of the present age. (a) They will be incorruptible—not merely destined never to decay, but not susceptible of corruption. By the certain action of physical laws our present body, as soon as deserted by the soul, is reduced to a mass of corruption so revolting that we hasten to bury our dead out of our sight. The future body will be liable to no such change; neither, as we learn from Scripture, will it be subject to those diseases and accidents which so often mar the beauty or destroy the energy of the bodies in which we now dwell. Being unsusceptible of decay, they will be incapable of suffering, or at least carefully preserved from it by Him who has promised to wash all tears from our eyes.

(b) The future body is to be immortal. This is something different from, something higher than incorruptible. The latter is negative, the other positive. The one implies immunity from decay; the other implies not merely immunity from death, but perpetuity of life. There is to be no decrepitude of age, no decay of the faculties, no loss of vigour, but immortal youth.

(c) The present body is sown in weakness, it will be raised in power. We know very well how weak we now are, how little we can effect, how few are our senses, how limited their range; but we do not yet know in what ways or in what measure our power is to be increased. It is probable that however high may be our expectations on this subject, they will fall short of the reality; for it doth not yet appear, it is not revealed in experience or in hope, what we shall be (1 John 3:2). We may have new senses, new and greatly exalted capabilities of taking cognizance of external things, of apprehending their nature, and of deriving knowledge and enjoyment from their wonders and their beauties. Instead of the slow and wearisome means of locomotion to which we are now confined, we may be able hereafter to pass with the velocity of light or of thought itself from one part of the universe to another. Our vision, instead of being confined to the range of a few hundred yards, may far exceed that of the most powerful telescope. These expectations cannot be extravagant, for we are assured that eye has not seen, nor ear heard, neither has it entered into the heart of man to conceive the things which God has prepared for them that love Him (1 Cor. 2:9).

(d) The body is sown in dishonour, it shall be raised in glory. Glory excites wonder, admiration, and delight. The bodies of the saints are to be fashioned like unto Christ's glorious body (Phil. 3:21). We shall be like Him when we see Him as He is (1 John 3:2). More than this cannot be said; what it means we know not now, but we shall know hereafter. . . . Let it suffice to say that as we have borne the image of the earthly, we shall also bear the image of the heavenly. Accordingly, the apostle well exhorts us not to mourn for the pious dead, for we are to see them again, arrayed in a beauty and glory of which we can now have no conception.

(e) It is sown a natural body, it is raised a spiritual body. When words are used thus antithetically, the meaning of the one enables us to determine the meaning of the other. . . . We know from experience what the former is; it is an earthly body made of the dust of the earth. The chemist can analyze it and reduce it to its constituents (hydrogen, carbon, etc.), and in the grave it soon becomes undistinguishable from other portions of the earth's surface. It is a body which, while living, has constant need of being repaired; it must be sustained by the oxygen of the air and by the chemical elements of its food. It soon grows weary and must be refreshed by rest and sleep. In a little more than seventy years, it is worn out and drops into the grave. The reverse of this is true of the spiritual body; it has no such necessities and is not subject to such weariness and decay. Unlike our present bodies, which are suited to the lower faculties of our nature (e.g., our sensibilities and appetites), the spiritual body is suited to the higher faculties of the soul (e.g., reason and conscience). . . . Even now the soul in one sense pervades the body, . . . giving to it a look and carriage which reveal man as the lord of this world. To a far greater degree the soul will permeate the refined and glorified body which it is to receive at the resurrection of the just, and will thus render it spiritual in its very nature. If the face of man formed out of the dust of the earth often beams with intelligence and glows with elevated emotions, what may be expected of a countenance made like unto that of the Son of God!

Since our future bodies are to retain the human form and thus be easily distinguished by those who knew and loved us on earth, since they are to be endued with an unknown power, since they are to be incorruptible, immortal, and spiritual, and since we are to bear the image of the heavenly, we ought to bow down with humble and joyful hearts and heed the exhortation of the apostle: "Therefore, my beloved brethren, be ye stedfast, unmoveable, always abounding in the work of the Lord, forasmuch as ye know that your labour is not in vain in the Lord" (1 Cor. 15:58).

[§2. History of the Doctrine]

Second Advent

§1. Preliminary Remarks

The second advent is a very comprehensive and very difficult subject. It is intimately allied with all the other great doctrines which fall under the head of eschatology. It has excited so much interest in all ages of the Church that the books written upon it would of themselves make a library. The subject cannot be adequately discussed without taking a survey of all the prophetic teachings both of the Old Testament and of the New. This task cannot be satisfactorily accomplished by any one who has not made the study of the prophecies a specialty. The author, knowing that he has no such qualifications for the work, purposes to confine himself in a great measure to a general survey of the Scriptural prophecies relating to this subject.

Before discussing the second advent of Christ, it is important to consider the true design of prophecy. Prophecy is very different from history. It is not intended to give us a knowledge of the future analogous to that which history gives us of the past. This truth is often overlooked. We see interpreters undertaking to give detailed expositions of the prophecies of Isaiah, of Ezekiel, of Daniel, and of the Apocalypse with the same confidence with which they would record the history of the recent past. Such interpretations have always been falsified by the event. . . . In prophecy, unlike history, details are subordinate to moral impression. The occurrence of important events is so predicted as to produce in the minds of the people of God faith that those events will certainly come to pass. Enough is made known of their nature, and of the time and mode of their occurrence, to awaken attention, desire, or apprehension, as the case may be, and to secure proper preparation for what is to come to pass. Although such predictions may be variously misinterpreted before their fulfilment, once they are fulfilled, the agreement between the prophecy and the event is seen to be such as to render the divine origin of the prophecy a matter of certainty. . . .

Prophecy, then, gives a general impression with regard to future events, but the details remain in obscurity. The Jews were not disappointed in the general impression made on their minds by the predictions relating to the Messiah. It was only in the explanation of details that they failed. . . . So we should be satisfied with the great truths unfolded by the prophecies of the second coming and leave the details to be explained by the event. This the Church has generally done.

§2. The Common Church Doctrine

The Church holds that there is to be a second personal, visible, and glorious advent of the Son of God. This second coming will be preceded by (1) the universal diffusion of the gospel or, as our Lord expresses it, the ingathering of the elect—this is the vocation of the Christian Church; (2) the conversion of the Jews—as their casting away was national (although a remnant was saved), so their conversion will be national (although some may remain obdurate); and (3) the coming of Antichrist. When these prerequisites have been fulfilled, Christ will return. Attending His second advent will be (1) the resurrection of the dead, both the just and the unjust; (2) the general judgment; (3) the end of the world; and (4) the consummation of Christ's kingdom.

§3. The Personal Advent of Christ

... There are a number of indications that the New Testament teaches a second visible and personal appearing of the Son of God:

(1) There is a close analogy between the first and second advents.... They are predicted in very nearly the same terms. Since Christ's first coming was in person and visible, His second coming must be as well. The two advents are often spoken of together, the one illustrating the other. He came the first time as the Lamb of God bearing the sins of the world; He is to come "the second time without sin unto salvation" (Heb. 9:28). God, said the apostle Peter, "shall send Jesus Christ, which before was preached unto you: whom the heaven must receive until the times of restitution of all things, which God hath spoken by the mouth of all his holy prophets since the world began" (Acts 3:20–21). Having been received up into heaven, Christ is to remain invisible until God shall send Him at the restitution of all things.

(2) In many places it is directly asserted that Christ's appearing is to be personal and visible. At the time of His ascension, the angels said to His disciples: "Ye men of Galilee, why stand ye gazing up into heaven? this same Jesus, which is taken up from you into heaven, shall so come in like manner as ye have seen him go into heaven" (Acts 1:11). His second coming is to be as visible as His ascension. They saw Him go, and they shall see Him come. In Matthew 26:64 Jesus says to Caiaphas, "Hereafter shall ye see the Son of man sitting on the right hand of power, and coming in the clouds of heaven." He had earlier told His disciples, "Then shall all the tribes of the earth mourn, and they shall see the Son of man coming in the clouds of heaven with power and great glory" (Matt. 24:30).

(3) The circumstances attending the second advent prove that it is to be personal and visible. It is to be in the clouds, with power and great glory, with the holy angels and all the saints, and with a shout and the voice of the archangel.

(4) The effects ascribed to the second advent prove the same thing. All the tribes of the earth shall mourn, the dead are to arise, the wicked shall call on the rocks and hills to cover them, the saints are to be caught up to meet the Lord in the air, and the earth and the heavens are to flee away at His presence.

(5) That the apostles understood Christ to have predicted His second coming in person does not admit of doubt.... Certain it is that they believed that He would come visibly and with great glory, and that they held His coming as the great object of expectation and desire. Indeed Christians are described as "waiting for the coming of our Lord Jesus Christ" (1 Cor. 1:7), "looking for that blessed hope, and the glo-

rious appearing of the great God and our Saviour Jesus Christ" (Titus
2:13), and expecting and earnestly desiring the coming of the day of
God (2 Peter 3:12). It is a marked characteristic of the apostolic writings that they give great prominence to the doctrine of the second
advent (see 1 Cor. 4:5; 15:23; 2 Cor. 1:14; Phil. 1:6; 2:16; 3:20; Col. 3:4;
1 Thess. 1:10; 2:19; 3:13; 4:15–17; 2 Thess. 1:7; 1 Tim. 6:14; 2 Tim. 4:8;
1 Peter 1:5–7; 4:5, 13; 5:4; 2 Peter 1:16; 3:10).

From all these passages and from the whole drift of the New Testament it is plain (1) that the apostles fully believed that there is to be
a second coming of Christ; (2) that His coming is to be in person,
visible and glorious; (3) that they kept this great event constantly
before their own minds and urged it on the attention of the people as
a motive to patience, constancy, joy, and holy living; and (4) that the
apostles believed that the second advent of Christ would be attended
by the general resurrection, the final judgment, and the end of the
world. . . .

§4. The Calling of the Gentiles

The first great event which is to precede the second coming of Christ
is the universal proclamation of the gospel. . . . Christ repeatedly taught
that the gospel is to be preached to all nations before His second
coming. Thus in Matthew 24:14 He says, "This gospel of the kingdom
shall be preached in all the world for a witness unto all nations; and
then shall the end come"; and in Mark 13:10, "The gospel must first
be published among all nations."

Accordingly, our Lord after His resurrection, in giving His commission to the Church, said: "Go ye therefore, and teach all nations,
baptizing them in the name of the Father, and of the Son, and of the
Holy Ghost: teaching them to observe all things whatsoever I have
commanded you: and, lo, I am with you alway, even unto the end of
the world" (Matt. 28:19–20). In Mark 16:15 the commission reads: "Go
ye into all the world, and preach the gospel to every creature." This
commission prescribes the present duty of the Church, one that is not
to be deferred or languidly performed until a new and more effective
dispensation be inaugurated. The promise of Christ to be with His
Church, as then commissioned, to the end of the world implies that
its obligation to teach the nations is to continue until the final
consummation. . . .

This ingathering of the heathen is the special work of the Church.
It is a missionary work. It was so understood by the apostles. Their
two great duties were the propagation and defence of the truth. To

these they devoted themselves. While they travelled hither and thither preaching the gospel through all parts of the Roman world, they laboured no less assiduously in defence of the gospel. All the epistles of the New Testament, those of Paul, Peter, John, and James, are directed towards the correction of false doctrine. These two duties of propagating and of defending the truth the apostles passed on to their successors. . . .

It is evident that the conversion of the Gentile world is the work assigned the Church under the present dispensation, and that it is not to fold its hands and await the second coming of Christ to accomplish that work for it: (1) This is the work which Christ commanded His Church to undertake. (2) He furnished the Church with all the means necessary to accomplish the task: He revealed the truth which is the power of God unto salvation; He instituted the ministry to be perpetuated to the end of the world, and promised to endow men from age to age with the gifts and graces necessary for the discharge of its duties, and to grant them His constant presence and assistance. (3) The apostles and the Church of that age so understood the work assigned and addressed themselves to it with such devotion and success that, had they been continued, the work would long ago have been accomplished. (4) There is no intimation in the New Testament that the work of converting the world is to be effected by any other means than those now in use. (5) It is to dishonour the gospel and the power of the Holy Spirit to suppose that they are inadequate to the accomplishment of this work. (6) The wonderful success of the work of missions in our day goes to prove the fact contended for. Barriers deemed insurmountable have been removed; facilities of access and intercourse have been increased a hundredfold; hundreds of missionary stations have been established in every part of the world; many thousands of converts have been gathered into churches. . . . Nations lately heathen have become Christian and are taking part in sending the gospel to those still sitting in darkness, and nothing seems wanting to secure the gathering in of the Gentiles but a revival of the missionary spirit of the apostolic age.

§5. Conversion of the Jews

The second great event which, according to the common faith of the Church, is to precede the second advent of Christ is the national conversion of the Jews. . . . The most decisive passage bearing on this subject is the eleventh chapter of the Epistle to the Romans. Paul had earlier taught that God had cast off the Jews because they as a nation, represented by the Sanhedrin, the high priest, the scribes and the Pharisees, by their rulers, and by the popular voice, had rejected Christ (cf. John 1:11—"He came unto his own, and his own received him not"). Therefore God rejected them as a nation. This rejection, however, Paul here teaches, was not entire. There was "a remnant according to the election of grace" (Rom. 11:5) who believed in Christ and were received into His kingdom. And as this national rejection of Israel was not entire, neither was it to be final. It was to continue until the bringing in of the Gentiles. God had made a covenant with Abraham that his posterity would be His people, and "the gifts and calling of God are without repentance" (v. 29). Therefore, although broken off from the olive tree for the present, they were to be grafted in again. Thus "all Israel shall be saved" (v. 26). Whether this means the Jews as a nation or the whole elect people of God, including both Jews and Gentiles, is doubtful. But in either case it is, in view of the context, a promise of the restoration of the Jews. There is, therefore, to be a national conversion of the Jews.

That this conversion is to take place before the second advent of Christ is clear from Paul's assertion that the salvation of the Gentiles is designed to provoke the Jews to jealousy (v. 11), and that the mercy shown to the Gentiles is to be the means of the Jews' obtaining mercy (v. 31). The rejection of the Jews was the occasion of the conversion of the Gentiles, and the conversion of the Gentiles is to be the occasion of the restoration of the Jews. . . .

The Scriptures, then, as they have been generally understood in the Church, teach that before the second advent there are to be an ingathering of the heathen (i.e., the gospel will be preached to all nations) and a national conversion of the Jews; but it is not to be inferred from this that either all the heathen or all the Jews are to become true Christians. In many cases the conversion may be merely nominal. Enough will remain unchanged in heart to be the germ of that persecuting power which shall bring about those days of tribulation which the Bible seems to teach are to immediately precede the coming of the Lord.

§6. Antichrist

That Antichrist is to appear before the second coming of Christ is expressly asserted by Paul in 2 Thessalonians 2:1–3: "We beseech you . . . that ye be not soon shaken in mind, or be troubled . . . as that the day of Christ is at hand. . . . For that day shall not come, except there come a falling away first, and that man of sin be revealed, the son of perdition." This is clear; but as to who or what Antichrist is, there is no little diversity of opinion.

1. Some understand by the term Antichrist any anti-Christian spirit, power, or person. The apostle John says, "Little children, it is the last time: and as ye have heard that antichrist shall come, even now are there many antichrists; whereby we know that it is the last time. . . . Who is a liar but he that denieth that Jesus is the Christ? He is antichrist, that denieth the Father and the Son" (1 John 2:18, 22; see also 4:3). And in 2 John 7 it is said, "Many deceivers are entered into the world, who confess not that Jesus Christ is come in the flesh. This is a deceiver and an antichrist." Our Lord Himself had predicted, "There shall arise false Christs, and false prophets, and shall show great signs and wonders; insomuch that, if it were possible, they shall deceive the very elect" (Matt. 24:24; see also 1 Tim. 4:1). These passages refer to a marked characteristic of the period between the apostolic age and the second coming of Christ. There were to be many antichrists, many manifestations of malignant opposition to the person and to the work of Christ, many attempts to cast off His authority and to overthrow His kingdom.

2. Besides this general reference to the anti-Christian spirit which was to manifest itself in different forms and with different degrees of intensity, many believe that there is yet to be a person in whom the power of the world shall be concentrated, and who will exert all his energies to overthrow Christianity and to usurp the place of Christ on earth. This is the Antichrist of prophecy, the person of whom it is assumed that Daniel, Paul, and John in the Apocalypse speak.

3. There is also a common opinion among Protestants that the prophecies concerning Antichrist have special reference to the papacy. This conviction is founded principally on the remarkable prediction contained in 2 Thessalonians 2. . . .

Whoever or whatever Antichrist may be, it is the common faith of the Church that the appearance of Antichrist is one of the great events which are to precede the second advent of Christ, the others being the universal proclamation of the gospel (or the conversion of the Gentile world) and the national conversion of the Jews.

The Concomitants of the Second Advent

The events which according to the common doctrine of the Church are to attend the second coming of Christ are (1) the general resurrection of the dead, (2) the final judgment, (3) the end of the world, and (4) the consummation of the kingdom of Christ.

§1. The General Resurrection

That there is to be a general resurrection of the just and of the unjust is not, among Christians, a matter of doubt. Already in Daniel 12:2–3 it is said, "Many of them that sleep in the dust of the earth shall awake, some to everlasting life, and some to shame and everlasting contempt. And they that be wise shall shine as the brightness of the firmament; and they that turn many to righteousness as the stars for ever and ever." This prediction our Lord repeats without any limitation: "Marvel not at this: for the hour is coming, in the which all that are in the graves shall hear his voice, and shall come forth; they that have done good, unto the resurrection of life; and they that have done evil, unto the resurrection of damnation" (John 5:28–29; see also Matt. 25:31–32; Acts 24:15; Rev. 20:12–13).

The uniform representation of Scripture on this subject is that this general resurrection is to take place "at the last day," i.e., at the second coming of Christ. The same form of expression is used to designate the time when the people of Christ are to rise and the time when the general resurrection is to occur. The Bible, if the doubtful passage Revelation 20:4–6 be excepted, never speaks of more than one resurrection. The dead, according to the Scriptures, are to rise together, some to everlasting life and some to shame and everlasting contempt. When Christ comes, all who are in their graves shall come forth, some to the resurrection of life and others to the resurrection of damnation. . . .

There are three types of passages in which the New Testament teaches that a general resurrection is to occur at the time of the second advent:

(1) In John 5:28–29 our Lord reiterates, as we have seen, Daniel's prediction that some will awake to everlasting life and others to eternal judgment. In Matthew 25:31–32 He says that when the Son of man shall appear in His glory, all nations shall stand before Him, and He shall separate the sheep from the goats (see also Rev. 20:12–13). And in 2 Thessalonians 1:7–10 it is taught that when the Lord Jesus is revealed from heaven, He will take vengeance on those who obey not the gospel and be glorified in all them that believe. In all these passages the resurrection of the righteous is declared to be contemporaneous with that of the wicked.

(2) A second class of passages teaches that the resurrection of the righteous is to take place at "the last day" and, therefore, not a thousand years before that event. Speaking of her brother Lazarus, Martha said, "I know that he shall rise again in the resurrection at the last day" (John 11:24). Our Lord in John 6:39 says it is the Father's will "that of all which he hath given me I should lose nothing, but should raise it up again at the last day." This declaration is repeated in verses 40, 44, and 54. In these passages "*the* last day" refers to a known and definite period. It is also to be remembered that what is predicted to happen on "*the* last day" is elsewhere predicted to happen when Christ shall appear in His glory.

(3) A third class of passages teaches that the resurrection of the saints is to take place at the day of judgment and in connection with that event. According to the common representations of Scripture, when Christ shall come the second time, all the dead are to rise, all nations are to be judged, and the present order of things is to cease. . . . Among those passages which connect the final judgment with a general resurrection are Matthew 24:30–31; 25:31–46; and 2 Thessalonians 1:7–10. . . .

The only passage which seems to teach that there are to be a first and second resurrection of the body, the former being confined to martyrs and saints, and the latter including "the rest of the dead," is Revelation 20:4–6. It must be admitted that that passage, taken by itself, does seem to teach two resurrections. But there are considerations against such an understanding of the text:

(1) It is a sound rule in the interpretation of Scripture that obscure passages should be so explained as to make them agree with those that are plain. It is unreasonable to make the symbolic and figurative language of prophecy and poetry the rule by which to explain the simple didactic prose of the Bible. It is no less unreasonable to take a multitude of passages out of their natural sense in order to make them accord with a single passage of doubtful import.

(2) The Apocalypse is an obscure book. This almost every reader knows from his own experience and from the endless diversity of interpretations to which the book has been subjected.

(3) The Bible speaks of a spiritual resurrection as well as of a literal resurrection. This figure of speech is used in reference to both individuals and communities. The sinner dead in trespasses and sins is said to be quickened and raised again in Christ Jesus (Rom. 6; Eph. 2). Whole communities when elevated from a state of depression and misery are in prophetic language said to be raised from the dead (Rom. 11:15; Isa. 26:19). . . . The first resurrection in view in Revelation 20 may be spiritual and the second literal.

(4) John does not say that the bodies of the martyrs are raised from the dead. He says, "I saw the souls of them that were beheaded for the witness of Jesus." The resurrection of the dead is never thus described in Scripture. . . .

(5) The common millenarian doctrine is that Christ shall come to reign in person upon the earth a thousand years before the end of the world. At the time of His return there is to be a literal resurrection of the saints, and they shall dwell here and share with Christ in the glories of His reign. But this seems to be inconsistent with what Paul teaches in 1 Corinthians 15:50: "Now this I say, brethren, that flesh and blood cannot inherit the kingdom of God; neither doth corruption inherit

incorruption." It is here expressly asserted that our bodies as now constituted are not suited to the state of things which shall exist when the kingdom of God is inaugurated. We must all be changed. From this it follows that the spiritual body is not suited to our present mode of existence; that is, it is not designed for an earthly kingdom. The renovated or transfigured body of necessity supposes a renovated earth. When the bodies of believers are changed, they are to be caught up from the earth and are to dwell with Christ in heaven. . . .

All this is said with diffidence and submission. Experience teaches that the interpretation of unfulfilled prophecy is exceedingly precarious. There is every reason to believe that the fulfilment of the predictions concerning the second advent of Christ, as well as the events which are to attend and follow it, will disappoint the expectations of commentators, as the expectations of the Jews were disappointed in the manner in which the prophecies concerning the first advent were accomplished.

§2. The Final Judgment

The Scriptures abound in passages which set forth God as the moral ruler of men and declare that He will judge the world in righteousness. The Bible represents Him as the Judge of nations and of individuals, as the avenger of the poor and the persecuted. It abounds also in promises and in threatenings and in illustrations of the righteous judgments of God. Nothing, therefore, is plainer than that men in this world are subject to the moral government of God. Besides this, the Bible also teaches that there is a future state of reward and punishment in which the inequalities and anomalies here permitted shall be adjusted. . . . The doctrine held by the Church universal on this subject includes the following points:

(1) The final judgment is a definite future event (not a protracted process) when the eternal destiny of men and of angels shall be finally determined and publicly manifested. That this is the doctrine of the Bible is proved by passages such as Matthew 11:24, "It shall be more tolerable for the land of Sodom in the day of judgment, than for thee"; Matthew 13:30, "Let both grow together until the harvest: and in the time of harvest I will say to the reapers, Gather ye together first the tares, and bind them in bundles to burn them: but gather the wheat into my barn"; and verse 49, "So shall it be at the end of the world: the angels shall come forth, and sever the wicked from among the just" (see also John 12:48; Acts 17:31; Rom. 2:5; and 1 Cor. 4:5). Since the word day is often used in Scripture for an indefinite period, it does

not follow from the use of this word that the judgment is to be commenced and ended in the space of twenty-four hours. Nevertheless, the way in which the word is used in this connection and the circumstances attending the judgment show that a definite and limited period, and not a protracted dispensation, is intended by the term. The appearance of Christ, the resurrection of the dead, and the gathering of the nations are not events which are to be protracted through years or centuries.

(2) Christ is to be the Judge: "The Father judgeth no man, but hath committed all judgment unto the Son: that all men should honour the Son, even as they honour the Father" (John 5:22–23); "[the Father] hath given him authority to execute judgment also, because he is the Son of man" (v. 27). . . . Paul in his speech on Mars' Hill tells the Athenians that God "hath appointed a day, in the which he will judge the world in righteousness by that man whom he hath ordained; whereof he hath given assurance unto all men, in that he hath raised him from the dead" (Acts 17:31). And in 2 Corinthians 5:10 he says, "We must all appear before the judgment seat of Christ." Our Lord represents Himself as saying to the wicked, "Depart from me, ye that work iniquity" (Matt. 7:23; Luke 13:27). Indeed, wherever the New Testament graphically describes the process of the final judgment, Christ is presented as the Judge. . . . It is especially appropriate that the man Christ Jesus, God manifest in the flesh, should be the Judge of all men. He has this authority committed to Him because He is the Son of man; that is, because He humbled Himself to be found in fashion as a man even though He was in the form of God and thought it no robbery to be equal with God. The prerogative of judging is part of the exaltation due to Him because He consented to become obedient unto death. It is meet that He who stood condemned at the bar of Pilate should sit enthroned on the seat of universal judgment. It is a joy and ground of special confidence to all believers that He who loved them and gave Himself for them shall be their Judge on the last day.

(3) This judgment is to take place at the second coming of Christ and at the general resurrection. Therefore it is not a process now in progress; it does not take place at death; it is not a protracted period prior to the general resurrection. Among the passages bearing on this point is the parable of the wheat and the tares (Matt. 13:36–43), in which we are taught that the final separation between the righteous and the wicked is to take place at the end of the world, when the Son of man shall send forth His angels to gather out of His kingdom all things that offend. This implies that the general resurrection, the second advent, and the last judgment are contemporaneous events. The Bible knows nothing of three personal advents of Christ: one at the

time of the incarnation, a second before the millennium, and a third to judge the world. He who came in the flesh is to come "the second time without sin unto salvation" (Heb. 9:28). "The Son of man shall come in the glory of his Father with his angels; and then he shall reward every man according to his works" (Matt. 16:27). Matthew 24:29–35 teaches that when the sign of the Son of man appears in the heavens, all the tribes of the earth shall mourn, and the elect shall be gathered in. Matthew 25:31–46 sets forth the whole process of the judgment. When the Son of man shall come in His glory, all nations shall be gathered before Him, and He shall separate them as a shepherd divides sheep from goats. Then shall He say to those on His right hand, "Come, ye blessed of my Father," and to those on the left, "Depart from me, ye cursed" (see also 1 Cor. 4:5; 2 Thess. 1:7–10; and 2 Tim. 4:1).

(4) The persons to be judged are men and angels. It is said that Christ is to come to judge "the quick and the dead" (2 Tim. 4:1), that all nations are to stand before Him (Matt. 25:32), that "we must all appear before the judgment seat of Christ" (2 Cor. 5:10), and that He "will render to every man according to his deeds" (Rom. 2:6). This judgment, then, is absolutely universal; it includes both small and great, and all the generations of men. With regard to the evil angels, it is said that God "delivered them into chains of darkness, to be reserved unto judgment" (2 Peter 2:4). . . .

(5) The ground or matter of judgment is said to be the deeds done in the body. Men are to be judged according to their works; the secrets of the heart are to be brought to light. God's judgment will not be founded on the professions or the relations of men, nor on the appearance or reputation which they sustain among their fellows, but on their real character and on their acts, however secret and covered from the sight of men those acts may have been. God will not be mocked and cannot be deceived; the character of every man will be clearly revealed not only in the sight of God, but also in the sight of the man himself. All self-deception will be banished. Every man will see himself as he appears in the sight of God. His memory will probably prove an indelible register of all his sinful acts and thoughts and feelings. His conscience will be so enlightened as to recognize the justice of the sentence which the righteous Judge shall pronounce upon him. All whom Christ condemns will be self-condemned. Moreover, there will be such a revelation of the character of every man to all around him, or to all who know him, as shall render the justice of the sentence of condemnation or acquittal apparent. Beyond this the representations of Scripture do not require us to go.

Besides these general representations of Scripture that the character and conduct of men are the ground on which the final sentence is to be pronounced, there is clear intimation in the Word of God that the destiny of those who hear the gospel depends on the attitude which they assume to Christ. "He came unto his own, and his own received him not. But as many as received him, to them gave he power to become the sons of God" (John 1:11–12). God manifest in the flesh came into the world to save sinners; all who receive Him as their God and Saviour are saved, while all who refuse to recognize and trust Him perish. They are condemned already, because they have not believed in the name of the only begotten Son of God (John 3:18). "He that believeth on the Son hath everlasting life: and he that believeth not the Son shall not see life; but the wrath of God abideth on him" (John 3:36). "Whosoever therefore shall confess me before men, him will I confess also before my Father which is in heaven. But whosoever shall deny me before men, him will I also deny before my Father which is in heaven" (Matt. 10:32–33). When the Jews asked our Lord, "What shall we do, that we might work the works of God?" His answer was, "This is the work of God, that ye believe on him whom he hath sent" (John 6:28–29). In the solemn account given of the last judgment in Matthew 25:31–46, the inquest concerns the conduct of men towards Christ. And Paul says, "If any man love not the Lord Jesus Christ, let him be Anathema Maranatha" (1 Cor. 16:22). The special ground of condemnation, then, under the gospel is unbelief, that is, refusal to receive Christ in the character in which He is presented for our acceptance.

(6) Men are to be judged according to the light which they have severally enjoyed. The servant that knew his Lord's will and did it not shall be beaten with many stripes, but he that knew it not shall be beaten with few stripes. "For unto whomsoever much is given, of him shall be much required" (Luke 12:47–48). Our Lord says that in the day of judgment it shall be more tolerable for Tyre and Sidon than for the men of His generation (Luke 10:14). Paul says that the heathen are inexcusable "because that, when they knew God, they glorified him not as God" (Rom. 1:20–21); and he lays down the principle that they who sin without law shall be judged without law, and they who have sinned in the law shall be judged by the law (Rom. 2:12).

(7) At the judgment of the last day the destiny of the righteous and of the wicked shall be unalterably determined. Each class shall be assigned to its final abode. This is taught in the solemn words: "These shall go away into everlasting punishment: but the righteous into life eternal" (Matt. 25:46).

How far the Biblical descriptions of the process of the last judgment are to be understood literally, it is useless to inquire. Two things about the prophecies of Scripture which have already been accomplished ought to be noted, however. The one is that the fulfilment has in many cases been very different from that which a literal interpretation led men to anticipate. The other is that in some cases they have been fulfilled even to the most minute details. These facts should render us both modest in our interpretation of those predictions which remain to be accomplished and satisfied that what we know not now we shall know hereafter.

§3. The End of the World

Several passages of Scriptures speak explicitly of the final consummation or the end of the world: "Of old hast thou laid the foundation of the earth: and the heavens are the work of thy hands. They shall perish, but thou shalt endure: yea, all of them shall wax old like a garment; as a vesture shalt thou change them, and they shall be changed" (Ps. 102:25-26); "Lift up your eyes to the heavens, and look upon the earth beneath: for the heavens shall vanish away like smoke, and the earth shall wax old like a garment" (Isa. 51:6); "Behold, I create new heavens and a new earth: and the former shall not be remembered, nor come into mind" (Isa. 65:17); "The world that then was, being overflowed with water, perished: but the heavens and the earth, which are now, by the same word are kept in store, reserved unto fire against the day of judgment and perdition of ungodly men. . . . The day of the Lord will come as a thief in the night; in the which the heavens shall pass away with a great noise, and the elements shall melt with fervent heat, the earth also and the works that are therein shall be burned up. . . . Nevertheless we, according to his promise, look for new heavens and a new earth, wherein dwelleth righteousness" (2 Peter 3:6-7, 10, 13; see also Luke 21:33; Rom. 8:19-21; Rev. 20:11; 21:1). . . .

It is clear that the destruction here foretold is not annihilation: (1) The world is to be burnt up, but combustion is merely a change of state or condition rather than a destruction of substance. (2) The destruction of the world by water and its destruction by fire are analogous events. The former was not annihilation; therefore the second is not. (3) The destruction spoken of is elsewhere called a regeneration (Matt. 19:28), a restitution (Acts 3:21), a deliverance from the bondage of corruption (Rom. 8:21). The apostle teaches that our vile bodies are not to be annihilated, but changed and fashioned like unto the glorious body of Christ (Phil. 3:21). A similar change is to take place in the world we inhabit. There are to be new heavens and a new earth, just as we are to have new bodies. . . .

This renovated earth, according to the common opinion, is to be the final seat of Christ's kingdom. This is the new heavens; this is the new Jerusalem, the Mount Zion in which are to be gathered the general assembly and Church of the first-born whose names are written in heaven, the spirits of just men made perfect. This is the heavenly Jerusalem, the city of the living God, the kingdom prepared for His people before the foundation of the world. . . .

§4. The Kingdom of Heaven

In the account given of the final judgment in Matthew 25:31–46, we are told that the King shall "say unto them on his right hand, Come, ye blessed of my Father, inherit the kingdom prepared for you from the foundation of the world." It had already been predicted in the Old Testament that God would set up a kingdom which was to be universal and everlasting. Of this kingdom the Messiah was to be the head. He is frequently in the Old Testament set forth as King (see Gen. 49:10; Num. 24:17; 2 Sam. 7:16; Pss. 2; 45; 72; 110; Isa. 9:6–7; 11; 52; 53; and Mic. 4). His kingdom is variously called the kingdom of God, the kingdom of Christ, the kingdom of the Son of man (Matt. 13:41), and the kingdom of heaven. The prophets describe it in glowing terms borrowed partly from the paradisiacal state of man and partly from the state of the theocracy during the reign of Solomon.

This kingdom belongs to Christ not as the Logos, but as the Son of man, the Theanthropos, God manifest in the flesh. Its twofold foundation, as presented in the Bible, is His possession of all the divine attributes and His work of redemption (Heb. 1:3; Phil. 2:6–11). It is because He being equal with God "humbled himself, and became obedient unto death, even the death of the cross, [that] God also hath highly exalted him, and given him a name which is above every name: that at the name of Jesus every knee should bow, of things in heaven, and things in earth, and things under the earth; and that every tongue should confess that Jesus Christ is Lord, to the glory of God the Father." All power in heaven and earth has been given into His hands, and all things (the universe) put under His feet. Even the angels are His ministering spirits, sent by Him to minister to those who shall be heirs of salvation.

This Messianic or mediatorial kingdom of Christ, being thus comprehensive, is presented in different aspects in the Word of God. Viewed as extending over all creatures, it is a kingdom of power which, according to 1 Corinthians 15:24, He shall deliver up to God the Father when His mediatorial work is accomplished. Viewed in relation to His own people on earth, it is the kingdom of grace. They all recognize Him as their absolute proprietor and sovereign. They all trust in His protection and devote themselves to His service. He rules in them, and reigns over them, and subdues all their and His enemies. Viewed in relation to the whole body of the redeemed when the work of redemption is consummated, it is the kingdom of glory, the kingdom of heaven, in the highest sense of those words. His headship over His people is to continue forever, and His dominion over those whom He has purchased with His blood shall never end. . . .

Although God has always had a kingdom upon earth, the kingdom of which the prophets speak began in its Messianic form when the Son of God came in the flesh. John the Baptist, the forerunner of Christ, came preaching that the kingdom of God was at hand. Our Lord Himself went from village to village, preaching the kingdom of God. . . . All those who profess allegiance to Christ as King constitute His kingdom upon earth. Nothing, therefore, can be more opposed to the plain teaching of the New Testament than that the kingdom of Christ is yet future and is not to be inaugurated until His second coming.

As to the nature of this kingdom, our Lord Himself teaches us that it is not of this world. It is not analogous to the kingdoms which exist among men. It is not a kingdom of earthly splendour, wealth, or power. It does not concern the civil or political affairs of men, except in their moral relations. Its rewards and enjoyments are not the good things of this world. It is said to consist in "righteousness, and peace, and joy in the Holy Ghost" (Rom. 14:17). Christ told His hearers, "The kingdom of God is within you" (Luke 17:21). The condition of admission into that kingdom is regeneration (John 3:5), conversion (Matt. 18:3), and holiness of heart and life. . . .

In the interval between the first and second advents of Christ His kingdom is to pass through many vicissitudes; it will have its times of depression and its seasons of exaltation and prosperity. There can be no doubt that this has been the case in the past. And prophecy sheds a sufficiently clear light on the future to teach us not only that this alternation is to continue to the end, but, more definitely, that before the second coming of Christ there is to be a time of great and long continued prosperity to be followed by a season of decay and of suffering, so that when the Son of man comes, He shall hardly find faith on the earth. In the preceding chapter we noted that all nations are to be converted, that the Jews are to be brought in and reingrafted into their own olive tree, and that their restoration is to be the occasion and the cause of a change from death unto life. Of this period the ancient prophets speak in terms designed to raise the hopes of the Church to the highest pitch. . . . This period is called a millennium because in Revelation it is said to last a thousand years, an expression which is generally understood in a literal sense. Some, however, think it means a protracted season of indefinite duration, as when it is said that one day is with the Lord as a thousand years. . . . During this period, whatever its length, the Church is to enjoy a season of peace, purity, and blessedness such as it has never yet experienced.

The principal reason for assuming a glorious state of the Church prior to the second advent is that the prophets represent the Church as being prosperous and glorious on earth. But we know that when Christ comes again, the heavens and earth are to pass away, and no more place will be found for them. The seat of the Church, after the second coming, is not to be the earth, but a new heaven and a new earth. Therefore, the Scriptural teachings that the kingdom of Christ is to extend over all the earth, that all nations are to serve Him, and that all people shall call Him blessed must refer to an era before the second coming of Christ. This era is described as one of spiritual prosperity—God will pour out His Spirit upon all flesh; knowledge shall everywhere abound; wars shall cease to the ends of the earth; and there shall be nothing to hurt or destroy in all God's holy mountain. This does not imply that there is to be neither sin nor sorrow in the world during this long period, or that all men are to be true Christians. The tares are to grow together with the wheat until the harvest. The means of grace will still be needed; conversion and sanctification will be then what they ever have been. What we are taught to anticipate in the millennium is only a higher measure of the good which the Church has experienced in the past. This, however, is not the end. After this blessed period and the apostasy which is to follow comes the consummation.

When Christ returns, He shall "be admired in all them that believe" (2 Thess. 1:10). Those who are then alive will be changed, in the twinkling of an eye; their corruptible shall put on incorruption, and their mortal shall put on immortality (1 Cor. 15:51–53). Those who are in the graves shall hear the voice of the Son of man and come forth to the resurrection of life, their bodies fashioned like unto the glorious body of the Son of God. Thus changed, both classes shall be ever with the Lord.

The place of the final abode of the righteous is sometimes called a house, as when the Saviour said, "In my Father's house are many mansions" (John 14:2), and sometimes "a city which hath foundations, whose builder and maker is God" (Heb. 11:10). Under this figure it is described as the new or heavenly Jerusalem (Rev. 21). Sometimes it is spoken of as "a better country, that is, an heavenly" (Heb. 11:16), a country through which flows the river of the water of life (Rev. 22:1-5). And sometimes the final abode of the redeemed is called "new heavens and a new earth" (2 Peter 3:13).

We know that the blessedness of this heavenly state is inconceivable: "Eye hath not seen, nor ear heard, neither have entered into the heart of man, the things which God hath prepared for them that love him" (1 Cor. 2:9). Nevertheless, there are certain general details which we are capable of understanding: (1) The incomprehensible blessedness of heaven shall arise from the vision of God. This vision beatifies and transforms the soul into the divine image, transfusing into it the divine life, so that it is filled with the fulness of God. This vision of God is in the face of Jesus Christ, in whom dwells the plenitude of the divine glory bodily. God is seen in fashion as a man, and this manifestation of God in the person of Christ is inconceivably ravishing. (2) The blessedness of the redeemed will flow from the manifestation not only of the glory, but also of the love of God—that love, mysterious, unchangeable, and infinite, of which the work of redemption is the fruit. (3) The future happiness of the saints will entail indefinite enlargement of all their faculties, entire exemption from all sin and sorrow, intercourse and fellowship with the high intelligences of heaven (patriarchs, prophets, apostles, martyrs, and all the redeemed), constant increase in knowledge and in the useful exercise of all their powers, secure and everlasting possession of all possible good, and outward circumstances such as will minister to their increasing blessedness.

[§5. The Theory of the Premillennial Advent]

§6. Future Punishment

Our Lord in His account of the final judgment says that the wicked shall go away into everlasting punishment, but the righteous into life eternal. The sufferings of the finally impenitent, according to the Scriptures, involve the loss of all earthly good, exclusion from the presence and favour of God, utter reprobation or the final withdrawal of the Holy Spirit, a consequent unrestrained dominion of sin and sinful passions, the operations of conscience, despair, evil associates, actual inflictions, and perpetuity.

There seems to be no more reason for supposing that the fire spoken of in Scripture is to be literal fire than that the worm that never dies is literally a worm. The devil and his angels, who are to suffer the vengeance of eternal fire and whose doom the finally impenitent are to share, have no material bodies to be acted upon by elemental fire. In the manner in which there are to be degrees in the glory and blessedness of heaven, as our Lord teaches us in the parable of the ten talents, so there will be differences as to degree in the sufferings of the lost: some will be beaten with few stripes, some with many.

A. The Duration of Future Punishment

. . . It is obvious that the question of the duration of future punishment can be decided only by divine revelation. No one can reasonably presume to decide upon any general principles of right and wrong how long the wicked are to suffer for their sins. The conditions of the problem are not within our grasp. What the infinitely wise and good God may see fit to do with His creatures, or what the exigencies of a government embracing the whole universe and continuing throughout eternal ages may demand, it is not for us worms of the dust to determine. If we believe the Bible to be the Word of God, all we have to do is to ascertain what it teaches on this subject and humbly submit.

It is an almost invincible presumption that the Bible does teach the unending punishment of the finally impenitent; all Christian churches have so understood it. . . . This is a doctrine which the natural heart revolts from and struggles against, and to which it submits only under stress of authority. The Church believes the doctrine because it must either believe it or renounce faith in the Bible and give up all the hopes founded upon its promises. . . .

The prophet Daniel says that the wicked "shall awake . . . to shame and everlasting contempt" (12:2). In Luke 3:17 it is said that Christ "will gather the wheat into his garner; but the chaff he will burn with fire unquenchable." In Mark 9:42–48 our Lord says that it is better "to enter into life maimed, than having two hands to go into hell, into the fire that never shall be quenched: where their worm dieth not, and the fire is not quenched." Three times in one discourse these awful words fell from the lips of mercy to give them the greater effect. Christ wept over Jerusalem. Why did He not avert its doom? Simply because it would not have been right to do so. In like manner He may weep over the doom of the impenitent wicked and yet leave them to their fate. It is no more possible that the cup should pass from their lips than that it should have been taken from the trembling hand of the Son of God Himself. The latter spectacle was far more appalling in the eyes of angels than is the lake of fire prepared for the devil and his angels.

The Judge on the last day, we are told, will say to those on the left hand: " 'Depart from me, ye cursed, into everlasting fire.' . . . And these shall go away into everlasting punishment: but the righteous into life eternal" (Matt. 25:41, 46). "Everlasting" and "eternal" are translations of the same Greek word, which obviously must have the same sense in both clauses. In John 3:36 it is said: "He that believeth on the Son hath everlasting life: and he that believeth not the Son shall not see life; but the wrath of God abideth on him." Paul teaches us in 2 Thessalonians 1:9 that when Christ comes, the wicked "shall be punished with everlasting destruction from the presence of the Lord, and from the glory of his power." Jude says that the angels which kept not their first estate are "reserved in everlasting chains under darkness unto the judgment of the great day. Even as Sodom and Gomorrah . . . are set forth for an example, suffering the vengeance of eternal fire" (vv. 6–7). He adds that "the blackness of darkness for ever" is reserved for apostates (v. 13). And according to Revelation 14:9–11 those who worship the beast and his image, or receive his mark, "shall be tormented with fire and brimstone in the presence of the holy angels, and in the presence of the Lamb: and the smoke of their torment ascendeth up for ever and ever: and they have no rest day nor night." Nearly the same words are repeated in Revelation 19:2–3, 20; and 20:10. . . .

B. Objections

It is urged that it cannot be consistent with the justice of God to inflict a really infinite penalty on such a creature as man. To this objection it may be remarked:

(1) We are incompetent judges of the penalty which sin deserves. We have no adequate apprehension of its inherent guilt, of the dignity of the person against whom it is committed, or of the extent of the evil which it is capable of producing. The proper end of punishment is retribution and prevention. Only God knows what is necessary for that end; and, therefore, the penalty which He imposes on sin is the only just measure of its ill-desert.

(2) If it be inconsistent with the justice of God that men should perish for their sins, then redemption is not a matter of grace or undeserved mercy. Deliverance from an unjust penalty is a matter of justice. Nothing, however, is plainer from the teaching of Scripture, and nothing is more universally and joyfully acknowledged by all Christians, than that the whole plan of redemption—the mission, the incarnation, and the sufferings and death of the Son of God for the salvation of sinners—is a wonderful exhibition of the love of God which passes knowledge. . . .

(3) The doom of the fallen angels teaches us that one act of rebellion

against God is fatal. It makes no difference whether all they have suffered since and will suffer in eternity is the penalty of that one act or the inevitable consequence of the condition into which that one act brought them.

A still more formidable objection is drawn from the goodness of God. It is said to be inconsistent with His benevolence that He should allow any of His creatures to be forever miserable. To this objection it may be remarked:

(1) . . . In view of the fact that God has permitted such a vast amount of sin and misery to exist in the world from the fall of Adam to the present time, how can we say that it is inconsistent with His goodness to allow them to continue to exist? How do we know that the reasons, so to speak, which constrained God to allow His children to be sinful and miserable for thousands of years may not constrain Him to permit some of them to remain miserable forever? If the highest glory of God and the good of the universe have been promoted by the past sinfulness and misery of men, why may not those objects be similarly promoted in the future?

(2) We have reason to believe that the number of the finally lost in comparison with the whole number of the saved will be very inconsiderable. Our blessed Lord, when surrounded by the innumerable company of the redeemed, will be hailed as the Saviour of men, as the Lamb that bore the sins of the world.

(3) We should be constrained to humility and to silence on this subject by the fact that the most solemn and explicit declarations of the everlasting misery of the wicked fell from the lips of Him who, though equal with God, was found in fashion as a man and humbled Himself unto death, even the death of the cross, for us men and for our salvation.

Study Questions

Expanding your knowledge of the Bible is essential for spiritual growth. Isaiah says, "And wisdom and knowledge shall be the stability of thy times, and strength of salvation" (Isa. 33:6). Conscientiously apply what you learn. True knowledge is the basis of a right relationship with God.

Share what you learn with others (Heb. 5:12–14). Remember that "unto whomsoever much is given, of him shall be much required" (Luke 12:48).

Pray for discernment and guidance each time you study. God will give you wisdom if you ask Him for it (James 1:5). Pray David's prayer: "Open thou mine eyes, that I may behold wondrous things out of thy law" (Ps. 119:18).

Preface

You should read the preface because it will familiarize you with Charles Hodge.

Chapter I

1. What is the difference between Biblical theology and systematic theology? (p. 24)
2. Briefly state four reasons why Biblical truths should be systematized. (pp. 24–25)
3. What is the difference between the speculative and mystical methods? (p. 26)

4. State the two rules by which the theologian and the physical scientist are to be guided in their research. (p. 28)
5. What is the proper method of theology? What are its main assumptions? (p. 31)

Chapter II

1. Define theology. (p. 34)
2. List five passages of Scripture that refer to natural theology. (pp. 36–37)
3. Natural theology is insufficient in what way? (p. 37)
4. Will infants who die go to heaven? Explain. (pp. 37–38)
5. What two things are essential for an adult to be saved? (p. 40)

Chapter III

1. Define rationalism. (p. 46)
2. List seven proofs that the Bible is the Word of God. (pp. 48–49)
3. Explain the proper spheres of reason and the senses. Note why it is inappropriate for spiritual truths to rest on the approval of our reasoning faculties. (pp. 52–53)
4. What are the three legitimate uses of reason in matters of religion? (pp. 54–57)
5. Define "impossible," and give several illustrations of things that are impossible. (p. 55)
6. Define "faith" by stating what it is not and what it is. (p. 57)
7. Christianity is equally opposed to two errors. Identify them. (p. 57)
8. Can the Bible contradict known facts? Explain. (p. 59)

Chapter IV

1. Define "mysticism," and state the main assumption of the mystic. (p. 64)
2. Give the three ways that mysticism differs from spiritual illumination. (p. 65)
3. The guidance of God for His children is composed of what three elements? (p. 65)
4. What two important doctrines of the Protestant Reformation are sometimes perverted by the mystic? (pp. 66–67)

5. What is the fundamental principle of Roman Catholicism concerning salvation? (p. 67)

Chapter V

1. What is the rule that determines the list of inspired Old Testament books? (p. 76)
2. What is the rule that determines the list of inspired New Testament books? (p. 77)
3. Define "inspiration" as it pertains to the writers of the Bible. (p. 77)
4. List the three ways that inspiration and spiritual illumination differ. (p. 78)
5. What is the "mechanical theory" of inspiration? Is it the accepted viewpoint? (p. 79)
6. What is the difference between revelation and inspiration? (p. 83)
7. What is "plenary inspiration"? What does it affirm and deny? (p. 85)
8. Did inspiration make its subject infallible in all areas? Explain. (pp. 85–86)
9. List four good answers to those who allege that there are discrepancies in the Bible. (p. 88)
10. State four important points in response to the allegations of historical and scientific error in the Scriptures. (p. 89)
11. Is the "partial inspiration" theory a true alternative for the Christian? Explain. (pp. 91–92)
12. What is meant by the completeness of Scripture? (p. 92)
13. Define "perspicuity" in reference to the Bible. (pp. 92–93)
14. Briefly state three important rules for interpreting the Scriptures. (pp. 94–95)

Part I

Chapter I

1. Define innate knowledge by explaining what it is not and what it is. (pp. 100–101)
2. Identify the two tests every primary truth (innate knowledge or axiom) must pass. (p. 100)
3. Explain the two proofs that support the claim that the knowledge of God is universal. (pp. 101–2)

Chapter II

1. Define theism in your own words. (p. 105)
2. Enumerate the four arguments for God's existence. (p. 105)
3. What is the ontological argument? (p. 105)
4. State the logical (syllogistic) form of the cosmological argument. (p. 106)
5. What does the cosmological argument prove? (p. 107)
6. State the syllogistic form of the teleological argument. (p. 107)
7. Define and give some examples of prevision. (p. 109)
8. Name three ancient philosophers who lauded the teleological argument, and give the syllogistic form used by the last one. (pp. 110–11)
9. Explain four ways in which the nature of the human soul evinces proof that it was designed for a higher state than that which is obtainable in this world. (pp. 112–13)
10. Explain how the moral judgments of man are independent. (p. 113)

Chapter III

1. Explain in what ways it is impossible and possible for a person to be an atheist. (pp. 117–18)
2. Define polytheism and explain how its representation as nature worship evolved. (p. 118)
3. Name and define the three general theories proposed to solve the great issues of life. (p. 119)
4. What two points satisfactorily refute materialism? (p. 119)
5. Explain how materialism denies three obvious facts of consciousness. (pp. 119–20)
6. State the one great exception to the general rule that pantheism has never taken hold on the hearts of common people, and explain the way it had to be altered in that one case. (p. 122)

Chapter IV

1. Explain the difference between knowing and comprehending God. (p. 126)
2. State the four sources of revelation through which God has made Himself known. (p. 126)
3. Name and define the three ways in which the mind forms its idea of God. (pp. 126–27)
4. Technically speaking, what is meant by worship? (p. 128)

5. How did the introduction of sin into human history demand the necessity of a supernatural revelation concerning the things of God? (pp. 129–30)
6. Explain the relationship of sense and reason to the truths of Scripture. (p. 130)

Chapter V

1. State the two extremes that must be avoided in explaining the relationship between God's essence and attributes. (p. 135)
2. Name and explain the three attributes of a spirit. (pp. 135–36)
3. Explain the difference between absolute and relative attributes, giving synonymous expressions. (p. 136)
4. Briefly explain what is involved in the statement, "God is a Spirit." (p. 138)
5. Explain the simplicity of God. (p. 139)
6. Explain how God can be infinite without being all. (pp. 140–41)
7. State and illustrate three possible modes of existence in space. (p. 141)
8. Briefly explain what Scripture teaches about God's eternity. (p. 143)
9. Explain the difference between God's immutability and His immobility. (pp. 143–44)
10. Explain how contingency (uncertainty) is not essential to free agency. (pp. 145–46)
11. Define and distinguish the decretive and preceptive will of God. (p. 147)
12. Explain the proper ground of moral obligation. (p. 148)
13. What is power? State the power human beings possess. (p. 149)
14. Define and give examples of *potentia absoluta* and *potentia ordinata*. (p. 150)
15. State and explain the two types of divine justice. (p. 152)
16. Distinguish punishment from chastisement and apply this to the Christian. (p. 152)
17. State the argument for God's justice as revealed in the Book of Romans. (p. 156)
18. Define and distinguish mercy and grace. (p. 157)
19. Why was sin permitted by God? (p. 161)
20. What is truth? How is God true? (p. 162)

Chapter VI

1. What is the design or goal of God in giving us His Word? (p. 165)

2. How is the doctrine of the Trinity the unconscious or unformed faith of all of God's people? (p. 166)
3. Describe the way Scripture relates titles and attributes to each Person of the Trinity. (pp. 166–67)
4. How can you prove that the Son and Father are different Persons? (p. 167)
5. How can you prove that they are at the same time perfectly equal? (p. 167)
6. Explain the subordination of one Person to another in the Trinity. (p. 167)
7. Explain the divine concurrence of each member of the Trinity in all the acts of the Trinity. (pp. 167–68)
8. Why are baptisms and benedictions important to the life of the Church and its knowledge of the Trinity? (p. 169)
9. What does "begotten of the Father" mean? (p. 171)
10. What did the Council of Constantinople (381 A.D.) say about the Trinity? (p. 172)
11. What creeds were formulated to help the Church define the doctrine of the Trinity? Why are these expressions important today? (pp. 172–73)

Chapter VII

1. Why must the Redeemer be both God and man? (pp. 175–76)
2. Explain the Protevangelium. (p. 176)
3. What are the two great truths intimated in Genesis? (p. 176)
4. Who is the Angel of Jehovah? (pp. 176–78)
5. Prove, from Psalm 2, that the Messiah is a divine Person. (p. 178)
6. Name and briefly describe the six major Old Testament prophecies concerning the coming Messiah. (pp. 179–81)
7. Briefly summarize the Old Testament teaching about the Messiah. (p. 181)
8. The divinity of Christ is seen from four aspects of His relationship to His people. Name them. (pp. 182–84)

Chapter VIII

1. What are the two reasons the Third Person of the Trinity is called the Holy Spirit? (p. 185)
2. What are the essential elements of a person or spirit? (p. 186)
3. List seven arguments proving the personality of the Holy Spirit. (pp. 186–88)
4. Relate four points describing the relationship that the Holy Spirit bears to the Father and the Son. (pp. 189–90)

5. List five aspects of the Spirit's work in redemption. (pp. 191–92)

Chapter IX

1. Explain and illustrate from the Bible what the final cause of all of God's decrees is. (p. 194)
2. What happens when we make the good of creatures the ultimate object of all God's works? (p. 194)
3. List some of the greatest questions and the one statement that answers them. (pp. 194–95)
4. Explain why an event occurs. (p. 195)
5. What Scripture passages prove that even our salvation is included in the eternal decrees of God? (pp. 195–96)
6. Prove why the decrees of God are immutable (unchanging). (p. 196)
7. Are animals' instinctive acts free acts? Explain. (pp. 196–97)
8. Explain what would be lost if we did not have hope that the decrees of God must come to pass. (p. 198)
9. State and briefly answer the four objections to the doctrine of God's divine decrees. (pp. 200–203)

Chapter X

1. Why is God's revelation the only reasonable source for explaining the origin of the universe? (p. 205)
2. What are the three elements of the Scripture's teaching concerning the origin of creation? (p. 206)
3. Distinguish mediate from immediate creation. (pp. 206–7)
4. What, according to Hebrews 11:3, is the great fundamental truth of all religion? Why is it so? (p. 208)
5. Why did God create the world? (p. 209)
6. What three ways have men interpreted Moses' account of creation? Which of these is the correct way? (p. 209)
7. Why must we distinguish between the *facts* of science and the *theories* of science? (p. 210)

Chapter XI

1. Define the works of God's providence. (p. 213)
2. Explain God's preservation. (p. 214)
3. Briefly summarize the three viewpoints concerning preservation, identifying the Biblical view. (pp. 214–15)
4. What are the four chief characteristics of God's government, according to the Scriptures? (pp. 215–16)
5. What relationship does God's providence have with "apparently fortuitous events"? (p. 219)

6. What relationship does God's providence have with nations? (p. 219)
7. What relationship does God's providence have with sin? (p. 220)
8. Distinguish God's *potentia ordinata* from His *potentia absoluta* and give examples of each. (pp. 224–25)
9. What extremes should we guard against when considering God's providence? (pp. 225–26)

Chapter XII

1. Define and describe a miracle of God. (pp. 227–28)
2. What tests should we use to prove if an alleged miracle is truly a work of God? (p. 228)
3. How can we distinguish between a true (divine) and false (demonic) sign or wonder? (p. 229)
4. How did God set His apostles apart from false apostles? (p. 230)

Chapter XIII

1. Repeat some of the ways that the Scriptures describe angels. (p. 231)
2. Describe the power of angels and list some things they cannot do. (p. 232)
3. Describe the state and rank of angels. (p. 232)
4. What are the three general employments of angels? (pp. 232–33)
5. Can angels communicate with us? How? (p. 233)
6. What danger must we guard against in thinking about angels? (p. 234)
7. Discuss the power and limitations of evil spirits. (p. 235)
8. Define demonic possession. Can this occur today? (pp. 235–36)
9. What is Satan's position in the world of demons? (p. 235)

Part II

Chapter I

1. What two truths are included in the account of the origin of man in Genesis 1:26–27? (p. 239)
2. Briefly list the four elements of Darwin's theory of evolution. (p. 240)
3. List Hodge's four refutations of Darwinism. (pp. 240–42)
4. The Scriptural doctrine of the universe includes what three basic points? (p. 242)
5. Explain why it is impossible to ascertain the chronology of the Bible with exactness and therefore the age of the earth. (p. 244)

Chapter II

1. Human beings consist of what two elements? (p. 247)
2. What three truths about our physical and mental constitutions are presented in the Scriptures? (p. 248)
3. What three facts concerning how the body and mind interact are important to remember? (p. 249)
4. What is trichotomy? (p. 250)
5. Briefly state four arguments against trichotomy. (pp. 250–51)

Chapter III

1. State and briefly describe the three theories concerning the origin of the human soul. (p. 253)
2. Briefly state the three main arguments in favor of the doctrine of creationism of the soul. (pp. 256–57)
3. Why is it dangerous to make a theory of the origin of the soul the foundation of one's understanding of original sin? (p. 257)
4. Explain what principles of traducianism (normally stated) are in opposition to plain and important doctrines of the Word of God. (p. 258)

Chapter V

1. Note the favorite assumption of skeptics concerning early mankind. (p. 261)
2. What is meant by the terms "immortal" and "impassible"? (p. 262)
3. What is the chief difference between man and animals? (p. 262)
4. What are the essential characteristics of a spirit? (p. 262)
5. Explain original righteousness. (p. 263)
6. Explain man's dominion. Has it ever been attained? (p. 264)

Chapter VI

1. According to the Scriptures, what are the only two methods of attaining eternal life? (p. 266)
2. Explain the two names of the covenant God made with Adam. (p. 266)
3. What was God's promise to Adam in the covenant of works? (p. 266)
4. What would have been included in the life promised therein? (p. 267)
5. What condition was set forth in the covenant of works? (p. 267)
6. What penalty was threatened in the covenant of works? (p. 268)
7. Who were the parties in the covenant of works? (p. 269)

Chapter VII

1. Note the four consequences of Adam's sin. (p. 271)
2. Give three arguments supporting the historical accuracy of the account of the fall. (pp. 271–72)
3. What were the three factors that led to the first sin? (p. 273)
4. What were the effects of the first sin on Adam and Eve? (p. 274)

Chapter VIII

1. What presuppositions does the Christian theologian assume when approaching the great challenge of defining sin? (p. 276)
2. What two sources of knowledge aid the Christian in defining sin? (pp. 276–77)
3. What four points were insisted on in the theological struggle over early heresies in the Church? (p. 277)
4. How did Pelagius describe "liberty of the will"? (p. 278)
5. Briefly summarize seven arguments against Pelagianism. (pp. 279–80)
6. Briefly summarize four of Augustine's conclusions based on the facts of consciousness and experience. (p. 282)
7. Define regeneration. (p. 283)
8. Why did the monks oppose Augustine? (p. 283)
9. Semi-Pelagians opposed Augustine in what three ways? (pp. 283–84)
10. What four conclusions may be drawn from the fact that the law demands entire conformity to the nature and will of God? (p. 287)
11. Sin includes what two elements? What do they relate to? (p. 289)
12. Define immediate imputation as it refers to Adam's seed. (p. 290)
13. Why is the penalty of Adam's sin imputed to his posterity? (p. 291)
14. Explain the chief argument in favor of the doctrine of imputation.
15. What three great truths were represented by the Old Testament sacrifices? (p. 294)
16. Define justification and state what it is not. (p. 294)
17. What three points are foundational to the doctrine of original sin as taught by Protestants? (p. 297)
18. Explain total depravity. (p. 298)
19. State two important principles that relate to answering objections against doctrinal truths. (pp. 303–4)

20. Explain the three general views that have been expressed in the history of the church concerning the ability of fallen man. (pp. 307–8)
21. According to the Scriptures, what is man's inability? (p. 308)

Chapter IX

1. What does the doctrine of fatalism teach? (p. 314)
2. Summarize the theory of certainty. (p. 315)
3. Explain the difference between "liberty of the will" and "liberty of the agent." (p. 315)
4. Define free agency and ability. (pp. 316–17)
5. Describe four doctrines that assume that free acts may indeed be certain as to their occurrence. (pp. 318–19)

Part III

Chapter I

1. What is the end (design) of redemption? Why is it important to understand this? (p. 324)
2. Briefly describe the supralapsarian scheme of the order of salvation in God's decrees. (p. 326)
3. Briefly describe the infralapsarian doctrine. (p. 327)
4. What are the major points of Arminianism? (p. 327)
5. What is the main difference between Arminianism and Augustinianism? (p. 328)
6. Briefly state the main points of Augustinianism. (pp. 329–30)
7. State the three main proofs of the truthfulness of the Augustinian position. (pp. 330–32)

Chapter II

1. Give two evidences that the plan of salvation is presented in the form of a covenant. (pp. 337–38)
2. State three reasons why the plan of salvation is of grace. (p. 339)
3. How do the two covenants relating to man's salvation differ? (p. 339)
4. Define the covenant of redemption. (p. 340)
5. What is the condition of the covenant of grace as far as adults are concerned? (p. 343)
6. Describe in what ways the plan of salvation has been the same under all dispensations of God's grace. (p. 344)

7. Describe precisely what the condition of salvation was under all eras of human history since the fall. (p. 347)
8. Enumerate and briefly describe the four dispensations of the covenant of grace. (pp. 348–50)

Chapter III

1. Name and describe the twofold constitution of human nature. (p. 352)
2. Explain the nature of the union between the soul and the body. (p. 352)
3. Explain what is meant by "communion of attributes." (p. 352)
4. What three main facts are taught in Scripture concerning the person of Christ? (p. 353)
5. State and briefly explain the four components of "the hypostatical union" in relation to Christ. (pp. 357–59)
6. What are the three consequences of this union in Christ? (pp. 359–61)

Chapter IV

1. How and where does the Bible teach that there was no other way for redemption to be accomplished except through Christ? (p. 363)
2. Briefly state the three necessary qualifications for the mediator between God and man. (pp. 364–65)
3. Could Jesus have sinned? Explain. (pp. 364–65)
4. What are the three offices exhibited by Christ in His mediatorial work? Give Scripture references from the Old Testament that predict these offices for the coming Messiah. (pp. 365–66)

Chapter V

1. What is a prophet? (p. 367)
2. How do preachers differ from prophets? (pp. 367–68)
3. In what four ways does Christ execute the office of a prophet? (p. 368)

Chapter VI

1. What are the three main elements of the priestly office? (pp. 369–70)
2. What constitutes a true consciousness of sin? (p. 370)
3. The author of Hebrews proves Christ's priesthood in what six ways? (pp. 370–71)
4. What three benefits accrue to us from Christ's priestly work? (p. 371)

5. Explain the connection between Old Testament priests (and their sacrifices) and the true priesthood of Christ. (p. 371)
6. Why is it inappropriate to call ministers of the gospel "priests"? (p. 371)
7. What is the satisfaction of Christ? (p. 372)
8. What is vicarious suffering? (pp. 374–75)
9. What is meant by guilt, and how is it removed? (p. 375)
10. Define redemption. (p. 375)
11. Define and distinguish expiation and propitiation. (pp. 375–76)

Chapter VII

1. What are the three main points in the doctrine of Christ's satisfaction? (pp. 377–79)
2. What is the chief lesson that the need for sacrifices teaches us? (p. 379)
3. What two great truths are revealed in both human nature and Scripture concerning God's justice? (p. 379)
4. List the five "great constituent principles of the religion of the Bible." (p. 380)
5. Describe the great condemning sin of people today. (p. 381)
6. In His work of redemption, Christ saves us from God's wrath and curse by functioning in what three ways? (pp. 381–83)
7. Why must the believer be redeemed from the law? (p. 384)

Chapter VIII

1. Distinguish the Augustinian from the anti-Augustinian position concerning the death of Christ. (p. 387)
2. What four points are not involved in this debate? (pp. 387–88)
3. Simply put, what is the main question in this debate? (p. 389)
4. Explain the connection between the doctrines of election and the redemptive work of Christ. (p. 390)
5. What four facts are clearly revealed in Scripture concerning the redemptive work of Christ? (p. 392)
6. How is the Augustinian doctrine to be reconciled with those passages which, in one form or another, teach that Christ died for all men? (pp. 392–93)
7. What is meant when Christ is called "the Savior of mankind"? (p. 393)

Chapter X

1. In what ways does Christ's work parallel that of the high priest in Old Testament times? (p. 397)
2. List the four activities involved in Christ's intercession. (p. 398)

3. Describe the two objects for whom Christ prays, and how His intercession differs for each of them. (pp. 398–99)

Chapter XI

1. For what four purposes did God enter into a covenant with Abraham, establishing His visible kingdom (Church)? (p. 402)
2. How long is Christ's dominion or kingdom to last, and what will become of it when its design is accomplished? (p. 405)
3. What are the terms of admission into Christ's kingdom, and what will not secure admission into it? (p. 405)
4. What are the basic laws required in Christ's kingdom? (p. 406)
5. What is the special law of Christ's kingdom? (p. 406)
6. What are the four characteristics of Christ's kingdom? (pp. 407–8)

Chapter XII

1. What particular circumstances "make the condescension of our Lord to pass all comprehension"? (p. 412)
2. Precisely what "law" was it that Christ subjected Himself to? (p. 412)
3. Christ's subjection to the law was both voluntary and vicarious. What is meant by these terms? (pp. 412–13)
4. Briefly describe the sufferings of Christ in relationship to His entire life. (p. 413)
5. What five elements constitute the "humiliation of Christ"? (pp. 411–14)

Chapter XIII

1. What four points prove the importance of Christ's resurrection to the Christian faith? (pp. 415–16)
2. What ten facts substantiate the resurrection of Christ as "the best-authenticated fact in the history of the world"? (p. 416)
3. Briefly describe the nature of Christ's resurrection body as it now exists in heaven. (p. 416)
4. What is definitely taught in Scripture concerning the ascension of Christ? (p. 417)
5. Give four reasons why the ascension was necessary. (pp. 417–18)
6. What four elements constitute the "exaltation of Christ"? (pp. 415–19)
7. Describe the rule and ground of Christ's judgment. (p. 419)

Chapter XIV

1. What is taught by Scripture concerning the parts played by the Father, Son, and Spirit in the work of man's redemption? (p. 421)
2. What Scripture texts represent the union of believers to Christ as the result of a divine calling? (p. 422)
3. What are the essential parts of the external call? (p. 423)
4. Discuss the internal (effectual) call and the external call as they relate to the concept of universality. (p. 423)
5. What is grace? (p. 425)
6. Explain what is meant by the statement "the gospel is a system of grace." (pp. 425–26)
7. What is common grace? (p. 426)
8. What are some of the effects of common grace? (p. 427)
9. What is the greatest calamity that can befall an individual, a church, or a people? (p. 428)
10. How can we grieve the Holy Spirit? (p. 428)
11. Discuss efficacious grace and common grace as they relate to the concept of irresistibility. (p. 429)
12. Describe the activity of the soul in regard to regeneration (i.e., effectual calling). (p. 429)
13. In what four ways does Scripture represent regeneration? (p. 430)

Chapter XV

1. What are the three major points of the evangelical doctrine of regeneration? (pp. 434–35)
2. What class of objects is not spiritually discerned by unrenewed mankind? (p. 435)
3. How does new life in Christ manifest itself? (p. 436)
4. Describe what is meant by a "new heart." (p. 436)
5. Summarize regeneration. (pp. 436–37)

Chapter XVI

1. State three reasons why it is absolutely necessary that we possess clear and correct ideas about faith. (p. 440)
2. Describe "truth." (p. 440)
3. Give Paul's two reasons why the apostles did not present their doctrines as propositions to be proved through human logic. (p. 441)
4. Present faith's object, ground, reception, and rejection according to 1 John 5:10–11. (pp. 441–42)

5. List four things that are not the ground for our faith. (p. 442)
6. State and briefly describe the three types of faith. (pp. 443–44)
7. What are the three chief functions of the Holy Spirit in this world according to John 16:8? (pp. 444–45)
8. What four things are taught in 1 John 2:20, 27? (p. 445)
9. Explain the different kinds of testimony and the types of faith they produce. (pp. 445–46)
10. Briefly state the relationship of knowledge to faith. (p. 446)
11. Distinguish implicit faith from real faith. (pp. 446–47)
12. Prove by three arguments that knowledge is essential to a true and living faith. (p. 447)
13. What are the three parts of saving faith? (p. 448)
14. State the two great principles that Protestants affirm. (p. 449)
15. Distinguish general faith from special faith. (p. 449)
16. List the six effects of saving faith. (pp. 450–52)

Chapter XVII

1. State six points that are necessary elements of a thorough definition of justification. (p. 454)
2. Contrast justification with sanctification. (pp. 454–55)
3. Contrast justification with condemnation. (pp. 455–56)
4. Explain the relationship between grace and justification. (p. 458)
5. Describe what is meant by the "righteousness of Christ." (p. 459)
6. Define imputation and its role in Christ's relationship with the believer. (pp. 459–60)
7. Explain what is and what is not meant by the statement, "God imputes righteousness to the sinner." (p. 460)
8. What does it mean that believers "are not under the law, but under grace"? (p. 461)
9. Describe the relationship between faith and justification. (p. 462)

Chapter XVIII

1. State six differences between justification and sanctification. (p. 464)
2. What two things are included in the assertion that sanctification is a work of God's free grace? (p. 464)
3. Discuss the place of "second causes" in the work of sanctification. (pp. 464–65)
4. What two things constitute the believer's sanctification? (p. 467)

5. The method of sanctification is carried out through what six channels? (pp. 467–69)
6. Give three consequences of the believer's union with Christ. (pp. 467–68)
7. List six or seven fruits of the inward work of the Spirit on the believer's mind. (p. 468)
8. Give four direct fruits of the kingly office of Christ within the believer. (p. 469)
9. In what three senses can a believer's works be called truly good? (p. 471)
10. Describe "living faith." (p. 471)
11. List four arguments against the teaching of perfectionism. (pp. 472–73)

Chapter XX

1. What are the three chief means of grace? (p. 478)
2. On what does a minister's success depend and not depend? (p. 480)
3. What four essential elements make baptism and the Lord's Supper sacraments? (p. 481)
4. Discuss three points established by the Reformed doctrine on the efficacy of the sacraments. (pp. 482–83)
5. Explain why the mode of baptism is not essential to the sacrament of baptism. (p. 483)
6. What are the three qualifications for adult baptism? (p. 484)
7. Name the eight points that underlie the Church's justification for baptizing infants. (pp. 484–90)
8. Discuss the relationship of parents to children in the sight of God. (p. 489)
9. Give several instances of household baptisms in the New Testament. (p. 490)
10. What are the three false doctrines opposed by the Reformed doctrine of the efficacy of baptism? (p. 491)
11. What five assertions does Reformed doctrine make regarding baptism's efficacy? (pp. 491–92)
12. Describe how baptism is a sign. (p. 492)
13. Describe how baptism is a seal or pledge. (p. 492)
14. Describe how baptism is a means of grace. (p. 493)
15. List the four designs of the Lord's Supper. (p. 494)
16. What are the three conditions for profitable communion in partaking of the Lord's Supper? (p. 494)
17. What does Matthew 26:28 teach about redemption? (p. 495)

18. Describe the presence of Christ's body in the Lord's Supper. (p. 497)
19. What is prayer? (p. 498)
20. What does prayer presuppose? (pp. 498–99)
21. What are the seven requisites for acceptable prayer? (pp. 500–502)

Part IV

Chapter I

1. State the Protestant doctrine of the state of the soul after death. To what doctrine is this opposed? (pp. 509–10)
2. Describe the soul and its relationship to the body. (p. 510)
3. Do human souls have a second chance to be saved after death according to the Scriptures? Explain. (p. 510)
4. Why is there no need for satisfaction to be rendered in the future life for the sins done in the body? (p. 510)
5. Contrast the believer's present life with what follows in the glorified state. (p. 511)
6. What is meant by the term "paradise" as used in Scripture? (p. 512)

Chapter II

1. What three texts of Scripture teach that our mortal bodies will be raised from the dead? (pp. 515–16)
2. Contrast the believer's present body with the future body. (p. 516)
3. What two negative statements about the resurrection body help us understand something about its nature? (p. 517)
4. What three things are plainly taught by Paul in 1 Corinthians 15:50? (p. 517)
5. State the four particulars the Bible teaches concerning the resurrected body. (pp. 517–19)
6. Explain the function of memory in the future state. (pp. 518–19)
7. Describe five ways in which the future bodies of believers will be unlike their present bodies. (pp. 519–20)

Chapter III

1. Explain the difference between prophecy and history. (pp. 523–24)
2. Discuss prophecy in reference to the themes of "general impression" versus "details." (p. 524)

3. What three events will precede the second coming of Christ? (p. 524)
4. What five things does the New Testament teach about a second visible and personal appearing of the Son of God? (pp. 525–26)
5. What, according to Mark 16:15, is the present duty of the Church? (p. 526)
6. What did the apostles see as their two great duties? (pp. 526–27)
7. State two arguments that support the view that the conversion of the Jewish nation must precede the second advent of Christ. (p. 528)
8. Describe three positions on the identity of the Antichrist. Do you have a preference? (p. 529)

Chapter IV

1. What passages imply a general resurrection of the dead? (pp. 530–31)
2. What text implies more than one resurrection of the dead? (p. 532)
3. What is the common millenarian doctrine, according to Hodge? Do you agree wit him that 1 Corinthians 15:50 seems to contradict those who believe in a literal 1000-year millennium? Why or why not? (pp. 533–34)
4. Notice the humble disclaimer that Hodge adds to this discussion (p. 534). What does he say about the interpretation of unfulfilled prophecy?
5. What seven points constitute the common doctrine of the final judgment? (pp. 534–37)
6. What two things about fulfilled prophecies of Scripture ought to be noted? (pp. 537–38)
7. In what way will the earth be "destroyed"? What will the renovated earth become? (pp. 538–39)
8. Describe the Messianic kingdom of Christ as it relates to all creatures, to the Church on earth, and to the whole body of the redeemed. (pp. 539–40)
9. What are the conditions for admission into Christ's kingdom? (p. 540)
10. What will the millennium be like? (pp. 540–41)
11. What will happen to all believers at the second coming of Christ? (p. 541)
12. What three details are known about the believer's heavenly state? (p. 542)
13. What will happen to the wicked and righteous at the judgment? (p. 542)

14. Will there be degrees in glory and suffering for the dead after this life? Explain. (p. 543)
15. What Biblical evidence is there that the duration of future punishment will be everlasting? (pp. 543–44)

Scripture Index

Subject Index

adult, 484; infant, 484–91, 493–94;
efficacy of, 491–94
"Beget," 244
Being, 134, 140
Benediction, apostolic, 169–70, 189
Benevolence, 156–57; and justice, 153–
54, 156
Bible. See Scripture
Biblical theology, 24
Birth, new. See Regeneration
Bishops, 68
Blindness, spiritual, 307, 308, 439–
40, 479
Body, 120, 247–51, 256, 306, 352–53,
510; as evidence of design, 108–9; of
Christ, 354, 357; Christ's resurrection,
416; resurrection of the, 515–17;
nature of the resurrection, 516–21,
534; and soul, 112
Branch of Jehovah, 179, 180
Breath of life, 240, 254, 256
Brotherly love, 406

Calling, effectual, 283. See also Vocation
Canon, 76–77
Causality (causation), 126–27, 136
Cause, 106–7, 120, 128
Certainty, 146, 147, 160, 197–98, 200–1,
203, 315, 317–19; of salvation, 452
Chance, 115, 215
Chastisement, 152–53
Chronology of the Bible, 244–45
Church, 401–2, 469; invisible, 405–6;
membership in the, 408, 485–90; prior
to the second coming, 541; and State,
407–8; visible, 407–8, 485
Circumcision, 488–89, 492, 493
Commercial satisfaction. See Pecuniary
satisfaction
Common grace, 66, 192, 425–28, 443
Communicable attributes, 136–37
Communion of attributes, 352–53,
359–60
Completeness of the Scriptures, 92
Comprehension, 54
Condemnation: of all, 38–40, 270, 296;
and justification, 455–56
Conditional nature of God's promises,
502
Conscience, 102, 113–14, 120, 129–30,
308
Constantine, 171

Constantinople, Council of, 172
Consummation, final, 538–39
Contingency, 146, 314–15, 317–19
Contradictions, alleged, 88–89
Contrary choice, 314. See also
Contingency
Control, 215
Conversion, 284, 307, 308, 333; of the
Jews, 524, 527–28
Corruption, 297. See also Depravity
Cosmological argument, 106–7
Covenant, 337–38, 340; with Abraham,
402, 486, 488; of grace, 302, 337–50,
467; of redemption, 339–42, 374, 389,
450–51, 461–62; of works, 265–70
Creation, 205–11, 214, 227, 326–27, 430
Creationism, 254–57, 258
Credibility, 55–56
Crime, prevention of, 153–54, 155
Crucifixion, 199, 202, 413
Curse, Christ as, 383–84

Darwin, Charles, 107, 240–43
David's Lord, 179
David's Son, 179
"Day," 210, 534
Dead faith, 443, 445–46
Death: as the penalty of disobedience,
268; soul after, 509–13; spiritual, 268,
274, 282, 284, 291, 296–97, 302, 427,
435; universality of, 303
Decrees of God, 193–203; order of the,
326–27
Decretive will, 147
Deism, 214
Deistical rationalism, 46–49
Demoniacs, 235–36
Depravity: hereditary, 257, 283, 296–97,
302; total, 298–300
Design, 146, 215; argument from,
107–11
Destruction of the world, 538
Development: law of, 196; theories of,
107, 240–43
Discernment, spiritual, 435, 444; lack
of, 308–9, 310
Discrepancies in Scripture, allegations
of, 88–89
Dispensations, 344–50
Dispositions, sinful, 287, 304, 305
Distributive justice, 152, 378

Edward N. Gross (M.Div., Faith Theological Seminary; D.Miss., Trinity Evangelical Divinity School), editor of this abridgment, is pastor of Pilgrim Presbyterian Church, in Philadelphia. He has served on the faculties of Faith Theological Seminary, Biblical Theological Seminary, and the Bible College of East Africa. Dr. Gross is author of *Miracles, Demons, and Spiritual Warfare; Christianity Without a King;* and *Will My Children Go to Heaven?* as well as a contributor to the *Evangelical Dictionary of World Missions.*